D1290152

The Arno Press Cinema Program

RESPONSE TO INNOVATION
A Study of Popular Argument
About New Mass Media

Robert Edward Davis

ARNO PRESS

A New York Times Company

New York · 1976

WILLIAM MADISON RANDALL LIBRARY UNC AT WILMINGTON

This volume was selected for the
Dissertations on Film Series
of the ARNO PRESS CINEMA PROGRAM
by Garth S. Jowett, Carleton University

Editorial Supervision: Sheila Mehlman

First publication in book form, Arno Press, 1976

Copyright © 1976 by Robert Edward Davis

THE ARNO PRESS CINEMA PROGRAM
For complete listing of cinema titles see last pages

Manufactured in the United States of America

Publisher's Note: This work has been reproduced
from the best available copy.

Library of Congress Cataloging in Publication Data

Davis, Robert Edward.
    Response to innovation.

    (Dissertations on film)
    Originally presented as the author's thesis, University of Iowa, 1965.
    1. Moving-pictures--Social aspects. 2. Mass media--Social aspects. I. Title.
PN1995.9.S6D3 1976   301.16'1   75-21430
ISBN 0-405-07533-2

HN90
.m3
.D38
1976

RESPONSE TO INNOVATION:

A STUDY OF POPULAR ARGUMENT ABOUT NEW MASS MEDIA

by

Robert Edward Davis

A dissertation submitted in partial fulfillment of
the requirements for the degree of Doctor of
Philosophy in the Department of Speech and
Dramatic Art in the Graduate College
of the University of Iowa

August 1965

Chairman: Professor Donald C. Bryant

192574

195274

for
J. B. D.
and
R. J. D.

ACKNOWLEDGMENTS

A number of persons deserve thanks for their contributions to this investigation. I am especially indebted to Professor Donald C. Bryant for his direction of the study. I wish also to acknowledge the guidance and encouragement given me by the members of my Committee: Professors H. Clay Harshbarger, Arthur M. Barnes, Samuel L. Becker, John Waite Bowers, and David Schaal.

TABLE OF CONTENTS

INTRODUCTION

The last three quarters of a century have witnessed the development of three new mass media: motion pictures, radio, and television. Each captured the public fancy and attention as few inventions had done before. Each was quickly adopted as the new mode for popular entertainment. Each was perceived to be capable of influencing the opinions, the attitudes, the values, and even the actions of its audiences. Consequently, wide ranging speculation about its influences accompanied the growth of each new medium. Promoters talked of the new machines as sources for information, education, culture, and diversion. The new media, they said, would do all that society wanted done. On the other hand, people suspicious of the new influences predicted that the mass media would damage culture, subvert values, and overturn respected institutions. Innovation, they said, would cause the evils society most feared. The effects of motion pictures, radio, and television, both real and predicted, have been the cause for lively and persistent controversy for some six decades.

That controversy is the subject of this study. This is not an examination of the effects of the media, but rather an analysis of what people said the effects would be. This is a study of agitation about new things; an appraisal of popular argument in a situation of innovation. In particular, the study examines the

patterns of discourse which developed as promoters sought to advance
the cause of the new media and critics sought to resist them. The
materials of the study are the arguments which appeared in the popular
periodical press between 1891 and 1955. Its purpose is to identify
and to describe the extent of the argument employed for advocacy
and attack and to isolate the lines of argument from which the web
of agitation was woven. Particular attention is paid to the persistent concerns of the arguers, to their recurrent themes, to
the common presumptions from which they draw support, and to the
values and institutions to which they appeal. The central questions are these: how does the advocate introduce the new so as to
make it compatible with the old, and on what grounds does the
opponent resist innovation. In the broadest sense, this investigation is of the general and particular topics in argument about
innovation. The primary organization of material I have employed
gives first prominence to the concern with modes, methods, classes,
and uses of arguments.

As a study of assault upon the public mind, this investigation
falls into a rhetorical tradition. This study is most like those
which trace discourse through time and across media in order to
improve our understanding of popular persuasion and at the same
time to illuminate a particular controversy. It is of the genre
of Leland Griffin's analysis of the anti-masonic persuasion in the

early nineteenth century.[1] It is similar to Donald Dedmon's examination of the twenty-five year congressional debate over the admission
of Hawaii to the Union.[2] It is akin to Todd Willy's study of the
agitation over the mission of General Charles George "Chinese" Gordon
to the Soudan.[3] Its purpose and theirs is the same: to add, as
Willy says, "to what is known about the nature of persuasion as it
appears in public discourse."

As a study of the development of argument through time and in
so far as it traces relationships among the media and between the
media and social institutions, this dissertation is historical.
The reader interested principally in the growth of the media, in
the controversies which surrounded them, and in the changes in the
public's perceptions and expectations of them, will find this kind
of material treated in the course of the analysis for argument.
Moreover, the viewing of history through the eyes of the arguers
provides a new perspective. Hence, this study should also add to
our understanding of the historical development of motion pictures,
radio, and television in America.

The focusing of this study on the arguments about the effects
of motion pictures, radio, and television removes it from the common
stream of research. Not much has been said about the argument as
argument. Much attention has been paid, however, especially in
the popular press, to the historical development of motion pictures,

radio, and television. I refer in particular to histories of the
motion pictures by Jacobs, Ramsaye, Vardac, and Knight, and to the
histories of broadcasting by White and Head.[4] Other studies have
dealt with regulation, both from outside agencies and from within
the industries. Representative of this approach are Moley's _The
Hays Office_, Schumach's _The Face on the Cutting Room Floor_, Emery's
Broadcasting and Government, and Morgan's dissertation on the
Television Code of the National Association of Broadcasters.[5] The
effects of the media have been of interest to many other writers.
Among these works are Mitchell's _Movies and Children_; Forman's
Our Movie Made Children; Siepmann's _Radio, Television, and Society_;
Schramm's _Television in the Lives of our Children_; and Klapper's
The Effects of Mass Communication.[6] Many of these works mention in
passing the arguments which provide the substance of the present
investigation, but none of them treats the arguments in depth.
Neither have papers in rhetoric dealt with the arguments about the
mass media. As far as I am able to determine, there has been neither
extensive popular treatment nor scholarly examination of the arguments by either historian, social scientist, or rhetorician

Since this study treats popular persuasion over a sixty-five
year period, certain limitations were necessary in the interests
of practicality and manageability. The first such limitation
related to the primary source material. Ideally, a study of this

kind would gather its data from as wide a variety of sources as possible: speeches, pamphlets, newspapers, sermons, books, and magazines. Such a wide range is hardly practical, however, if the study is to cover in depth argument over a number of years. Therefore, the decision was made to focus the investigation on the main stream of discourse as represented in the national periodical press. From Theodore Peterson's Magazines in the Twentieth Century I established a comprehensive list of periodicals ranging from the mass-circulation, general-interest magazines to special-interest, limited-circulation journals. Since nearly all of the magazines on this list were indexed in the Readers' Guide to Periodical Literature, I used the Readers' Guide to find the individual articles from the periodicals on the Peterson list. In a few cases, Readers' Guide also led me to other articles which were especially relevant to the study but which lay outside the periodicals which constituted the principal sources.

Further limits were imposed by the varying interests of the magazines. Many of them did not discuss except occasionally the social effects of movies, radio, and television; they dealt mostly with features about the industries, biographies of stars, reviews of pictures, and so on. Attention was consequently focused on those magazines which did argue about the social impact of the media. In all, some 1000 major articles from seventy different magazines were gathered to form the primary body of material. At least double this number was examined, however, before the final selection was made.

The scope of the study was further limited by eliminating from consideration those articles which dealt primarily with censorship or some form of regulation. That is, arguments about censorship as a solution to the problem of the movies and regulation as a means for controlling radio and television, although interesting in themselves and excellent material for another study were deemed outside the province of this investigation. Similarly arguments about aesthetics, about strictly economic problems within the media, about technical changes (with the exception of the sound picture) are dealt with only incidentally.

This investigation therefore is concerned with arguments about the social influences of the new mass media. The effects of innovation, as viewed by advocates and attackers, is the burden of this paper.

The period of the study is from 1891 through 1955. The opening date was set by Harper's Weekly which announced on June 13 of that year Edison's completion of the motion picture machine. The ending date was chosen arbitrarily. It represents, in a general way, the end of the first major wave of argument about television, climaxed by the report of the Senate Subcommittee on Juvenile Delinquency under the chairmanship of Estes Kefauver. The argument did not end then as current periodicals demonstrate; there was merely a lull in the controversy. The argument about the influence of the mass media remains current, but one has to stop somewhere, and 1955 dates a significant change of phase.

The organization of the study reflects the genres of argument apparent in the discourse. Various patterns of development are available, but the following four divisions seem best to character- ize the bases and methods of argument in this controversy: argument from cause, from comparison, from association, and from definition. In the first chapter I trace in outline the history of the contro- versy through its successive stages both as each medium developed and as one medium succeeded another. In Chapters Two through Eight, as will be evident from the Table of Contents, I present my analyses of the arguments under the four classes named above. In the final chapter I offer my conclusions.

In the interests of completeness and intelligibility in citing the very large number of sources which it has been necessary to use, I have modified the standard forms and practices of footnoting. In general, a single footnote refers to all the sources for material within a given paragraph, except that extended quotations are identi- fied individually. Hence, in a typical paragraph in which an ex- tended quotation and several other references appear, the footnote number for the quotation refers the reader to the source for that quotation. The second footnote number in the paragraph refers to the other articles in which the argument may be found. Hence, a

reader interested in the relative frequency of given arguments
is supplied with an exhaustive list of occurrences. The notes will
be found at the ends of chapters.

Notation of periodicals follows a simple code. HW, 30 Jl '10,
p. 12. refers to Harper's Weekly, July 30, 1910, p. 12. As far as
is practicable, the authors and titles of articles and the sources
for arguments are indicated in the text. Periodical titles are
abbreviated as follows:

AAA	Annals of the American Academy
AC	American City
Amer	America
AmMag	American Magazine
AmMerc	American Mercury
Atlan	Atlantic Monthly
BHG	Better Homes and Gardens
Bookm	Bookman
CC	Christian Century
CCom	Charities and The Commons
Cent	Century
ChgT	Changing Times
CL	Current Literature
CO	Current Opinion
Col	Collier's
Comm	Commonweal
Dial	Dial
Educa	Education
Etude	Etude
EvM	Everybody's Magazine
Forum	Forum
GH	Good Housekeeping
HB	House Beautiful

HM	Harper's (Monthly) Magazine
HW	Harper's Weekly
Ind	Independent
IW	Illustrated World
LA	Living Age
LD	Literary Digest
LHJ	Ladies' Home Journal
Life	Life
Lip	Lippincott's Monthly Magazine
LJ	Library Journal
Mus	Musician
MusAm	Musical America
NAR	North American Review
Nat	Nation
NB	Nation's Business
NC	Nineteenth Century and After
NO	New Outlook
NR	New Republic
Nwk	Newsweek
Out	Outlook
Over	Overland Monthly
ParM	Parents' Magazine
PE	Photo-Era
PMech	Popular Mechanics Magazine
PW	Publisher's Weekly
RD	Reader's Digest
Rot	Rotarian
RR	(The American) Review of Reviews
SA	Scientific American
SAS	Scientific American Supplement
Scrib	Scribner's Magazine
SD	Science Digest
SEP	Saturday Evening Post
SG	Survey Graphic
SNL	Science News Letter
SR	Saturday Review (of Literature)
SS	Senior Scholastic (Scholastic)
SSoc	School and Society

Sur	Survey
TA	Theatre Arts
TM	Theatre Magazine
Time	Time
TW	Technical World
USN	United States News & World Report
WHC	Woman's Home Companion
WT	World Today
WW	World's Work

Notes

1. Leland M. Griffin, "The Anti-Masonic Persuasion: A Study
of Public Address in the American Anti-Masonic Movement, 1826-
1838" (unpublished Ph. D. dissertation, Cornell University, 1950)

2. Donald N. Dedmon, "An Analysis of the Arguments in the
Debate in Congress on the Admission of Hawaii to the Union" (unpublished Ph. D. dissertation, University of Iowa, 1961).

3. Todd G. Willy, "The Agitation in Parliament and England
over Charles George 'Chinese' Gordon and His Mission to the Soudan,
January, 1884, to February, 1885" (unpublished Ph. D. dissertation,
University of Iowa, 1962).

4. Lewis Jacobs, The Rise of the American Film (New York:
Harcourt, Brace and Company, 1939); Terry Ramsaye, A Million and
One Nights (New York: Simon and Schuster, 1926); A. Nicholas Var-
dac, Stage to Screen (Cambridge: Harvard University Press, 1949);
Arthur Knight, The Liveliest Art (New York: Macmillan, 1957);
Llewellyn White, The American Radio (Chicago: University of Chicago
Press, 1947); Sydney Head, Broadcasting in America (Boston: Houghton-
Mifflin, 1956).

5. Raymond Moley, The Hays Office (New York: Bobbs-Merrill,
1945); Murray Schumach, The Face on the Cutting Room Floor (New
York: Morrow, 1964); Walter B. Emery, Broadcasting and Government:
Responsibilities and Regulations (East Lansing: Michigan State
University Press, 1961); Robert Shepard Morgan, "The Television
Code of the National Association of Broadcasters: The First Ten
Years" (unpublished Ph. D. dissertation, University of Iowa, 1964).

6. Alice Miller Mitchell, Children and Movies (Chicago:
University of Chicago Press, 1929); Henry J. Forman, Our Movie Made
Children (New York: Macmillan, 1933); Charles A. Siepmann, Radio,
Television, and Society (New York: Oxford University Press, 1950);
Wilbur Schramm, Television in the Lives of Our Children (Stanford:
Stanford University Press, 1961); Joseph T. Klapper, The Effects
of Mass Communication (Glencoe, Illinois: Free Press, 1960).

7. Theodore B. Peterson, Magazines in the Twentieth Century
(Rev. ed.; Urbana: University of Illinois Press, 1958).

CHAPTER I

HISTORY OF THE CONTROVERSY

The controversy with which this study is concerned begins in 1891 and is traced through 1955. The arguments grow out of the introduction of motion pictures, radio, and television. Since the special emphasis of this investigation is on patterns of argument, and since the study is organized around them rather than chronologically, it is desirable to look to the history of the controversy before beginning the analysis. This chapter, therefore, traces briefly the development of the arguments about the three media. This is not intended to be a history of the media themselves, but rather a history of agitation about them. Hence, particular attention is paid to those events in time and alterations in course which gave rise to argument.

Motion Pictures

The active promotion of motion pictures was begun in the early summer of 1891. In an article for Harper's Weekly of June 13, George Parsons Lathrop, the son-in-law of Nathaniel Hawthorne and a prominent magazine writer of the nineteenth century who had done earlier pieces on Edison's inventions, announced that Edison had invented the kinetograph, a combination of the moving picture machine

and the phonograph. It was, said Lathrop, a device "to set down and
permanently record exact images of men walking, trees waving in the
wind, birds flying, machinery in active operation--in fine, to secure
pictures of any or everything that is going (i. e. in motion), and
then to show us a complete representation of these objects with
their movement, just the same as though we were looking at reality."
Although it was at first necessary to look at the pictures through a
peep-hole, the arrangement was only temporary: "The usual and most
effective manner of using the kinetograph will be to project the
figures from /the7 lens greatly enlarged, upon a screen, where they
may be shown, if need be, as of life size." The uses of the machine
were obvious. It would provide "a great fund of entertainment,"
repeating

> in life-like shadow-play all sorts of dances, the rhythmic
> whirl of ball-rooms, scenes from the theatre, or exciting
> debates in Congress. Military processions, camp scenes,
> street scenes (with their accompanying noise and stir),
> horse races, prize fights, athletic games, famous base-
> ball players batting or catching, college crews swinging
> with a racing stroke in their boat, and the contortions
> of acrobats, will all be material for the kineto-phono-
> graph.[1]

Moving pictures would also be instructive "in sundry directions."
Not only could actors study their own art, but the public might
see for themselves "the majestic tumult of Niagara. . . . a loco-
motive with rods and wheels in full swing of motion. . . . and
the animated presence of far-off peoples!" There was no doubt,

Lathrop concluded, that "the kinetograph may yet play a part of incalculable importance in human life."[2]

This first article, with its emphasis on the dual nature of the moving picture, set the tone for future promotion of the medium. Movies were not merely a new form of amusement, said their advocates, they were also a means for education, a business, an adjunct to the stage, a resource for religion, and a great new social force.

But the movies prospered as amusement. The Columbian Exposition of 1893 featured nickel-in-the-slot movie machines. The Atlanta Exposition of 1895 had projected pictures until the tent burned down. Vaudeville houses began showing short films as part of their programs in 1896. Store front movie houses, some of them "shacks in the rear yard of a tenement" in which "the price of admission and entertainment for from fifteen to twenty minutes is a coin of the smallest denomination in circulation west of the Rockies," catering to immigrants and the "lower classes," were opened after 1899. The Nickelodeon, the movie house whose name became a generic term for the new amusement, opened its doors in Pittsburgh in 1905 and played to standing room only for weeks on end. As many as 100,000 people a day came to the nickelodeons in Chicago in 1907. Pictures, said their promoters, offering "harmless diversion for the poor," were "a nightly amusement ground of the masses. . . . a recreative school for the whole family, . . .

the academy of the working man, his pulpit, his newspaper, his club."[3]

By 1909 the movies were well established; they had taken over as the preeminent national amusement. No longer could they be dismissed merely as entertainment for the masses or simply as cheap diversion. Walter Prichard Eaton, the theatrical critic, put it well when he said that

> when you first reflect that in New York City alone, on a Sunday, 500,000 people go to moving picture shows, a majority of them perhaps children, and that in the poorer quarters of town every teacher testifies that the children now save their pennies for picture shows instead of candy, you cannot dismiss canned drama with a shrug of contempt. It is a big factor in the lives of the masses, to be reckoned with, if possible to be made better, if used for good ends. Eighty percent of present day theatrical audiences in this country are canned drama audiences. Ten million people attended professional baseball games in America in 1908. Four million people attend moving picture theaters, it is said, every day. $50,000,-000 are invested in the industry. Chicago has over 300 theaters, New York 300, St. Louis 205, Philadelphia 186, even conservative Boston boasts more than 30. Almost 190 miles of film are unrolled on the screens of America's canned drama theaters every day in the year. Here is an industry to be controlled, an influence to be reckoned with.[4]

Spokesmen for other amusements were some of the first to complain about the influence of the movies. The pictures had taken over part of the audience for the theatre and were threatening to replace the saloon as the haven of the working man. Even respected institutions which depended upon popular support were reported to be feeling the pinch of the nickelodeon. At the same time, the movies

were labeled dangerous to health. The flickering, scratched films
were hard on the eyes and the ill-ventilated show rooms were harbors
for disease. But these were not the most serious of the complaints.
Above all, movies were held to be immoral. Children, attackers said,
wanted so much to see the pictures that they stole the price of
admission; once inside the theater they were exposed to scenes of
violence and debauchery. From the pictures, audience members not
only learned how to commit crimes but they were inspired to imitate
the deeds they saw on the screen. The moving picture, said one of
its opponents in 1910, "is the crown and summit of all the influences demoralizing the youth of the country today, not even the
saloon being an exception."[5]

There was no organized response in the periodical press to
these attacks. Advocates continued to point to the beneficial
social influences of the movies, to compare them to familiar and
respected social institutions, and to point to their place in "the
education, diversion, and development of a great mass of the people."[6]

The motion picture industry, however, did respond. Motion
picture makers represented by the Motion Picture Patents Company
asked the People's Institute of New York to establish a committee
to preview and approve new films voluntarily submitted to it by
the manufacturers. This committee, known first as the National
Board of Censorship of Motion Pictures and after 1914 as the National

Board of Review, was originally made up of representatives of the
People's Institute, Y. M. C. A., Y. W. C. A., the Children's Aid
Society, Woman's Municipal League, the S. P. C. A., the Purity
League, the W. C. T. U., and various other charitable, civic, and
private organizations interested in the morality of the motion
picture. The National Board began its work in March of 1909.[7]

One of the Board's first tasks was the publication of a list
of subjects to be avoided by film makers. The World To-Day offered
this summary of the prohibitions:

1. All obscene subjects.

2. 'All crime pictures showing gruesome details or tending to
teach the techniques of crime, are voted against. The suggestion
is too strong, even where the picture brings out a strong lesson.
The minds of the young today are too fertile to trust such pictures
to and we believe the same lessons can be shown effectively in
other ways.'

3. 'All suggestive crime, that is, crime like arson or suicide, is
taboo. We do not object to a Shakespearean suicide. But we do
object to a picture which shows a man or woman jumping off the
Brooklyn Bridge into the East River. That picture would possibly
be the cause of several people trying such a leap for themselves.'

4. 'Unmitigated sensationalism and malicious mischief we do not
believe should be exploited. We are not prudes in this direction,
however. We even encourage innocent mischief.'

5. No offense to religion was condoned. Religious films were
not to be censored for historical innaccuracy, however.

6. 'We discourage pictures dealing with the subject of marital
infelicity. But in some cases we do not condemn them. We believe
that the problem play is all right, if it is presented in the
proper manner.'

7. 'Kidnapping pictures we do not like and seldom pass. In New Jersey there is a law against producing them. Also, pictures which show wanton cruelty to animals, even hunting scenes, we cut out, except in remote cases where there is a moral pointed that could not be shown in any other way.'

8. Prize fight films were approved 'if there was nothing extremely brutal shown and where the persons who took part were of a better grade.'

This form of self-regulation of films was labeled by Harper's Weekly

> a stirring example of successful voluntary cooperation between vast business and the ethical sense of the public. It has grown in life with the growth of business. It has not been exacting. The business has prospered and the public has been protected.[9]

The arrangement apparently satisfied the attackers, too, for the argument about morality was abandoned for a time after the establishment of the National Board.

Sound motion pictures were a recurring topic with promoters, particularly Edison, from the beginning of the agitation. Scientific American, for example, reported Edison's intent to demonstrate at the Brooklyn Institute in 1893 a picture machine "by which a moving image is projected on the screen simultaneously with the production by a phonograph of the words or the song which accompany the movements pictured." In the demonstration itself, however, neither was the film projected nor was the sound attachment displayed. Again in 1894 and 1896 Edison told about his plans for sound pictures. In 1908 and 1909, both World To-Day and Photo-Era reported that pictures with phonograph recordings for accompaniment were being used in vaudeville houses, although as _Photo-Era_ said, the results were "grotesque and a travesty of the real thing."[10]

Edison's sound pictures were successfully demonstrated in four New York vaudeville theaters on February 17, 1913. The program consisted of two films. In the first one, remarkably like the first Vitaphone demonstration film thirteen years later, it was reported that "a man discusses with many oratorical flourishes of voice and limb the history and future of the invention, and then illustrates the possibilities of the kinetophone by breaking plates, blowing horns and whistles, and by the introduction of a singer, a pianist, a violinist, and a barking dog." The second film was of a "minstrel troupe in full cry."[11]

On the basis of the demonstration Edison and his representatives predicted that great drama and opera would be taken to the masses, that "the political orator can appeal to thousands while remaining at his own fireside; the world's greatest statesmen, actors and singers can be heard and seen in even the smallest hamlet, not only today, but a hundred years hence." Moreover, the talking picture opened new vistas for the use of films in education. Writers not so certain of the desirability of the invention, however, suggested that "the complete rout of human actors from the stage and the concert hall seems no longer an impossibility."[12]

The sound pictures did not prove to be popular at this time, however, and arguments about them fell victim to the controversy over the white slave films. The release of Traffic in Souls in 1914 and other films on the same theme prompted renewal of the arguments about morality in pictures. This time, however, there was more emphasis on the sexual implications of pictures than there had been in the previous controversy. The work of the National Board of Review was labeled ineffective, and individual states, beginning with Pennsylvania, established their own censorship boards. In addition, there was proposed in 1914 a Federal Motion Picture Commission which would

> license every film submitted to it and intended for
> entrance into inter-state commerce unless it finds that
> such film is obscene, indecent, immoral, or depicts a
> bull-fight or a prize-fight, or is of such a character
> that its exhibition would tend to corrupt the morals
> of children or adults or incite to crime.[13]

This proposal failed when presented to Congress, but the agitation continued. The reaction of the industry was the formation in 1916 of the National Association of the Motion Picture Industry and the creation in 1917 of the Motion Picture Art League with D. W. Griffith as its first chairman. Both organizations served to publicize the position of the film makers and to oppose censorship. With the coming of the First World War, however, arguments both for and against movies disappeared from the periodicals.[14]

After the war, advocates of pictures began again to tell how movies were both entertaining and educational, how they had proved valuable to the church, and how they had helped the war effort. Opponents on the other hand talked about the moral problems of the movies. The agitation, which culminated in the passage of new censorship laws in several states, was accurately characterized as a fight against crime, sex, and nudity in the motion pictures.

The response of the film industry to the renewed calls for censorship and the charges of immorality was the creation of the Motion Picture Producers and Distributors Association, the M. P. P. D. A. Will H. Hays, former Postmaster General, was hired, as a writer for Outlook put it,

> hokum aside--to block additional Governmental supervision, to tame radical spirits among the producers, to prevent trade practices which cause expensive litigation, to use his influence as an important politician of the party in power, and, it is said, to prevent the Actor's Equity Association from organizing motion picture actors and extras.[15]

In his inaugural statement, Hays said his purpose was "the attaining and maintaining, for the motion picture industry, a high educational, moral, and business plane." He stressed particularly the responsibility of the motion picture industry to children, commenting that

> above all . . . is our duty to youth. We must have toward that sacred thing, the mind of a child, toward that clean and virgin thing, that unmarked state--we must have toward that the same sense of responsibility, the same care about

the impression made upon it, that the best teacher, or
the best clergyman, the most inspired teacher of youth,
would have.[16]

Hays became "the buffer between industry and the public," and the

spokesman for the motion picture industry. His office, beginning

in 1922, undertook a vast campaign to better the image of the

motion picture.

The Hays Office campaign stressed the importance of the motion

picture in the national life. Movies were, he argued, a great

institution of service, a national amusement, one of the largest

industries in the country, and "an instrument and means of immeasur-

able education and moral influence." Better pictures were promised.

A committee on Public Relations was founded on which were represented

most of the organizations which had been invited to participate in

the National Board in 1909. The help of civic organizations and

betterment groups was solicited. Parents were reminded of their

responsibility to supervise the movie going of their children and

of their obligation to patronize the better films produced at their

request. In addition, the office drafted and administered the

familiar Motion Picture Production Code, and provided other stra-

tegically timed evidence of self-regulation in practice.[17] The Hays

campaign was successful, for arguments against the motion picture

disappeared from the periodical press for nearly ten years.

Sound pictures were introduced for a second time in 1926. On
the first program, audiences watched a filmed speech by Will Hays,
saw and heard demonstrated the remarkable versatility of the machinery, and watched John Barrymore act Don Juan with printed subtitles
and accompaniment, via Vitaphone, by the New York Philharmonic.
Magazine writers predicted that the new device would revolutionize
movies, bring the greatest actors and actresses to every hamlet,
add a new dimension to education, and spread culture across the land.
Others said Vitaphone would kill the silents, destroy the art of
pantomime, halt the artistic development of the motion picture, and
ruin the stage. Public response, at first, was lukewarm. The next
year, on October 6, 1927, Al Jolson opened in The Jazz Singer and
the talkie was established. The silents were dead by 1930.[18]

The Hays Office campaigns and the distractions provided by the
introduction of the talking pictures gave the industry a respite
from published attack on the morality of films. The publication
in 1929, however, of Alice Miller Mitchell's Children and Movies,
a study of the influence of motion pictures in the lives of 10,052
Chicago children, served as the catalyst for new attacks. Reform
groups, never satisfied with the work of the Hays Office and never
convinced that movies had truly reformed, renewed the arguments
which had lain idle for nearly a decade and embellished them with
new evidence.

In January of 1930, Christian Century began a campaign to clean up the films. The principal writer for this series, and the series three years later, was Fred Eastman, Professor of Religious Literature and Drama, Chicago Theological Seminary. In some of the most vituperative attacks since the first decade of the century, Eastman argued that motion pictures dealt too much with crime and sex, corrupted youth, and misrepresented the United States abroad. Naming the movies a menace to the mental and moral life of America, Christian Century called for support of legislation to establish a federal motion picture commission to supervise production, to revise the block booking system, and to give the State Department the power to preview all films sent abroad. By October of 1931, Christian Century reported, some forty national religious and educational groups had adopted resolutions calling for some form of federal regulation, which Christian Century called "social control," of the motion pictures. None of the bills or resolutions to control the movies was reported out of committee, however.

The year 1933 was marked by the publication of the Payne Fund studies of motion pictures and youth, by the formation of the Legion of Decency, and a new campaign by Christian Century. The second crusade by Christian Century was based, for the most part, on Henry James Forman's Our Movie Made Children, a popular summary of the individual Payne Fund monographs. Arguing that movies were

the cause of crime, delinquency, and sexual misconduct among youth,
Eastman provided his readers with vivid and spectacular examples
of moral lapses caused by the motion picture. At the same time,
the Legion of Decency campaign was joined by the Federal Council of
Churches of Christ in America and by the Central Conference of
Jewish Rabbis. The battle for movie morality was carried on by
the Legion of Decency after the Christian Century attacks tapered
off, but the work of the Legion was never given extensive coverage
in the general periodicals nor were their arguments widely publicized.

The motion picture industry, through the Hays Office, reacted
to the Legion of Decency campaign, which was called grim, business-
like, and effective, by creating a Production Code Administration
headed by Joseph Breen. It was Breen's task to supervise all motion
pictures from scenario through final release, a solution proposed
by the reform groups as a federal function. From Breen's office
in Hollywood were issued certificates of approval, 1115 of them
the first year, attesting to the moral purity of the Hollywood
products.[19]

The arguments about the effects of motion pictures subsided
after 1935. Movies continued to be a major form of public entertainment, but they inspired little sustained controversy after that.
There were occasional disputes, as when gangster pictures were

revived in the late 1930's and when The Outlaw was re-released in
1946, but never was the argument so bitter or so long lasting as
in the earlier agitation.

The latest argument about the movies began after the advent
of television. Here, however, the concern was about the impact
of innovation on the motion picture industry, and not about the
influences of movies in society. The focus of the argument had
shifted. The new concern was television.

Radio

The second of the new media to be introduced was radio. Its
practicality having been demonstrated by Marconi in 1895, radio
telegraphy, wireless, was brought into the United States in 1899
as a new method for point-to-point and ship-to-shore communication.
In that year, Scientific American commented on the medium as a method
for communication and predicted that it would be valuable in prevent-
ing collisions at sea. By 1902 there were reports of radio telephony, voice communication, having been used to span distances up
to three miles. Radio at this stage was considered only a medium
for communication, and this view of it was typical of the periodical
press for the next two decades. Most of the writers who talked about
broadcasting referred to it only as a method for establishing voice
communication between distant points when wired circuits were unavailable.[20]

A few people, however, speculated about radio broadcasting as something more than a communication service. One of the first of these was Lee DeForest, who in 1906 had broadcast the opening night of the Metropolitan Opera with Caruso singing _Cavalleria Rusticana_. _Review of Reviews_ reported this summary of DeForest's ideas about radio in 1907:

> The great and universal appreciation of music reproduced by gramophone, telharmonium, or other device has suggested to Dr. DeForest that radio-telephony has also a field in the distribution of music from a central station, such as an opera house. By installing a wireless telephone transmission station on the roof, the music of singers and orchestra could be supplied to all subscribers who would have aerial wires on or near their homes. The transmission stations for such music would be tuned to an entirely different wave length from that used for any other form of wave telegraph or telephone transmission, and the inventor believes that by using four different forms of waves as many classes of music can be sent out as desired by the different subscribers.[21]

In 1913, a writer for _Collier's_ told how the wireless telephone might be used "to distribute news and messages of all sorts from central stations to an enormous number of subscribers." Not only that, but

> we shall talk with our friends at sea or from sea to land, or from New York to Peking almost as freely as we now talk to our neighbors in the next block. An opera performance in London or Berlin will be caught by this new transmitter set about the stage and thrown into the air for all the world to hear.[22]

The most complete development of this view of radio broadcasting was articulated in 1916 by David Sarnoff, then assistant traffic

manager for American Marconi in New York. In his "music box memo"
Sarnoff spoke of a radio receiver for home use, operating on several
wave lengths, which could be used to pick up music and for

> receiving lectures at home, which can be made perfectly
> audible. Also events of national importance could be
> simutaneously announced and received.
>   Baseball scores could be transmitted in the air by
> the use of one set installed in the Polo Grounds. The
> same would be true of other cities. This proposition
> would be especially interesting to farmers and others
> living in outlying districts removed from cities. By
> the purchase of a radio music box they could enjoy con-
> certs, lectures, recitals which might be going on in the
> nearest city within their radius.[23]

The line of development predicted by these writers led to
commercial radio broadcasting. Their comments about the possible
uses of the medium accurately foreshadowed not only the form radio
was to take but also the lines of advocacy undertaken by its promoters.

Broadcasting as we know it is commonly dated from KDKA's
coverage of the Harding-Cox election returns on November 2, 1920,
although several stations were on the air before that. The periodical
press took occasional note of news, weather reports, and time signals on the air in 1919, but the promotion of broadcasting did not
begin until 1921. In June of that year, Scientific American told
of the programs carried by the Westinghouse station.

> Concerts are given nightly from this station, and they
> are heard over an area of three million square miles.
> In this territory there are hundreds of thousands of
> persons who hear these concerts. The program for the

> evening usually consists, in the main, of phonograph
> music and national and international news. . . . The
> program for each night is carefully considered and a
> selection is made of instrumental and vocal, classical
> and popular /music/.24

Moreover, there were church services to be heard on Sundays and

whenever possible, speeches by prominent men. The programs were

already good, said the writer of the article, L. H. Rosenberg, but

they were going to be even better.

> Soon in radio you will be able to get popular music
> if you desire, or classical music, or church services,
> or speeches, or crop reports or news. These will all
> be sent out at the same time, and it will merely be a
> question of 'looking in the proper direction' for the
> reception of your choice.25

For the next two years the national press carried frequent

articles about "that greatest of all public services of the new

era--the radiophone broadcasting of education, culture and democ-

racy." These articles, like the one noted above, explored the

vast potential of radio. Its advocates told how broadcasting would

bring a variety of material into the home, how it was already being

used by schools and churches, how it would end isolation and unify

the nation. Radio was named second only to the movies as the new

national amusement, and, like movies, radio educated while it

entertained. Advocates promised that "news, entertainment, music,

culture, education, everything that can be made available will

literally be on the air, ours for the taking."26

At the same time, advocates offered reassurance that familiar institutions, other forms of communication, and tradition itself were safe from the encroachment of broadcasting. Innovation, they argued, would not be damaging to familiar things. Still, however, some writers expressed their fears that radio would take audiences away from other amusements, that the church would find its congregations shrinking, that newspapers would be faced with new competition from the broadcasting of news. Radio, said those suspicious of innovation, was but another complicating and disrupting force in society.

The use of radio in the national political campaigns of 1924 provided a new basis for assessment of the medium. Prediction tapered off, and the periodicals turned to evaluation. Radio, said its friends, was shown by experience to be a valuable instrument for politics; radio, said its enemies, was dangerous, not only to politics but to other institutions as well. With the coming of each new campaign, the argument about broadcasting and politics was renewed. The arguments about radio and other institutions were equally repetitive.

A second recurrent theme in the evaluation of radio was introduced in 1924: program quality was said to be falling short of the standards promised by advocates in their promotion of the medium. For the next twenty years there was a persistent murmur of discontent about the quality of radio's offerings. Broadcasting, for the

most part, was a medium for entertainment. Never did radio work
as well for culture, for education, or for enlightenment as critics
thought it should or as promoters said it would.

Related to the complaints about program quality were arguments
about advertising. The growing commericalism of broadcasting
after 1924 provided fuel for the attack. Stuart Chase, for example,
complained in 1928 about the use of radio for direct advertising
messages. Radio, he said, "is trying to live on advertising, and
being poisoned by it." Other writers, including Lee DeForest,
voiced frequent complaints about the use of radio for commercial
purposes over the years.[27] This was another of the recurrent themes
in the agitation over broadcasting.

Spokesmen for broadcasting responded periodically to the complaints of the opposition. Advocates' answers, like the charges
which prompted them, are to be found spaced throughout the agitation. The flurries of controversy is some cases were related to
significant changes in the structure of broadcasting, the formation
of networks for example, but most commonly advocates responded to
the charges of the critics. In the main, defenders spoke to the
present uses of radio in public service, education, culture, and
entertainment, and predicted an even better day to come. Radio,
they said, complemented society's values and strengthened its
institutions. The future, however, would be even better than the
present.

Questions about regulation and censorship of broadcasting were raised occasionally, but were never major topics in the agitation. From the beginning, the federal government had undertaken to grant licenses to broadcasters and to assign them frequencies. Both advocates and critics viewed this function as one of maintaining order, and so apparently accepted the role of the government without strenuous complaint. The radio acts of 1927 and 1934, for instance, inspired comment in the periodicals, but neither was the cause for serious controversy. Moreover, radio, perhaps taking warning from the example of the movies, avoided the kinds of sex themes which had brought about the frequent calls for censorship of the earlier medium. Radio, however, was attacked in 1933, 1937, and 1945 for its treatment of crime and violence, particularly in the children's programs.

In March of 1933, at the same time motion pictures were being indicted on the basis of the Payne Fund reports, a group of mothers in Scarsdale, New York, objected to 35 of the 40 current children's shows on the grounds that the programs had a harmful effect on the emotions of the young listeners.[28] The attack was soon extended by other writers to include objections to the programs' emphasis on crime. After formal complaints about the programs were published by such organizations as the American Legion Auxiliary and branches of the various Child Study Associations, the networks revised their policy for children's programming, suspended some of the objectionable programs, and the attack subsided.

The attack was renewed in 1937, and this and the third wave of argument in 1945 emphasized the influence of the crime programs on the behavior of children. The 1937 attack focused on the "blood and thunder" programs and for the first time labeled their effects a problem of morality. Objections were raised at this time, too, to the aura of commercialism that surrounded the "juvenile radio racket." The arguments which began in 1945 stressed the influence of radio as a cause of juvenile delinquency.[29] Here radio was charged with providing youth with both method and inspiration for criminal acts. In the later period the networks again responded by eliminating the programs which were most attacked, and the argument in the periodicals ended in 1947.

After the Second World War, the periodicals which formerly talked about radio were taken up mostly with articles about television. As had happened with motion pictures, the focus of the argument about radio shifted; concern was voiced that radio would be supplanted by television. The topics which had characterized the agitation about radio were transferred to television.

Television

Primitive forms of television, devices for sending still and moving pictures by wire, were given occasional attention in the periodical press in the last years of the nineteenth century and in the first decade of the twentieth.[30] It was not until 1912, however, that a form of television resembling the one we know today was proposed. S. C. Gilfillan, writing in Independent, told of the "electric theater," a system of distributing motion pictures into the home over telephone lines. With such a device, he said, "a whole nation will be able actually to see an inauguration, a launching, a ball game, or a first performance." Education, culture, art, and entertainment would be brought into the home. But such advantages would not be achieved without cost.

> To make room for its own life the home theater will strike right and left among our institutions. The theaters and nickelodiums /sic7, of course, and orchestras, will almost all go, as already the melodrama houses have been practically abolished by the 'pictures.' The novel and the short story will fall from their pinnacle, the all-story magazines are already feeling the motion pictures' competition. The schoolhouse Edison is preparing to invade with his educational films--how far will these replace the teacher when to sight are added speaking and color, depth and perfection? What about churches, the rural ones especially, in competition with national churches which offer glorious music and the best preachers in the land? What will happen to our political forms when a candidate must appeal directly to all the electorate, revealing his personality by his close range appearance and normal voice? Will representative government survive this nation-wide extension of the neighborhood in which a man can be known?[31]

In twenty years, said Gilfillan, the country would know, for by then
the home theater would be as familiar as the telephone.

The first general promotion of television began ten years
after the Gilfillan article appeared, and extended for another
fifteen years. During this time various new television systems
were introduced, discussed, and evaluated. In April of 1927, for
example, a television demonstration via a wire system was conducted
by Bell Laboratories. Part of the test consisted of a speech by
Secretary of Commerce Herbert Hoover which was originated in Washington and viewed in New York. Scientific American was pleased with
the performance of the medium because "all facial characteristics,
the play of emotions and in fact every detail at the Washington
terminal were plainly seen by the watchers in New York." In 1928
C. Francis Jenkins claimed to be broadcasting "radio movies" on the
air every Monday, Wednesday, and Friday evening. By 1932, Review of
Reviews claimed, there were twenty stations broadcasting television
programs. Scientific American, however, said television was not
yet practical mainly because most screens were little larger than
a postage stamp. In 1936 the BBC went on the air with a regular
schedule of television programs, and RCA demonstrated its latest
camera system. In May of 1938 Time reported that NBC was on the
air several hours a week with television programs. New York University used a closed circuit television system for a lecture-

demonstration in science at the beginning of the new school year.
In 1939 television was used to open the New York World's Fair. The
age of television, said some, had begun.[32]

These demonstrations and experiments with the medium prompted
supporters of television to speak in glowing terms of its future.
David Sarnoff, for example, told in 1926 about a new development
in radio. "We call it television. At present we hear by radio.
But the time will come when we shall also see by radio." Like many
others in this early period, Sarnoff considered television a natural
extension of radio, and not a new or separate medium. It was therefore his opinion that when television arrived, "we shall have
reached the Golden Age of radio broadcasting, the day when not only
the human voice but also the image of the speaker can be flashed
through space." Other promoters predicted that television would
bring grand opera, theatre, sports, political events, educational
talks and demonstrations, and advertising into the home. As Jenkins
said after his demonstration of radio movies in 1928, "By the next
presidential election in 1932 men and women from Maine to California
can, in the comfort of their homes, watch the face of the President
elect as he delivers his inaugural address." Ten years later,
Gilbert Seldes promised that television would bring into the home
in the next year or so "a blackboard for the mathematician, a
laboratory for the chemist, a picture gallery for the art critic,

and possibly a stage upon which the historian can reenact the events
of the past, or a news commentator the headlines of today." Television was named "the most fantastic of all the scientific miracles,"
the ultimate goal of communication.[33]

While promoters spoke of the prospects for the medium, other
writers warned that the new device could damage the theatre, inter-
rupt the growth of movies, and destroy radio. In 1928, for example,
Lee DeForest called the predictions of almost immediate television
"the veriest bunk," and said that "in the interest of fact, common
sense, and on behalf of theater owners and sincere purveyors of
motion-picture entertainment, some of whom are actually panicky
concerning the future, such pipe dreams should be conscientiously
discouraged." On the other hand, Seldes commented that when television did arrive radio manufacturers "will be trying to sell electric light bulbs and kerosene lamps over the same counter."[34] Promoters responded with assurances that television would neither
damage nor displace the amusements and institutions with which
people were familiar.

For a time after the introduction of television at the World's
Fair, its spokesmen, presuming that the medium was underway, undertook to evaluate its accomplishments. Saturday Evening Post, for
example, asked in a major article, "Now what can we do with television?" and others told about the television programs which were

then on the air. In February 1940, the FCC authorized limited

commercial operation of television for the purposes of further

experimentation and field testing. By the fall of 1940, however,

it was apparent that TV was not catching on as rapidly as its

promoters had said it would. Not many people had bought receivers,

and the ones who had them were reported to be dissatisfied with the

limited number of programs available and with the program quality.

As Saturday Evening Post said, "Too much prophecy has made the

magic box something of an anti-climax." In May 1941, the FCC

authorized full commercial operation of television. There were

six stations on the air and about 10,000 receivers in use when

the Second World War began. Most of the technical work on tele-

vision was curtailed and the manufacturing of sets was suspended

after early 1942. But even before the war began, some of the

periodicals, Saturday Review among them, were beginning to ask

what had happened to the new medium for which so much had been

promised.35

From 1942 until the middle of 1947 the promotion of television

depended principally upon predictions about the future of the

medium. Writers talked of the many areas of the national life

in which TV might serve, of the many good things it would bring

into the home, and of the kinds of programs people might expect

after the war. Set manufacturing was resumed following the war,

new stations began to go on the air, and by 1946 from twenty to forty
hours of programming a week were available in New York, Chicago,
Philadelphia, Washington, and Los Angeles. In July of 1947, Nation's
Business reported that the television boom which had been predicted
for the last eight years had arrived.[36]

The argument turned to evaluation in 1948, the year which
marked the emergence of television as a mass medium and the beginning of the FCC freeze on new station construction. Speculation
about the impact of television on other amusements, on business,
on social life, on education, on health, on society's institutions
and its values became a national pastime. Friends of the medium
claimed it helped all of the things people held dear. Opponents
warned that what served good could also serve evil, and told how
television had hurt radio, conversation, reading, and the patterns
of family living. The tone of the argument was investigative,
exploratory, and evaluative. In general, the comments, if not
wholly laudatory, were at least friendly to the medium.

The denunciation of television began in 1949. Reinhold Niebuhr,
the theologian, was one of the first to comment. The immediate
effect of television, he said, will be "a further vulgarization
of our culture. . . . Much of what is still wholesome in our life
will perish under the impact of this new visual aid." Gilbert
Seldes warned that TV was going the way of the media of the past.

Television's great ingenuity and technical capacity was wasted,
for the substance of its offerings was "stale, unrewarding, contrived, and imitative banality." The strongest of all the attacks,
however, came from Norman Cousins in Saturday Review for December 24,
1949. It was his contention that out of this "most magnificient of
all forms of communication, . . . the supreme triumph of invention,
the dream of the ages" has come "such an assault against the human
mind, such a mobilized attack on the imagination, such an invasion
against good taste as no other communications medium has known, not
excepting the motion picture or radio itself." Television, moreover,
had become a prime mover "in juvenile misconduct and delinquency."
It was Cousins' conclusion that "in any event, all speculations
over the future of television must begin with the hard truth that
right now it is being murdered in the cradle."37

For the next five years the patterns of the argument were
similar to those we have observed in the other media. Friends of
television pointed to its potential in education, politics, religion,
culture, and entertainment. Attackers charged that its entertainment, if not harmful, was plodding and dull; its culture nonexistent;
its service to religion and education negligible; and its influence
in politics damaging. Crime and violence, said its enemies, were
television's mainstays, and children its victims. Television, like
movies and radio before it, was at the same time praised and damned.

Although motion pictures, radio, and television developed over the span of half a century, the patterns of agitation surrounding them are similar. All were introduced with glowing predictions. Promoters promised that the new inventions would make possible the brave new world for which men were presumed to seek. Opponents at the same time resisted innovation on the grounds of possible dangers arising from the coming of the new. Progress, at this stage in the controversy, was opposed with tradition, the uncertainty of the future was weighed against the security of the present.

With the media in operation, both advocates and opponents turned to evaluation. The performance of the new inventions was tested against the predictions made about them. Moreover, the media were assessed on the basis of what the arguers perceived their effects to be. Writers for both sides referred to the same topics: education, culture, politics, health, religion, and entertainment. Judgments about the new media were made on the basis of their real or supposed influences on things and ideas society held to be good and valuable.

I referred above to the stages of the argument. In general, prediction came first, followed by evaluation. This pattern was repeated not only in the introductions of the media themselves, but whenever new developments arose within a given medium. For

example, when a new method of sound recording was introduced, writers
first talked about it predictively and turned later to evaluation.
This movement through stages, apparently, is typical of argument
about innovation. This, however, is but one of the patterns apparent
in the total agitation over motion pictures, radio, and television.
Others are examined in the chapters which follow.

Notes

1. HW, 13 Je 1891, p. 447.

2. HW, 13 Je 1891, pp. 446-447. For a discussion of Edison's development and promotion of the motion picture machine see: Gordon Hendricks, The Edison Motion Picture Myth (Berkeley: University of California Press, 1961).

3. WW, F '11, p. 14020; HW, 24 Ag '07, p. 1246; CCom, 8 Je '07, p. 295; WT, O '08, p. 1053. For a discussion of the growth of the motion picture see: Terry Ramsaye, "The Rise and Place of the Motion Picture," Mass Communications, ed. Wilbur Schramm (Urbana: University of Illinois Press, 1960), pp. 24-38; Lewis Jacobs, The Rise of the American Film (New York: Harcourt, Brace and Company, 1939), pp. 3-21, 52-66.

4. AmMag, S '09, p. 498.

5. GH, Ag '10, p. 184.

6. HW, 16 S '11, p. 6.

7. WT, O '10, p. 1135.

8. WT, O '10, pp. 1136-1137.

9. HW, 19 D '14, p. 577.

10. SA, 20 My 1893, p. 310; CO, My 1894, p. 442; CL, Jl 1896, p. 78; NAR, S 1896, p. 377; WT, O '08, p. 1052; PE, N '09, p. 228.

11. Out, 8 Mr '13, p. 517; TW, Mr '13, pp. 16-21.

12. TW, Mr '13, p. 20; CO, Ap '13, p. 297; Lip, Ag '13, p. 194.

13. Out, 20 Je '14, p. 388.

14. CO, Mr '17, p. 185.

15. Out, 11 Ap '28, p. 576.

16. Out, 11 Ap '28, p. 576.

17. RR, Ja '23, p. 65; NAR, D '39, p. 506.

18. SA, Jl '26, pp. 53-54; Out, 18 Ag '26, p. 526; SA, S '26, p. 209.

19. Nwk, 17 Ag, '35, pp. 16-17; NAR, D '39, pp. 505-506. For the Christian Century campaigns see: CC, 15 Ja '30, pp. 75-78, and following issues of the periodical until March 1934. For a discussion of censorship and the Legion of Decency see: Ruth Inglis, Freedom of the Movies (Chicago: University of Chicago Press, 1947).

20. SA, 1 Jl 1899, p. 5; SA, 19 Jl '02, p. 37; SA, 15 My '15, p. 450; SA, 15 My '20, p. 540; RR, My '19, p. 500; LD, 28 Je '19, p. 25; Ind, 5 Jl '19, p. 11. For a discussion of the growth of radio in the United States see: Llewellyn White, "The Growth of American Radio," Mass Communications, ed. Wilbur Schramm (Urbana: University of Illinois Press, 1960), pp. 39-42; Sydney W. Head, Broadcasting in America (Boston: Houghton-Mifflin, 1956), pp. 91-124.

21. RR, Je '07, p. 685. See also: SEP, 30 Je '28, p. 10.

22. Col, 25 O '13, pp. 22-23.

23. SEP, 7 Ag '26, p. 145.

24. SA, 4 Je '21, p. 449.

25. SA, 4 Je '21, p. 449.

26. Col, 8 Ap '21, p. 4; LD, 10 Je '22, p. 27.

27. Out, 18 Ap '21, p. 619; NR, 3 F '47, p. 10.

28. Nwk, 11 Mr '33, p. 30; LD, 18 Mr '33, p. 32.

29. Nwk, 8 N '37, p. 26; AmMerc, 6 Jl '38, pp. 294-296; Rot, N '38, pp. 11-12, 59-60; BHG, N '45, p. 23.

30. RR, Jl 1898, p. 93; RR, Jl '07, p. 98.

31. Ind, 17 O '12, p. 890.

32. SA, Je '27, p. 385; PMech, N '28, p. 822; RR, Ja '32, p. 44; SA, My '32, p. 284; Nat, N '36, p. 567; Time, 23 My '38, p. 25; SSoc, 1 O '38, p. 431; Col, 18 Mr '39, p. 12.

33. AmMag, Mr '26, p. 170; SEP, 27 Jl '29, p. 12; Atlan, My '37, p. 539; Scrib, Jl '29, p. 1.

34. PMech, N '28, p. 822; Atlan, My '37, p. 531.

35. SEP, 20 My '39, p. 20; SEP, 6 My '39, p. 8; Col, 18 My '39, pp. 12-13; SEP, 28 S '40, p. 24; SR, 21 F '42, pp. 3-4.

36. Nat, 30 N '46, p. 618; NB, Jl '47, p. 37.

37. Time, 7 F '49, p. 70; Atlan, Mr '49, p. 36; SR, 24 D '49, p. 20.

CHAPTER II

ARGUMENT FROM CAUSE: VALUES

Advocacy

Statements intended to change men's minds, it has been pointed
out a number of times in the past, must proceed from those things
the men addressed already believe. That is, effective argument is
necessarily related to the auditor's value system, those shared
judgments about what is "good and bad, right and wrong, desirable
and undesirable, pleasant and unpleasant, worthwhile and worthless,
efficacious and non-efficacious, allowable or non-allowable, beautiful or non-beautiful, adequate or inadequate, promising or non-
promising."[1] Since the introduction of the new mass media promised
both advantage and threat to the established order, the arguments
growing out of innovation, as should be expected, were strongly tied
to society's prevailing values.

Advocates and attackers alike sought to demonstrate that motion
pictures, then radio, and finally television were related, either
beneficially or harmfully, to those things and ideas which were commonly held to be necessary, worthwhile, and desirable. Often, the
values, while implicit in the foundation of the argument, were not
exposed to immediate view. Rather, they served as the presumptions
upon which the argument was grounded, the reference points in the
belief system, but were not explicit in the argument itself. For

instance, it might be presumed that a knowledge of their world, a

consequence of education, is desirable for all children; the immediate

argument, however, relates to television's facility for showing scenes

of historic interest. At other times, the argument depended upon the

establishment of a close, clear, direct, and causal connection

between innovation and some part of the value structure. Here the

statement of the value system became an explicit part of the argument,

as when motion pictures were asserted to be an important new means

for education.

In the four chapters following I shall deal with arguments

which depended upon this direct, explicit connection between inno-

vation and value. First to be considered will be those arguments

which suggested that innovation would in some way benefit, extend,

strengthen, or enhance the accepted values. Such arguments are

exemplified by the assertion that radio will extend democracy. Then,

in Chapter Three, I will explore those arguments which were employed

to demonstrate various dangers to the value system growing out of

innovation. Here will be found, for example, statements which con-

nected the new media with a rising crime rate. In Chapters Four

and Five I will discuss arguments which pointed to a causal con-

nection between innovation and the institutions which society had

established to realize the value system. Such relationships as the

impact of the media on the schools, the effect of innovation on the church, and the changes in the political structure fostered by the new mass media will be considered in these chapters.

Two characteristics of the arguments treated in this section need to be pointed out before beginning. First, the arguments are causal. If the causal connections were not made explicit by promoters or critics, they were clearly implied, for writers on both sides were concerned with the impact of innovation on the value system. The new media were presumed to influence the body of beliefs and concepts which formed the working basis of this society. Second, the values are frequently expressed vaguely, are referred to in abstractions, and lose their force when made explicit and precise. Hence the argument often is cast in god and devil terms which elude rigid definition, but which generate contexts of meanings which in turn serve to characterize the value which the writer sought to express. When the argument shifts from the values themselves to the institutions, much of the clarity is restored, for the notion of "teaching in the public schools" permits much more satisfactory definition than does the concept of education.

Entertainment

Motion pictures, radio, and television are, in popular terms, the mass media of entertainment. Public response to them in this capacity has been spectacular. Hence, it would be sensible to expect that the new media would be introduced and defended on the basis of

their unusual capabilities as mass entertainers. In reality, however,
though it was common for promoters to describe the media in terms
of the entertainment offered, they were notably hesitant to depend
upon arguments from entertainment alone. Never was entertainment
for its own sake--that is, the presentation of material solely for
the amusement of the audience and for no other purpose--used as the
foundation of the defense. Never did advocates argue that simply
because the media offered amusement and diversion they were valuable
in society.

This is not to say that entertainment, as one function of the
media, was ignored. Various writers talked of the amusement to be
found in motion pictures, on radio, or on television. In fact, the
article in Harper's Weekly which introduced the motion picture spoke
of the possibilities of the combined picture machine and phonograph
for both instruction and entertainment. Speaking of the latter
the author, George Parsons Lathrop, said that

> the resources /the kinetograph/ opens in the way simply
> of amusement are very large. Mr. Edison's minute inch
> and half-inch photographs reproduce in action every little
> muscular movement of the face, can show people laughing,
> smiling, crying, and so may be used to exhibit the gestures
> and changing facial expressions of orators, humorists, and
> actors. By means of them, too, we shall be able to repeat
> in life-like shadowplay all sorts of dances, the rhythmic
> whirl of ballrooms, scenes from the theatre, or exciting
> debates in Congress. Military processions, camp scenes,
> street scenes (with their accompanying noise and stir),
> horse races, prize fights, athletic games, famous baseball
> players batting or catching, college crews swinging with
> a racing stroke in their boat, and the contortions of acro-
> bats, will all be material for the kineto-phonograph. And

even the kinetograph alone, by presenting some of these
things in the dumb-show, without voices, holds itself
a great fund of entertainment.[2]

When pictures became popular fifteen years later, they were

described as a new form of dramatic entertainment, a great contri-

bution to amusement, and the nightly amusement ground of the masses.

Later, following the First World War, movies were said to be "a

great American Institution . . . our pre-eminent national amusement,"

an invention which had "thrown open the prison doors of domesticity"

and released the American public to new-found amusement.[3] When Will

Hays undertook to defend the picture industry he emphasized its

place as entertainer. Writing in 1927 Hays said that

the importance of motion pictures is measured by the
imperative necessity of entertainment for the people.
    Accepted almost as a habit, motion pictures have
become the chief amusement of the great majority and
the sole amusement of millions.
    . . . .

    We do not make any mistake about the importance
of amusement. The demand for entertainment and recreation is as old as man. It is natural, it is right,
and to combat it is to oppose nature.[4]

Radio was also introduced as a new entertainer. Even early in

the century, when the possibilities of radio were only speculative,

DeForest suggested that sometime in the future it might be possible

to send out music from a central radio station, thus furnishing to

the home musical entertainment of a type never before possible. Some

fifteen years later, with radio broadcasting an actuality, the new

medium was described as providing "both useful information and a

varied program of entertainment."[5] From then on, nearly every writer

who discussed the place of radio in society mentioned, at least in
passing, its function as an entertainer.

Television too, was named as a new means for amusement. S. C.
Gilfillan predicted in 1912 that a form of television which depended
on telephone wires for distribution might revolutionize entertainment
by bringing plays, speeches, lectures, music, or dance into the
home. In 1913 another writer promised that the time was not far
off when music, plays, and pictures would be broadcast from central
television stations to enormous numbers of subscribers. A similar
theme was stressed in 1929, when The Saturday Evening Post carried
a report of the spectacular entertainment--theatrical performances
and grand opera--which would be available to the public with the
coming of television. R. E. Sherwood predicted in Scribner's that
within five years the entire evening's entertainment would be
presented on television. Television was to be "the magic eye that
could bring the wonders of entertainment, information, and education
into the living room."[6]

Despite the frequency with which entertainment was mentioned
in connection with the media, and despite the public's willing
acceptance of the entertainment offered, advocates considered entertainment the weakest justification of the new devices. Characteristically, in the discussion of the media entertainment was named as only
one of the ends of the innovation. Usually entertainment was linked

with some more comfortably acceptable end such as education. Just
as television was described as bringing "entertainment, information,
and education," into the living room, so the earlier media were most
·commonly said to provide "entertainment and education," "entertainment and culture," "entertainment and instruction." Thus the most
common function of the media could be recognized, and at the same
time they could be given stature by reference to other praiseworthy
ends.

Unquestionably, there existed a deep-seated suspicion of entertainment as a worthwhile product of the mass media. Various comments
illuminate an underlying attitude, perhaps a reflection of Puritan
tradition, which forced advocates to avoid relying primarily upon the
value of entertainment. For example, in 1912 the editor of The
Independent, having described motion pictures as a new form of
drama, a new method of journalism, a means for scientific invention
"comparable in importance to the telescope and microscope," concluded that "it is wrong to regard such an instrument as this as a
mere means of entertainment." Likewise, the editor of Current
Opinion, writing ten years later, claimed that the potential power
of one of the greatest social forces in America, the motion picture,
was almost entirely wasted because not five per cent of the films
were anything more than entertainment.[7] In 1938, the film critic
for the New York Times was quoted in The Christian Century as saying
that

the pictures highest in quality . . . are those which are
providing something beyond entertainment . . .. If a great
industry with the inherent power and virility of the movies
devotes its talents 'hollowly to the task of being insip-
idly entertaining,' it may succeed only in making an ass
of itself.[8]

Even the animated cartoon was subject to the prescription that the

mass media should do more than merely entertain. A writer for

Scribner's, having described the complexity of cartoon production,

argued that

it is high time that someone in authority should perceive
the possibilities of this marvelous and practically unused
new medium and emancipate it from the narrow limits of the
merely funny, the groove in which it happened to start and
the one in which it has been running ever since. There are
a thousand other directions which it might as easily ramify
--toward knowledge, toward beauty, toward social satire,
symbol, and allegory, or pure imaginative fantasy like
'Little Nemo in Slumberland,' in contradistinction to the
warmed-over fantasy of Grimm and Mother Goose . . .. But
the only use which has been made of this medium thus far
is as a vehicle for slap-stick comedy.[9]

Other comments indicate that radio and television, too, were

expected to do more than entertain if they were to be acceptable.

A writer quoted in The Review of Reviews, for example, observed

that to serve the public interest, convenience, and necessity (the

touchstones of the radio act of 1934), radio would have to give the

nation something that would help solve the practical problems of

everday life, and not just entertainment. Charles Siepmann, writing

at the beginning of the Second World War, said that radio, in order

to live up to the responsibility thrust upon it in wartime, and in

order to prepare for the new responsibilities which would come with peace, must learn that "to provide distraction for a weary world is not enough."[10]

Television had been preceded by some twenty years of prediction which promised that this ultimate means of communication would not only be amusing but would serve society in ways never before dreamed possible. The expectation that TV would do more than merely entertain was made explicit in a 1951 statement from FCC Commissioner Frieda Hennock, who said that

> television can do either tremendous good or incalculable harm. In five years, Americans have bought more than 10 million television sets. TV has quickly won the public's fancy and has literally captured the imagination of our children. In their interest, we must see to it that this powerful medium is also used for cultural advancement --for education as well as entertainment.[11]

Recognizing that any invention which was introduced as serving principally to entertain would be viewed with suspicion, advocates either avoided naming entertainment as a worthy single end of the mass media or sought to demonstrate that while the media did serve to amuse, the recreation was socially useful. That is, promoters argued that movies, radio, and television brought entertainment to groups formerly denied amusement, improved the quality of existing entertainment, or made recreation democratic.

The mass audience entertained

Since motion pictures could be distributed widely with ease, cost the consumer little to attend, and were highly popular with audiences, they were therefore named a new means for entertainment of the mass audience, the lower classes of society for whom organized, commercial amusements had not been available before. As long as the mass audience remained in favor, the argument retained its popularity.

It was presumed during the two decades preceding the First World War that mass audiences should be provided with organized and socially acceptable entertainment, and that the new moving pictures provided the means. Films, said the Superintendent of the Chicago Relief and Aid Society in 1907, fulfilled the need for amusement in lower class sections of large cities.[12] Independent put it like this in 1908:

> The moving picture drama furnished entertainment for the millions, literally reproducing comic, tragic, and great events to some 16 million people a week at a nominal cost of a nickel or a dime. The effect of this new form of pictorial drama on the public is without parallel in modern history . . .. The moving picture is drama for the multitude, attracting thousands who never go to the theater, and particularly appealing to the children. In the poorer sections of the cities where innumerable foreigners congregate, the so-called 'nickelodeon' has held pre-eminent sway for the last year.[13]

A writer for The Outlook said, in 1911, that for the poor the movies meant

> opportunity--a chance to glimpse the beautiful and strange things in the world that you haven't in your life; the gratification of the higher side of your nature; opportunity which, except for the big moving picture book, would be forever closed to you.[14]

Thomas Edison, who promoted his moving pictures for twenty years

on the grounds of their value to working people, said in 1913 that

for a dime the common man would be able to see great plays, grand

opera, and spectacles performed by the world's greatest players.

The movies meant to Edison that "entertainment that has heretofore

been possible only at a prohibitive cost will be provided for the

masses." Motion pictures were, then, "the greatest contribution

in history to the brightening of the lives of the masses."[15]

This argument was employed only in connection with motion

pictures, however. Following the First World War, there was a

marked decrease in concern for the entertainment of the masses,

probably because of the changing character of the population and a

decrease in the number of immigrants, who formerly had provided a

large segment of the so-called low-class audience. By the time

radio and television developed, not only was it assumed that movies

provided well enough for the entertainment of the masses, but there

was growing concern voiced over the influence the mass audience

had on the quality of filmed entertainment. When entertainment

was no longer a gift to be given the mass audience, but rather

was dictated by the whims and wishes of the general population,

the argument that movies were good because they gave amusement

to the mass was no longer employed.

New quality in entertainment

Writers seeking to justify the new mass media on the grounds of
entertainment also argued that motion pictures, radio, and television
would make it possible for the mass audience to enjoy entertainment
of a quality formerly unavailable to them. Audiences were promised
grand opera and legitimate plays, as well as lighter entertainment
from vaudeville and musical comedy. This was a favorite theme of
Thomas Edison in his comments about the movies. In 1894, for example,
he said that with his new kineto-phonograph, as yet undeveloped, it
would be possible "to see and hear grand opera by stereopticon."
Then again in 1912 he predicted that with his new speaking pictures
"the working man will be able, by laying down his dime at the modern
theater of cinematography, to enjoy grand opera and dramatic productions, with sound, dialogue, color, and action, all scientifically
produced." Later it was promised that the Vitaphone would bring
grand opera to all communities, making available to them, for example,
Der Meistersinger accompanied by Toscanini and the Philharmonic.
Once talkies were established, grand opera was said to be on its
way to hundreds of opera houses in America which had never presented
an opera although this was their builders' dream.16

Equally high quality entertainment was promised from both radio
and television. As early as 1913 Collier's reported that when the
wireless telephone was perfected it would mean that opera performances
could be broadcast from London or Berlin for all the world to hear.

Thirty years later, Milton Cross was able to give radio credit for having introduced people to opera who had hever heard it before and would never have been exposed to it except for radio. When television was discussed in 1912, it was predicted that this medium would mean that the plays of Shakespeare would become the chief recreation in the lives of the people, with grand opera second in popularity. In 1937 Etude again predicted that television would make it possible to broadcast an entire opera directly into the home. Television was still defended with this argument in 1951 when a writer in American Mercury commented that television had given people all over the country a chance to see opera, which was normally unavailable outside of New York City. Opera, she wrote, was something "only television can take into every American home."[17]

Opera, apparently considered to represent ultimate quality in entertainment, was not the only kind of quality amusement promised from the mass media. (It was, however, mentioned sixteen times in the twenty-two times this argument was employed.) Other forms of entertainment considered to be of sufficient quality to support the argument were legitimate plays reproduced on film, the best in comedy performances, some vaudeville, all great drama, some of the top radio programs (reproduced on television), symphonies, and cer-tain of the outstanding talking pictures.

Support for innovation was gained by arguing that those forms of entertainment usually thought to be of highest quality would be

found in the new media. This justification sought to link the
new with those things of acknowledged superiority which were widely
praised, generally revered, but sparsely attended. Another group of
advocates developed a similar argument, but named the media as con-
tributors to "culture." A discussion of this argument begins on
page 90 below.

Entertainment to the small town

Not only did the new mass media promise to bring a new quality
of entertainment to the theaters and into the home, they were also
expected to bring low cost, high quality amusement to the small
towns where such recreation had not existed previously. This was
the argument of Robert Grau, writing in Lippincott's in 1913.

> The 'talking pictures' are here, and they are worthy
> of a far more dignified name . . .. It is not too much
> to predict that where heretofore only five per cent of
> the nation's population could afford to hear and see the
> best plays and operas at the prevailing prices, another
> year may record the astonishing fact that ninety-five
> per cent of the people of the civilized world may hear
> and see the very best in music and the drama. And mark
> you, the people in 'Podunk,' as /Thomas Edison/ the
> Wizard expressed it, would enjoy the blessing on the
> same day that the New York's public does, and at the
> same low price.[18]

Science, as D. W. Griffith put it in 1916, had "come to the rescue
of those typical Americans in small places." Movies had brought
amusement to the "parched American deserts of small towns and
villages."[19]

Radio and television also were to bring new recreational opportunities to out of the way places. Nation said radio meant that
"Smith's Four Corners is in listening distance of Broadway," and
David Sarnoff predicted that with the coming of television the
backwoodsman, far from the major centers of culture, would be able
to see the nation's leading artists.[20] The new mass media promised
to relieve the monotony of the small town, bringing to the hamlet
the advantages of the city at a price low enough so that the entire
population could afford to be amused.

Equality of entertainment

The provision of entertainment for the mass audience and to
small towns was described by the advocates of the mass media as
evidence of a new democracy of entertainment springing from the new
inventions. Here, in entertainment, was to be found the same
equality of opportunity which characterized the national democracy.
Both motion pictures and radio were promoted through this play on
democracy.

Thomas Edison was one of the first to use the argument. It is
to be found in his advocacy of the early talking pictures, but it
was American Magazine which labeled pictures the "art democratic."[21]
The phrase "democracy of entertainment," or an equivalent notion,
was commonly used to describe the movies. One of the most complete
developments of the argument appeared in 1926 in an article in

Photo-Era Magazine. The author, C. B. Neblette of the "Division

of Photography, A. M., College of Texas," held that motion pictures,

more than any other agency of amusement, fostered the democratic

tradition of equal opportunity for all.

> Democracy in educational, cultural, social and economic
> advantages, as well as democracy in a political sense,
> has always been a characteristic of the American people.
> Consequently, the educational, social and economic history
> of the American people has been toward a more equitable
> distribution of these advantages among the people, of
> finding agencies to bring together on one common ground
> of mutual interest all of the classes of people in all
> parts of the country and rendering available to every
> citizen opportunities equal to those of every other
> citizen.

It was the motion picture which continued the tradition. Therefore,

> because it filled a long-felt need admirably and completely;
> because it brought to the rank and file of the American
> people the dramatic entertainment which had been beyond
> their reach; because it bridged one more point of cleav-
> ance between the large cities and the small towns and rural
> sections; the motion picture, even in the crude state of
> its early beginnings, had a powerful and magnetic fasci-
> nation for the American people.[22]

This argument on equality of entertainment, with its implied

contribution to the democratic tradition, was also used by the advo-

cates of radio. Owen D. Young, Chairman of the Board of R. C. A.,

said in 1921 that the possibilities of radio for progress were

almost infinite because through radio "we can share thought and

culture and knowledge, rich as well as poor, farmers as well as

the city dwellers." Five years later, the President of R. C. A.,

General James G. Harbord, named radio broadcasting "the greatest

force yet developed by man in his march down the slopes of time"
because, among other things, radio was characterized by equality
of opportunity. Broadcasts were equally available to the humble
citizen and the millionaire.[23]

Escape through entertainment

Among the other advantages of motion pictures and radio was
their capacity to provide the audience with entertainment which
allowed them to escape from the reality of daily life.

In pictures, it was said, the lower classes found an opportunity to visit new worlds, to see things formerly forbidden them,
to escape, at least for the moment, the harshness which characterized their daily lives. Twenty-five years later, in the midst of
attacks on the morality of pictures, movies were defended by a
speaker at the 9th International Congress of Psychology at Yale
on the grounds that they afforded "healthy escape from drabness, to
adult and child alike. Radio was named a new medium of escape in
1928, a means by which the listener could go any place in the world
with a sense of spiritual freedom. During the depression, radio
was judged successful because it provided escape from the mental
and physical suffering of the times.[24]

Obviously, motion pictures, radio, and television were important
new means for entertainment. This was, in fact, their most common
function. Aware that amusement for its own sake was hardly an

acceptable basis for advocacy, promoters of the media employed the
strategy of naming the new in connection with generally accepted
good things. Entertainment was thus linked with social service,
democracy, equality, cultural growth, and even healthy escape.
Entertainment, because of the association, became a good thing.
Thus sanctioned, the new media could be publicly supported, justified, and defended.

Acquisition of Information

Spokesmen for motion pictures, radio, and television argued
that the new media offered benefits to society in making new information available to the public, in making acquisition of knowledge
easier and more attractive, and in bringing the individual into
new contact with the events and people of his world. It was from
the media that a new kind of education was to be derived, a kind of
learning not contained in books, but equal in quality to that gained
from the schools. Advocates spoke of widening horizons, of formerly
narrow and restricted worlds enlarged. One defender said, for
instance, that motion pictures had

> opened many minds to a larger understanding of the bigness
> of the world, and transformed insular creatures into cos-
> mopolitans, putting a magic telescope to the vision of the
> farmer boy, townsman, and city-hemmed in folks. The movies
> have opened minds, and with them opened, people are forced
> to keep ahead of the intelligence thus awakened, and the
> imagination thus aroused.[25]

The mass media were characterized as offering the public a broad,
yet informal, education which, as Will Hays said, involved "art,
letters, sciences, and . . . every other human activity," and which
would lead to world progress by combatting the evil generated from
ignorance.[26] This was the vision of the media created by their
defenders.

New places

Motion pictures made it possible for the mass audience to see
parts of the world which would otherwise be forbidden them. The
article which announced the beginnings of moving pictures noted
that with the new medium the audience could see pageants and cele-
brations, the natural wonders of the land, and object lessons from
"foreign lands of literally moving sights or accidents, and the
animated presence of far-off peoples!" How else might an east-
side youngster see "a bear hunt in Russia," scenes from an Indian
Reservation, or "pictures of the dredging machines at work on the
Panama Canal?" When Independent began running movie reviews, and
was criticized for doing so, it defended its action by reminding
critics that "those who by means of the moving film have been with
Scott to the Antarctic, with Rainey in Africa, with Curie in the
laboratory, with Sienkiewicz in Rome, with Ditmars in the reptile-
house, with Dante in the Inferno or with Homer in Ilium, will
appreciate the importance of motion pictures as an educational

factor."[27] In 1923 Will Hays argued that motion pictures

> enable millions to enjoy the benefits of travel in the
> wildest regions, without risk and at negligible expense.
> All the world is being filmed, and the pictures are bring-
> ing home to us, as nothing else could except an actual
> trip, the appearance of the various countries, the life
> of the inhabitants, their customs and manners.
> We have an enormous advantage in this respect over
> the people who lived before motion pictures were invented.
> There is scarcely a boy or girl who does not now have
> a vivid and fairly accurate idea of numerous places of
> which he had only a vague conception until he saw them
> in motion pictures. The life of the Indians of the Ama-
> zon country of South America and the Indians of the
> picturesque Acoma pueblo in New Mexico have been filmed
> recently; and an expedition has gone to take motion pic-
> tures of Tibet and its famous Hidden City of Lhasa,
> together with things sacred to Buddha.[28]

Ten years later he said that sound pictures

> permit you to become companions of Arctic adventurers
> and African explorers; they lead you to jungles and
> deserts and mountain ranges upon which folk have never
> gazed; and they render you as familiar with the temples,
> cathedrals, and social life of Asiatic and European
> cities, as you are with the churches, streets, and neighbors
> or your own home town.[29]

A new acquaintance with the world was one of the benefits of

radio. Its programs were called a liberal education, a means for

reaching out to places and people unknown before. With radio, a

listener could go anywhere that sound could travel. Listening,

youngsters gained a clearer understanding of their world.[30] Even

from afternoon serials, which had been soundly condemned by parents'

groups and uplift societies, the children learned good things.

According to the Director of Women's and Children's Activities for

ABC,

Jack Armstrong has taught the need for schooling in
science, geography, mathematics, and at the same time
telling the listeners much about the people, industry,
and culture of Australia and other far places . . ..
Terry and the Pirates has taken its followers to China,
India, and Burma. Captain Midnight has performed a
similar service with regard to South America and the
Pacific Islands.[31]

Television was named a window on the universe. Like the motion

pictures of Will Hays, it was to bring the wonders of exploration

to the general public, but in even more spectacular fashion, tele-

vision was predicted to allow a man, in his own home, to see the

world at the pressing of a button. In 1931, Nation's movie critic

said that the time was not far off when "television tours will be

conducted through the most inaccessible parts of the world, and we

shall be watching the life of the jungle, the desert and the deep

sea as today with the help of newspapers we watch the happenings in

the capitals of Europe." In retrospect, in 1955, television was

said to have served to take viewers "vicariously into strange and

fascinating spots and situations" where they probably would not have

been able to go had they been on their own.[32]

This argument, that the mass media broadened the horizons of

the public, taking them places where they could not otherwise go,

and, in effect, bringing the benefits of travel into the home at

minimum expense and with no effort to speak of, persisted through-

out the discussion of the new media. Not only was it applied to

each one of them in turn, it was also repeated in virtually the

identical phrasing for television that had been used for the moving picture.

Personalities and performers

Just as motion pictures, radio, and television allowed audiences
to visit strange and inaccessible places, so they also brought
famous people to the audience. Through films, the great personalities of the times first became familiar to the mass audience.
By 1911, it was possible for World's Work to report that millions
had seen the funeral cortege of Edward VII, and that "hardly a
crowned head or historical event of the last three years or a
branch of human ingenuity or a characteristic landscape in any
land has evaded the moving picture camera." With this new talking
film, Edison promised that "the world's greatest statemen, actors,
and singers can be heard and seen in even the smallest hamlet."[33]
Will Hays echoed Edison's statement in 1932, when he said that

> All great and unusual men and women sooner or later
> march through the lens of a sound-recording camera to
> appear and talk to all the peoples of earth.
> Everybody everywhere by grace of motion picture
> enterprise eventually can meet face to face every living
> person of interest or importance.[34]

Radio, too, promised to bring famous people to the home audience.
Saturday Evening Post expected that in the 1924 election radio would
permit every town and hamlet in the country to hear the final arguments of the nominees in nation-wide campaign speeches. Radio,
its advocates argued, would permit even the President to speak to

boys and girls in school; bring great opera and concert singers into new relationship with the audience; and, in retrospect, had allowed millions to hear the voices of Presidents, scientists, lawyers, professors, a thousand and one experts, who would never have been heard otherwise.[35]

Television, even in 1928, held out the possibility that presidential candidates would soon be reading their speeches. Like motion pictures, television would permit the greats and near greats to be seen by all who wished to watch. Looking back, twenty years later, a writer for Good Housekeeping confirmed that television had done just that, had brought the great personalities of the time into the home.[36] This was another service of the new media which provided a basis for advocacy for some forty years.

Current events

For man to keep abreast of the happenings in his world is generally acknowledged to be a good thing. The mass media were, therefore, judged to be of value because of their coverage of current events. All had the capacity to reproduce and distribute information in such a way as to allow many people to witness a variety of events which they otherwise would not be able to see. Antonia and W. K. L. Dickson's article for Century in 1894, in which they discussed Edison's invention of the motion picture, stressed the importance of the device as a reporter of the contemporary scene.

No scene, however animated and extensive, but will eventually be within reproductive power. Martial evolutions,
naval exercise., processions, and countless kindred exhibitions will be recorded for the leisurely gratification
of those who are debarred from attendance or who desire
to recall them.[37]

In early 1908, a writer for Independent, discussing the place and

purpose of the new motion pictures, pointed out that audiences had

seen the Jefferies-Sharkey fight at Coney Island, could see "impor-

tant events of the day"--shipwrecks, trainwrecks, new buildings

under construction, all in the moving pictures.[38]

By 1916, the reporting function of films had been taken over

by the newsreels, and the argument from then on focused on the

news film. Kenneth Macgowan reported for Collier's, for example,

that the newly formed newsreels had already carried to viewers many

remarkable scenes--the burning of Hankow, the Ohio flood, the

Titanic victims photographed the day following the disaster.

Thomas Edison predicted in 1919 that there would soon be a daily

news film of world events which could be shown in both theaters

and schools.[39] Will Hays later gave the newsreels great credit as

recorders of history, as public educators, and as reporters of

current happenings. Of the latter function he said this:

How many of you realize that the admission ticket /to the
newsreel7 is railroad and steamship transportation around
the world? The Mississippi River, the towering Alps, the
Pyramids of Egypt, the girls in the Maine salmon packing
houses, the latest invention, the train wreck in the far
West, the Smyrna horror, the Chilean earthquake, the
Facista uprising in Italy, the burial of a stateman, an

inauguration of a President, a political convention, this
and that event, at home or 10,000 miles away, all are
there before us.[40]

Movies were a good and interesting reporter of the current scene,
but they were slow; news films were commonly shown a week after the
event had been reported by the newspapers, and it was the rare
happening--the inauguration of a President--which permitted the
immediate processing and distributing of news films for next-day
showing. Hence radio was described as offering improvement in the
methods of reporting. As early as 1913, a writer for Collier's
had predicted that wireless telephony would be used, in the future,
"to distribute news and messages of all sorts from central stations
to an enormus number of subscribers," but it was not until the early
1920's that listeners could hear, in their homes, the farewell of
Clemenceau as he left New York for France, a speech by Steinmetz,
the World's Series with Grantland Rice, various other sports events,
an amazing variety of current happenings, including even a burglary
in progress.[41] But the important consideration in all this was
radio's ability to put the listener in instant touch with the event
in progress. But radio offered no pictures.

This changed with television, for the newest of the media
offered instant sound, and pictures, too. Television was predicted
to be an even greater reporter than either the newsreels or radio.
It would mean, said David Sarnoff, that

> by means of radio television, we shall see, as well as
> hear, our future Presidents being inaugurated. We, even
> here in America, may witness a coronation in London, a
> royal Durbar in India, a dance of savages in Africa. The
> possibilities are almost limitless.[42]

Marconi predicted in 1927 that television would bring great sports

events to the whole world, insuring "those beholders at a distance

. . . every advantage of ring-side seats and none of the inconven-

ience of actual attendance." It would mean, too, that every great

spectacle--coronations, Presidential inaugurations--would be available

to all who wanted to see them. With the coming of nationwide tele-

vision, the advantages of the medium, while not as great as some

had predicted, were greater than the realists had hoped. Advocates

quickly pointed out the accomplishments of television as a national

news reporter. A typical comment was carried by Senior Scholastic,

which noted that because of television school children had been able

to watch the U. N. in session, had seen a variety of special events

from the scene, and were consequently better informed about current

events than any students before them.[43] This function of the media

as reporter thus served as one of the primary defense arguments.

Information service

Apart from their value as reporters, both radio and television

were introduced as new sources for a variety of useful information.

Various defenders of radio argued that the medium could provide, or

had provided, crop reports for farmers, frost warnings, farm market

reports, other generally valuable farm information; market and business reports, information about prices of goods and sale notices.
From the radio, too, housewives could obtain the kind of material
which would make them generally better informed as citizens. The
stands of the various legislators could be widely publicized.
Information on national issues could be sent out over the entire
nation. Television was likewise expected to bring general information
to the mass audience. It was praised for having made more people
aware of national issues than had ever known about them before and
for having introduced new and useful products to the public.[44]
This capacity of the two media was used as a frequent basis for
advocacy.

Participation in history

The new mass media were admitted to be excellent reporters
of the contemporary scene, but another of their peculiar capacities
was even more intriguing to their defenders. It was suggested that
radio and television, and the movies to some degree, in their
reporting of historic events made the listener or viewer a virtual
participant in history in the making. Newsreels were defended in
1925 on the grounds that they made the observer a participant in the
historical moment,[45] but it was radio and television with their live
coverage which made the auditor feel a party to the action itself.

It was noted in Saturday Evening Post in 1924 that radio's
remote broadcasts, originating on the scene, not only brought major
events to the public at the time of their happening, but allowed
the listener to become, in fact, a part of the event, a witness
present at the presidential speech, at the concert in the auditorium,
at the sports event. H. V. Kaltenborn argued that "the opportunity to
have school children participate in such great public events as the
inauguration of a president, a political convention, a program that
marks some great holiday observance or historic occasion cannot be
neglected." He believed that "through radio we participate personally and instantly in man's great adventures."[46] Radio made the
listener a participant in history.

If radio was good in this respect, television was even better;
with television the audience member was visually linked to the
events as they unfolded, even if they were to occur a thousand miles
away. It was suggested, as Kaltenborn had done with radio, that
for school use, "current topics of an educational character may be
shown and discussed as they take place, the same as though the class
were actually present and taking part in these happenings.[47] This
capacity to observe events while they happened was stressed as one
of the great contributions of television.

Advocates of television suggested that one of the primary
advantages of television over film was that, with TV, the outcome

was known. One writer who observed that television could combine
live and filmed action was concerned with this possibility, for
the combination of the known with the suspenseful lessened the
excitement of the unexpected happening, which was an ever present
possibility with live programming.[48] It was David Sarnoff who
said that

> television will finally bring to people in their homes
> for the first time in history, a complete means of instan-
> taneous participation in the sights and sounds of the
> entire outer world. It will be more realistic than a
> motion picture because it will project the present instead
> of the past.[49]

One writer even predicted that television would allow people at
home to participate in history being made on the battlefield.
Evidence of television's value in live coverage of events was
supplied by the crash of a bomber into the Empire State Building
in 1945. NBC went on the air with the scene, live, and this coverage was noted as exemplifying the kind of work television could
do. Here the viewer became, as the argument put it, a participant
in history.[50] The viewer, or even the listener, could not help
but become involved in the life of his times.

Things usually unseen

The capability of motion pictures to enlarge small objects
and be taken almost anywhere; the ability of radio to amplify
sounds out of normal proportion; the power of television to look
at the common thing from an uncommon point of view all provided

substance for arguments in their behalf. It was pointed out very

early that moving pictures would allow audiences to see a variety

of things which they could not have seen except at considerable

inconvenience or expense. Antonia and W. K. L. Dickson commented

in 1894 on the power of film to bring to view normally elusive

sights, and spoke of the difficulty of the accomplishment.

> We have yet to speak of the microscopic subjects,
> a class of especial interest, as lying outside the unaided
> vision of man. In the treatment of these infintesimal
> types, much difficulty was experienced in obtaining a
> perfect adjustment so as to reproduce the breathing of
> insects, the circulation of blood in a frog's leg, and
> other similar processes of nature. The enlargement of
> the animalculae in a drop of stagnant water proved a
> most exacting task, but by the aid of a powerful lime-
> light, concentrated on the water, by the interposition
> of alum cells for the interception of most of the heat
> rays, and by the use of a quick shutter and kindred
> contrivances, the obstacles were overcome, and the final
> results were such as fully to compensate for the expen-
> diture of time and trouble. . . . A series of inch-large
> shapes then springs into view, magnified stereoptically
> to nearly three feet each, gruesome beyond power of
> expression, and exhibiting an indescribable celerity
> and rage. Monsters close upon one another in a blind and
> indiscriminate attack, limbs are dismembered, gory globules
> are tapped, whole batalions disappear from view. Before
> the ruthless completeness of these martial tactics the
> Kilkenny cats fade into insignificance. A curious feature
> of the performance is the passing of these creatures in
> and out of focus, appearing sometimes as huge and dis-
> torted shadows, then springing into the reality of their
> own size and proportions.[51]

As film makers continued to explore the capabilities of the

motion picture in revealing the microscopic and the obscure, advo-

cates continued to point to the value of films in such application.

With a moving picture it was possible to see a crystal grow, to see
insects and even germs magnified on the screen, to watch moving
X-rays, to see birds and animals in their native habitat, undisturbed
by the presence of man. Pictures allowed man to see those things
not usually visible to him. With stop-motion photography it was
possible to compress the normal life cycle of plants into a few
minutes; all the changes of a season in the life cycle of a cow-
pea were shown in a three minute film, for instance. Slow motion,
on the other hand, was said to permit new kinds of analyses of
sports, industrial processes, the operation of machinery. A writer
for The Outlook, having seen a picture being shot, speculated that
films might be useful in the analysis of human behavior, particularly if the pictures were made without the subject knowing about
it.[52]

These arguments were most frequently employed to point out
the surprising capabilities of the motion picture, but are also
to be found in connection with radio and television. A writer
for Scientific American, for example, pointed out that with radio
it would be possible for the listener to hear sounds normally outside his range; he had in mind particularly the amplification with
radio equipment of sounds within the human body. Collier's, at
the time when television was used to open the 1939 New York World's
Fair, surveyed the capabilities of the new medium and pointed with
some awe to the fact that "television can take you into the

laboratory and let you look through microscopes or up in the air for a bird's-eye view.[53] The worth of the new media was thus assessed, in part, on the basis of what could be done with them that was outside the normal range of man. Their ability to stretch the limits of human experience, and consequently of knowledge, was counted in their favor.

Closeness to the source

Since motion pictures, radio, and television provided a vehicle through which materials were communicated more or less directly from the source to the auditor, their spokesmen argued that the new media allowed more accurate transmission and judgement of information than had previously been possible. It was the contention of the advocates that with the new media there would no longer be need for interpretation of information by reporters. The audience member would be permitted to see for himself, as it were. And it was presumed that if the individual had the chance to see first hand, the assessment would be more accurate. Such was the basis for the argument.

This argument was used only occasionally, but was applied to each medium. The Dicksons explained that with respect to the picturing of current and historically important events on film,

> the advantages to students and historians will be immeasurable. Instead of dry and misleading accounts, tinged with exaggerations of the chroniclers' minds, our archives will

> be enriched by the vitalized pictures of great national
> scenes, instinct with all the glowing personalities
> which characterized them.[54]

Writers about radio said that the machine provided entertainment and

information direct from the source. As General Harbord, President

of R. C. A. put it, no longer would people need to make political

decisions on the basis of hearsay; rather, with radio the infor-

mation could be obtained directly from the candidates themselves.

A writer for Collier's was somewhat more colorful in making the

same point: "Everybody is inhaling recitals, recitations, time

signals, market reports, jazz music and Presidential messages through

the ears direct from the source." It was suggested of television,

too, that one of the advantages of the new instrument was that it

brought news and information to the viewer more quickly and more

directly than was possible with printed sources. No longer was

there a need to wait for papers and pictures, nor was the viewer

to be subjected to the interpretation usually found in print.[55]

Here advocates relied upon the presumed fear of slanted or

interpreted news to give weight to their argument, and they played

upon the hope of each viewer or listener that he might be permitted,

in fact, to "see for yourself." At the same time the advocates

ignored the possibility that interpretation was surely as much a

part of the film and electronic media as of the papers which had

borne the burden of the criticism.

The National Good

Another major category into which arguments can be grouped is best labeled "the national good." Here the defenders sought to demonstrate that innovation exerted a beneficial influence on various aspects of the national life. In simplest terms, the arguers proposed that if the new media were good for those parts of the national life which were thought to be valuable, then the media themselves were worthy of acceptance. In support of this proposition, the writers pointed to various ways in which the nation stood to benefit from the introduction of motion pictures, radio, and television.

Democracy strengthened

Much of what the media did or were capable of doing could have been interpreted to mean that democracy--that is, the existing form of national government--would be strengthened. In much of the argument, the conclusion that the government or democracy would benefit was left to the reader. Advocates played upon the impact of the word "democracy," however, and argued that because of the new mass media democracy was strengthened.

The movies were said to have strengthened democracy, to have reaffirmed democratic priniples, or to have awakened public interest in democracy. The means of these various yet similar ends were patriotic short subjects, films dealing with the development of the democratic ideal in America, and feature films on patriotic or war themes. In each argument, the force grew from the conclusion that democracy, never-defined, had been strengthened by the motion pictures.[56]

Radio was suggested to have more varied means by which the end might be accomplished. A writer for Collier's, who described radio as having in it "the promise of a new democracy of thought and culture and universal contact," predicted that the new medium, by drawing us closer together as a nation while destroying the long-standing sectional lines, would be a "powerful factor in perfecting our democracy." Others argued that radio, by providing the mass audience with more information than was previously available to them, thus creating a more intelligent and cooperative citizenry who were unwilling to accept panaceas and easy formulas, would lead to stronger democratic government.[57] This end was to be accomplished, others said, by simply allowing the general public exposure to political candidates. Following the 1924 Presidential election, the Chairman of the Board of R. C. A. said that

> no citizen of this great country need say that he has
> not heard the pronouncements of the presidential candi-
> dates of the two great national parties. . . . What a
> great hope for democracy![58]

As long as both sides had their say, another writer commented, radio would remain "an implement of democracy." It was suggested, finally, that because of radio, the public "accustomed to hearing frequent discussions, from all sides, of important political issues, may decide to make real uses of those who now are only theoretical public servants."[59]

The explicit connection **between** television and a strengthened democracy was made less frequently than with any of the other media. Seldom was the end of television said to be an enhancement of democracy. However, when discussion began as to the wisdom of televising Presidential press conferences supporters of the proposal argued that such exposure represented a step toward the extension of intelligent democracy.[60] So, just as motion pictures and radio had been defended as means of aiding a valued concept, when an innovation involving both government and television was proposed, it was defended by reference to the hope for a stronger democracy.

Ideal democracy restored

Writers envisioned an eventual perfection of the democratic form of government and offered the new mass media as a means of accomplishing the goal. For instance, when radio was evaluated in 1929 by the president of N. B. C., he predicted the medium to be a means for "making our country what it was theoretically supposed to be when its government was established--an ideal democracy."[61]

Those defenders who attempted to describe the form of idealized
democracy turned to one of two images, the Athenian forum or the
New England town meeting, both of which represented   long-sought
but yet unrealized ideals of governmental operation. In 1924, 1925,
1929, and 1936 radio was described as allowing the electorate to
judge the political candidate in person as had been possible when the
speaker presented himself before the entire electorate. The New
Republic said in 1924 that

> potentially the radio gives every member of the electo-
> rate the possibility of a direct reaction to the candi-
> dates themselves. It does reproduce to some degree, for
> the first time in the United States, the conditions of
> Athenian democracy where every voter, for himself could
> hear and judge the candidates.[62]

School and Society in 1936 described radio as making practical the
former rule that "no city-state should be larger than a group of
citizens within the range of a herald's voice." The ideal of
democracy could be realized through the new medium for

> through the telescoping of time and space the radio is
> able to compress a great continental democracy as if
> within the confines of a market place. One voice can
> reach the whole nation, and that must be important in
> government.[63]

A second form of idealized democracy was the town meeting,
characterized by face to face debate among candidates and between
candidates and audience. Radio and television were both presented
as offering a means for returning to this ideal on a national scale.
Even before broadcasting was formally begun, on the grounds of

successful voice communication between the United States and Hawaii in 1915, Independent predicted that radio would mean that "the old New England town meeting system of government is not limited to those who can be gathered into one room, but may be extended to include those who can talk together in a common tongue and work together under a common flag." When in 1950 Thomas E. Dewey used a TV marathon in his campaign for the governorship of New York, spending eighteen hours in the television studio answering questions telephoned in by viewers, Christian Century, characterizing the technique as another far-reaching consequence of the technological revolution, asked, "Has TV brought the longed for equivalent of town-meeting democracy?" Four years later, a Reader's Digest article noting the revolution in politics caused by television, went on to comment that "television may be providing a substitute for the old-fashioned town meetings which kept the New England villages reasonably pure, through a combination of conscience and basti-nado."[64] Again, the mass media were held out as a new hope for remedy of weaknesses perceived in the present, and as a dream for restoration of the ideal.

Class distinctions leveled

Related to the hope for strengthening or restoring democracy was an argument which appeared only twice, but which suggested that the nation would be made better if the new media destroyed

distinctions between classes. One of the first articles to evaluate
the impact of radio on the national life introduced the idea of
leveling class distinctions through radio. Arguing that the present
stratification of American society was due to differences in opportunity for information and culture, a writer in Collier's proposed
that radio, since it meant equal opportunity for all listeners
to get information and participate in cultural activities, would
mean destruction of the informational-cultural barriers which
presently separated the population. A similar justification of
motion pictures was published in 1932 by Albert Shaw in The Review
of Reviews. Speaking of the accomplishments of the movies, Shaw
suggested that motion pictures were a valuable part of the nation's
life not only because they were "so dynamic in their influence and
so universal in their appeal," but also because they reached everybody, thus sweeping away class distinctions, removing the sting of
poverty, and reducing the pride of wealth.[65] Assuming that such
leveling of distinctions was generally thought to be good, these
two authors attempted to show that radio and motion pictures would
help secure its accomplishment.

National unity

One of the promises of radio, motion pictures, and television
was that of creating greater national unity. Advocates of radio
predicted that the new medium would not only bridge the distances

which separated the American people, but would also create a new
"sense of national solidarity in all parts of the country, and
particularly in remote settlements and on the farm." The argument from national unity was used typically by a Collier's writer
in 1922. He predicted that radio could "do more than any other
agency in spreading mutual understanding to all sections of the
country, to unifying our thoughts, ideals, and purposes, to making
us a strong and well-knit people."[66]

Variations on the argument were applied in single instances
to both television and motion pictures. C. B. Neblette, who commented regularly on motion pictures for Photo-Era Magazine, assessed
the place of the motion picture in American life in 1926. It was
his contention that pictures served a major function in distributing entertainment to the small towns which dotted the country.
When the same pictures appeared at all the little towns, films
created a new feeling of oneness throughout the nation. Moreover,
the pictures drew Americans together by opening their eyes "to the
romantic history of the North American continent." Films such as
"Miles Standish," "America," "The Birth of a Nation," "The Covered
Wagon," and "The Iron Horse" awakened in the American people "a
new interest in their own country, in its romance and its history,
and /were/ instrumental in developing a new sense of national
consciousness." Television was mentioned in a similar connection

in a 1955 survey undertaken by U. S. News and World Report. Seeking
to determine "what TV is doing to America," the publication surveyed
the impact of television on national life. One of a number of conclusions about the values of television was that this new medium
was "breaking down regional barriers and prejudices, ironing out
accents, giving people in one part of the country a better understanding of people in other parts."[67] Although this argument
appeared in connection with both pictures and television, it was
never employed as a major part of the defense of either one.

Isolation ended

Another major argument employed by the advocates of radio was
related to radio's ability to establish communications over great
distances. Various writers presented radio as a new means for
ending the isolation of persons separated from the main stream of
civilization either by physical distance or by physical incapacity.
Just as it was earlier argued that motion pictures brought entertainment to the small community, so now radio was defended on the
grounds that it brought contact with the outside world to people
who were distant from it.

Advocates suggested, first of all, that radio would end the
isolation of physical distance. Stanley Frost, writing in Collier's
in 1922, said that with radio

no one of us, whether at home or in a city flat, a village
residence, a farmhouse, or a mountain cabin or camp, need
ever be shut in behind the barrier of our resources. News,
entertainment, music, culture, education, everything that
can be made audible will literally be on the air, ours for
the taking. It will give to all of us according to our
several tastes and abilities.[68]

Floyd W. Parson, writing in The Saturday Evening Post in 1922,

stressed the importance of radio in ending the isolation of the

farm family.

One great value of radio is that it will bring its message
to the group in the isolated farmhouse as quickly and
satisfactorily as to the dwellers in the heart of a great
city. The members of a family living miles from a railroad and receiving mail but once a day will likely profit
most of all from the development of the radio-telephone.[69]

With radio, the farm family could have entertainment, news, agri-

cultural reports, and even church services brought into the home

when weather prevented their going out to church. More spectacu-

lar, however, was the report of a forest ranger in the Temagami

Forest Reserve who wrote for Collier's that he became reacquainted

with the world through radio. Listening at night, with his dog

by his side, he heard the news, concerts, prize fights, church

services, and, in a land without women, "a low-toned, cultured

feminine voice speaking to a multitude of homes." He was, he wrote,

no longer apart from the world--"I may be at 'the back of beyond,'

but the whole world has marched right up to the edge of the little

copper switch at my elbow." Another writer believed radio would

be such a power that the trapper, farmer, and logger would be

brought together with the rest of the world and that, because of
radio, "there will be no more young Lincolns, tramping miles for
a book and reading it painfully by firelight."[70] Pauline Frederick,
writing in Good Housekeeping, argued that radio would be of great
benefit to the woman isolated in the home, bringing her diversion,
amusement, entertainment, and instruction throughout the day. This
would be of more than passing benefit, for, according to this
writer,

> isolation, whether mental or geographical, has been the
> cause of much of woman's restlessness and has done more
> to retard her progress than any other one factor. And
> now the radio comes as a sort of panacea to cure all the
> ills which isolation brings forth.[71]

Radio, in serving to end isolation, whether physical or mental,
of various groups in the population performed a national service.

A variation on the argument that radio ended physical isolation
was introduced in 1922, when a writer for American Magazine told
how much the radio had helped relieve the isolation of patients
in a tuberculosis hospital near Pittsburgh. The following year
a member of the medical staff at Mt. Sinai hospital in Philadelphia
also reported that radio had helped cheer and entertain the patients.
By 1924, radio was characterized as a great boon to shut-ins, and
thereafter, it was common to find the two arguments presented
together. That is, radio brought the world to those isolated
either by distance or by some physical incapacity.[72]

Motion pictures were of course defended on the grounds that
they brought entertainment to small towns and out-of-the-way villages.
Seldom, however, were they defended on the basis of putting an end
to isolation as radio had been said to do. One of the few to use
this defense was the Mayor of Los Angeles who adopted the argument
for his brief for motion pictures in 1922, a year after the argument was introduced in connection with radio. He contended that the
motion picture served not only "to bring joy to the hearts of young
and old," but it also ended the loneliness of those far from civilization for "it invades the most distant desert districts and
links them in knowledge and understanding with the most favored
metropolis."[73] Will Hays presented a somewhat more lengthy development of the argument in his 1927 defense of the motion pictures.
He contended, first, that motion pictures were more than a medium
for recreation. As evidence, he pointed to the use of films in
education, in medicine, and in ending the isolation both of the ill
and those far distant from the centers of civilization. Motion
pictures, he wrote,

> are entertaining and giving happiness to hundreds of
> thousands of helplessly shut-in men and women and
> children in the hospitals, orphanages, prisons, and
> homes for the aged. Even the lonely leper in the
> Pacific is not deprived of his share in the world's
> fun on the screen. The other day a letter came to me
> signed by a group of children in Alaska telling me that
> they had traveled fifty miles to see pictures we had
> sent them. 'We had always heard of West Point Cadets,'
> the letter read, 'but this was our first opportunity
> to see our future national defenders.'[74]

It was only these two times, however, that this argument was applied to the motion picture.

Neither was the argument used in defense of television. Perhaps it was so generally assumed that television, extending the functions of radio, would end isolation that it was not necessary for the argument to be made explicit. Perhaps the argument was simply believed to no longer have currency. Nevertheless, it was not employed in the predictions of television except in a brief report on the use of television for amusement of the sick and aged, people "who are cut off from active life and normal contacts with families and friends."[75] In this context, television was reported to have been a great boon.

Rural life made attractive

Radio's capacity to bring information and entertainment to isolated areas provided substance for a few writers who argued that radio would provide the necessary impetus to stem the tide from the farm to the city, restore the attractiveness of farm life in America, and perhaps attract new residents to the farm. Mention of benefits to the farm were common in the discussions of radio as a means of ending isolation, but only an occasional writer proposed that radio would serve to create a new interest in farm living.

The argument was popular for a two year period. Literary Digest said in 1924 that the radio had become as much of a necessity for the farmer as the automobile, then went on to argue that radio might come to the aid of the "back to the farm movement" and so serve to popularize rural life, halting the exodus from the farm while at the same time attracting new people to farm living. Radio would supply the human touch which was lacking in the other mechanical conveniences.

> The roads may be bad, with the movie show, the church or the social miles away; the telephone lines may be down; and the mail-carrier unable to complete his circuit; but news and entertainment are always in the air, to be caught by the adequate receiving set, to inform, to instruct, to amuse.[76]

The argument was then repeated in The Century Magazine six months later, but the back-to-the-farm movement was not mentioned. In the latter instance, the writer commented first that radio would create new national solidarity, and then went on to say that radio

> may even be the final factor needed to make rural life attractive to young people, and to stop that herding into the cities which is now going on at the rate of 1,200,000 a year, and is causing students of American social conditions much alarm.[77]

In 1926, David Sarnoff offered a slightly different version of the argument in an interview with Mary Margaret McBride published in Saturday Evening Post. Sarnoff contended that radio would bring information to the farm which would offset the cultural advantages of the city. But more than that,

keeping on the farm the boy and girl already there is the
ultimate service the radio will render to rural communities. It is too early to call for statistics, but they
will show, I am convinced, that the new movement has
already begun.[78]

During this period of freshened interest in rural life, radio

offered a means for implementing part of the plan for renewed

rurality. Radio was a way to realization of the dream. Innovation

in this case was adopted by the spokesmen for a cause, and the

cause was adopted briefly by the spokesmen for radio.

Speech habits improved

A further beneficial influence on both radio and motion pic-

tures was predicted to lay in their improvement of the speech habits

of the American people. Assuming that the common speech needed

improvement, advocates of radio tentatively presented the new device

as a means to that end. It was H. V. Kaltenborn, for example, who

made this prediction in 1925:

> In the course of a few years, the radio will do
> much to improve the slovenly speech habits of the Aver-
> age American. Every listener-in learned long ago how to
> pronounce the names of all important composers; and by
> hearing the country's best speakers, the radio audience
> is becoming indifferent or hostile to platform mediocrity.[79]

Another writer in The North American Review some eleven years later

listed the goods radio might accomplish in America. Among them

was that "radio will markedly affect the common speech."[80] He

apparently meant that radio would improve the common speech, although the meaning cannot be ascertained with certainty from the brief assertion.

Improvement of national speech habits was also named as one of the benefits to be derived from the introduction of talking pictures. The argument was applied to talkies soon after they were established as the new form of motion picture drama. It was in 1929 that William DeMille wrote in Scribners that if the talkies achieved their full potential, one of their great contributions would be that they would "become a standard of speech for the whole people," and DeMille assumed that the standard of speech of the talkie would be a high standard. The same year, Cecil B. DeMille was supposed to have predicted that within a year or so everyone would be speaking perfect English because of the influence of the talkie. Other writers presumed that the talkie would provide the entire country with a desirable and uniform standard of speech, which would be copied by the auditors, to their benefit. Hence, through pictures, as a country philosopher's comment put it in Collier's, even the inmates of Brooklyn, Jersey City, New York, and New England might begin speaking English.[81]

A national forum

Again calling upon the ability of the new media to communicate with large groups of people, advocates of motion pictures and radio said the machines would serve as a national forum. The

argument first appeared in an article about motion pictures in
1908. The author, talking of a future combination of pictures
and telegraph which would provide nearly instant pictures of the
world on the screen in motion picture theaters, said that

> inventors behold in the nickelodeon the future forum
> of the race. With the progress of science it is des-
> tined to replace the lecture platform, the pulpit, books
> and the newspaper. It will become an institution where
> the people may pause to rest for a few moments, a quiet
> orderly little hall where silence is wholly enforced
> and where, on a huge screen, the human activity of the
> world is being shown about simultaneously with the action
> of the events, with the very shouts, the cries, the
> speeches or what not, all transmitted by telephotography.[82]

These predictions anticipated those common to television some
twenty years later.

Writers dealing with radio envisioned their forum to be a
place for discussion of contemporary issues rather than merely a
source for information. Speaking of the place of radio in politics,
a writer in New Republic said in 1924 that never before did we have
such a national forum as radio had provided. David Sarnoff at the
same time described radio as the bar of public opinion for great
causes, an "illimitable forum."[83] These few, at least, saw radio's
function as that of making public formerly private opinion, and
providing a national common ground for discussion of a variety of
national concerns.

The war effort is aided

It was common to describe the new mass media as great forces for good or evil, their eventual use dependent upon the men who managed them. Periodically, when the nation was at war, the media were defended on the grounds of their contribution to the war effort. (At other times their contributions to peace were stressed.) Motion pictures, then radio, and finally television, their advocates pointed out during the two World Wars, had contributed greatly to the nation's war efforts.

During the First World War, the press took note of the contribution of the motion pictures to the national effort. It was reported that training films, 1500 of them, were shown to troops. Illustrated on the camp screens were warfare in practice, modes of attack and defense, methods of personal and camp hygiene, the nature of the enemy, and the type of terrain over which the fighting would take place. Films were also used at home, said Current Opinion, to demonstrate graphically the realities of war, to keep the public informed about the war effort, to inspire the home folks in their war work, and to stimulate the various Liberty Loan drives.[84] Films were used by both sides for propaganda purposes, reports said. The Germans made feature films stressing national pride, and used them to further the efforts on the home front. The Americans made films to demonstrate to their allies the might of the nation, and prepared filmed answers to German propaganda in order to refute the German

claims. Of the latter films, Current Opinion said:

> Such pictured facts cannot be denied or ignored. Further,
> pictures headed with striking captions, set forth the
> causes of our going to war.[85]

The reports of the part motion pictures played in the war

were a clear demonstration of the value of the new medium. There

was little need for advocates to point to the obvious values to be

derived from the use of films in the war. Conversely, the sug-

gestion could hardly be ignored that a medium of so much value to

the nation at war was a medium valuable for its similar capacities

in peacetime.

When motion picture spokesmen sought grounds for defense of

the medium following the First World War, one of the items called

upon was films' war record. One writer, building a case for the

motion picture in 1919, recalled that during the recent war, films

were given preferential status.

> We have seen recently, as America mobilized her forces,
> civilian and military, for war, in what an agony of
> suspense millions waited to learn whether or not the
> movies had been declared an 'essential industry.' Until
> this was settled, the country could not face the future.[86]

Two years later, another writer, this time defending the film against

charges of artistic and moral failure, called attention to the good

that pictures had done in mustering the nation to war and in helping

to sell bonds.[87] Will Hays also argued that since the motion picture, specifically the newsreel, had been of value during the

war, the entire industry was worthy of encouragement. To support

his assertion, Hays reminded his readers of the service films had

performed during the war.

> When the German troops marched into Brussels in 1914,
> an American motion-picture man filmed the event. First he
> pictured the movements of the German troops, then those of
> the Belgian, trying to get both sides. Finally he was
> shot by the Germans as a spy. Many will remember, too,
> that the German super-submarine, thought to be a phantom
> only, was eventually shown to be a reality by motion
> pictures. A daring American motion-picture man took
> these pictures from a port-hole in a Dutch steamer carrying
> him from Holland to England, which had been stopped by the
> submarine. When he reached England his pictures were
> developed; and for the first time the British Admirality
> --and later Americans--saw, through motion pictures, the
> much discussed but previously invisible German super-
> submarine.[88]

Finally, William A. Brady, former theatrical producer turned

movie producer, argued that motion pictures had actually saved

the world during the First World War. The Germans, he wrote, had

launched a great propaganda drive in France, intended to convince

the nation that the United States would not and could not come

to her assistance in the war. The seemingly truthful German

assertions could not be answered by statesmen, and hopelessness

gathered in France. What was needed was a means of reaching the

French masses with the truth about America's capacity and her

intent.

> In its five thousand recorded years humanity has con-
> trived only one device to make such an exposition

possible: The Motion-Picture. Not thousands but millions
of feet of film were rushed across by our government, and
were shown in all parts of France simultaneously. . . .
/The French saw/ gun-works like Krupp's, or their own
Creusot's, roaring through the day, blazing through the
night. Shipyards, with great carriers building in quar-
tets and octets. Shell-factories, with literal miles
or workers. Army camps, with hundreds of thousands of
splendidly-drilled troops. Small-arms factories the
like of which are nowhere. The vast organization of army
and navy, actually at work in Washington. The conser-
vation of food for every part of the world except Kaiser-
dom--France saw a moving, living, rushing negative of
every vicious argument Wilhelm's agents had put forth.
France drew a long breath. It smiled. It cinched up its
belt. And--with its American brothers--it began to give
their answer to the Germans at Chateau-Thierry. That is
how the motion picture saved the world.[89]

When the Second World War began, motion pictures were again

defended on the grounds of their contribution to the war effort.

In 1941, for example, a writer for Christian Century recalled the

service performed by films in the First World War, and predicted

that the service in the present war would be even greater. Three

years later, it was possible for a writer in New Republic to cite

the contributions of motion pictures in "entertaining troops, sell-

ing bonds, and instructing new factory workers." The next year,

The Nation also praised Hollywood for its part in the war effort.[90]

Films once again had come to support the effort of the nation in

time of war.

Radio was very much in the experimental stage at the time of

the First World War. Nevertheless, Literary Digest took note, in

1919, of the uses to which the wireless telephone had been put

during the recent war. Most directly related to the war was the use of wireless telephone in communication with airplanes and

between ships. The new device was also used at home to stimulate

the war effort.

> Having done its bit in winning the war, the radio tele-
> phone was given the task of inspiring the Victory Way
> crowds /in New York City7 to put their dollars into
> bonds to help pay for victory. It performed its task
> with great success.[91]

At the beginning of the Second World War, radio was praised

for its excellent coverage of the war news, and Charles Siepmann,

among others, saw the war as an excellent opportunity for radio

to prove itself a genuine public service.[92] When Norman Corwin

assessed the place of radio in the war effort in 1942, he said

this:

> The duty and responsibility of American radio is
> obvious and simple and urgent: to explain to the people
> the nature of fascism and why we are fighting it; to
> explain what we stand to lose by defeat and gain by
> victory; to face squarely the issues of this war instead
> of ducking them; to hammer away at, to reiterate, to
> follow through with the truth no matter how many appeasers
> and editors and weary intellectuals resent and resist the
> truth; to inform the people instead of selling, coaxing,
> scaring, upbraiding, or exhorting them.[93]

When radio's service during the war was evaluated, its defenders

pointed to the news service provided, its handling of public infor-

mation, its presentation of national messages in both announcements

and drama, its promotion of the various bond drives. A writer for

Saturday Review said that

> there is no denying that the public has been enlightened,
> unified, and heartened by radio. Public energy has been

> directed into channels where it can do the most good.
> And that's important.[94]

As had been the case with motion pictures, radio was said to have made a significant contribution to the efforts of the nation at war.

Television was only predicted at the time of the First World War, and even when the second war began was only in very limited use. There was, nevertheless, some discussion all along of possibilities for the medium in war service. An inventor of a new television system, C. Francis Jenkins, spoke in 1929 of the ultimate possibilities of the new medium. Apart from its entertainment value, Jenkins saw television as having value in war. That is, television might be used by a naval commander to watch the progress of a sea battle, or a camera could be mounted in an airplane so a military commander might look at enemy fortifications from the air while sitting at his desk.[95] At the beginning of the Second World War, a writer for Saturday Review argued that television could contribute substantially to the war effort, if it were only put to that use. He suggested that television could be used to teach bandage rolling to large groups of people, and also

> could be utilized to teach the conservation of fuel,
> of food, of clothing, of any number of materials
> affecting civilian life, a project which the news-
> papers and radio have attempted, but not successfully.
> And consider the army and navy training programs. With
> sets in barracks and camp meeting halls, whole regiments
> could be taught intricate gunnery manipulations practic-
> ally simultaneously.[96]

The possibilities had not been realized, he concluded, because

"the powerful interests in the press, the movies, and the radio

put /television7 as far back on the shelf as they could because

they saw it as a threat to the status quo."

 This accusation brought an immediate response from Gilbert

Seldes, then director of television programs for C. B. S. Seldes

argued that television, limited in air time though it was, had

contributed substantially, and would continue to contribute, to

the war effort. He cited the 240 news programs, the 38 analyses

of war situations, the 33 programs devoted to Red Cross first aid

instruction, the defense bond sales over television, the program

on war geography, and the broadcasts of the President which had

been carried since December 7, 1941. Within the scope of its limi-

tations, the medium was serving the war effort.[97]

 The involvement of the country in each war resulted in the

mass media being defended vigorously on the grounds that they had

contributed, or in the case of television could contribute, to the

national effort. Again, the apparent purpose of the argument was

to show that the new media were valuable in connection with the

current national effort. With their beneficial influence demon-

strated in the context of the war effort, it was to be presumed

that they also had more wide-ranging potential value. It must be

noted, too, that this argument had currency only at the times when

the nation was at war; between the wars, as will be discussed later,

advocates were concerned with demonstrating the influences for
peace which were to be derived from the media.

History recorded and preserved

Motion pictures were presented by their advocates as a new
means of preserving the history of the nation. Thus, events in
which the present generation took pride could be saved for those
who were to come later. Although this argument was not used to
defend either radio or television, it appeared often in connection
with motion pictures.

George Parsons Lathrop introduced the argument in his article
announcing Edison's combination of the motion picture machine and
the phonograph. Lathrop said that, in addition to other applications,
"by preserving for future ages vitalized pictures of each passing
generation or of historic events, the kinetograph may yet play a
part of incalculable importance in human life."[98] As time passed
the argument was amplified, and in some cases made more explicit,
but suffered no fundamental change. The defenders of films continued to argue, as Will Hays did in 1932, that

> our children's children will attend the next presidential
> inauguration, see the Chief Justice administer the oath
> of office, and listen to the President's actual address.
> They will watch Byrd sail for the South Pole and witness
> Lindbergh begin his flight into immortality.[99]

History, formerly a transient thing which often eluded the grasp
of man, would now be preserved by the motion picture.

In presenting the argument, advocates appealed not only to the pride of each generation in its own accomplishments and to its desire for immortality, but also played upon the desire to see the great personalities of the past and to relive great events of history which had gone unrecorded. For instance, in the filmed afterpiece appended to one of the early Edison films demonstrating the new combination of picture and sound, the filmed lecturer asked the audience to "consider the historic value of a kinetophone production of George Washington, if it were possible to show it now, and you will realize the splendid opportunity for future generations to study the great men of today."[100] Speaking of the same demonstration Outlook said that

> the value of the kinetophone is too obvious to be emphasized or discussed. What would we not give for such a record of the Gettysburg Address! [101]

And Kenneth Macgowan, speaking of the advent of news films, held that these films would mean for future generations what films of great events of the past would mean to the present readers. Captions for those pictures of the past might read:

> Pheidippides wins the first Marathon, 490 B.C. Christians burn Rome during one of Nero's chamber concerts. Thebes. Egypt. Wild scenes occur in the wheat pit when Joseph, a young broker, puts over his first corner.[102]

It is worth noting, too, that the argument appeared whenever there was a new development in motion pictures which demanded justification. That is, when pictures were announced, they were

introduced as a new means of recording and preserving material of
historical value. As Edison promoted his revised sound films in
1913, the argument was used again. When newsreels were introduced,
the argument served to show their usefulness. When a film library
was established in the state of Iowa, the argument was employed
to justify the new department. When films needed defense against
charges of immorality, readers were reminded that the medium deserved
praise rather than blame because of "its great and thrilling everyday service as history's handmaiden, in such vivid recording of
events as has never before been possible." When a new method of
motion picture sound recording was announced in 1923, Scientific
American said the system had "a definite application in recording
speeches, songs, and other sounds for future generations." And
when the talking pictures were finally a reality, Will Hays said
this was the "instrument with which the speaking likenesses of
centuries will be preserved."103

Pictures were held to be valuable in recording history not only
because they preserved a likeness of the present for the future.
Some writers pointed to the value of such a record in the teaching
of history. (Others stressed the use of dramatic recreations of
historical events for teaching purposes.) Using films of the past,
the student would be able virtually to project himself into the
context of the time since passed. When, for example, a film library

was established as a part of the Iowa Department of History, Harper's

Weekly commented that

> a generation hence the young people of Iowa will study
> the history of their state with the aid of the kineto-
> graphic art, as the result of the founding of the first
> moving picture library for purely historical purposes.
> . . . School children fifty years from today will be able
> to understand more clearly present-day customs and manners
> when they see thrown upon the screen some of the many
> events that held the attention of their forefathers . . .
> /The future student of history would thus be able/ to
> visualize the important happenings of the present history-
> making epoch in Iowa.[104]

Films, used in this fashion, would serve not only to record, but also

to teach.

Artistic immortality

The preceding argument suggested that pictures were useful

in society because of their function in recording the history of

the nation. A major variation on the argument pointed out the

importance of motion pictures as a means for preserving events of

artistic significance. It was asserted that the invention of the

moving picture allowed the preservation for all time of the great

acting and dramatic performances of the age. Because of the motion

picture, Edison said, "the world's great statesmen, actors and

singers can be seen and heard in even the smallest hamlet, not

only today, but a hundred years hence." Leading actors and

actresses of the present could be seen in their most famous roles.

Just as it would be interesting for the generation of 1913 to see

the greats of the past--Siddons, Forrest, Macready, Booth, Kean,
Jenny Lind, Frisi, Piccolomini, Rosa, and Patti--so future generations would be able to see, and hear, Sothern, Marlowe, Maude
Adams, Viola Allen, Faversham, Lecouvreur, Rejane, Mounet-Sully,
and Bernhardt. With the motion picture and phonograph combined,
"the next generation of stars will not die with their artistic
deaths." Even Bernhardt, when she finished filming Queen Eliza-
beth, was said to have exclaimed, "I am immortal! I am a film!"
She was given, said one commentator, "an opportunity to be vis-
ualized to all nations for all time." George Bernard Shaw said
that because of films one need no longer hear of the "fugitive fame"
of the actor's art. "The Hamlet of Forbes Robertson, for instance,
filmed and recorded, may delight posterity, generation after generation." In a similar vein, the singer Feodor Chaliapin described
the screen, in 1929, as the repository for the great performances
of the world. The great singers and actors, he said, would see
their art preserved for the ages.[105] Emil Jannings, too, named
sound films the salvation of actors trained in theatre. Speaking
of the differences between stage and screen Jannings said this:

> The theatre is the most perishable of all arts. Its
> great moments are born in the twinkling of an eye and
> vanish as rapidly. . . . How different it is in the
> film, where our achievement is recorded for all time
> as permanently as the printed works of any writer. For
> the first time since man ever strode upon a stage the
> actor at last feels that, with the films, the words
> 'gone by' hold no more terror for him.[106]

A further variation on the argument was used in 1939 in connection with television. In an article which took the form of prognostication about the future, the science editor of the New York
Times, Waldemar Kaempffert, suggested that as an outgrowth of
television it would be possible electrically to record pictures
of people for future replaying, thus assuring what he called
"electric immortality."[107] The argument was not generally used
to support television, however.

It was presumed by those who used the argument that there
was benefit to be derived not only from the preservation of the
historical record of the nation but also from the saving for posterity of the best artistic products of the age. The good things
of the present could now be preserved for the future. Motion pictures provided the means to this desirable end.

The American image spread abroad

As American motion pictures became a primary export and were
distributed around the world, promoters were quick to note that
films thus served to propogate America's image abroad. Harper's,
for instance, in 1926 commented that American motion pictures had
achieved in the world, "unwittingly, what different powers in
different times have built navies, levied taxes, intrigued, coerced,
and slaughtered in order to achieve."[108]

Operating on the presumption that it was a good thing to
spread widely the American image, writers argued that silent motion
pictures sold America abroad as had never been possible. As evidence of the widespread influence of American pictures, a Saturday Evening Post article quoted a piece from a Paris paper which
said that even if the American tourist stayed home and the diplo-
matic corps were sent home,

> America's citizens, problems, its towns and countryside,
> its roads, motor cars, counting houses and saloons would
> still be familiar in the uttermost corners of the world.
> . . . The film is to America what the flag was once to
> Britain. By its means Uncle Sam may hope someday, if he
> is not checked in time, to Americanize the world.[109]

In another article the Post pointed out that motion pictures created
an image of America as a great progressive nation, and in so doing
caused foreigners to want to live like Americans. Not only that,
but because of the pictures American "ideals, culture, customs,
and traditions" were said to be undermining those of other nations,
creating not a little resentment of American films on the part of
foreign governments. With some pride in the impact of American
films abroad, William deMille wrote in 1927 that "foreign nations
are worrying about the influence of American pictures upon their
innocent populations, and if their complaints are justified, it
would seem that the American movie is destined to upset the world
as much as our part in the late war has upset Europe."[110]

When talking pictures were introduced in America, and consequently abroad, the influence of the movies, as well as their
problems, was said to be increased enormously. The Saturday Evening
Post argued in 1930 that

> a world war is on--of talking pictures. The issue at
> stake is not the fortunes of any country's film indus-
> try. The issue is nothing more or less than the cultural
> progress of the world. The influence of the new machines
> of sight and sound upon the world's mass millions may not
> be minimized.[111]

Armed with the new weapon of sound, it was predicted that "Hollywood will prove, as never before, a potent factor in shaping civilization." Looking back over the years of American influence abroad,
Samuel Goldwyn said in 1954 that motion pictures had shown the
world all sides of the American life, leaving it up to the people
to draw their own conclusions about us. And, said Goldwyn,

> I think it /American life as represented in pictures7
> is pretty darned good. So far it is better than some of
> the other countries we read about.[112]

Assuming that America prospered because of her image spread
abroad by pictures, Goldwyn and others defended films on their
international publicity value. The world knew the United States
by its movies.

Foreign trade stimulated

As a consequence of the exportation of American motion pictures,
their spokesmen argued, a new demand for American goods was created
abroad. Seeing a variety of American products in our motion pictures

caused foreign viewers to want similar items, resulting in increased

sales for American businesses. A writer in The Independent said

in 1926 that "the film is a silent salesman of great effectiveness,

and by that method much trade is being diverted to America."[113]

The extent of the influence of American pictures as salesmen was

inferred by a writer in Photo-Era on the basis of the concern about

the problem in England. He wrote:

> That the British realize the seriousness of the situ-
> ation as it affects their industry and trade is evident
> from the more or less recurrent attention given the
> matter in Parliament. Evidence has more than once been
> brought forward to show that the presence of the American
> film in the Colonies and even at home has led the people
> to demand the American products illustrated in the films
> in preference to those of the Mother Country. . . . So
> serious is the matter from the viewpoint of British
> industry that all sorts of alternatives have been dis-
> cussed in Parliament, even to the extent of barring
> American films from the country.[114]

The concern of England thus served to demonstrate the importance of

American pictures as a source of new business to the United States.

To support their claim that American films had, in fact,

served to sell goods abroad, the defenders pointed to specific

instances of things sold because of motion pictures. One writer

said there was evidence of autos, sewing machines, player-pianos,

armchairs, and clothing having been ordered from China, Peru,

Japan, and England following the exhibition of American films there.

Another pointed out that cash registers had been bought for a

Paris cafe after the cafe owner had seen them in an American picture.

He was the one, too, who implied that American films had increased
the sale of plumbing equipment in France, at the same time denying
he made the connection: "I would not presume to trace it directly
to the pictures, with their unconscious propaganda for products of
the most sanitary nations on earth." Added to these examples was
the estimate of the Department of Commerce, quoted in an encomium
for the Hays office in Review of Reviews, that every foot of film
sold abroad returns a dollar of income from other exports. Such was
the evidence that writers concluded the "American movie is the
spearhead of a new trade offensive, sinister if you happen to be
on the wrong end of it."[115] On the right end, the evidence supported the argument that the motion picture was a valuable national medium because it increased American business abroad.

English promoted

The hope that English might become the language of international
communication and commerce was rejuvenated with the introduction
of radio, talking pictures, and television.

In connection with radio and television, the argument explicitly concerned the destruction of international language barriers,
but English was promoted to the universal tongue. For example,
the science editor of the New York Times argued in 1924 that one
of the benefits to be derived from radio was the breaking down of
international language barriers. Because of radio, in which the

United States and Britain had taken the lead, he contended that
English must become the dominant world tongue, the new universal
language. As he put it, radio could do more in a generation toward
making English universal than any other medium could do in a century. DeForest likewise predicted that a universal language,
English, would be the eventual result of television's introduction.[116]

When talking pictures were introduced commercially in 1927 and
the exportation of sound films was begun, advocates interpreted
this to mean that, since the motion picture had an important influence in the world, the English language would become more widely
understood and eventually the universal tongue. Implicit in the
argument was the nation's pride in its mother tongue and the notion
that English was the proper mode of international communication.
Jesse Lasky, commenting on the new talking pictures in 1929, asserted
that the new movies would result not in a loss of foreign market as
some had predicted, but would instead "encourage a better understanding of English the world over." A writer for Independent and
Outlook developed a similar argument when he said that because of
motion pictures, "absurd as it may sound at first, there does indeed
seem to be some truth in the suggestion that all the world will
some day learn English--or what is more likely, that the world will
settle on three or four languages and cast aside its dialects and
local lingual idiosyncrasies." Like radio, talkies were predicted

by their supporters to "have an international influence in lessening the barriers of language."[117] Again, pictures were defended on the grounds that they promoted something which was of benefit to the United States.

It is interesting that when talking pictures were introduced in England, the same argument was used in their justification. In an article in Living Age, the President of British International Pictures, John Maxwell, said that the film Blackmail, the first British talkie, had led to a reawakening to the fine qualities of the English language. It was his contention that films would thus cause Englishmen to appreciate their language again.[118] So, just as films were considered valuable in America because they fostered the spread and understanding of the native language, they were raised to serve a similar function in England and were defended there, too, on that basis.

Valuable national business

Another area on which the defense of motion pictures, radio, and television was built was their contribution to the economic life of the nation. One line of argument that was employed with respect to all three media stressed their importance to the total national economy. It was argued, in effect, that the new media had caused the nation to prosper; assuming that national prosperity

was a virtue to be cultivated, the media were judged to be valuable
because they were the creators of the prosperity.

When this argument first appeared, the emphasis was on the
value of the motion pictures to the individual exhibitor. The
new amusement allowed businessmen to make a profit, said the advocates, and was therefore valuable. The Independent said, in 1908,
that motion pictures were cheap to operate and returned a good profit.
"The field thus offers golden opportunities for those who can induce
the multitudes to pay their nickels and dimes to witness up-to-date
entertainments." That same year, a writer in Photo-Era described
the nickelodeons as having "proved veritable gold-mines for their
owners." Scientific American pointed out that the new moving pictures had allowed the managers of formerly destitute "opery houses"
to turn a handsome profit,[119] and Lippincott's Magazine summarized
the experience of one company as evidence for its contention that
the movies were indeed a good business.

> One company rents two buildings /on Broadway in New York/
> for which they pay ninety thousand dollars a year, yet
> the profits, after taking out the royalty for film service,
> salaries of employees, and all other outlay, were twenty-
> five thousand dollars last year--and not a single admis-
> sion cost over five cents.[120]

With individual profit and good business defined as material values,
the movies, which caused the prosperity were judged valuable.

While pictures were most often defended in the early days on
the grounds that they brought their exhibitors profit, it was

occasionally pointed out that the industry was valuable nationally.
The emphasis in the argument, on these occasions, was shifted from
the benefits to the individual theater owner or exhibitor to the
benefits accruing to related industries and to the general business
climate of the nation. For instance, when Lucy France Pierce discussed the growth and place of the nickelodeon in 1908, she argued
that the new entertainment was also a valuable new business.

> It has been roughly estimated that the profits to American
> manufacturers of films and projecting machines amounted
> last year to $75,000,000. The middlemen, or rental agents,
> buy annually from the manufacturer $4,000,000 worth of
> films, from which they derive a rental from the nickelodeon
> of $8,000,000. It requires an army of ninety thousand or
> more persons to conduct the rental agencies and the theaters
> proper. It is estimated that four times that number are
> employed in the manufacturing corps. In the season just
> past, $65,000,000 were spent in paid admissions to the
> nickelodeon in the United States alone.[121]

Another writer in 1910 also pointed to the wide-ranging character
of the business arrangements in the movie industry and concluded
that "if, by some inconceivable chance the moving picture business
should be suddenly stopped, sixty thousand men and women, at the
most conservative estimate would be thrown out of work."[122] These
arguments were the exception in the early period, however. But it
was from these arguments that the later defense of the three new
media evolved, for rather than arguing the individual profits to
be derived from the industries, advocates stressed the national
economic importance of the media.

When the defense of motion pictures was undertaken by the
MPPDA under the leadership of Will Hays, argument from national
profit was given major emphasis. It became common to promote
pictures on the grounds that they were an important national industry which had vital influence on the rest of the nation's business.
Hays argued that not only was the motion picture industry important
in the national economy because of the "$50,000,000 paid annually
in salaries and wages, $200,000,000 spent annually in production,
and possibly $600,000,000 taken in each year for admissions," but
that the movies also did much business with related industries,
thus stimulating their economy. For example, Hays estimated that
the picture industry spent $12,000,000 a year on materials related
to advertising, so "the newspaper, magazine, advertiser, printer,
engraver, typesetter, photographer, lithographer, artists, book-
binders, ink and paper manufacturers, bill-posters, and their help
are all benefitted by these immense sums spent." But more than
these workers profited indirectly from the motion picture industry.

> Whole cities are built for motion pictures. The
> items for material and labor in 'sets' will reach over
> $5,000,000 annually. Millions of feet of lumber are
> used, from pegs to palaces. Thus the lumberman, car-
> penters, builders, and architects come in for benefits.
> The clothing trade benefits to nearly $1,000,000 in the
> wardrobes of the studios. All manner of costumes, modern
> and medieval, are kept and made. The drapery depart-
> ments contain rare fabrics, priceless tapestry, and
> modern textiles. Furniture of every period is made or
> the originals purchased. Wild and domestic animals and
> birds are kept, and plant nurseries are maintained; for

everything must be true to form in motion pictures. The
railroads and hotels receive almost $5,000,000 annually
through travel expenses of the industry. Hundreds of
thousands of metal cases are used for shipping films,
benefitting the metal trade, not to mention the cameras
and projecting machines. Cost of transporting films by
express and parcel post is enormous, and the insurance
runs into large sums. Real estate and rents figure in
an important way, both in ground and buildings of the
producing plants and in the theaters. The electrical
trade, the coal industry, the electric power companies,
the telegraph and telephone, the optical trade, and the
automobile industry all participate in the benefits.
The film industry furnishes not far from one billion
feet of films annually to the motion-picture producers,
enough to encircle the earth eight times.[123]

Hence, motion pictures were, in Hays' argument, connected to many

facets of the national economy, and of primary importance in the

national business life. By implication, Hays suggested that if the

motion picture industry suffered economic harm, the economy of the

nation which depended directly or indirectly upon the movies for

support would also be hurt.

This argument was also used in connection with radio and

television. In 1925, for example, a writer for Review of Reviews

pointed out that not only were the sales of radio sets important

to the national economy, but that the radio industry employed,

directly or indirectly, some one-half million people. Moreover,

the growth of radio had prompted the development of a whole new

field of publishing which specialized in radio news, radio hand-

books, and radio schedules. Similar things were said about TV.

The sale of sets was a booming business: "The first six months of 1950 upward of 3,000,000 sets were sold at an average price plus

installation costs of over $300 each."[124]   By 1955, U. S. News and

World Report was able to say that

> industrially, TV is big business. Forty nine companies
> produce TV sets. There are more than 100,000 TV repair
> men, and many thousands of other people make a living
> in the sale and servicing of TV.[125]

At the same time, said U. S. News, the broadcasting side of tele-

vision was reported to be solvent, "a vast enterprise, still grow-

ing." Some 461 television stations were on the air, and 123 others

were under construction.[126] Television and radio were important

national industries.

Employment provided

Some of the arguments just examined suggest that the new media

were valuable because, at least indirectly, they provided more

opportunity for employment than had existed before. Promoters

also made the argument explicit.

When the matter of employment in motion pictures was injected

into the argument, it first referred to actors who were given a

new place to work. In 1907, for instance, Barton Currie in Harper's

Weekly said that one of the benefits of the new motion pictures,

in addition to the entertainment provided, was that for their pro-

ductions picture makers employed "great troops of actors and /took/

them all over the world to perform." Harper's Weekly reported

that Longacre Square, the traditional meeting place for out of work

actors, had been nearly decimated by the demands of motion pictures.
And by 1912 it was reported that motion picture companies had in
their employment over 400 actors.[127] Because of the chance to work
in pictures, actors were offered new security. (At the same time,
as critics pointed out, the theatre was damaged by this loss of
personnel.)

After the First World War, the argument was enlarged to refer
to all employment in motion pictures, and not only to actors. Hays
suggested, of course, that general employment was supported by the
widespread business demands of motion pictures. But, more directly,
the Mayor of Los Angeles argued in 1922 that the motion picture was
a valuable asset to the nation not only because it was the fourth
largest industry in the country, but because it provided employment,
both directly and indirectly, for some 1,000,000 people. In 1926,
a writer for Photo-Era placed the figure at 300,000 persons directly
employed in the industry. During the depression, pictures were
again assessed as valuable to the nation because they gave employment to "several hundred thousand people in these hard times."[128]

Radio, too, was defended as a new source of employment for
artists, specialized personnel, and technicians. For instance,
radio was said to have indirectly stimulated employment for people
who appeared on the air; exposure on the radio created a demand
for personal appearances for various artists. Moreover, the need
of radio for musicians created a demand for concert artists on the

air and provided a new source of income for musicians. Friends
argued that radio also furnished new employment for thousands of
engineers and technical people. The employment figures, directly
or indirectly due to radio, were placed at "close to one-half million
people."[129]

During the time that television was predicted to be on the
way, its advocates linked it with new job opportunities. Looking
ahead to television, a Collier's article in 1939 predicted that

> television broadcasting, even more than sound broadcasting,
> will be a great consumer of art. It will constantly demand
> more and better writers, musicians, actors and scenic
> designers--new thoughts, new words, new songs, new faces,
> new backgrounds. Unlike a play on the stage or a motion
> picture which may run for a year, the television program,
> once it has been shown to a national audience, is on the
> scrap heap. It is finished. Television will call for a
> whole new generation of artists. It should help materially
> to solve the unemployment problem.[130]

The new medium was expected to provide new job opportunity quite
directly by hiring new people to fulfill its demands.

The predictions continued following the Second World War and
the introduction of TV on a limited scale. For example, in 1945,
the science editor of the New York Times predicted that there
would be many new opportunities for employment in television,
matching or outstripping any such development witnessed in the
growth of motion pictures, radio, or the automobile. To him,
television and its supporting industries, would be an important
new source of jobs. In 1949 a writer for Etude sought to reassure

piano teachers that the advent of television would not mean the
end of music lessons. In fact, said Etude, there would no doubt
be music lessons on TV; this would create a new army of players
and singers, and a consequent demand for teachers of music. In
total, the lot of the music teacher would be improved by television,
not damaged.[131] Like its predecessors, then, television was predicted to be a new source of employment, at a time when employment
was viewed as a societal good.

Aid to business

Operating on the presumption that sound business was good for
the nation, and that what aided business indirectly supported the
national economy, defenders of motion pictures, radio, and television
pointed out the relationship of the new media to the business
world. All of the media were said to be of aid to business, although
the specific ways in which the aid was generated varied.

Motion pictures, for example, were described by Scientific
American in 1901 as "an instrument of practical utility in the
great world of commerce." What the writer meant was that the new
films could be used to show samples of goods not handily trans-
ported or demonstrated--locomotives, pile-drivers, fire extinguish-
ers, and blasting powder--and to "recall to prospective purchasers
the operation of complicated devices." In this fashion, business
would be allowed even greater chance to make use of the axiom

that seeing is believing. Other writers suggested that pictures could aid business through slow motion studies and through filmed analysis of industrial operations.[132] Will Hays again presented the most extensive treatment of this argument. In 1923 he wrote that

> motion pictures are used to demonstrate machines and inventions to prospective buyers who sit in their office chairs and view the projection of the apparatus on the screen, which they will not go miles to see in actual operation. Every 'movie' fan is acquainted with the slow-motion effect that can be obtained in pictures, which enables the eye to see the most minute movements of every intricate mechanism. Instead of spending three days in inspecting properties upon which a bond issue was to be floated, representatives of important bond houses recently spent three hours seeing the properties in motion pictures and then purhcased the bonds. A stock breeder clinched his deal with his prospects through motion pictures.[133]

Certainly, promoters suggested, a medium which was of this much benefit to business, must be of value to the nation as a whole.

Radio was defended on similar grounds. When wireless communication was reported to have been established between European capitals and New York, one of the first uses suggested was that of relaying business messages between the cities. Then again in 1928, when the importance of radio to the country was surveyed, one of its great contributions was said to be that it could "get a single piece of business news to millions of people instantly and at low cost."[134]

Television, too, was predicted to be of assistance to business.
As early as 1907, when Review of Reviews reported that pictures
had been successfully transmitted by wire, it suggested that this
new invention would have important consequences for the nation,
one of which was that signatures could be transmitted by wire,
thus providing business with nearly instantaneous means of authenti-
cating transactions.[135]
Much later, television was praised as having been

> the biggest thing that's happened to the bar-and-tavern
> business since the free lunch. Often when a hot fight
> or a tight ball game is being televised, bewildered but
> beaming publicans have to lock their doors against late
> comers to keep their television-equipped establishments
> from bursting at the seams.[136]

These applications of the new media to business were, of
course, separate from the function of the media in advertising.
Both radio and television were defended on the grounds that they
gave business a new means for advertising, although there was also
much objection on the basis of this function. Early in 1922, it
was predicted that advertising would soon be on the air, for the
new medium, said a writer for Illustrated World, was certainly
too cheap, too popular, too striking to escape the keen eye of the
advertiser. After radio advertising had become accepted as fact,
Roy S. Durstine, of B. B. D. and O., evaluated radio advertising
as a method of building "an extraordinary fund of good will," a

way of attracting listeners to an advertising message, and a means
of stimulating listeners to read related forms of advertising.[137]

On the basis of the performance of radio in advertising,
television was predicted to have even greater potential as a salesman in the home. Having seen a demonstration of television in the
laboratory, a writer in Reader's Digest was enthusiastic about the
quality of the picture he had watched. "Imagine," he asked his
readers, "what such reproduction will mean to visual broadcast
advertising when the time comes."[138] After television had been in
nationwide operation for five years, the predictions of the earlier
writers were confirmed. U. S. News and World Report, for instance,
said in 1955 that

> TV has had a phenomenal success in advertising. Since
> 1948, revenues to TV networks from advertising have
> risen from about 1 million dollars to 444 million in
> 1954.[139]

Such figures served to add evidence to the earlier assertions that
"television's capacity for showing and demonstrating products in
use makes it highly suited to the advertising and merchandising
of all manner of goods and services.[140] Like the radio before it,
television became the newest and most powerful means of reaching
a vast public with a sales message; like its predecessor, television was a servant of business.

Law enforcement aided

Very early in their history, motion pictures were attacked
as a cause of crime. Later this accusation was leveled against
both radio and television. In response to this charge, defenders
of radio and television sought to show that these media were of
value in law enforcement. For instance, it was argued that radio,
because of the rapidity of communication possible with it, would
assist the police in capturing criminals.[141]

When pictures by wireless were announced in 1907, Review of
Reviews predicted that among their uses would be work with law
enforcement; not only could pictures of criminals be sent over the
wire to aid in their capture, but the picture would promote justice
by helping to prevent innocent people from being prosecuted as
criminals. Twenty years later David Sarnoff predicted that television would diminish crime by instantly showing pictures of criminals on the air. The Saturday Evening Post in 1940 reported that
thumb prints of criminals had been put on television in the Los
Angeles area, and that "from these wireless motion pictures, seven
sheriffs were able to identify the criminal immediately."[142] Thus
the new media were predicted to be a weapon in the fight against
crime. The advantages to society were obvious.

Other benefits

    In addition to the lines of argument which have been discussed, arguments about the national good which appeared only once or twice should also be noted. These, like the more popular arguments, reflect the attempt of advocates to associate the new media with accepted values and to establish a causal connection between the new and the valued. At the same time, the arguments cited here reflect special interests and particular concerns.

    For example, movies were praised by Outlook as a new method for promoting traffic safety; were named as having raised public morale in the depression; and were said to be "teaching immigrants to be good Americans." Radio helped to prevent crime; to promote "social justice;" and to give minorities fair representation. Television kept youth from "the dangers of cheap dance halls" while Superman "exercised his unique gifts, such as X-ray vision, long distance hearing, supersonic speed and the ability to fly, on behalf of interracial tolerance and against juvenile delinquency and school absenteeism."[143]

    In many ways the new media served the national good. Promoters sought to link television, radio, and motion pictures with a wide range of improvements in the life of the nation. If the media served well there, their worth was amply demonstrated.

World Peace

Advocates of motion pictures, radio, and television held in common the vision of the media they supported leading to a peaceful world. Except for times when the nation was at war, when spokesmen for the media talked of contributions to the war effort, a major item in the repertory of advocacy was the assertion that movies and broadcasting would create an international climate conducive to peaceful cooperation among nations. For instance, Gerald Swope, the president of General Electric, was quoted in Outlook in 1924 forecasting that radio would be "a means for general and perpetual peace on earth."[144] The means varied from writer to writer, but the end, peace on earth, they held as a common dream.

New understanding

Most of the writers discussing the media as a way to world peace presumed that war resulted from simple misunderstanding among the people of the world. Consequently, if the people of the many nations could get to know each other, could become familiar with each others' customs and cultures, the new-found understanding would bring an end to war. It was the function of the mass media to create that new understanding.

The argument was introduced in the announcement of Edison's sound pictures in 1891. There Lathrop said that the new pictures would be useful in "sundry directions," one of them being to acquaint

Americans with the people of foreign lands: "What object-lessons
might it not bring to us from foreign lands of literally moving
sights or accidents, and the animated presence of far-off peoples!"
Then in 1910, Review of Reviews quoted Thomas Edison as saying the
motion picture "will wipe out narrow minded prejudices which are
founded on ignorance, it will create a feeling of sympathy and a
desire to help the down-trodden people of the earth, and it will
give new ideals to be followed." The American Magazine in 1913
argued that in pictures the mass man "sees alien people and begins
to understand how like they are to him." However in 1919, Edison,
prompted by the war situation, made explicit the connection between
the understanding created by pictures and the end of wars. It was
his argument that only universal education could prevent future
fighting, and that "the best schoolhouse is the screen; the best
teacher is the film."[145]

After this, the argument that pictures would lead to peace
through understanding was commonly used in praise of the medium.
For example, when D. W. Griffith talked about the future of movies
for Collier's he said that in a hundred years films would have
helped eliminate wars by demonstrating to men that they were like
all other men around the world.[146] When newsreels were introduced,
Independent carried a statement by the editor of the Fox News Reels
that films would

break down the barriers of ignorance that separate nations
by showing half the world in intimate detail the life of
the other half. A great force for universal peace, teaching
by the power of fact, the universal brotherhood of man.[147]

Will Hays adopted the argument and used it repeatedly in his promo-

tion of the medium. He developed the argument in this fashion in

1927. Because of motion pictures, he wrote,

provincialism is being wiped out and the world brought
into closer contact with increased knowledge and understanding. I do not think I am too visionary when I say
that the motion picture is the greatest agency yet given
to man to bring about more cordial relations between
nations. When we know each other we do not hate; when we
do not hate we do not wage war.[148]

Finally, the talking pictures were also introduced as offering

new possibilities for greater understanding on the international

level. A writer for Photo-Era, held that

what the motion picture and radio have accomplished toward
bringing the world closer together, the talking picture,
which unites the advantages of both, can be utilized to
expand and further. Properly utilized, it can be made of
the greatest service in the furtherance of international
understanding and the development of good will among
nations.[149]

Each of these writers saw the medium they lauded as offering new

possibilities for realizing the dream of world peace through

understanding.

Similarly, the spokesmen for radio hailed this invention as

aiding the cause of peace. Early in 1922 a reporter for Illus-

trated World, prompted to comment by the use of wireless in the

Washington Peace Conference of 1921, predicted that radio would

be one of the great means of eliminating misunderstanding among
nations. "The handmaiden of peace," he wrote, "in other words,
is the wireless." Later radio was characterized as the greatest
civilizer the world had ever known because it could help every man
become acquainted with the culture of every other man. David
Sarnoff, recalling that a radio minister opened a sermon by addres-
sing his "fellow human beings," asked, "On a day when we can all
be addressed as fellow human beings may we not hope that something
finer and more tolerant will come into our attitudes, one toward
the other?" And a writer for Review of Reviews, noting the founding
of the International Broadcasting Union, dedicated to international
understanding and good will, argued that the radio, by creating a
feeling of international familiarity through the exchange of music,
history, and culture, was the best means through which to achieve
international harmony and the peace that accompanies it.[150]

As radio before it, television was also predicted to exert a
beneficial influence in world affairs by creating new understanding.
As early as 1928, when TV was still only predicted, Literary Digest
told readers they could use the new medium to see people in other
lands and to observe how they lived. "And we shall not look forever
and not sympathize," the article concluded. Etude described the
late 1940's as the Television Age, an era when the thoughts and
ideals of all people would be brought into harmonious understanding
and peace. And a vice president of R. C. A. in 1952 argued that

television might foster world peace by carrying bits of information

and culture from nation to nation, helping people to understand

other people. Thus television on an international level would

spread friendship throughout the world and serve as an antidote

to recurrent threats of war.[151]

International unity

Spokesmen for the new media talked of another dream which

could be realized through international communication. Lee DeForest

was one of the early proponents of the notion as he talked about

the way in which radio had served to link the whole world in a new

kind of international kinship. In H. V. Kaltenborn's terms, because

of radio "space has disappeared and all mankind speaks and listens

in unison." Radio was to him a magic instrument of unity and power

destined to link nations, to enlarge knowledge, to remove misunder-

standing, and to promote truth." Saturday Review called upon

Tennyson's vision of "earth at last a warless world, a single race,

a single tongue," to express its hope that the new forms of broad-

casting might serve to achieve international unity.[152]

A similar hope was held out for television. Like radio, it

also made distance seem less, caused the world to appear smaller,

brought mankind into closer touch. Looking ahead, Independent

predicted in 1928 that one day television would allow "a comfort-

able citizen ensconced in his bathtub in San Francisco /to/ watch

without embarrassment the inauguration of a President in Washington."
What would all this mean? Television, said Independent, was not

> a thing which will rock the earth or solve the problems
> of all mankind, but it may, in a year or two, develop
> into a valuable and spectacular convenience. It is one
> of those inventions which editors will commend as 'cement-
> ing the friendship of nations' by annihilating space and
> 'placing the capitals of Europe in your back yard.'[153]

Seeing each other at this range, or hearing each other, the
peoples of the earth might not only gain a new understanding of each
other, but might begin to think alike, to talk about the business
they had together, and even to sense that discussion of international
problems could be brought into the open. The world might be unified,
as a family is unified. This was the goal of the new media. As
Floyd Parsons wrote in Saturday Evening Post in 1922, "It is not too
much to say that the radiophone will tend to develop the people of
a nation into one family and will serve effectively in removing such
obstacles to international amity as the boundary lines that separate
nations."[154] Because of the new mass media, the people of the world
would think together and act together in peace and harmony, undisturbed by the artificial barriers erected between them.

Persuasion by example

It was further argued by the advocates of motion pictures and
television that these two media, by supplying audiences with scenes
of war and battles, would lead the viewers to desire peace. W. D.
Howells first argued in Harper's that through viewing filmed scenes

of war, school children would be taught to strive for peace. With

the motion picture,

> a modern battle with smokeless powder may be taught to
> rage before their eyes, with every detail of heads and
> legs blown off that they /the school children/ may realize
> how glorious war is at close range. Towns burning n the
> background and women and children flying for all their
> lives will fill the perspective. A sea-fight, with
> armored battle-ships sinking one another, could be as
> easily rendered if the films were recovered from the
> body of some witness representing an enterprising metro-
> politan journal in the engagement.[155]

The children, Howells thought, could hardly desire war, having seen

its effects first hand. Twenty years later, both Living Age and

The Commonweal reported the results of experiments in which school

children were exposed to war films, and calculated the attitude

changes resulting. In both instances, the war films were said to

cause children to dislike war. In one case, 97% of the viewers,

said Commonweal, were made

> determinedly contra-war by the films. This seems to
> us to be a very fine score for the movies and a solid
> achievement for realism.[156]

A similar argument was employed with regard to television.

Literary Digest in 1928 surveyed opinion about television's impact.

One writer held that TV would create greater international under-

standing by showing people in other lands, and then went on to say

"nor is it easy to believe that if we once see a battle and what

comes after, we shall go on forever believing that 'war is a part

of human nature,' and we will always have it."[157]

Peace in the world was assumed to be man's worthy goal. The new mass media, according to their advocates, would help him achieve it. Hence, motion pictures, radio, and television were again promoted through their association with values men were presumed to respect and goals they were thought to seek. The new media were characterized as the servants of unity, understanding, goodwill, and peace, the enemies of dissent, misunderstanding, and war. New inventions would cause to be done the things man held to be good. Innovation would allow mankind to achieve the ends which have so far eluded him.

Culture

Spokesmen for motion pictures, radio, and television argued that the new media would prove beneficial to the cultural life of the nation. That is, some advocates simply labeled the new media cultural; the persuasion was effected by the general image of goodness surrounding the term. Other writers dealt with what they believed to be the constituents of culture; certain benefits, they said, derived from the movies, radio, or TV which in turn would bolster the cultural life of the community. In either case, the media contributed to something understood to be good and desirable.

A general cultural argument was employed in connection with each of the new media. Television's first contribution to culture was predicted in 1912, as Gilfillan argued that pictures in the home would bring to the family entertainment and education. But, he

went on,

> outside of education lies culture, the appreciation of
> beauty in ideas, aspects, sounds and gestures. The
> home theatre will impart culture--remember that we shall
> be awakened from sleep by Hoffmann playing, to wander
> through the Louvre with Chase, and in the evening sit
> at the feet of Maeterlinck, or before the great artists
> of the stage.[158]

Later, in 1922, when a writer for Collier's listed the advantages

of radio, he argued that radio would spread culture everywhere.

That is, he said, changing the definition of culture from an empha-

sis on the aesthetic to a broadening of knowledge, radio would

"give everyone the chance and the impulse to learn to use his brains."

Will Hays, speaking of the talking pictures, assumed that no defi-

nition of culture was needed and listed it with various other goods,

asserting that the motion picture "is more than a business, far more

than an industry; above everything else, it is a servant of happi-

ness, of enlightenment, of culture, of human brotherhood."[159] Then,

in 1941, when David Sarnoff surveyed the future of television, he

predicted that the new medium would lead to a higher cultural stan-

dard, just as radio had already raised the cultural level of the

nation.

> We have seen how the general level of musical taste
> in this country has been raised by the widespread radio
> broadcasting of good music. People to whom such privi-
> leges as grand opera and symphonic music were unknown
> fifteen years ago are becoming increasingly familiar with
> them. With television, a similar widening cultural develop-
> ment in appreciation of the best in drama, the dance,

> painting, and sculpture may be expected. Through television,
> coupled with the universal increase in schooling, Americans
> may attain the highest general cultural level of any people
> in the history of the world.[160]

Hence, one of the promises of each of the new media was that of

improving in some fashion the cultural life of the times.

Other writers focused on particular constituents of what they

defined as cultural, and argued that these areas would be enhanced

by the new media. First of all, various writers argued that the

new media led to a new exposure to culture among the mass audience.

From the beginning, there were reports that in the moving picture

houses the auditor might see not only the various places in the

world formerly closed to him, but also filmed versions of "poems,

scenes from novels, Bible history," plays such as "East Lynne,"

"Camille," "The Rivals," and "great spectacular melodrama such as

'Quo Vadis' and the Passion Play of Oberammergau." This exposure

meant, said a writer for The New Republic, that from pictures

Americans were "getting the rudiments of a spiritual education."

From the exposure, too, came a new understanding of dramatic art.

"The motion picture," wrote C. B. Neblette in Photo-Era, "has given

to the American people an understanding of the drama, of stagecraft,

of acting which they would never had without it."[161] As Walter

Prichard Eaton put it in The American Magazine in 1909, the motion

pictures were

> real dramas, with real actors portraying real emotions.
> Considering who the people are that frequent moving

picture shows, their effect cannot fail to be for good;
they make for the elevation of taste, for a better understanding of theatric art.[162]

The argument that there was cultural value to be derived from

the exposure of the public to drama was used both in connection

with motion pictures and radio. Sarnoff's comments about radio

already have been noted above. Before Sarnoff, others argued that

radio had served to expose the mass audience to materials formerly

unavailable to them. For example, Charles D. Isaacsson in Theatre

Magazine asked his readers to consider the good done by radio.

Think of the millions who have listened to opera airs
for the first time in their lives! Think of the millions
who have heard speeches on intellectual subjects for the
first time in their lives![163]

Both motion pictures and radio were thus defended on the grounds

that they contributed a new dimension to the cultural exposure of

the mass audience.

Offering a modification of the previous argument, other writers

maintained in support of the media that they had not only served

to expose the public to culture, but had created a new and broader

interest in things cultural among the general audience. Isaacson

argued that radio, through exposure of the audience to a variety

of arts, "is in the long run, . . . the best booster for the new

ideals and hopes of the theatrical, musical and literary world

that has ever come into being."[164] In a similar vein, radio was

held to have been responsible for the musical revival of the late

1930's. The Secretary of the National Piano Manufacturers Association was reported by The Etude to have declared

> after a careful and dispassionate study of the nearly
> 300% increase in piano sales during the past twelve
> months, radio must now be considered one of the major
> reasons for this increase. Millions of listeners, who
> otherwise might never have attained an appreciation
> of music, are manifesting an interest in musical culture
> and endeavoring to become participants themselves.[165]

Motion pictures, said School and Society, had created a new interest in music among children, and the movie director Monta Bell said films had inspired public interest in the legitimate stage and in the use of dialogue. Television was also defended on the basis of its contribution to a new interest in culture. In articles which maintained that TV programs had inspired people to take up music, and in the predictions that television would lead to a new interest in art, making the latter so attractive that "people may even come to look at pictures without expecting to have them explained, discussed, and commented on till they vanish,"[166] television was said to have come to the aid of culture.

A further hope held out for the motion pictures by their advocates was that this new medium would come to the aid of beauty. George Bernard Shaw, for instance, argued in 1914 that "the cinematograph, by familiarizing us with elegance, grace, beauty, and the rest of those immoral virtues, which are so much more important than the moral ones, could easily make our ugliness look ridiculous." Some time later, a writer for Scribners argued that the movies were the fulcrum which could be used to move the world and make it not only wiser, but "more universally beautiful . . . than our present-day minds can conceive." A variation on this argument proposed that the awakening to beauty which could take place through color motion pictures would serve to counterbalance the damage which had been done children by too frequent exposure to films.[167] In each argument, the aim was to support beauty; the means was the motion picture.

Good taste

An argument closely related to the influence of the media on the culture was one on their influence on taste. There was general dissatisfaction, apparently, with the level of public taste, for both advocates and attackers made reference to its low level. Advocates, however, argued that the mass media offered a means of raising public taste while the attackers argued, as I shall demonstrate later, that the media either caused the bad taste, pandered to it, or failed to raise taste to the anticipated level. Interestingly, neither side defined what it was they meant by "good taste."

The taste argument, as it related to the movies, was primarily an argument of attack. Only twice was it used by the defenders. It was introduced by Walter Prichard Eaton who, as I have already noted, argued that motion pictures could not help but raise the level of public taste when considered in the light of the audiences

which attended films in the first place. It was his position that
with the mass audience, taste could move only in an upward direction. The second writer to employ the argument was Albert Shaw,
who in 1932 argued that the motion picture had a highly beneficial
influence on the American public, and in the future would be even
better. It was his contention that the pictures would in the
future exert direct initiative and leadership in elevating the
average standard of manners and taste and would lead to improvement
in the artistic good taste of the public.[168] In neither case did
the writers supply any support for their assertions.

It was also predicted that radio would serve to raise public
taste. In 1923, Floyd Parsons predicted in a Saturday Evening Post
story about radio that one of its functions would be to "uplift
the popular taste in music and the spoken drama."[169] Some evidence
was available to support a similar assertion in 1938. Then it was
argued in The North American Review that over a ten year period the
effect of radio on musical taste had been beneficial.

> Ten years ago Edgar's Salut d'Amour and Chopin's E-Flat
> Nocturne meant classical music to the public. The story
> is different today. The radio has acquainted millions
> of listeners with the works of Beethoven and Bach. The
> concert audience is demanding whole programs devoted
> exclusively to the works of a single master--a step for-
> ward in the maturity of American music lovers, which
> concert masters can only explain by the fact that radio
> broadcasting has elevated public taste.[170]

Further evidence of the change was inferred from the changing
behavior of radio advertisers over a ten year period. While in the

early history of broadcasting advertisers most often supported
programs of blues, one defender noted a distinct shift to support
of classical music among advertisers in the later 1930's. Surveys
of audience preference confirmed the observation that there had
been a shift in program preferences among listeners. The conclusion from this evidence was that "the taste of the American public
has improved so during the last ten years that businessmen, looking
for profit, seek the ally of great music." Recall, too, that in
his 1941 predictions about television David Sarnoff had based his
argument on similar presumptions about the influence of radio on
the level of musical taste among the public.[171] Although radio was
credited with having improved public taste in at least one area,
and the experience used to predict the influence of television,
the argument on taste was not employed by spokesmen for television.

Culture, vaguely defined and variously interpreted, was another
of the good things which was to be enhanced by the new mass media.
Culture, related to education, beauty, good taste, serious music,
and proper manners, was not only a god term, but a social goal.
As such, it became referent in the class built by advocates.

Morality

A major area of attack on motion pictures, radio, and television
involved the influence of the media on morality. Defenders consequently also dealt with moral issues, but with less frequency

and far less vigor than did the opposition. Both sides agreed that
the media exerted a moral influence; the disagreement centered in
the direction of that influence. While attackers argued that the
media undermined the conventional system of morality, caused children
to indulge in illicit sexual adventure, and were a primary influence in stimulating criminal behavior, the defenders held that the
media taught useful moral lessons and might be used to substitute
for real life in the learning of ethical precepts.

As early as 1907 motion pictures were charged with having
corrupted children and with having been a haven for pickpockets.
In answer to the charges, a writer for Harper's Weekly, Barton
Currie, argued that not only would criminals find lean pickings
in the pockets of picture show audiences, but that seeing the films
might lead to the criminal's moral reform. Even burglars, wrote
Currie, could learn a lesson from the pictures,

> for most of the slides offer you a quick flash or melo-
> drama in which the villain and the criminals are always
> getting the worst of it. Pursuits of malefactors are
> by far the most popular of all nickel deliriums. You
> may see snatch-purses, burglars, and an infinite variety
> of criminals hunted by the police and the mob in almost
> any nickelet you have the curiosity to visit.[172]

Other writers adopted and expanded this defense. In later years
readers were to be told that movies not only frightened criminals
into lawful pursuit, but also served "to encourage goodness and
kindness, virtue and courage;" to teach "lessons of honesty, decency,

courage, manliness, industry, sobriety, and good citizenship generally;" and, in 1929, to be "perhaps the most useful of all the
present mediums of expression in the inculcation of generally
accepted standards of morality and behavior."[173]   One defense position thus focused on the use of the movies to provide lessons in
acceptable moral behavior.

A variation of the argument on morality asserted that the
motion picture provided a substitute for real life in the learning
of moral behavior.   The learner, gaining his experience through
viewing films, was spared the harsh consequences of moral lapses
in real life.   This was one of the arguments Thomas Edison used to
justify motion pictures.   On one occasion Edison proposed that with
film a National University of Experience could be created which
would teach lessons in honesty, for example, by exposing the "economic absurdity that any enduring success or happiness could be
built on trickery or fraud or deceit."   Several years earlier he
had argued that "one of the most valuable educational features of
the film is that it actually shows the moral reward to scholars;
it shows them the effect of doing wrong and of doing right."[174]
The argument was amplified further in 1930 when the DeVry School
Films Company proposed "to teach social reform and higher ethics
to our children" through motion pictures.   Explaining the method,
Photo-Era said that

children cannot grasp abstract notions of morals and
ethics until they begin to experience them. Normally,
a child must lie in order to experience the abstraction
and have us discuss it clearly to his understanding and
intelligence. But in the movies we don't have to wait
until the child actually lies. A story may be built
up to show a situation where a lie may be used, and moral
conduct deducted therefrom. Equally, matrimonially inclined,
the natural process of marrying through natural impulse,
and its consequences--or, on the other hand, of marrying
through a proper conception of companionship. This form
of education, this heading off domestic difficulties
before they arrive, is a wholly new form, with the field
of investigation not even scratched. It treats the patient
before he gets into trouble. All forms of moral reactions
may thus be placed, not only before the children from
primary to college, but before parents. It may be made
to include all ethics, domestic and international.[175]

The specific films would help overcome the immediate problem of

moral education, and the end result would be, the argument implied,

the strengthening of the national moral fibre.

I commented before that the defense offered moral arguments

much less frequently than did the attack. The disparity becomes

clear when it is recognized that only eleven times did the defense

argue that motion pictures would influence morality beneficially,

whereas the attack argued from morality at least five times more

frequently.

Arguments on morality were occasionally offered in defense

of both radio and television. For example, the daytime radio serial

was defended in 1945 on the grounds that it supported the conven-

tional moral system and demonstrated "to its listeners the fact that

ultimately good must overcome evil." In similar fashion, television was defended with the argument that it would support the ethical

commonplace that good would triumph, right would win. For example,

a writer in Good Housekeeping argued in 1950 that "psychiatrists

or no, I'm convinced that a generation of Western-movie fans will

grow into adulthood . . . firmly believing in the triumph of right.

It was on this basis that Elliot Roosevelt also argued that tele-

vision would "raise . . . the ethical standards of our people."

Finally, a writer in Saturday Evening Post contended that tele-

vision might improve the national moral standard simply by showing

people in public places. Hence, individuals who did not want to

be seen engaging in behavior of which they might later be ashamed,

or who did not want to be seen in places they believed they should

not be, would be discouraged from the activity by the threat of

exposure on TV. In this fashion, their personal moral standard,

and the general moral standard of the nation, might be improved.[176]

The argument on morality, however, was never a serious means of

defense for either radio or television although such argument did

play a significant role in the attack on both of the media.

Health

Questions about the influence of motion pictures, radio, or

television on the health of audience members were one of the first

sources of attack on the new media. Presuming that people were

concerned about their health, and opposed to things which threatened

their good health, critics argued that the nickelodeons were ill-
ventilated spreaders of disease and that the pictures shown in
them were hard on the eyes. Radio was charged with discouraging
active play among children, thus making them sedentary and soft,
and with frightening young listeners into nervous disorders. Television combined the ill-effects of both movies and radio.

Proponents of the new media, who could hardly avoid acquaintance with the charges, took one of three courses in dealing with
them. Most of the advocates simply ignored the attacks, operating on
the assumption that the best defense was silence. Some of the spokesmen for the media dealt with the health problem indirectly. That is,
they talked about the way in which movies were being sent "over swamp,
valley, and hill to explain to the people the menace of dirty dairies
and of the disease-carrying fly, the proper care of the baby, and
other things that will aid people to become healthy." They told how
radio and television could be used to diagnose disease over long distances and how, because of radio, no ship at sea would need be without
medical advice in the future. Or they wrote of the valuable training
medical students received through filmed lectures or televised demonstrations.[177] A few others attempted to demonstrate that the new
media, if not good for health, were at least not damaging to it.
These arguments will be considered now.

Spokesmen who chose to deal with the health issue first of all
denied that any damage to the eyes resulted from either movies or
television, and offered readers reassurance about the safety of

their eyesight. A symposium of doctors, for example, writing originally in The Medical Times and quoted in 1915 by Literary Digest,
were of the opinion that if the eyes were strong and normal they
would not be damaged by motion pictures.[178] John Crosby, telling
readers not to worry about their eyesight because television would
not hurt it, answered charges to the contrary with a story about
a dog.

> There was, it's true, a dog in Greenwich, Conn., who
> got eyestrain from staring at television. I suspect
> he had weak eyes to begin with. Or else he didn't
> have much sense.[179]

The same year a member of the faculty in the medical college,
Cornell University, commented that while every new invention had
caused "the timid to fear a danger in what is really a forward
step," there was no more danger to the eyes from television than
from other normal activities--watching movies, reading, sewing,
or driving a car.[180] Television might, however, cause eye fatigue
if improperly viewed, but this would leave no permanent injury.

Other advocates argued that if movies or television did cause
eye discomfort, this was a good thing, for the discomfort served
to reveal formerly unknown eye defects. This argument was first
used in 1915 in connection with pictures. It appeared again, 35
years later, in the defense of television. Science Digest, for
example, quoted the Executive Director of the National Society for
the Prevention of Blindness who said that while television made the

eyes work harder than other visual activities, it normally did not cause eye defects. Television served only to show up pre-existing conditions which needed treatment.[181] These advocates presented a kind of silver lining argument, asserting that even what appeared at first to be an evil led to good results.

Some of the spokesmen for movies and television laid the responsibility for any eye damages to the viewer himself, contending that if used properly the media were harmless. This was the position of the Director of the psychological laboratory at Colgate University who said in Scientific American that if eye problems did result from movies it was probable simply because the viewer sat too close to the screen. A writer for Parent's Magazine said about the same thing of television. She claimed that children's eyes hurt because they sat too close to the screen and had difficulty focusing on the picture. It was up to the parents to see they used the set properly.[182] Here, then, the responsibility was shifted from the medium to the auditor or someone responsible for him.

Finally, occasional defenders of television argued that the medium could be used to correct certain eye defects in children. It was Time which first mentioned this application of television. Reporting a study by a doctor from Philadelphia's Pennsylvania State College of Optometry, Time said TV could be used to treat a child's squint or crossed eyes. "By covering the healthy eye, a youngster's 'lazy' eye can be painlessly strengthened while it is focused happily

for an hour or more on Hopalong Cassidy and Captain Video." This
use for TV was confirmed by the faculty member from Cornell.[183]
The medium had a direct and beneficial medical application.

This was the extent of advocates' arguments from health.
Those who talked about health denied the damage, asserted that any
harm was really good, shifted the responsibility from the media
to the viewer, and linked television with medical treatment. They
presumed, as had attackers, that good health was highly valued, and
sought to show that the new media were not responsible for any
defects in either eyesight or general well-being. The arguments
from health, however, were primarily the property of the critics.
A significant part of their attack was based on this issue. Most of
the defenders chose simply not to respond to it.

The arguments which have been surveyed in this chapter stress
the positive and beneficial relationship between innovation and the
prevailing value system. Advocates contended that the new media
had influenced, or would influence in a salutary fashion those things
and ideas generally held to be necessary, worthwhile, and desirable.
Motion pictures, radio, and television were therefore presented
as new modes of useful entertainment, as new means for acquiring
knowledge, as new sources of benefit to the nation, as new influences for peace, as new instruments of culture, as reinforcement
for the ethical system, and as aids to good health. In effect,

promoters argued that the newly arrived media would do those things
society most wanted done, and would support those ideas held most
dear.

Notes

1. Joyce Oramel Hertzler, American Social Institutions (Boston: Allyn and Bacon, 1961), p. 36.

2. HW, 13 Je 1891, p. 447.

3. CO, S '08, p. 328; PE, N '08 p. 231; WT, O '08, p. 1052; HM, Ja '19, pp. 183, 185.

4. RR, Ap '27, p. 393.

5. RR, Je '07, p. 685; RR, Ja '22, p. 102. See also IW, F '22, p. 835; RR, Ja '23, p. 52.

6. Ind, 17 O '12, p. 886; Col, 25 O '13, p. 22; SEP 27 Jl '29, p. 134; RR, Ag '29, p. 78; SR, 24 D '49, p. 20.

7. Ind, 11 Ja '12, p. 110; CO, D '22, p. 707.

8. CC, 27 Ap '38, p. 520.

9. Scrib, Jl '34, p. 43

10. RR, Mr '37, p. 72; NR, 12 Ja '42, p. 48.

11. NR, 26 F '51, p. 18.

12. CCom, 8 Je '07, p. 295.

13. Ind, 6 F '08, p. 306.

14. Out, 24 Je '11, p. 447.

15. Ind, 17 Jl '13, p. 142; CO, Ag '18, p. 99. See also HW, 16 S '11, p. 6; WT, O '08, p. 1052.

16. CL, My 1894, p. 443; RR, Mr '12, p. 335; Out, 3 N '26, p. 308; NAR, F '35, p. 145.

17. Col, 25 O '13, p. 23; Etude, S '43, p. 558; Ind, 17 O '12, p. 889; Etude, Je '37, p. 359; AmMerc, Jl '51, p. 115. See also, Cent, Je 1894, p. 214; CL, Jl 1896, p. 78; SA, 25 Ap '08, p. 292; AmMag, S '09, p. 499; Lip, O '09, p. 454; Ind, 17 Jl '13, p. 142; PE, O '26, p 176; LD, 18 My '29, p. 27; RR, S '30, p. 65; Scrib, F '37, p. 64; NR, 13 D '48, p. 28; TA, Ja '49, p. 28; AmMerc, Jl '51, p. 115.

18. Lip, Ag '13, pp. 191-192.

19. Ind, 11 D '16, p. 448; HM, Ja '19, p 185. See also, PE, O '26, p. 175.

20. Nat, 29 M '22, p. 362; SEP, 14 Ag '26, p. 103. See also, NAR, S 1896, p. 378; CO, Je '15, p. 411; NR, 15 F '19, p. 80; SA, S '26, p. 209; LD, 25 S '26, p. 28; Col, 2 Jl '27, p. 17; Col, 25 Ag '28, p. 48; NR, 12 Je '29, p. 97; RR, D '30, p. 78.

21. TW, Mr '13, p. 21; AmMag, Jl '13, p. 105.

22. PE, O '26, pp. 175-176.

23. Col, 8 Ap '21, p. 4; RR, Ja '26, p. 33. See also, AmMag, Jl '13, p. 105; Lip, Ag '13, p. 194; Nat, 28 Ag '13, p. 193; RR, Ap '27, p. 393; Scrib, My '28, p. 624; Scrib, Ag '28, p. 160; Col, 8 Ap '21, p. 4; NO, S '33, p. 26.

24. NO, 24 Je '11, p. 447; Nat, 18 S '29, p. 291; SEP, 9 Je '28, p. 167; RR, O '35, p. 29. See also, HM, Ja '19, p. 186.

25. Col, 28 F '20, p. 16.

26. RR, Ap '27, p. 395. See also, Out, 24 Je '11, p. 441; HW, 16 S '11, p. 6; WW, My '13, p. 39.

27. HW, 13 Je 1891, p. 447; AmMag, S '09, p. 498; CO, Je '14, p. 438.

28. RR, Ja '23, p. 74.

29. RR, Mr '32, p. 34.

30. AmMag, Je '22, p. 13; Scrib, Ap '23, p 414; Col, 14 Je '24, p. 20; Educa, D '36, p. 216; Rot, N '38, p. 13.

31. BHG, N '45, p. 73.

32. Etude, Je '49, p. 341; SEP, Ag '26, p. 103; SEP, 30 Je '28, p. 130; Nat, 18 Mr '31, p. 305; USN, 2 S '55, p. 36. See also, SA. 17 Ap 1897, p. 250; CO, Jl 1896, p. 78; HW, 24 Ag '07, p. 1246; Ind, 6 F '08, p. 310(; RR, Jl '14, p. 103; NR, 1 My '15, p. 329; Ind, 11 0 '15, p. 44; HM, Ja '19, p. 189; CO, Mr '23, p. 331; LA, 22 S '23, p. 569; SEP, 28 Mr '25, p. 47; LD, 11 Ag '28, p. 8; RR, Ap '27, p. 398; SEP, 27 Jl '29, p. 134; ParM, D '48, p. 67; GH, N '50, p. 263; SR, 25 N '50, p. 10' USN, 5 Mr '54, p. 41; USN, 2 S '55, p. 46.

33. WW, F '11, p. 14030; TW, Mr. '13, p. 20.

34. RR, Mr '32, p. 34.

35. SEP, 15 Ap '22, p. 7; LD, 10 Je '22, p. 27; RR, F '25, p. 170; RR, S '30, p. 66.

36. LD, 1 S '28, p. 19; NR, 23 0 '29, p. 259; GH, N '50, p. 263. See also, Ind, 6 F '08, p. 310; Educa, Je '13, p. 625; PE, S '27, p. 164; Col, 25 Ag '28, p. 48; AmMag, Ap '29, p. 125; Cent, Je '29, p. 218; Mus, Je '29, p. 17; Out, 4 Je '30, p. 179; RR, N '32, p. 52.

37. Cent, Je 1894, p. 214.

38. RR, D '08, p. 309.

39. Col, 1 Ap '16, p. 27; CO, Ap '19, p. 234.

40. RR, Ja '23, pp. 70-71.

41. Col, 25 0 '13, p. 22; Scrib, Ap '23, pp. 412-414.

42. AmMag, Mr '26, p. 170.

43. SEP, 3 D '27, p. 46; SS, 20 S '50, p. 21. See also, Ind, 6 F '08, p. 309; WW, F '11, p. 14030; Ind, 12 Jl '19, p. 64; SA, 4 Je '21, p. 449; Scrib, Ap '23, p. 413; SEP, 28 Mr '25, p. 47; SEP, 7 Ag '26, p. 103; Ind, 25 Feb '28, p. 172; Out, 4 Je '30, p. 179; RR, Jl '30, p. 90; RR, N '32, p. 52; Atlan, Mr '36, p. 357; GH, 0 '45, p. 24; NR, 17 F '47, p. 44.

44. SA, 4 Je '21, p. 449; LD, 9 Jl '21, p. 23; IW, F '22, p. 834; SEP, 15 Ap '22, p. 141; SEP, 7 Ag '26, p. 98; LD, 15 Ap '22, p. 29; AmMag, Je '22 p. 72; Col, 10 Je '22, p. 18; Forum, Je '24, p. 768; RD, Mr '54, p. 144; USN, 2 S '55, p. 37.

45. SEP, 28 Mr '25, p. 47.

46. SEP, 17 My '24, p. 102; Cent, O '26, p. 671; Scrib, My '31, p. 498.

47. Col, 23 Jl '27, p. 43; SSoc, 1 O '38, p. 432.

48. SEP, 6 My '36, p. 9; SEP, 20 My '39, p. 106. See also, Col 19 Mr '39, p. 12.

49. PMech, S '39, p. 322.

50. SD, Ja '46, p. 8; HM, N '52, p. 27. See also, LD 11 Ag '28, p. 8; Atlan, My '37, p. 534; SS, 18 Mr '46, p. 3.

51 Cent, Je 1894, p. 214

52. WW, F '11, p. 14030; Educa, Je '13, p. 623; CO, Mr '17, p. 185; WW, Je '06, p. 7690; Ind, 6 F '08, p. 307; Ind, 24 Ja '20, p. 152; Out, 1 N '13, p. 495.

53. SA, 15 My '20, p. 554; Col, 18 Mr '39, p. 12.

54. Cent, Je 1894, p. 214.

55. RR, Ap '29, p. 88; Col, 6 F '26, p. 8; Scrib, Jl '29, p. 4.

56. CC, 8 Mr '39, p. 310; Nat, 8 Ap '39, p. 399.

57. RR, Mr '37, pp. 3-4; Col, 10 Je '22, p. 18; SEP, 15 Ap '22, p. 144; Forum, Ap '29, p. 216; SSoc, 22 Ag '36, p. 235.

58. NR, 19 Mi '24, p. 91.

59. NAR, Mr '36, p.56; HM, Ap '33, p. 559.

60. Comm, 4 F '55, p. 469.

61. RR, Jl '29, p. 142.

62. NR, 19 Mr '24, p. 91.

63. SSoc, 22 Ag '36, p. 233. See also, NR, 3 S '24, p. 9; Forum, Ap '29, p. 214.

64. Ind, 1! O '15, p. 44; CC, 22N '50, p. 1381; RD, Mr '54, p. 143. See also, SR, Ag '52, p. 20; HM, N '52, p. 27.

65. Col, 10 Je '22, p. 18; RR, Mr '32, p. 31.

66. Col, 10 Je '22, p. 18. See also, Ind, 11 O '15, p. 44; Col, 8 Ap '22, p. 4; SEP, 15 Ap '22, p. 144; Forum, Je '24, p. 772; Cent, Je '24, p. 149.

67. PE, O '26, p. 177; USN, 2 S '55, p. 36.

68. Col, 8 Ap '22, p. 4.

69. SEP, 15 Ap '22, p. 141.

70. Col, 29 Ap '22, p. 18; Col, 10 Je '22, p. 18.

71. RR, Ag '22, p. 202. See also, SA, 4 Je '21, p. 449; IW, F '22, p. 835; IW, Mr '22, p. 37; Nat, 29 Mr '22, p. 362; LD, 15 Ap '22, p. 29; IW, Je '22, p. 502; AmMag, Mr '24, p. 60; SEP, 6 D '24, p. 74; SEP, 14 Ag '26, p. 145; RR, N '27, p. 521; SEP, 9 Je '28, p. 165; RR, Jl '28, p. 88; AmMag, Ja '29, p. 15; SEP, 23 Ag '30, p. 6.

72. AmMag, S '22, p. 65; LD, 17 Mr '23, p. 27; SEP, 17 My '24, p. 107; SEP, 6 D '24, p. 74; RR, N '27, p. 521.

73. CO, Ap '22, p. 507.

74. RR, Ap '27, p. 398.

75. USN, 2 S '55, p. 48.

76. LD, 12 Ja '24, p. 26.

77. Cent, Je '24, p. 149.

78. SEP, 7 Ag '26, p. 98.

79. Ind, 23 My '25, p. 584.

80. NAR, Mr '36, p. 49.

81. Scrib, Ap '29, p. 373; LD, 17 Ag '29, p. 19; Col, 23 N '29, p. 11. See also, RR M '32, p. 31.

82. WT, O '08, p. 1055.

83. NR, 19 M '24, p. 93; Nat, 23 Jl '24, p. 90.

84. CO, Je '18, p. 403; CO, D '17, p. 391.

85. CO, Je '18, p. 403.

86. HM, Ja '19, p. 183.

87. Out, 26 Ja '21, p. 136.

88. RR, Ja '23, p. 73.

89. CO, F '19, p. 98.

90. CC, 24 S '41, p. 1172-1173; NR, 3 Ja '44, p. 20; Nat,
27 Ja '45, p. 93.

91. LD, 28 Je '19, p. 25.

92. NR, 12 Ja '42, p. 46.

93. SR, 4 Jl '42. p. 6.

94. SR, 19 F '44, p. 29. See also, Nwk, 29 M '43, p. 59;
SS, 18 M '46, p. 20; NR, 14 Jl '47, p. 23.

95. SEP, 27 Jl '29, pp. 133, 134.

96. SR, 21 F '42, p. 17.

97. SR, 14 M '42, p. 13.

98. HW, 13 Je 1891, p. 447.

99. RR, Mr'32, p. 34.

100. TW, Mr'13, p. 20.

101. Out, 8 Mr'13, p. 517.

102. Col, 1 Ag '16, p. 27.

103. HW, 13 Je 1891, p. 447; CL, My 1894, p. 443; Cent, Je 1894, p. 214; SA, 17 Ap 1897, p. 249; Ind, 6 F '08, p. 307; TW, M '13, p. 20; Out, 8 Mr '13, p. 517; Col, 1 Ap '16, p. 20; SA, 26 Ag '16, p. 193; HM, Ja '19, p. 184; SA, Ja '23, p. 71; RR, Mr '32, p. 34.

104. HW, 25 D '15, p. 620.

105. TW, Mr '13, p. 20; CO, Ap '13, p. 297; Ind, 17 Jl '13, p. 143; Col, 12 Ap '13, p. 11; CO, Je '15, p. 411; Out, 24 Ap '29, p. 663.

106. LA, 1 Jl '30, p. 554.

107. AmMag, My '39, p. 31. See also, Ind, 29 S '10, p. 715; RR, Mr '12, p. 336; CO, Jl '19, p. 32; LD, 25 S '26, p. 28.

108. HM, Ja '26, p. 161.

109. SEP, 7 N '25, p. 12.

110. SEP, 5 Je '26, p. 221; Ind, 12 Je '26, p. 669; Scrib, Mr '27, p. 311.

111. SEP, 19 Jl '30, p. 124.

112. USN, 5 Mr '54, p. 41.

113. Ind, 12 Je '26, p. 669.

114. PE, O '26, p. 178.

115. SEP, 5 Je '26, p. 221; SEP, 7 N '25, p. 13; HM, Ja '26, p. 161.

116. Forum, Je '24, p. 771; SEP, 30 Je '28, p. 130.

117. Col, 25 My '29, p. 48; Out, 23 O '29, p. 292; RR, Mr '32, p. 31.

118. LA, Ap '31, p. 208.

119. Ind, 6 F '08, p. 310; RR, D '08, p. 744; SA, 12 Ag '11, p. 56.

120. Lip, O '09, p. 456.

121. WT, O '08, p. 1056.

122. HW, 30 Jl '10, p. 12.

123. RR, Ja '23, pp. 69-70.

124. RR, F '25, pp. 168-169; Out, 31 D '30, p. 693; SR,
26 Ag '50, p. 7.

125. USN, 2 S '55, p. 50.

126. USN, 2 S '55, p. 50.

127. HW, 24 Ag '07, p. 1247; HW, 13 N '09, p. 8; RR, Mr '12,
p. 332. See also, Ind, 6 F '08, p. 308; AmMag, S '09, p. 500;
Lip, O '09, p. 458; HW, 13 N '09, p. 8; RR, Mr '12, p. 72, Lip,
Ag '13, p. 194; AmMag, O '14, p. 96.

128. CO, Ap '22, p. 507; PE, O '26, p. 176; RR, Mr '32, p. 3

129. SEP, 17 My '24, p. 102; NAR, S '38, p. 309; HM, Ap '33,
p. 554; RR, F '25, p. 168.

130. Col, 18 Mr '39, p. 72.

131. SG, Ag '45, p. 350; SEP, 9 Mr '46, p. 10; Etude, Je '49,
p. 341.

132. SA, 30 Mr '01, p. 196; SEP, 7 Ag '20, p. 34.

133. RR, Ja '23, p. 68.

134. RR, F '13, p. 147; Scrib, My '28, p. 631.

135. RR, Jl '07, p. 98.

136. Col, 27 S '47, p. 28.

137. IW, Je '22, p. 503; Scrib, My '28, p. 631.

138. RR, Je '35, p. 54; RD, F '36, p. 43. See also, SD, Jl '45,
p. 36.

139. USN, 2 S '55, p. 49.

140. SR, 26 Ag '50, p. 29.

141. IW, Je '22, p. 501; RR, D '25, p. 646.

142. RR, Jl '07, p. 97; SEP, 14 Ag '26, p. 103; Col, 23 Jl '27, p. 43; SEP, 28 S '40, p. 37.

143. Out, 4 F '25, p. 184; NO, S '33, p. 22; RR, Ap '27, p. 398; Nat, 18 S '25, p. 291; Nwk, 1 D '34, p. 27; Etude, Je '49, p. 341; BHG, N '45, p. 23; Cent, Je '24, p. 153; NR, 3 Mr '47, p. 15.

144. Out, 19 Mr '24, p. 466. See also, CC, 4 N '34, p. 1447.

145. HW, 13 Je 1891, p. 447; RR, S '10, p. 317; AmMag, Jl '13, p. 105; CO, Ap '19, p. 234.

146. Col, 3 My '24, p. 7.

147. Ind, 18 S '26, p. 326.

148. RR, Ap '27, p. 398.

149. PE, S '27, p. 164. See also, CO, Je '15, p. 411; Ind, 11 O '15, p. 43; Ind, 24 Ja '20, p. 152; Col, 2 D '22, p. 11; Scrib, S '24, p. 231; SEP, 7 N '25, p. 154.

150. IW, M '22, p. 40; Col, 10 Je '22, p. 18; SEP, 7 Ag '26, p. 97; RR, F '37, p. 40. See also, Scrib, Ap '23, p. 414; RR, M '26, p. 229; RR, Jl '29, p. 142; RR, N '32, p. 52.

151. LD, 1 S '28, p. 19; Etude, Je '49, p. 339; SNL, 27 S '52, p. 200.

152. SEP, 30 Je '28, p. 10; Scrib, My '31, p. 498; SR, 19 F '44, p. 30. See also, Ind, 29 Mr '24, p. 172; Forum, Ap '29, p. 216; SSoc, 3 D '38, p. 724.

153. Ind, 25 F '28, p. 172.

154. IW, F '22, p. 948; IW, Mr '22, p. 37; RR, N '32, p. 52; RR, F '37, p. 39; SEP, 15 Ap '22, p. 144.

155. HM S '12, p. 636.

156. Comm, 13 Ja '32, p. 285; LA, 1 Ag '30, p. 665.

157. LD, 1 S '28, p. 19.

158. Ind, 17 O '12, p. 890.

159. Col, 10 Je '22, p. 18; RR, Mr'32, p. 34.

160. AAA, Ja '41, p. 151. See also, TA, F '51, p. 48.

161. Lip, O '09, p. 457; WT, O '08, p. 1054; NR, 15 F '19, p. 80; PE, O '26, p. 176.

162. AmMag, S '09, p. 500. See also, CO, Mr'17, p. 185; NAR, Jl '20, p. 90.

163. CO, Ap '23, p. 457.

164. CO, Ap '23, p. 457.

165. Etude, F '38, p. 72.

166. SSoc, 3 D '38, p. 723; NAR, O '28, p. 430; NB, Je '49, p. 74; Atlan, D '45, p. 130.

167. CO, Ag '14, p. 106; Scrib, Ag '28, p. 160; Out, 3 D '10, p. 768.

168. AmMag, S '09, p. 500; RR, Mr'32, p. 31.

169. SEP, 15 Ap '22, p. 144.

170. NAR, Summer of '38, p. 309.

171. NAR, Summer of '38, P. 310; AAA, Ja '41, p. 151.

172. HW, 24 Ag '07, p. 1246.

173. WW, Mr'13, p. 40; Educa, F '15, p. 351; Nat, 18 S '29, p. 291.

174. Col, 3 Ja '25, p. 40; CO, Ap '19, p. 234.

175. PE, Ja '30, p. 60. See also, HW, 2 Ja '15, p. 8; NR, 15 F '19, p. 81; Scrib, S '24, p. 231; NO, S '33, p. 26.

176. LJ, 15 F '45, p. 175; GH, N '50, p. 264; NR, 1 N '54, p. 13; TA, F '51, p. 48; SEP, 14 My '49, p. 132.

177. WW, My '13, p. 20; AmMag, Jl '21, p. 32; RR, N '22, p. 553; SD, N '45, p. 32. See also, Chapter 4, Medical Education.

178. LD, 31 Jl '15, p. 209.

179. HB, F '50, p. 127.

180. HB, Ag'50. p. 80.

181. LD, 31 Jl '15, p. 208; SD, Je '49, p. 31. See also, SA, Mr '30, p. 201; SD, Je '49, p. 31.

182. SA, Mr '30, p. 201; ParM, N '49, p. 45.

183. Time, 1 My '50 p. 34; HB, F '50, p. 127.

CHAPTER III

ARGUMENT FROM CAUSE: VALUES

Attack

Writers protesting the introduction of motion pictures, radio,
and television, like the advocates of the new media, sought sanction
in the prevailing values of society. Pessimists about the influence
of new machines, representatives of established modes of entertainment and information, defenders of existing systems of regulation,
and proponents of new ones, contended that innovation represented
a threat to the established order. Because of the new media, things
and ideas held to be necessary, worthwhile and desirable were destined to be changed, twisted, replaced, or destroyed. These were
the grounds on which an important part of the attack was built.

In looking at the arguments devised by the opposition it is
both convenient and revealing to turn again to the general categories established in the preceding chapter for the analysis of
arguments of advocacy. It is clear that there was no fundamental
disagreement about what was good and desirable, but that there was
a considerable shift in emphasis. Never did attackers deny that
the new media represented progress in communication, nor did they
spend much time arguing about dangers connected with entertainment,
the acquisition of information, international relations, or culture.
Instead, they focused on things which promised greater rhetorical

impact--matters of morality, health, and the national good--and argued
that motion pictures, radio, and television threatened the nation's
reputation and the traits of character which had long distinguished
its citizens, that the new media endangered health, and that innovation was responsible for increasing crime and growing sexual
laxity among the nation's youth. Moreover, attackers talked explicitly of the value system, something advocates had not discussed
per se. Just as advocates had promised that the new media would do
the things we as a nation most wanted done, so attackers predicted
that motion pictures, radio, and television would cause the evils
we most feared.

The Value System

Although advocates of the new media based their arguments on
beliefs with which they presumed most readers would agree, they
did not usually suppose a systematic or functional collection of
values. That is, defenders did not use the words value system
as a term in the argument. Opponents did. One, for example, took
exception to "the whole scale of values that seem to be dominant
in Hollywood studios."[1] Writers who argued from violations of the
value system said, first, that the values represented in the movies
and on radio or TV contradicted generally accepted standards, goals,
and ideals. Presuming that people adopted the values offered them
by the mass media, attackers went on to argue that motion pictures,

radio, and television were causing impressionable members of the audience, mostly children whose value systems were not yet fully established, to accept new and often false values. The traditional teachings of home, school, and church were being undermined, and long standing systems of beliefs and guides for action were in danger of being discarded because of the pressures exerted by the mass media. New values were being offered for old, and the children of the nation suffered for it.

From the time motion pictures were established as a popular amusement their opponents were concerned about the things children saw on the screen and the lessons they learned from the entertainment. Numerous complaints are to be found regarding the preoccupation of films with crime and violence, their distortions of reality, their unconcern with death and disaster, their exploitation of sex, their choices of heroes and heroines. Much too frequently, said their detractors, film stories represented as acceptable beliefs and courses of action which were, in fact, in conflict with society's standards. Writers had talked about these things for twenty years, without labeling them values; rather, they spoke of "the lapses from the old, established customs and ideas of society, . . . this revolt of youth against long established precedents." In the 1920's, however, this collection of guidelines was named a value system. By 1927 New Republic, concerned about the same problems as the previous writers and reflecting changing nomenclature, argued that movie makers had proved to be vendors of "corrupt and glamorous values" for the mass audience.[2] About the same time other writers began to talk of the influence of motion pictures on the value system.

This became a popular argument in the <u>Christian</u> <u>Century</u> repertory. At the beginning of their first campaign for regulation of motion pictures, writers for <u>Christian</u> <u>Century</u> argued that while the character of the movies was shady, their morals a mess, and their pull downward, "worst of all, they are educating millions of young people daily in false standards of taste and conduct, false conceptions of human relationships."[3] The charge was made more explicit a half-year later in an editorial which asserted that

> the cesspools of Hollywood are being piped unchecked to the minds of children everywhere. Their poison consists not in the bathing beauties, who are comparatively harmless, because so dumb, but in the movies' sentimentality, their false views of life, their glorification of the acquisitive instincts, their financial rewards for virtue, their never-ending portrayal of stupid and mean people doing stupid and mean things to one another.[4]

Another time, <u>Christian</u> <u>Century</u> charged that the movie industry had developed its own ethical system which was "at variance with the standards of enlightened public opinion" because it subscribed to "the standards of the jungle, with criminality, lust and unbridled greed the dominant forces."[5]

This line of argument was further amplified in <u>Christian</u> <u>Century's</u> campaign of 1933. There Fred Eastman, the principal author for the series, developed this attack:

The most subtle influence of the movies . . . does not
arise from overemphasis on the crime and sex pictures,
pernicious as those may be. It comes rather from the
whole scale of values that seem to be dominant in Hollywood studios. The values that you as a parent and your
school and church have tried to implant in your child's
mind might roughly be suggested by certain adjectives
--unselfish, courageous, honest, hardworking, competent,
faithful, poised, restrained, patient, thrifty, good,
kind. These are not the adjectives that describe Hollywood's values. Hollywood has a different set, something
like this: smart, sophisticated, daring, bold, clever,
rich, thrilling, big stupendous, exciting, passionate,
dazzling. Between the two sets of values represented
by these adjectives there is a great gulf fixed.[6]

The Hollywood values, said Eastman, misrepresented America; rejected

the teachings of church, school, and home; and ignored "the exper-

ience of the human race." The child was caught between the two

systems in his own struggle to develop individuality and character.

At home and school and church he sees one set of values
upheld as the secret of a desirable life. At the movies
he sees another set presented with all the power and glamor
of strong emotional stimulus. Two results are possible:
he will either be confused and vacillate between one set
of values and the other, or he will choose one and scrap
the other. May heaven--and his parents--help him to
choose rightly![7]

Christian Century feared that having seen the values of Hollywood

expressed in the highly persuasive climate of the movie world

"poor, beglamored, unprepared adolescents may be moved to imitate

them and to their heavy cost."[8]

The argument remained current following the Second World War,

reflecting a continuing concern about the kinds of values children

were exposed to. A clergyman writing in the Annals of the American

Academy in 1947 charged that motion pictures presented the child

with a false view of the world and of life as it really was. Founded

on a value system which supposed that "one can get everything

through money and glamor," which glamorized the gangster and made

"the good man a colorless pussyfooter," the influence of most films

on the child's character and values was judged to be negative.[9]

At the same time Raymond Spottiswoode in Saturday Review contended

that even the animated cartoon contributes harmfully to the value

system being developed by child viewers. He argued that "today's

film cartoon implants a ferociously distorted picture in children's

minds," for

> more violence and trickery is packed into ten minutes of
> cartoon than into ninety minutes of feature film. From
> Bugs Bunny downward--and it is significant that he has
> long supplanted Walt Disney's characters in popular esteem
> --the moral is always the same" 'if you can't trick the
> world into doing what you want, you'll surely get left
> behind.'[10]

For a number of years, then, movies were blamed for presenting

children with values inconsistent with those traditionally upheld,

and influencing them to adopt the new standards.

Radio and television were also charged with warping the values

of their audiences, but the arguments here were neither so frequent

nor so vehement as those used in connection with pictures. In 1947,

for example, Lou Frankel argued that radio programs had proved

detrimental to children's values by reversing the normal standards

of goodness in men. In radio, he said,

invariably the hero is a run-of-the-mill individual with
rough edges, a heart of gold, and plenty of strength
and staying power. The villain is sophisticated, educated,
and speaks precisely and fluently. How this determines
a child's attitudes requires no expert to interpret.[11]

At the same time the superintendent of schools in Dover, Delaware,

argued that movies, radio, and the press together had created value

systems which competed with those upheld by the schools. Speaking

of the media, he argued that the "new out of school channels of

education are not so much the old time 'school of life' as they

are another interpretation of life; not so much supplementary to

our schools as contradictory; not so much adding reality as estab-

lishing a different reality; not so much an objective evaluation

of life as a deliberate creation of a counter set of values."[12]

With the growth of television, arguments about influences on

the value system were transferred to the new medium. Again children

were said to be too much exposed to ideas and situations which served

to break down long-standing beliefs about man and his relationships

with other men. A writer for Theatre Arts said television caused

children to develop faulty ideas about what was good in literature

because TV depended upon mediocre material rather than that which

was generally agreed to be the best. On yet another occasion, in

1952, television was said to ignore the basic values of the general

audience, offering it instead the delights of the chase; action

instead of ideas; intrigue instead of character; sex but no love;

resolution by coincidnece; one-dimensional heroes whose primary attributes were great physical stamina and cunning--all of this connected with dialogue consisting of grunts, snorts, growls, and yaps. These were the new standards offered man for his adoption. Conspicuously lacking were former ideals, wisdom, cultivation, or the gentle decency of good men.[13]

When television was examined as a possible cause of juvenile delinquency in the 1950's, opponents of the medium argued that the distortions of values offered by television might be substantial enough to influence criminal behavior. One writer for Good Housekeeping said, for example, that "so many hours of television are devoted to murder that children who are allowed to watch will inevitably become calloused to violence and death."[14] Contending that television distinctly changed the attitudes and values of children, Walter Goodman quoted a psychiatrist that

> seeing constant brutality, viciousness and unsocial acts results in hardness, intense selfishness, even in mercilessness, proportionate to the amount of exposure and its play on the native temperament of the child. Some cease to show resentment to insults, to indignities, and even cruelty toward helpless old people, to women and other children.[15]

And the Senate Subcommittee on Juvenile Delinquency concluded from its hearings that "repeated exposures to scenes of crime and violence may well blunt and callous human sensitivity to, and sympathy for, human suffering and distress."[16] Grown accustomed to violence on television, children no longer rejected it as a course of action. Seeing crimes committed as entertainment, young viewers became hardened to them in real life. Exposed to human suffering as part of their amusement, children were no longer moved by it. Delinquency became acceptable, a mode of behavior consistent with the values demonstrated on television. So, like its predecessors, television was charged with having damaged the values of its audience.

This line of argument, while it appeared occasionally in news magazines, digests, special interest publications, and general circulation periodicals, was most frequently used by writers for religious magazines and opinion journals. That is, for example, Christian Century, Commonweal, New Republic, Outlook, Nation, and and Saturday Review account for 60 per cent of the appearances of the argument.[17] In general, these were the same periodicals which were involved after 1930 with the morality issue. Their argument, because of their specialized audiences, was directed to a relatively small segment of the total population. They served, however, to formulate and lead the attack on the issues of damage to the general value system and subversion of morality.

Speaking in opposition to motion pictures, radio, and television, writers for these periodicals charged that the new media tampered with fundamental notions of good and evil. Insinuating by example that the old ways of doing things were no longer valid, that formerly revered beliefs had outlived their usefulness, the mass media offered the malleable audience new values for old. Threatened were the basic rules by which men governed their behavior.

Opposed by innovation were the fundamental beliefs which had traditionally served as the governing themes of society. In threatening
the value system the new mass media menaced society's foundation.

In terms of the total attack relatively few of the periodicals
discussed the value system as such. More commonly, attackers
developed their arguments from the same categories as the advocates.
The first of these was entertainment.

Entertainment

In one sense, nearly all of the arguments surveyed in this
chapter are arguments about entertainment. Writers who argued
that the new mass media damaged things and ideas valued by society
were concerned first of all about the entertainment side of motion
pictures, radio, and television. The educational features were
seldom sources for complaint, news programs were generally approved,
good music was recommended. When writers talked of moral dangers
associated with pictures, however, they referred specifically to the
entertainment films. When radio was accused of damaging the health
of children, it was the entertainment programs which were blamed.
When television was labeled dangerous because of its preoccupation
with crime, attackers spoke of the entertainment programs. Hence,
much of the argument about innovation could be considered argument
about entertainment. This kind of classification is so general,
however, that it serves little useful purpose in analysis. It is

more fruitful to look at some of the specific arguments about entertainment which were devised by the attackers.

The mass audience

Promoters of motion pictures had argued that the medium was a valuable addition because it provided entertainment for the mass audience, who were formerly without commercial amusement. Authors less friendly to the mass media did not see this as a virtue. Instead, they argued that it was the mass audience which had prevented any of the media from reaching an artistic level, that it was the mass audience which stifled intellectual development in either pictures or programs, that it was the mass audience which prevented fulfillment of the media's cultural potential.

Where defenders of motion pictures praised the medium for its service to the general audience, the phrase mass audience or even mass medium became a term of denigration for the opposition. All three of the media were evaluated on the basis of the audiences to which they appealed. Very early, in 1913, a writer for Harper's Weekly questioned the apathy of the movie audience; she had presumed that any entertainment of value could move the audience to some kind of visible response. Instead she found the movie audience--three quarters of them men, even in the middle of the day, and the rest "shirking housewives and truant children"--"Indifferent and relaxed; its jaws moving unconcernedly in time with the endlessly reiterated ragtime ground out by some durable automaton; . . . its dull eyes unresponsively meeting the shadowy grimaces on the flickering film." Other writers characterized movie watchers as "mental oysters;" spoke of their "jaded eyes and shallow brains;" called them idle, vulgar, ignorant, lazy; and sneeringly named them "the great heart of human-ity." When radio and television arrived their audiences were known collectively as "the mass." The objects of audience interest were called "the chewing gum of the masses," "enervating daydreams wrapped in cellophane," or, depreciatingly, "the mass media."[18] The worth of the new media was measured by the quality of the following they attracted.

The fact that the media did appeal to the mass was never questioned, and the effects of such a relationship were said to be debilitating both for the medium and for the audience. Pictures were first said to have to appeal to the mass audience because they cost too much to be made solely for the intelligent minority.[19] So they reflected the desires of their auditors. William Allen White put it like this in 1926:

> The best books, the best music, the best plays are written
> frankly for the discerning and the wise. The best in
> all the other arts is conceived, produced, sold, and
> lives or dies solely and with brutal frankness for the
> approval of the intelligent; in all the other arts except
> in the movies. There, no artists, no producers, no
> theatres, are set apart to please people of understand-
> ing.[20]

The movies said White, provided "little that is much better than a glittering toy for an imbecile giant." The guiding philosophy, give the audience what they want, produced mass entertainment which was, to Nation, the antithesis of art.[21] The motion picture, said its detractors, appealed to the lowest common denominator of the mass audience, offered the mass neither stimulation nor hope for improvement of its state, and so perpetuated mediocrity. The effect was circular; films influenced the audience and the audience imposed its standards on the film.

When objections were raised to the low level of the entertainment provided by radio, a writer for Harper's argued that the cause was broadcasting's "surrender to the current standards of mass public taste." The level of music on the air was said to be unnecessarily low for the same reason; broadcasters depended upon the public favor as expressed by fan mail. Because it appealed to the mass audience, radio was found wanting in quality.[22]

When television was still in the speculation stage, the executive director of the Theatre Guild predicted that, like movies, television would become "the new Goliath, guilty of the same evils of mass appeal" which had separated motion pictures from legitimate theatre. Gilbert Seldes, even in 1949, argued that television must divorce itself from the fallacy of the mass audience, must strive to regain the spark of creativity which had characterized its productions during the war years, when only a few people had sets and when there

was no necessity to appeal to a mass audience. In 1951, Charles
A. Siepmann, Chairman of the Department of Communications at New
York University and a frequent commentator about the role of the
mass media, argued that the present, 1951, was the golden age of
television, for in the future sponsors would be driven to the
lowest common denominator of programming to capture audiences.
Television would then become mass entertainment, he said, and
the former quality would be lost. Commonweal also feared that
the "American masses" would "inexorably . . . determine the content of our television programs," and in so doing restrict quality
entertainment.23 Each of these arguments exposed the same con-
cern--the mass audience would effectively prevent television from
achieving its greatest potential as a medium of artistic, educational,
and entertaining communication.

The mass audience, thought of at one time as deserving higher
quality entertainment than it had been accustomed to, was later
named by attackers a threat to the quality of the new mass media.
Making pictures to attract the mass audience, devising programs
to sell it goods, motion pictures, radio, and television failed to
produce the kind of programs and stories acceptable to their critics.

The mass audience exchanging its role of beneficiary for one
of power, became a threat to the new mass media.

The quality of entertainment

I have already pointed out that the opponents of motion pictures, radio, and television believed that because of the attempts of the media to serve the mass audience the quality of their products was inferior. This was but one effect of the mutual attraction of the media for the mass and the mass for the media. The argument also answered promoters predictions that the movies, radio, and television would lead to a new quality of entertainment for the nation. The prediction, according to attackers, was unfulfilled in practice.

Objections to the quality of entertainment offered are implicit in most of the arguments developed by writers seeking changes in the media. Many of the complaints became explicit, however, and are to be discovered in a variety of statements about motion pictures, radio, and television. Here, for example, was C. H. Claudy's description of the motion picture in 1908: "A great agent for good, a means of education unrivaled, a source of much innocent and inexpensive pleasure, the moving picture show has come to mean, as a rule, a pandering to the lowest tastes, a misrepresentation of life as it really is, as harmful and more accessible than the dime novel, and the telling of a lie, constantly and universally, not only in the fake pictures it produces, but in the way which the true pictures are run." In 1930, Outlook and Independent wrote that "the inferior work of mediocrities predominates in present-day broadcasts," and that the air is filled with "blather and bunk, ignorance and vulgarity." Later, Lee DeForest, often

called in the press the father of radio, complained that "nine-

tenths of what one can hear is the continual dribble of second rate

jazz, sickening crooning by degenerate 'sax' players, interrupted

by blatant sales talks."[24] The case against television was put

most succinctly by Norman Cousins in his opening attack on the new

medium in December of 1949:

> Here, in concept at least, was the most magnificent of
> all forms of communication. Here was the supreme triumph
> of invention, the dream of the ages--something that could
> bring directly into the home a moving image fused with
> sound--reproducing action, language, and thought without
> the loss of measurable time. Here was the magic eye that
> could bring the wonders of entertainment, information,
> and education into the living room. Here was a tool for
> the making of a more enlightened democracy than the world
> had ever seen.
> Yet out of the wizardry of the television tube has
> come such an assault against the human mind, such as a
> mobilized attack on the imagination, such as an invasion
> against good taste as no other communications medium has
> known, not excepting the motion picture or radio itself.
> In the one year since television has been on an assembly
> line basis, there has been mass produced a series of
> plodding stereotypes and low-quality programs. Behind
> it all, apparently, is a grinding lack of imagination
> and originality which has resulted in the standardized
> formula for an evening's entertainment: a poisoning,
> a variety show, a wrestling match.[25]

Others, afterwards, said many of the same things about television,

but never was the charge put more clearly than Cousins put it in

1949.

In addition to these comments, the dissatisfaction with motion

picture, radio, and television entertainment is also apparent in

other arguments. Consider the discussions of morality and the
mass media. Here attackers charged that the entertainment offered
was not only of low quality, but that it constituted a danger to
the moral life of the nation's children. These arguments will be
discussed later in this chapter. Consider, too, the comparisons,
both implicit and explicit, between the potential of the new media
and the use to which they were put in practice. Here again, the
entertainment quality was said to be unacceptable. These arguments
will be found in Chapter Six.

In all of these discussions the controversy centered in the
quality of the entertainment. This quality, in turn, was determined
by the audience for whom the media were intended. In their efforts
to reach the largest possible audience, the media failed to provide
quality entertainment.

Intellectual damage

Another influence of the mass audience was perceived in the
intellectual level of the new media. It had been the hope of advocates that each new medium would in some fashion come to the aid
of the intellectual life of the nation. This would never happen,
according to attackers, and charges that the media had failed intellectually were ubiquitous. In addition, opponents of motion pictures, radio, and television argued that even if damage to the
intellect could not be demonstrated, the media did nothing to
foster intellectual growth.

There was hope in the beginning that motion pictures would be something of an intellectual medium, but disappointment on that score was articulated within five years of their spread across the nation. Writers soon discovered that with pictures "no degree of intelligence is necessary, no knowledge of our language, nor convictions, no attitude of any kind, reasonably good eyesight being indeed the only requisite." The outcasts of the movies, said William Allen White and others, were the intelligent people; the movies had no message for them. In similar fashion, Commonweal in 1932 repeated the charge that "the overwhelming majority of films are illiterate when they are not emotionally or morally primitive."[26] The movies themselves, then, failed to measure up to the standards of intelligence demanded by their critics.

The effects of this minimal intellectual capacity were predicted to be widely felt. Films were expected to impose their standards on their audiences. A writer for North American Review, for example, claimed that "as a snare to intellect . . . the danger of the movies cannot be overdrawn." The movies, she argued, had so undermined the power of audiences to think that both church and education had found it necessary to adopt films "in the struggle for survival." Not only were these films used to draw crowds to church and as substitutes for Scripture, but teachers were even using films so that

> lessons may amuse the pupil's eye instead of exercising
> the pupil's mind. . . . Children whose intelligence has
> already been undermined by the movies out of school, are
> to be further debauched by them in what should be hours
> of study. No wonder that the man with eyes to see is
> now watching with dismay the human race as it advances
> briskly along the highway back to illiteracy, fast draw-
> ing near the day when the movies will deliver it even
> from the alphabet, and when the ultimate glory of the
> twentieth century culture will be the return to the pic-
> ture writing in vogue before letters were invented.[27]

An anonymous film producer writing in Collier's claimed that "the
intelligence, the standards of taste and character and morality,
of the whole country are being gradually undermined by /the/ unend-
ing stream of stupid photoplays, watched by millions, open-mouthed."
Christian Century claimed that, "according to testimony of teachers
and psychologists," motion pictures caused the mental ability of
students to be retarded. And it was the contention of Frances
Taylor Patterson in New Republic that the eventual effect of the
non-intellectual talkie would be to reduce all entertainment to the
lowest common denominator of intelligence."[28]

Both radio and television were also charged with intellectual
inferiority, and the effects were predicted to be as damaging as
those of the movies. Radio serials were said to be "geared to low-
grade mentalities," and Lee DeForest said that because radio had
been resolutely kept to the average intelligence of thirteen years,"
it was "a laughing stock of intelligence." Christian Century, commenting on the removal of Kukla, Fran, and Ollie from television,
argued that this was but one more evidence of the "commercial drive

to cut down or abandon intelligent programs." This trend was
judged to be as much a threat to the child audience as "plunging
necklines, off-color jokes, and too much blood and thunder."
Clifton Utley argued in Commonweal that television could well
lead to "functional illiteracy," that is, to "people who can read,
but don't."29 Like the movies, radio and television were judged
intellectually inferior, and their opponents feared they would
pass the inferiority along to their followers.

Arguments such as these on the topic of entertainment did
two things. First of all, they reflected and reinforced the notion that entertainment for its own sake was not a worthy end of
the public arts. Recall, it was this attitude which prevented the
advocates of the new media from building a defense on the things
the new media did best. Second, these arguments countered the
assertions of advocates that the entertainment provided by the
media was socially useful. The entertainment, said the attackers, was not socially useful, it did not mean better quality amusement, it did not help those groups who most needed help. Instead,
the entertainment threatened qualities and values which were a
fundamental part of the social system.

Acquisition of Information

When motion pictures, radio, and television were new, their friends represented them as valuable sources for acquiring new information. Because of the media audiences could become acquainted with new places, could see the important personalities of their time, could gain a new perspective on the world and its doings, and could, in effect, become participants in history in the making. Never did opponents challenge the capability of the media as sources of information; they challenged the honesty and morality of the information transmitted. Debate centered not on the means of transmission, but on the content of the transmission.

Opponents of the new media said, in essence, "These are wonderful new ways of transmitting ideas, far better than anything we had in the past. They have great potential for good. But look at the way in which they are used. Instead of dealing with what is good and true, they play on the worst part of life, and teach our children lessons from which we have tried to protect them." Attackers argued that much of the information transmitted by the new media was in itself a violation of what society believed to be good and right. As I shall point out later, the most common argument was one from morality, with attackers taking the position that the media served to propagate information inconsistent with the best interests of a moral society and also served to inspire immoral behavior. But there

were also other objections to the information provided by motion
pictures, radio, and television.

Attackers challenged the honesty of the media as sources for
information. On two occasions it was pointed out that even in
newsreels seeing was not necessarily believing, for faked scenes
and recreations had been presented as the real thing. The first
objection on this score was raised in 1908 when C. H. Claudy charged
in _Photo-Era_ that newsreels were so skillfully faked that the falsification could be distinguished only by an expert. Claudy cited
this example.

> Take a scene from the Japanese war. The picture shows
> you a column of marching Japs. They halt, get their
> dinner, go to sleep, get up, march on and act just like
> the real thing. As they are the real thing, it would
> be strange if they didn't so act. Then you see those
> same Japs go into battle and, stranger yet, they are
> shooting right at you, in the audience. Some woman
> right behind me once said: 'Wasn't that picture-man
> brave to get out there and get those pictures with
> all those bullets flying?' He certainly would have
> been, if the bullets had been there. As a matter of
> fact it was a joined film,--the first part real, the
> second part faked; and the artfulness of it comes from
> the fact that the general public cannot say when the
> real leaves off and the fake commences.30

Nearly thirty years later, Gilbert Seldes commented on a similar
problem in the talking newsreels. He argued that the greatest
disaster of talking pictures, after five years of them, was the
newsreel, which offered far too many recreated events in place of
the action shot from life.31 Both of these arguments directly

challenged the assertions of advocates that the newsreel represented the highest use of the motion picture as a source of information.

Other attackers questioned both the handling of news on radio and the balance between information and other programs on television. Shortly after the Second World War, Llewellyn White argued in _Atlantic_ that not only was at least 20 per cent of the nation unable to receive radio news, but that where broadcasts were available there was insufficient commentary on the news, too frequently opposing points of view were not reported, and that minorities had far too little chance to be heard on controversial issues. Television, which boasted of its ability to keep even children informed of world affairs, was challenged on this score in 1952. Writers for _Parents Magazine_ argued that programming for young viewers tended mainly to westerns and cartoons. During a typical week of New York programming for children, "only three hours could be labeled 'for information and instruction.'"[32] Broadcasting therefore was failing to do the very thing its spokesmen said it did best.

Reflection of reality

The mass media, even though dealing in a fictionalized and often idealized vision of the world, were expected to conform to certain conventions relating to reality and to present a "true" picture of the world. Some opponents of motion pictures, radio, and television contended that the view of the world presented by the media was

faulty, that the world on the screen was an inaccurate reflection
of the world as it really was. This was the equivalent of giving out
false information, and was predicted to have serious consequences.
Of special concern was the predicted damage to children who were
presumed to structure their world from the lessons presented in
movies, radio, and television. Confronted too frequently with
lies about the world, children would soon be unable to separate
the real from the unreal and would emerge from their experience with
a flawed perception of reality.

The ideal against which the new mass media were measured was
entertainment which was "real," which reflected a proper and correct
version of life. (The standards of propriety and correctness were
assumed to be agreeable to all and to be consistent throughout
society.) This attitude is apparent in a comment about motion
pictures which appeared in Photo-Era for April of 1909. The author
held that the best films were the real films, and that

> the greatest film ever produced was that of a train
> robbery, and . . . it was great not only because well
> acted, but because there was only one 'fake' scene in
> it; the rest was real--real country, real horses, real
> trains, real engine, real everything. It was so natural
> that it convinced.[33]

And it was this presumption about art and reality which conditioned
many of the comments about motion pictures and the two later media.
Writers who argued from the reality of entertainment would have
found no disagreement with the writer for Collier's who argued that

"in the theaters, as amusement, the film should give correct ideas
of human life, of human character, and of human emotion."[34] Violations of this standard led to criticism of the new media.

Such violations became evident almost as soon as the motion
pictures offered their first public entertainment. Even in 1909,
C. H. Claudy was disappointed in the motion pictures in which all
manner of bad behavior was presented as true to life, "no matter
how false it may actually be." From them, youth got "a distorted
view and a poor perspective" on life. And this was the same basis
on which the white slave films were condemned in 1913. Outlook
claimed that the films might even attract young girls into prostitution because they failed to show the real facts of the case,
failed to show what happened to girls who had been prostitutes.
The movies were labeled "the world's worst failure" in 1921, again
because of their "absolute failure to present truthfully the fabric
of the cosmic drama which we call life." The continuing call was
for reality in pictures, and Hollywood's productions were frequently
condemned because they failed to deal with what their critics defined
as reality, failed to accurately reflect the ways of polite society,
suffered from inaccuracy, lacked "realism," and in effect spread
falsehoods about "real life."[35]

Radio was charged with similar violations of reality. The
children's programs and the soap operas were considered particularly
offensive on this score, for their characters and situations were

usually even more unreal than those in the normal run of radio

drama. There was even objection to the "Bobby Benson" program because

the part of the hero, "a supposedly sub-adolescent, . . . is read

on the radio by an eighteen-year-old midget who enjoys considerable

prestige as a juvenile star of the air." Writers who said they

would not go so far as to assert that the children s programs

"encourage vicious habits among their listeners," still argued

that there was damage to youth in listening to programs on which

the characters lacked shading as in real life and in which there

was violence past all resemblence to reality. These programs were

criticized because they were "distortions, negative and disturbing

when they should be positive and beneficial."[36] The programs ignored

real life for the sake of excitement and suspense.

Like radio, television stories were said by their critics to be

isolated from the real world. For example, Ruth A. Inglis in

American Mercury argued that

> the great volume of violence and crime in television pro-
> grams for children cannot be defended as being 'helpful
> in orienting the child to his social surroundings.' We
> do live in violent times, and crime is on the increase,
> but the picture given by television (as well as comic
> books and movies) bears no relation to real life.[37]

This was also the position taken by the national associations for

better radio and television. Found wanting, too, but on the grounds

of oversimplification of reality, were the shows like "Medic."

When it was proposed that the program would begin dealing with more

complex medical situations such as "homosexuality and insanity after
childbirth in which moral issues will be added to the medical,"
Christian Century published this statement: "We shudder to think
of the results if the same heavy-handed oversimplification is
accorded to ethical and moral issues as has been given the medical
side."38 The argument still reflected the presumption that entertainment must truly reflect its world, no matter if the intent is
merely to amuse. Writers were fearful of violations of reality.
Apparently the twenty or so writers who used this argument believed
that if the mass media would only stick to the real world everything would be all right.

A variation on this general argument about reality dealt with
the distortions of fictional works which had been adapted for movies.
It was charged in Current Opinion in 1915 that great works of literature had been so changed in filming that they appeared in public
"sterilized, emasculated, completely innocuous," stripped of any
social purpose for which they had been written. Outlook argued in
an editorial that it was undesirable "for the child to learn through
moving pictures the changed and sometimes viciously altered versions
of the classics and history that they frequently present."39 Mothers
objected because, they said, Hollywood's changes in classic stories,
and sometimes the industry's penchant for utter realism in the
visualization, made them unfit for the children who saw them.

How many people have gone to see a classic, with happy
memories of the book and author, and found to their sad
disappointment, immortal scenes and situations desecrated
and mutilated beyond recognition! How many mothers have
sorely regretted taking their impressionable eight and
ten year olds to see Robert Louis Stevenson's 'Treasure
Island'! A similar experience was in store for those
mothers who hopefully trotted their youngsters over to
the theater to see 'Jack and the Beanstalk'. A child's
sense of justice may be satisfied at having the giant's
head cut off, but the effect of visualizing this on the
screen proves quite disastrous to its mental equilib-
rium.[40]

And even educational pictures, for which all but the most immovable

critics usually had high praise, were charged with offering dis-

torted versions of well known tales. <u>Outlook</u> offered the movie

of 'The Man Without a Country' as evidence.

In it the magnificently worked out theme is almost entirely
subverted to a 'heart interest' including Philip Nolan's
marriage and the doings of his children to the third and
fourth generations. The children liked it? Yes. But
were they interested and impressed by the theme of Hale's
'Man Without a Country'? No. Is it desirable that they
should be impressed by and interested in that theme? If
so, this 'movie' fails. And in this, as in many of the
historical pageant productions, so much of the real argument is lost in either an attempt at 'propaganda' or the
fixed determination to glorify still further some more or
less miscast 'star.'[41]

In this distortion of literature, the attackers maintained, the

motion picture industry was engaging in the same process which

resulted in the distortions of reality which characterized other

films. Truth to the source was sacrificed for other ends.

Their ignorance of reality and their distortions of literary

classics were in themselves sufficient reasons for disapproving of

the new media, but writers involved with this line of argument
went on to predict that these practices would have other ill effects
on auditors. If nothing else, children would come from the movies
misunderstanding great literary works. But there were more serious
influences. Presuming that the movies, radio, and television contributed much to the child's perception of his world, several writers
argued that because of the media the child would get a mistaken
impression of the world and a distorted picture of life. The situations and solutions portrayed on the screen and over the air were
too likely to be accepted as true reflections of the way the world
worked. Just as other writers were afraid children's values would
be warped by the movies, these authors feared that the child's
image of the world would be cast away.[42] The particulars, however,
were left up to the reader; each one was permitted to measure the
performance of the media against his own perception of the reality
and to create his own vision of the dangers of violation.

At other times writers tried to spell out more precisely what ill
effects were likely to result from distortions of reality by the media.
Outlook said, for example, in 1916 that if children were continually exposed to the exaggerated idea of life contained in the movies,
they would be bored with reality. The New York Tribune, quoted
in Current Opinion, objected to the distortions of life and the
"bogus information on manners and customs" that children got from

the movies. The Tribune believed that while "loading young minds
with misinformation may not lead their owners astray, . . . it is
going to subject them to stern disillusionment by and by and make
their character-forming fight with the wolf even harder to win."[43]
A professor of psychology writing in Collier's argued there was a
clear and grave danger in too much exposure to "mental lotus eating" in films.

> There seems little doubt that in course of time the boy
> or girl movie fan gets out of the habit of thinking with
> facts, and into the habit of thinking pleasantly. This
> develops a type of person who is necessarily out of touch
> with his surroundings, essentially unhappy, for whom the
> world must be out of joint because it cannot be made over
> to his impossible wishes. An overdose of movies is a
> distinct menace to the young.[44]

The Nation was concerned because movies, in their concentration
on non-reality, were perpetuating "the old and false identification
of goodness with institutional allegiance" and leading to the dangerous end of moral conformity. Alexander Bakshy, also writing
in Nation, feared that oversimplification of problems in the movies
would lead to an eventual hypocriscy about the true evils of our
society. Llewellyn White, in Atlantic, concluded that the danger
of children's radio was that the programs never really served to
clarify the goals and values of society, but preserved standards
most often measured "in box tops or soap chip sales." The result
of television was named "narcotic disfunction," which meant, said
U. S. News, that "more and more men come home in the evening, drop

into a chair in front of the TV set after supper and slip into a
dream world of unreality."[45] All of these dangers were said to be
present in the distortions of reality perpetuated by the mass media.
The movies, radio, and television in providing their picture of the
world constituted a threat to the audience in its realistic perception of its surroundings. The general influence was a weakening of man's ability to cope with his world.

The new media were thus labeled failures as purveyors of
information, not because they weren't good at it, but because the
material propagated was deemed unacceptable. The position of the
advocates was denied, and opponents of the media contended that if
the information presented on the screen and over the air was not a
lie, then it distorted reality to such a degree that it threatened
the viewer's orientation to his world.

The National Good

Their advocates had predicted that motion pictures, radio,
and television would prove beneficial to the national good. That
is, the media would serve to reinforce democratic ideals, would
promote national unity, would aid business, and in so doing would
help make the United States a strong, progressive nation. Opponents
took issue with this position and argued that the new media would
not only damage national traditions, weaken the national economy,
and distort the national image, but would debilitate those traits

of character which had long distinguished the American citizen.

Moreover, they claimed the media already threatened the development

of the younger generation, the nation's future leaders.

The image of America: immigrants

Motion pictures were assumed to play an important role in the

Americanization of immigrants. People newly arrived from other

countries, said both advocates and attackers, got many of their

first lessons about American life and American ways from the movies.

It was the position of writers suspicious of the influence of films,

however, that the newcomers were given a false, even dangerous,

introduction to their new land.

As long as immigration continued, this was one of the grounds

on which motion pictures were attacked. In 1916, Outlook combined

the appeal of children and immigrants by arguing that movies were

particularly dangerous for the immigrant child who could not learn

about America from his parents and so turned to the movie for

instruction.

> The version of life presented to him in the majority of
> moving pictures is false in fact, sickly in sentiment,
> and utterly foreign to the Anglo-Saxon ideals of our
> nation. In them we usually find this formula for a hero:
> He must commit a crime, repent of it, and be exonerated
> on the ground that he 'never had a mother' or 'never
> had a chance'--or perhaps that he was born poor. The
> heroine is in most cases the familiar, passive, persecuted
> heroine of the melodrama.[46]

The lessons failed to portray America accurately, and the immigrant

child was the victim of the misinformation. The adult immigrants

were also said to be taught falsely, not by the instructional films
shown them on shipboard to acquaint them with American institutions,
but by the crime pictures they saw as soon as they attended the
commercial threaters.[47] In 1923, Outlook again called attention
to the education immigrants received from the pictures they saw.
Of particular concern were the standards of sexual behavior upheld
by the movies.

> Many of the foreign boys have sent back to the old
> country for their fiancees, who have joined them here.
> There are always a few weeks or months before the mar-
> riages take place, the girls usually living with some
> relative. The boys have been most anxious that the
> girls become 'American.' It has been painful to listen
> to these boys as they tell that they take the girls to
> the 'movies' (or vaudeville) every week, 'so they can
> learn how American girls act and be real Americans.'
> Those of them who have come from a civilization that
> supposes some reserve and self-control in the more
> intimate relations of human beings receive rather severe
> shocks.[48]

This argument was not used after 1923, nor was it applied to
either radio   or television. But for a time, it served
to refute promoter's contentions that movies were a valuable asset
in the Americanization of the immigrant.

The image of America abroad

Not only did people coming to the United States get a false
impression of this country from the movies; people in other nations
also were misinformed about us from our motion pictures. Films
which were exported, said their opponents, carried with them a
distorted picture of America and its life.

This argument was introduced as a part of the general attack on films which started after the First World War. The New York Times Magazine, as quoted in Current Opinion, concluded after an analysis of the plots of five pictures slated for overseas release in 1924 that all the films presented distorted views of American life and American aspirations, and were especially objectionable because of their heavy emphasis on crime and violence.[49] Collier's in 1925 collected a number of statements about America which reflected impressions of this country gained from movies. Foreigners believed, said Collier's, that

> Every American woman can have three husbands.
> She's hot stuff, the American wife.
> American girls wear clothes only when they're bored.
> An affair a day while the husband's away is the regular thing in America.[50]

Because of movies, America as viewed from abroad was a "Never Never Land, a phantasmagoria, a nightmare country." Harper's in 1926 devoted a long article to the problem of American films abroad. Repeated were the charges that motion pictures sent abroad were distortions of reality. "Lust, greediness, infidelity, murder, malevolence, depravity--the wide world is invited to believe that the Statue of Liberty holds a red light and that the tenderloin ends where the West begins." Quoted was this statement of Charles Evans Hughes:

> I wish, indeed, . . . that that important educational instrument, the moving picture, was not so frequently

used in foreign countries to give forth impressions of
American life. It is most discouraging to reflect upon
the extent to which the best efforts of educators and
men of public affairs are thwarted by the subtle influence of a pernicious distortion among other peoples with
respect to the way in which our people live.[51]

Having surveyed its evidence, Harper's concluded that "the American

movie is caricaturing us cruelly enough to lay the basis for a

libel suit."

Christian Century picked up the line of argument, adapted

it for its attack on motion pictures, and repeated it seven times

from 1930 to 1934. In this time the substance of the argument

went unchanged--motion pictures misrepresent America and damage

her good name abroad--but a variety of examples were provided for

support. Several times opinions of English writers were quoted,

as in this listing of objectionable materials contained in Ameri-

can pictures: "the crude imbeciles of wild west drama; the raw-

ness of industrial production and business adventure; of cocktail

parties, night clubs, the duel of sex, and the degredation of

marriage; of bootleggers and highjackers, the high-powered car in

robbery, revenge, double-crossings, and juvenile debauchery--mean

and abominable people incessantly doing mean and abominable or

farcical things, with a lawless and lunatic waste of money, and

against a background of luxury and indulgence such as the peoples

of the old world have known about from this American revelation

alone."[52] A conclusion which Christian Century adopted as representing its position about American pictures abroad had first appeared in

London's New Statesman.

> Americans should realize that so long as the United
> States travesties and profanes herself before the whole
> world by the loathsome pictures that pour steadily from
> Hollywood, there is little excuse for complaining if other
> people think America ridiculous . . . and not only ridic-
> ulous but obscene and trivial. . . . America sometimes makes
> excuse for Hollywood on the ground that foreign nations
> must enjoy these pictures, or else they would not patro-
> nize them! . . . It is an argument that could be used
> equally well by the keepers of brothels. People willing
> to traffic in a certain line of goods can always do a
> lively business with the unhappy human race, but they
> should be content with gold for payment and should not
> clamor for respect![53]

If America's reputation abroad was endangered, the motion picture

bore full responsibility for the damage. Foreigners gained much

of their knowledge of America from Hollywood's productions, and

the image presented there was false.

The line of argument remained viable following the Second

World War. Added to former concerns, however, was the new threat

of Soviet propaganda which played upon the image of America fostered

by the movies. Norman Cousins, in a three-part editorial in Satur-

day Review in early 1950, argued that American movies pictured us

"as a nation consisting largely of quick killers and quick kissers,

with a collective intelligence at ceiling zero and practically no

contact with civilized values."[54] This "costly libel" grew out of

the same kinds of misrepresentation to which Christian Century

had objected two decades earlier. As Cousins said,

the fact is that movies do not accurately reflect America
and Americans. We have more than our share of humanity's
faults, but we do not monopolize them. Nor are we pre-
dominantly a nation of murders, gangsters, idlers, dead-
beats, dipsomaniacs, touts, tarts, and swindlers, as
Hollywood would have us appear. We don't all work in
swanky buildings with private offices large enough to
house a small army. We don't all live in plush duplex
apartments with elaborate cocktail bars and retinues of
servants. We don't all sleep in kingsize beds with
silk topsheets, nor do we all arise languidly at noon
for breakfast in bed. Some of us find something to do
with our hands other than to drape them around long
cocktail glasses, expensive cigarette holders, or
smoking revolvers. Some of us even read a book
occasionally and find something to talk about other
than a scheme to murder our wives or our business
partners. And, while we like to hold our own in
discussion or debate, it isn't true that the only
rebuttal is a sock on the jaw.[55]

While Americans might take all this to be harmless, playful, Holly-

wood distortions of life, these same scenes were too frequently

"soaked up by Frenchmen or Englishmen or Italians or any other

people who know little of America outside of what they see on the

screen."[56]

It was unpleasant enough for the United States merely to be

misrepresented by its own products, but Cousins argued that the

falsification had international ramifications. First of all, the

movies established shallow and inaccurate criteria for the measure-

ment of democracy. Nations lacking experience with a democratic

form of government could not learn from movies that

democracy is much more than deep-freeze units, duplex
apartments, and dynaflow. It is more than the zoot
suit, the latest bebop recording, the bubble gum. And
by thus emphasizing and exalting the materialistic and

superficial aspects of democracy, Hollywood is actually
weakening the cause of free government abroad.[57]

Selling democracy abroad was made doubly hard because of the image

created by the movies. But more than this, movies played into the

hands of Soviet propagandists who sought to blacken the American

image abroad. Cousins said that "Soviet propaganda against the

United States was not nearly as damaging as the grotesquely distorted

view of the American people being created abroad by our own motion

pictures." The United States, spending millions each year on its

own information services, found it "impossible to catch up with all

the harmful impressions of America being mass-produced for export

by Hollywood." Because of the movies, the United States found

itself "on an absurd treadmill: it is spending millions of dollars

abroad to counteract Soviet propaganda against us, but much of the

damage is being spun off our own movie reels."[58] American movies

not only misrepresented us abroad, but had become a threat to the

place of the nation in international affairs.

America was thus badly, even dangerously misrepresented by

the movies it exported. Foreigners saw us in the worst possible

light, and lacking experience at first hand, were unable to separate

truth from fabrication. The nation's reputation was endangered,

democracy was represented badly to other nations. In the post-war

propaganda battle, both the prospects for democracy and the position of the United States were further weakened by the movies. This, without doubt, was inconsistent with the national good.

Speech and language damaged

The new media were predicted by their opponents to cause damage both to the nation's language and to the manner in which it was spoken. Where advocates had predicted that the media would add words to the vocabulary and provide a high quality of model for imitation in speaking, opponents envisioned opposite effects. Speech standards would continue to drift downward, and the precision, beauty, and flexibility of the language would suffer because of the movies, radio, and television.

Writers who argued that the new media damaged speech assumed that viewers and listeners copied the language of the screen and adopted it for their own. As a result, Outlook in 1916 argued that the English learned from film titles was "incredible," and that there was "no end to the strange lingua misapprehension" flashed on the screen. It was, Outlook said, English written "by one who knows it not," in which "Jim extols his brother not to" perform some act, and heroines were asked to "wear this for a sentiment of me." It was hardly an acceptable model for imitation. When films were exported, English writers were quick to file similar complaints, arguing not only that American pictures perpetuated the worst of the language but that they also introduced American slang and "cinemese" to further clutter the mother tongue.[59]

Similar complaints appeared in connection with radio, the talkies, and television. All were accused of damaging the language and the speech habits of the nation. Mothers argued in the 1930's that radio shows were teaching children bad grammar because the characters on the air used bad grammar. One father, writing for Scribner's, was particularly upset because his son had begun to speak like the gangsters who appeared in the children's programs.[60] Other writers asserted that if radio speech were substandard, it could in turn influence the common speech of the nation, leading to wuz for was, avenoos for avenues, boids for birds, and Gawd for God. Where speakers before the advent of radio could address, at most, thousands, and influence only this many at one time, the radio orator could reach millions, "and as his speech is, so will theirs be." Just as radio speech reached great numbers of people, the speech in talkies not only reached many but was repeated again and again,

> and if the speech recorded in the dialogue is vulgar
> or ugly, its potentialities for lowering the speech
> standard of the country are almost incalculable. The
> fact that it is likely to be heard by the less discrimi-
> nating portion of the public operates to increase its
> evil effects; for among the regular attendants at moving
> picture theatres there are to be found large groups from
> among our foreign-born population, to whom it is really
> vitally important that they hear only the best speech.[61]

Economic damage

The motion picture had been hailed as a great source of revenue for a number of related industries, and pictures were indirectly a business asset to the nation as a whole. When the talking picture

was introduced, attackers argued that this new development would
lead to financial damage for the movie industry itself, and eventually for the entire nation. If the movie industry, which was said
to be one of the nation's largest industries, was hurt, the national
economy was bound to suffer some depression as a secondary effect.

This argument was generated by the introduction of talking
pictures, and was applied only to talkies. Shortly after Jolson
led the sound picture into prominence, The Nation, speculating
about the impact of talkies, suggested that with the coming of
sound the international market for American pictures would be
lost, and Hollywood would lose a source of income on which it depended. Outlook and Independent added the fact that the foreign market
accounted for 40 per cent of Hollywood's revenue, and it became
common in discussions of the new talking films to note that now
facing the industry was the prospect of a 40 per cent drop in revenue, for talking pictures would not sell in nations which did not
speak English. The injury to the industry was immediately apparent
and it was predicted that "unless the foreign language film problem
is solved quickly the American motion picture industry will soon
be in a very bad way indeed." With the coming of the depression,
writers blamed the talkies, "a grotesque and colossal failure at
the box office" both at home and abroad, for many of the financial
troubles of the industry.[62] Implicit in this argument, which was
used fourteen times between 1928 and 1933, was the clear implication

that if the movie industry suffered, the nation's economy was

likely to be hurt, too. In this fashion, a change in the industry

itself was tied to the prospects for the nation's economic life.

By pointing to the threat of the nation, the attackers could trans-

fer suspicion to the innovation.

This argument on the falling off of the foreign market for

talkies also suggested another kind of damage to the national

economy. If it were true, as the defense had suggested, that exported

pictures stimulated sales of American goods abroad, then this source

of income might also suffer with the curtailment of the flow of

pictures out of the country. The prospects of reduction in exports

of American films thus presented a varied threat to the national

economy.

Invasion of privacy

Writers seeking to denigrate television also played on the desire

of individuals for privacy and anonymity, for they suggested that

this medium would intrude on the individual's private world. It

was apparently a fairly common notion in the 1930's that if one had

a television set he could not only see the world, but could be seen

by it. This notion did not become a part of the argument, but several

writers were prompted to comment in introducing television that it

would not expose men to their fellows. For instance, Nation in 1936

assured readers they need not fear a new terror in their brave new world for television would not be equipped with keyhole and vest

pocket cameras. And a writer for Collier's in 1939 commented that

so much had been promised about television that some people were

afraid it would see too much. "No one is going to see you or your

wife in the bath tub," he assured readers. "We might as well get

this straight right away."63

But two writers, both of them in 1949, played upon this concern

and developed an argument from it, before broader experience with

television demonstrated that the problem was really not going to

be significant. Robert M. Yoder in Saturday Evening Post said that

television would create new problems by picking up embarrassing

scenes in crowd and reaction shots at public affairs. Home audiences

might see a girl fixing her garter in the crowd, a man using obvious

profanity, or even someone out with a woman not his wife. Yoder

concluded that

> TV is the most remarkable tattletale of all time, a fact
> that makes no one happy. Inevitably it is going to pro-
> duce many a schmozzle.64

The problem was not merely one of simple embarrassment of unfortu-

nates in the audience. It was suggested that the invasion of

privacy at public events might be serious enough to cause legal

problems for the stations originating the programs. But the prob-

lem never materialized in practice, perhaps because alert television

directors, aware that embarrassment could bring suit, kept away from

the obviously revealing or embarrassing picture, and the argument
faded out.

As writers sought to demonstrate that motion pictures, radio,
and television threatened the national welfare on all levels, they
turned to the impact of the media on the traits of character said
to be typically American. If Americans were traditionally hard
working, television was accused of making them lazy; if Americans
were normally sympathetic, movies hardened them to human suffering.
The new media were said to be wearing away the foundations of the
national character; if the media continued their work, the traditional descriptions would no longer be acceptable.

A nation of spectators

Presumably, Americans were active people; the passive role was
foreign to them. Yet television demanded passivity; one could
hardly participate in any of the programs except, perhaps, some of
the how-to-do-it or physical fitness shows. Consequently, there
was concern lest the nation become a spectator nation in contrast
to the tradition of active participation. This was a special
danger for children, for they were often trapped into watching
television at times when former generations were engaged in active
play or were busy participating in sports. Not only did this
convert the children to the spectator's role, said the attackers,

but it also prevented them from learning many of the basic skills which former generations had learned from both free play and organized recreation.[65]

A nation made lazy

If Americans were formerly hardworking, industrious people, television threatened to make them lazy. In 1937 Scribner's, surveying the prospects for television, predicted that the medium would not harm the rugged individuals in America who could resist its temptations, but that it would threaten the average, less self-sufficient man. He who was unable to withstand the promises of television would become lazy, intent on his leisure time, "the most interesting part of his day," and accustomed to having information and entertainment available "to him, his wife, and his children by the mere twisting of another dial." Television was expected to make his life too easy. In retrospect, a similar conclusion was drawn after ten years experience with television on a national scale. U. S. News reported that critics commonly thought that television made people "lazy and sodden."[66] In yet another way television was linked with the erosion of the national character.

Individuality lost

It was a persistent concern that radio and television, since they did provide the same information for many listeners, would cause people to hold the same opinions, to approach problems in a similar fashion, to give up their individuality in favor of mass

thinking. Because of the persistent buffeting of the media, individuality would be lost and more than ever men would seek conformity
as a goal. Writers who surveyed the impact of radio on American
society, H. V. Kaltenborn among them, saw this as one of the dangers
of radio; it was his concern that Americans would eventually have
uniform, machine minds. For all the good things that radio had
done, Kaltenborn argued that its greatest threat lay in the possibility of "making people think in unison." Radio, he said, was
"doing more than any other agency to develop the lock-step in public opinion."[67]

People who wrote about television were concerned about the
same influence, but they called it something else--standardization
of taste. John Crosby, in 1950, warned readers of yielding to the
conformity advocated and subtly promoted by television. He contended
that

> as individuals, more particularly as a nation of indi-
> viduals, what we have to guard against most from tele-
> vision is standardization of taste. Television is going
> to be a powerful force toward dictating to housewives
> and to teen-age kids, who occasionally grow into adults,
> how they should look, what they should think, how they
> should talk, what they should wear.[68]

Crosby's phrase, a standardization of taste, was adopted to describe
the phenomenon as it related to television. This was one of the
further intrusions of broadcasting on the values which had long
been a part of the American ideal;[69] because of the media the nation
would lose its individuality and its thought process would be shaped
by its broadcasters.

Imagination damaged

Just as individuality was a quality admired by Americans, so too was imagination respected. Both talkies and television were said to cause damage to the imagination, and this was pointed to as another of the dangerous effects of the media. At the transition between silents and talkies, it was common for writers to compare the two and evaluate them. Silent films were to evoke an imaginative response from audience members because the story was not made explicit on the screen. Sound films substituted conversation for this exercise of imagination. No longer was the mind free to react to the stimulus of the screen. As Gilbert Seldes predicted in 1928, the talking picture

> will make a minimum appeal to the imagination. For the
> effect of speech in the movies is definitely to check
> the imagination by preventing it from going free.[70]

When Christian Century sought to demonstrate that the motion picture was dangerous to the child in all his associations and in all his experiences, it argued that one of the influences of the movie was to tarnish, if not to destroy the wholesome imagination of the child. Because of movies, the purity of the child's imagination was corrupted, and substituted was a fascination with blood and thunder, crime and sex, the topics of the movies.[71]

Arguments from the effects on imagination were also used in connection with evaluations of television in the early 1950's.

That most television programs offered no stimulation for imagination was the contention of the critics, and the lack of stimulation constituted damage.[72] Hence, further evidence of the damage inflicted by the movies and television was supplied by those suspicious of the new media. Not even the imagination was safe from their influence.

Influences on children

Not only was the general national good threatened and the national character undermined by the new mass media, but the nation's future was endangered because of what children were exposed to in the movies, on radio, or on television. If anyone in the audience were likely to be hurt, it would be those most impressionable members. Critics argued that through the media children were exposed to experiences which violated social norms and that they tended to imitate what they saw or heard. The media, in effect, provided instruction in values, some of which, as we have already observed, conflicted with those encountered in more conventional sources. The child's belief system, not yet fully structured, was being warped in the making by the mass media; children were exposed to things they should not see, they learned things they should not learn. And this was dangerous because the beliefs of children eventually became the common beliefs of the nation.

This kind of danger was a concern for various periodicals, but the leader in the attack on this issue was Christian Century.

Again and again, <u>Christian Century</u> warned of harm to children,
stressing that no part of the child's life was free from the influence of the mass media. Most commonly, attackers spoke of threats
to morality, but they were also concerned about other kinds of
damage, not defined as moral, which could also result from exposure
to the new media. These latter arguments will be discussed now:
morality will be treated in a later section.

Oversophistication

Conventionally, the child's world was a simple world, a world
devoid of adult complications. All three media were charged with
destroying this simplicity, leading the child to a kind of sophistication which was unbecoming and unnatural. This was one of several
items in the indictment of radio programs drawn up by the mothers
of Scarsdale in 1933. They said, specifically, that children's
radio programs set a standard of "affectation and sophistication
that some girls of junior-high-school age love to adopt." Less than
a half-year later, <u>Christian Century</u>, which joined the attack on
every issue, supported its campaign against motion pictures with
the same charge, quoting from a psychological study of motion
pcitures and children the conclusion that "unnatural sophistication"
resulted from exposure to movies. Television was said to have the
same influence, when Robert Lewis Shayon in 1950 wrote of the influence of "the pied piper of video."[73]

The argument, in essence, said that the mass media caused children to be something they were not supposed to be. This could be taken to be harmful not only to the children involved, but damaging to the society in which the children lived.

Dangerous imitation

Writers who believed children to be endangered by the mass media argued that the examples presented by films, radio, and television caused children to imitate behavior which was frequently not childlike and occasionally dangerous. All kinds of examples were offered to show how the influence extended from the medium to the child. For instance, children dressed like their motion picture, radio, and television heroes, which meant that their costumes ranged from the undress of Clara Bow in the days of the flapper to bundling in black Hopalong Cassidy outfits in the hottest of TV summers. Christian Century, in all of its attacks, drew upon autobiographical materials in the studies of movies and children, to demonstrate that children had been influenced to imitate behavior ranging from merely foolish to violently anti-social. And New Republic in 1947 printed the complaint of a woman who said "her neighbor's child became so zealous after listening to Superman's cry of 'Up, Up . . . and AWA-A-Y!' that he forthwith climbed on the garage roof and attempted to take off, with disastrous results."74

Whether the behavior was dangerous or foolish, ludicrous or vicious, it was inspired by the new media. Children, said the attackers, were caused to do things they would not otherwise have thought of. Their behavior was unacceptable in the adult world, even if not dangerous to the child himself.

Children frightened

When mothers' groups objected to children's radio programs in 1933 and 1934, one of the grounds chosen for argument was that children were frightened by what they heard on the air. Those who used this argument presumed that all parents felt as they did, and wished to protect their children from unnecessarily frightening experiences. In developing their attack parent groups asserted that the programs created bad emotional effects by frightening children, that programs for children served to "shatter their nerves, /and/ stimulate emotions of horror." This argument was used as one of the stock issues in the first attack on children's radio, but was then dropped as the attackers found more effective grounds on which to build their cases.[75]

This argument was also picked up by Christian Century for its first attack on the movies. In May of 1933, Fred Eastman, discussing the effects of motion pictures on children's health, argued that by frightening children the movies represented a health hazard. Support for his position came from studies of the fears children had as a result of movies, and from the statements of a neurologist who

claimed that the scenes of horror might injure sensitive children

in a fashion akin to shell shock. It was Eastman's conclusion

that

> the excitement of horror pictures--especially if often
> repeated--may sow the seeds of future nervous disorders.
> You may laugh at his /the child's/ fears and try to
> reassure him, but his nerve cells do not laugh. Down
> in their depths they store away impressions, fear, and
> terrors that are never wholly obliterated. Some day they
> may rise up and smite him.[76]

Part of the objection to radio and motion pictures was related

to their frightening children, which in turn was suggested to be

damaging to their health. As the health of children suffered, so

suffered the welfare of the nation.

Sense of humor damaged

Critics were worried about children's sense of humor. Assuming

that humor could be plotted along a continuum which ranged from

"acceptable" or "real" humor to "perverted humor," writers for

Outlook argued that real humor and wholesome fun were virtually

non-existant in motion pictures. From the situation came a

> perversion of humor. In almost all the shows the things
> at which the people laugh are pretty generally the things
> that are silly, or that so clearly betoken human weak-
> ness or human frailty that pity or disgust would be a
> more fitting response. On such a foundation how can
> simple kindness and an appreciation of real humor be
> taught?[77]

In still another way, in the warping of their sense of humor, were

children threatened by the movies they saw.

False heroes

Writers who attacked motion pictures and television argued that children made heroes of the people they watched on the screen, and that many of the heroes seen there were unworthy of emulation or imitation. Christian Century, for example, quoted a study conducted by N. Y. U. which indicated that in congested city areas youths held as their heroes the gangsters seen in motion pictures. Twenty years later, mothers complained after watching four hours of children's programs on television that "not one episode, not one character, not one emotion did we see evoked that the children might emulate to their gain."[78] The presumption in both cases was the same; the mass media should give children something worthy of imitation. The media failed their child audiences in the kinds of heroes offered. Implicitly, the argument accused the media of leading to anti-social behavior in children.

Bad manners caused

Writers opposed to pictures went on to suggest that the movies were responsible for the bad manners of children. This charge was offered first by the ubiquitous Christian Century in a reader's letter which asserted that motion pictures gave "lessons in bad manners to children." A similar assertion appeared in Commonweal in 1939, when Blanche Jennings Thompson held that movie favorites such as the Dead End Kids and the Little Tough Guys were a bad

influence on the manners of the children who watched their pictures.[79]
Once again, motion pictures were claimed to be the cause of a fault
observed in children.

Decision making damaged

Ability to make decisions on the basis of reasoned consideration
of alternatives was also said to be threatened by television. Children long exposed to the medium might find decision-making even more
difficult than it had been in the past. The argument was developed
by Dallas W. Smythe, of the University of Illinois Institute of
Communications:

> The function of the school in developing pupils who will
> grow into logical thinking adults faces a highly dangerous
> potential in TV, . . . because of the exposure of juvenile
> TV-viewers to powerful influences affecting public opinion.
> Techniques of communications may shortly mature into
> reliable and efficient methods for engineering public
> opinion in the interest of those able to command the
> means of communication, regardless of what the identity
> of these persons or institutions may be.[80]

Television, beginning to manage the thinking of children, might
lead eventually to a decline in rational decision making. This
was a further threat of the medium, and children were again the
group most susceptible to influence.

In various ways the mass media threatened the youth of the
nation. Children were made less childlike, were caused to be
disrespectful, to be ill-mannered, were frightened, and tempted
to foolish and dangerous acts. Even if their morality went unharmed,

the future citizens of the nation suffered damage from the new
inventions.

These were the major objections to the new media on the grounds
of their influence on the national good. There were, however, other
incidental arguments which pointed to unique dangers arising out
of the innovations. Individual writers charged, for instance, that
movies damaged race relations, soldiers were portrayed disrespectfully,
that minorities were not adequately represented on the radio, that
radio stations practiced the very censorship they denounced, that the
art of salesmanship was debased by television, that the growth of
the media represented the latest step in the replacement of man
by the machine, and that the "flood of cheap and untruthful and
melodramatic entertainment /was7 literally, with its unhealthy
influence on American ideals and character, undermining America."[81]
All of these predicted dangers were further illustrations of the
vast damage of which the new media were capable. In threatening
beliefs long held and virtues traditionally admired; in weakening
traits of character which had long distinguished Americans; in
corrupting the youth of the nation the new media were cast in
opposition to the national good.

World Peace

Defenders of motion pictures, radio, and television had argued
that the media would serve the cause of world peace by creating new

limates of understanding among nations, by eliminating some of the
ong-standing sources of international friction, and by offering
triking and persuasive examples of the horrors of war. Attackers,
while agreeing that the goal of world peace was a desirable one,
argued that the new media, particularly the motion picture, would
 not contribute to peace; rather, the movies might well lead to
greater international misunderstanding and act as a catalyst for
nternational conflict.

Attackers began to talk of the international influence of movies
n the early 1920's. They contended that the motion picture kept
nations from achieving a full measure of understanding, and that
o eliminate the danger, films must be strictly regulated. When
he Christian Century attacks were launched, the argument from
peace was one chosen to illustrate the dangers arising out of the
movies. Arguments about the effects of pictures on international
ffairs had been incidental prior to the first Christian Century
eries; with the opening of that series argument on this topic
doubled. Each time this argument was used, the writer called for
egulation of the motion picture industry in order to eliminate
he danger to world peace.

nternational misunderstanding

Both defense and attack apparently agreed that the elimination
of international misunderstanding would do much to preserve peace.

It was the contention of the attackers, however, that movies rather than helping people understand each other better actually were a new source of international friction, disagreement, and misunderstanding.

This argument appeared first in the general assertion that "cheap, silly moving pictures" were "a most fruitful source of misunderstanding between the United States and Japan, China, and India." Later, England, New Zealand, Turkey, France, Spain, and South America were included in the list of those resentful of the American motion picture, and the specific sources of friction were spelled out. Foreigners were said to object to the immorality of American pictures, to their "sensuality, trashiness, and lack of realism,"[82] and to resent the importation of such material into their homelands under the guise of entertainment. A further source of dissatisfaction was the extreme nationalism exhibited in American pictures. A writer for Harper's noted that in the American films

> heroes spring from native soil; 'foreigners' supply its villains. It knows one flag and one flag only. That flag must wave if any waving is in order. When 'Peter Pan' was done at Hollywood, Peter did not wave--as Barrie had him wave--the Union Jack. Peter waved the Stars and Stripes, like a good naturalized American.[83]

Others spoke particularly of the treatment of foreigners in films.

Resentment of the nationalistic focus of American films was intensified with the coming of the talkie, for this new dimension represented a further intrusion of American values in other nations.

Saturday Evening Post reported this reaction to American talkies

in England:

> It was bad enough to have the United Kingdom swamped with
> American pictures, with the exploitations of American
> life, dress, customs, and manufacturers, but now to have
> American speech, with its execrable slang and twang,
> foisted upon the people, especially the younger genera-
> tion, was intolerable.[84]

Then, having spelled out the particulars, Christian Century, which

sustained this argument for the longest period, reverted to the

assertions that the American movie had a bad effect "upon inter-

national relations" and that they caused "resentment toward America

because of misrepresentation of the life of other countries;"[85] the

reader, familiar with the specifics of the charge, was left to

draw any more explicit conclusion he might desire.

The force of this argument depended upon acceptance of the

notion that resentment of the motion picture was transferred from

the movie itself to the nation producing it; films must be thought

of as having great persuasive impact. It followed that nations

dissatisfied with American films were antagonistic toward America

as a nation. Hence, attackers sought to link the American movie

with threats to international harmony. The films, rather than bring-

ing together the peoples of different nations, were broadening the

gulf of resentment and misunderstanding. It was in this light that

Christian Century concluded films worked to "poison the minds of

Europeans against American culture," and so labeled motion pictures "ambassadors of ill will."[86]

Films a cause of war

Implicit in the arguments about the international frictions and misunderstandings generated by the motion picture was the suggestion that the movies might lead the world closer to war, for war, as the defense had often pointed out, was a product of misunderstanding. The attackers were for the most part hesitant to predict war as a consequence of dissatisfaction with motion pictures. Christian Century, however, in 1933 discussed the possibility of the motion picture leading to war.

A dispatch from the magazine's Tokyo correspondent commented on the film "Men Must Fight," recently shown in Tokyo. In it, America declared war on "Eurasia," treaties were forgotten, and troops were sent into the field. Having seen the film, Christian Century's correspondent found himself "joining his many Japanese friends of peace and internationalism in looking with concern and even with suspicion upon the nation which permits such pictures to be made and distributed at home and abroad." It was his conclusion that "the scandal of the American movies is not limited to looseness in sexual morality; part of the bill for damages to the cause for international good will, already so badly strained, in the far east, may ultimately be paid for by American blood."[87]

The motion picture was finally named as a major contributor
to the complete breakdown of international relations.

War given approval

If motion pictures did not lead directly to war, they still
provided in their subject matter a kind of tacit approval of war.
This was the concern of two writers in the decade of the 1930's;
motion pictures might either arouse a desire for war in viewers,
or might make war appear glamorous and exciting.

The Living Age first expressed concern about the attitudes
toward war which children might gain from motion pictures. In its
report of a study of the reaction of French children to war pictures,
the magazine reported that although films were the most efficient
means of conveying the horrors of war to young audiences apart from
exposing them to real fighting, it was "always unwise" to show war
films to children because of the danger of "awakening dormant war-
like propensities" in them.[88] Christian Century at the end of the
decade expressed concern that recent movies were making war attractive and glamorous. Some of the new features cited stressed the
excitement and romance of war rather than its horror and dangers.
The magazine feared that the movies might break down the national
resistance to war and give a kind of approval to fighting which
was out of keeping with the American tradition. Again, motion pictures were contributing, this time indirectly, to the danger of war.

White men degraded

In yet another fashion the motion picture contributed to
international tension; the reputation of the white man was undermined
by the the motion picture. It was the contention of a writer for
Harper's in 1926 that the American film "actually impairs the safety
of empires . . . by lowering the prestige of the white man in the
orient." Evidence of the concern came from an article in the
London Daily Chronicle which had warned of

> the far-reaching consequences of inferior $\sqrt{}$motion picture$\sqrt{}$
> productions which are neither healthy nor patriotic. It
> is here that the Bolsheviks are said to enter into the
> equation: using cheap melodrama to undermine the prestige
> of white governments at home. What could be more silly,
> they are supposed to say to India, and Syria, and Malay,
> than to let yourselves be ruled by duffers who spend
> fortunes on their clothes, have no god but money, indulge
> in every form of inane folly, have no home life and use
> axle-grease to smooth their hair?[89]

Christian Century incorporated this argument into its attacks
on the motion picture in both 1932 and 1933. In the first instance,
the testimony of Lord Irwin, retired Viceroy of India, was quoted.
It was Irwin's argument that three factors were responsible for the
lowering of the prestige of white men in the East. Included were
the defeat of Russia by the Japanese, the reports of Eastern soldiers
about Western life they had seen during service in the World War,
and, finally, the movies. Of the latter, Christian Century said:

> Nothing is operating more constantly, more insidiously,
> to make the east contemptuous of the west, to offset
> all the constructive and friendly services of diplomacy,

commerce and religion, than the movies. How long is this
international trouble breeding to go on unsupervised and
unchecked?90

When the magazine renewed its attack on pictures in 1933, the charge,

and Irwin's statement, were repeated. One of the dangers of the

motion picture was still said to be its undermining of the prestige

of the white men in non-white nations.

In still another fashion the movie contributed to international

misunderstanding and ill will. In this case, there was also a danger

of conflict, for it was the implied belief of these writers that

peace in non-white nations, and progress, were benefits imposed by

the white man. Without the leadership of the white, not only would

the non-white suffer, but the stability of the world would be lost

as the great empires were disrupted.

Motion pictures were in these ways presented as threats to world

peace. Where defenders had argued that the world could expect to

find progress and cooperation increased because of films, the

attackers argued that movies were a source of conflict and mis-

understanding. To those who opposed films, the innovation posed a

threat to the peace of the world.

Culture

Motion pictures, radio, and television were promised by their

advocates to offer a new stimulus to the cultural life of the nation.

Here was to be a new opportunity to expose the mass audience to the
great symphonies, the great works of art, the great ideas reflecting
the best that man could be. Such exposure would in turn lead to
a new appreciation of beauty and to an improvement in taste, both
concomitants of culture. The potential was never realized, however,
and attackers pointed to the failures of the media in the very
areas for which the defense had held such high hopes.

The impact on culture

Just as advocates had dwelt upon the potential cultural influence of the media, the attack pointed to the failure of the media in
providing cultural material. This argument was not made explicit
in the charges against motion pictures; the critics, however, pointed
to the kinds of material supplied by pictures, none of which represented cultural attainment. With respect to both radio and television,
attackers pointed specifically to the damaging influence of the media
on the cultural life of the nation. For example, a writer for
Saturday Review argued in 1950 that programming decisions in radio,
which determined the cultural content of the medium, were "made
on crass commercial grounds, and that the advertisers have thus
captured and bastardized the great cultural force of radio."[91]
Radio was accused of not having attained its cultural promise, and
the cause of the failure was spelled out. When television was promised, it too was advertised as a new force for cultural growth. But

this was not a universal prediction; some writers who looked to the

place of the new medium argued that it would be harmful to culture.

For example, the theologian Reinhold Niebuhr said in 1949 that the

immediate effect of television would be

> a further vulgarization of our culture. . . . Much of what
> is still wholesome in our life will perish under the
> impact of this new visual aid.92

In the same year that Neibuhr made this comment, Norman Cousins

also spoke of television's place in the national life. It was his

position that television's potential as a cultural medium had

never been, and probable never would be realized. For each of

the "truly magnificent public service features," which in other

contexts were labeled cultural, Cousins claimed there were "num-

berless time-fillers whose only function seems to be to keep the

animated commercials from running together."93 Here, then, television

violated its cultural potential simply by not doing what it could

to stimulate culture; its sin was one of omission.

Using the same categories established by the advocates, attackers

pointed to the failures of the new media. Not only did the movies,

radio, and television sometimes offer a direct and clear-cut chal-

lenge to culture, but more frequently served to degrade and damage

cultural life simply by refusing to give it the support needed to

sustain life. Culture, a predicted end of the new media, was not

served by them.

Beauty lacking in films

Some of the defenders of motion pictures, George Bernard Shaw
among them, suggested that films might lead audiences to a new
awareness and appreciation of beauty. Writers opposed to films
saw no beauty in them, however. It was the argument of two of the
attackers that films were characterized by a lack of beauty. It
was the contention of C. H. Claudy in 1909 that films should not
be judged on the basis of their beauty, for

> nobody will contend--unless, indeed, it be the manufac-
> turers of moving picture film--that most of such films
> have much claim to beauty of any kind. They aim to
> excite, to interest, to be funny, to be tragic, to rouse
> the emotions and to draw a crowd; but their appeal is
> seldom, if ever, the appeal of beauty. Nor will any words
> of mine make them so. The field of the moving-picture
> is not that of the satisfaction of the craving for all
> that is beautiful, any more than the daily paper is
> intended to satisfy a desire for good literature.[94]

If the movie had no beauty, it was doubtful that it could inspire
audiences to appreciation of beauty. This evaluation of pictures
as a medium of entertainment, reduced by mechanical limitations
to "the level of bare incident, without intellectual appeal and
without the glorifying touch of literature, of beauty," was carried
at least through 1915.[95] If the quality to be admired in films
was beauty, and if the example of beauty created a new appreciation
of beauty, the motion picture lacked grounds for defense. Beauty,
according to detractors, was not one of the distinctive characteristics of the motion picture.

Poor taste

Both critics and promoters were dissatisfied with the level of

taste they saw in the public. Operating on the presumption that

public taste could be improved, the defenders argued that this was

one function of the new media. The opposition, however, argued

that it was the motion picture, and later television, which had

caused the poor taste in the first place.

Attackers argued that the movies created public taste; that is,

motion pictures provided standards of judgment by which audiences

evaluated their surroundings. This argument was first used in the

attack in 1915, when Literary Digest reported the charge that

> the movies are of immense importance. They are making
> the taste of the millions. They are making it bad,
> execrable taste--bad and execrable, because it is based
> solely on sensation, and is to that extent wholly animalis-
> tic.[96]

George Jean Nathan repeated the assertion in 1920, arguing that

the motion picture was one of the chief factors in reducing the

taste, sense and general culture of the American nation. The

charge was repeated five times in the next five years; each time

the writer assumed that his readers understood his use of the term

"taste," and each time the argument was presented as a new indict-

ment of the motion picture.[97]

A variation was introduced in the argument in 1927 when Gilbert

Seldes explained why it was that high quality pictures were often

box office failures. He wrote, "I have felt for many years that

the reason good films fail, particularly outside of New York, is
that unimaginative and meretricious films have spoiled the public
taste."[98] The chain of influence of bad pictures was thus lengthened;
not only did films prove hurtful to good taste, but in so doing prevented any improvement in the general quality of film production.
The motion picture, because of its failure to raise the public
taste, was in essence killing itself.

Television was also charged with damaging good taste. Even though
its proponents had not predicted that it would raise the general
level of taste, attackers were disappointed when it failed to demonstrate any influence in that direction. And like the movies, television was also said to have been the cause of a decline in taste.
Norman Cousins said in 1949, for example, that television had
instigated "such an invasion against good taste as no other communications medium had known." By this he meant that on television
there had been

> mass-produced a series of plodding stereotypes and low-
> quality programs. Behind it all, is a grinding lack of
> imagination and originality which has resulted in the
> standardized formula for an evening's entertainment: a
> poisoning, a variety show, a wrestling match.[99]

All too infrequent was any "truly magnificent public-service feature
such as the televising of the sessions of the United Nations or
the NBC symphony or the round-table forums of the Roy K. Marshalls
or the Ivan Sandersons or the book-author programs." This was the

charge when nationwide television was but a year old; the charge

was intact and viable six years later when U. S. News reported

concern that television had taught the children of the nation poor

taste.[100] Good taste, an end desirable in itself, was destroyed

by the newest of the mass media.

Good taste, beauty, culture--none were served by the recently

invented means of communication and entertainment. The attackers

pointed to the failures of the mass media to fulfill the predictions

of their promoters, and argued that the new constituted a threat

to the cultural life of the nation. A further desirable quality

was threatened by the media.

Morality

The most frequent and persistent arguments about motion pictures,

radio, and television dealt with the moral influences of the new

media. From 1906 through 1955, whenever writers wished to drama-

tize the spectacular dangers of innovation, whenever proponents

sought to support the need for new regulation of the media, when-

ever defenders felt it necessary to justify existing systems of

censorship, they turned to arguments from morality. Never was the

line of argument discarded, nor was it changed substantially through

the years. From the beginning attackers argued that the entertain-

ment provided by the media was taken up too much with crime, violence, and (in motion pictures) sex. Such amusement, they argued, violated acceptable moral standards, weakened the moral fibre of audience members, and sometimes inspired auditors to immoral acts reflecting the stories they had seen on the screen or heard on the air. From the beginning, too, critics held that while it could hardly be good for anyone to be fed a steady diet of crime and sensuality for amusement, it was the children in the audience, whose standards of behavior were yet in the process of formation, who were most likely to be hurt by what they saw or heard. Along these general lines the argument from morality provided substance for the attack for half a century.

Seeking the strongest available category for attack, opponents named the new mass media moral problems. Thus the movies, radio, and television could be denigrated either by associating them with the context of evil surrounding the term immoral or by contrasting them to the god term morality. In each new attack, and for each new generation of readers, arguers made certain that the audience was aware that in dealing with the mass media they were involved in a moral controversy.

Objections to the movies on the grounds of their moral influence was reported as early as 1906, and the Chicago City Council ordered that the police prohibit all pictures which showed crime or other "immoral scenes." Then in 1908 an editorial in Photo-Era

asserted that movies had "reached the stage of actually impairing
the morals as well as the health (eyesight) of the people." And
in 1910 Review of Reviews argued that when an enterprise as vast
as motion pictures "gets into the field of morals, something serious
is bound to happen."[101] When Christian Century undertook its campaigns to clean up the movies and establish governmental control
over them, it argued the move was necessary because

> the movies are so occupied with crime and sex stuff and
> are so saturating the minds of children the world over
> with social sewage that they have become a menace to the
> mental and moral life of the coming generation.[102]

In similar fashion, the work of the Legion of Decency was justified on the grounds that "it is necessary to apply to the cinema
a supreme rule which must direct and regulate the greatest of art
in order that it may not find itself in continual conflict with
Christian morality or even simply with human morality based upon
natural law." Again in 1954, America reasserted the Catholic
position that "movies do have a moral effect upon people." As it
said, "movies and morals go together. The movie shapes a person's
moral standards, moves a person to imitate and to sympathize, and
stimulates an emotional response."[103] In comments such as these,
movies and morality were linked throughout the argument.

Broadcasting was less commonly described in moral terms, although
its opponents talked often of its emphasis on crime, violence, and
brutality. The significant difference, for purposes of argument, lay

in broadcasting's treatment of sex. Because of the restrictions
imposed both by government regulation and advertiser preference,
sex themes were played down or eliminated from radio and television.
This omission staved off the kind of full-fledged, vituperative
attack on moral grounds which had been mounted against films.
Neverthless, broadcasting was still believed to influence morality.
For example, it was said of radio that "the moral standards of the
nation" were being set "by a little clique which judges the effectiveness of programs by its own warped standards." By 1952 television
programs were under fire because of their moral tone,[104] and in
1954 Christian Century, speaking of movies and television together,
argued that

> these mass entertainment giants go far toward determining
> the moral climate of the nation. The record of their
> attainments is being daily written in the life of the
> nation. Part of it is inscribed on the rolls of divorce
> courts, on police blotters, on the admission cards of
> homes for juvenile delinquents and hospitals for alco-
> holics.[105]

In 1955, U. S. News reported that people in general believed that
television tended to "loosen morals."[106]

When opponents turned from definition to cause, three basic
lines of attack developed. First, they objected to the exposure
of children to stories of crime and sex. Implicit here was the
fear that auditors would imitate what they saw on the screen or
heard over the air. But even if behavior was not altered, even if
the stories were presented merely in fun and for amusement, critics

still objected to children being exposed to them. Children were
to be sheltered as long as possible from violence and sensuality.
The second line of attack pointed to the possibility of children
learning about the methods of criminals from the stories they saw
and heard. Critics wanted to avoid such criminal instruction.
Finally, attackers made explicit the causal connection between
scenes of crime for entertainment and criminal acts in real life,
arguing that because of the media auditors were moved to immoral
or anti-social behavior. Movies, radio, and television were named
causes of crime, violence, or promiscuity. Consider first the arguments about exposure to crime and sex.

Exposure to crime and sex

Speculation about the influence of films followed close on
the heels of the nickelodeon. One of the first writers to name
motion pictures undesirable because of their subjects was Sher-
man C. Kingsley, who asserted that in movies children were introduced to "objectionable features . . . such as robberies, suggestive
jokes, hold-up scenes." Along with the ten cent theaters, where
the show was live, and the penny arcades, the five cent movies caused
children who were "aroused by hold-up scenes, shoplifting episodes,
or fascinated by stage life and the influence of unscrupulous actors
and actresses, . . . to get into trouble." Other writers recalled
that in the past, before censorship regulations had eliminated the

problem, the motion picture was "often a carnival of vulgarity, suggestiveness, and violence, the fit subject for police regulation." And police departments, reacting to agitation by "press, pulpit, and laymen alike" which did not appear in the periodicals, prohibited all "representations of criminal acts, violent scenes, or questionable social incidents calculated to arouse harmful emotions."[107] These comments appeared between 1906 and early 1908, but the popular argument about the moral influence of films began in earnest late in 1908.

The first major argument involved crime stories filmed for nickelodeons. C. H. Claudy, writing in Photo-Era in December, 1908, contended that such movies were too often "taken up on the bad side" of life, and that violent scenes of crime were damaging to viewers.

> To be specific, I recently attended three such shows
> in an evening, all within three squares of each other.
> In each show the principal attraction was a tragedy!
> In one the famous James Brothers murdered, robbed and
> set fire to their heart's content; in another an Indian
> took revenge on a white man for a wrong, in manner highly
> satisfactory to the audience; and in the third some
> ruffians kidnapped a child and were killed in the end.
> . . . The constant picturing of crime in any form, even
> if the punishment is shown at the end, is a harmful and
> degrading thing, especially when a large percentage of
> the patrons of such theaters is made up of minors, or
> adults without the education and point of view which will
> enable them to see things as they are.[108]

Three months later, allowing on the basis of the "vigorous protests from one quarter, and from other quarters equally vigorous condemnation" that the subject was popular and that his earlier article had "touched someone's sore elbow," Claudy renewed his attack on pictures. Again he entered objections to the brutality of pictures, to the "blood and thunder, detective, murder, battle, and sudden-death films . . . in which men were shot and women abducted and, presumably, mistreated with utmost abandon." In addition, he condemned the "vulgar, the loose-moraled and the uncivilizing films" so often shown. That is, he was disturbed by the sexual implications of the films, but like other writers of the period was hesitant about making his argument explicit. He made his point, however, by describing one of the "disgusting films" he had seen recently. This story of illicit love

> depicted the vacation of a husband. He packs his bag
> --in about three seconds--says good-by to his wife in
> a snap-shot, and flies for his train. On the train he
> makes friends with a girl, and kisses her as he goes
> through a tunnel. Then a letter to his wife is thrown
> on the screen in which he expresses his disgust with his
> stupid and uneventful journey. He goes to the theater
> in the town of his destination, flirts with a chorus
> girl, takes her to supper, and the film ends as he takes
> her on his lap and has a vigorous kissing match with
> her. Ugh! Following this is another letter to the
> deceived wife, who is told what a stupid time he is
> having, and how anxious he is to get home. Next a bar-
> room scene, in which Hubby drinks, is robbed, fights
> and is hailed down to the police station where his wife
> finds him, and where he makes up with her in a most
> touching manner, with winks to the audience on the side.[109]

If this man were to serve as an example of behavior, then this was hardly a proper lesson to reinforce society's codes. This sort of thing could not be dismissed as mere entertainment, therefore

harmless; it did influence moral behavior. This was Claudy's
argument, and he developed it after conceding that the film was
harmless,

> possibly, to you or to me. We have reached reasonable
> years of discretion; we know what society thinks of this
> class of man; and we recognize that while humans are humans
> vice will be vice. But what of its effects on the two
> callow youths who sat in front of me, with the two girls
> of fifteen or thereabouts who sat with them? What per-
> spective had they on life to judge the true from the
> false? The audience laughed heartily at the deceived
> wife, and at the antics of the husband, and at the readi-
> ness with which he was able to make all right with her
> again. Is this the sort of moral teaching to produce
> good men and women?[110]

The two major concerns about the movies were thus stated: films
dealt too much in criminal behavior and presented a false standard
of sexual conduct, which in turn influenced the moral standards
of audience members.

These two charges were commonly linked in the rest of the
argument. Attackers talked of crime and sex in the movies. Another
example of the early treatment of the argument is provided by
William A. McKeever, professor of philosophy at Kansas State
Agricultural College, writing for Good Housekeeping in August of
1910. McKeever said that movies were objectionable because in
them the viewer would find

> depicted again and again, in living form, all sorts of
> acts of a criminal and depraving nature. And around
> it all is thrown a sentiment such as to give the minds
> of plastic youth a tendency to regard the coarser forms
> of conduct as a common thing in our daily walks of life.

There he learns precisely how robberies, holdups and
murders are committed; how officers of the law, such
as policemen, are false to their oath of office and to
the demands of plain, everyday duty; how divorces are
originated and how the various members of the family
violate the most sacred laws that bind together the home
circle and give it its charm and perpetuity.[111]

From pictures the young viewer could also learn how policemen protect and aid criminals; how men get drunk in saloons and mistreat their wives; how a person, "while he is out in the night . . . gets into the company of others of criminal minds and does unnamable things"; how "girls learn to flirt and take up with vulgar men;" "how girls go with men to questionable places . . . and receive all sorts of questionable treatment." The movie could well have said to the youth,

I will also give you a few lessons showing you just how
to deceive your mother and make her think you have gone
to the young people's prayer meeting, while at the same
time you slip out into this company. There will be pictures to show every scene and every movement, so that
you can remember it as long as you live, and think about
it as you go about your daily affairs.[112]

It was McKeever's contention that the entire moral code was violated by the motion picture, and that children were exposed by it to vice and wrongdoing of a range and scope presented by no other agency. He argued that in pictures the viewers would

not only unlearn all the moral lessons of the schools,
but learn directly many of the immoral lessons that were
once confined to the worst centers of our largest cities.
In fact, the motto of these moving-picture organizations
might be this: 'A red-light district in easy reach of
every home. See the murder and the debauchery while you
wait. It is only a nickel.'

Hence, "if the citizens of any community should assemble with the
purpose of laying plans and devising means whereby to teach immorality, obscenity and crime, I can think of no better way definitely
and certainly to bring about such results than the use of the moving-
picture show as it is now conducted."[113]

McKeever's attack on films was the most extreme of those to
be found in the early period. But the argument that motion pictures
served to expose youth to the worst side of human nature and make
them conversant with the ways of crime and sensuality was continued
in the periodical press. American Magazine objected in 1913 to
scenes of robbery, violence, cheating, shooting, assault, and abduc-
tion; to the silly love stories; to the examples of ladies smoking;
to the emphasis in pictures on "some element of the bad side of
life." All of this, it said must wear some "ruts and grooves" in
the brains of the youngsters who populated the theaters. Readers of
Outlook whose letters were published as an article argued that the
white slave films which appeared just before the First World War
unnecessarily exposed children to sex. They protested the "exhibition to young, immature, and easily influenced minds of pictures
which suggest a life which, though it may apparently end tragically,
is extremely alluring to the youthful mind."[114] A writer in Education
objected not only to the crime and violence which characterized
films, but to the frequent erotic appeals, and to the nudity

of female stars. He recalled recent pictures of one actress which

showed her

> seated before her dressing table clad in the intimate
> lingerie of her bedroom, with a bountiful display of
> her nether limbs. It does not require the insight of
> a psychologist to predict the new crop of standards
> that will arise within the minds of the coming genera-
> tions.[115]

After the war the periodical carried frequent complaints about

the amount of sex and crime in pictures and their treatment of it.

It was argued that children became too knowing, hardened against

the normal relationships between men and women from watching motion

pictures, which they took as standards for their own behavior.

Outlook said in 1921 that the sex picture situation was worse

than ever before.[116] A typical comment on the dangers of sex

pictures for children was published that year.

> How many times, mothers, have you found yourselves
> sitting in a motion picture house, with your youngsters
> beside you, absolutely ashamed of being there--unable
> to give your child a satisfactory explanation of what
> the picture was all about? You and Dad wouldn't talk
> of these things in the presence of your children--would
> you? You want your children to grow up with wholesome
> concepts of life. You want them to have faith in sim-
> ple, everyday values. You face the problem of sex tremu-
> lously. You yearn to instill your child with a reverence
> for sacred relationships. As they grow older, you become
> even more anxious to guard your boys and girls from the
> pitfals that surround adolescents.
> The evils are so apparent to all that argument on
> the question seems almost unnecessary.[117]

Then in 1924 a writer for Ladies Home Journal reiterated the argu-

ment that "sex problems of various kinds, stories of passion and

violence, above all suicides, are not proper subjects for nervous
children to see." And in 1926 another writer, objecting to vamps,
to "vivid picturization of lustful abandon," to the "increased
portrayal of violent sensuality in films," argued not only that
there had been "recent releases more likely to undermine accepted
moral standards than anything the writer has observed in fifteen
years of special interest in motion pictures," but that enough
evidence had been gathered through the years "to suggest that the
motion picture has affected /sic/ and will continue to vitally
affect the moral conduct particularly of the young."[118]

In 1930 and again in 1933 <u>Christian</u> <u>Century</u> undertook campaigns
to promote Federal "social control" of motion pictures. Arguing
that the movies had not cleaned up since the founding of the Hays
Office, and that films remained a moral threat, writers for the
periodical asked that the government assume control of the industry.
The arguments used to support the need for such action were some
of the most vituperative in the history of attacks on pictures.
These arguments reflected the traditional charges against motion
pictures. The primary author of both series, Fred Eastman, mentioned
at the beginning of his first article, that he had read "every
important article and book published on this subject /motion pic-
tures/ during the last five years."[119] In addition to refurbishing
and amplifying traditional arguments, the articles also introduced

some of the most recent investigations on the effects of movies.
In particular, the first series made use of Alice Miller Mitchell's
Children and Movies and the second drew from several of the mono-
graphs prepared under the sponsorship of the Payne fund.

In twenty-eight articles between January of 1930 and November
of 1934, Christian Century argued that motion pictures were "a
menace to the mental and moral life of the community" because of
their continuing emphasis on "blood and thunder, crime, gun play,
lasciviousness, sentimentality, and inanity." Movies had come
to "menace our youth and America's good name across the seas."[120]

The periodical characterized this objectionable content as
"thousands of scenes of filth and garbage," contained in "coarse
and dirty films." In motion pictures children saw drinking scenes,
women smoking, "breaking homes and broken morals," suggestive and
vulgar "educational" materials, "horrible night life," "underworld
pictures of crime and lust, of triangle love of the most disgusting
type," and in at least one case "the almost complete nudity of the
principal female character most of the time." The movies presented
children with "drastic revisions of the religion taught in the
home and in the church." Film makers were "piping the cesspools
of Hollywood through the motion picture theaters and into the
minds of children."[121]

Christian Century objected most frequently to exposure of
children to "crime and sex" stuff through motion pictures.

In support of their contention, Christian Century writers
presented tabulations of the numbers of crimes found in pictures,
a technique which had not been used before in the argument. For
example, in the 1930 series Fred Eastman cited a report of the Child
Welfare Committee of the League of Nations which, having analyzed
250 films in 1926, found in them 97 murders, 51 cases of adultery,
19 suicides, 22 abductions. He referred, too, to the work of the
Chicago Censorship Board in eliminating from 788 pictures 1811
assaults with guns, 175 assaults with knives, 129 assaults with
other weapons, 231 hangings, 173 scenes of horror (clawing out
eyes, biting off ears, etc.), 757 immoral attacks on women, 929
scenes of nudity and semi-nudity, and 31 jail break scenes.[122]
Figures for the 1933 series were taken from Edgar Dale's analysis
of the content of motion pictures, a study supported by the Payne
Fund. Eastman informed his readers that

> the shift in recent years has been away from the love
> stories and toward sex and crime pictures, so that of
> the 500 features produced in 1930, 137 had crime as
> their major theme, 44 were primarily devoted to war,
> horror, and mystery, . . . and 70 centered around sex.
> . . . Only one picture in the entire year was made
> especially for children. Thus more than 50 per cent of
> the average child's movie diet that year consisted of
> pictures chiefly concerned with sex or crime or vio-
> lence of some sort. In 115 pictures taken at random
> from recent productions, 406 crimes are committed: in
> 35 pictures there are 54 murders; in 12 pictures are
> 17 holdups; in 14 pictures are 21 kidnappings. Of the
> murders the heroes committed 13, the villains 30,
> others 11.[123]

he motion picture was thus convicted as a significant source of

nformation potentially damaging to the child viewer.

Christian Century commonly linked crime and sex in its

rguments, objecting to both as subjects for the entertainment

f children. At times, however, the argument stressed the

ictures' preoccupation with sex as worse than crime as a threat

o children. When Dale's analysis was published, it was quoted

n the second Christian Century series to confirm previous assertions

hat films dealt too much with sex. Using the Dale monograph as a

ackground Christian Century said that

> one picture out of seven is built around sex as its
> dominant feature. In the 115 pictures which Dr. Dale
> selected at random he found that 43 per cent of them
> seemed to be set largely in bedrooms; at least the bed-
> room figures as the largest single heading under a
> classification of settings. In 22 pictures illicit
> love appears as the 'goal' of thirty-five leading charac-
> ters, including the heroes and heroines. 'Perhaps one
> of the most dangerous aspects of the situation,' says
> Dr. Dale, 'is that colorful and attractive stars are
> commonly given roles depicting women who lose their
> virtue.[124]

he motion picture was thus a source of education about sex, but

ne which undermined the standards of morality which Christian

entury espoused.

The kinds of pictures that children saw--lascivious, lewd,

exy, suggestive, immoral--weakened the traditional standards which

erved to guide and regulate sexual behavior. The movies, said

hristian Century, were a school, a school in which children learned

of the wrong side of life, a school which educated "millions of
young people daily in false standards of taste and conduct, false
conceptions of human relations." Because of exposure to stories
about "gangsters and rum runners, crooks, prostitutes and wastrels"
in which "crime, sex, and violence" were the major themes, youth
had gained a "terrible sophistication," a worldliness, a surprising
breadth of erotic understanding from which they would have been
shielded had it not been for the movies. Because of their exposure
to stimulating films, the children of 1930 were said to be more
"sex-wise, sex-excited, sex-absorbed" than the children of any
previous generation.[125] Endangered were traditional and accepted
standards of behavior, gone were former notions of modesty and
chastity, lost was regard for the sacredness of marriage. Standards
of sexual behavior were changing and the cause of the change was the
motion picture. This, to Christian Century, was the menace of the
movies.

While motion pictures were under attack by Christian Century
for their undue emphasis on crime and sex, other writers were worried about the content of radio programs, particularly those programs intended for children. It has been asserted that radio
escaped attack on moral grounds. In a sense the observation is
accurate, for radio was never charged with inciting sexual misconduct, and the number of writers naming radio a cause of crime
were relatively few. On the other hand, writers were much concerned

about the amount of crime and violence on the children's programs.
Exposure to this kind of material, they argued, could not be good
for children.

The first attacks on radio's children's programs came in 1933
when a committee of Scarsdale mothers objected to overly exciting,
criminally oriented mystery thrillers. Rating programs, this group
classed as very poor such programs as "Skippy," "Little Orphan
Annie," "Detectives Black and Blue," "Myrt and Marge," "The Shadow,"
and "Howard Thurston, Magician." Rated poor were "Paul Wing,"
"Uncle Don," "Betty Boop," "Just Plain Bill," "Boy's Club," "The
Marx Brothers," "Charlie Chan," "Chan du," "Eno Crime Club," and
"Bobby Benson." [126] All of these programs were so rated because
of their dependence upon criminal violence. A writer for Scribner's
explained his objections to Little Orphan Annie this way:

> Annie, the leading character, is an orphan, and the esca-
> pades which comprise the child's day-by-day life approxi-
> mate a high degree of sadism. She has been kidnapped,
> chloroformed, rendered unconscious by a deliberate blow
> on the head, held prisoner several times, pursued over the
> countryside by the law, imprisoned in barns and hovels and
> freight cars. She has trailed and captured bank thieves.
> She has been forced to spend several nights in a deserted
> shack in the woods to avoid being taken back to a sadistic
> orphan asylum which is under the direction of a shrew. She
> has been taken back to the orphan asylum through a procedure
> obviously unjust, if not illegal, and there has been made to
> scrub floors and perform the labors of a sub-menial.
> When I last tuned in, her constant boy companion
> was with her aboard the clipper ship belonging to her
> foster father. He was financing a search for a Pacific
> island treasure. The owner of the map was an aged half-
> wit with a blood-curdling laugh. Down in the hold was

a stowaway villian. He was fast lining up the crew for
mutiny. He planned to kill or drown the rich foster
father, Daddy Warbucks, grab the map and the ship and
seek the treasure.[127]

It was this kind of intrigue, suspense, suggested crime, and
anticipated violence which gave rise to the arguments about the
exposure of children to radio programs. Opponents contended that
not more than three or four of the twenty five juvenile radio programs broadcast in 1933 were "free of crime and planned felony,
either by subtle suggestion or actual commission." Analysis of
individual programs revealed radio's emphasis on kidnapping, pyro-
mania, sadism, double-crossing, robbery, attempted murder, arson,
revenge, dope addiction, blackmail--"all the skulduggery conceivable
to the human brain." Arthur Mann summarized the basic objection
to children's radio when he said, "I have listened carefully, and I
can say without fear of contradiction that every form of crime known
to man is either committed or suggested in the majority of juvenile
programs on the radio today."[128]

A second wave of attack on children's radio was launched in
1937. Gore and violence, threatening death and daredevil escape,
the gruesome details of bloodshed, crime, violence, and skulduggery
were radio's topics. Its characters were the gangster and the
G-man, the corpse, the ghost, "the ogre-like monster with one flaming
eye," its stock-in-trade the mystery and horror serial.[129] Children
were frightened by the programs, made nervous by then, but still
they listened. As American Mercury said,

come five o'clock every week-day afternoon, millions of
American children drop whatever they are doing and rush
to the nearest radio set. Here, with feverish eyes and
cocked ears, they listen for that first earsplitting
sound which indicates that the children's hour is at
hand. This introductory signal may be the wail of a
police siren, the rattle of a machine-gun, the explosion
of a hand grenade, the shriek of a dying woman, the bark
of a gangster's pistol, or the groan of a soul in purga-
tory. Whatever it is, the implication is the same:
Radio has resumed its daily task of cultivating our
children's morals--with blood-and-thunder effects.[130]

Following the Second World War there was renewed concern

about the content of radio. Complaints once again centered in

the "blood and thunder shockers," "detective dramas, ostensibly

designed for adult ears," but heard most frequently by children

"the chiller-diller juveniles," and the "dubious excitement of

pulp-written violence." Variety was quoted as saying that the

children's serials made up "a carnival of sluggings, muggings,

shootings, murders and tortures--a veritable paradise for sad-

ists."[131] There was apparently little real change in the content

of the radio programs between 1933 and 1947, and the objections of

opponents reflected a continuing concern about the entertainment

to which children were exposed. Writers argeed that much of radio's

entertainment was not proper for children. As one father explained

in 1933,

I do not believe that boys and girls should be guarded
in sweet simplicity until they are in their late thir-
ties, but on the other hand I should like to see my
children more or less in the dark on the subject of
counterfeiting until they are about ten years old.
I should like to postpone my children's knowledge of

how to rob a bank, scuttle a ship, shoot a sheriff, the
emotional effects of romantic infidelity, jungle hazards,
and the horrors of the drug habit for a few more years
at least.[132]

Critics continued to argue that hearing about violence and
crime must have some influence, probably a harmful one, on the
values of the auditor. Their assertions were supported by some
of the earliest studies of radio which indicated that it did influence the behavior of children. The Nation in 1947 feared that
radio might leave children "with a perverted sense of moral values,"[133]
and create in them "an unappeased appetite for violence." In response
to protests such as this, one network outlawed on their children's
programs

any appearance of making a hero of a gangster, criminal
or racketeer; disrespect for parents or other proper
authority; cruelty, greed, and selfishness; action arousing
harmful nervous reactions; conceit, smugness or an unwarranted superiority of anyone over others less fortunate;
recklessness; unfair exploitation of others; exalting
dishonesty and deceit.[134]

There was fair evidence to indicate that the programs did
make some children nervous, and had frightened many who listened.
But there was nothing firm on which to base any conclusion about
the effects of the programs. As a writer for Rotarian said in
1938, "Some partial and special studies have been made of radio's
effects on children's minds, nerves, and general health and outlook, but as yet there has been none, so far as I know, sufficiently
general, thorough, and authentic to support broad conclusions or

wholesale indictments."[135] With this kind of uncertainty about the
influence of the medium, it was not unusual to find people concerned
about the content of radio, certain that it must have some unhealthy
influence, but unable to specify the particulars of the charge.
Hence, it was charged that radio was damaging to the morality of
children, and the reader was left to supply the details of the
damages. The thing certain in the argument, however, was the presumption that radio's violence could not be good for anyone who
listened to it.

Concern about the amount of crime and violence on television
was articulated in the periodicals when the medium was in its first
year of nationwide operation. Norman Cousins opened the attack
in print in 1949, arguing that children were unnecessarily exposed
to crime and violence on television. "For every Kukla, Fran, and
Ollie, which stimulates rather than stultifies the imagination of
children," he wrote, "there are countless unskilled and ear shat-
tering kiddie shows and an even larger number of terror and tor-
ture specials." Following this opening there were numerous reports
of anxiety about crime on television. In 1950, Robert Lewis Shayon
reported that expressions of horror at the allegedly evil effects
of television upon out children, dire prophecies, urgent calls
for action rise in unremitting chorus from parents, teachers,
editorial writers, Government officials, bankers--yes, even advertising executives!" Parents were said to think television programs

too violent and too stimulating. When the Senate Subcommittee on Juvenile Delinquency opened its hearings in 1954, the chairman said his group had received "thousands and thousands of letters from parents expressing their fear about the adverse influence of television on their children." Through 1955, the periodicals carried stories of the continuing concern about children getting "wrapped up in the violent programs, blood and thunder stuff, stories of international intrigue."[136] The belief persisted that witnessing crime, violence and brutality, even as part of amusement, must have an adverse influence on the auditor.

In summary, attackers argued that children, who watched television between 20 and 30 hours a week, were too much exposed to crime and violence by the medium. As a writer for Saturday Review said in 1950, "Never has a generation of impressionable youngsters been instructed in the best ways to commit murder, mayhem, and bank robbery as demonstrably as they have of late on television. The favorite kind of evidence to demonstrate the extent of the problem was tabulation of crimes on television for a given period. Such lists were compiled by a number of agencies and were published frequently between 1950 and 1955. For example, Saturday Evening Post in an editorial in 1951 reported that the last week in May had seen 692 crimes committed in the television programs broadcast by seven Los Angeles stations. The crimes included 127 murders, 101 "justifiable killings," 357 attempted murders, 93 kidnappings,

11 jail breaks, and 3 hot iron brandings of men. What concerned

the Post was that 82 per cent of this violence appeared in the

children's programs; the violence, for all practical purposes ended

at bedtime.[137] In 1954, the National Association for Better Radio

and Television, NAFBRAT, reported itself

> dismayed over the volume of crime and the degree of
> violence which dominate television programs for child-
> ren. . . . Today, crime programs are being produced
> specifically for television in a volume approximately
> four times greater than in 1951.[138]

Saturday Evening Post, again in 1955 reported another tabulation of

television crime, this one compiled by a group of Chicago parents

who watched during Christmas week. Available to the children during

this period were 77 murders, 53 shooting, 30 gunfights, 7 kidnappings,

59 fist fights, 2 knifings, 22 sluggings, 3 whiplashings, 2 poison-

ings, 2 bombings, 3 murders by poisoned darts, 1 attempted lynching,

1 man thrown over a cliff, "and various other grisly events, such

as panic on a burning ship." It was difficult to avoid evidence

that television did, in fact, present a variety of crimes at times

when children could watch. Interestingly, though, apart from iso-

lated objections to vulgarity among comedians and to abbreviated

costumes on the variety shows, television was free from attack on

its treatment of sex.[139]

Attackers agreed that the presentation of crime for entertain-

ment could not be of benefit to audiences, but there was disagree-

ment about specific effects. Some argued that television was a cause of juvenile delinquency, as I will show later. Others, less

certain of the results, again classified the danger as generally

relating to "morality." For instance, a writer for <u>Nation</u> argued

in 1950 that

> programs like CBS's 'Suspense' and NBC's 'Martin Kane'
> --to single out only two of the rapidly multiplying
> crime stories now on the air--deal in detail with first
> degree murder week in and week out. People are killed
> with ice picks, axes, and poison in these all too graphic
> shows, and the effect on the youthful mind can hardly
> be salutary.[140]

Walter Goodman in <u>New Republic</u> said "no critic has suggested that

a crime story will instantly turn a clean-cut American lad into a

razor-wielding sadist," but he implied unnamed dangers in his con-

trasting question: "But do our present TV shows satisfy the child-

ren's needs in the happiest way?" <u>American Mercury</u> said that

"the effect of various kinds of violence and crime shows upon child-

ren of various ages, experience, and temperament is up to the

parent's imagination."[141] Parents were quoted as saying of tele-

vision in 1952 that

> it's not healthy. All day long it's machine guns, murders
> and gangs. You can't tell me children don't get dangerous
> ideas from TV.[142]

And in 1955 <u>U. S. News</u>, in this statment from a parent, presented

what is probably the most accurate characterization of the general

attitude toward the influence of television: "The casual display

of crime, sex and anger is an insidiously evil force and this gene-

ration is bound to suffer morally."[143] In general terms, then, television could be named a danger to the moral life of the nation because it exposed children to crime, violence, and brutality.

The continuing concern over the exposure to scenes of crime and violence--and in motion pictures, to sex--is apparent in the argument over half a century. Parents did not want their children exposed to obvious contradictions of the value system, and attackers employed this adversion to their advantage. Underlying the argument was the presumption that undue exposure to action and ideas in conflict with the moral system constituted a moral danger It was on this basis that part of the argument proceeded. The threat was non-specific, but its force was generated by threatened damage to morality, a concept which in its very generality provided sustenance for the argument. Arguments on exposure to immorality made up one part of the attack. Extending this argument, other attackers argued that the danger lay not in the mere exposure of the child to crime or to sex, but that what children saw or heard inspired them to imitation. In this manner, the new media were a direct inspiration to anti-social behavior, a cause of crime and the stimulus for sexual experimentation.

Instruction in criminal methods

One of the dangers of the new media was that children could learn from them how to commit various kinds of crimes, that the media constituted a kind of school of instruction in criminal methods. A youngster might learn how to perform a variety of crimes

simply by watching them performed on the screen. This argument
appeared in connection with each new medium.

Motion pictures, which often dealt with crimes and criminals,
were early accused of providing such instructions. In 1910, a
writer in Good Housekeeping said that from the pictures boys learned
"precisely how robberies, holdups and murders are committed."
Drawing on his own experience with films, another author recounted
how he and his wife in one afternoon at the movies learned how to
set a wheat field on fire with lumps of phosphorus, how to open a
safe, how to cut telephone lines, how to use a car for a getaway,
and how to use a pistol in committing crimes. These same lessons
were also available to the children who attended the movies. As
a writer for World's Work put it, the showing of such scenes "may
be instructive to those who may see the ease and entertain the
advisability of imitating the feat." It was the opinion of Outlook and Independent that "one evening spent looking at a talking
picture like Underworld gives . . . more information about the ins
and outs of crime than a week of patient study under Al Capone."[144]

Both radio and television were also said to provide lessons
in how to perform criminal acts. Even though it was more difficult
to get such instruction through radio programs--the learner could
not simply sit and watch the action take place and thus see how
to do it--one writer for Commonweal asserted that on radio the
listener could learn his lessons from the criminal, and a writer

in Saturday Review argued that the juvenile radio programs demonstrated "to listeners all the latest developments in the arts of treachery, venality, and crime."[145] Television, of course, again allowed the viewer to learn about crime simply by watching the actions unfold. This was taken into account in the argument. Norman Cousins, for example, argued that viewers had been given by television both inspiration to commit crimes and specific instructions in how to go about it. As evidence he recounted a lesson learned from TV.

> In Los Angeles, a housemaid caught a seven-year-old boy in the act of sprinkling ground glass into the family's lamb stew. There was no malice behind the act. It was purely experimental, having been inspired by curiosity to learn whether it would really work as well as it had on television.[146]

Lessons in crime was a facet of television explored in the Senate Subcommittee investigations of 1954. It was the conclusion of the committee, after testimony on the influence of television on youth, that

> scenes of crime and violence may well teach techniques of crime. (The police chiefs of Boston, New Haven, and other cities told the Subcommittee of children taken into custody who claimed they picked up their ideas and techniques from watching crime shows.)[147]

Over this century, then, there was continuing suspicion that the new mass media were not only inspiring the impressionable viewer to anti-social acts, but were providing an effective course of study in the necessary methodology. The media could both make the viewer want to commit a crime and give him the techniques for doing it.

Influences to crime

Attackers all along argued generally that children would copy the crimes which they saw, but the causal connection was implicit in their statements. Others during the period from 1907 through 1955 argued explicitly that the new media had caused youngsters to commit crimes. This argument hit all the media, but was used most frequently against the moving picture.

Some of the earliest of these arguments asserted that children committed crimes in order to get money to pay admission to the movie houses. In 1907 Charities and Commons called attention to a new threat to youth: children were so captivated by movies that they had stolen the nickels needed to get in. The argument was repeated in 1909,[148] and in 1910 Review of Reviews said that

> recent records show that three Brooklyn lads committed burglary to get the price of admission to unlimited 'Wild West' pictures. To obtain free tickets from the criminals who run shows in sections of large cities, many boys and girls have been led into all sorts of vice.[149]

Again in 1913, when a writer for Harper's Weekly sought to demonstrate that the motion picture was an important influence on the national life she suggested that movies had launched children on their first steps in a life of crime:

The overpowering desire felt by the youthful East Side
citizens to see certain celebrated 'movies' has more
than once led them into tragic difficulty. Not many
months ago, just after a much advertised prizefight,
two little boys, whose uncontrollable longing for the
admission fee to a picture hall had led them to upset
a grocer's display and barter his goods independently,
were brought to Children's Court. 'The price of admit-
tance was five cents?' enquired the judge, examing them.
The smaller boy, who was very small indeed, quickly raised
his thin, tense face. 'Oh, but it was ten cents to see
the big fight, judge!' he cried hoarsely, the tremendous
intensity of his manner and expression at once defining
the almost irresistable character of his temptation and
what he felt to be the manly magnitude of his crime.[150]

This argument, which was used by attackers to demonstrate
the powerful attraction of the movies during their first few years,
disappeared as pictures grew out of their novelty stage. Later
writers held that children got into trouble not so much because
of heir desire to go to the movies but rather because of what they
saw once they were inside the theater.

Critics who used this argument in the period before the First
World War envisioned a rather simple connection between movies and
crime: viewers either simply imitated the crimes shown on the
screen or they were inspired by the pictures to some other kind of
generally unacceptable behavior. This charge was first published
in a defense of films carried by The World To-Day in 1908. There
Lucy France Pierce, who held that the nickelodeon served as "a
recreative school for the whole family" (because of strict police
censorship), mentioned that while French pictures had been found
immoral from "a social standpoint, American ones have often been

found to encourage violent crimes and daring deeds of robbery and
brigandage." The argument was carried no further at this time but
it appeared again in 1910 when Review of Reviews, arguing in support
of the National Board of Censorship, surveyed the impact of the motion
picture on the national character. Three examples were provided to
substantiate the assertion that motion pictures caused crime. First,
"two Pittsburg youths tried to 'hold up' a street car after viewing
a train robbery enacted on a moving picture screen."[151] Further
evidence was supplied in a story from a "last month's newspaper."

> 'Charles Judson witnessed a 'suicide' scene last night
> in a motion picture show at Newark. Then he went home
> and copied the plan of the picture heroine. His body
> was found in his gas filled room this morning.
> 'The suicide was nineteen years old. The picture
> that he saw last night showed a young woman going through
> all the preliminaries to suicide by gas, finally reclining
> on her bed and awaiting death calmly.
> 'What was thrown on the screen Judson copied to
> the last detail, even to the stuffing of the cracks of
> the windows and doors.'[152]

Finally, Review of Reviews quoted another newspaper story relating
to

> a tragedy in Philadelphia. A clerk, unreasonably jealous
> of his wife, went with her to a moving-picture melodrama.
> It showed a home disrupted by a friend's attentions to
> the wife. The suggestion of fancied wrongs fanned the
> clerk to a murderous rage. The next morning this clerk
> shot his wife dead in the presence of their seven-year-
> old son. The police had no trouble in learning the
> immediate incitement.[153]

In each case it was the motion pictures which was said to be directly
responsible for the violations of societal codes. Consequently,

Review of Reviews upheld recent efforts "for the suppression of
moving pictures calculated to increase crime."

Following the stories in Review of Reviews other periodicals
--Good Housekeeping, Outlook, and Harper's Weekly--carried stories
which linked films with undesirable behavior, reinforcing the apparently common notion that movies were a criminal influence. This,
of course, was one of the grounds on which the so-called "white
slave" films were opposed; attackers argued that such pictures
would lead impressionable girls to prostitution. In support of the
latter assertion Mrs. Barclay Hazard, the head of the New York
branch of the National Florence Crittenton Mission for unfortunate
women, argued that if the motion picture, even with punishment
shown at the end of the film, could lead youth to criminal acts,
as she presumed the films had done, then the white slave films
could as easily lead girls to protitution. In support of her
argument Mrs. Hazard submitted

> the analogous case of films showing holdups, railway
> wrecks and cowboy fights, etc., the heroes of which are
> occasionally led even to the electric chair. But even
> their final destination does not in the smallest degree
> discourage their would-be imitators among the boys of
> the community. Hardly a week passes that some enter-
> prising boys are not arrested as runaways, having started
> out to capture and annihilate the wild Indians, with the
> somewhat inadequate equipment of two dollars and forty
> cents and a rusty revolver. Did their activities end there,
> the amusing interest might be the one most obvious; but
> these same children have been known to tie younger and
> weaker comrades to the stake and light bonfires, which
> have so injured the victims that several deaths are the
> record of this species of entertainment.[154]

On the grounds that motion pictures had lured children to criminal
acts in the past, she opposed the white slave films for fear they
would have the same influence: "We protest . . . against an exhibition to young, immature and easily influenced minds of pictures
which suggest a life which tho it may apparently end tragically,
is extremely alluring to the youthful mind."

For at least ten years it was generally accepted that a clearly
defined causal connection existed between movies and criminal
behavior; it was presumed that viewers simply imitated what they
saw on the screen or were inspired to some action like that which
they had watched. This presumption was first challenged in 1914,
when the Chairman of the National Board of Censorship of Motion
Pictures, the voluntary screening agency which later became the
National Board of Review, argued that the voluntary system was
more desirable than a proposed system of Federal control. He contended that the flexible policy of the National Board was necessary
since it was impossible to measure and trace the educational, social,
or moral influences of pictures, just as "no one can be sure of the
moral effects of any book, drama, or portrayal of fact or fiction
that is not obviously vulgar, suggestive or alluring." A year
later, Harper's Weekly reported that not even the National Board
knew how films exercised their influence nor how much real effect
they had on "public sentiment and private morality." Nevertheless,
it was still held that the movies did have an influence although the

way in which the influence worked was not fully understood. By late
1915 Outlook said it was "well recognized . . . that the effects
of motion pictures on children are not fully understood."155 Statements such as these reflect a growing sophistication in thinking
about the effects of the mass media; the formerly satisfactory
causal assertions no longer were accepted without qualification.
It was becoming apparent to some that the relationship was neither
simple or direct.

The growing refinement in thinking about the connection between
movies and behavior was not reflected in the argument. Attackers
continued to stress the clear, simple, and direct link between the
movies and crime, and sought to prevent qualification and restriction from intruding upon the causal line established. This was not
argument generated by the lunatic fringe, but was a standard part
of the attack in a variety of circumstances and from a variety of
respectible resources. Those who called for censorship following
the First World War argued that the movies had caused crime. Among
them was the General Secretary of the Big Brother movement who said
he wished movie producers and writers "could visit the criminals
they have made." The judges of Kings County, New York, in 1925
labeled vicious and improper movies a cause of crime. Christian
Century at the close of its 1930 series on movies concluded that
"the manner in which the moving pictures have directly stimulated
juvenile delinquency and crime, both in the United States and abroad,

is too well known to require evidence." The Knights of Columbus
in 1931 passed a resolution which stated that the gang film "creates
a criminal instinct in our youth," a conclusion with which the
editor of Commonweal expressed agreement.[156] The second Christian
Century series, based principally upon new studies of motion pictures and behavior, continued to argue that movies were a primary
causal factor in the growing crime rate. The Legion of Decency
incorporated the line of argument in its crusade for morality in
films. And the argument even turned up occasionally after the
Second World War, when most people were interested in television.

The line of argument was not changed significantly between
1907 and 1955; attackers throughout the period depended upon the
presumption that crime and violence in entertainment caused crime
and violence in real life. There was, however, a change in the
pattern of evidence after 1915. Before that, support for the contention came mainly from examples of crimes which seemed to be
inspired by films and from assertions by those who argued. Attackers
recognized that this connection was tenuous, and sought more substantial support. It came first in the form of testimony from
people in penal institutions. For example, the Chairman of the
Pennsylvania Board of Motion Picture Censors, Ellis P. Oberholtzer,
supported his assertion that pictures caused boys to become amateur
highwaymen, with the comment that "keepers are told by the inmates
of reformatories and penitentiaries that they were prompted to wrong

doing by looking at motion pictures."[157] The General Secretary of

the Big Brother Movement quoted interviews with boys in the reforma-

tory in support of his case.

> One said, 'It was the movies that got me in here.'
> I asked, 'Do you mean that you stole in order to get
> money to go to the movies, or that you saw pictures that
> made you want to steal?'
> 'I saw pictures that made me think of stealing.'
> 'But didn't the pictures show that the thief always
> gets caught and punished?'
> 'Oh, yes, but I thought I was wise and wouldn't get
> caught. I thought I wouldn't make the mistake he did and
> get caught.'[158]

Also quoted were opinions of psychologists, one of whom was A. T.

Poffenberger of Columbia University. It was his belief that young

people and adults of low mentality were led to crime by motion

pictures, accounting for the growing involvement of young people

in the crime wave sweeping the nation in 1921. He wrote that

> motion pictures, containing scenes vividly protraying
> defiance of laws and crimes of all degrees, may by an
> ending which shows the criminal brought to justice and
> the victory of the right, carry a moral to the intelli-
> gence of the adult; but that which impresses the mind
> of the mentally young and colors their imagination is
> the excitement and bravado accompanying the criminal
> act, while the moral goes unheeded. Their minds cannot
> logically reach the conclusion to which the chain of
> circumstances will drive the normal adult.[159]

There was a proliferation of evidence in support of the attack

as more studies became available and more people became concerned

about the influence of motion pictures in society. Christian Cen-

tury made broad use of the available sources, citing reports of the

League of Nations Committees; reports of censorship boards;

testimony from criminoligists, sociologists, teachers, and readers
of the magazine; and drawing heavily upon Alice Miller Mitchell's
Children and Movies in 1930 and upon the Payne Fund studies in
1933. In addition to expert testimony, a favorite kind of evidence
was the autobiographical accounts by criminals, contained primarily
in Mitchell, in Movies and Conduct by Herbert Blumer, and Movies,
Delinquency, and Crime by Blumer and Philip M. Hauser, both of the
latter monographs sponsored by the Payne Fund. For example, in
1930, drawing the material from Mitchell, Christian Century quoted
a fifteen year old reformatory inmate who said movies had caused
his attempt at crime. In the boy's words,

> movies sorta coax a feller. You know, you see them in
> the movies doing things, looks so easy. They get money
> easy in the movies, hold-ups, rob, if they make a mis-
> take they get caught. A feller thinks he won't make a
> mistake if he tries it. I thought I could get the money,
> put it in a bank for a long time and then use it later.[160]

Again in 1933, the primary author for Christian Century, Fred
Eastman, quoted a statement from a delinquent which blamed the
movies for his downfall.

> 'I think that the movies are mostly responsible
> for my criminal career. When I would see a crime pic-
> ture and notice how crime was carried out it would make
> me feel like going out and looking for something to
> steal. I have always had a desire for luxury and good
> clothes. When I worked the salary was so small that I
> could not buy what I wanted and pay the price for good
> clothes. When I would see crime pictures I would stay
> out all night, stealing. I have quit six or seven jobs
> just to steal.[161]

On the basis of stories of this kind, gathered from recently published investigations of motion pictures' influence on young viewers,
Christian Century argued that the movies were a cause of crime. The
motion picture was named as a degrading moral influence by its
attackers, and the argument was sustained principally by the additional material provided by the Payne Fund investigations.

The Christian Century campaigns were the last major attack
to focus so specifically on movies as a cause of crime. The Legion
of Decency campaigns which followed in 1934, characterized as an
attack "against the degrading influence of vile and crime-breeding
motion pictures" and as "a rabid crusade to remove sex, love and
crime as subjects for motion picture treatment," did not focus
so sharply on crime in films.[162] Rather, the emphasis was on
general moral damage, and the charges were carried primarily in
League publications and through church related organs; the League's
position often explained in the general periodicals with which this
study deals. Moreover, the reactions of Hollywood blunted the
attack, for some of the demands of the crusades were met, in token
form, by the motion picture industry. All of these factors served
to reduce the intensity of the attacks on moral grounds.

Nevertheless, the notion that motion pictures were a cause of
crime did come to the surface periodically from the late 1930's
until 1955. Various events prompted commentators to recall once
again that movies were a cause of crime. One such incident was

reported by Literary Digest late in 1937. Following the showing

of the movie Dead End, some 40 children in one New York neighborhood

appeared "with identical marks on their faces--angry red stripes

ranging from pin scratches to minor knife cuts that ran diagonally

from the middle of the cheek to the chin." The cause was said to

be the movie, in which was featured a similar "mark of the squealer."

As Literary Digest said,

> how much of the powerful and tragic social lesson of the
> picture impressed itself upon these East Side youngsters
> is uncertain. One lesson they did learn--how to inflict
> the mark of the squealer.[163]

The release of celebrated "immoral" or "indecent" films--The Outlaw,

The Miracle, The Moon Is Blue--also prompted recollection of the

argument immediately after the Second World War: in conjunction

with some of the criticism of these films, commentators commonly

noted that one of the bases for their present concern was the

past influence of movies on criminal behavior. Other specific

incidents also renewed the argument; the commission of a crime

might inspire assertions about movies as a cause of crime. For

example, Catholic Digest reported in 1955 that a young office worker,

having seen the film Violated, became sexually aroused and went

in search of a woman.

> Driving home early in the morning after an unsuccessful
> search, the youth sees Elaine Gallagher, 21, walking to
> her home on Gladys Ave., Lakewood. He gets out of his
> car, hits her with a wrapped brick. She screams. He
> runs. Police catch him. He says, "I never had anything
> affect me like that before. The movie was about a sex
> maniac who murders three or four women. I wanted to go
> out and do the same thing.[164]

Then when Samuel Goldwyn called for a re-evaluation and possible

revamping of the Motion Picture Code in 1954, Christian Century

feared that any change would lead to a lowering of moral standards

in pictures. It was their contention that movies, and television,

had already done enough damage, that

> the record of their attainments is being daily written
> in the life of the nation. Part of it is inscribed on
> the rolls of divorce courts, on police blotters, on
> the admission cards of homes for juvenile delinquents
> and hospitals for alcoholics.[165]

The presumption that motion pictures were a cause of crime remained

intact; it was cast into argument on a variety of occasions when

the moral influence of motion pictures came under scrutiny.

Radio's first attack in connection with crime came in 1933,

when mothers objected to exposure of their children to crime and

violence through radio programs. The main concerns about radio

at this time, however, were that children heard too much about crime

and violence, became overly excited because of it, and were pre-

vented from participating in more worthwhile activities A few

writers suggested that radio programs might also cause crime. One

of these was James Balan, New York Police Commissioner, who said in

1933 that crime stories on the radio were "liable to give dangerous

ideas to young America."[166] Evidence for the contention was similar to that employed in some of the early argument about crime and movies; a recent crime reflected a recent piece of entertainment. New Outlook explained that

> the drive against the broadcast shockers reached a new
> peak when wome critic pointed out that the Eno Crime
> Club's shocker of February 21-22, 1933, contained a
> story much like the kidnapping of the little McMath
> child from a school on Cape Cod, and might well have
> suggested the method of the crime to the half-wit who
> seized the girls and has since been sent to an asylum.
> . . . That was the incident that elicited Commissioner
> Balan's disapproval of aerial crime yards.[167]

This type of charge was uncommon in connection with radio, in the period before World War II. Only occasionally did parents complain about the influence of radio on behavior. Late in 1937, however, Newsweek carried a report of parental complaints to the FCC about radio crime programs; the objection arose out of the belief that programs influenced "the minds of children to such an extent that their play life becomes an embryo crime life."[168]

Following the Second World War, writers seeking to explain the causes of the rising tide of juvenile delinquency turned to radio and its continuing emphasis on crime and violence. A writer in Commonweal analyzed the situation in this fashion in 1945:

> People used to say bad children were the product of pov-
> erty, neglect, broken homes. But that does not cover
> the case now; because I know many who come from pros-
> perous families; they lead sheltered lives. These young
> vandals are out for excitement. When they deface a school,
> a church, or rob a filling station, its just for the hell
> of it. What leads them on? Several things: the comics,
> the movies, the radio--mostly the radio: all those crime
> stories coming over the air.[169]

Two years later <u>Saturday Review</u> reported that "in several large
cities, recently, police officials have suggested that the almost
complete focusing of young people's programs on murder, mayhem,
violence, and crime in such shows as 'Superman,' 'Dick Tracy,'
'Captain Midnight,' 'Tom Mix,' etc., is contributing more than a
little to the problem of juvenile delinquency."[170]   Radio, like
the movies, was thus charged with causing youth to violate society's
codes.   This argument about radio as a cause of crime was dropped
from the periodicals, unresolved, when television caught the public
fancy.   As television expanded across the country attention shifted
to it, and arguers looked to it for new explanations for the rise
in delinquency.

The initial assertion that television was a cause of crime
came from Norman Cousins in 1949.   He wrote, in <u>Saturday Review</u>,
that "the terror comic strips were bad enough, but they are rapidly
on the way to playing a squeaky second fiddle to television as
prime movers in juvenile misconduct and delinquency."   As evidence
of television's disintegrating influence Cousins presented three
samples of juvenile behavior which had been inspired by the medium.
In one of them he told how

> in a Boston suburb, a nine-year-old boy reluctantly
> showed his father a report card heavily decorated with
> red marks, then proposes one way of getting at the heart
> of the matter: they could give the teacher a box of
> poisoned chocolates for Christmas.   'It's easy, Dad, they
> did it on television last week.   A man wanted to kill his

wife, so he gave her candy with poison in it and she didn't
know who did it.[171]

Cousins was unusual in that he named television as a cause of
delinquency; most writers avoided such a direct statement of the
connection between television and crime and instead talked of the
vast amounts of time devoted to crime and violence on the medium
and left the obvious conclusion to the readers. The audience,
conditioned by forty years of argument over movies and crime,
twenty years of concern about radio's influence on the crime rate,
and operating on the presumption that witnessing crime and violence
bred delinquency, were fully capable of completing the chain. That
there was concern about the influence of television on delinquency
is apparent in comments elicited from readers by U. S. News. One
of the "widely held convictions" of the public about television
was that it "causes juvenile delinquency." Moreover, there was
published in 1955 the report of the Senate Subcommittee to Investigate Juvenile Delinquency. Having taken testimony in 1954 and
1955, the committee expressed concern over the subjects chosen
for television entertainment, but concluded that it had been "unable
to gather proof of a direct causal relationship between the viewing of
acts of crime and violence and the actual performance of criminal
deeds." On the other hand, the Committee reported that it had not
found "irrefutable evidence that young people may not be negatively
influenced in their present-day behavior by the saturated exposure

they now receive to picture and drama based on an underlying theme of lawlessness and crime which depict human violence." The report concluded that "in the light of the evidence that there is a calculated risk incurred through the repeated exposure of young boys and girls, even of tender age, to ruthless, unethical forms of behavior, the Subcommittee believes it would be wise to minimize this risk insofar as possible."[172] The argument stood unresolved in 1955, but the report of the Subcommittee confirmed the position of those who had expressed concern about the influence of television on behavior.

All of the new media were accused of fostering crime and violence by their examples. The argument, explicit in relation to motion pictures, remained below the surface of discourse much of the time in connection with both radio and television. The same fears were apparent, however. All the mass media were leading youth to violate the codes by which society governed itself.

Sexual experimentation

As I have already pointed out, attackers suggested indirectly that motion pictures were a source of undesirable sex information and unwarranted sexual stimulation, particularly for young viewers. In this argument, the connection between sensuality in pictures and sexuality among audiences, while often hinted at, was usually left unmade; the reader was encouraged to supply the missing elements in the argument. In one line of attack

however, the charge was made explicit; motion pictures were a cause
of sexual experimentation and sexual indulgence among adolescents.

This argument appeared very early in the attack on pictures,
but in the beginning was handled with great caution and indirection,
for explicit discussions of sexual matters were apparently deemed
improper for the periodicals. Recall, for example, that John Collier
in 1908 had named pictures "a carnival of vulgarity, suggestiveness,
and violence," and William Inglis in 1910 charged nickelodeons with
being "breeders of crime and immorality." William McKeever, the
boldest of the early attackers, argued that movies which showed
"how the various members of the family violate the most sacred
laws that bind together the home circle and give it its charm and
perpetuity," were teaching "immorality, obscenity, and crime."
He contended that the motto of the picture might well be, "A red-
light district in easy reach of every home. See the murder and
debauchery while you wait. It is only a nickel."[173] Characteristically the language was indirect, euphemistic, slightly shocking
but still polite; the idea was sufficiently clear to make the point.

Less inhibited were the authors who wrote against Traffic In
Souls and the other white slave films which followed it after 1914.
Predictably, there was concern that seeing the films might lead
"weak and unmoral" girls to lives of prostitution. Such girls
because of "vanity, love of luxury, and craving for excitement"

saw only the glamour of the life depicted in the films and so were said to be "willing to run any risks to attain the results." Having carried her argument this far, one writer was unwilling to be more specific and concluded that

> as to the effect . . . it is perhaps not best to go into it here. Suffice it to say that any physician with experience among such cases will testify to the immediate and serious physical results of this auto-suggestion.[174]

Speaking of the same motion picture, A Traffic In Souls, the Secretary of the Mason City, Iowa, Y. M. C. A. argued that boys were sexually stimulated by the film and moved to experiment along lines suggested by the story. Hinting at perversion, he said that boys had, "with the motion picture drama as a basis, carried out and extended in their own minds and with themselves as the principals the idea of the scenario to include imagined acts astonishingly degrading."[175] More clearly were arguers connecting films with sexual misconduct.

Following the First World War, while sex in entertainment films became a more common topic for comment, writers still avoided discussing the details of sexual relationships and commonly built their cases by indirections. The Secretary of the Pennsylvania Board of Motion Picture Censors, outspoken about films as a cause of crime, said in reference to sex in films only that

> adolescents are fed upon sex stories and are incited to sensuality and passion. The pretty innocence of young womanhood, the chilvary of young manhood are swept away.[176]

When in 1924 the Ladies Home Journal quoted Professor Patrick of
Iowa State University on the damage to children from movies, it
said only that certain films aroused feelings "best let slumber"
and fostered "emotivity to a rather serious extent." In 1926,
analyzing the influence of motion pictures on changing moral standards, Harmon B. Stephens suggested that children became sexually
aroused in films which contained scenes of violent sensuality and
"vivid picturizations of sadistic, lustful abandon."[177] Such
scenes were said to teach children a standard of sexual conduct
inconsistent with society's norms and were hinted to have been
influential in increasing the number of rape and assault cases.

It was Christian Century which made the most spectacular use
of this line of argument. Attempting to demonstrate the magnitude
of the moral dangers inherent in motion pictures, Fred Eastman
chose examples which were explicit in both language and detail.
He argued that movies caused children to become sexually aroused,
inspired them to sexual play, and often served as a prelude to intercourse. The charge was supported in the first campaign primarily
with autobiographical material from Alice Miller Mitchell's Children
and Movies. Quoted both in Christian Century and in a later article
in Parent's Magazine was a statement from a 16 year old delinquent
girl who said that

> those pictures with hot love making in them; they make
> girls and boys sitting together get up and walk out,
> go off somewhere, you know. Once I walked out with a

boy before the picture was even over. We took a ride.
But my friend, she all the time had to get up and go
out with her boy friend.[178]

Arguing that movies have "stimulated . . . the sex impulses" and

"demoralized standards of modesty and social conduct" in America's

children, <u>Christian Century</u> from 1930 through 1932 supported pro-

posals for "social control" of the motion picture industry.

New evidence supporting this line of argument was made availab le

by the Payne Fund studies and it was incorporated into the 1933

articles. Again Eastman argued that movies destroyed the traditional

notion of "a decent restraint between the sexes" and led to a break-

down of sexual morality in adolescents. First, he said, children

copied the standards of behavior and patterns of conduct seen in

pictures. From Blumer's <u>Movies and Conduct</u>, Eastman reported this

statement from a seventeen year old high school senior who said

that from movies

> I have learned how to flirt, and how to 'handle'em.'
> I have also learned different ways of kissing, and what
> to say when made love to. I have had all kinds of chances
> to use what I've learned from moving pictures, and I've
> taken advantage of them.[179]

Having provided a knowledge of technique, the movies were a source

of sexual stimulation. Evidence of this influence came from other

autobiographical statements contained in Blumer, among them this

one from a sixteen year old boy:

> I like some love pictures, like Charles 'Buddy' Rogers
> plays in. When you see these hot love pictures it makes

> you feel like going out and having **sexual relations**.
> A guy was out in a garden with a girl and after he had
> become a father he left the girl. Pictures like that
> make a guy feel like going out and doing things. I took
> a girl to one of these pictures and we followed the
> picture and did everything they did in the picture. I
> got what I was after later.[180]

In his next Christian Century article, Eastman again maintained

that movies led to delinquent behavior and particularly to sexual

conduct which violated the conventional societal codes. As evidence

he cited other statements gathered by Blumer. A seventeen year

old delinquent girl said, for example:

> I like to see men and women fall in love in the movies and
> go out on parties, etc. It teaches me how to do the same.
> I also like to see them kiss, love, drink, smoke, and lead
> up to intercourse. It makes me get all stirred up in a
> passionate way. Love pictures, wild west pictures, mur-
> der cases are the pictures I like best, because I like
> to love, myself, and I know others want to do the same.
> After I see them I get out and love and have sexual inter-
> course and go on parties and only do worse. Movies teach
> me how to treat my men and fool them.[181]

The assertion that movies led girls to intercourse was sustained

by Blumer's conclusion that "of 252 delinquent girls, most of them

14 to 18 years of age, 25 per cent acknowledged 'engaging in sexual

relations after becoming sexually aroused at a movie.'"[182] Movies

were thus linked by Christian Century to a breakdown in moral stan-

dards and were named a cause of sexual misconduct in youth.

The concern about movies as a cause of sexual misbehavior

continued after the Christian Century campaigns. It was one of

the major themes of the Legion of Decency crusade, and comments about

this influence may be found in isolated instances following the
Second World War. But never again was the charge made as explicitly
as it had been in the Eastman interpretations of the Payne Fund
reports; for the most part the later argument reverted to discussions
of "obscenity" or "immorality" in films and readers were left with
their own interpretations.

Violence approved

Even if motion pictures, radio, or television did not cause
children to overtly abandon the codes of behavior recommended by
society, certain of the authors feared that because of the media
children would be reoriented to violence. That is, seeing constant violence for entertainment, children were likely to develop
an abnormal appetite for this kind of excitement.

This argument was first applied to motion pictures. It developed out of a survey conducted in Cleveland before the First World
War to determine what children liked in films. When subjects
reported in essays that they liked best the pictures of war, burglary, love, and vaudeville, American Magazine concluded that
children should not be permitted this kind of entertainment because
the craving for "this kind of excitement" was "not so easily allayed"
and "not likely to fade out." In a similar vein, a writer assessing
the impact of movies on children for Education argued that films
had caused children to develop "a craze and an abnormal appetite for
the sensational, the grotesque, and the bizarre."[183]

Both radio and television were said to have the same kind of an influence on children. Speaking of radio, one writer claimed that children's programs were helping "breed a race of neurotic impressionables" who would be unaware of non-violent amusement and another predicted that the shows would "create an unappeased appetite for violence." When television began to spend much of its time exploring the violence in life, one writer said that "so many hours of television are devoted to murder that children who are allowed to watch will inevitably become calloused to violence and death." Certainly, said another, the amount of crime and violence shown on television could not be defended as being good for the child.[184] In yet another instance, the mass media were offering amusement which violated society's ideas about normal and proper behavior; it was presumed that such exposure would have a damaging influence on impressionable viewers.

One place where the damage became apparent in behavior, apart from crime and promiscuity, was in the child's play. Because of the new media, children's play was said to be more violent than in the past and in many cases to be dangerous to the participants. Movies and television both caused an increase in cowboy and Indian play. One writer in 1914, using the analogy to point to potential dangers in the white slave films, argued that movies had caused children to "tie younger and weaker comrades to the stake and light onfires, which so injured the victims that several deaths are the

ecord of this species of entertainment."[185] Christian Century

uoted the autobiographical account of a young man who recalled that

fter seeing a movie he and his playmates, then much younger,

> tied one of our members to an oak tree, and notwithstanding
> his frantic cries, proceeded with a boisterous war-dance
> about the victim. The struggling boy was almost strangled
> by the numerous coils of rope about his neck before his
> frenzied mother appeared to secure his release.[186]

here are also the stories associated with television, possibly

pocryphal for they are difficult to document, of the burnings at the

take by children which were inspired by scenes on the tube. Radio,

nlike the other two media, was blamed only with increasing the

mount of gun play among adolescents.

Even the play of the child, supposed to be exciting but not

angerous, reflected the violence of its model. All areas of the

hild's life were threatened by his entertainment.

ther moral influences

Drinking, smoking, divorce, and immodesty in dress were also

efined as moral problems by writers who discussed the impact of

he new mass media. In all of the areas just named, motion pictures

nd occasionally television were said to damage traditional beliefs

nd standards.

Objections to alcohol developed along two lines: first, children

ere exposed to scenes of drinking , and, second, they were persuaded to begin the use of alcohol. Scenes of drinking in films were cited

as bad examples as early as 1910 when Good Housekeeping objected

to children learning from films "how to get drunk in a saloon."[187]

Later, other writers complained that in films, if nowhere else,

children would become acquainted with liquor. Christian Century,

as would be expected, objected on this count. Speaking of drink-

ing in films, Fred Eastman had this to say in 1933:

> Does your child see drinking at home? If he doesn't,
> he must think your home quite unusual, for he sees it in
> most of the movies. In fact, 78 per cent of all pictures
> contain liquor situations. Drinking is usually shown as
> the accepted thing and drunkenness often as funny.[188]

Writers who used this argument presumed that motion pictures were

one of the determiners of social behavior and that if drinking were

shown in films then film audiences, especially children, would come

to accept the use of alcohol as having social approval.

Films, and in one instance television, were also said to cause

children to begin the use of alcohol. Christian Century quoted

the testimony of young delinquents who said they mimicked what they

saw in the motion picture and thus began drinking. Later the same

publication argued that the use of certain kinds of alcohol in

pictures, i. e. pink champagne, resulted in a "phenomenal increase"

in customer requests for the beverage. Moreover, said Christian

Century the effect of drinking in films was to influence the youth-

ful audience "unconsciously to assume that if they are to be up to

ate, to enjoy the pleasure and assurance which the admired film
haracters seem to gain from this procedure, they must go and do
ikewise." Thirteen years later, the pastor of the Mount Holly-
ood Congregational Church, commenting in the Annals of the American
cademy on the influence of movies said that "incidentally but not
nsignificantly, the doctrine will be deftly slipped into the uncon-
cious mind /of the child/ that to be socially acceptable one has
o alternative but to drink." Similarly, another Christian Century
riter in 1949 argued that television was subtly causing children
o drink because the beer commercials were so "effective and fasci-
ating."[189] Moving pictures and television were thus both accused
f influencing children to begin the use of alcoholic beverages,
n some eyes a moral offense.

Similar objections were raised to smoking. Those who used the
rgument considered the use of tobacco, particularly cigarettes,
moral offense. American Magazine, for example, objected to movies
s a harmful moral influence in 1914 because in them children saw
omen smoking, something to which the writer presumed children were
ot normally exposed.[190] Christian Century readers commonly used
e phrase "drinking and smoking" to name related moral abuses, and
e of them whose letter was published in 1930 said this about
lms:

> Almost every one of the present day movies shows drinking
> scenes, indulged in by both men and women, and in practically

> every one, women are shown smoking cigarettes and drinking
> high-balls and cocktails, so that the average youth of
> today between the ages of eight and sixteen has the impres-
> sion that he most certainly will have to drink and smoke
> when he becomes of legal age.[191]

Again in 1933 Christian Century argued that movies had started

youth on a dangerous moral path by exposing them to smoking, and

consequently influencing them to take up cigarettes. The movies

caused youth to believe it was "smart to smoke," in direct violation

of the traditional standards upheld by family and church.[192] Motion

pictures were again responsible for violations of the moral code.

Other moral dangers were also seen to lurk in the entertain-

ment provided by the moving picture. By example, said Christian

Century the traditional standards of modesty in both dress and

social conduct were being restructured through the moving picture.

Children were led to believe that exposure of the body was desirable,

and that immodesty in behavior was permissable. Good Housekeeping

in 1910 objected to pictures because in them children learned "how

divorces are originated," and in 1926 Harmon B. Stephens argued in

the Annals of the American Academy that motion pictures had "encour-

aged or intensified a number of changes in moral conduct" and that

"as an example of a change in moral standards we may cite the

steadily mounting divorce rate."[193] And a writer for Ladies Home

Journal suggested in 1924 that suicides in movies

> are not proper subjects for nervous children to see. Young
> folks at ever younger and younger years are the victims of

the tendency to self destruction, which is a feature of
modern civilization. The suggestion of suicides as
exhibited on the screen may prove, in a moment of intense
discouragement or depression, an incitement to imitation
of the act which may prove unescapable in a nervous individual.[194]

Just as in 1910 Review of Reviews had argued that a young boy learned

the method of suicide from a movie[195] so there was still concern

about this influence of pictures fourteen years later. In these

recurring arguments moving pictures were said by their detractors

to damage the moral life of the nation.

All areas of the nation's moral life lay within the sphere

of influence of motion pictures, radio, and television. In all

decisions about good and evil, the mass media played their role.

Children, yet uncertain about what was right and wrong, accepted

the lessons from screen and radio and were moved to crime and to

promiscuity. Former notions of behavior were discarded in favor

of the new models provided by innovation. Traditional ideas of

man's relationship with other men were changed because of pressures

exerted by the media. The moral structure was in danger of being

warped beyond recognition, if not toppled, by movies, radio, and

TV.

Health

Presuming that men in general favor those things which promote

their good health, and disfavor those which threaten it, both

promoters and critics argued from the effects of motion pictures,
radio, and television on the health of their audiences. Promoters
as I pointed out in Chapter Two, made less of the issue of health
than did the attackers. If promoters dealt with the question at all,
they tended to handle it indirectly and to gloss over the prospects
of damage. Critics, however, particularly when the new media first
were introduced played upon the fear that they might prove harmful
to health. New health hazards, they said, accompanied each new
medium. The line of argument was introduced in connection with motion
pictures, and was used subsequently in the evaluation of both radio
and television.

Objections to movies on the grounds of their potential damage
to health grew out of a legitimate concern for the welfare of viewers.
First of all, there was a danger of fire; the film stock was highly
inflammable, the machines erratic, and the operators careless.
Scientific American in 1905 spoke of the dangers of the movies:
"The increased use of moving-picture apparatus for exhibition purposes in recent years has been accompanied by a large number of more
or less serious fires traceable to the moving-picture apparatus or
to the wires used for supplying electric current for the apparatus."
The importance of the problem was "clearly shown by the occurrence
within six weeks of fires due to moving-picture exhibitions in
Haverhill, Salem, and Lynn, /Massachusetts/, which resulted in damage

mounting to $60,000 and caused many persons to be seriously injured.
hree years later, an article from The Electrical Review quoted in
iterary Digest reported that safety legislation and licensing had
ot reduced the dangers of the movie houses. "Serious fires caused
y machines for the exhibition of moving pictures have not been
ncommon." For one thing, when New York municipal authorities
urveyed the picture houses, "it was discovered that one of the
undred and eighty places where these moving-picture machines were
perated, over ninety per cent were kept by foreigners and incom-
etent people, seventy-five per cent of this ninety-five per cent
eing apparently unable to read and comprehend the printed instruc-
ions which were issued at the time of issuing their licenses.
he Electrical Review repeated the suggestions made earlier by
cientific American that fireproof projection booths be constructed
n theaters and that a "fireproof magazine for the film supply reel
nd a similar magazine for the take-up reel" be used. New city
egulations governing picture machine operation, the location of the
rojection equipment, and the number of entrances and exits to the
heaters were also noted. Literary Digest concluded that "if these
urther restrictions do not eliminate the danger of life and property,
he moving-picture exhibits will be closed up altogether."[196]

The new regulations, stricter enforcement of the licensing
aws, better projection equipment, and greater care on the part of
perators apparently worked together to reduce the number of fires.

With the danger diminished, warnings about fires in picture houses
disappeared from the periodicals.

More persistent were the warnings about exposure to disease
in the movie houses. From 1910 through 1924, opponents of the new
amusement called attention to the poor ventilation in the picture
shows, the crowding together of many people in closed rooms, and
the inadequate cleaning of the theaters. They told how people were
"subjected to the dangers of disease from foul and germ-laden air
in the theaters"; how audiences sat "breathing in contamination
from the breath of others and from the lack of cleanness in the
place"; how people coughed without precaution, thus spreading "any
bacilli that may be in their mouths or in their lungs"; how audience
members did "not hesitate to expectorate on the floor, usually near
the angles of seats or along the iron supports, just where it is
most difficult to secure its thoro /sic7 removal"; how close contact
with sick people at the movies served to "facilitate distribution
of infectious diseases."197

Critics warned that people who went to the movies under these
conditions were not only exposing themselves generally to "infectious diseases of various kinds," but also to   tuberculosis,
"coughing and serious colds," and "epidemics in winter." If nothing
worse happened, audience members were apt to leave the theaters
groggy, tired , almost hypnotized because of the poor ventilation.

But most opponents played upon the concern that people might catch
something at the movies. As a writer for Education said in 1919,
suggesting that even children who watched educational films in
school might be harmed, "Continued confinement in a semi-darkened
room must produce an undesirable effect."[198]

The attitude about the motion pictures as a threat to health
is clearly demonstrated in an editorial from The Independent in 1910.
There the author contended that every new form of amusement created
new dangers to health, but that the motion picture was the worst
of them all.

> It is a well known rule that every new form of popular
> amusement brings with it special dangers to health. The
> roller skating rink with its dust and exercise in a con-
> fined space, the bicycle with its tendency to accidents,
> the automobile emphasizing even this and adding the
> dangers from dust and exposure, are all typical examples.
> Recently it has been pointed out that the latest form
> of popular entertainment, the moving picture show, is
> liable to be more of a menace to health than any of the
> popular amusements of recent years. This is all the
> more serious because of the wide vogue that the moving
> picture show has obtained in the last year. . . . It is
> probable that the fad will die out in the course of the
> next few years, but in the meantime it is evident that
> great harm to health may be worked by them, for they are
> maintained as a rule under the worst possible hygenic
> conditions and nearly everything about them favors the
> spread of disease.[199]

This line of argument remained viable for about 15 years.
As long as the theaters were small, dirty, and crowded, the argument retained its credibility. It was dropped by critics in the

mid-1920's, when the movie houses became elaborate and luxurious showplaces, carpeted, upholstered, and chandeliered.

Most frequent of all, however, were warnings about damage to the eyes. This was a favorite topic of critics in the early years of the movies. C. H. Claudy and others complained in 1908 of the flicker, the blurring, the "jerky, spasmotic movements. . . that one is accustomed to see at the vaudeville moving picture show," which worked to "ruin the eyes."[200] By 1913 eye specialists were said by Outlook to have isolated a new illness, "'moving picture eye,' an already well-developed optical phenomenon." Outlook told readers that

> the consensus of opinion of oculists is that a man with
> normal eyesight can safely endure four sittings of
> thirty minutes each per week with but little or no
> unpleasant symptoms and no permanent ill-effects. But
> the 'movie' fan lays himself open to overtaxed eye nerves,
> with the consequent headaches, indigestion, and general
> nervous complaints.[201]

The Journal of the American Medical Association, quoted by Scientific American Supplement, argued that "it has been shown that a number of disorders of the eyes are caused by this form of entertainment /the movies/." Frequently, however, the complaints--"headache, nausea, and fatigue of the eyes, followed by vomiting, sleeplessness, and lack of energy"--were not traced soon enough to the movies, not were they called to public attention. Until the First World War critics argued that one of the dangers of the motion picture was damage to the eyes.[202]

This line of attack, like the ones discussed above, died out as movies became more sophisticated technically. The quality of both films and projection improved, people became accustomed to watching movies, and experience demonstrated that eye damage was not a significant side effect of the movies. The argument, a major source of attack for about ten years, was abandoned by 1920.

When the arguments about fires, disease, and eye strain ran out, critics turned to predictions about psychological damage caused by movies. This line of attack coincided with the growing interest in psychology which developed in the 1920's and so permitted critics to relate the movies to problems which had only recently become a popular concern. Moreover, discussions of psychological problems permitted attackers greater freedom for speculation than did the former arguments about physical effects. That is, it seemed to be easier to demonstrate, either experimentally or by lay observation, a connection between movies and mental health. So critics began talking about the effects of movies on the minds of the audience.

A suggestion of this kind of argument is contained in an article for Outlook in 1921. There a mother objected to movie serials because there were "too exciting--many of the kids go home and dream about the episodes at night "203 This sort of thing, she presumed, was not good for the mental health of the child. Then in 1924, Ladies Home Journal warned against exposing "nervous children" and infants to the stimulation of motion pictures. Drawing upon

"recent psychological studies," the Journal argued that

> the taking of infants to the motion picture auditorium
> is of course inexcusable. The ill ventilated auditorium,
> the alternating bright and dark lights, the clang of
> music, possibly liberal portions of candy to keep the
> youngster quiet, followed perhaps by a ride in an auto-
> mobile homeward late at night--this is the price many
> infants pay for their mother's desire for entertainment.
> That it certainly will result in serious damage to the
> nervous systems of those children goes without saying,
> since it is a perfect orgy of over-stimulation.[204]

With damage suggested by the periodical, the audience was left to

supply the particular details. With effects implied, readers

could fill out the argument with their own special concerns and

fears. The technique is reminiscent of the attacks on morality.

Christian Century revived the health arguments for its articles

in 1930 and 1933. In the first series, the comments were similar

to the ones quoted above. That is, movies were dangerous because

they caused children to get too excited and made them nervous.[205]

In the second series, Fred Eastman stressed the psychological

effects of movies, drawing his evidence from the recent Payne Fund

studies. In one article, "The Movies and Your Child's Health,"

he argued that films damaged health by causing children to sleep

restlessly, which led in turn to physical and emotional disturbances.

Movies were likewise judged responsible for children's fears and

bad dreams. In addition, the stimulation of pictures was suggested

to be dangerous for children with heart trouble. In "The Movies and Your Child's Emotions" Eastman reported evidence that children

did react more emotionally to films than adults did. From movies,

in the words of one of the studies quoted by Eastman (the deletions

are his),

> profound mental and physiological effects of an emotional
> order are produced. . . . Unnatural sophistication and
> premature bodily stimulation . . . result. The emotions
> are widely known in the psychological literature for
> their extensive and intensive grip on mind and body.[206]

Movies on this basis were judged harmful to the physical and mental

health of their audiences. Eastman left his readers with this

warning:

> Here then is something for you as a parent to ponder:
> the sleep impairment and fatigue produced by movies tends
> to weaken your child's inhibitions and his control over
> his temper and conduct. They increase his nervousness
> and irritably. The excitement of horror pictures--espec-
> ially if often repeated--may sow the seeds of future
> nervous disorders. You may laugh at his fears and try to
> reassure him, but his nerve cells do not laugh. Down in
> their depths they store away impressions, fears, and
> terrors that are never wholly obliterated. Some day they
> may rise up and smite them.[207]

The Christian Century articles ended the discussions of movies

and health. Radio was the second medium to be tested for its influ-

ence on health.

Radio could not be connected readily with damage to physical

health, although one doctor did argue facetiously that the radio

programs he disliked caused his blood pressure to rise to dangerous

levels.[208] Critics sometimes argued, as I pointed out earlier, that programs frightened children or that radio caused youngsters to give up needed exercise. Commonly, however, when radio and health were linked, attackers contended that it was the child's mental health which suffered.

Arguments about the psychological dangers of children's radio began in 1933 and continued until 1947. Individual writers objected to the programs because of their "bad emotional effects;" because they kept "the children in emotional suspense;" because they caused fingernail biting, a sign of emotional distress; because they were leading to "a race of neurotic impressionables;" or, as Lee DeForest said, because "children are rendered psychopathic by . . . bedtime stories."[209] There were, however, two common concerns. First, parents complained radio programs caused children to sleep rest-lessly and to have bad dreams. For example, this situation was reported in 1938:

> A New York doctor recently reported on the case of a youthful patient who suffered from 'night terrors.' Each night the boy would awake, sweating and sreaming, his face contorted, his muscles stiff. After essaying various treatments without success, the doctor cross-examined the child. The boy appeared reluctant to discuss his case. Finally he confessed that some weeks earlier, he had listened to a children's radio program which involved a corpse, two ghosts, a haunted castle, and an ogre-like monster with one flaming eye. Each night as he lay in bed, the boy disclosed, his last waking thoughts dwelt upon the monster. The result was a nightmare of the most virulent type--mentally and physically harmful. . . . Was it for this that Marconi invented the wire-less?[210]

econd, the programs made children nervous. This was one count,

ιattered nerves, on which the Scarsdale mothers objected to radio.

ther parents reported "increased nervousness" in their children,

ιd objected to the effects of "overstimulating programs on immature

ιrves."[211] Radio, judged on these grounds, the same on which movies

ιd been condemned, could hardly be considered good for the child

ιstener.

Some writers claimed that radio was equally harmful to the

ιotional stability of adults. New Republic, for example, said

ι 1945 that psychologists were concerned about soap opera listeners

ιcause they identified themselves so closely with the programs,

ιing so far as to send radio characters cakes and baby clothes.

ιo years later, New Republic reported that radio's soap operas

ιd led some listeners, who saw themselves in the programs, to

ιpochondria. At the same time a psychiatrist was quoted to the

ιfect that soap opera devotees underwent "tachycardia, arythmia,

ιofuse perspiration, tremors, gastrointestinal disturbances, emo-

onal instability and vertigo while listening to the programs."[212]

ιdio, while it might disturb the listener's physical well-being,

ιs most commonly accused of fostering mental instability. Radio,

s critic warned, was in its own way a health hazard.

Television's critics reverted to arguments about damage to

ιewer's eyes. The complaints began as soon as television became

popular. In 1949 Science Digest reported widespread concern that
TV might harm the eyes. Just as people forty years earlier had
complained about "moving picture eyes," so now viewers talked about
a new malady, "television eyes." Parent's Magazine warned that
unless children were carefully supervised, their eyes might be damaged by watching television. Television viewing rules were published.
The proper viewing range was from 6 to 12 feet away from the set
with some light on in the room. Sitting on the floor to watch was
prohibited because the angle of vision could cause eye strain.
The screen should be properly focused at all times. "Dark glasses
are not recommended." Adults were warned that since the eyes
suffered about a 40 per cent loss of night vision after watching
TV, "after an evening in front of the neighbor's television set, a
guest should sit for at least 20 minutes in a darkened room before
driving home."213

By 1950, television or its effects were held to account for
about 10 per cent of the nation's eye troubles. A writer for
Education warned again that "there is a decided effect upon the
eye sight of youngsters that spend too much time watching a partially
focused screen." At the end of the year Robert Lewis Shayon reported
in Saturday Review that children who got television in their homes
displayed the effects of eye strain almost immediately.214 While
these arguments were in progress, supporters of the medium were

defending the position that there was no more danger to the eyes
in television than in movies, reading, sewing, or driving a car.

Most of the flurry about the eyes was over in about two years.
Perhaps the arguments of the advocates prevailed; more likely, as
people got accustomed to television experience proved that the
problem was not as severe as opponents had predicted. Still,
however, as late as 1955 U. S. News reported that "some eye specialists . . . point out that TV watching adds just one more stress to
those placed on eyesight by bright lights and movies, and thus
increases the likelihood of eye trouble."[215]

Writers suspicious of the medium continued to argue that there
was a danger to the health of the child who sat hunched in front of
the television, watcing for as much as five hours a day. Some said
the danger lay in the child's lack of exercise. Children became
soft because they simply sat and looked: television "keeps /children/
from play such as baseball and hopscotch, which will help exercise
and develop their eyes and the co-ordination between eyes, hands,
and feet." Other writers returned to themes which had been used in
attacks on both movies and radio: children didn't get enough sleep
because they sat up watching television; when they did get to bed
they slept restlessly; as a consequence they were nervous and
irritable during the day.[216] The argument had fallen back upon
predictable topics.

Arguments about health thus became commonplaces in the repertory
of attack. Each new medium was greeted with predictions that it
would damage the good health, physical or mental, of those who used
it. In some cases, as with motion picture fire hazards, the fears
were justified and the argument subsided as the danger diminished.
In other areas, opponents continued the argument as long as it
remained plausible, even when there appeared to be little substantial
base for their assertions. Often no one really knew whether the
media were harmful to health or not. Critics therefore played upon
the doubts and upon the fears that the media might be hazardous. It
is interesting that both movies and television were attacked first
on grounds of physical damage, and that when this line ran out the
concern shifted to the less certain areas of emotional or psychological damage. Radio was charged only with the latter kind of
damage in the periodicals I surveyed, but undoubtedly there were
attackers who pointed to the dangers of electrical shocks from radio
sets, if nothing else. Worth noting, too, is the continuing concern
for the mental stability of children. Just as attackers were most
often worried about the influence of the new media on the morality
of youth, so also were they fearful of psychological damage to the
coming generation. Thus all the media were tested against man's
goal of good health. It was the contention of the opponents that
this valued state was threatened by innovation.

It was not good health alone which faced debilitation by the new media. All those things considered worthwhile, useful, or beneficial, all those ideas thought to be necessary, proper, or desirable were endangered. Motion pictures, radio, and television threatened the prevailing system of values. The fundamental ideas which society held in common, said the opponents of the-media, were likely to suffer because of the new forms of, communication. Just as the defense of the media had been built on the value system, so too was this part of the attack founded there. Where the defense had argued that the influence of the new would be beneficial, the attack held that it would be damaging. The case of the attackers was built on this proposition: things and ideas of value were threatened with extinction because of the introduction of motion pictures, radio, and television. This was the threat of innovation.

Notes

1. <u>CC</u>, 24 My '33, p. 689.

2. <u>PE</u>, 0 '26, p. 179; <u>NR</u>, 8 Je '27, p. 62.

3. <u>CC</u>, 15 Ja '30, p. 77.

4. <u>CC</u>, 22 0 '30, p. 1271.

5. <u>CC</u>, 18 Je '30, p. 775.

6. <u>CC</u>, 24 My '33, p. 689.

7. <u>CC</u>, 24 My '33, p. 689.

8. <u>CC</u>, 3 My '33, p. 593.

9. <u>AAA</u>, N '47, pp. 95-96.

10. <u>SR</u>, 13 N '48, p. 60.

11. <u>Nat</u>, 26 Ap '47, p. 481.

12. <u>SG</u>, Mr '47, p. 187.

13. <u>Time</u>, 3 Mr '52, p. 70; <u>TA</u>, My '51, p. 43; <u>TA</u>, Je '52, p. 46.

14. <u>GH</u>, N '50, p 265.

15. <u>NR</u>, 1 N '54, p. 12.

16. <u>USN</u>, 2 S '55, p. 75.

17. The argument was used 16 times in the periodicals named, and twice the material from Christian Century was used in other magazines. See: Christian Century, 15 Ja '30, p. 77; 22 Ja '30, p. 112; 18 Je '30, p. 775; 22 O '30, p. 1271; 3 My '33, p. 593; 24 My '33, p. 688; 7 Je '33, p. 751; 14 Je '33, p. 781: Commonweal, 13 Ag '30, p. 381; 17 N '33, p. 78: New Republic, 10 N '26, p. 343; 8 Je '27, p. 62; 1 N '54, p. 12: Outlook, 26 Jl '16, p. 694: Nation, 26 Ap '47, p. 481: Saturday Review, 13 N '48, p. 60: Parent's Magazine, N '31, p. 20: Annals of the American Academy, N '47, p. 95. The argument appeared in other periodicals 12 times. See: Photo-Era, Mr '09, p. 124; O '26, p. 179: Current Opinion, O '15, p. 244; Mr '21, p. 320; Ag '18, p. 99: Theatre Arts, My '51, p. 43; Je '52, p. 46: American Magazine, Ag '13, p. 93: Survey Graphic, Mr '47, p. 187: Good Housekeeping, N '50, p. 265: Time, 3 Mr '52, p. 70: U. S. News, 2 S '55, p. 75.

18. HW, 18 Ja, '13, p. 20; HW, 6 Je '14, p. 20; NAR, Jl, '20, p. 82; LA, 11 Mr '22, p. 619, NO, F '35, p. 14; Col, 16 Ja '26, p. 45; Nat, 9 F '46, p. 171.

19. Ind, 31 Ja '25, p. 115.

20. Col, 16 Ja '26, p. 6.

21. Nat, 9 F '46, p. 170. See also, Scrib, Mr '37, p. 16; Comm, 23 O '53, p. 65.

22. HM, N '31, p. 720; Nat, 1 F '33, p. 130. See also, NR, 19 F '40, p. 236; NR, 3 F '47, p. 10.

23. NAR, Summer '37, p. 242; Atlan, Mr '49, p. 36; NR, 26 F '51, p. 20. Comm, 14 S '51, p. 20; Comm, 19 D '52, p. 271; Amer, 26 Je '54, p. 329.

24. RR, D '08, p. 161; Out, 16 Jl '34, p. 435; NR, 3 O '34, p. 201.

25. SR, 24 D '49, p. 20.

26. HW, 18 Ja '13, p. 22; Col, 16 Ja '26, p. 5; Comm, 29 Je '32, p. 230. See also, LA, 11 Mr '22, p. 619.

27. NAR, N '21, p. 626.

28. Col, 7 O '22, p. 13; CC, 21 My '30, p. 646; NR, 5 F '30, p. 298.

29. Comm, 26 Ja '40, p. 299; NR, 3 F '47, p. 10; CC, 26 D '51, p. 1499; Comm, 14 N '48, p. 138. See also, Col, 14 Je '24, p. 20; TA, Je '52, p. 46.

30. RR, D '08, p. 164.

31. Scrib, F '35, p. 84.

32. Atlan, Ap '47, pp. 64-65; ParM, D '52, p. 36.

33. PE, Ap '09, p. 173.

34. Col, 2 D '22, p. 11.

35. PE, Mr '09, p. 119, 123; Out, 14 F '14, p. 350; Out, 19 Ja '21, p. 104. See also, Out, 23 F '21, p. 292; Col, 11 F '22, p. 22; CC, 18 Je '30, p. 775; Comm, 13 Ag '30, p. 381; CC, 17 Mr '34, p. 326; Nat, 9 F '46, p. 170.

36. LD, 18 Mr '33, p. 32, Nat, 5 Ap '33, p. 362; Scrib, My '33, p. 314; NR, 3 F '47, p. 10; Rot, N '38, p. 59.

37. AmMerc, D '54, p. 83.

38. CC, 19 O '55, p. 1198.

39. CO, O '15, p. 244; Out, 26 Jl '16, p. 695.

40. Out, 24 Ag '21, p. 660.

41. Out, 16 My '23, p. 883. See also, Out, 19 Ja '21, p. 104.

42. CC, 22 Ja '30, p. 112; CC, 21 My '30, p. 646; CC, 13 Ag '30, p. 978; CC, 22 O '30, p. 1271; NR, 26 F '45, p. 298; SR, 13 N '48, p. 60; SR, 25 N '50, p. 10.

43. Out, 26 Jl '16, p. 694; CO, Ap '22, p. 506.

44. Col, 24 My '24, p. 5.

45. Nat, 18 S '29, p. 292; Nat, 21 Ja '31, p. 80; Atlan, Ap '47, p. 67; USN, 2 S '55, p. 38.

46. Out, 26 Jl '16, p. 695.

47. WW, Ja '21, p. 257.

48. Out, 16 My '23, p. 883.

49. CO, Jl '24, pp. 74-75.

50. Col, 17 O '25, p. 14.

51. HM, Ja '26, p. 160. See also, SEP, 5 Je '26, p. 26.

52. CC, 29 Ja '30, p. 145.

53. CC, 13 Ap '32, p. 482. See also, Comm, 13 Ag '20, p. 381; CC, 13 Ag '30, p. 987; CC, 29 Ap '31, p. 570; CC, 7 Je '33, p. 750; CC, 17 Mr '34, p. 325.

54. SR, 4 F '50, p. 22.

55. SR, 21 Ja '50, p. 25.

56. SR, 21 Ja '50, p. 24.

57. SR, 28 Ja '50, p. 20.

58. SR, 28 Ja '50, p. 20; SR, 4 F '50, p. 22.

59. Out, 26 Jl '16, p. 694. See also, LD, 17 Ag, '29, p. 19; LA, 1 Ap '30, p. 188.

60. LD, 18 Mr '33, p. 32; Nat, 5 Ap '33, p. 362; Nwk, ' D '34, p. 27; Scrib, My '33, p. 313; Comm, 14 Ap '39, p. 686.

61. Comm, 10 Ap '29, p. 653.

62. Nat, 26 S '28, p. 286; Out, 5 D '28, p. 1272; Out, 23 O '29, p. 292; NAR, Ag '33, p. 145. See also, NAR, O '28, p. 430; HM, N '28, p. 709; Col, 23 F '29, p. 42; AmMag, Ap '29, p. 125; Col, 25 My '29, p. 48; SEP, 15 Je '29, p. 50; PE, Ag '29, p. 74; Comm, 22 Ja '30, p. 333; Out, 17 Je '31, p. 206; SEP, 23 Ja '32, p. 90; NAR, My '32, p. 446.

63. Nat, 14 N '36, p. 567; Col, 18 Mr '38, p. 12.

64. SEP, 14 My '49, pp. 29, 131. See also, NB, Je '49, p. 74.

65. SS, 20 S '50, p. 20; SR, 25 N '50, p. 10; SSoc, 15 D '51, p. 369; USN, 2 S '55, p. 37.

66. Scrib, F '37, p. 65; USN, 2 S '55, p. 36.

67. RR, N '27, p. 523; Cent, O '26, pp. 675-676.

68. HB, F '50, p. 125.

69. GH, N '50, p. 264; USN, 2 S '50, p. 36.

70. HM, N '28, p. 712. See also, SEP, 21 S '29, p. 22.

71. CC, 3 My '33, p. 591.

72. TA, Je '52, p. 46.

73. LD, 18 Mr '33, p. 32; CC, 17 My '33, p. 654; SR, 25 N '50, p. 10.

74. Out, 16 My '23, p. 883; CC, 24 My '33, p. 668; Comm, 4 Ag '50 p. 406; SR, 26 Ag '50, p. 7; SR, 25 N '50, p. 9; USN, 2 S '55, p. 36. CC, 15 Ja '30, p. 75; BHG, Mr '37, p. 78; NR, 3 Mr '47, p. 15.

75. LD, 18 Mr '33, p. 32; Nat, 5 Ap '33, p. 362; Scrib, My '33, p. 313; Nwk, 1 D '34, p. 27.

76. CC, 10 My '33, p. 622.

77. Out, 16 My '23, p. 883.

78. CC, 31 My '33, p. 719; Time, 3 Mr '52, p. 70. See also, CC, 14 Ap '39, p. 686.

79. CC, 15 Ja '30, p. 76; CC, 14 Ap '39, p. 687.

80. SD, My '50, p. 36.

81. Out, 16 Jl '10, p. 541; CC, 15 Ja '30, p. 75; RR, Mr '37, p. 72; CC, 5 O '32, p. 1190; USN, 2 S '55, p. 37; CO, Ap '13, p. 297; Scrib, F '37, p. 65; Col, 18 N '22, p. 9.

82. CO, My '21, p. 652; Comm, 13 Ag '30, p. 383.

83. HM, Ja '26, p. 160.

84. SEP, 19 Jl '30, p. 33; CC, 29 Ja '30, p. 145.

85. CC, 21 My '30, p. 646.

86. CC, 29 Ja '30, p. 147. See also, CC, 18 Je '30, p. 775;
C, 7 Je '33, p. 752.

87. CC, 4 O '33, p. 1248.

88. LA, 1 Ag '30, p. 669.

89. HM, Ja '26, p. 160.

90. CC, 29 Jl '31, p. 965.

91. SR, 26 Ag '50, p. 29.

92. Time, 7 F '49, p. 70. See also, Comm, 24 Mr '50, p. 621.

93. SR, 24 D '49, p. 20.

94. PE, Ap '09, p. 171.

95. AmMag, D '15, p. 64.

96. LD, 18 S '15, p. 592.

97. CO, O '15, p. 244; CO, Je '20, p. 794; Bookm, Mr '19,
. 43; NAR, N '21, p. 624; CoT, 16 S '22, p. 4; CoT, 7 O '22, p. 13;
C, 22 O '30, p. 1271.

98. NR, 27 Jl '27, p. 256. See also, CC, 22 O '30, p. 1270;
Comm, 19 D '52, p. 271.

99. SR, 24 D '49, p. 20.

100. USN, 2 S '55, p. 41.

101. CCom, 8 Je '07, p. 296; PE, N '08, p. 236; RR, S '10,
. 316.

102. CC, Ja '30, p. 110.

103. Nat, 21 Jl '36, p. 33; Amer, 5 Je '54, p. 278. See also,
E, Mr '09, p. 120; CO, Ag '18, p. 99; Out, 23 F '21, p. 292;
CO, Mr '21, p. 320; CC, 15 Ja '30, p. 75; CC, 29 Ap '31, p. 571;
C, 13 Ap '32, p. 480; Comm, 23 Mr '34, p. 565.

104. CC, 12 Ap '50, p. 453; SEP, 2 F '52, p. 102.

105. CC, 13 Ja '54, p. 37.

106. USN, 2 S '55, p. 36.

107. CCom, 8 Je '07, p. 295; CCom, 11 Ap '08, p. 74; WT, O '08, p. 1053.

108. RR, D '08, p. 744.

109. PE, Mr '09, pp. 120-121.

110. PE, Mr '09, p. 121.

111. GH, Ag '10, p. 184.

112. GH, Ag '10, p. 185.

113. GH, Ag '10, p. 184.

114. AmMag, Ag '13, pp. 92-93; Out, 14 F, p. 349.

115. Educa, D '19, p. 209.

116. CO, Mr '21, p. 362.

117. Out, 24 Ag '21, p. 660.

118. LHJ, F '24, p. 40; AAA, N '26, pp. 152, 153, 157.

119. CC, 15 Ja '30, p. 75.

120. CC, 15 Ja '30, pp. 75, 78.

121. CC, 31 D '30, p. 1617; CC, 15 Ja '30, pp. 76-77; CC, 31 D '30, p. 1617.

122. CC, 22 Ja '30, p. 110.

123. CC, 3 My '33, p. 592.

124. CC, 3 My '33, p. 593.

125. CC, 15 Ja '30, p. 77; CC, 24 My '33, p. 688; CC, 22 Ja '30, p. 111.

126. Nwk, 11 Mr '33, p. 30.

127. Scrib, My '33, p. 314.

128. Scrib, My '33, pp. 313, 314-315.

129. AmMerc, 6 Jl '38, p. 294; Rot, N '38, pp. 11, 60; LHJ, p '39, p. 4.

130. AmMerc, 6 Jl '38, p. 294.

131. Nat, 26 Ap '47, p. 481.

132. Scrib, My '33, p. 315.

133. Nwk,6 Jl '35, p. 26; Nat, 26 Ap '47, p. 481.

134. Rot, N '38, p. 61.

135. Rot, N '38, p. 59.

136. SR, 24 D '49, p. 20; SR, 25 N '50, p. 9; AmMerc, D '54, . 80; USN, 2 S '55, p. 45.

137. AmMerc, D '54, p. 80; USN, 2 S '55, p. 40; SR, 26 Ag '50, . 29; SEP, 7 Jl '51, pp. 10, 12.

138. Nat, 15 0 '55, p. 232.

139. SEP, 12 Mr '55, p. 33; Nat, 22 Jl '50, p. 87; USN, 2 S '55, . 41.

140. Nat, 22 Jl '50, p. 87.

141. NR, 1 N '54, p. 14; AmMerc, D '54, p. 83.

142. ParM, D '52, p. 37.

143. USN, 2 S '55, p. 41. For other objections to the exposure of children to crime, violence, and sex, in addition to those already cited, see: WW, Ja '21, p. 294; LHJ, F '24, p. 40; CO, Ap '14, p. 290; Out, 14 F '23, p. 296; Out, 16 My '23, p. 883; CC, 29 Ja '30, p. 144; CC, 5 F '30, p. 173; CC, 12 F '30, p. 202; Out, 16 Ap '30, p. 612; CC, 21 My '30, p. 646; CC, 16 Je '30, p. 774; CC, 12 Ag '31, p. 1015; Comm, 13 Ag '30, p. 381; CC, 13 Ag '30, p. 987; CC, 22 O '30, p. 1270; CC, 28 Ja '31, p. 127; CC, 25 Mr '31, p. 395; CC, 29 Ap '31, p. 570; CC, 21 O '31, p. 1301; CC, 13 Ap '32, p. 480; CC, 31 My '33, p. 718; CC, 7 Je '33, p. 752; CC, 14 Je '33, p. 779; NR, 18 Ap '34, p. 273; LD, 18 Mr '33, p. 32; NR, 26 F '45, p. 296; SR, 8 F '47, p. 26; Nwk, 26 D '49, p. 36; Time, 3 Mr '52, p. 70; CC, 14 Ja '53, p. 36; SR, 14 Ag '54, p. 25; Time, 1 N '54, p. 64; USN, 2 S '55, pp. 36-38, 76; Comm, 24 Je '55, p. 294.

144. GH, Ag '10, p. 184; CO, Mr '21, p. 321; WW, Ja '21, p. 257; Out, 29 Jl '31, p. 399. See also, Bookm, Mr '19, p. 43; Comm, 10 Je '31, p. 143; LD, 13 My '33, p. 16.

145. Comm, 14 Ap '39, p. 686; SR, 8 F '47, p. 26.

146. SR, 24 D '49, p. 20.

147. USN, 2 S '55, p. 76.

148. CCom, 8 Je '07, p. 295; Scrib, Jl '09, p. 122.

149. RR, S '10, p. 316.

150. HW, 18 Ja '13, p. 22.

151. WT, O '08, p. 1056; RR, S '10, p. 316.

152. RR, S '10, p. 316.

153. RR, S '10, p. 316.

154. CO, Ap '14, p. 290.

155. Out, 20 Je '14, p. 413; HW, 2 Ja '15, p. 8; Out, 8 D '15, p. 830.

156. Bookm, My '21, p. 243; Ind, 31 Ja '25, p. 114; CC, 13 Ag '30, p. 987; Comm, 10 Je '31, p. 143.

157. WW, Ja '21, p. 251.

158. Bookm, My '21, p. 242.

159. RR, My '21, p. 555.

160. CC, 22 Ja '30, p. 112.

161. CC, My '33, p. 718.

162. Comm, 29 Je '34, p. 225; NAR, D '39, p. 506.

163. LD, 11 D '37, p. 4.

164. Catholic Digest, D '54, pp. 69-70.

165. CC, 13 Ja '54, p. 37.

166. BHG, Mr '37, pp. 78, 96-98; NO, Jl '33, p. 20.

167. NO, Jl '33, p. 20.

168. Nwk, 8 N '37, p. 26.

169. Comm, 19 O '45, p. 14.

170. SR, 8 F '47, p. 26.

171. SR, 24 D '49, p. 20.

172. USN, 2 S '55, p. 36; USN, 2 S '55, p. 75. For additional comments about the media as a cause of crime see: GH, Ag '10, p. 184, Out, 13 Jl '12, p. 598; CC, 12 Ag '31, p. 1015; Out, 29 Jl '31, p. 398; ParM, N '31, p. 20; CC, 24 My '33, p. 688; CC, 31 My '33, p. 4; Scrib, My '33, p. 313; Comm, 14 Ap '39, p. 686; Nat, 26 Ap '47, p. 481.

173. CCom, 11 Ap '08, p. 74; HW, 30 Jl '10, p. 13; GH, Ag '10, p. 184.

174. Out, 14 F '14, p. 348; CO, Ap '14, p. 290.

175. Out, 14 F '14, p. 346.

176. WW, Ja '21, p. 251.

177. LHJ, F '24, p. 40; AAA, N '26, p. 151.

178. <u>CC</u>, 22 Ja '30, p. 112; <u>ParM</u>, N '31, p. 20.

179. <u>CC</u>, 24 My '33, p. 689.

180. <u>CC</u>, 24 My '33, p. 689.

181. <u>CC</u>, 31 My '33, p. 719.

182. <u>CC</u>, 31 My '33, p. 719.

183. <u>AmMag</u>, Ag '13, p. 93; <u>Educa</u>, D '19, p. 206. See also, <u>CO</u>, Ap '22, p. 506.

184. <u>AmMerc</u>, 6 Jl '38, p. 294; <u>Nat</u>, 26 Ap '47, p. 481; <u>GH</u>, N '50, p. 265; <u>AmMerc</u>, D '54, p. 83.

185. <u>Comm</u>, 4 Ag '50, p. 406; <u>CC</u>, 24 My '33, p. 688; <u>Out</u>, 14 F '14, p. 349.

186. <u>CC</u>, 24 My '33, p. 688.

187. <u>GH</u>, Ag '10, p. 185.

188. <u>CC</u>, 3 My '33, p. 593. See also, <u>Educa</u>, Je '13, p. 625; <u>AmMag</u>, Ag '13, p. 92; <u>CC</u>, 15 Ja '30, p. 75; <u>CC</u>, 22 Ja '30, p. 593; <u>CC</u>, 24 My '33, p. 689; <u>CC</u>, 17 Mr '34, p. 325.

189. <u>CC</u>, 24 My '33, p. 689; <u>CC</u>, 17 Mr '34, p. 325; <u>AAA</u>, N '47, p. 96; <u>CC</u>, 2 F '49, p. 143.

190. <u>AmMag</u>, Ag '13, p. 93.

191. <u>CC</u>, 15 Ja '30, p. 75.

192. <u>CC</u>, 24 My '33, p. 689.

193. <u>CC</u>, 22 Ja '30, p. 112; <u>CC</u>, 21 My '30, p. 646; <u>GH</u>, Ag '10, p. 184; <u>AAA</u>, N '26, p. 151.

194. <u>LHJ</u>, F '24, p. 40.

195. <u>RR</u>, S '10, p. 316.

196. <u>SA</u>, 5 Ag '05, p. 334; <u>LD</u>, 7 Mr '08, p. 334.

197. AmMag, Ag '13, p. 93; Ind, 17 Mr '10, p. 592; SAS, 2 My '14, p. 288.

198. Ind, 17 Mr '10, p. 592; AmMag, Ag '13, p. 93; LD, 22 S '17, p. 27; LD, 31 Jl '15, p. 209; Educa, 17 Mr '10, p. 591. See also, LHJ, F '24, p. 40.

199. Ind, 17 Mr '10, pp. 591-592.

200. PE, 0 '08, p. 164.

201. Out, 5 Ap '13, p. 784.

202. SAS, 2 My '14, p. 288; LD, 31 Jl '15, p. 208; LD, 22 S '17, p. 27.

203. Out, 24 Ag '21, p. 660.

204. LHJ, F '24, p. 214.

205. CC, 22 Ja '30, p. 112; CC, 21 My '30, p. 646.

206. CC, 17 My '33, p. 654.

207. CC, 10 My '33, p. 622.

208. RD, My '47, p. 29.

209. Nat, 5 Ap '33, p. 362; Nwk, 11 Mr '33, p. 30; Nwk, 8 N '37, p. 26; AmMerc, 6 Jl '38, p. 294; NR, 3 F '47, p. 10.

210. AmMerc, 6 Jl '38, p. 296. See also, Nwk, 11 Mr '33, p. 30; LD, 18 Mr '33, p. 32; NO, Jl '33, p. 20; Nwk, 8 N '37, p. 26.

211. Nat, 5 Ap '33, p. 362; Nwk, 8 N '37, p. 26; LHJ, Ap '39, p. 4.

212. NR, 26 F '45, p. 297; NR, 14 Jl '47, p. 21.

213. SD, Je '49, p. 31; ParM, N '49, p. 45; SD, 0 '49, p. 24; Time, 1 My '50, p. 34.

214. Time, 1 My '50, p. 34; Educa, 0 '50, p. 127; SR, 25 N '50, p. 10; GH, N '50, p. 265.

215. USN, 2 S '55, p. 41.

216. USN, 2 S '55, pp. 36, 41; ParM, N '49, p. 56; SSoc, 15 D '51, p. 369; SD, O '49, p. 25; CC, 26 D '51, p. 1499; USN, 2 S '55, p. 48.

CHAPTER IV

ARGUMENTS FROM CAUSE: INSTITUTIONS

Advocacy

Another significant part of the total causal argument dealt
with the influence of motion pitures, radio, and television on
existing social institutions. Promoters and critics alike maintained
that educational, political, religious, familial, and recreational
institutions, which served to implement society's notions about the
good and the desirable, would be influenced by innovation. The
direction and desirability of the influence were the points in
contention.

To writers agreeable to innovation, the changes fostered by
the new mass media portended good for society's institutions. Their
arguments in support of this position developed along three broad
lines. First, advocates offered reassurance. Frequently readers
were told that although motion pictures, radio, and television did
in fact represent social change, the change presented no threat
to familiar institutions. The telephone and telegraph, for example,
were in no danger because of radio. No disruption of the established
order was foreseen. Second, promoters of the media as well as
spokesmen for schools, churches, and political parties told how
established institutions would profit because of the new media.
They argued that innovation would cause institutions to be stronger,

more efficient, and more effective than ever before. Finally,
promoters employed variations on an argument from concession.
Agreeing that the new media might compete with and possibly dis-
rupt the old order, they argued that the ultimate effect would be
good: competition might force desirable changes; the damage would
be temporary and the institution would emerge stronger than ever;
certain undesirable features of the institution would be eliminated
and the desirable features of the institution would be eliminated
and the desirable would remain unscathed.

These were the positions established by the advocates. Consider
first their attempts to reassure readers that no damage would result
from innovation.

Reassurance

As promoters wrote of the possible applications of the new
media in the work of social institutions and of the potential
influences of innovation on the existing order, they repeatedly
asserted that nothing presently valued, nothing familiar, would
be damaged by the introduction of motion pictures, radio, or television. This became one of the major arguments of the advocates,
and was repeated in connection with each new medium.

Motion pictures were a strong competitor of the legitimate
theater. Crowds which formerly sat in the galleries of the legitimate houses were by 1910 patrons of the nickel motion picture. Even

so, promoters of the movies assured readers that the theatre, presumed

to be of value to society, would never be destroyed by the new enter-

tainment. To illustrate, _Outlook_ argued in a 1915 editorial that

although there was concern that the theatre was sinking, "On the whole,

we are inclined to believe that there will always be plenty of room

for both the 'legitimate' and the 'movies.'" When Carl Holliday

proposed that motion pictures be used in churches, he assured readers

of _Independent_ that the pictures would take over none of the present

activities of the church. Rather, pictures were "simply a powerful

auxiliary for the machinery already existing and a new attractive

force in the hands of a moral worker."[1] When Edison spoke in 1919

of the possibilities of a daily news film of world events, he was

quick to offer reassurance that films would not replace the familiar

newspaper.

> But the daily news film will never, in my opinion, supplant
> the daily newspaper, at least in America. This is the
> land of the newspaper; we are a nation of newspaper readers.
> The newspaper is the university of the masses. The film,
> however, will become the most important and valuable
> pictorial supplement to the newspaper.[2]

These three situations varied somewhat, but the pattern of the

argument here, and in similar circumstances, was consistent. Pro-

moters sought to demonstrate the compatibility of the new with the

old; the new was defended on the grounds that it was no threat to

the established order.

This kind of argument appeared whenever a new medium was introduced or whenever a major innovation appeared within a medium.
Hence, promoters of talking pictures assured readers that talkies
would not "supplant the present silent pictures," and that talkies
would not destroy familiar silent stars, the theatre, the foreign
market, religion, vaudeville, or education. Similarly, the intro-
ductipn of radio prompted Literary Digest to comment that "the
commercial telephone is not going to be put out of commission and
the land service of the telegraph will continue in full importance."[3]
When educational radio became a topic for discussion again in the
late 1930's, a writer for Education argued that the medium would
not replace teachers.

> In general one criterion must be kept in mind: the radio
> should do what the teacher cannot do; it ought not to do
> what the teacher can do better. However radio may develop,
> I cannot conceive of the time when a good teacher will not
> continue to be the most important object in any class-
> room.[4]

And in addition, the theatre, the educational system, reading,
lecture programs, adult education, political oratory, motion pictures, and newspapers were all said to be safe from harm by radio.
Again with television, promoters spoke of familiar institutions
which would not be damaged: the theatre, motion pictures, religion,
radio, live concerts, newspapers, reading, sports, teachers, and
education. Gilbert Seldes, for instance, called attention to society's
orientation toward visual communication and predicted that since

"the visualization of facts and ideas is the natural basis of education in television" the medium would not "revolutionize education any more than we will revolutionize art or entertainment by a new medium." C. Francis Jenkins, who developed an early television system, claimed that instead of damaging radio, television meant that "radio has found its eyes."[5] The advocate's argument was stated most succinctly by The Nation which said in 1944 that television

> is something totally new and unique and original. It will
> not displace or replace anything else. It will grow on
> new soil where nothing ever grew before.[6]

All of the advocates were concerned lest the new media be labeled disruptive, intrusive, damaging to familiar and comfortable institutions. They therefore worked to assure readers that this was really not the case at all. The media were compatible with the status quo, would fit with little discomfort into the patterns already laid down. The argument was used not only to prepare the ground for innovation, but to answer the kinds of objections which proponents were sure would come. It was a justification thought necessary to promote acceptance of innovation, and a favorite argument of the promoters of motion pictures, radio, and television.

Beneficial Influences

The second broad line of advocacy stressed the direct and
beneficial influences of motion pictures, radio, and television
on social institutions. There was no suggestion here that the
relationship between new and old was one of mere compatibility.
Instead, promoters traced the causal line in bold strokes, arguing
that the new media had a distinct and valuable place in the institutional structure, that the media would reinforce respected institutions and help them do their work more effectively, that the media
would give society new vitality by strengthening its institutions.
Advocates envisioned a variety of means by which the institutions
would profit from innovation.

New Audiences

Since movies, radio, and television reached vast numbers of
people, promoters argued that if the media were employed by social
institutions, the institutions would have available to them all
the advantages of new and widespread audiences. According to the
advocates, any institution which depended for support upon public
attention or attendance would profit from the use of the new media.
Hence, the theatre, various musical endeavors, the church, the
newspaper, recreational reading, politics, and even poetry were
to receive help. This line of argument obviously helped build a

case for the advocates, but at the same time it worked to deny
frequent assertions by attackers that the new media were destroying
established institutions by taking over their audiences. So the
argument was both a means of promotion and a form of refutation.

Institutions were to benefit in at least three ways from this
accumulation of audiences. First, the media were offered new
possibilities for dissemination of the institutional message. This
potential was first noted by the proponents of motion pictures.
With movies it became possible to reach larger groups of people
than had been gathered into one audience previously. This meant,
as one writer pointed out in 1908, that the "Passion Play," recently
put on film, would be witnessed by greater crowds than ever before.
When talking films were proposed, they were judged of value because
with them a political orator could reach thousands of people from
his own fireside. Forty years later it was again noted that film,
this time films made by Congressmen for broadcast by local TV stations, allowed the legislators to be seen by more people than they
could reach in person if they served in Congress for forty years.7
And movies meant, too, that entertainment, both praiseworthy and
objectionable, reached wider audiences than ever before.

Compared to films, radio was spectacular. Even its supporters
were awed by the vast number of people who could be gathered into
one audience. Radio, said Scientific American in 1921, allowed

Herbert Hoover to talk to thousands of people at one time, where
formerly he could talk at most to a few hundred in a hall. By 1924
the President could be heard by one-fifth of the nation. And Bruce
Barton predicted that "the time may come--and soon--when the President of the United States in the White House can sit at his own
desk and, talking in an ordinary telephone instrument, be heard
by every household in the nation where there is a radio set."
Church services broadcast from Wichita, Kansas, elicted letters
from listeners in Texas, Colorado, and Iowa. The radio preacher,
said Dr. S. Parkes Cadman, could reach more people in one afternoon
on the air than he could reach in a lifetime of conventional preaching. Once it was predicted that radio would eventually permit the
Pope to speak to all Catholics at the same time. Madam Galli-Curci
in 1922 sang before the largest audience ever assembled at one time,
established at 100,000 or more radio listeners. Three years later,
John McCormack sang for 8,000,000 listeners, and received as many
letters in response to his concert as there had been people in
Galli-Curci's entire audience. Radio "offered new kingdoms of
musical riches for the multitudes," awakening an enormous public
to music they didn't know existed. Because of radio, the orator
could speak to millions, the teacher in a radio university serve
as many pupils as there were in schools, the national leader spell
out political issues to as many of the electorate who would listen.[8]

As North American Review said in 1936,

> the nature of the medium has given radio the widest
> audience ever reached by speeches, poems, news, and
> drama in audible form. The power of the spoken word
> has never been so great.[9]

Television carried on where radio left off, adding to the
sounds the sights of the world. Following the successful demonstration of a wired television system in 1927, Literary Digest
declared that television had in fact arrived, which meant that
"in time millions of people may watch and listen to a Presidential
inauguration, a championship football game, or even the clash of
armies on a battle field."[10] The possibilities of large audiences
through television were never as impressive to the advocates as
had been the potential audience of radio. By the time television
arrived, there was no longer fascination in the accumulation of
startlingly large audience figures; such audiences were apparently
taken to be a normal consequence of broadcasting. Nevertheless,
when network television was finally extended across the country
in 1951, a writer in The Nation called attention to the size of
the potential audience.

> More people now watch television than attend all our
> schools and universities. The speech of a Presidential
> candidate, a session of the United Nations, the signing
> of the Japanese peace treaty, may be witnessed by more
> Americans than voted in the Presidential election.
> Uncle Miltie, Studio One, or the Pulitzer Prize plays
> may be seen by more people in one hour than attended all
> the motion picture theaters in the country during a
> whole week of 1951.[11]

And when Der Rosenkavalier was broadcast on television in 1952,
Theatre Arts commented that "this lovely work was heard and seen
in one performance by more people in this country than have witnessed all the other performances in the United States."12

All institutions were served equally by the new mass media.
Preacher, poet, publisher, and politician all found new audiences
for their wares through movies, radio, or television. All were
given the chance to appear before more people than had ever been
assembled before.

Certainly there was advantage to simply exposing the public
to the institutional message through the media. But promoters
went further than this in their argument. They predicted that if
the public were once exposed to plays, good music, poetry, or
politics through some sort of mechanical reproduction, then the
newly exposed audience would seek some active means of participation
in the institution. That is, the patrons of the nickel movies
might become theatre-goers, radio's jazz fans would be educated
to appreciate opera, and people formerly uninterested in politics
would be led to vote. The media served to introduce the public
to the institution, or to some form of it, and the charismatic
qualities of the institution led to involvement. This was the
second way in which the media were said to help established institutions, by leading new audiences to use social institutions. The

argument was most often used in connection with the theatre, politics, and reading, but was also applied to newspapers, concerts,
the church, and poetry.

Implicit in this argument when it was applied to theatre was
the presumption that the living stage was in some way superior
to mechanical amusements. The movies were spoken of as leading
up to the theatre. Charles Frohman, who had recently formed his
own motion picture company, argued from this presumption in 1913.

> The moving picture is contributory and educational and
> will help the attendance in theatres. That has been
> proved in the case of Bernhardt. We feel certain that
> nothing can ever supplant the living actor in the liv-
> ing play. The pictures are never the real thing, no
> matter how fine they may be. Rather, they make count-
> less auditors for the actor; create an interest in him.
> People, for instance, who see Hackett for the first time
> when he appears on the screen will want to see him in
> life. The shadow on a screen will only stimulate inter-
> est.[13]

The same year Robert Grau argued, in response to Edison's proposal
that drama and opera might be presented in talking films, that the
mechanical theater would never replace the stage. In fact, he
claimed motion pictures created new patrons for drama from the
masses who had never before been in any kind of a theater. These
newcomers to theatrical entertainment, once they tired of "scientific stimulation," would turn to the legitimate theatre where "it
is hoped the superiority of the performance on the real stage
will tend to hold them fast thenceforth!" Similarly, in 1924,
radio was said to have created new interest in seeing as well as

hearing favorite performers, and had thus stimulated theatrical
business.[14] Had radio kept people from the theatre?

> No, radio isn't doing that. It's sending them--in the
> long run its the best little booster for the new ideals
> and hopes of the theatrical, musical and literary world
> that has ever come into being.[15]

And talkies, too, were defended as having drawn new patrons to
Broadway shows. Speaking of the new audiences, the producer Edgar
Selwyn said that "when now they see famous Broadway players in a
form of amusement not far removed from the stage production, the
desire to see what the original is like sends them flocking to
Broadway."[16] In each of these arguments, the predicted effect was
the same; the new media had served to stimulate a fresh audience
for the theatre.

Another variation on the basic argument was used in connection
with the media and politics. Here the desired end was political
participation, and radio and television were credited with leading
to this involvment by making politics a public concern. Collier's
said in 1924 that for the first time "at least 20,000,000 of us are
getting our politics first-hand this year, direct from politicians."
The result was predicted to be thirty to forty million votes cast, compared to a past record of some twenty seven million. During the 1928
campaign Collier's argued that "science, through the radio, has
found a way of filling the very air with our political problems,
and whether we desire it or not, it is inevitable that millions of

us who have never before reached political decisions will find ourselves taking sides in political controversy." The result, said
Graham McNamee, would be more votes cast than ever before. In 1933,
Deems Taylor named radio an "extraordinarily effective means" for
arousing public interest in political questions, and commented that
never before had there been such public involvement in the campaign. Following the 1952 campaign, New Republic concluded that
"there is little doubt that television--the new and revolutionary
medium of American politics--contributed to the unusually heavy
turnout of normally non-voting citizens."[17] The new media, by
extending the sphere of active politics, helped the institution
achieve an end desired for it.

These arguments about theatre and politics are typical of
this line of advocacy. Other authors, those who were primarily
interested in reading, music, religion, newspapers, motion pictures or poetry, said the same kind of thing about these media-
institutional relationships.[18] In each case, the media introduced
the institution to new segments of the general public who in turn
became involved with the activities of institutions. A new audience,
a new involvement, a new relationship was created and both the
public and the institution profited. Thus, in this second way
the new media served to strengthen social institutions.

Finally, a few of the promoters argued that education, churches, and taverns would profit from the unique capacity of the new media to attract a crowd. People sought out education when it was presented in movie form. For example, Survey noted in 1911 that where audiences had ignored conventional messages stressing public health, they came eagerly to summer programs to see films such as The Man Who Learned, "an impressive story of the danger from a dirty dairy," and Fly Pest, which gave "the life cycle of a fly and how it carries contagion." This meant for churches that congregations swelled when movies were shown as part of the worship service, that social halls filled when a radio was brought in, and that the parish house became competitive with the corner saloon when the television set arrived.[19] As one minister explained, with films

> I preach the Gospel as nearly as I know how, or at least
> as well as I should be preaching it if I had no picture.
> And I preach it to one thousand or twelve hundred people
> instead of a handful.[20]

Another preacher argued that the congregations drawn first by films often became habituated to religious services and returned even when no pictures were shown, that he had more people joining the church than ever before, and that for the first time in history his church was out of debt.[21] To these writers there was little question of the value of motion pictures in the work of the church.

Similarly, television served to attract new patrons to taverns, particularly in the early days when it was more common to find a

set in a bar than in the home. Collier's reported in 1947 that the
introduction of television in a bar meant "a 30 to 60 per cent
increase in business" and that "one innkeeper headily estimated
his trade had quintupled." Said Collier's:

> Television is the biggest thing that's happened to the
> bar-and-tavern business since the free lunch. Often
> when a hot fight over a tight ball game is being tele-
> vised, bewildered but beaming publicans have to lock
> their doors against late comers to keep their television-
> equipped establishments from bursting at the seams.[22]

American Magazine reported a similar situation in 1948, concluding that "it is to the corner bar that television has drawn its
biggest audiences."[23] The attraction of the medium was thus employed
with equal success by society's competing institutions.

Various institutions which depended upon public support were
said to have gained strength because of the influence of motion
pictures, radio, and television. Friends of the media and spokesmen for the institutions alike argued that here was evidence of
the benefits to be derived from innovation. But there were other
ways in which valued institutions also stood to profit from the
new media. Advocates took these into account in the argument.
Consider, for example, the influence of the new media on education.

Education

Each new medium was said by its promoters to be of value in
education. With the introduction of motion pictures, radio, and

finally television, advocates hurried to associate their cause
with that of education, for they could safely assume that there
would be no objection to any new device which promised to serve
this respected institution.

Some of the arguments, general in nature and similar in tone,
appeared at the introduction of each new medium and whenever there
was need to justify it. For example, the argument that motion
pictures would serve education appeared in the article which introduced Edison's picture machine. There, in 1891, George Parsons
Lathrop predicted that "the kinetoscope may become very useful
for instruction in sundry directions." As the nickelodeon movement
was gathering momentum, Photo-Era reminded readers that "for educational purposes /the movie's/ value is acknowledged." During the
clamor for censorship of films after the First World War, one of
their defenders argued in Harper's that even the worst enemies of
films must admit their educational value. Radio was described by
Owen D. Young, Chairman of the Board of R. C. A., as "the greatest
potential educator and spreader of culture that has ever been
dreamed of." And in 1929 Graham McNamee said radio had revised
the traditional picture of education--Abe Lincoln lying on his
stomach in front of the fire studying. Now, he argued, education
was symbolized by the farm boy listening to his radio, for "with
a little radio set in one corner of the farm house, . . . the plow

boy of 1929 has the world at his feet." The first time television
was mentioned its advocates predicted there would be "enormous
educational value in the home theater," and a decade and a half
later Lee DeForest asserted that the medium would eventually make
practical man's goal of universal education. Still later, with
television on the brink of full operation, Senior Scholastic confirmed that TV was "set to open a whole new age of entertainment and
education."[24]

There was no attempt in any of these arguments to define
education. No one was interested in the particulars of the case.
The argument served its function in calling attention to some
potential association between the new and the respected. The
statement that the new media were good for education became one
of the commonplaces of advocacy, an expected part of the introductory rhetoric.

Teaching aids

When promoters of motion pictures, radio, and television turned
to the specific applications of the new media to education, they
first thought in terms of classroom teaching. Each of the new
devices, they argued, could be used to supplement the teacher in
the classroom; could be used to bring the world to the student;
could be used in the creation of new instructional methods and
materials.

There were occasional comments about pictures in teaching from 1891 on, but the line of argument was not widely used until 1910, after the moral character of the movies had come under fire and after manufacturers began turning out educational features. In September of 1910, for example, The Review of Reviews, disturbed by evidence of moral decay caused by motion pictures, asked, "Is there any reason why so compelling a force /as the movies/ cannot be thrown entirely to the aid of education and inspiration?" The answer, of course, was that the films could be used for these higher ends; the motion picture could be "a tremendous vital force of culture as well as amusement." Already available, according to the manufacturers' catalogs, were filmed lessons in "agriculture, aeronautics, animal life, bacteriology, biography, biology, botany, entomology, ethnology, fisheries, geography, history, industrial, kindergarten studies, mining and metalurgy, microscopy, military, naval, natural history, ornithology, pathology, pisciculture, railroad, religion, scenic, travel and zoology."[25]

Thomas Edison took up the cause of educational films in 1911, and for the next fourteen years, until 1925, when he apparently abandoned his educational film project, Edison was one of the principal promoters, repeatedly asserting that films had an important place in the classroom. His argument was introduced in 1911 in an interview published in Harper's Weekly. Asked if he had any new ideas for education Edison replied:

'I have, . . . education by moving pictures. Teach the
children everything, from mathematics to morality, by little
dramas acted out before the cameras and reproduced in the
school room at very low cost. Sort o' swing the education
in on them so attractively that they'll want to go to
school. You'll have to lick 'em to keep 'em away.[26]

In this new scheme for education Edison proposed to teach the

alphabet, history, mathematics, physics, nature study, and geog-

raphy. Most of the lessons would be presented dramatically. Here,

for example, is Edison's description of his lesson on the alphabet:

'Take the alphabet. . . . You remember how hard it
was to learn the letters? Why? Because it was dry and
uninteresting. Lord, how dry! But now see what we'll
do: Suppose, instead of the dull solemn letters on a
board or card, you have a little play going on that the
littlest youngster can understand--oh, as small as that,
and the wizard's hand shot down to his knee. 'The play
begins with a couple of lively little fellows who carry
in a big letter T. They put it down, and it stands there.
Then they carry in an H. Then a little cuss comes in,
hopping and skipping and turning sommersaults, and '--
both hands were whirling in the air now--' as he takes
his place next to the H you see he is the letter I.
Next to him they put down an S. There you have the
word 'This.' In the same way they bring in the letters,
or the letters run in and dodge into place, until the
sentence stands there. 'This is a man.' Then a hand
appears pointing, and up marches a man for it to point
at. Of course, the teacher gives the children the name
of each letter and pronounces each word as they go along.
You can see how eagerly the youngsters will watch every
movement on the picture-screen, for there will be something going on there every moment. Nothing like action
--drama--a play that fascinated the eye--to keep the
attention keyed up. I don't think it'll taken them long
to learn the alphabet that's lively and full of character.'[27]

In other subjects, the lessons would be taught through recre-

ations of historic scenes, photographed in costume on the locations

where the original action took place. Pictures would provide the
primary substance of education, less and less teaching would come
from conventional books and lectures. Edison was even quoted in
1914 as having said that

> books will soon be obsolete in the public schools. . . .
> Scholars will be instructed through the eye. It is
> possible to teach every branch of human knowledge with
> the motion-picture. Our school system will be completely
> changed inside of ten years.[28]

It was Edison's position that "as an aid to education moving pictures
can do more than any of the usual agencies, books, magazines, newspapers, and talk."[29]

Edison's basic proposal was expanded in 1919, when he said
that

> the best schoolhouse is the screen; the best teacher is
> the film. Human teachers will be needed only to help
> guide and direct the minds of the pupils, but the pic-
> tures will do the instructing. One of the most valuable
> educational features of the film is that it actually
> shows the moral reqard to scholars; it shows them the
> effect of doing wrong and of doing right.

Again in 1925, Edison argued that the film could be used to establish a "national university of experience," in which students would
be exposed to the actual workings of business and to practical
training through motion pictures.[31] Although he had abandoned his
educational sound film experiments--"When the educators failed
to respond I lost interest."--Edison still argued that with motion
pictures the educator has

not only an opportunity to teach directly from a busy
world at work but with all the atmosphere of adventure,
romance, achievement.
    We could teach history, of course, in much the same
way, and literature, and biology--and in our advanced
courses chemistry, geology, physics. There is no limitation to the camera. It is simply a matter of the
right direction.[32]

Edison, obviously, was not the only spokesman for motion pic-

tures in the classroom. Whenever promoters needed to say some-

thing good about motion pictures, whenever they needed to demon-

strate the importance of the medium, whenever they needed to defend

the movies they turned to the use of films in teaching. Promoting

the use of films in education, Carl Holliday argued in 1913 that

the use of film

    means a revolution in pedagogy. It means vividness where
    vagueness has reigned before. It means a true visuali-
    zation and realization of life where hitherto only an
    indefinite printed description of it was acquired.[33]

Surveying the educational future of movies, Review of Reviews

quoted a member of the faculty of the Cleveland Normal School who

said that "with its alluring, shifting scene, its compelling reality,

its limitless range of subject matter, it /the motion picture/

represents the most highly evolved educational instrument which

the present century has bequeathed." Current Opinion predicted

in an editorial in 1922 that before many years every classroom

would have its projector, that textbooks would be produced on film,

and that evening courses for special education would be handled through motion pictures.[34] Will Hays, defending the motion picture

industry in 1923, assured his audience that the industry was not

hostile to the educational film.

> The producers want to serve America. They know that there
> is no more important and lasting service they can perform
> than to aid in educating the youth of the country by this
> means, and they propose to make a very definite contribu-
> tion to the pedagogic forces of the world.[35]

As evidence of the industry's good intentions, Hays suggested

that the National Education Association "appoint a committee made

up of the foremost educators, which would meet with the great pro-

ducers and-together study the whole program of the use of the

motion picture as a direct pedagogic instrument and together find

the means of making classroom pictures which would be scientifi-

cally, psychologically, and pedagogically sound."[36] When East-

man Kodak went into the business of producing educational films

in 1929, a writer for Scientific American echoed an argument which

had first appeared twenty years earlier. She predicted that

> within a few more years films will be available for all
> branches of learning. . . . It is now certain that motion
> pictures will assume an increasingly important role in
> education. Their worth in the classroom has been proved;
> their future is assured.[37]

When Literary Digest explored the use of films in education in 1934

it had this to say

> The educational talking picture brings the world into
> the classroom. Mechanical progress has provided the
> school with a powerful new instrument for overcoming the
> obstacles of time and space. The modern student can

> explore the seas, skies, and earth; penetrate ocean depths,
> or forests and jungles; visit far-off lands to become
> acquainted with other customs; scrutinize the animal and
> plant kingdoms, the inner workings of the human mecha-
> nism, or observe the world's social and economic pro-
> gress.[38]

Quoting the former United States Commissioner of Education, George

F. Zook, the Digest concluded that "potentially, the motion picture

is one of the chief contributions of science to education." And

fifteen years later, readers of American Mercury were still reading

that motion pictures were one of the most effective means of teach-

ing ever devised.[39]

Radio's promoters also argued that the medium would be use-

ful and valuable in classroom teaching. A writer for Radio Globe,

quoted in Literary Digest in June of 1922, said that the "educa-

tional uses of the radio are virtually without limit." Quoting the

New York Superintendent of Schools, he went on to say that the

greatest value for the school was radio's potential teaching of

subnormal and blind children, who found attendance at classes

particularly difficult.[40] H. V. Kaltenborn in 1926 feared that

radio had escaped   notice by educators. It was his belief that

in education

> lies radio's greatest opportunity. Education comes
> more easily through the ear than through the eye. Like
> the correspondence course, radio delivers education to
> the pupil in his easy-chair. But it supplements the
> imperfect contact between the student and teacher, made
> by the written exercise, with the appeal of voice and
> personality. The size of the class makes it possible

> to have the best teachers in every subject. Courses
> in literature, oral English, foreign languages, history,
> and music are particularly well adapted for radio pre-
> sentation, but any subject that does not require appa-
> ratus or laboratory work can be taught on the air.[41]

In addition, schools could use broadcasts of current events to

supplement classroom study of history, government, and civics,

with these subjects "given a new meaning by judicious relation

to properly selected radio programs." It was Kaltenborn's con-

clusion that "it will be only a short time before a receiving-set

with proper amplification will be a part of the equipment of every

school-house in the United States." When Walter Damrosch went on

the air with his music programs for school children, his work was

taken to be evidence of what radio could do in classroom education.

Speaking of this new venture in broadcasting in 1929, M. H. Ayles-

worth, the President of N. B. C., said that "we have only made a

beginning in the adoption of radio to the field of education and

yet it seems inevitable that the future will see a radio in every

school-room in the United States, with the very best educational

programs possible."[42]

Television was also promoted as a new method for supplementing

traditional classroom teaching. With television yet untried,

Christian Century predicted that it would carry on the educational

work of radio, for with visual demonstration added to oral instruc-

tion, "there is no reason why this form of teaching should not be

as effective as any classroom." In 1938 N. B. C. and New York
University presented a televised lesson for 250 science students.
The educational director of N. B. C., Dr. James Rowland Angell,
former President of Yale, pronounced the experimental program a
great success and went on to say that "five years from now I expect
to see television used frequently in the classroom."[43] The faculty
member who taught the televised course said this:

> When television becomes a wide-spread and common prac-
> tice in the United States it will have great educational
> possibilities. These values will be, it seems to me,
> in bringing into the classroom programs by experts and
> masters in many fields that cannot possibly be provided
> otherwise. Also, many other programs on topics of timely
> interest may be used to enrich the curriculum, and appeal
> to student interest in his school work. In addition,
> current topics of an educational character may be shown
> and discussed as they take place, the same as though the
> class were actually present and taking part in the hap-
> penings. This is, indeed, an effective method of teach-
> ing.[44]

Following the Second World War, predictions about television
were renewed. Readers of Nation's Business learned that television
would be the "biggest classroom the world has ever seen," and The
Etude promised, in addition to music of all kinds, lectures on
science, art, geography. Senior Scholastic, noting that television
had been used in the classroom in 1950, argued that television
extended the classroom "out into the world," and promised that
"history will leap from the pages of textbooks through the dramati-
zation of past events and through the direct viewing of current

events as they take place." Education said that with television
"constructive as well as instructive programs may be presented with
a vividness impossible to equal in a classroom." When the Federal
Communications Commission began hearings on Educational Television
Channels, the United States Office of Education took the position
that such channels must be granted because TV was an essential
medium for the classroom. Then when Educational Television, ETV,
was launched, the medium was again defended on the grounds that
there was "an important place and a growing demand for wisely
planned non-commercial programs" intended to expand and supplement the work of the classroom.[45]

In a variety of situations, promoters of motion pictures,
radio, and television associated the new media with beneficial
changes in classroom instruction. They argued that the inventions
would be a valuable adjunct to traditional educational methods,
that the new would improve the familiar institution. At the same
time, they bolstered the position of the new media, for it might
reasonable be presumed that if motion pictures, for example, were
good enough for use in the school, then the medium itself was
worthy of public support. Using this argument from improvement
of the established institution, advocates gained support for innovation from two directions.

The advantages of the new media for education were not limited
to supplementing classroom instruction. Advocates argued that
motion pictures, radio, and television could serve to better the
educational system. Long standing problems could be made less
severe; institutional goals could be achieved more efficiently.

Education made interesting

Education was commonly presumed to be a dull and uninteresting
process. Advocates of motion pictures argued that this need not
be so, and proposed that the use of films in education would make
learning interesting and would serve to keep pupils in school.

This was a favorite argument of Thomas Edison. In 1911 he commented on the dry, dull, and uninteresting manner in which schooling
was normally conducted. In contrast, he suggested that motion
pictures would make learning interesting, would leave children
"crying for more," would eliminate the truant office because "every
little toddler in the district will just want to scoot to school!"[46]
Again in 1919 he argued that school held little interest for most
pupils simply because it had not changed since he, Edison, was a
boy.

> But make every classroom and every assembly-hall a movie-
> show, a show where the child learns every moment while
> his eyes are glued to the screen, and you'll have one
> hundred per cent attendance. Why, you won't be able
> to keep boys and girls away from school then. They'll
> get there ahead of time and scramble for good seats,

and they'll stay late begging to see some of the films
over again. I'd like to be a boy again when film-
teaching becomes universal.[47]

Still in 1925, he repeated his belief that pictures could eliminate

much of the drudgery from the classroom, could replace the "color-

less, standardized lessons of the textbooks" with interesting, yet

substantial lessons.

Others echoed Edison's statements. W. D. Howells, for example,

said in Harper's that "learning might be turned from the dry stock

which now revolts the youthful mind" and be given new life with

filmed lessons. When the University of Wisconsin established a

film library, the Dean of the Extension Division justified the new

undertaking on the grounds that the films would provide a "means

of stimulation, especially for the sluggish pupil," and would help

the pupil learn without trying and in spite of himself. In addition,

the use of films in school would help solve the problem of truancy,

for with films being shown, "how many times a week will the boys

cut this kind of school?"[48] Outlook said in an editorial that

education would come to life when history was committed to film.

> History under the skillful touch and dramatic genius of
> moving picture artists may for all of us thus become a
> present fact. The school boy of tomorrow may read his
> Caesar with eyes fixed upon the soldiers of Vercingetorix,
> may watch the campfires along the Roman wall, may see
> Michael Angelo building the defenses of Florence, may
> march with bloddy Alva through the stricken Netherlands,
> follow the forces of Hudson to the north, suffer hardship
> with Marion the Swamp Fox, or camp with Grant at Appomattox.
> History, a thing alive will come to him out of the brains of

scholars, a ray of prisoned light and a flickering pro-
cession of ghostly shadows thrown upon a whitened screen.[49]

When another writer for <u>Outlook</u> defended motion pictures against the

charge that they had failed the public, he asked his audience to

recall that films had added new life to education and had helped

to relieve both "pedagogical mediocrity and class-room indiffer-

ence."[50] All of these writers, and others, gave films credit for

having added new interest to the process of education, thus cor-

recting a fault of the traditional system.

The argument in this specific form was seldom applied to

television and was not used in connection with radio. A varia-

tion on it is suggested, however, in the recurring statement that

the new media would bring the world into the classroom, would bring

information not formerly available, would allow students to free

themselves of traditional textbook methods.

Increased efficiency in education

The educational system was held by Thomas Edison, and others,

to be inefficient in its teaching. Students did not learn as much

as they should as quickly as should be possible. The motion pic-

ture promised to increase the efficiency of the system.

Edison predicted that eventually teaching in schools would

be done without books. Nevertheless,

the pupils will learn everything there is to learn, in
every grade from the lowest to the highest. The long years

now spent in cramming indigestible knowledge down unwilling
young throats and in examining young minds on subjects
they can never learn under the present system, will cut
down marvelously, waste will be eliminated, and the youth
of every land will at last become actually educated.[51]

The school system as constituted, he argued, was not delivering

enough in either teaching methods or in content. Moreover, the

textbooks were, on the average, only 2 per cent efficient.[52] The

educational motion picture, more interesting and more efficient,

would serve to eliminate the problem, and restore educational

efficiency.

It was Edison who also reported one of the early studies of

the use of films in education. In his case, the investigation

concerned retention or memory training, and Edison reported that

by gradually speeding up the presentation of filmed materials

a 25 to 30 per cent increase in memory was achieved.[53]

Other writers used similar studies as evidence that motion

pictures provided a more efficient means of education than other

methods commonly used in the schools. For example, in 1925 the

United States Commissioner of Education, Dr. John J. Tigert, asserted

that "students have a higher degree of knowledge of those subjects

which are presented to them in motion pictures than those which are

presented through lectures." Scientific American reported in 1929

that in an experiment involving some 10,000 students in twelve

major cities half of the students taught with films supplementing their class work learned from 15 to 33 per cent more than the equivalent group taught without films. The film classes were judged by another writer to have been "superior in their achievement and attitude to non-film classes." Literary Digest reported another study in 1934, this one indicating that students taught with films learned 20 per cent more on the average in general subjects, and an average of 35 per cent more in a limited field in which fact relationships were specifically dealt with, than they did from conventional teaching.[54] Just as Edison had asserted earlier that films made education more efficient, the same conclusion could be drawn from these studies although the argument was not couched in terms comparable to those of Edison.

Great teachers

A further advantage of the new mass media involved the quality of teaching available to students. The traditional system of education limited the student to the teacher who happened to be assigned to his room. Motion pictures, radio, and televison promised that the greatest teachers in every subject would be available to all students.

All of the new media made it possible to circulate the work of the most prominent men in each field. C. B. Neblette argued in Photo-Era that

> the possibility of recording lecture-demonstrations by
> great scientists appears to the writer to be one of the
> great fields open to the talking picture. . . . Such
> productions lack nothing essential. Not only do they
> reproduce the exact words of the speaker, but they show
> likewise his demonstrations and are able to capture
> something of that elusive quality known as personality,
> the effect of which on undergraduate and graduate students
> is often as great as the actual matter absorbed.[55]

Arguing that the educational possibilities of radio were unlimited,

Floyd W. Parsons predicted that with the new instrument "the real

masters among us will be able to talk to the multitude." Bruce

Barton said that radio meant "the little red schoolhouse at the

cross-roads can receive the lectures of the greatest teacher of

physics, or of history, or of biology in the state, in the lec-

turer's own voice." Television, too, was introduced as a means

of allowing all who wished to do so to learn from the great masters

in the various fields. David Sarnoff predicted in 1941, for instance,

that "the school system will probably make increasing use of tele-

vision as part of the educational program; for with this medium

it will become possible for the best teachers in the land to give

carefully prepared and illustrated lectures simultaneously to

millions of children."[56] In still another way, then, the new mass

media promised to improve the present educational system.

University of the air

When it became apparent that radio and television could be

used to provide educational materials for large audiences, promoters

suggested occasionally that the new media would permit the establishment of a national university of the air. H. V. Kaltenborn suggested
that a possible development out of radio was "the creation of an
endowed radio university, consisting of a super-power broadcasting
station and a special staff of educators selected for their ability
to make a wide popular appeal by the lecture method." Walter
Damrosch's broadcasts were taken by Graham McNamee to be the beginning
of this "great University of the Air," the agency "which will bring
the culture of the world and of the age to our people as vividly
and perfectly as radio now brings a prize fight, a political convention or a world series."[57]

While the dreams for a University of the Air were never realized,
various Schools of the Air, with radio lessons designed for elementary and secondary students, were begun after 1925. Most prominent
among these were the Ohio School of the Air, the California School
of the Air, the Wisconsin School of the Air, and the American School
of the Air. In addition, educational programs for classroom use
were broadcast by the networks, a number of individual commercial
stations, colleges and universities, state and territorial departments of public instruction, county school systems, and individual
public schools. The existence of the Schools of the Air and the
educational programs never played a significant role in the general
evaluation of radio, however. Advocates usually avoided the topic,

probably because, as attackers pointed out on occasion, school
broadcasts had never worked out as well in practice as either
radio people or educators hoped they might.[58]

With television still in the laboratory, David Sarnoff predicted
in 1926 that eventually this new form of radio with pictures would
broadcast illustrated courses and perhaps grant degrees through
a radio-television university to students who had taken written
examinations.[59] In a 1929 editorial New Republic amplified the
idea of a television university.

> No one will go to Siwash when by turning a switch he can
> bring Harvard into his living room. . . . No one will
> study medicine at a second rate school when he can have
> the Mayo Clinic of Johns Hopkins before his eyes. For
> certain supremely important species of education and
> diversion a half dozen geniuses can take the places now
> held by thousands of the barely competent. We shall need
> only one university.[60]

The creation of the radio university would mean disruption of the
existing forms of education, but the changes were justified on the
grounds they would be of significant benefit to the educational
system.

Adult education

The new media were also presented by their promoters as offering
new possibilities for adult education. That is, the movies, radio,
and television made it possible to reach adults who were past school
age with educational materials. This kind of teaching came eventually

to be called adult education, but the idea was common in the early discussions of motion pictures.

When promoters spoke of the educational possibilities of the movies they assumed that the pictures would be shown, first of all, in theaters, where the audience was composed of both children and adults. This was often, in effect, a form of adult education. For example, Clapp spoke in 1913 of the uses of films as "a ready means of instructing masses of children or adults." Holliday also wrote of films distributed by the University of Minnesota "showing thousands of farmers how to handle cream and butter, how to make the Babcock test, how to mix cattle feed, and how to cook a wholesome meal." Gregory Mason wrote in Outlook of how "in a hundred ways, the motion picture is utilized for educational purposes in the United States and abroad," many of them involving instruction of adults.[61] Advocates of motion pictures were thus talking of adult education, but not identifying the process with this term.

The term adult education became popular in connection with radio. At first, writers talked of the prospects for colleges and universities broadcasting "extension courses which will encourage home study." In 1929, however, Graham McNamee wrote of expanding radio programs for adult education, based on past experience with lectures on citizenship. In 1936 William J. Donovan, writing in School and Society, argued that radio must be used to reach the

76,000,000 adults who had not yet finished high school. A strong

program of adult education was proposed.[62]

Television also promised aid to adult education. _Saturday_

Review said in 1950 that

> educators are keenly aware that television removed in
> one fell swoop most of the mechanical barriers to cor-
> respondence-school efforts to widen adult or nonclassroom
> education and thus makes it possible, in the language of
> the pulp-magazine ads, to 'get a college education at home.
> Via television it is possible to project almost any sort
> of educational subject matter--lectures, exhibits, demon-
> strations, and even field trips and examinations--outside
> the classroom.[63]

When the University of Michigan instituted adult education courses

by television in 1950, _Time_ quoted its dean: "We are entering a

new era in adult education and the university is in it to stay."

When a representative of RCA talked of television's potential in

1952 he also referred to adult education, predicting that the

medium would create "a pattern of adult education that surmounts

evening classes and correspondence courses in convenience and effec-

tiveness." The argument was applied finally to ETV, and adult

education was named as one of the areas in which the new system

of non-commercial broadcasting would have great potential appli-

cation.[64]

Medical education

A specialized branch of education   predicted to benefit

from motion pictures and television **was** medical education. Advocates

argued that films and television would offer distinct advantages
to medical schools. Students could use films to observe symptoms
of disease and use moving pictures for case study. No longer would
live patients be required for instruction, with perhaps no sample
of a particular disease available when it was being taught. Films
would also permit more precise description than could be obtained
in print; students would be able to see the thing itself rather
than being allowed only to read about it.[65] Particularly important, however, was the opportunity for medical students to observe,
on film or on television, various operations, often as performed by
the leading surgeons in the field. C. B. Neblette, writing in
Photo-Era in 1929 said that

> no longer is the /medical7 student required to draw
> on his imagination to fill out what he is unable to
> see perfectly; for with the motion picture film there
> will be unfolded before him every detail of the tech-
> nique employed, the reaction of the patient, the movement
> of the surgeon's hands, the exact nature of the operation
> --in short, every detail that constitutes the technique
> employed by that surgeon in such operations. Surgical
> operations difficult to describe can be appreciated in
> a few moment's view of the film. By the use of slow
> motion, many movements which will not be caught by the
> average student may be slowed down so that he is able
> to catch their significance. Furthermore, the use of
> motion pictures allows a given operation to be reviewed
> as many times as is thought desirable. . . . Any opera-
> tion, however infrequently it may be met within the
> clinic, may be repeated over and over until the student
> has mastered every detail.[66]

This statement is a thorough summary of the arguments offered in
support of the motion picture in medical education.

When television was becoming operational in 1945, a spokesman
for RCA said this to the Erie County Medical Society:

> Great surgeons and medical instructors of our day may
> be seen as well as heard in actual demonstrations by
> medical students wherever they may be. Moreover, these
> students, grouped around large-screen television receivers,
> will be able to see and hear much better than those at
> the scene of the demonstration.[67]

In effect, supporters of the media argued that the new machines
placed the small medical school on an equal plane with the greatest
of teaching institutions, for through the use of film or television
all had equal facilities and knowledge at their disposal.

This argument was repeated periodically between 1906 and
1955. Although it was never a major argument in terms of the
number of appearances, it was significant in that it was a persistent
concern of the promoters, who apparently believed that it retained
its rhetorical force for the entire period. In addition, the argument served as an indirect refutation for attacks on the grounds
that motion pictures and television were damaging to the health
of viewers. Promoters used the benefits to medical education to
balance predicted health damages caused by the media.

Politics

Friends of radio and television, politicians, and political
commentators expected broadcasting to have a beneficial influence
on politics. They argued that radio and television were, first of

all, useful tools for the politician. But more than this, the media were effective means for modifying and strengthening politics as practiced. To them innovation offered politics another chance, a new opportunity to serve democratic government. Their hopes for the political system are reflected in their arguments about the projected influences of the new media.

As I have already suggested, arguments about politics were limited, for the most part, to radio and television. Only occasionally did anyone speak of the application of pictures to politics. Scientific American said in 1891 that motion pictures would allow political orators to analyze their own performance, and others suggested later that talking films gave speakers a precise model for imitation. World's Work in 1910 saw no reason why pictures might not be used in political campaigns, and in 1911 reported that "last autumn the Democrats arranged displays of Tammany cartoons in 300 moving picture theatres in New York City as campaign arguments." George Bernard Shaw said in 1915 that filmed political speeches would work "for the benefit of democracy;" New Republic in 1928 claimed that talkies gave Hoover an advantage in the campaign because he looked better on the screen than in real life; Readers Digest in 1936 gave filmed newsreel interviews credit for helping defeat Upton Sinclair in his bid for the governorship of California; and Life in 1940 carried a picture story about the

current Republican campaign film, with the comment that "its Republican sponsors expect A New Tomorrow to be a potent fund-raiser and
vote getter."[68] These comments are typical of what was said about
movies and politics. From them it was apparent that little sustained
or substantial argument was developed from the use of films in politics either by advocates of motion pictures or spokesmen for politics.

From the start, however, broadcasting was predicted to have
important applications in politics. Whenever promoters of radio
or television talked of institutions which would profit from the
introduction of the media, politics was named. Some of their arguments have already been covered in the discussions of the use of
the mass media to create new audiences for established institutions.
The others will be considered here.

The public informed

Writers concerned with broadcasting and those primarily interested in politics agreed that an interested and well informed
public was essential to the institution. At the same time, these
writers presumed that the public fell short of the ideal; they
were neither as interested in politics as they should be nor were
they well enough informed. Radio and television offered a chance
to change all this. The public could now participate in politics
with greater freedom than was ever before possible and could learn
as much about politics as they wished to know.

It became commonplace for supporters of the media to mention
that radio, then television, had made available more information
about politics than had ever been available before. Moreover,
they said, the broadcasting of politics created new public interest
in the institution. David Sarnoff, for example, defended radio
on the grounds that it would create new political interest by air-
ing debates and would create, in the same way, a more politically
intelligent populace. Elliot Roosevelt argued in 1951 that television "is having and will continue to have an enormous effect
. . . on the political complexion of our country," primarily because
the political education provided had led to increased political
awareness.69 The argument that radio and television provided more
political information than had ever been available before became
one of the standard topics in the promotion of the new media.

In yet another sense the media were sources of political
information. For the first time, with the beginning of radio
coverage, the general public was permitted to participate in the
workings of the political conventions. This participation was
revealing. New Republic said that the result of broadcasting the
1924 conventions "was one to dismay the most hardened political
cynic," for the public listened "fascinated, horrified, and finally
amused" to empty speeches, hours of inanity and monotony, learning
all the while what really constituted a political convention.

Graham McNamee predicted that as a consequence of broadcasting the
1928 conventions "four years from now, we shall see some very
extensive changes in the scenarios of the national conventions,
and they will be made principally to meet the tastes and hold the
attention of the great radio audience."[70] When the conventions
appeared on television Saturday Review claimed the meetings had
been revealed for what they were, organized fanfare.

> To the spectator, sitting solitary or in a small group
> before his instrument, the boisterous excitement of
> the convention floor was inevitably revealed in its
> true light, as in great part manufactured and super-
> fluous, a sort of mass emotion produced in part by delib-
> erate efforts of party leaders and in part by self-
> hypnosis, a calculated demonstration, saved by the Ameri-
> can tradition of democracy from dictatorial spirit but
> akin, no matter how distantly, to the pressurized displays
> of a Hitler Germany or a Mussolini Italy. Americans
> have had a lesson in practical politics in these past
> weeks, thanks to television and radio, such as they have
> never had before, a concrete exposition of the give-and-
> take of politics, of its methods and stratagems, its
> stresses and strains, which must have been a revelation
> indeed to that large part of the nation which habitu-
> ally takes its political information in newspaper head-
> lines alone.[71]

Harper's and Nation agreed that television had revealed much about
the national political system through coverage of the conventions;
more than this, the revelation pointed up clearly the need for
political reform.[72] The media had not only provided new information
about politics, but had served to initiate changes in the institution.

The candidate and the public

The introduction of radio and television into political campaigning was expected to change the way in which the candidate
communicated with his supporters. Traditional campaign methods
were no longer sufficient; established ways of doing things quickly
became obsolete. While some writers were highly suspicious of such
changes, the promoters of the media and many of the political
commentators argued that the modifications were a good thing for
politics and that the institution would profit because of them.

In the first place, advocates argued, radio and television
established a new and close relationship between the candidate and
the public. No longer was the candidate known mainly through newspaper reports; no longer did only those of the electorate who
happened to hear a speech know the candidate at first hand. For the
first time the candidate was able to represent himself, in his
own words, virtually in person, to vast sections of the nation.
As New Republic put it in 1924, the first campaign in which radio
was used extensively,

> for the first time in history the nominees will have the
> opportunity to be judged out of their own mouths. The
> radio overcame four barriers between the candidate and
> the voter. The barrier of distance, the barrier of time,
> the barrier of inertia, and, most important, the barrier
> of crowd psychology. It gives the voter the candidate's
> exact words, intonations, hesitations, hems and haws
> --reveals the timbre of his voice. If he has a charming
> chuckle it will be heard. If he is worried or dubious
> or a pussyfooting straddler upon issues, the intent ears

of the nation's radio owners will detect it. 'The voice
with a smile' is probably going to win--for once.[73]

But television even more than radio brought the candidate to
the public, made him a person as well as a political figure. The
new closeness between candidate and public, the new ability of the
candidate to represent himself almost as if in person, had important implications for politics. Saturday Review, for example,
argued in 1952 that

> television and radio have introduced an enormously
> effective factor into the political arena, for they
> have turned candidates into men, not names, into persons
> in their habits as they live, with all their traits of
> manner and speech, their glances and their quips. Gene-
> ral Eisenhower and Governor Stevenson, Senator Nixon and
> Senator Sparkman, the many figures who held the rostrum
> in both Republican and Democratic conventions, smiling,
> gesticulating, talking, caught in asides and unexpected
> poses, have become flesh-and-blood beings to the public
> instead of mere pictured figures as in the past. Never
> before in the history of the country have its political
> personages become as familiar as his neighbors to the man
> in the street, never before have their voices and their
> words been heard by such enormous numbers. What this
> materialization of political personality into person
> implies is easy to see. That vast public which is too
> untutored or too indifferent to apply itself with assid-
> uity to evolving a clear conception of a candidate from
> his speeches as reported in the press is now able to
> follow his course through political events with the
> least possible effort over television and radio. The
> America of 150,000,000 souls is nearer today to the era
> when politicians and people met face to face than in
> many a long decade.[74]

Because of the new media, then, politicians were better known
than ever before and politics assumed a new kind of personal quality.

Consequently, advocates said, there was less chance of the politician's ideas being garbled in transmission, less chance for
the public to misunderstand what the speaker meant, and greater
public involvement in political affairs. No longer was the message
filtered through a newspaper report; instead, the audience would
have a chance to hear for themselves, and so be better able to
judge accurately the message. Politics was given both a new personality and a new clarity by radio and television.

Even though the candidate spoke directly to the voter over
the radio or on television, most supporters of the media recognized
that the broadcasting of a speech was not a duplication of the live
speechmaking situation and thought that personality would not show
on the air. The candidate could not establish the same rapport
with his audience on radio or television that was possible face
to face. Some of the commentators glossed over the apparent disadvantage by explaining this was beneficial to politics for it
eliminated the persuasion exerted by the speaker's personality,
and restored good sense and logic to political judgments. New
Republic, for example, said in 1924 that on radio "the speaker's
'personal magnetism,' if he has any, is enormously diminished in
its power to affect the judgment of his auditors. Critical standards
are preserved which are a useful assistance to independent thinking."
A writer for Saturday Evening Post called up the example of William

Jennings Bryan as evidence of radio's effect on personal magnetism.
Bryan, he said, had great personal magnetism and charm in the
studio, but none of this on the air. On the radio "his talk was
simply reduced to effects producible on the ear alone--one-sense
effects, as the radio folks put it." James G. Harbord, President
of RCA, predicted that logic would be restored to political judgments because on the air the orator's personal magnetism was cooled,
his impassioned gestures unseen, his flashing eye unnoticed, and
his purple periods faded. And television was expected to exert
the same influence. There again, personality was not expected to
be transmitted in full, and the effect on politics was judged
salutary. The candidate on television could not be judged solely
on the basis of his personality.[75]

Advocates of radio and television also argued that political
decisions would be freed of the influence of the audience, freed
from so-called mob appeals, when speeches were carried on the air.
The listener alone in his home was no longer a part of an audience,
no longer susceptible to influence from his fellow audience members.
He was, as it were, insulated from the reactions of the crowd.
Radio listeners, said Saturday Evening Post after the 1924 Democratic national convention,

> follow the speech with one sense only. There is nothing
> to distract their attention. They do not share in the
> excitement and movement of the meeting, nor does the per-
> sonality of the speaker register with them.[76]

A writer for Century Magazine believed this to be an advantage for

politics, but a problem for the speaker.

> A problem for the politicians is the fact that a radio
> audience has a psychology utterly different from that
> of a crowd assembled in one place. The mob spirit, with
> its factitious enthusiasm, is of course entirely lacking.
> There is no applause to let the speaker know what is his
> most popular 'line.' His ideas will therefore have a
> better chance of being weighed for what they are really
> worth.[77]

Mob emotion, "the glamour of mob enthusiasm," was to be eliminated

from politics because of radio. When writers spoke of the same

influence from television, they spoke of the "objectivity" of the

medium, but they meant that at home the pressures of the audience

were eliminated.[78] In eliminating the persuasion of the audience,

politics was restored to the rational base so admired by the com-

mentators. The new media offered still another prospect for making

politics what they thought it should be.

Radio and television were advanced by their supporters as

instruments for analysis and evaluation, not only of political

discourse but of performance in general. Advocates argued that

the new media exposed that which was false, insincere, or incom-

petent in its true light, revealed flaws in thought and performance

which previously had gone undetected. Where it might be possible

for a skilled speaker to deceive most members of a live audience

or for a second rate performer to get by in a live concert, such

things would not be acceptable in broadcasting. Performance on the air was stripped of all but the essentials, revealed for what it was, made to stand on its fundamental merit, to be judged by an audience free of distraction and attentive to the message offered.

This argument was used first in connection with politics on radio. As I have already pointed out, radio was praised for permitting candidates to speak for themselves. Audiences were presumed to be able to make more reliable judgments of a radio speaker than of the same speaker in a face to face situation. This meant, said James G. Harbord, that politics had been "debunked."

> The microphone and the moving picture combined divest
> leadership of all legend and myth. The man who speaks
> while millions listen cannot hide paucity of ideas with
> a brilliant oratorical style. The path to political
> preferment is no longer confined to those who can talk
> glibly, but it is open to every man or woman who can
> think.[79]

On another occasion Harbord commented that radio had "revealed the characteristics of personality of the outstanding candidates intimately to the calm and calculating judgment of the millions of their constituents from coast to coast.[80] By revealing the false, radio forced attention to be paid to the real and the sincere.

Television was predicted to be even more revealing than radio had been. When C. Francis Jenkins talked of his television system in 1929 he said that in politics the new instrument would render its ultimate service to mankind, by allowing the nation to see the candidate as if in person, and not limited to acquaintance by voice

alone. In 1946, Alva Johnston argued in <u>Saturday</u> <u>Evening</u> <u>Post</u> that
television was an important medium of communication because with it
reality could not be distorted, no one could kid the viewer who
could see for himself. In 1948 a writer for <u>American</u> <u>Magazine</u>
spoke of the "merciless realism" of which television was capable,
and suggested that the willingness of politicians to expose themselves to the probing of the medium was a giddy sort of courage.[81]
A writer for <u>Good</u> <u>Housekeeping</u> spoke of the impact personalities
had on television, when they were not judged by voice alone.

> When we see them on television we judge them for what
> they are. Television is a revealing medium, and it is
> impossible for a man or a woman appearing before those
> cameras to conceal his or her true self.[82]

John Crosby argued that when applied to politics television forced
the political candidate to know what he was talking about and to
answer questions fully and honestly. Looks did not matter.
"The candidate, I'm convinced, could be ugly as a hedgehog; it is
not his looks that television puts under scrutiny--it is his ability "[83] Another time, Crosby noted that television had an unusual
ability to show up the political phoney, and consequently placed
a premium on sincerity and ability, qualities impossible to feign.
Crosby phrased his argument like this:

> In the long run, though, television is likely to be an
> unparalleled blessing to the voter. The phonies, the
> stuffed shirts, the liars, the crooks will have to look
> the camera straight in the eye and talk fast. We'll see
> the politicos as they are, warts and all. If, after so

stringent a test, the political hacks survive, we have
only ourselves to blame.[84]

There was still admiration for this ability of television in 1955.

Leonard W. Hall, for example, told the National Federation of Repub-

lican Women that television had changed the course of the political

campaign, for it was pitiless at exposing anything that smacked

of being phony.[85] The service to politics was obvious; the ideals

of sincerity, honesty, and intelligence could be restored to poli-

tics because of the force of television in revealing their oppo-

sites.

Just as the radio and television broadcasts were capable of

revealing the phony and the fake, so, supporters of the media argued,

could they eliminate the political demagogue. The process was the

same; the demagogue would be stripped of his tools and his tech-

niques. The President of RCA used this argument in his justification

of radio in 1929. He claimed that radio freed democracy of the danger

of the demagogue, which arose in the past because "the devices of

the orator, the mystery of personal magnetism, the gift of leader-

ship, and the contagion of mob feeling have swayed the crowd."

Radio, he argued, had eliminated mob feeling from the political

audience, and had separated the listener from the contagion of the

crowd. Consequently, because of radio, "only the logic of the

issue which the orator presents can move him," the listener.

Elliot Roosevelt, John Crosby, and Leonard Hall used the same

argument in discussing the applications of television in politics.
Roosevelt, for instance, asserted that television presaged the end
of both the political machine and the demagogue. "We have already
seen them start to disintegrate," he wrote, "and as television
keeps spreading across the country and it reaches into every home,
just so fast will come the end of the political machine, and of
demagogery." Crosby recognized the argument that television might
be an excellent medium for the demagogue, but countered it with the
assertion that "this is extremely doubtful. Television exposes
phoniness and would probably just make a demagogue look foolish."[86]
Again in this argument, these supporters of radio and television
connected the new medium with changes they believed desirable in
politics.

Political speaking

Proponents of radio and television predicted that the new media
would cause beneficial revisions in traditional political speaking.
The kind of speechmaking usually associated with politics would no
longer be acceptable when speeches were broadcast; the orators
themselves would be cast in a new image because of the particular
demands of broadcasting. This argument was reintroduced with each
new political campaign and appeared regularly in discussions of
both radio and television.

Writers who sought revisions in political speechmaking argued
in 1924 that for too long "a good personality, a musical voice, a
power of dramatic gesture have served to cover up baldness of thought
and limping phraseology." The stereotype of the political orator,
"the spellbinder, gesticulating, pounding, striding up and down,
stirred to frenzy by the applause of his audience," was unacceptable
on the radio. It was John Crosby's hope twenty years later that
television would eliminate "the normal pomposites of political
rhetoric." To him, Sam Rayburn was an "excellent example of the
type of politico who will have to modify sharply /his/ florid
prose style and arm flailing delivery for the skeptical and intimate cameras." Earlier, of course, other writers had commented
that "no man, or woman, either, can be oratorically eloquent over
the precise and matter-of-fact radio."[87]

The vision of radio and television as tools for analysis, as
revealers and debunkers, was carried over into this argument about
political oratory. Supporters of the media argued that the old style
of oratory was made invalid by broadcasting because its fakery, false-
hood, and insincerity were exposed to all who listened or watched.
Saturday Evening Post, for example said in a 1924 editorial that
the politician's protective coloration was stripped away by radio
because it was

> uncompromising and literal transmission. The listeners
> follow the speech with one sense only. There is nothing

to distract their attention. They do not share in the
excitement and movement of the meeting, nor does the
personality of the speaker register with them. It is
what he says and the words he uses in saying it which
counts with them. If he rushes into such phrases as
'of which I am a proud member of,' the unerring forces
of Nature transmit the expression exactly as it falls
from his lips to the listening thousands or tens of
thousands, as the case may be. Somehow the spread-eagle
sort of thing and all the familiar phrases and resources
of the spellbinder sound very flat and stale over the air.
Radio constitutes the severest test for speakers of the
rough-and-ready, catch-as-catch-can school, and reputations
are going to shrink badly, now that the whole nation is
listening in. Silver-tongued orators whose fame has been
won before sympathetic audiences are going to scale down
to their real stature when the verdict comes from the
radio audiences.[88]

Collier's said that

by means of radio more than one old-time politician this
year /1924/ will dig himself into political quicksands,
at the microphone, without knowing what he is doing.
He won't have sense enough to stay away from the microphone. He will think that it is only a means of further
spreading his wonderous oratory. . . . He will have suffocated himself in his own blah.[89]

With radio, and later television, the orator was forced to stand

before an impartial audience whose critical faculties were thought

to be unimpaired by the distractions of the political meeting or

even of political affiliation. He approached them through a medium

which itself was revelatory, which served to cut away fraud and

deception. He stood exposed to judgment in a way which had never

been a part of politics before. The persuasion of personality no

longer worked, and the political speaker was forced to fall back

upon the substantial power of logic.

As a result, a new kind of political oratory was predicted to develop. Audiences, said supporters of the media, would no longer be satisfied with traditional political speechmaking and would demand improvement in the art. The new motto for politicians, said a writer for Collier's, would be this: "Cut out the blah." Another predicted that the new oratory would be characterized by "substance not sobs." In essence, the new oratory, as supporters of the media envisioned it, would be made of all that was admired in public speaking. Speakers would be factual, logical, reasonable, intelligent, sensible, thoughtful, candid, fair, earnest, and sincere. Moreover, they would be brief. New Republic pointed out, for instance, that as soon as radio audiences gained any sophistication at all with the medium, they found long speeches wearisome; a quarter hour on the radio was judged to be the equivalent of an hour in the lecture hall.[90] The media, and the same hopes were held out for both radio and television, would help make speechmaking what critics wanted it to be.

As a consequence of the demands on the medium, and the audience, a new kind of politician was also envisioned. On radio he was to be the kind of man who could sit in a quiet room and speak to the entire country. This, said Christian Century,

would not be the death of oratory. It would be the birth of a new type of oratory which could contain all the warmth of emotion the candidate's personality is capable of, and which would also put a premium on intelligence.[91]

The politician on television would also have access to the voter
in his living room. As David Sarnoff said in 1935, the television
politician would have to "make it appear to that man that he is talking to him personally." Television of course would make it possible
for the politician to make use of visual evidence he could not use
on the radio, but the major change would have to come in the speaker's relationship with his audience. Television, even more than
radio,   made the politician a guest in the home of the viewer.
Elliot Roosevelt said, for example, that in the television campaign
the candidate would be brought into the living room to sell himself to the voters gathered there, and "his ability to sell himself
--just as an actor must do on a stage--will become all-important
to the politician in the future."[92] The new politician, the television politician, would be faced with the new problem of meeting
an audience composed of thougtful, interested, well-informed individuals, or perhaps small groups, in homes rather than the traditional meeting hall crowds. The change, said the supporters of the
medium, would be good for politics.

Two additional modifications of the current mode of political
discourse were also predicted by writers concerned with radio and
television. First of all, a small group who believed that oratory
had suffered a decline in the twentieth century saw the new media
as means for the restoration of both oratory and political rhetoric

to their rightful places. This argument was used initially to justify
the Future Home Theater, primitive television, in 1912, its defender
asserting that with the coming of television "oratory /will/ be
reborn when for the first time in history it will be worth while
for a really great man to give his genius to a speech intended for
ordinary people, not legislators." Similarly, the science editor of
the New York Times argued in 1924 that because of radio "perhaps
oratory may flourish again as it did in the days of Greece and Rome.
What a success Demosthenes would have been in the days of broadcasting!" Review of Reviews predicted in 1928 that radio might restore political stump speaking to the place of importance it had
been losing gradually through the years. In 1937, New Republic,
recalling that earlier political battles--the Lincoln-Douglas debates
among them--were fought with oratory but that political speechmaking
had declined in influence, commented that "the radio, it might be
said, has returned rhetoric to its place as a political instrument."[93]
It was predicted, secondly, that television might restore face-to-face
debate to politics. This was an argument developed by Elliot Roosevelt, who claimed that the ultimate goal of television in politics was
to bring the candidates face to face, as Lincoln and Douglas had been,
so

> we will be able to measure the worth of their ideals,
> their principles, and their integrity. . . . There will
> be no ducking of issues, because each candidate will be
> right there to catch the others.[94]

In each of these modifications of current practice, the political institution as well as the voting public stood to benefit from the influence of the new media.

The political campaign

Many of the arguments I have already discussed could be applied to political campaigning. Supporters of the media, however, also referred specifically to improvements in campaigning which would result from the introduction of radio and television. Two kinds of influence were predicted. First, certain undesirable features of the campaign might be eliminated, and, second, new and more effective campaign techniques were introduced.

In general, writers objected to the nonsense and foolishness traditionally associated with campaigns. Radio and television were supposed to eliminate this. That is, radio was to "knock the nonsense out of politics," eliminate the influence of meaningless crowd enthusiasm on political decision making and candidate selection, and in effect "revolutionize the political campaign in this country, and render the political rally an anachronism." Television was to do the same kind of thing. John Crosby, for example, said the cameras would cut down on parades and monkey shines at conventions, "partly to save time, partly because the delegates look asinine milling around the aisles," and would reduce the amount of general campaign oratory because "experience has shown that the

wind-filled phrase seems especially empty on television." With
political hokum lacking on the air, only one course was open to
the political campaigner--"full frontal attack. In the absence
of subterfuge, the campaign will have to relapse to natural candor."95 Hence, with the foolishness, the crowd fervor, the empty
oratory, the meaningless rallies eliminated from campaigning, politics would better serve democratic government. Those who employed
the argument offered radio and television as a means to this end.

Broadcasting also offered some relief to the campaigning
politician. No longer would it be necessary for him to travel around
the country, appearing at political meetings and county fairs.
Instead, with radio, "a carefully prepared speech . . . can now
be made to reach the public with more telling effect and without
any strain upon the physical vitality of the candidate."96 Review
of Reviews went so far in 1928 as to suggest that if President
Wilson had had radio available to him, he would have been spared
the strain of his western tour on behalf of the League of Nations.

> There is reason to think that his strength would not
> have failed, and that his life would have been spared.
> . . . One speech with our present radio facilities,
> delivered quietly in Washington, would have been ten times
> more effective that the Western trip, and would have
> involved no strain whatever.97

Television, of course, offered the same possibilities to the candidate. The public could be reached with a minimum of effort and in
general the business of campaigning would be made easier.98

Political campaigns could also be shorter after the advent
of television, for no longer was the task of reaching voters necessarily a long or difficult one. That it was both possible and
practical to shorten national campaigns was the conclusion of a
writer for New Republic who surveyed the use of broadcasting in
the 1952 campaign. Three years later, looking forward to the 1956
campaign, Walter Goodman argued that with barnstorming no longer
necessary, the campaign would be shortened in 1956 with the National
Conventions held a month later than in 1952.[99] The influence of
television on the campaign was thus demonstrated as well as predicted.

It became apparent soon after the introduction of radio that
the medium made available to the politician a variety of new campaign methods. No longer was he limited to speechmaking, personal
appearances, and the press. Eunice Fuller Barnard suggested in
New Republic in 1924 that while the radio speech "might eclipse
even the hearty handshake as a vote getter," before long the public might find radio press agents on the air for the candidates,
bedtime stories about the candidate's boyhood, "tenors expanding
on his favorite lullaby, radio orchestras playing his special
march directly after the Star Spangled Banner, even the voice of
his aged mother now and then quavering out a tribute." A writer
for Saturday Evening Post, speaking in a more serious vein in 1929,

recommended that politicians make more use of a variety of program

formats, for speeches alone, even on the radio, were boring.[100]

Television more than radio promised new techniques for the

politician. Gilbert Seldes predicted in 1937 that when television

came to be used extensively in politics "the astute politician will

want to be sure that his audience will have something agreeable,

but not distracting, to look at--which, in nine cases out of ten,

eliminates the speaker himself." When Thomas E. Dewey ran for

re-election as Governor of New York in 1950 he made extensive and

unusual use of television. But far from eliminating himself from

the screen, Dewey engaged in an 18 hour telethon the day before the

election, answering questions telephoned into the studio by the

viewing public. Christian Century said the new technique "worked

so well it is sure to be copied," and John Crosby argued that

Dewey's innovation had revolutionized thinking about television

as a political instrument.[101] In 1951, with Dewey's experience

as a jumping off point, Robert Lewis Shayon predicted in Saturday

Review that

> television will make it insufficient henceforth for
> candidates to be laudable. They will have to be view-
> able. This means daring TV exploitation of new politi-
> cal communication techniques--the discussion, the docu-
> mentary, perhaps even the variety show.[102]

Shayon even wondered why the sketch, songs, and ballet could not

be used for campaigning on television. He concluded that "the

timate would be the relegation of the argument to the status of
e commercial--in jingle form."103

The 1952 campaign furnished considerable evidence that Shayon's
edictions were not mere fantasy. In this year when television
ame to national politics in full bloom, the Republicans opened
ith television coverage of their Madison Square Garden Rally, an
vent judged by Crosby to have consisted of "too much hoopla and
ot enough enlightenment." The medium was credited with having
reated the public image of two of the leading candidates and
ith having inspired the public clamor for Estes Kefauver to enter
he race.104 As New Republic said,

> within four months a man unknown to the American public
> became, largely by virtue of television, a celebrity
> in his own land. (The same, incidentally, could have
> been said of Senator Richard Nixon and of his dog Check-
> ers.)105

en days before election the Republicans undertook a spot advertising
litz on both radio and television, saturating 50 key counties in
2 states with material for Eisenhower. The night before election
here was another half-hour Republican rally on the networks. When
he results were in, one Stevenson supporter is reported to have
ommented, "Chalk this one up for B. B. D. & O." Television was
escribed as "the new and revolutionary medium of American poli-
ics."106

There was no question but that television would play an important role in the 1956 campaign. Walter Goodman in New Republic
wrote in May of 1955 that "whether or not it is the absolute political weapon that some enthusiasts maintain, television has, since
1948, come to be valued as a potent vote-getter by experienced
tacticians of both parties." It was Goodman's prediction that
"everybody in the national scene--from the first term Representative up to the President himself--will be competing for the choice
TV hour in 1956." The chief of Newsweek's Washington Bureau reported
that the campaign would be adapted to television, the conventions
geared to the medium. In addition, both parties were devising
new means of reaching voters--issues dramatized in cartoons, docu-
mentaries, interviews, testimonials from voters, and a modified form
of "This Is Your Life" for candidates.[107] Television not only
offered the politician new techniques for reaching the voter, but
also served to influence traditional methods of campaigning.
Supporters of television argued all this was beneficial for politics.

In these various ways, supporters of radio and television
sought to link the new media to improvements in politics. It was
their contention that innovation would strengthen the machinery
which made government work, and finally bring the institution in
line with its theoretical potential. The qualities which had long
been sought for politics and politicians, but never achieved, were

now to be realized. The institution, because of radio and television, was to become what men had long hoped it might be. At the
same time, the case for the media was strengthened in the demonstration. If radio and television could serve politics well, the
media were indeed valuable to society.

Religion

The principal contribution of motion pictures, radio, and
television to religion lay in dissemination of information and
in creation of a new audience for the church. But promoters of
the media also sought to demonstrate that religion would benefit
in other ways from the innovation.

As was typical in other situations, promoters first argued
that the media were applicable in matters of religion. That is,
they proposed that movies and broadcasting could be employed with
good results by religious institutions. For example, in 1913
Carl Holliday, former head of the English Department at Vander-
bilt University, argued that motion pictures had an important
place in the work of the church. He concluded that

> here is a movement that cannot be ignored by the pro-
> gressive church. Every agency is ready; cheap and safe
> projecting machines are now on the market; highly suit-
> able church auditoriums relieve the institution of all
> rental expenses; practical artistic and eminently suit-
> able films are available, and certainly a most willing
> and receptive audience is at hand. This new form is
> entering silently but effectively into the character of

public education and modern life, and no student of the
American social conditions as they really are can afford
to be ignorant of its power or ignore its potentialities
in economic, social, intellectual and moral uplift.[108]

Christian Century said this of radio:

Radio offers an unparalleled opportunity to the religious teacher to adapt his message to the need and understanding of the man in the market place. Religion has
in abundance the very material radio uses best: music,
drama, emotional appeal, vital news, inspiration, human
interest stories, mystery, universal interest, biographi-
cal data, family appeal. Religious leaders must learn
how to utilize these resources for radio instead of complaining that radio is a competition for the people's
interest or looking upon it as a toy of doubtful value
to the church.[109]

Newsweek commented in 1949 that the new religious programs on tele-

vision marked the "beginning of a vast religious undertaking, com-

plicated with problems of denominational, technical, and financial,

but which in time can bring the churches new means of evangelism

and comfort for the millions they seek to bring to God." The hope

of all faiths, said Newsweek, was "that the video medium will

become for the churches a new light of the world burning right

in the home."[110] Established in this fashion was the notion that

the media could be used in connection with religious undertakings

and would prove profitable for the institution.

Not many of the writers who talked about the relationships of

the media and religion suggested that the church would be improved

with the addition of movies, radio, or television. They were per-

haps unwilling to argue explicitly that there was need for change

in such a venerable institution. But for whatever reason, the kind
of causal argument which was used in connection with other institutions was much less frequent with respect to religion. Instead,
as I will demonstrate in a later chapter, supporters of the media
were inclined to rely upon associative argument. That is, they
maintained that since the established and respected institutions,
the church, used the new media, the media were worthy of public
consideration. Still, however, there was limited argument from
the beneficial effects of the media on religion, and these will
be considered now.

Supporters of the new media, and church people who wrote of the
uses for the media in religion, argued that movies, radio, and
television would help make the good works of the church even better.
Carl Holliday, for example, argued in 1913 that movies could be
used to dramatize for the public the concerns of the church. He
wrote that "in the battle against child labor, white slavery,
labor conflicts, and vice development, in spreading knowledge of
the Bible and Biblical lands, in the teaching of patriotism and
brotherhood, in the general education and developing of the public
conscience, it /the motion picture/ apparently is destined to play
an enormous part." Since these were also the concerns of the church,
then the movies, he argued, had a rightful place in the institution. In 1929 the pastor of the First Congregational Church in

Los Angeles said that even feature pictures could be used as sup-
plements to the sermons to point up object lessons and to give the
theme of the sermon a vitality which was lacking in words alone.[111]
The Saturday Evening Post took a simpler view in an editorial in
1948, arguing that Biblical pictures could make the lessons of
religion vital and interesting for children.

> What youngster who saw a screen version of the fight
> between David and Goliath would ever forget it? What
> boy would not be thrilled by the adventures of Daniel
> in the lion's den?
>   The career of the Apostle Paul, from his part in
> the stoning of Stephen to his trial before Festus and
> King Agrippa, contains episodes which would thrill the
> moviegoer, to say nothing of informing him on a vital
> chapter in early Christian history.[112]

All of these authors suggested that the work of the church would
be advanced if the motion pictures were used to supplement traditional teaching. They at no time denied that the institution was
doing good things, but clearly implicit in the argument is the
assumption that the work could be made better.

Radio and television were also said to have a place in the
work of the church, but their contribution to the institution was
thought to relate primarily to the work of the church in dissemination of its message. For one thing, radio could effectively
serve pastorless churches, bringing to them services from other
places. No church needed to be without a pastor, and the shortage
of ministers could be relieved in some measure. More than this,

owever, broadcasting offered every church the possibility of
aving its message delivered by the greatest preacher in the land.
he prospect that all worshipers might participate in the services
f famous churches was held out by David Sarnoff in 1941. He wrote
hat "religious broadcasting will rise to new spiritual levels,
or with television large audiences can participate intimately
n the services of the great cathedrals; they will not only hear
he ministers and the music, but they will see the preacher face
o face as he delivers his sermon, witness the responsiveness of
he audience, and observe directly the solemn ceremonies at the
ltar." It was even possible, said New Republic, that because of
he new media only one church would be needed for each denomina-
ion.113

When specific objections to the conduct of religion did appear
hey centered in preaching. Just as commentators about politics
ere dissatisfied with political oratory, so some of the writers
bout religion were unimpressed with pulpit speaking. A Univer-
alist leader quoted by Literary Digest in 1924 said that in a
ocal church he visited the prayer was "an insult to the Creator
nd a slander to the congregation," while the sermon was "noisy,
illy, unpractical, weak, and worthless." Radio, he argued, would
t least allow the parishioner to avoid this sort of ineptitude.
ther writers, however, thought that radio might improve the general

quality of preaching. <u>Christian Century</u> argued that radio broad-casting would cause ministers to shed their "professional piety," to drop "the professional tone of voice which many preachers have unconsciously and unfortunately acquired." The editor of <u>Review of Reviews</u> predicted that talkies would improve pulpit speaking by giving ministers a better model of speaking for their imita-tion. And <u>Literary Digest</u> suggested the radio might develop a new class of preacher, the ecclesiastical orator, who would spec-ialize in broadcasting and leave other pastoral work to those who did less well at speaking.[114] Radio thus offered religion an opportunity to bolster the weak places in its structure.

In the discussions of religion and the new media, proponents again sought to show how the innovation would serve the respected institution. They presumed that if the media could be demonstrated to have a salutary influence on religion, then the worth of the innovation was made clear.

The Family

Home and family were other institutions promoters said would benefit from the introduction of motion pictures, radio, and tele-vision. Two general lines of influence were predicted: first, family bonds would be strengthened as the members enjoyed the

media together; second, families would profit from the kinds of
materials appearing in the media.

Assuming that family participation in activities was a good
thing, promoters sought to identify the new media as family entertainment. Recall, for example, that Lucy France Pierce described
the movie as "a kind of recreative school for the whole family"
in her 1908 defense of the nickelodeon,[115] and that Will Hays
defended moving pictures in 1927 with this argument:

> That motion-picture entertainment is wholesome is
> proved by the fact that its success has been built upon
> family patronage. Fathers, mothers, children attend
> the motion-picture theater together. It has become their
> gathering place, allowing the family, as a whole, its
> first indoor recreation together. And this is tremen-
> dously important at a time when we hear so much about
> the disintegration of the American home.[116]

Radio listening too, was described by Bruce Barton in 1922 as the
means for bringing the family together at night, and by H. V.
Kaltenborn in 1931 as a social function for the family group clus-
tered around the receiver. Another time, the success of radio
was attributed to the fact that broadcasts were received in the
home, "and Americans are home-loving people."[117]

The argument that the media would preserve the home was used
most frequently in connection with television, however. When the
first promotion of television appeared, In 1912, the writer of the
piece in Independent asserted the medium would "tend powerfully to
preserve the home," presumably because family members would gather

to watch the events as they were projected. The argument was
repeated as other writers talked of the coming of television,
Robert Sherwood for example predicting in 1929 that television
would cause people to enjoy being home by bringing into the home
everything the theatre could offer, "and much that the theatre
could offer, "and much that the theatre has never been able to
offer in the past." In 1945 former Federal Radio Commissioner
Orestes H. Calwell said "the American family will find new occasion
for getting together and getting better acquainted again, in the
coming age of television." With television established, writers
continued to speak of its healthy influence in the family. An
article in Parent's Magazine in 1949 said this of TV: Certainly
it has brought back the family circle in the living room." But
whether or not the family circle was viable became a question in
1950. John Crosby, for one, noted that although the family might
come together for a time with the new television, they had little
to say while together and soon drifted on to other pursuits. Then
in 1954 Ruth Inglis commented that "although families spend more
time together around the television set, conversation is discouraged
except during the commercials." By 1955, Science News Letter concluded that the new togetherness in the family was passive.[118] Television had served to fulfill the dream only in part.

A variation on the preceding argument was employed by a few
writers who argued not only that greater physical togetherness was
achieved through television, but that families were given new
common interests and new subjects for conversation by the medium.
It was Dorothy McFadden who asked readers of Parent's Magazine
in 1949 to "think of the family dinner table discussions promoted
by watching one of WNBT's Navy programs, direct from the aircraft
carrier 'Leyte,' with the cameras showing every angle of the ship,
the catapulting of planes, their disappearance on the ship's ele-
vators, the excitements of landings on deck." U. S. News concluded
in 1954 that the medium not only kept the family in the same room,
but also stimulated new conversations among the family members.119

The second general line of argument stressed the good to come
to the family when a great variety of educational, cultural, and
informational features were brought into the home. Underlying
the argument were several important assumptions, apart from the
obvious one that it is good to learn new things in a comfortable
and convenient fashion. First, it had to be assumed that some
of the family at least would be home to hear or see the programs.
Hence, the argument strengthened the presumption about family
unity growing out of the introduction of the media. In addition,
writers relied upon the god terms home and family to lend force
to their arguments. Stressed often was the notion that the new

media reached people <u>in the home</u> or <u>with their family</u>. Although the argument suggested that the home would be influenced by the media, still the media were given respectability by these associations with the home. Finally, the argument reflected a great faith in the good taste and judgment of the public. If people allowed the media in their homes and enjoyed them, then the media must be worthwhile.

Proponents expected radio and television to bring entertainment, education, culture, and information into the homes of all, thus giving the home new life and making available to the family vast new resources for pleasure and for learning. Typical of the general comments about this function of the media are these:

> Television will finally bring to people in their homes, for the first time in history, a complete means of instantaneous participation in the sights and sounds of the entire outer world.

> ⎣Television portends⎦ a glowing future when we will all have an educational, cultural, and entertainment device in our homes ten times as effective as anything we have now.[121]

To put these prospects into particular terms, advocates of the media often spelled out the kinds of things they expected to see and hear in the future. Sports--especially boxing and football--and movies were the entertainment most often mentioned. But in addition to these, readers were told they would see and hear poetry, religious services, drama, musical comedy, opera, variety programs, music, news, politics, speeches, and even television broadcasts of favorite radio programs in the comfort of their own homes.[122]   Such fare, said promoters of the media, could not help but make the home more lively and attractive.   The home would become the center of the family's cultural life, the source of much of their education and amusement.   The media would in effect, restore an idealized function of the home.

There were also hints that the home had influenced the form and function of both radio and television.   Because the new media did come into the home, they were somewhat limited in the kind of material they could deal with.   The implication was clear: because radio and television did serve the home, both were "cleaner" than were the motion pictures which operated under no such limitations. The specific statement of this notion appeared twice.   The first time was in connection with the proposal for the first primitive television system, the home theater.   The advocate of this new medium argued that

> the moral tone of the home theater will be excellent.
> For the electric form, like the motion pictures, but
> in much greater degree, will be supported by family
> audiences.   And . . . the inevitable concentration of
> the producing industry will make easy the protection
> of the innocent public.   Some such body as the present
> National Board of Censorship for Motion Pictures will
> be given legal power to review all productions and either
> delimit or forbid their circulation.[123]

A similar argument appeared in connection with radio in 1936, as
a writer for Education explained why radio had never been charged
with immorality. He claimed that radio had so long been a tenant of
the home that society had "from the very beginnings imposed a severe
restriction on subject matter and treatment."124 Hence, the influence was not directed solely from the media to the home; in addition,
the home influenced the new mass media.

Entertainment

I have already discussed two of the lines of argument which
proponents used to show the influence of the new media on existing
forms of entertainment. Recall, first, advocates' assurances that
the status quo would remain undisturbed by innovation; nothing
presently valued, they said, would be replaced by new inventions.
In addition, these writers argued that motion pictures, radio, and
television would in fact strengthen institutions, indirectly, by
furnishing them new audiences. Both of these arguments were applicable to the usual forms of amusement.

Proponents were not satisfied to rest their case on these
grounds. They apparently felt compelled to demonstrate that the
new media had, or would have, a direct and beneficial influence
on other entertainment. In so doing they were no doubt reacting
to the common presumption that the new media would compete with

all other forms of amusement. And it is true that on first view the case apparently lay with the opposition. It seemed reasonable that the introduction of new media would mean damage for the old when the functions of both were similar. What experience there was seemed to bear this out; writers who opposed innovation or who defended the status quo pointed to numerous instances in which harm had come to established amusements because of the competition of both motion pictures and broadcasting.

In comparison, the advocates had little to go on. It was difficult for them to demonstrate that the old amusements had been improved by the new, or even that the old were safe in light of the new competition. They were in the position of trying to explain that extreme and direct competition was a good thing for the institions most clearly threatened. Advocates, in addition, were uncertain about the kind of influences which might be expected from the new media, or even which of the usual amusements might be helped or hurt. Hence, each author did his best to explain how the new would benefit the old. This resulted not only in a great variety of argument as many areas were touched, but also in a lack of concensus among the advocates, and in the tendency for their comments to be highly speculative, diffuse, and shallow. The argument about the beneficial influences of movies, radio, and television on other forms of entertainment was an uncomfortable one for friends of the new media.

The legitimate theater was expected to benefit in a variety of ways. Some of the proponents argued that the new media were really the beginning of a new kind of theatre, which would serve to augment and supplement the existing legitimate companies without damaging them. For instance, silent pictures were described in 1908 as "the beginning of a true theater of the people," radio was said to have created a new theater in 1925, and talkies were said in 1929 to "make a real national theatre possible." Others said talkies and radio would create entirely new forms of dramatic expression, these also supplementary to the regular theatre. But in addition, pictures were predicted to influence the kind of dramatic writing common on the stage; plays, following the example of the movies, would concentrate on action and so eliminate the boredom of great stretches of dialogue. New sound recording methods growing out of talking pictures were said to have an obvious application to the stage. Pantomime was to be revived by the silent films and restored to its rightful place among the arts of acting. Broadway was to find new financial life in the backing of plays by the movie companies. The technical facilities of the legitimate theaters were to be expanded and enhanced by the introduction of new motion picture and radio production techniques. William DeMille argued that the technical capacity of the theatre was so increased by motion pictures that "not since Shakespeare's day has the dramatic

form been so fluid." George Parsons Lathrop even predicted in 1896
that motion pictures might be used, with a kind of rear-screen
projection, to provide stage scenery and so "take an important
position in heightening theatrical verisimilitude."125

Like the theatre, the actor also was to have new prosperity
because of innovation. But again, a variety of effects were predicted. Supporters of pictures argued that in films the actor would
not only be paid better than on the stage, but would have year
around work without the bother of traveling on the road. Actors
would gain valuable publicity from their appearances both in films
and on the radio. Actors in films, said George Bernard Shaw, could
concentrate on the creation of new roles; no longer would the actor
spend most of his time repeating old parts. With the coming of the
talkies, promoters asserted that finally the actor was getting
the recognition he deserved, and that the new medium would create
a great new demand for the stage-trained, technically proficient
actor. Radio, on the other hand, promised that actors would no
longer have to be handsome in order to be popular. Finally, advocates
of motion pictures--both silent and talkie--held out the hope that
performance on the screen would cause a return to what they called
a natural style of acting.126 Hence, while attackers of the media
agreed that the theater would be decimated, its actors stolen by

the newcomers, supporters of the movies and broadcasting stressed the benefits to actors and to the art of acting.

Both supporters of the media and writers interested primarily in music argued that the musical life of the nation would benefit from movies, radio, and television. Silent films were said to have introduced audiences to good music from the pit orchestras; to have opened new sources of income for musicians, and to have given valuable experience to young performers. The start of radio and the beginning of talkies were held to be even more beneficial to music and musicians. The musical film was called a new mode of musical expression. More music was used in dramatic films than ever before, and picture audiences were increasingly exposed to good music. A new musical consciousness was created among the public both by picture sound tracks and music broadcasts, and new work for conductors, musicians, and teachers was the result. Moreover, music teachers found their jobs easier because of the new musical intelligence of their pupils; the names of composers were less frequently mispronounced; and the sale of musical instruments seemed to reflect the new general interest in music. New symphonies were formed by broadcasting companies; great old songs became popular again; and people read more books about music than ever before.[127] In these many ways music prospered because of innovation.

A relatively large number of writers spoke of the beneficial
influence the media would have on opera. Thomas Edison predicted
that his talking pictures would permit the performance of an entire
grand opera on film. Radio News boasted that broadcasts had stimulated sales of opera recordings. Musical America told how radio
had brought in new money for the Metropolitan Opera while causing
it to become a more democratic art. Radio, talkies, and television
were all said to offer opera new technical freedom in staging and
performance, and television was said to be particularly good for
opera because of the eye appeal of the performance. In addition,
all three of the new media were said to make possible a new genre
of opera, commonly called intimate opera. Here the works would be
shorter, written particularly for the screen or for the air, and
intended to play up the unique capabilities both of opera and the
transmitting medium. Speaking of this form of opera, a writer for
North American Review said that with operas written for radio,
lovers no longer need to "bawl out tender sentiments at the top of
their lungs." Instead, composers could make use of the crooner,
"who gets closer to his audience than any concert singer. Then,
too, many singers with small, although beautiful voices would with
the intimate opera on radio "have the opportunity they have thus
far lacked."128 The application to opera would be obvious, and
the change was viewed by proponents as an improvement of the art form

Related to the influence of the media on music were comments about their expected influence on musical composition and on dramatic writing. Current Literature reported in 1908 that because of motion pictures "a new career has been opened to dramatists who are well received by the motion picture makers." But most commonly promoters expected musical composition to be stimulated. The need for new music for the talkies was predicted to stimulate new composition, and the prospect of filmed operas was thought to be a stimulus for the composition, by American composers, of new operas in English. Radio, said North American Review, had stimulated new compositions by young composers by playing their works on the air and by commissioning new works. And the promise of having their operas on television offered even greater stimulation to American composers.[129]

Promoters of the media also argued that radio and television, and occasionally movies, would have an important place in most sports. The association of the media with sports was natural, said some of the promoters, pointing as far back as 1899 when 198,000 feet of film was shot on the Jeffries-Sharkey fight at Coney Island. The American people were great sports fans, radio could give them scores and play by play reports, television brought them a ring side seat. Recognizing the objections which had been raised to radio in connection with sports, defenders argued that

radio would not hurt the gate, but instead would draw even more
spectators than had attended before broadcasts were initiated.
After nearly ten years association of television with sports,
promoters conceded that broadcasting had hurt some sports--minor
league baseball especially--but had proved to be an advantage to
sports in general. Finally, it was even suggested that sports
broadcasting might help the slumping movie industry by attracting
new spectators, at increased admissions, to theater TV coverage
of important sports events.130

While most of the writers concerned with the relationship
between silent and sound films and between sound films and television predicted in each case the old would be damaged or destroyed
by the new, a few of the promoters saw the relationship as beneficial.
For example, some writers argued that the introduction of sound
saved the motion picture from financial disaster, almost immediately
increasing attendance as much as twenty-five per cent. Others
said that sound had raised technical and artistic standards of the
movies. The public expected more of the talkies, and the industry
sought to meet the expectation. Television was likewise said to
have come to the aid of the motion picture industry by attracting
new audiences to some special pictures, for instance the Hopalong
Cassidy films which had been reintroduced on television; by stimulating new foreign business for motion pictures; and by forcing

the motion picture industry to higher artistic standards. In addition
to this, television also brought new income to the picture industry
through theater TV, in the re-runs of past Hollywood productions,
and in the use of Hollywood facilities for the production of filmed
television programs. Finally, television provided still another
source of income for the picture studios, for as <u>Saturday</u> <u>Evening</u> <u>Post</u>
commented in 1952, various picture companies were in the process
of buying up television stations.[131]

Some of the same arguments were used in connection with the
impact of television on radio. At one point in 1931, when radio
listenership was low, <u>Christian</u> <u>Century</u> suggested that perhaps
the new novelty, television, might revive audience interest in
broadcasting in general. Later, after television was established,
<u>Changing</u> <u>Times</u> argued that the competition of television had been
good for radio, despite the apparent damage, for it had forced radio
people to re-evaluate their medium and had led them to begin doing
what was unique to radio and what television could not do as well.
In effect, television forced radio to find its place in society.[132]

These, then, were the arguments which appeared when defenders
of motion pictures, radio, and television tried to demonstrate that
traditional entertainment would benefit from innovation. As I have
pointed out before in other contexts, these arguments reflect, as
much as anything else, the hopes of the writers for the established

institutions. The new media offered another chance for existing

forms to be improved, for them to be made into what their supporters

hoped they might become. At the same time, by showing that movies,

radio, and TV did have a good influence on respected institutions,

advocates gained support for the objects of their concern. The new

was linked in praiseworthy fashion to institutions which, in reflect-

ing society's goals, had long been accepted as worthwhile and valu-

able. Innovation, said its friends, truly served to make good things

even better.

Concession

Soon after motion pictures, radio, and television were intro-

duced, it became clear that they were not only strong competitors

for established amusements but were potential sources of trouble

for other social institutions as well. Attackers called attention

to the obvious competition in their arguments. Consequently, advo-

cates were obliged to account for the apparent damages if they were

to pursue their former line that innovation was good for social

institutions. To meet the objections of the opposition, both

implicit and explicit, and to account for the fact that the new

media did cause modification in established institutions, some of

the advocates turned to arguments from concession. That is, they

agreed that movies, radio, or television had caused changes in social institutions, but went on to argue either that the changes were only temporary or that they would be ultimately beneficial. Three variations on this pattern were employed.

Temporary Damage

In the simplest of the concession arguments, advocates asserted that while institutions might have suffered because of the new media, the damage was only temporary, and once the novelty of the new wore off, the institutions would return to normal operation. These arguments appeared during the early stages of each medium, at a point when there had been time enough to observe that the medium was influential, but before sufficient time had passed to determine what the long range effects would be. The writers who used this line of argument represented both the new media and the threatened institutions. They were confident that the new media would not permanently damage established forms, and in effect offered audiences a kind of reassurance about the safety of tradition.

The line of argument was first used in connection with the influence of motion pictures on the stage. In 1911, after commenting that the theatre had reached its lowest point in thirty years, Robert Grau argued that while pictures were at first hurting "legitimate style drama," they would eventually train new audiences for the living stage and become the salvation of the theatre.

Varying the substance of the argument, Alfred Kuttner argued in
New Republic in 1915 that while pictures had caused a temporary
deterioration in the quality of legitimate plays as authors tried
to imitate motion picture technique on the stage, the theatre would
soon discard the innovations and return to its former high standards.
Speaking of the influence of radio on the church, a Presbyterian
paper quoted in Literary Digest in 1922 conceded that while congregations might shrink for a time after religious services were put
on the air, they would soon come back to the church because to
hear a service only would "not fulfill to any soul conscious of
its spiritual needs the ministry of the congregation of the house
of God." The executive director of the National Music League offered
similar reassurance to readers concerend that radio would permanently
deplete concert audiences, arguing that while the broadcasts might
mean a temporary dwindling of patronage, listeners would soon realize
that radio did not replace the real thing "and the concert halls
will fill again with an audience many times larger than before."[133]
When talking pictures arrived, concern was expressed that the new
device, if it did not kill the silent screen, would at least limit
the freedom and the expressiveness of the former mode. One answer
to the fear was this one from Helena Huntington Smith in Outlook
and Independent:

> Temporarily, beyond a doubt, talking has destroyed the
> screen's incentive to visual expression and just so far

it has superseded the art of the screen. But I am unable
to see how this state of things will last. For the
law of all dramatic expression, whether for stage or
screen, it to tell the story in terms of action first.
. . . Nearly all the flexibility of the old medium can be
restored, once the producers get over their present idea
that nothing matters except talk. . . . In the movie of
the future, as in real life, people will not need to
talk their heads off.[134]

And television seemed to pose the greatest threat of all, to all

institutions. Advocates and institutional spokesmen hurriedly

assured all interested that the damage was only temporary. Once

the novelty of television wore off, they said, people would return

to reading books, to attending concerts, to going to movies, to

watching baseball games at the ball park, and even to talking to

each other.

In this argument promoters explicitly recognized that the

theatre, reading, sports, family activities, conversation, the

church, even motion pictures and radio, and virtually all other

activities in which people engaged for amusement, relaxation, or

profit were apt to be upset to some degree by innovation. The

danger, however, was to be only temporary. Once accustomed to the

new, people would return to former pursuits, institutions would

regain strength, and things in general would return to normal.

Hence, promoters of the media, and spokesmen for threatened insti-

tutions offered assurances of the stability of familiar things.

Moreover, they contended, there was a strong, but only temporary

attraction to that which was new and unusual. In the long run the
mechanical reproduction of familiar arts and amusements would never
satisfactorily substitute for the real thing.

Weakness Eliminated

In the second argument from concession, advocates and institutional spokesmen argued that innovation would cause, or had
caused, damage only to those institutions, or parts of institutions,
which were undesirable in the first place. That is, they said in
effect that what was harmed was bad to begin with and was, consequently, no great loss. On the other hand, they continued to offer
assurance that nothing valuable, nothing of substance, nothing
good had been hurt. Innovation served to prune away dead wood,
eliminating both trees and branches which should have gone long
before. The effect, ultimately, was beneficial, and desirable
institutions were strengthened as a result of innovation.

This was the argument used to justify the influence of motion
pictures on saloons. The defenders of movies, presuming that it
was better for the working man to spend his nickel in the nickelodeon than for beer in the corner saloon, contended that pictures
had served society well by reducing the patronage of bars. As
early as 1907 Barton Currie in Harper's reported approval that
"even now some of the saloon-keepers are complaining that they

/̶m̶o̶t̶i̶o̶n̶ ̶p̶i̶c̶t̶u̶r̶e̶s̶/ injure their trade."135 The next year Lucy

France Pierce argued that

> in three years' time the nickelodeon has in truth become
> both a clubhouse and an academy for the workingman.
> Saloonkeepers have protested excitedly against its perma-
> nent establishment as a menace to their trade. The
> saloon has lost its hypocritical and pious cloak as the
> workingman's club. The nickelodeon now beckons to the
> saloon's former patrons with arguments too strong to be
> withstood.136

In 1910, William Inglis defended pictures by quoting Professor

Simon N. Patton who

> after much study gave his opinion that the nickelodeons
> were 'the first cheap amusement to occupy the economic
> plane that the saloon has so long exclusively control-
> led. . . . To close the moving picture theatre would
> be to leave the fivecent pleasure-seekers with no alter-
> native but the saloon or the street.'137

This line of argument became one of the common defenses for

silent films, and was repeated regularly between 1910 and 1926

in Independent, Outlook, Harper's Monthly, New Republic, Current

Opinion (in an editorial), and Photo-Era. The writers who used

it agreed that movies had hurt the saloon, but concluded that the

damage was beneficial to society. This statement from Photo-Era,

although longer than some of the other comments, will illustrate

the kind of argument which later defenders employed.

> With further reference to the social influences
> of the motion picture, an incident may be mentioned
> which took place in a conversation with a man who has
> charge of a motion-picture theater in a small town in
> the ranching country of western Texas. He said, 'Tell
> 'em the movies are here to stay. Look up the street

there. You can still see the signs on two or three
buildings which were used as saloons or gambling-
places. There were several more, but the buildings
have been occupied by others who have torn down the old
signs. Before I opened up this show, those were the
only places in this place a man could go when the day's
work was over. When I opened this place, men who had
never been keen about saloons or gambling-places, but who
had frequented them because they were the only places
to go, began coming here instead. Others followed and
soon all but a certain set were coming more or less
regularly. Even before the War and prohibition some of
the saloons had to close down because they didn't get
enough trade to keep a'going and I think this show had
a lot to do with it. Yes, sir. You can tell 'em that
the movies are here to stay.[138]

Movies were thus defended by reference to damage they had

caused. In this case, however, the institution hurt was one looked

upon with distaste by the writers who employed the line of argument.

The argument was essentially causal in nature, but in the implicit

comparison contained in the substance movies were judged to be of

greater worth than the saloons they replaced. Benefits to society

as a whole resulted from damage to one of its parts.

But the line of argument was not limited to discussions of

the impact of innovation on undesirable institutions. It was

available to any advocates of the media who needed to justify apparent

damages to valued institutions, and to spokesmen for institutions

who needed to rationalize changes caused by innovation. These

writers interpreted as beneficial many of the changes which attackers

described as hurtful. Hence, instead of bemoaning the death of melo-

drama, John Collier in 1908 argued that the principal effect of the nickelodeon had been to drive out the old time crass melodrama, a distinct improvement in terms of theatre. Robert Grau praised the movie because it had "driven mediocre theatrical companies off the road." D. W. Griffith argued that through the motion pic- ture science had "come to the rescue of those typical Americans in small places" by freeing them from dependence on "a chilly theater and a backward play . . . /with/ inadequate scenery" for entertainment. Still other writers contended that movies had ended the theatre's dependence on popular business, popular plays, and the mass audience, all of which they termed beneficial. By luring away some of the actors and producers, movies were said to have freed the theatre from the encumbrance of poor actors, incompetent performers, and quick moneymakers. And Jesse Lasky argued in 1920 that movies had served theater well by eliminating the fourth class road companies which got "$2.00 a seat in Keokuk," and by killing the road shows of Broadway failures which made money in one night stands only because the audience did not know how bad the show was until they had seen it.[139]

The same argument was used with respect to other institutions. When sound pictures overran Hollywood, their promoters argued that talkies signalled the end of incompetent acting, the shiek types who had gained popularity with the silents, the title cliches such as "Came the Dawn," and the troubles connected with exporting

motion pictures. Television was praised by some for having eliminated both the B pictures and the mass audience. John Crosby,
generally somewhat more moderate in his predictions, still argued
in 1950 that just as silent pictures had cut off the road companies,
melodrama, "and the rest of the riff raff which the movies could
supply cheaper," so television would have the same effect on talking
pictures and possibly also on books, magazines, and newspapers.
But, he emphasized, television would destroy none of the older
media even though it did eliminate some of their functions. When
attackers expressed concern about the influences of radio and television on reading, advocates contended that only light, pastime,
or marginal reading would suffer. Non-fiction and "good reading"
would survive.[140] Saturday Review went so far as to argue that
no respectable publication would suffer, but that the light stuff
would merely move to radio thus freeing available space for weightier
materials.

> In all probability the radio--pocket, auto, and
> library table--will eventually take over much, though
> by no means all, so-called light fiction of the rental
> library variety, leaving the better books a freer field
> to attract good readers. Many Westerns, many boy-and-
> girls stories, many detective stories, most sermons on
> economics and politics, most books that comment on cur-
> rent events, most popular science, all simple lyric and
> narrative poetry, will find a happy home on the radio.
> What would be left would be real books. The radio
> can talk about them, but not give them. They must be
> written--and read.[141]

If any reading suffered, said Good Housekeeping, it would be only

the comics, abandoned in favor of TV. Among newspapers, the new

mass media menaced only those which served headline readers, for

example, the "800,000 'readers' of the Daily News in New York, in

which there is nothing to read." Similarly, all that was to be

eliminated in music were mediocre and incompetent musicians along

with old-fashioned operas. Nor were two of radio's stalwarts

--the mediocre comedian and the daytime serial--to survive the

advent of television.[142]

All of the things which were hurt, promoters argued, were

institutional millstones. If they disappeared as a result of

changes forced by innovation, they would none of them be missed.

Innovation was therefore damaging only to the worst elements of

social institutions; what was good in them would survive unscathed.

The basic function and character of the institution would remain

unchanged.

Institutional Revision

A third type of argument from concession recognized the prospect

of broad and often basic changes in the structure and function of

certain established institutions. The anticipation of these drastic

changes distinguished these arguments from the ones studied before.

There, advocates assured readers that institutions would retain

their familiar character despite pressure from the new. Here,
however, writers expected that innovation would result in fundamental
changes in the nature of the theatre and radio broadcasting. Still,
they argued, the ultimate results would be good.

This line of argument was used most frequently in connection
with theatre. Spokesmen for both the media and the theatre recognized that the competition of new amusements had caused extensive
changes in the traditional role of the theatre. No longer, after the
beginning of motion pictures, was the theatre the nation's popular
amusement. The mass audience had turned to other entertainment.
There was talk, which I will discuss in the following chapter, of
the theatre's going under. In this situation advocates still argued
that the introduction of the new media would prove beneficial to the
old art.

There are two views of the situation. First, some of the
writers, especially those who considered the theatre an aristocratic
institution which should have limited popular appeal, believed
that the loss of the mass audience would leave theatre free to
develop what they called the true art of the drama. Others--theatre
businessmen, some critics, and media representatives--held that the
new circumstances forced the theatre to seek new fields lest it
die. Nevertheless, both groups offered similar proposals for
adaptation to the new circumstances.

First, the theatre could turn to intellectual drama which was
unavailable in other amusements. This was proposed by Walter
Prichard Eaton in 1914, who said that in the face of the competition from silent films the theatre should "more and more concentrate
upon modern realistic plays with an intellectual drift, or upon
poetry." That is, the theatre should concentrate upon the plays
of "Shaw and Barrie and Galsworthy and a hundred other modern
dramatists /whose work/ can no more be adapted into films than gold
can be transmuted into tin." A year later, Eaton argued that the
result of the competition was "bound to be that the theater will
become more intellectually aristocratic, more a pastime of the
educated, while the movies will more definitely segregate the
masses." George Bernard Shaw said in 1915 that films were so
successful in their competition with theatre that they would drive
the spoken drama "to its highest ground and close all paths to it
except those in which its true glory lies--that is, the path of
high human utterances of great thoughts and great wit, of poesy and
of prophecy, or as some of our more hopelessly prosaic critics
call it, the Path of Talk."[143] Robert Anderson, writing in _Illus-
trated World_ in 1916, wondered how much longer the theatre might
survive.

> The answer is that in the places where the legitimate
> drama competes directly with the celluloid, the legiti-
> mate drama must surrender. That is the decision of the
> box office balance sheet. The truth of the matter is that in

the places where there is such competition, the movie
has already gained a large ascendency, the transformation
being in the main painless. Theaters have merely shifted
over to being moving picture houses, and there has been
little fuss or flurry connected with it.[144]

Left for the legitimate theatre was the drama of intellectual appeal,

the works of Ibsen, Strindberg, Synge, Shaw, and Galsworthy, writers

who depended upon the play of ideas rather than plot action.

Talkies were expected to be even more damaging to the theatre

than the silent films had been. Again, writers proposed that the

theatre either would be free for intellectual plays, or forced to

them. Richard Dana Skinner, for example, argued in 1929 that because

of talkies "the entertainment industry . . . is definitely passing

from the stage to the screen, leaving the true art of the theatre

a new freedom for development and an audience of its own." Like-

wise, Brooks Atkinson expressed satisfaction that the movies had

taken over the job of entertaining the masses. The theatre, he

argued, would be left free for better things. Nation, in 1929,

predicted that movies "may compel the theater to confine itself

to those things with which Hollywood and celluloid cannot compete,

and perhaps that would be just as well." And Jesse L. Lasky wrote

in Collier's that just as silent films had reduced the scope of the

legitimate theatre, so talkies would change the function of the

stage. In his view, "the so-called legitimate stage will, in the

new order of things, become even more of a strictly metropolitan institution than it is now," and as such would be doing "opera and those classics which are not attempted by the movies."[145]

A second possible course of action for the theatre was to turn to expressionistic or experimental drama, leaving realism and melodrama to the movies. This was proposed as another alternative by Eaton in 1914, who wrote that, in regard even to scenery,

> just because the camera can be carried so easily far
> afield, to show mountains and gorges, rivers and caverns,
> deserts and jungles, which all people love to look upon
> and which the pasteboard stage of the theater can never
> hope to depict with a thousandth part of the camera's
> realism, it is more than likely that the old-fashioned
> spectacular play will fall more and more into disrepute,
> and the drama will more and more concentrate upon . . .
> that form of scenery which is not realistic but consci-
> ously artificial, calculated to achieve a decorative or
> suggestive effect.[146]

New Republic argued that because talkies had taken over much of the audience, the theatre was finally left free for experimentation.[147] Nation explained the situation in this fashion:

> If the legitimate stage is to survive (as we think it
> will), it will have to appeal to a more intelligent
> audience than the talkies and it will have to take much
> greater commercial risks. In brief, it will have to
> become 'experimental,' to bear much the same relation
> to the talkies as an institution as the Theatre Guild
> was originally intended to bear to the ordinary commer-
> cial theatre on Broadway.[148]

Similarly, Theresa Helburn argued in 1937 that the future of the theatre lay along experimental lines. She contended that

> the silent movies did not encroach on the theater to
> any great degree, but with the invention of 'talkies,'
> the preeminence of the theater was doomed. As a business

it fell to second place, and, with the rise of radio
to third. Today the theater is bad business and an
increasingly difficult one. Its only hope is as an
art.[149]

The theatre, then, was faced with a changing function due to the

pressures of the new mass media. One possibility for its continu-

ation lay in empahsis on intellectual drama, the other in experi-

mental drama. Both forms, advocates thought, would appeal to the

limited audience left for the living stage.

There was still a third possibility. John Dos Passos argued

that since the theatre of 1930 actually served as "a laboratory

and a try-out place for the talkies," it should turn to social

commentary. Perhaps, he said, it would be good if the old theatre

died, good if the financial crisis wrecked Broadway entirely, for

then a new theatre of social concern could be begun. Then,

> through the theatre socially constructive ideas could
> reach the wider field of the talkies. By socially con-
> structive ideas I don't mean little bedtime readings
> from Marx and Engles; I mean the new myth that's got
> to be created to replace the imperialist prosperity
> myth if the machinery of American life is ever to be
> gotten under social control. If the theatre isn't a
> transformer for the deep high-tension currents of his-
> tory, it's deader than cock fighting.[150]

Out of the ashes of the conventional theatre, through the medium

of the talking picture, there might grow a theatre of social utility.

Just as other writers expressed their dreams for the theatre in the

arguments they devised in defense of it, so Dos Passos proposed

another alternative mode of action for the drama.

This type of argument from concession was also used by supporters
of radio who said the same kinds of things which had been said about
theatre. For example, Business Week in 1953 argued that television
had killed radio as a national pastime, forcing it to turn to local
programming. But the changes had added new strength and vitality
to the medium. Howard Becker in New Republic contended that when
the big money and the big audiences deserted radio, control eased
also and performers gained new freedom of expression. This meant
to him that "the announcers and disc jockeys are allowed a large
amount of freedom in what they say and play."[151] Walter Goodman
broadcasting critic for New Republic, said that television was
a catastrophe for radio, for radio had too long depended on the
very kinds of things that television did much better visually.
But there was hope in catastrophe.

> Unable to compete in the big-time entertainment circuit,
> radio may look into its own potentialities for the things
> it can do better than the other media but has never had
> to do before. Hooper ratings have lost their charm,
> radio will be able to direct its appeal to more limited
> but more particular audiences. The ingredients: music
> of all sorts, technically superior and intelligently
> varied, with fewer interruptions for commercials; talks
> on subjects which a medium catering to mass audience
> whims could ever dare to touch; imaginatively conceived
> dramatic shows, written to be heard, not seen; prose and
> poetry readings by ugly or camera shy actors.[152]

Radio, no longer saddled with the masses, could turn for support to
a small but superior audience who sought intellectual stimulation
rather than mere entertainment. Advocates thus chose explanations

for the changing status of radio which permitted them to maintain their position that despite the damage caused by it, innovation was in the end a good thing.

Three general lines are apparent in the case built by the advocates. First, they offered reassurance that familiar and valued institutions would not be destroyed by innovation. Tradition would be preserved despite changes. Second, promoters argued that society's institutions, in which were reflected its values, would be strengthened by the new mass media. Innovation might result in change, but the change served to benefit the institutions. Good things, they said, would be made better. Finally, advocates conceded that damage had been done to institutions by the new media. But even the damage, which might be only temporary, would be ultimately beneficial. Because of the changes wrought by innovation, the deadwood was eliminated from institutions, they were freed from past encumbrances and elevated to higher purposes. If damage did occur, the results were worth it. Innovation, everything taken into account, was good for society's institutions.

Notes

1. Out, 3 Mr '15, p. 499; Ind, 13 F '13, p. 356.

2. CO, Ap '19, p. 234.

3. LD, 18 Mr '22, p. 13.

4. Educa, D '36, p. 217.

5. Educa, Je '40, p. 654; SEP, 27 Jl '29, p. ;2.

6. Nat, 29 Jl '44, p. 127. See also, RR, Je '07, pp. 680, 685; AmMag, S '13, p. 60; RR, D '14, p. 726; Educa, F '15, p. 361; Out, 3 Mr '15, p. 499; SAS, 14 S '15, p. 147; IW, Ja '16, p. 662; NAR, My '17, p. 450; CO, Je '20, p. 794; NAR, Jl '20, pp. 86, 92; Ind, 12 Jl '19, p. 64; LD, 9 Jl '21, p. 23; SEP, 15 Ap '22, p. 6; IW, Je '22, p. 500; AmMag, Je '22, p. 70; Col, 10 Je 22, p. 9; RR, Ag '22, p. 167; RR, S '22, p. 307; SA, Ja '23, p. 19; CO, Ap '23, p. 457; Col, 3 My '24, p. 28; Cent, Je '24, p. 154; LD, 9 Ag '24, p. 11; NR, 8 0 '24, p. 136; SEP, 6 D '24, p. 82; AmMag, M '26, p. 170. SEP, 14 Ag '26, p. 103; LD, 25 S '26, p. 28; Ind, 9 Jl '27, p. 34; NR, 26 0 '27, p. 251; RR, N '27, p. 520; Ind, 25 F '28, p. 172; SA, Mr '28, p. 247; Scrib, Mr '28, p. 628; NAR, 0 '28, p. 433; PMech, N '28, p. 822; SEP, 9 Mr '29, p. 132; Col, 25 My '29, p. 8; SA, Je '29, p. 527; SEP, 15 Je '29, p. 10; PE, Jl '29, p. 46; Scrib, Jl '29, p. 2; TA, S '29, p. 636; SEP, 21 S '29, p. 136; Comm, 7 Mr '30, p. 23; NR, 7 My '30, p. 314; LA, 15 My '30, p. 349; Nat, 27 Ag '30, p. 216; Out, 31 D '30. p. 693; RR, M '32, p. 31; SA, Mr '32, p. 284; Col, 30 N '35, p. 10; SR, 15 F '36, p. 8; NAR, Mr '36, p. 54; Scrib, F '37, pp. 64-65; NAR, Summer '37, p. 241; Etude, Je '37, p. 359; Nat, 5 F '38, p. 155; SEP, 20 My '39, p. 104; Nat, 6 Ap '40, p. 448; SD, Ja '46, p. 9; AmMerc, Ja '47, p. 341; CC, 10 S '47, p. 1079; Etude, Je '49, p. 342; SA, S '49, p. 26; HB, F '50, p. 126; Educa, Je '51, p. 601; SEP, 7 F '53, p. 35; ChgT, F '54, p. 41; SEP, 12 Mr '55, p. 33; Nat, 5 N '55, p. 378.

7. Ind, 6 F '08, p. 308; TW, Mr '13, p. 20; SEP, 14 F '53, p. 112.

8. SA, 4 Je '21, p. 449; LD, 9 Jl '21, p. 23; Cent, Je '24, p. 153; AmMag, Je '22, p. 72; AmMag, Jl '21, p. 32; RR, F '25, p. 203; Col, 10 Je '22, p. 18; Col, 8 Ap '22, p. 3; SEP, 18 Ap '25, p. 185; NAR, Summer '38, p. 300; LD, 3 N '28, p. 29; Scrib, Ap '23, p. 410; AmMag, Ja '29, p. 15.

9. NAR, Mr '36, p. 55.

10. LD, 23 Ap '27, p. 7.

11. Nat, 13 O '51, p. 297.

12. TA, D '53, p. 88. See also, WW, F '11, p. 14031; CO, Mr '17, p. 185; LD, 11 Ag '17, p. 26; CO, Ag '18, p. 99; LD, 4 F '22, p. 32; RR, Ap '22, p. 339; IW, Mr '22, p. 37; CO, My '22, p. 649; RR, S '22, p. 306; RR, Ja '24, p. 3; NR, 19 Mr '24, p. 92; SEP, 17 My '24, p. 109; Out, 23 Jl '24, p. 427; CO, Ag '24, p. 202; LD, 9 Ag '24, p. 11; SEP, 23 Ag '24, p. 20; RR, S '24, p. 237; NR, 8 O '24, p. 135; RR, F '25, p. 170; SA, Jl '26, p. 53; Col, 3 Jl '26, p. 16; SEP, 7 Ag '26; p. 103; LD, 25 S '26, p. 28; Scrib, My '28, p. 631; RR, Jl '28, p. 88; RR, N '28, p. 555; RR, F '29, p. 132; Col, 25 Mr '29, p. 72; Mus, Je '29, p. 18; Nat, 5 Je '29, p. 671; RR, My '30, p. 92; LA, 1 Jl '30, p. 554; Comm, 2 Jl '30, p. 266; RR, S '30, p. 66; LA, Mr '31, p. 95; Comm, 30 N '34, p. 139; NAR, F '35, p. 145; Nwk, 1 D '34, p. 27; NAR, S '35, p. 278; SSoc, 22 Ag '36, p. 231; Atlan, My '37, p. 541; Etude, S '43, p. 557; SS, 18 Mr '46, p. 20; GH, Ja '49, p. 143; MusAm, F '49, p. 11; Nwk, 18 Ap '49, p. 78; CC, 11 My '49, p. 591; Etude, Je '49, p. 341; ParM, D '52, p. 300; USN, 2 S '55, p. 44; Nat, 5 N '55, p. 378.

13. Col, 12 Ap '13, p. 11.

14. Ind, 17 Jl '13, p. 143; AmMag, Mr '24, p. 60.

15. CO, Ap '23, p. 457.

16. TM, Ja '30, p. 30. See also, AmMag, S '09, p. 500; Lip, Ag '13, p. 191; AmMag, S '13, p. 60; HW, 6 Je '14, p. 20; AmMag, O '14, p. 96; Col, 28 F '20, p. 16; SEP, 6 D '24, p. 82; CO, Mr '25, p. 330; Scrib, Ap '29, p. 373.

17. Col, 23 Ag '24, p. 10; Col, 24 S '27, p. 32; AmMag, N '28, p. 15; HM, Ap '33, p. 559; NR, 1 D '52, p. 13. See also, SEP, 2 F '29, p. 141; Forum, Ap '29, p. 215; HM, N '52, p. 28.

18. Educa, Je '13, p. 625; Col, 28 F '20, p. 16; LD, 29 Ja '21,
p. 35; CO, My '22, p. 649; AmMag, Je '22, p. 72; CO, O '23, p. 471;
CO, Ag '24, p. 202; Nat, 24 D '24, p. 700; NAR, O '28, p. 431;
PE, Ja '29, p. 103; PE, Jl '29, p. 46; PE, Ja '30, p. 48; Out,
31 D '30, p. 692; NR, 19 F '40 , p. 237; SR, 8 Je '40, p. 12;
SR, 19 F '44, p. 28; NB, Je '49, p. 42; PW, 6 Ja '51, p. 38; LJ,
15 F '52, p. 305; Nat, 5 N '55, p. 379.

19. Sur, 21 O '11, p. 1060; AmMag, Jl '22, p. 64; PE, Jl '29,
p. 46; LD, 27 Ja '33, p. 35; Nwk, 27 O '47, p. 82; CC, 2 F '49,
p. 143.

20. PE, Jl '29, p. 46.

21. AmMag, Jl '22, p. 65.

22. Col, 27 S '47, p. 28.

23. AmMag, Mr '48, p. 105.

24. HW, 13 Je 1891, p. 447; PE, N '08, p. 231; HM, Ja '19,
p. 184; Col, 8 Ap '22, p. 4; AmMag, Ja '29, p. 15; Ind, 17 O '12,
p. 890; SEP, 20 Je '28, p. 130; SS, 18 Mr '46, p. 3. See also,
PE, O '08, p. 162; WT, O '08, p. 1052; WW, My '10, p. 12876; Col,
12 Ap '13, p. 11; WW, My '13, p. 35; Out, 17 Ja '14, p. 121; Nat,
6 Ag '14, p. 154; Out, 22 Ag '14, p. 970; RR, D '14, p. 725; Educa,
F '15, p. 355; CO, O '18, p. 234; PE, Ap '19, p. 178; CO, Ap '19,
p. 234; RR, Ap '22, p. 401; LD, 10 Je '22, p. 27; Cent, O '26,
p. 670; Out, 11 Ap '28, p 576; Scrib, Ag '28, p. 160; RR, N '28,
p. 555; HM, N '31, p. 724; RR, Mr '32, p. 32; LD, 21 Jl '34, p. 24;
SSoc, 3 D '38, pp. 723, 724; ParM, N '49, p. 58; Schlastic Teacher,
1 N '50, p. 21T; NR, 26 F '51, p. 18; Educa, Je '51, p. 600; Nat,
13 O '51, p. 297; USN, 2 S '55, p. 36.

25. SA, 21 Mr '08, p. 199; SAS, 30 Ja '09, p. 76; RR, S '10,
pp. 316, 317.

26. HW, 4 N '11, p. 8.

27. HW, 4 N '11, p. 8.

28. RR, D '14, p. 725.

29. Out, 22 Ag '14, p. 968.

30. CO, Ap '19, p. 234.

31. Col, 3 Ja '25, p. 14.

32. Col, 21 F '25, pp. 20, 21. See also, WW, My '13, p. 39; Educa, Je '13, p. 625.

33. WW, My '13, p. 40.

34. RR, D '14, p. 726; CO, D '22, p. 708.

35. RR, Ja '23, p. 78.

36. RR, Ja '23, p. 77.

37. SA, Je '29, p. 527.

38. LD, 21 Jl '34, p. 24.

39. LD, 21 Jl '34, p. 24; AmMerc, Ja '47, p. 36. See also, HW, 13 Je 1891, p. 447; SA, 20 Je 1891, p. 393; SA, 21 Mr '08, p. 199; SAS, 30 Ja '09, p. 76; RR, S '10, p. 317; WW, F '11, p. 14031; CO, Ag '14, p. 105; Nat, 6 Ag '14, p. 154; Ind, 5 F '17, p. 218; RR, Jl '20, p. 108; PE, Ap '19, p. 178; PE, S '29, p. 161; PE, Ja '30, p. 59; RR, Ap '27, p. 398.

40. LD 10 Je '22, p. 27.

41. Cent, 0 '26, p. 670.

42. Cent, 0 '26, p. 671; Cent, Je '29, p. 218. See also, RR, F '25, p. 170; RR, Ap '26, p. 434.

43. CC, 15 Ap '31, p. 512; SSoc, 1 0 '38, p. 432.

44. SSoc, 1 0 '38, p. 432

45. NB, Jl '47, p. 74; Etude, Je '49, p. 342; SS, 20 S '50, p. 21; Educa, 0 '50, p. 127; Scholastic Teacher, 1 N '50, p. 21T; SEP, 12 Mr '55, p. 136. See also, USN, 2 S '55, pp. 40, 42.

46. HW, 4 N '11, p. 8.

47. CO, Ap '19, p. 235.

48. HM, '12, p. 636; Ind, 19 Ja '14, p. 104.

49. Out, 27 Je '14, p. 445.

50. Out, 26 Ja '21, p. 137. See also, Ind, 17 0 '12, p. 890; WW, My '13, p. 42; Educa, Je '13, p. 625; LD, 4 0 '13, p. 576; Out. 22 Ag '14, p. 970; Ind, 28 F '16, p. 311; PE, Ap '19, p. 178; LD, 29 Ja '21, p. 35; Col, 21 F '25, p. 21; PE, 0 '26, p. 177; PE, F '29, p. 103.

51. CO, Ap '19, p. 234.

52. Col, 2 Ja '25, p. 14.

53. Col, 21 F '25, p. 21.

54. Out, 25 N '25, p. 424; SA, Je '29, p. 527; PE, S '29, p. 161; LD, 21 Jl, '34, p. 24. See also, Out, 22 Ag '14, p. 970; CO, Ap '19, p. 234; Col, 3 Ja '25, p. 14.

55. PE, S '27, p. 164.

56. SEP, 15 Ap '22, p. 7; AmMag, Je '22, p. 70; AAA, Ja 41, p. 152. See also, Cent, 0 '26, p. 670; AmMag, Ja '29, p. 101; NR, 23 0 '29, p. 259; RR, S '30, p. 66; SSoc, 1 0 '38, p. 432; USN, 2 S '55, p. 42.

57. Cent, 0 '26, p. 671; AmMag, Ja '29, p. 15; RR, S '30, p. 67.

58. An excellent survey of the Schools of the Air is contained in Carroll Atkinson, Radio Programs Intended for Classroom Use (Boston: Meador Publishing Company, 1942), pp. 11-93. Typical comments about educational broadcasting may be found in, CC, 8 Ap '31, pp. 478-479; SSoc, 22 Ag '36, pp. 225-231; Educa, D '36, pp. 214-217.

59. SEP, 7 Ag '26, p. 103.

60. NR, 23 0 '29, p. 259. See also, Col, 10 Je '22, p. 9; RR, '25, p. 127; Cent, 0 '26, p. 671; AmMag, Ja '29, p. 100.

61. Educa, Je '13, p. 620; WW, My '13, p. 40; Out, 22 Ag '14, p. 936.

62. SA, D '22, p. 379; AmMag, Ja '29, p. 101; SSoc, 22 Ag '36, p. 235.

63. SR, 26 Ag '50, p. 29.

64. Time, 21 Ag '50, p. 44; SNL, 27 S '52, p. 200; SEP, 12 Mr '55, p. 137; Col, 10 Je '22, p. 9; RR, F '25, p. 127; SSoc, 1 O '38, p. 432; NR, 26 F '51, p. 18.

65. LD, 21 Jl '06, p. 80; SA, 21 Mr '08, p. 199; PE, F '29, p. 101; LD, 17 Ag '29, p. 36; PE, F '30, p. 64.

66. PE, F '29, p. 101.

67. SD, N '45, p. 32. See also, LD, 29 Ja '10, p. 185; HW, 25 D '15, p. 620; Col, 20 S '47, p. 20; USN, 2 S '55, p. 48.

68. SA, 20 Je 1891, p. 393; RR, Mr '32, p. 31; WW, My '10, p. 12876; WW, F '11, p. 14031; CO, Je '15, p. 411; NR, 23 My '28, p. 7; RD, Ag '36, p. 4; Life, 29 Ap '40, p. 36.

69. SEP, 7 Ag '26, p. 98; TA, F '51, p. 47. See also, LD, 9 Ag '24, p. 11; RR, Jl '28, p. 87; RR, Jl '29, p. 142; RR, S '30, p. 66; RR, Ap '32, p. 12; SR, 9 Ag '52, p. 20; Nat, 16 Ag '52, p. 131; HM, N '52, p. 33; Amer, 26 Je '54, p. 329; USN, 2 S '55, p. 37.

70. NR, 3 S '24, p. 9; AmMag, N '28, p. 156.

71. SR, 9 Ag '52, p. 20.

72. Nat, 16 Ag '52, p. 131; HM, N '52, p. 30. See also, Nat, 25 Mr '25, p. 325; HM, Ap '33, p. 559.

73. CO, My '24, p. 731.

74. SR, 9 Ag '52, p. 20. See also, NR, 19 Mr '24, p. 91; Scrib, My '28, p. 631; Cent, Je '24, p. 153; Forum, Ap '29, p. 214; SEP, 15 Je '29, p. 10; HM, N '52, p. 28; RD, Mr '54, p. 144; USN, 2 S '55, p. 37.

75. NR, 8 O '24, p. 135; SEP, 17 My '24, p. 11; RR, Ap '29, p. 88; SR, 9 Ag '52, p. 20.

76. SEP, 23 Ag '24, p. 20.

77. Cent, Je '24, p. 153.

78. NR, 23 My '28, p. 7; Forum, Ap '29, p. 215; SR, 9 Ag '52, p. 20.

79. RR, N '28, p. 496.

80. Forum, Ap '29, p. 215. See also, NAR, Mr '36, p. 56.
This line of argument was also applied twice to music, the writers
contending that radio and movies revealed the fundamental nature of
musical performances just as it revealed the true character of the
speaker. See, LD, 18 My '29, p. 27; LD, 7 Ja '33, p. 16.

81. SEP, 27 Jl '29, p. 134; SEP, 16 Mr '46, p. 23; AmMag, Mr
'48, p. 107.

82. GH, N '50, p. 263.

83. RD, J '51, p. 5.

84. AmMag, Ap '52, p. 111.

85. Nwk, 14 Mr '55, p. 28. See also, CO, My '24, p. 731;
TA, F '51, p. 48; Col, 13 O '51, p. 74.

86. Forum, Ap '29, p. 215; RR, Ap '29, p. 88; TA, F '51, p. 48;
AmMag, Ap '52, p. 111. See also, SEP, 20 My '39, p. 106; Nwk,
14 Mr '55, p. 28.

87. SEP, 23 Ag '24, p. 20; Forum, Ap '29, p. 215; RD, Ja '51,
p. 4; AmMag, Ap '52, p. 109; SEP, 2 F '29, p. 9.

88. SEP, 23 Ag '24, p. 20.

89. Col, 23 Ag '24, p. 11.

90. Col, 23 Ag '24, p. 10; SEP, 2 F '29, p. 9; NR, 23 My '28,
p. 7. See also, CC, 30 N '32, p. 1461.

91. CC, 30 N '32, p. 1461. See also, Cent, Je '24, p. 153.

92. Col, 30 N '35, p. 10; SEP, 20 My '39, p. 106; Atlan, My
'37, p. 538; TA, F '51, p. 48.

93. Ind, 17 O '12, p. 889; Forum, Je '24, p. 768; RR, O '28,
p. 340; NR, 17 Mr '37, p. 189.

94. TA, F '51, p. 48. See also, SA, 20 Je 1891, p. 393;
LD, 9 Ag '24, p. 11; NR, 3 S '24, p. 9; SEP, 22 My '26, p. 185;
SEP, 14 Ag '26, p. 98; RR, N '28, p. 496; RR, Ap '29, p. 88; RR,
S '30, p. 66; RR, Mr '32, p. 31; RR, Ap '32, p. 12; HM, Ap '33,
p. 559, NR, 17 Mr '37, p. 189; SR, 9 Ag '52, p. 20; Nwk, 19 S '55,
p. 39.

95. Col, 23 Ag '24, p. 10; CC, 30 N '32, p. 1461; HM, Ap '33, p. 559; AmMag, Ap '52, p. 111; NR, 3 S '24, p. 9.

96. RR, O '28, p. 340.

97. RR, O '28, p. 341.

98. HM, N '52, p. 14; NR, 9 My '55, p. 13.

99. NR, 1 D '52, p. 14; NR, 9 My '55, p. 13.

100. NR, 19 Mr '24, p. 93; SEP, 2 F '29, p. 141.

101. Atlan, My '37, p. 538; CC, 22 N '50, p. 109.

102. SR, 6 O '51, p. 37.

103. SR, 6 O '51, p. 37.

104. AmMag, Ap '52, pp. 21, 110.

105. NR, 1 D '52, p. 13.

106. NR, 1 D '52, pp. 12-14.

107. NR, 9 My '55, p. 15; Nwk, 19 S '55, p. 40. See also, RD, Ja '51, p. 4; TA, F '51, p. 47; HM, N '52, p. 28.

108. Ind, 13 F '13, p. 356.

109. CC, 23 Ag '44, p. 974.

110. Nwk, 18 Ap '49, p. 78; RR, Mr '32, p. 32; CC, 28 N '45, p. 1308.

111. Ind, 13 F '13, p. 356; PE, Jl '29, p. 46.

112. SEP, 25 S '48, p. 172.

113. LD, 27 Ja '33, p. 35; LD, 23 Ag '24, p. 31; RR, S '30, p. 66; AAA, Ja '41, p. 152; NR, 23 O '29, p. 259.

114. LD, 23 Ag '24, p. 31; Out, 28 My '24, p. 132; RR, Mr '32, p. 31; LD, 27 Ja '33, p. 35. See also, Out, 17 Ja '14, p. 122; CO, My '22, p. 649; Forum, Je '24, p. 259; SEP, 14 Ag '26, p. 97.

115. WT, O '08, p. 1052.

116. RR, Ap '27, p. 395.

117. AmMag, Je '22, p. 13; Scrib, My '31, p. 489; RR, Ja '23, p. 52.

118. Ind, 17 O '12, p. 891; Scrib, Jl '29, p. 8; SD, Ap '45, p. 27; ParM, N '49, p. 58; HB, F '50, p. 125; AmMerc, D '54, p. 81; SNL, 26 N '55, p. 344. See also, LD, 1 S '28, p. 19; SEP, 16 Mr '46, p. 92; ParM, D '48, p. 65; ParM, Ja '49, p. 26; Etude, Je '49, p. 341; SA, S '49, p. 26; SSoc, 20 S '50, p. 21; WHC, N '50, p. 71; GH, N '50, p. 263; SSoc, 15 D '51, p. 369; SEP, 23 Ap '55, p. 12; USN, 2 S '55, p. 36.

119. ParM, Ja '49, p. 27; USN, 2 S '55, p. 36. See also, GH, N '50, p. 263; SSoc, 15 D '51, p. 369.

120. PMech, S '39, p. 322.

121. SR, 21 F '42, p. 17.

122. PE, Jl '27, p. 49; Col, 23 Jl '27, p. 43; LA, 15 N '27, p. 993; SEP, 30 Je '28, p. 129; LD, 1 S '28, p. 19; SA, O '28, p. 358; PMech, N '28, p. 820; SEP, 27 Jl '29, p. 12; SEP, 21 S '29, p. 140; RR, Jl '30, p. 89; RR, S '30, p. 65; RR, Je '35, p. 54; Col, 30 N '35, p. 10; PMech, S '39, p. 322; SEP, 28 S '40, p. 25; Nat, 25 D '48, p. 723; ParM, J '49, p. 27; Atlan, M '49, p. 35. See also, RR, Je '07, p. 685; RR, Ja '23, p. 52; CO, Ap '23, p. 457; Scrib, Ap '23, p. 411; Cent, Je '24, p. 150; Nat, 23 Jl '24, p. 90; SEP, 7 Ag '26, p. 103; LD, 11 Ag '28, p. 8; Nat, 10 O '28, p. 360; Col, 20 O '28, p. 40; PE, Ag '29, p. 70; Out, 4 Je '30, p. 179; Nat, 18 M '31, p. 305; LD, 27 Ja '33, p. 35; NO, Jl '33, p. 17; Comm, 28 S '34, p. 499; Scrib, F '37, p. 61; Etude, Je '37, p. 359; NR, 19 F '40, p. 236; AAA, Ja '41, p. 145; SR, 21 F '42, p. 3; NB, Jl '47, p. 36; HB, O '47, p. 275; USN, 7 Ja '49, p. 24; Nwk, 18 Ap '49 p.   ; SR, 24 D '49, p. 20; SR, 17 Je '50, p. 9; HB, Ag '50, p. 80; HM, N '52, p. 27; SR, 6 D '52, p. 17; Nwk, 14 Mr '55, p. 28; NR, 9 My '55, p. 13.

123. Ind, 17 O '12, p. 890.

124. Educa, D '36, p. 214.

125. CCom, 11 Ap '08, p. 75; SEP, 18 Ap '25, p. 182; Scrib, Ap '29, p. 373; CO, O '23, p. 471; Forum, Je '24, p. 769; HW, 6 Je '14, p. 21; SA, Ja '23, p. 71; Out, 3 Mr '15, p. 498; Educa, D '19. p. 136; NAR, Mr '36, p. 52; Ind, 11 D '16, p. 448; Scrib, Ap '29, p. 372; NAR, S 1896, p. 378.

126. HW, 24 Ag '07, p. 1246; Ind, 6 F '08, p. 306; AmMag, S '09, p. 493; Lip, O '09, p. 454; HW, 13 N '09, p. 8; RR, M '12, p. 372; Lip, Ag '13, p. 194; AmMag, O '14, p. 96; LA, 1 Jl '30, p. 554; CO, Je '15, p. 411; SEP, 6 D '24, p. 74; Ind, 1 S '28, p. 210; NAR, O '28, p. 432; Forum, Je '24, p. 769; NR, 14 Ag '15, p. 51; Ind, 11 D '16, p. 448; HM, N '28, p. 708.

127. Out, 23 Jl '24, p. 471; CO, Ag '18, p. 95; Out, 3 N '26, p. 308; SSoc, 3 D '38, p. 732; LD, 7 Ja '33, p. 16; Col, 13 D '30, p. 311; Etude, Je '49, p. 342; Etude, S '31, p. 616; Comm, 4 Ag '50, p. 406; NAR, Summer '38, p. 306; RR, N '28, p. 555; Etude, N '40, p. 740; SEP, 14 Ag '26, p. 103; AmMag, J '29, p. 100; Etude, F '38, p. 72.

128. Col, 21 F '25, p. 20; CO, M '25, p. 331; MusAm, F '49, p. 10; Out, 24 Ap '29, p. 675; NAR, S '39, p. 278; Scrib, Ap '23, p. 410; Etude, Je '49, p. 342; HB, Ag '50, p. 98; NR, 13 D '48, p. 28; NAR, M '36, p. 50.

129. CL, S '08, p. 328; CO, D '15, p. 405; Out, 24 Ap '29, p. 663; LD, 18 My '29, p. 27; NAR, F '35, p. 145; NAR, Summer '38, p. 309; TA, D '53, p. 88.

130. Ind, 6 F '08, p. 307; SEP, 28 S '40, p. 37; AmMag, M '48, p. 107; Etude, Je '49, p. 342; SEP, 15 Ap '22, p. 141; AmMag, Jl '21, p. 32; SA, D '22, p. 379; SEP, 3 D '27, p. 46; ParM, Ja '49, p. 27; Comm, 4 Ag '50, p. 406; LD, 16 Jl '32, p. 32; USN, 2 S '55, p. 43; SR, 5 Je '48, p. 6.

131. SEP, 9 Mr '29, p. 132; TA, S '29, p. 652; Nat, 22 Ja '30, p. 106; Comm, 21 My '30, p. 73; USN, 14 O '49, p. 21; SR, 17 Je '50, p. 38; SEP, 19 Je '52, p. 72; Atlan, O '53, p. 58; USN, 2 S '55, p. 43; Nwk, 20 N '50, p. 102; SEP, 26 Je '52, p. 120; Scrib, Jl '29, p. 6.

132. CC, 11 Mr '31, p. 340; ChgT, F '54 pp. 41-42.

133. RR, Mr '12, p. 334; NR, 14 Ag '15, p. 51; LD, 4 F '22, p. 32; LD, 3 N '28, p. 29.

134. Out, 5 D '28, p. 1272; SEP, 6 D '24, p. 78; NAR, O '28, p. 434; AmMag, Ap '29, p. 125; Mus, Je '29, p. 40; LA, N '30, p. 299; Etude, S '31, p. 615; SR, 15 F '36, p. 8; Col, 27 S '47, p. 32; USN, 7 Ja '49, N '50, p. 265; SEP, 2 F '52, p. 102; Nat, 5 N '55, p. 378.

135. HW, 24 Ag '07, p. 1247.

136. WT, O '08, p. 1052.

137. HW, 30 Jl '10, p. 13.

138. PE, O '26, p. 180. See also, PE, Mr '09. p. 123; Lip, O '09, p. 454; GH, Ag '10, p. 184; Ind, 13 F '13, p. 354; Ind, 28 F '16, p. 311; Out, 20 Je '14, p. 413; Ind, 5 Mr '17, p. 426; HM, Ja '19, p. 185; NAR, Jl '20, p. 80; CO, Ag '22, p. 156; CO, Mr '23, p. 330.

139. CCom, 11 Ap '08, p. 73; Lip, Ag '13, p. 191; Ind, 11 D '16, p. 447; Nat, 28 Ag '13, p. 193; HW, 6 Je '14, p. 20; AmMag, O '14, p. 98; CO, Je '15, p. 411; CO, D '15, p. 405; AmMag, D '15, p. 64; NAR, Mr '17, p. 456; NAR, Jl '20, p. 87; NAR, Jl '20, p. 90; LD, 11 Ag '28, p. 9; NAM, Mr '29, p. 306; Col, 25 My '29, p. 10; SEP, 20 Jl '29, p. 82; TA, S '29, p. 636; Comm, 18 S '29, p. 507; LA, 15 My '30, p. 350; Nat, 27 Ag '30, p. 216; Scrib, Mr '37, p. 16; NAR, Summer '37, p. 234.

140. LD, 11 Ag '28, p. 9; SEP, 15 Je '29, p. 50; Col, 23 N '29, p. 11; Comm, 21 My '30, p. 71; HB, F '50, p. 126; SR, 17 Je '50, p. 34; Nat, 13 O '51.

141. SR, 15 F '36, p. 8.

142. GH, N '50, p. 264; Nat, 24 D '24, p. 700; SA, S '26, p. 209; NAR, Mr '29, p. 307; Mus, My '29, p. 34; GH, Ja '49, p. 143; MusAm, F '49, p. 10; SR, 19 F '44, p. 29; Etude, Je '49, p. 342.

143. AmMag, O '14, p. 98; AmMag, D '15, p. 64; CO, Je '15, p. 411.

144. IW, Ja '16, p. 661.

145. Comm, 18 S '29, p. 507; Scrib, Mr '37, p. 16; Nat, 27 Mr '29, p. 365; Col, 25 My '29, p. 9.

146. AmMag, O '14, p. 98.

147. NR, 5 F '30, p. 299.

148. Nat, 27 Ag '30, p. 216.

149. NAR, Summer '37, p. 231.

150. NR, 1 Ap '31, p. 175. See also, CO, D '15, p. 405; NAR, Jl '20, p. 87; TA, S '29, p. 636.

151. BW, 27 D '52, p. 27; NR, 28 N '55, p. 20.

152. NR, 26 Ap '54, p. 22.

CHAPTER V

ARGUMENT FROM CAUSE: INSTITUTIONS
Attack

Writers who opposed the new media and who supported established institutions against the encroachment of innovation maintained a single broad line of argument. Change, they said, was undesirable. Movies, then radio, and later television caused new problems for society, threatened respected institutions with undesirable modification and possible displacement. The damage which opponents predicted to follow innovation affected all of society. It ranged from the depletion of the audience for traditional amusements to disruption of children's play. The intrusion of the new meant that orderly patterns of the past were disrupted, that settled ways of doing things were undone, that traditional functions of the old were taken over by the new. The writers who took this stand, many of them representatives of threatened institutions, argued not only from vested interest, but also from the presumption that it was desirable to maintain things as they were, that customary modes of thought and action should be preserved. Theirs was argument from tradition, argument which played upon unwillingness to disturb the existing order.

In examining the attack, I shall use the general categories
established in the preceding chapter insofar as they are applicable.
The two which will not be found here are arguments from reassurance
and from concession, neither of which were used by opponents. I
shall begin with arguments concerning the loss to the new media
of institutional audiences and then turn to the effects of innovation on the institutions themselves.

The Audience Depleted

All of the institutions which depended upon public support
faced a common threat from motion pictures, radio, and television
--the loss to the new media of their patrons, congregations, or
audiences. As attackers were quick to point out, the new media
were popular, they were cheap, and they drew audiences as nothing
had ever done before them. One writer said of television that it
is the "most amazingly effective distraction man has ever produced."[1]
The same thing might have been said about either motion pictures
or radio some years earlier. People gave up their former amusements,
deserted their usual sources of information, and even modified
their patterns of church attendance in favor of the new media.
This was a matter of major concern to spokesmen for social institutions, and they argued that the changes they saw going on augured
ill for society. The threat was seen first in the rise of the
motion picture.

Movies became "a factor to be reckoned with" in public entertainment after 1907. In that year, Chicago nickelodeons were reported drawing 100,000 patrons daily. Two years later New York movies were attracting 250,000 people a day, and by 1910 the national daily attendance at motion pictures was estimated at 5,000,000.[2] The first of the old amusements to feel the impact of the new entertainment was the legitimate theatre, and its defenders pointed to motion pictures as the source of the theatre's troubles. Lippincott's Magazine, for example, said in 1909 that

> one of the results of the moving picture show is the decrease in box office receipts at the legitimate and vaudeville theatres and the disbanding of theatrical companies. You do not need the proof of the decline in attendance if you count the empty seats where the nickel competitor is in the vicinity. The gallery in the home of Thespis is usually most deserted as the 'gods' are strongly tempted to the tragedy and comedy of the camera, but there is no doubt that nearly every class of those whom we term theatregoers have been lured from their former haunts.[3]

Watching former patrons leave the theatre in favor of the nickelodeon, noting that movies were prospering while the legitimate houses were losing money, writers concluded that "the silent-moving-picture drama has come to rival the living talking actors." After 1910 there were regular reports of the pictures' "terrific inroads upon the support of the regular theatre." The traditional mode of dramatic entertainment was giving way to the movies; familiar patterns of amusement were changing because of innovation. Watching the process, the theatrical producer William A. Brady predicted in 1915 that "if pictures go on as they have been going in the last ten years, it will mean the death of the spoken drama."[4]

Radio, talkies, and television were each in turn perceived to threaten the theatre by taking away its audience. When radio appeared, William A. Brady, who had predicted the death of theatre because of silent films, said radio constituted

> the gravest menace the theatre has ever faced. . . . Plays emerge very badly over the radio, and I am sure that such performances keep many people from the theatre.[5]

Talkies, which had become firmly established by 1930, were first predicted to empty the playhouses, and later were named a cause for theatre's decline.[6] For example, Theresa Helburn, the executive head of the Theatre Guild, said both sound films and radio had attracted the audience away from the theatre. She argued that

> with the invention of 'talkies,' the preeminence of the theater was doomed. As a business it fell to second place, and, with the rise of radio, to third. Today the theater is bad business and an increasingly difficult one.[7]

Television, said R. E. Sherwood in 1929, would continue the work of the other media, reducing theatrical crowds even further, until the time would come when most Americans would "see the inside of a theatre, movie or otherwise, only rarely."[8] The silent films, because they were the first to compete with the theatre for public attention, were considered the gravest source of danger to the stage. But each new medium added to the theatre's problem, for each one attracted a greater share of the audience. Thus the theatre, the most prestigious of all the amusements, was faced with loss of its audience because of the competition of the new mass media.

Silent films, radio, and talkies, since they also depended upon the audience for support, were each faced with debilitation when a new, competitive medium was introduced. The arguments in behalf of movies and broadcasting were the same as those used in defense of other institutions, for by the time any of the new media was threatened it was, in fact, part of the established order, and its loss was to be deplored. When, for instance, the movies were challenged by the talkies, the silent pictures were twenty years old, the primary entertainment of the mass audience, an accepted part of the amusement scheme. Given a taste of talkies and Jolson in combination, audiences flocked to the new amusement. Talkies were, even in 1928, a box-office smash, and the invention was predicted to double motion picture attendance.[9] By 1929, Jerome Beatty said in Saturday Evening Post that

> talkies have taken hold--there is no doubt about that
> --and no producer dares offer a picture that has not
> at least an accompaniment of music and effects--the
> effects being all sound except talking. Most of the
> pictures contain a reel or so of talking.[10]

Nation said the mass audience had indicated in no uncertain terms their preference for the talkies, and Jesse Lasky credited public response to the talkie with making business jump "by leaps and

bounds." At the end of 1929, Creighton Peet, motion picture re-

viewer for the New York Evening Post, said it was clear that "we

will never go back to the silent film any more than we will go back

to the pony express."11 The pattern of amusement was changed again;

silent films were dead. The audience had moved to the latest

development in the line.

Talkies, in turn, were threatened both by radio and television.

Radio offered the first major competition for the talkies during

the depression when the public sought free entertainment. As Gilbert

Seldes and others pointed out, people simply did not have the money

to go to the movies, and radio was free. Radio continued to be a

major source of entertainment into the war years. J. P. McVoy

argued, for example, that radio was one of the causes for the decline

of films in the early 1940's. For evidence he pointed to "Fortune's

survey that 79 per cent would give up movies rather than radio."12

The major argument, however, related to television's influence on

the motion picture audience.

Movie attendance began to give way to television in 1948 as

new set owners stayed home to watch the broadcasts. Researchers

verified attackers' predictions in 1949, reporting that movie-going

did in fact decline following the purchase of a television set.

Arthur Mayer claimed that motion picture attendance dropped 15 per cent during television's first full year. Spyros Skouras of 20th Century Fox increased the figure to 30 per cent the following year and named the cause "this great new medium, television." In 1952, Saturday Evening Post reported that "current estimates of box office recession vary from 20 to 40 per cent."[13] Defenders of the movies continued to report dwindling attendance figures, and argued that television was causing drastic alteration in the pattern of national entertainment. Looking back at the situation, U. S. News commented in 1955 that

> in its early years, television almost wrecked the movie
> industry. Attendance dropped wherever TV came in. For
> last year, weekly attendance at movie theaters was at the
> rate of 50 million, little more than half the size of
> the movie audience in 1946, the movies' best year and
> also the year that TV came generally on the scene.[14]

Like the silents before them, talkies lost a share of their audience to the newest entertainment.

Radio was faced with the same kind of competition from television. Its defenders argued, from 1946 on, that radio's audience would disappear, that the medium would suffer drastic changes, if not extinction, because of TV. It was Lou Frankel who commented in Nation that broadcasters were surprised that television had caught the public fancy so quickly, and disappointed that FM, the other innovation in broadcasting, had not caught on. It was Frankel's contention that "since either FM or television will tend to kill the broadcasters' existing audience, they know they may have to switch to

one or the other, and those with limited resources would naturally
prefer it to be FM." By 1948 many former radio listeners were to
be counted among the television audience. American Magazine reported
a CBS survey in which more than half of the respondents said there
was no radio program they preferred to television, and Newsweek
concluded that "already the /television/ shows are good enough to
cut radio listening to a minimum." A survey conducted the following
year found 92.4 per cent of the respondents listening to radio less
frequently than they had before getting television. Milton MacKaye
pointed to the striking changes in radio program ratings as evidence
of the impact of television. Listeners were no longer concerned
with radio; they were now viewers. And U. S. News, as late as 1955,
confirmed the earlier reports. Radio listening for the person in
Fort Wayne, Indiana, it said, dropped from a pre-TV average of 122
minutes a day to a post-TV average of 52 minutes.[15] Radio had been
displaced by television; much of its audience had moved, for a time
at least, to the competition.

The theatre, movies, and radio were obviously not the only
institutions faced with depletion of their audiences because of
innovation. Spokesmen for other institutions told of the same
problem. The associate rector of St. Thomas Episcopal Church in
New York, for example, reported in Literary Digest that clergymen
blamed radio for their dwindling congregations. People stayed home

to listen instead of attending services in person. The editor
and publisher of Musician, speaking to the convention of the West
Virginia Federation of Music Clubs, argued that radio had taken
the audience from the concert hall. Professional athletic events
were taken off radio for a time in 1929 because of the medium's
suspected encroachment on live audiences. Colleges banned radio
reports of football for the same reason in 1932. Later, according
to their spokesmen, both professional and collegiate athletics were
similarly damaged by television. By 1955, minor league baseball
was acknowledged to have been one of the victims of television.
And even the circus banned television coverage to save its audience.
As John Ringling North said, "We won't give away our entertainment."16

The common danger faced by all of the established modes of
entertainment, and by any of the institutions which depended upon
an audience for support, was loss of patronage. The new media
were attractive, popular, and cheap. Audiences flocked to them,
usually at the expense of formerly popular amusements. Consequently,
spokesmen for the status quo, fearful that the effects of innovation would be permanent, warned that good things of the past
were threatened, that respected institutions were in danger of
going under. Such cries of danger themselves became something of
a tradition. Every time a new medium appeared, the prophets appeared
with it, foretelling the end of something good. In the case of
silent films they were right. The rest of the time, however, the

situation was never as bad as attackers predicted it would be.
Although familiar things were hurt for a time, as movies were with
the coming of television, or forced to change their former mode
of operation, as radio was, they survived. There was, after all,
audience enough to go around. Nevertheless, the warnings of danger
to valued institutions, commonplaces in the repertory of attack,
were repeated in each new situation of innovation.

Migration of the audience was only one of the problems said to
attend the introduction of new media. Writers who upheld the old
and opposed the new predicted that movies, radio, and television
held potential danger for nearly all of society's institutions.

Education

Since promoters of motion pictures, radio, and television
argued frequently from the direct and beneficial influences of the
media in education, attackers might be expected to maintain the
opposing ground, arguing there was danger to the institution in
innovation. To an extent they did this. As I shall demonstrate,
some held the media weakened education because their use was inconsistent with current educational theory; some believed the media
caused new problems for schools already overburdened; and others
contended that movies, radio, or television caused children to do
poorly in their studies. More commonly, attackers avoided discussions of causality and talked instead of the unfulfilled promise

of the media in education, asserting that although movies, radio, and television had great potential for classroom teaching and adult education as advocates had said, the media had been badly used for such purposes. This kind of argument comparing potential and practice is the subject of a later chapter. The discussion here will be limited to causal argument.

Educational theory

A few writers implied the new media were dangerous to education because the way in which they presented materials was not compatible with contemporary educational theory. That is, movies and radio stressed acquisition of factual knowledge while educational theory stressed the child's participation in the learning process.

This concern was first expressed as a reaction to Edison's proposal for teaching elementary subjects in motion pictures. Leonard P. Ayres of the Russell Sage Foundation, for example, warned against using movies "for the mere imparting of facts," the funnelling of knowledge into children who did not understand what it meant.[17] John Dewey of Columbia University expressed similar reservation about educational films.

> I was . . . imprest by the fact that, after all, seeing things behave is rather a vicarious form of activity, and that there is some danger of the better becoming an enemy of the best. I mean that a wide-spread adoption of motion pictures in schools might have a tendency to retard the introduction of occupations in which children themselves actually do things.[18]

When radio was proposed as a new educational tool, Bruce Bliven's questions in an article for Century in 1924 reflected a similar concern about the compatability of the medium and education.

> Is radio to become a chief arm of education? Will the
> classroom be abolished, and the child of the future
> stuffed with facts as he sits at home or even as he
> walks about the streets with his portable receiving-
> set in his pocket?[19]

Then in 1930 New Republic asserted that most attempts at education by radio had failed, possibly because the trend in education was away from merely listening. And a year later, Christian Century argued that educational radio had failed because there was confusion about the value of radio in the classroom. Educators of the period were in favor of "project" teaching, and the authoritarian voice from the radio did not fit into current educational philosophy.[20]

This was the extent of the line of argument. Never was it fully developed, never was it used for any firm attack on the media. Instead, the nagging suspicion lingered that if movies and radio were used for teaching, they might well retard the application of modern educational methods in the schools. The media were made to seem opposed to progress.

The line of argument was never applied to television in this form. A variation on it which suggested that television teaching did not fit into contemporary patterns of education was used, however. Opponents argued that the materials of television education were transitory, the medium lacked any form of inter-communication between teachers and students, the lessons were rapidly paced and took no account of the slow learner, and that there was no way for the teacher to discover at the time of presentation if her lessons were getting across to the students.[21]   None of these objections were developed into substantial causal argument, but the statements implied a danger to conventional teaching from the intrusion of a new device. The medium was made to seem opposed to a tradition. At the same time, the comments hinted that a machine could never educate a child as well as a classroom teacher could.

Education by air is dull

Indirectly, educational broadcasting was detrimental to education as a whole in yet another way. As advocates had often pointed out, classroom education as practiced was dull. Opponents occasionally argued that radio education was equally dull, offered the listener little stimulation, and consequently reinforced hearers' disenchantment with learning.

James Rorty claimed in Harper's Monthly in 1931 that educational broadcasting was perceived by commercial interests as "the incompetent, prolix mouthing of educational dodoes, completely lacking in showmanship." Gilbert Seldes, generally favorable to all ventures of the new media, mentioned in Atlantic in 1937 that "the great fault of educational programmes so far has been not so

much that they were too serious or too informative: they simply
were not as skilfully and interestingly presented as the sponsored
material." And Harriet Van Horne, writing for Saturday Review
in 1944, concluded that whenever radio tried deliberately to be an
educator, it was dull.22

Once again, causal relationships were not made explicit. But
radio was demonstrated to be no asset to education. If anything,
the very dullness of broadcast lessons was detrimental to the
institution. The new medium was open to the same criticism which
advocates had made of the present system.

New problems for the schools

The introduction of the mass media created new problems for
an already overburdened school system. That is, opponents said,
movies, radio, and television took students away from school activities, the disruptive influence of television extended into the classroom, and schools were forced to take on new responsibilities to
compensate for the influences of television. Instead of helping
solve existing problems, innovation made things worse.

School activities, once the most common recreation for students, were replaced by new amusements growing out of innovation.
That is, as Survey Graphic reported in 1947, the new pastimes of
American youth were "listening to the radio, going to the movies.
and riding in an automobile, and watching athletic events."23 The

school, because of the new media and other attractions, was losing its place of importance in the life of the student. Tradition was upset.

Motion pictures and television caused disruptions in the normally sedate process of education. For one thing, children who went frequently to movies and those who watched television were badly behaved in school. A writer for Better Homes and Gardens argued in 1937 "we've found that the movie children average lower deportment records, do on the average poorer work in their school subjects, are rated lower in reputation by their teachers, are less cooperative and less self-controlled as measured both by ratings and conduct tests, are slightly more deceptive in school situations, slightly less skillful in judging what is the most sensible thing to do, and are somewhat less emotionally stable." In 1950, Robert Lewis Shayon supported his claim that television caused children to be unruly in school with a letter from a private school operator who said that after her children got television in November of 1949 their behavior changed. There was more playing with guns--" a group barricades itself in the doll house; another group, armed to the teeth, gallops up and attacks them"; drawings appeared on the wall referring to "the Clutching Claw"; students were tired "nervously, physically, emotionally, mentally"; children lost their values, their sense of wonder, their interest, and their stability.

Paul Witty repeated in 1951 the charge that television had caused
school children to be restless and irritable in class, and went on
to argue secondly, that the medium damaged the morale of teachers.
One New Jersey teacher, he said, quit her job because she was tired
of competing for attention with television.[24]

Finally, television forced the schools to take on new tasks
thus increasing their work load. Clifton Utley argued in 1948 that
when television arrived, the schools would be faced with the task
of implanting in students enough intellectual curiosity, enough
desire to read, so that after a decade of television they would still
seek knowledge. Teaching with this end in view would not be simple.
In 1950, Dallas W. Smythe predicted that not only would schools
have to compensate for "the lack of active play in children's lives
whose time free from school is spent in passive TV viewing rather
than in outdoor recreation, pursuing a hobby or reading," but they
would need also to expand the teaching of logical decision making
in order to counter "the exposure of juvenile TV-viewers to powerful
influences affecting public opinion."[25] Because of television,
the school would be forced to assume greater responsibility for the
lives of the students.

To some extent, these arguments served to answer claims made
by advocates about the place of the media in education. But they
were incidental to the critics' total argument, for as I have

already pointed out, opponents of the media chose other grounds
on which to build their primary case. In only one area was causal
argument sustained; opponents argued that the new media caused the
school work of children to deteriorate.

Children in school

The most persistent attacks on the new media in education were
related to their influence on the children's school work. Attackers
maintained that because of motion pictures and radio, but especially
television, children did badly in their studies. After 1949, this
line of argument became the principal ground for attacks on television as it related to education. Through its use, attackers
suggested that the media were not only harmful to children but
detrimental to all of education.

One of the first charges against motion pictures in connection
with education named movies a cause of truancy; children went to
the movies instead of to school. Other writers argued that children
learned the wrong things from films. But it was not until 1930,
in the Christian Century campaign, that pictures were accused of
causing children to do badly in school. On the basis of statements
from teachers and principals, collected by the department of sociology at the University of Chicago, Fred Eastman argued that movies
interfered with school work, retarded the mental development of
students, lowered their vitality, rendered them nervous and excitable,

weakened their initiative and their ambition. Readers of <u>Christian</u>
<u>Century</u> agreed that "movies have a bad educational influence on
many children."[26]

Radio was also named as a cause for children neglecting their
studies. At one point, <u>Collier's</u> country philosopher, Uncle Henry,
commented that "I've noticed that children can't seem to study
their lessons any more without havin' the radio an' phonograph
goin' full tilt, a scientific fact that may help to explain some
of the peculiarities of the younger generation." Later, in 1937
and 1938, other writers argued that a major problem of radio was
that children listened instead of studying and could not be lured
away from the loudspeaker to do their homework.[27]

Beginning in 1949 this argument was applied to television
and became one of the commonplaces of the attack on the medium.
<u>Science Digest</u> reported in October of 1949 that teachers complained
that students were not doing their homework because of television.
Three months later, the principal of the Clifton, New Jersey,
grammar school expressed alarm in <u>Newsweek</u> at the "television
profile" of his students, "the nodding heads and the drooping
eyelids," and noted that after television "homework, if it was
prepared at all, was increasingly sloppy." In a year the percentage of students doing unsatisfactory work had risen from 9 per
cent to 30 per cent, and "almost all the failures had television

sets in their homes." More than half of the parents surveyed agreed
that "video was harmful to school work."[28]

For the next five years television was blamed frequently for
students' failures. Critics said students' grades dropped because
of too much television and not enough homework; their class performance suffered because they were tired from having watched the
late shows; their reading skills either were not developed or
deteriorated through lack of practice; and their interest in school
was transferred to television. In 1955 U. S. News reported gin-
gerly that "excessive viewing seemed to be connected with substandard
school work."[29]

These arguments about the adverse influences of television on
the schooling of children constituted one of the major attacks on
the medium. As had happened before, opponents sought to demonstrate that valued institutions would suffer at the hands of innovation. The schools were forced to take on new duties to make up
for the damage inflicted by the media, schools were displaced as
centers for student activities, and children were caused to do badly
in their studies. Education, presumed to be desirable both as an
end and as institution, was threatened by innovation.

Politics

Politics were also threatened by innovation. Where advocates
of radio and television had argued that the new media could be

employed to advantage in politics, opponents believed the institution would suffer if the media were used. Familiar political
traditions would be changed if campaigns were carried on by radio
or television, new complications would be added to the party nominating conventions, candidates would be judged by new standards
and would face new problems in communication because of microphones
and cameras. The revisions caused by radio and television were
judged to be disruptive and dangerous. Opponents of broadcasting
in politics stood as defenders of traditional and familiar political
practices.

The candidate: new criteria

Opponents of broadcasting in politics argued that the use of
the new media would change the criteria for selection of candidates. Ideally, the men chosen for elective office were honest,
sensible, experienced, public spirited, and personable. Radio and
television, critics said, would substitute less desirable attributes, namely personality and appearance, for the substantial
qualities formerly demanded for men seeking office. A man of
lesser quality, they implied, would be chosen for public office
if the media standards were employed.

A suggestion of this line of argument appeared in New Republic
in 1924, the first year that radio was used in the campaign. The
writer commented that the candidate's personality might become more

of a factor in the campaigns of the future, and she wondered if
"a good presence, so to speak, might not even eclipse the hearty
handshake as a vote getter." The candidate selected for his strong
radio personality might catch uncommitted voters via radio. What,
she speculated, would have happened if Teddy Roosevelt had had
access to radio in 1912? Although she did not go on to attack
personality as a valid criterion for candidate selection, it must
be remembered in considering this argument that writers were generally suspicious of decisions made on the basis of "personality"
or of persuasion effected by this means.[30] The implication of
new dangers was clear.

The argument about new criteria was never important in the
discussions of radio, but it was used more frequently in connection
with television. When television was used, in a limited fashion,
in the 1950 state campaigns, U. S. News said that as a result of the
experience "candidates may be picked for photogenic appeal as well
as voice appeal."[31] Commonweal believed television would change
the basis for candidate selection, that more and more a "pleasing
countenance and well modulated voice are requirements for politicians." Presuming that good looks and intelligence were attributes not usually found together, the writer for Commonweal concluded that

> one more product of Yankee ingenuity has come along to
> affect our political life. To hold major political office,

> it will be increasingly necessary to have an effective
> radio voice, a face that can be made presentable and
> an even higher bankroll--although the latter can con-
> tinue to be supplied by wealthy friends or a well-heeled
> political machine. The attributes intellect, training,
> and a certain public spiritedness fall still further
> down on the list.[32]

After 1952, New Republic reported a study of voting behavior which

revealed that "election decision lay more in the realm of person-

alities than in any difference in platform planks or candidate

proposals." And in 1955 Commonweal again argued that because of

television parties would seek out as candidates those men who were

already widely known and who had a national following.[33] The use

of television in the campaign had placed a premium on the good

looks and personality of the candidate, two factors which writers

rejected as valid criteria for the selection of political leaders.

They did not believe, apparently, that a man could be both good

looking and a good politician. Traditional standards for candidate

selection, and by extension good government by competent men, were

threatened by innovation.

The demagogue

Advocates of radio and television had argued that the revela-

tory powers of the media would serve to eliminate demagoguery by

stripping false politicians of their power to deceive. This was

not necessarily true said opponents. There was no reason why the

444

demagogue could not use the media as well as any other man, and use it to effectively deceive.

The assertions of advocates were challenged on speculative grounds as early as 1939, before television got into operation. Then Alva Johnson, surveying the prospects of television for Sat-urday Evening Post, argued that the medium did not necessarily give the honest man an advantage, as advocates said it would. Johnson reminded readers that the con-man, the demagogue, could usually beat an honest man at looking and sounding sincere. Tele-vision would merely transmit the message. It would not reveal anything about the truth or lack of it in the communication.[34]

After several years of experience with television, other writers also challenged the validity of the advocates' position. For example, Edward R. Murrow asked in 1952,

Does it /television/ sort out the charlatan from the statesman? Are we sure that Father Coughlin and Hughie Long wouldn't have been even bigger with the help of television? You can't stop the picture and say, 'Go look at his voting record.'[35]

Gilbert Seldes, after watching the 1952 conventions said the use of the medium this way made it possible for television to become eventually the natural tool of the demagogue. While it did reveal truth about men, at the same time television could be used by the charlatan who would not be revealed for three months, too late in politics. When a filmed and edited version of the Presidential

press conference was televised in 1955, <u>Commonweal</u> objected to the
practice on the grounds that it could make the President into a
demagogue. With the program manipulated by the "ad men who plan his
TV," the President might become too familiar to the people, too
democratic, too much the flawless leader who spoke only with "wisdom,
assurance, conviction." And <u>U. S. News</u> reported in 1955 the common
belief that television had handed demagogues a new weapon.[36] The
medium, these writers believed, was not the means for ending demagoguery, but merely another tool which might be used by men of
false purpose.

Political speaking

The revisions in political speechmaking envisioned by promoters
of the new media were spectacular. The old style political oratory, they said, would end, speakers would return to reason for their
persuasion, a new type of politician would emerge because of radio
and television. Writers opposed to the media in politics ignored
most of these predictions. They neither attempted to refute the
advocates nor offered defense for political speaking as it was
practiced. In general, they had little to say about speechmaking
in politics, agreeing, apparently, that it was not all that it
should be, but unwilling to bring the issue to any greater public
attention.

When they did talk about political speechmaking, however, critics failed to develop a consistent line of attack. Most of their comments were related to the new problems the media caused for the speaker. For example, Review of Reviews said in 1924 that radio would make it difficult for the politician to judge the response of his audience. Harper's said in 1952 that television made it hard for the political speaker to adapt to both the audience in the hall and the audience at home. The Brooklyn Eagle, quoted in Literary Digest, regretted the elimination by radio of the speaker's personality. (This was one of the advantages of the medium seen by advocates.) New Republic commented that radio meant more work for the politician, for no longer could he simply give the same speech at each whistle-stop. And both Literary Digest and Harper's thought the elimination of the speaker's personal touches, his comments to individuals and his handshaking, would be disadvantageous.[37] The task of the speaker was thus made more difficult by the addition of microphones and cameras. No longer did he have available to him the personal touches, the marks of individuality which helped him make his case. Political speechmaking, opponents implied, was likely to suffer as a result.

Political conventions

Advocates had praised radio and television for bringing the conventions to larger audiences than ever before, and for pointing

up the need for reform in the proceedings. Writers critical of the
medium, agreeing that television had indeed revealed the workings
of the conventions, questioned the value of this intrusion into the
meetings. For example, after the Republican convention of 1952
Time said that "some of those watching were beginning to wonder if
television and its ubiquitous reporters had not managed to turn
what was essentially a serious meeting into a sort of vaudeville
act," and the delegates into actors in the show.[38] The same year,
a writer for Nation argued that television had revealed too much.
He was convinced that "Republicans and Democrats alike were simply
doing their best to camouflage steam rollers to look like band
wagons and phony drafts to look like spontaneous calls to service,
all for the benefit of the television audience." Politics was turned
into a

> fatuous exhibition of phoniness. Politics was only play-
> acting after all, not reality. The climaxes were care-
> fully plotted; the eloquence was thoroughly rehearsed;
> the denouement was inevitable from the start.[39]

The effect of the revelation was disillusionment: "I shall have
to be confronted with a great mass of evidence before I can erase
from my mind the doubts about American democracy raised by my
participation through television in this year's nominating conventions."[40]

Furthermore, there was some question about television's ability
to draw the crowds advocates had predicted. Walter Goodman, for one,

noted that when rating services indicated the conventions had at
best 32 per cent of the audience and at worst 17 per cent, I Love
Lucy, on at the same time, had 62 per cent of the audience. And
even if the crowds were there, the question of whether television
did in fact influence voting behavior remained.[41]

Reference was made occasionally to television's interference
with the normal operations of the conventions. There were comments
about changes in dress demanded by the cameras, and the revisions
Democrats made in format and seating after watching the coverage
of the Republican meeting in 1952. But more serious was the hint
that television might manipulate the proceedings to create more
interesting viewing. Gilbert Seldes brought up the possibility
in 1952 as he warned readers that the introduction of television
into the campaign also meant the introduction of new problems.
He recalled John Crosby's report that at the 1948 convention the
N. B. C.-Life reporters staged moving pictures of the Southern
delegates ripping off their badges after walking out of the convention. If this happened in the comparatively simple times before
TV, what would happen when the coverage was greatly expanded, asked
Seldes. "Who will draw the line between effective showmanship and
the good little undiscoverable fake?"[42]

The campaign

Some of the problems of the political campaign have been illuminated already in the comments about candidates and conventions. But writers suspicious of broadcasting as a campaign medium also talked of inequities caused by radio and television coverage, of shabby campaign methods, and of the rising costs of campaigning by TV.

Television, said those skeptical about its use in politics, violated the tradition that all candidates should have an equal chance to lay their cases before the electorate. The medium, by nature and by application, gave some candidates an unfair advantage. When a television studio was proposed for the Senate Office Building, for example, U. S. News pointed out that this would give the man in office a distinct advantage over the man seeking office, for the Senator or Congressman could prepare filmed material for release at home for half the usual cost.[43] Senator Richard Neuberger argued that some of the usual paraphernalia of television--teleprompters, makeup, and professional advisors--gave television campaigners an advantage over their opponents. For example, he said,

> here is a man who may sit in the White House, the President's Cabinet, or in the United States Senate. Before the TV camera he seems to be chatting away off the cuff about the gravest of topics--taxes, the armed forces, diplomacy, civil liberties. Yet he has been tutored in this relaxed and easy manner by Hollywood stars. He is reading from the teleprompter the speech written for him by political

> counselors or an advertising agency. Artfully used
> creams and powder pare a dozen years off his normal
> appearance.[44]

The Senator said he intended to introduce a bill providing that

"any television broadcast of an address by or on behalf of a candi-

date for any public office shall include an announcement of whether

the speaker is speaking extemporaneously or from prepared material

and what facial make-up, if any, is being used by the speaker while

making the broadcast." When the parties announced that conventions

would be later than usual in 1956, Commonweal argued that while

this would not hurt the established candidates who were well-known

anyway, it would be disastrous for the little man, not widely known,

who would be forced to spend large sums for television coverage,

the only means by which he could become known in a short time.[45]

Television thus increased the opportunity for inequity in politics,

said its opponents. In so doing TV violated the spirit of fair

play which was supposed to characterize American politics. The

medium, when turned over to special interests, with its special

gadgetry employed to make things seem different from what they

were, did not give all men an equal chance to be heard under equiva-

lent conditions, did not give the public an opportunity to become

equally familiar with all sides and all issues. Television under

these circumstances did not serve, as its critics had hoped it

would, as an instrument for getting at the truth. It was used to

present a blemished image of reality.

Radio and television, moreover, were accused of bias. That is, said their detractors, the electronic media favored the Republicans in the campaigns in which they were used. New Republic, for example, had this to say in 1928:

> It is generally believed that the radio played an impor-
> tant part in the campaign of 1924. Just what effect it
> had, no one can be sure; but many persons have seen a
> connection between the overwhelming vote for Mr. Coolidge
> and the fact that the Republicans practically controlled
> the radio in that year. Because of larger financial
> resources, and for other reasons, their orators were
> heard on the air at least three or four times as much
> as those of the Democrats, and probably eight or ten
> times as much as the supporters of LaFollette.[46]

The new media cost money, the Republican party had more money to spend than the other parties had, and the Republican candidates thus gained greater exposure than their opposition. This was the argument, but at the same time the media were held responsible for the bias. Again in 1952, New Republic noted that Republicans got twice as much air time as the Democrats in the campaign. Looking forward to the 1956 campaigns, Senator Neuberger concluded that "the Republicans have developed political make-believe into a fine art because they have funds with which to pay for it."[47] The new media seemed to give the Republican party an unusual advan-tage in the campaigns because the party had more money to invest in their use. Opponents pointed to this as evidence of the bias of the media.

Television, when it became available as a campaign tool, led politicians to violate the spirit of reason, candor, and sincerity in the selection of public officers, and to substitute for it the appeals of the propagandist, the techniques of the huckster. For example, U. S. News was concerned that politicians had found straight speeches to have little appeal on TV. Consequently, the magazine said, TV was all too likely to bring out the politician with an unusual dramatic flare, just as "radio brought to the Senate such men as Glen H. Taylor, the banjoist from Idaho, and W. Lee O'Daniels, the flour salesman from Texas."[48] After the 1952 election, Saul Carson argued in Nation that Republicans had conducted an ad man's campaign, capped with an hour-long show the night before election.

> It was a mammouth production. It was done with vast
> skill. It was a monstrous, patent fraud. It was ex-
> cellent propaganda. Along with other factors, it worked.
> Eisenhower is the victor.[49]

Paul Seabury of the Columbia University law faculty argued in New Republic that in the same campaign, as in Nixon's Checkers speech, television had made emotions more important than political scientists would like. It was his concern that "turned to sordid expediency, sloganeering, and manipulation, /television/ can do great damage to our political processes."[50] Television thus permitted, if not encouraged, the use of persuasive techniques which both critics and advocates objected to in politics.

All these arguments contributed to the general impression the opposition sought to leave: the new media, television and radio, were harmful to politics. They exposed to public view workings of conventions which were best left hidden. They disturbed the orderly and traditional procedures of candidate selection. They created new hardships for political speechmakers. They worked to the advantage of special interests. They increased the opportunities for fraud and chicanery. They injected new and undesirable modes of persuasion into the campaigns. They were biased in their coverage. Innovations such as these served neither politics nor the democratic process.

In addition, television brought new financial complications to politics. This was the favorite theme of the critics. U. S. News phrased their concern most aptly with its comment that television was making politics "a rich man's game." Comments about increasing costs appeared as soon as television was introduced into politics. U. S. News predicted in 1950 that "costs of political campaigns then /with television/ are bound to skyrocket." Commonweal said campaigning on the air cost as much as $200 per minute. New Republic said in 1951 that while campaign costs had multiplied four or five times since the first use of radio, "the growing use of television guarantees another violent inflation in the political expenses next year." John Crosby reported that the Democrats had earmarked a million dollars for TV in 1952, an increase of $985,000 over 1948.[51]

After the 1952 election was over, campaign expenses were assessed. The cost of radio and television coverage of the conventions alone was placed at $6,000,000, and the total campaign was estimated to have cost $20,000,000 for radio and television. The Republican spot announcement blitz the last ten days of the campaign--up to 130 one-minute announcements in a single day in New York City, described by Gilbert Seldes as "the greatest saturation ever achieved for any purpose"--was said to have cost local and state committees and the Citizens for Eisenhower groups $1,500,000. But this was not the end; costs for the future campaigns were predicted to rise even higher. The two major parties were said to have earmarked six million dollars for television in 1956, and the broadcasting industry estimated it would cost between thirty and fifty million dollars to cover the 1956 campaign.[52]

The obvious conclusion was that if television were to be used in the campaign, as it most certainly would be, politics was going to cost a considerable amount of money. Writers saw dangers in this emphasis on financing the campaign. For one thing, as I have already mentioned, candidates with substantial backing or private means were presumed to hold an advantage. Some of the critics believed the power of television to be such that the candidate had only to appear on it enough times and he would be assured of victory. Seldes, for one, explained that in 1952 "already the feeling persists that he who spends the most money wins."53 This of course would change both the qualifications for candidacy and the role of the political party. Commonweal argued that

> there are already those who think that dependence upon TV makes the transformation of political debates into a gigantic fund-raising contest almost inevitable. We do not, and certainly the eventuality cannot be considered a healthy development in a democratic society.54

There was a second disadvantage to the increasingly costly campaign: some candidates could not afford a full scale effort. New Republic pointed out that if a man wanted to run for the Senate or for a major office in most large states in 1952, and intended to use radio and television, he would need access to at least one or two million dollars for support of his campaign. And most candidates did not have much choice in connection with television; if one used it, all used it. As Commonweal noted in 1955, if the candidate cannot raise money for frequent television appearances, "he will face an almost insuperable handicap." This was the point of Estes Kefauver, who said in February of 1952 that his campaign would be curtailed because he could not afford the expense of much work with television.55

Finally, the involvement in the campaigns of such large sums raised anew the spectre of corruption. This was a concern of

Senator William Benton, who asked in 1952, "How can party leaders take care of legitimate expenditures without getting eye-brow deep in the old corrupting game of favors and protection?" New Republic, which carried Benton's statement, argued that "if the 1952 election is not to be run under circumstances conducive to corruption of the candidates and the parties by those with easy money to offer," the government would have to step in to regulate spending. The same year, John Crosby, commenting on the beginning of advertiser sponsorship of political programs, reminded readers that "whenever such impressive sums change hands, there is possibility for corruption."56 Once again one of the perennial fears about politics was articulated. This time, television was held to be responsible if indeed corruption did find nourishment in politics.

Hence politics was another of the institutions endangered by innovation. Again critics of the new were fearful lest the old and familiar be disturbed. But in the case of politics not only were old ways threatened, but radio and television were predicted to bring dormant problems once again to life, and to create new evils within the institution. Politics, never very stable in the first place, was more likely to be hurt by the new media than to be helped by them.

Religion

Most of the arguments about the damaging effects of the new
mass media on religion have already been examined. Assertions
that movies, radio, and television caused congregations to dwindle
were handled at the beginning of this chapter. Charges that the
media had undermined morality, thus contradicting the teachings
of the church, were treated in an earlier chapter. The arguments
which remain to be discussed here are minor, but they reflect the
continuing concern that the new media would damage respected institutions.

For one thing, supporters of the church feared that movies,
radio, and television might be looked upon as substitutes for
attendance at religious services. The media might serve, in effect,
to replace the church. The substitution of pictures for church
services was suggested in the comment by Lucy France Pierce in 1908
that "on Sunday with its religious subjects it /the motion picture/
takes the place of the sermon." Objections to radio on the same
grounds appeared in Current Opinion in 1923. Bishop Coadjutor
Stearly of Newark argued that radio, and other amusements, had
undermined "the habit of churchgoing," and Cardinal Dubois of
Paris reminded "the faithful that the radio cannot convert sinners
and that people must come to church." Then in 1949, Catholics
in New York City were warned that watching the Mass on television

was not an acceptable substitute for personal participation in a church.[57] The mass media, even when involved with religion, were still merely means for the mechanical reproduction or transmission of a message. They were not the thing itself, but only a representation of it. Therefore, they did not replace, in the eyes of churchmen, the service of worship.

Advocates proposed that films be used in church to draw crowds or to supplement the service of worship. Church people agreed this might be done, but objected to the kinds of pictures which were offered as appropriate for use in church. When a life of Christ was filmed in 1914, for example, Current Opinion noted that church spokesmen reacted adversely to it. For example, one theologian argued that motion pictures were not an appropriate vehicle for sacred subjects.

> Such efforts to depict the life of Jesus must always fail, as the movie cannot convey the religious convictions or edify the soul. Only the formalistic and crude religious ideas and ideals of the Oriental church can favor such methods of picturing Christ and his work.[58]

A Baptist preacher, who incorporated films in his services, argued that there were simply too few pictures which could be used in a church. For example, he said, there were only two films on the Bible available in 1922, and most others were not appropriate for a religious meeting without extensive editing.[59] What advocates had said might be done was not practicable.

Early in the history of movies, Day Allen Willey argued that church buildings had been taken over for motion picture theaters. He said

> it is a fact that two churches in good locations for machine entertainemnt were bought at a high price from their congregations, and the phonograph took the place of the organ, while the dialogue of the play is now heard as a substitute for the sermon. In one of the churches the pulpit was left standing as a platform on which to place the picture machine.[60]

Not only was the incongruity of the situation important in the argument, but Willey implied desecration of the church building by the motion picture.

Finally, spokesmen for the church also pointed to potential danger in the broadcasting of church services, which might do religion more harm than good. Outlook warned in 1924 that intolerant sermons ought to be avoided when broadcasting because they sounded "doubly intolerant over the radio, for the mysterious voice in the air cannot bring with it the face and the gesture of the speaker." Moreover, radio broadcasts might also leave a false impression of professional piety in the minister unless he were careful to adapt to the medium.[61]

Motion pictures, radio, and television, even when their subject matter was religious, were not satisfactory substitutes for church attendance. Watching or listening did not excuse church members from their obligation to participate in worship. The claims made

for the use of films in the church were not fulfilled in practice.
Church buildings were desecrated when turned into picture houses.
And radio broadcasts were apt to give the public an uncomplimentary
impression of ministers and of the religion they represented.
These, in addition to complaints about congregations lost to the
media and morality undermined by amusement, were critics' objections to the new devices in religion. The venerable institution
did not stand to profit from the introduction of television, radio,
or movies.

The Family

Where promoters of the media argued that home and family
would be strengthened by motion pictures, radio, and television,
opponents contended that the new media threatened to subvert the
institution. Critics pointed to two areas of principal danger.
Motion pictures fostered attitudes that conflicted with beliefs
on which family life was founded. Radio and television, which
became an intimate part of home life, disrupted household routines
and family relationships. In either case, the strength and serenity
of the home was vitiated because of the new media. In addition,
the influence of television was predicted to extend even to home
decoration.

Motion pictures were competition for the home because, if for no other reason, they were shown in theaters. Even if the family attended as a group, they were drawn away from the home, the former center of family recreation. But more important than this, attackers argued that what they saw in the pictures caused people, particularly children, to change their attitudes about home and family. The movies served to destroy traditional conceptions of the home and its function. This was an early concern. Recall, for example, McKeever's argument from 1910 in which he charged that from movies children learned "how divorces are originated and how the various members of the family violate the most sacred laws that bind together the home circle and give it its charm and perpetuity." Again in 1917 attackers argued that movies not only kept people from staying at home, but also undermined family relationships within the home.[62] Children saw exemplified in films modes of conduct which denied the virtues commonly held to be a part of home life.

Christian Century adopted this line of argument, and amplified it, for the campaigns of the 1930's. In January of 1930 Fred Eastman argued that motion pictures had undermined the teachings of the home and the church, that movies had caused children to lose respect for the home, and that pictures had "engendered disregard of marriage ties."[63] The argument was expanded in 1933. Quoting from statements by delinquents, Eastman argued that movies had caused children to resent parental restraint, to look upon

their homes as drab and dull, to want to run away, and to seek

freedom from parental control. Eastman asked,

> Is the family the basis for our civilization? Does the
> integrity of the family depend upon monogamy and the
> faithfulness of husband and wife in the marital rela-
> tionship? Does beauty in this relationship depend in
> any measure upon a decent restraint between the sexes?
> If so, any conduct pattern which established a differ-
> ent conception is an enemy to family life.[64]

To Eastman, motion pictures established such a pattern and were,

therefore, the enemy of family life. By causing revision in tradi-

tional attitudes about the home, motion pictures had caused the

institution to suffer harm.

Radio and television entertainment in the home created another

kind of problem. It upset the normal order of the household,

caused old routines to be discarded and new ones adopted, and

created dissension within the family. This line of argument was

introduced in connection with radio. Some writers argued that

all their children did was listen to the radio. Nation claimed

radio had ruined the peace and quiet of the home. Forum said

that instead of providing entertainment, the instrument had dis-

integrated in most homes into "a mere excuse for failing to enter-

tain."[65] And television was judged to be worse than radio. Not

only did it ruin the peace of the home, and change patterns of

entertainment, it seemed to crowd out most other family activity.

As one new set owner explained in U. S. News,

> When we first got the set, all my hobbies, stamps, model
> trains, were dropped. My wife is a great seamstress.
> She practically gave up sewing. Now we're both getting
> back to our former activities. TV has kept us home
> from the movies. We used to go regularly to the local
> movie unless a picture was known to be particularly
> bad. But now it's the reverse. We only go if the pic-
> ture is outstanding.[66]

Other writers argued that television had disrupted meals. Robert
Lewis Shayon, for example, told of an advertising executive who
complained "bitterly that he must eat dinner in the dark so the
family can watch TV." Surveys of the impact of television on
the family indicated that after TV became available to them, children
were harder to get to bed than formerly, and that "the TV kids
went to bed 20 minutes later than did the non-TV ones."[67] Finally,
television proved to be a new source of disagreement among families. When asked by U. S. News how programs were selected by his
children, one father replied:

> Usually, it's who shouts loudest, if we're not
> there.
> When we are, we make the decision, and it usually
> pleases only the one who wanted that program. 'Disney-
> land' is the only program on which they and we all agree.
> When there's boxing on, our children go to the neighbors
> to watch, while the parents come over and join us. TV
> definitely causes dissension in the family.[68]

Critics of TV also commented on what was supposed to be the
new togetherness growing out of family viewing. They argued that
the family gained little from sitting silently in front of a lighted

screen. As Ruth Inglis said in American Mercury, "although families spend more time together around the television set, conversation is discouraged except during commercials." The new togetherness was almost totally passive. Charles Siepmann, responding to claims of advocates, argued that one did well to "question whether a family grouped in silence around a television receiver is in any true sense favorably affected in terms of family relationships."[69]

Home decoration, as well as family relationships, was expected to be changed by the introduction of television. Alva Johnson predicted in 1946 that television would cause

> a revolution in domestic architecture, resulting in the modern home being built around the television room. Interior decorators have already come out with designs for new furniture to arrange the family and guests in concentric half circles in front of the television screen.[70]

Such prognostication was popular, for again in 1949 Harlan Manchester told readers of Nation's Business that the new living room would focus on the television screen, with furniture grouped in theater style. Perhaps, he said,

> luminous paint may be used to indicate hazards in the dark and keep viewers from breaking their necks. Luminous silverware and dishes are also proposed, and a supply of small tables for eating.[71]

Millard Faught repeated these predictions a year later in Saturday Review and added that "architects are already redesigning houses to make the living rooms more like 'theatres' than parlors; . . .

the office swivel chair is being adapted for home use so that viewers can easily swerve back and forth between watching the screen and keeping an eye on the kids and an ear cocked to whatever conversation is able to survive TV's competition."72 Whether these changes constituted a danger to the home was a matter open for speculation.

Nevertheless, home and family, like education, politics, and religion, were to be changed because of the introduction of the new mass media. In the first place, the coming of motion pictures meant that the home lost its primary position as the center of family entertainment. But critics objected more strongly to the changes in traditional attitudes caused by films. Children lost their respect for family relationships and became discontented with their home environment. Television and radio, which brought entertainment back into the home, were also new sources for disruption and discontent. And not even home decoration was safe from the changes inspired by television. Opponents of the media held these modifications of home and family life, the changes in attitudes and relationships to be undesirable. The institution, they said, was threatened by innovation.

Entertainment

Motion pictures, radio, and television were powerful rivals of other forms of entertainment. The extent of their competition was demonstrated very early as the public, much taken with the new forms, deserted their usual amusements in favor of the new media. This influence, as I have shown, was decried by supporters of traditional recreation. But the defenders of the status quo did not expect the influence to end with piracy. They argued that the new media would lay waste the traditional forms of entertainment, that established patterns of amusement would be disrupted, and that respected institutions would suffer irreparable damage. None of the common forms of entertainment were thought to be safe from the influence of innovation.

Theatre

Supporters of the theatre argued that not only was this institution threatened with loss of its audience, but that motion pictures were forcing upon it new and restrictive patterns of operation. The changes they saw arising out of innovation represented a threat to the very life of the theatre and to dramatic art. It was their position that if theatre were damaged, society was the poorer because of it.

The silent picture grew at the expense of the legitimate theatre. From the early 1900's into the period of the talkies, spokesmen for the theatre told how the movies were crowding out the drama and taking over former playhouses. Day Allen Willey first called attention to the phenomenon. He said, in 1909,

> the fact is that in many cities it is a common occurrence to enjoy amusement by machinery in what was once a regulation play-house. The Academy of Music, the largest theatre in Baltimore; and the Grand Opera House of Evansville, Indiana, are instances of this.73

World's Work, the next year, added other names to the list.

> In New York the biograph manager has driven vaudeville and the old fashioned, first class drama from the Manhattan Theatre, the Union Square, the Lincoln Square, the Circle, the Majestic, the Yorkville, the Savoy, Keith and Proctor's 23rd Street Theatre, and the Harlem Opera House, among others, and threatens to occupy even the Academy of Music. When the great hall which long served the metropolis for an Opera House, and in which New York gave its ball to the Prince of Wales-- when so famous a place echoes the click of the moving-picture reel, something is taking place that merits attention.74

In 1911, the same magazine claimed that pictures had driven theatrical performances from 1,400 former playhouses. The next year Robert Grau announced that motion pictures had breached New York's legitimate theatre zone. Charles H. Ford had leased Mendelssohn Hall on West 40th Street for a movie house.75 By 1915, movies had possession of more than half of the largest auditoriums in New York, and a similar situation was said to exist around the country.

A writer for Illustrated World told of the hypothetical salesman,

in New York from Ohio, looking for theatrical entertainment.

> Our friends from Ohio moved along the familiar routes
> in the mad search for amusement. And they found nothing
> --movies, everywhere, and that was all. Of the nineteen
> largest theatres in town, only three were giving shows
> that were at all possible--and two of them were in Yid-
> dish.[76]

The first confrontation was over by the beginning of World

War I, and the argument disappeared for a time. Then with the

coming of talkies defenders again began to talk of the movies'

infringement on the theatre. Nation, for example, predicted in

1929 that one-half to two-thirds of the New York legitimate theatres

would be turned over to the talkies in the next three to four years.

Others commented periodically on the loss of theatres to the motion

pictures, and in 1937 Arthur Hopkins argued that because of the

movies, the nation's theatre had been reduced to a few blocks in

Manhattan and forced to fight for economic survival. What hope,

he asked, was there for any "social or cultural significance" for

theatre under these circumstances?[77] The argument was over, and

movies were judged the victor.

Motion pictures and radio were attacked on the grounds that

they had also destroyed ancillary forms of the theatre. For instance,

Robert Grau reported in 1912 that in a single week in December of

1911 seventy traveling theatrical companies were forced to close

for the season. The cause, he suggested, was the motion picture.

In 1924, Saturday Evening Post quoted the playwright Augustus
Thomas on "cancellation of road-company plays because those plays
had already been heard over the radio." And in 1937, Arthur Hopkins argued that it was the motion picture which had eliminated
the theatrical touring company. Similarly, motion pictures were
named responsible for the demise of the "vaudeville theatres of
Broadway and Main Street," and were said to have "quite annihilated
the popular-priced circuits where melodramas like 'Bertha, the
Sewing Machine Girl' and moth-eaten Broadway successes like 'The
Old Homestead' had flourished." In addition, even local theatrical
companies were said to have folded because of the motion pictures.[78]
The introduction of new media, said defenders of the status quo,
caused damage in all levels of theatre.

There was still another way in which motion pictures were
said to damage the stage. Richard Dana Skinner explained it in
1930, arguing that motion pictures lured actors away from the
stage by paying them more money, by eliminating long rehearsals,
and by reducing the uncertainties of the actor's life. The influence was subtle, but the damage was serious.[79]

Skinner did not originate the argument; it appeared first when
Robert Grau listed the stage personnel who had deserted theatre
for films.

> Mabel Taliaferro received more money for posing for
> the 'Cinderella' pictures for the Selig Company, than
> she has earned as a star for an entire season's efforts.

> Among other celebrities in this country who have become
> allies to the cameraman, may be named McKee Rankin,
> Sydney Booth, Mildred Holland, Nat C. Goodwin, Charles
> Kent, Mary Fuller, and others.[80]

Three months later, Grau reported that the lure of films extended

to other stage personnel. He wrote in _Overland_ in June of 1912

that "today the very best players, producers, and authors are avail-

able to the film manufacturer, for here they will get their sala-

ries with clock-like regularity, with engagements for fifty-two

weeks in the year, and such a thing as tie-walking is unknown

where the cameraman rules."[81] William A. Brady, the theatrical

producer, argued in 1915 that movies had created a dirth of actors

for the stage. He predicted

> the actor will die out because the movies offer induce-
> ments and the drama doesn't. Through active connection
> with the theatre I find where ten years ago there were
> twenty young men ambitious for a stage career, to-day
> there is not one. In another year there will be no
> actor.[82]

Walter Prichard Eaton, concerned about "actor-snatching" by the mov-

ies, provided another list of the players who had gone to work for

film makers. Included were Charlotte Walker, Geraldine Farrar who

went to "play Carmen for the camera," Raymond Hitchcock, Fanny

Ward, Flora Zabelle, Julian Eltenge, Laura Hope Crews, Harry Wood-

ruff, Blanche Ring, Frank Reicher, Theodore Roberts, Pedro deCordoba,

Donald Brian, William Elliot, DeWolfe Hopper, Eddie Foy, Billie

Burke, "and the lovely Alexandra Carlisle." Then in 1920, Kenneth

Macgowan, writing for the New York _Globe_, argued that "the celluloid serpent is casting its coils around the legitimate drama,
. . . buying up Broadway, buying up plays, buying up theaters,
buying up managers, buying up playwrights, buying up actors."[83]

The introduction of talkies placed an even greater premium
on the stage trained actor and on other stage personnel. Consequently, _Variety_ was said to have predicted "that many of the
legitimate producers will find themselves hard pressed next year
when they come to cast their productions." _Saturday Evening Post_
explained in 1929 that if plays were poor for a couple of seasons
it was because most of the playwrights--Sidney Howard, Arthur
Richman, Charles McArthur, Ben Hecht, and George Abbott among them
--had been lured to Hollywood. Supporters of theater continued
to assert that movies had hurt the stage by causing a scarcity
of acting and production talent for legitimate drama.[84] It was
the conclusion of Edgar Selwyn, himself a producer, that

> motion-picture moguls have combed the stage of its good
> players, have baited the best with juicy contracts and
> have left the Broadway mart as dry of excellent actors
> as a glass eye.
>   This, to me, is the greatest blow Hollywood has
> rendered Broadway.[85]

In addition to these main lines of attack, supporters of the
theatre also wrote of other damages to the stage. These arguments
were incidental, but need to be noted in order to demonstrate the
range of the attack. When motion picture companies began backing

legitimate plays, attackers argued this would weaken the theatre.
When motion pictures bought the rights to legitimate plays, critics
warned that this was but another way for movies to subvert the
drama. Both Brooks Atkinson and Alexander Wolcott attacked talkies
on the grounds that they "will ruin the stage and leave in its
place a harsh, mechanical monstrosity that can never aspire to
good entertainment." Theresa Helburn argued that the stage was
forced to compete with movies in lavish productions. As a result,
the theatre was suffocated in production costs. And Arthur Hopkins
held motion pictures responsible for the advent of the long run on
Broadway.[86]

The theatre, one of society's valued institutions, was challenged by innovation. It's supporters argued that the changes
forced upon it by motion pictures were damaging in the extreme.
Because of movies, the theatre was likely to die, and if not to
die, was assuredly toppled from its position of preeminence in
entertainment.

Silent films

The introduction of commercial motion pictures with synchronized music and speech represented another disruption of tradition.
By 1926, even though they were attacked as detrimental to the
theatre, silent pictures were generally accepted as part of the
established order, and defenders of silents argued against innovation.

Their defense of the medium was similar to that devised by spokesmen for the theatre.

Defenders of the silent screen argued, first, that the coming
of sound meant the end of the silent film, the latter presumed by
them to be an asset to society. Gilbert Seldes, having seen one
of the sound pictures released before Jazz Singer, predicted that
"in the future, efforts will be made to introduce speech into the
regular narrative movie, at which point the death of the pure movie
will be only a matter of time." In 1928, the movie director Monta
Bell suggested that motion pictures would be "thrown into a veritable
hurly-burly of inartistic experiment with noise and speech--at the
very time when the silent cinema art is reaching notable heights
of beauty and power as pantomine only." Nation said that the
talkie was "bound to oust and supplant, in the field of popular
entertainment, both the silent picture and the theater of living
actors." Seldes commented on talkies again in 1928, claiming this
time that they threatened "the life of both the silent picture and
the stage." By the end of the year, a writer for Independent and
Outlook was moved to comment that "it is too late to do anything
for the silent drama but mourn." To her there was "no doubt that
the talkies have set back the swift and exciting growth of this
infant art a good many years, even if, as there is reason to hope,
they have not arrested it permanently."[87]

Spokesmen for the silents described them as a medium for
artistic expression, pure in form, which had reached in Murnau's
The Last Laugh "the culmination of cinematic technique." It was
therefore no mere hour's entertainment which would end with the
death of the movies; talkies meant the death of an art, the substitution of a new medium "neither silent drama nor proper spoken
drama, but a misbegotten mixture of the two." Talkies were not a
transition to a new art, but an interruption of an old one.
As Richard Dana Skinner said, they were not an improvement, but an
innovation.[88]

The introduction of talkies ruined all that was pleasing in
silent films. Defenders of the displaced medium argued that the
art of pantomine, admired because it served to connect the movies
with the theatre, would disappear when silents ended. Even Scientific American regretted the loss, commenting that "by reproducing
the speech of the actor the fine art of pantomine would be brought
to naught and an element of the commonplace, a jarring note, would
often be introduced." Outlook and Independent thought talkies
would unnecessarily disturb the quiet of the movie theater, but
"unfortunately something even more important that this is threatened along with it, and that is pantomimic art."[89]

Actors and acting were predicted to suffer along with the
silents. Gilbert Seldes argued, with little regret, that

> a serious displacement of moving picture favorites is
> . . . likely to occur. Probably a more intelligent type
> of player will be required and the young woman who looks
> well in a close-up or a young man who expresses 'it' by
> jumping over six-foot fences, will receive less fan mail
> than those whose voices register warmly and clearly and
> who learn the new technique of acting which the talking
> film requires.[90]

But more seriously affected were those actors and actresses of

foreign birth who handled English with difficulty. Emil Jannings,

Conrad Veidt, Greta Garbo, "and the new horde of Russians," were

all thought to be in trouble. Former silent stars, untrained in

speaking, also stood with "their backs to the brink of oblivion."

Actors, in addition, lost their former close relationship with the

audience. That is, as Alexander Bakshy explained in Nation, in

silents the great actors transcended their screen characters,

became larger than life, and seemed to come into direct contact

with the audience. Lost was the intimacy and magnetic force that

had flowed from actor to audience in the silents.[91]

The universal appeal of the silent film ended with the addition

of sound. No longer was pantomine, the universal language, the

medium of communication. No longer were films understandable,

despite variations in national language. A new barrier had been

erected. Mary Pickford explained that not only did American actors

lose their world-wide audiences, but America had lost its silent

ambassadors.[92]

Movement, the chief resource of the silent film, was suddenly limited with the beginning of sound production. The camera, shrouded to prevent its noise leaking into the sound track, lost its mobility for a time, and the actor, limited to the pickup range of the microphone, lost his freedom to move within the scene. The limitation was apparent on the screen, and opponents of talkies contended the new mode of operation was one of the unfortunate consequences of innovation. Seldes argued that film would be hindered until directors learned to work within the new restrictions. Even then, he continued, there were times that speech must be subordinate to action:

> whenever the essence of the movie is pure movement, speech becomes an interruption. It becomes, in fact, merely spoken titles, the character is immobilized, the rhythm broken as it was by subtitle or by close-ups.[93]

Outlook and Independent charged film makers with having paralyzed action, and a writer in Saturday Evening Post argued that talkies were a hybrid art. To him, the art of the screen called for the story to be told in action, in motion. The introduction of dialogue changed the fundamental appeal of the film.[94] The strength of the past, the film's reliance on movement for communication, had been discarded for the novelty of the immediate present.

Two other admired qualities of silent pictures were also said to be destroyed in the introduction of dialogue. Welford

Beaton argued in Saturday Evening Post that speech added an un-

necessary intellectual distraction to the movies.

> The motion picture gives us motion without noise and
> excitement, and can convey impressions to us without
> involving our intellects. The appeal of the silent
> picture is straight to our emotions, without reference
> to our intellects. It is precisely the appeal that
> music has.[95]

This appeal was lost with the addition of talk. Also lost with the

introduction of talkies was the old slapstick comedy. Gilbert

Seldes took this stand in 1930, arguing that the new sophistication

accompanying dialogue, the new emphasis on the witty and the humor-

ous, as opposed to the comic, spelled the end of the slapstick.[96]

Finally, defenders of silent movies argued frequently that

talkies revolutionized production techniques to the detriment of the

industry. Nation predicted in 1928 that if the movies were replaced

by talkies, "entirely new techniques of production would have to

be evolved."[97] Monta Bell confirmed in North American Review that

this was in fact true, even in 1928. New production techniques

were already in practice. Movies were now rehearsed as if they

were a stage play, players were limited in their movements, and

no longer could the director simply talk his actors through their

scenes. The studio likewise was changed and soundproofed.

> There can be no more sunshine; no open air. The studio,
> rather, is like a padded cell on a large scale, enclosed
> and sealed to keep out all other sound.[98]

Neither was there supposed to be any possibility for cutting or editing a picture after the film was completed. It was Bell's conclusion that because of the changes in technique required by sound, "talking and synchronized pictures today are where motion pictures were fifteen years ago." Motion picture making became a much more difficult task once talkie production was undertaken. Concomitantly, production costs rose. Bell, for example, reported that "some of the best informed technicians estimate that intro- duction of sound will raise the production costs of feature pictures as much as half a million dollars."99

According to defenders of the present system, the advent of talkies spelled the end of the silent film, and the beginning of new problems for the motion picture industry. But as the industry gained more experience with the medium, even the critics recognized that talkies would find a place in the scheme of entertainment. A statement from North American Review in 1932 is a fitting epi- logue to this phase of the argument.

> The talking screen has been experimented with and tried out. Its adaptability to certain forms of entertainment has been demonstrated, as well as its lack of adaptabil- ity to others, notably musical comedy. The frantic out- burst of chattering which characterized the earlier talking pictures has given way to a soberer blending of speech and action. Generally speaking, the pendulum has come to rest at a point much nearer the art of the silent screen. The picture industry has learned that no matter how much talk you put on a screen, it remains a screen and primarily a visual medium. Although the present

trend is to reduce dialogue, there is no thought of
return to the silents. The talkies are definitely here
to stay.[100]

Talking pictures

Talkies, which were "here to stay" in 1932, were in turn

threatened by television. Their spokesmen turned to familiar

lines of argument for the defense, contending, in general, that

sound pictures, a good and valuable institution, were threatened

by innovation.

Predictions of a coming clash between television and motion

pictures began about the time that talkies were introduced. The

Boston Globe, for example, predicted in 1928 that movies would

have a tough nut to crack with the coming of television.[101] In

1929 R. E. Sherwood said that when television arrived, within

five years,

> a considerable number of theatres are destined to close
> their doors. . . . They will have fulfilled their earthly
> mission as palaces of diversion, and they will either
> be destroyed or converted to more profitable uses.[102]

The same year, Gilbert Seldes, who defended in turn each of the

institutions threatened by innovation, said that "the talkies, as

a successful entertainment, are only two years old and already

they are threatened in turn." He referred to the home sound movies

and to "comparatively inexpensive mechanisms, now being perfected,

which will throw on a small screen set up beside the home radio

set a moving picture projected from a central broadcasting station"
as the antagonists. Again in 1935 Seldes warned that talkies must
begin producing significant entertainment if they were to survive
in the light of the "continued threat of television escaping from
the research laboratories." Review of Reviews cautioned in 1936
that the advent of television would probably mean the "to-let
sign for motion-picture theaters." And when FCC Chairman James
Lawrence Fly saw the television programs broadcast into Newburgh,
New York, in 1940 he predicted, "This is going to kill the movies."[103]

By 1947 the long predicted TV boom had arrived, and Nation's
Business said that it, and others, did not see how movies could
survive the competition. Newsweek said television programs were
already good enough "to send chills through the Hollywood movie
factories."[104] Some writers, Milton MacKaye in Saturday Evening
Post, for example, offered assurance that the movies would survive,
even though changed in compass and in form. Recalling the past,
he argued that

> when talking pictures came in, there were Jeremiahs who
> foresaw the death of the legitimate theater. It got
> pretty sick, but survived. It is the belief of this
> reporter that movies and movie theaters will also sur-
> vive, although there may be fewer feature films and fewer
> theaters. The pattern of national entertainment may be
> different, but there are never enough talented enter-
> tainers to go around.[105]

Most others, however, who were suspicious of the influence of television on the motion pictures talked of specific ways, in addition to loss of audience, in which the movies would be hurt.

Just as defenders of the theatre had called attention to the playhouses closed because of movies, so defenders of movies pointed to picture houses closed because of television. Spyros P. Skouras, for example, told stockholders of 20th Century Fox that from 1949 to 1951, 134 movie houses in Southern California had closed. The cause, he said, was "this great new medium, television." A writer for Saturday Evening Post compiled other figures of closings caused by television. Among them was the notation that 126 movie houses had closed in the Los Angeles vicinity alone, 70 in Pennsylvania, 61 in Massachusetts, 64 in Chicago, and at least 75 in metropolitan New York. Charles Skouras, president of the 20th Century Fox Theater chain, "predicted that television would eliminate 50 per cent of the movie theaters now existing in the United States." Spokesmen for independent theater chains said the loss would be between 25 and 33 per cent.[106] No one knew how serious the damage would be, but there was consensus that the business was hurt by television.

Movie spokesmen contended, furthermore, that television had forced the motion picture industry to undesirable compromises. That is, some said the movies, cutting production costs and corners

in order to compete with television, were turning out a cheapened
product. Others argued that television had forced the industry to
turn to gimmicks such as 3D and Cinemascope and to spectacular and
expensive productions in an attempt to lure the audiences back into
the theaters. Both courses were judged debilitating. Moreover,
television was held to be responsible for the end of both the B
picture and the double feature.[107] This, most said, was an undesirable break with tradition.

Finally, television was also said to have reduced employment
in Hollywood, and to have diminished the importance of the movie
industry. U. S. News reported in 1949, for example, that while
television prospered, employment in the film industry dropped 25
per cent from the 1946 peak. Affected, too, were film actors and
actresses, who were reported to be losing their status as entertainers along with their box office appeal. Television, on the
other hand, was creating new stars, and former film stars were reported moving to the competition. Milton MacKaye explained in
Saturday Evening Post that "a brand new audience is about to be
born, brand new stars will blaze in the night, and, in the interest
of survival, Hollywood actors and actresses know that they, too,
must be seen and heard." What was the effect of all this on Hollywood? Harland Manchester argued in Nation's Business that television
would "close thousands of theaters, reduce salaries of producers,
directors and stars, and ultimately deglamorize the Hollywood legend

which has done so much to shape the tastes, habits and dreams of millions."[108] Before experience demonstrated that talkies would survive even the threat of television, critics of innovation feared the end of another prized institution.

Radio

For a number of years, television was promoted as a new system of radio broadcasting with pictures. Literary Digest, for example, spoke in 1928 of "the movie and radio in combination." Recall, too, that Seldes talked in 1929 of television as "a small screen set up beside the home radio set." C. Francis Jenkins, the inventor of a television system, said that with his invention radio would find its voice, and that moving pictures would be viewed at home in a small cabinet like a radio receiver, except that "it will have an opening with curtains resembling a miniature stage." Review of Reviews said in 1935 that when television arrived the radio chains would simply add pictures to the sound they carried already.[109] For these writers, television offered radio no competition. It was merely the extension of a present system.

As television approached broadcast capability, defenders of radio began to talk about the dangers of innovation. Gilbert Seldes in 1937 noted that engineers spoke of television as "the natural and inevitable fulfillment of radio," and that promoters of televsion described it as supplementary to radio. Radio

manufacturers, he said, aware that television would not long remain
supplementary, knew the time would come "when they will be trying to
sell electric light bulbs and kerosene lamps over the same counter."
Review of Reviews put it more bluntly, commenting that "when practical television arrives it means the dump-heap for radio sets."
After television had been shown at the World's Fair, Saturday
Review predicted it would replace radio in all but the most isolated
areas of the country.110

The beginning of the television boom after World War II,
stimulated defenders of radio to renewed predictions of disaster
A writer for Nation's Business reported predictions that television
would make a dead duck of radio in six years. John Crosby, surveying events of 1948, said that the year marked "the beginning of
an epoch and the end of another." Amplifying Crosby's remark,
Newsweek argued that "1948 marked the beginning of the long, slow
descent of radio against the spiraling ascent of television, even
though the latter is still unavailable to much of the country."
Christian Century said in 1949 that "persons high in the radio
industry declare it /television7 will supplant radio within three
years."111 Saul Carson wrote in New Republic in 1950 that radio
and television, handled in joint operations by CBS, NBC, and ABC,
seemed to be "unable to decide whether they are man and wife engaged
in a single family project or a pair of brothers trying to outsmart
each other." He predicted, however, that when the showdown came,

when the internal competition gets really rough--perhaps
three years from now, certainly not more than five--one
of the media will almost certainly assert its supremacy.
Since the greater investment will be in television,
radio is more likely to be moved to the annex.[112]

Looking back on the growth of television, Walter Goodman wrote in

1954 that

if television has not been with us long enough to make
clear just what changes it will wreak upon the country,
cultural, educational, entertainment-wise, it has, by
the very fact of its existence, already cast a pall over
the once shining spirits of radio. As the dusk deepens
for the former champions, they will find themselves
among the first to change, growing thin, pale, and bent
as they scrabble for a niche, however modest, in the
life of a nation of TV-viewers.[113]

Radio's spokesmen, like those for theatre and the movies, saw dis-

aster in the changes forced by innovation. And once again, the

patterns of their arguments traced familiar lines.

The loss of its audience was the most serious damage done

radio by television. But defenders also argued that other harm

had come to radio. First, the sale of radio receivers dropped

sharply as did the sale of time for radio advertising. But more

important, the configuration of the industry changed. Robert

Landry said in Nation in 1948 that television would place too much

power in the hands of the networks, and eventually eliminate the

local broadcaster. The situation was reversed in radio, however.

There the networks lost ground because of television. Local radio

stations became restive about the amount of time network programs consumed, and so turned to the greater profits of local advertising and programming. In addition, the patterns of desirable program times shifted because of the nighttime competition of television. No longer were evening hours prime time. Instead, radio began to concentrate on local programming for the daylight hours, from early morning through early evening. Because of the competition of television, radio became a medium of local rather than network service and turned to local instead of national advertising business as the primary source of revenue.[114] Radio was changed by the pressure of innovation, but it was not, as critics had predicted, eliminated by television. There was room, broadcasters found, for both services. Like the talkies, radio also survived television.

Music

Various musical events suffered a loss of audience because of the introduction of new forms of entertainment, and defenders of music were quick to point this out as they talked of the damage caused by innovation. But they talked of other damage, too.

The introduction of talking pictures caused attackers to talk again of the replacement of man by the machine. For example, when the first Vitaphone production was released, with the musical score recorded, Perceval Reniers argued in Independent that this was but "the latest contribution of the scientists to the robotism of the films," and the replacement of man as a performing artist.

Maurice Mermey, noting that most movie houses did away with their orchestras, organists, or pianists with the coming of sound, said "it does not seem unreasonable to predict that the movies will have canned orchestral accompaniment--music turned out by a group of a few hundred artists in canning factories in New York or else-where to supply a nation's movie-music needs." The machine, ex-emplified by the motion picture sound track, was feared to be rapidly pushing man from the scene. This was the point of Joseph N. Weber, International President of the American Federation of Musicians, the musician's union, when he argued that "with the development of machines that will synchronize action with words and music we have reached a development in which efforts are made to have machine productions supersede the personal services of artists in public performances of all kinds."115

Unemployment was the theme of other spokesmen for music. For example, The Musician warned readers that the coming of sound pictures meant that

> the organ as an accompaniment to the picture will more or less fade out of the picture. That may mean that some organists will have to become brick-layers or else be good enough or ambitious enough to become musical directors for picture producers.116

Jerome Beatty told in Saturday Evening Post how orchestras that cost $2,850.00 a week had been fired, along with their $350.00 a week leader, with the coming of talkies. And the editor and publisher of Musician spoke of the music teachers, the song writers, and the performers who had been thrown out of work by radio. He also argued that radio had caused a sharp decline in the number of touring concert companies, and concluded that those artists who did not have a contract with the opera or radio did not know where they would find work.[117] Machines had reduced demand for the live performing artist.

Other writers were concerned that radio and motion pictures caused the sale of musical instruments, sheet music, and phonographs to drop off. One of the attackers also feared that radio would make us a nation of passive listeners instead of performers.[118] And the head of the musician's union, equating music with culture, argued that the mechanical reproduction of music would eventually cause a shortage of musicians and a loss of culture, for with little prospect for work, people would avoid the field.

> Surely . . . if machine made music displaces the presence
> of the artist in hundreds, nay, thousands of instances
> the incentive for any individual to perfect himself, so
> necessary for progress in all art, is minimized, and
> music will no longer have the cultural value it formerly
> possessed. Any art is dependent upon the number of its
> executants, and when their activities are replaced by
> machine productions, then in time their numbers will be
> greatly reduced, and we will thus have a restriction
> in the art itself, and consequent reduction of its cul-
> tural value.[119]

Music, like other good things, was threatened by innovation. Its predicted debilitation was regretted both by its promoters and by opponents of the new media.

Reading

Reading, both for recreation and for acquisition of knowledge, is highly valued in our society. The ability to read, and an interest in doing so, is taken to be a demonstration of learning. Consequently, opponents of the new media argued that reading would be damaged by innovation, and pointed to this influence as-evidence of the disruption caused by movies, radio, and television.

Motion pictures and radio were first accused of damaging reading. In 1915, a writer for Education called attention to statistics which contradicted advocates' arguments that movies were a beneficial influence in education. A survey of high school students indicated that pictures based on books neither took the place of reading nor encouraged subsequent reading. In 1919, the writer of a letter to Bookman, arguing that motion pictures caused children to lose interest in books, predicted that "the flashing screen" might well "replace the printed page." New Republic contended in 1926 that movies were not an adequate substitute for reading, and in 1947 Survey Graphic reported a study by Witty and Kopel which concluded that listening to radio, going to movies, riding in automobiles, and watching athletic events all took the place of reading for youth.[120] While these scattered reports suggest continuing concern about the effect of the media on reading, there was little substantial argument from the concern.

The major argument about the mass media and reading began with the coming of television. Bennett Cerf charged in 1948 that television had already put a crimp in the sale of books and magazines, which could be interpreted to indicate a decline in reading. He concluded that

> publishers and authors can only hope that they will be able to get a small cut of the gravy--and that after the novelty of television has worn off, people again will prefer a good book, to the spectacle of two unknown prize-fighters staggering around a ring, or a syrupy-voiced huckster proclaiming the virtues of Dinkelspiel's Deodorant.[121]

When 1,580 New York families were surveyed in 1949 to discover the impact of television on them, researchers learned that 58.9 per cent of the respondents claimed to read fewer books after getting television. The basic argument about television and reading was summarized by Millard Faught in Saturday Review. "Welcome or not," he worte, "these new visual guests /on television7 are demanding --and receiving--millions of family hours of attention daily that were formerly devoted to reading, visiting, movie-going, and to the consuming of a long list of leisure-time goods that must now compete with this new monopolist of people's attention and money."[122] Put most simply, a great number of people watched television instead of reading, and the loss was deemed regrettable.

After 1950, the charge that television limited the amount of time both children and adults spent in reading became common in any attack on the medium. Then in 1955 U. S. News surveyed studies

of the influence of television on reading, only to conclude that

"in the mass, the TV set keeps people away from the printed word."[123]

That this was a matter of concern is indicated by responses to

interviews conducted by U. S. News. Asked if television had influ-

enced her children's school work, one mother answered that

> I am afraid it has set them back, especially in reading.
> Bill, who is 9, has a terrible time at school. He can't
> seem to learn to concentrate. At home, he even has to
> ask me what the newspaper headlines say. He just doesn't
> seem to want to learn to read.[124]

A housewife replied that television

> practically ruins my reading, and I am a reading person.
> I used to read as many as four, five books a month.
> Reading has always been the main interest in my life,
> and TV has cut it down to practically nothing.[125]

Another father claimed that because of having given most of their

free time to television, his children could not read.

> And I mean that they literally cannot read--or, if at
> all, just barely. My 13-year-old boy doesn't know how to
> read hardly at all.[126]

Reading, a highly valued activity, was threatened with dis-

placement by television, an unsatisfactory substitute. While both

children and adults would suffer from the change, it was the children

who would be hurt most. Captured by television before they learned

to read, children would develop neither the desire to read nor

basic reading skills. Hence, they would be handicapped both in

recreation and in their future education. The impact of television,
and earlier movies and radio, on reading thus had serious implications
for society.

Related to the arguments about educational and recreational
reading were those about newspapers. Predictably, some writers
argued that the advent of the new media meant the death of the newspaper. For example, Isabelle Keating said this in Harper's Monthly
in 1934:

> When economic conditions are ripe it /radio/ will play
> its ace-in-the-hole, televison, and the fight will be
> over. For with television the newspaper as it is at
> present constituted cannot compete. By means of it radio
> will be able to send not only news bulletins but news-
> reels of the events described in those bulletins into our
> homes; it will be able to show us animated advertisements
> of goods on sale at the neighboring department store and
> in the neighboring town. It will be able to perform most
> of the functions of the newspapers in a form which has
> been demonstrated to be more appealing to the American
> public than the printed page.
>   When that time comes those newspapers which have
> had funds and foresight enough to acquire radio stations
> will remain solvent by using their papers to supplement
> their radio programs, as they now use radio to supplement
> their news columns. The others--well, the experience
> of the weekly papers when dailies entered the field may
> be an index to the fate of the others. Some of the week-
> lies turned to interpretative material and continued to
> exist. Others belong to the ages.[127]

In addition to charging that movies, radio, and television
had taken over the basic function of the newspaper--the gathering
and reporting of news--and had diverted advertising revenue formerly
available to papers, attackers argued that the new media caused

readers to give up their papers. Time, for example, in 1949 reported that television caused a 24 per cent decrease in newspaper reading in homes surveyed in New York. Six years later a study by NBC concluded that newspaper reading fell off 20 per cent when television was purchased. The basic trend after the advent of television, said U. S. News, was toward less reading of newspapers.[128] Like the decline in recreational reading, this too was called damaging to society.

Sports

The major influence of the new media on sports centered in loss of audiences for the various events. Occasionally, however, writers mentioned other possible areas of damage. For example, Commonweal implied that television would be harmful for college athletics by asking,

> how can larger educational institutions keep athletics in its properly subordinate role when teams know they will be performing before half a million spectators? It will be likewise difficult for college administrators to maintain a good perspective when large sums are dangled before them by TV representatives.[129]

Three times in 1951 Commonweal asked the same questions. Each time it implied that television would influence athletics in some undesirable fashion, possibly related to the honesty of players, but the charges were never made explicit nor were the questions answered.[130]

Children's recreation

Attackers of radio and television charged that the new media
were so attractive to children that they gave up former amusements
and patterns of recreation in favor of either listening or watching.
Neither radio nor television required any effort for participation,
and as a result children became sedentary. This was one of the
problems of radio, according to Saturday Review. It was also a
danger in television. John R. Harmon explained in Education that
the child who became entranced with television failed to pick up
the pre-TV recreational routine, "which might include an afternoon
of sports, or a trip to the 'Y'," and so did not develop the kinds
of recreational skills important today. The United Parents Association of New York objected to television on the grounds that because
of it children had "less interest in active outdoor play, arts,
and crafts."[131] Television, in sum, changed the patterns of children's play.

Other entertainment

The influence of the new media extended into nearly all recreational activities. In addition to those already mentioned, other
attackers claimed that radio and television had curtailed conversation and had taken time formerly devoted to visiting. Finally,
one of the early researchers interested in the effects of television on family recreation found that dining out, dancing, and

evenings out decreased as soon as the family television set was
purchased.[132]

None of the familiar forms of recreation seemed to be safe
from the competition of the new media. Critics charged that movies,
which had attracted crowds away from the theatres, also took over
theatre buildings and lured away stage personnel. Radio cut into
the time people had once had for movies, for concerts, for reading
or for sports. Talkies in turn laid waste the silent films, replac-
ing them entirely in half a decade. Television, finally was labeled
the greatest competitor of all. It threatened to drive out or to
cripple nearly everything which had gone before. Movies, radio,
reading, sports, concerts, conversation, and even children's games
were influenced by it. Each new invention, said its opponents,
posed a threat for the amusements which had preceded it.

The strategy which critics employed to counteract the threat
of innovation in entertainment is familiar. Arguing from the
presumption that it is good to preserve well known and comfortable
things, playing on uncertainty about change and fears of the unknown future, endowing the old with the sanction of tradition,
their opponents charged the new media with breaking down familiar
and respected forms of amusement, with destroying easy and habitual
patterns of entertainment. The argument played upon the audience's
committment to the notion that "this is how we've always done it,

it therefore must be good." Hence it not only served in defense
of entertainment of high status, the theatre and concerts, but
could also be used in behalf of former villains, movies and radio,
when they were threatened by television, for by then they were
firmly established in the existing order, a part of the tradition
which critics sought to preserve.

Much of what I have said about entertainment could also be
said about the arguments over threats to other institutions. In
every case, critics denied that the advantages promised by advocates were truly advantageous. The new media would not do the good
that their promoters had promised. Moreover, said opponents, the
introduction of television, radio, and movies raised new problems
which would cause damage to familiar institutions. Instead of
profiting from innovation, social institutions would suffer because
of it. The presumption lay with the existing institution and on the
side of tradition.

This, then, was the case of the opposition. Just as advocates
had maintained that society would benefit from the new media through
improvement of its institutions, attackers argued that the changes
fostered by motion pictures, radio, and television would prove
damaging to education, politics, religion, family, and recreation.
The good things society had constructed to implement its visions
were threatened with ruin. Theirs was argument for tradition,

argument for the preservation of the status quo in the face of new invention. Their resistance reflected a fear of change, a desire for stability, and a vested interest in those parts of the social order susceptible to the influence of the new mass media. To the attackers, innovation was indeed the counterpart of improvement.

This ends the discussion of argument from cause. In the past four chapters I have examined arguments presented by advocates and critics, related both to social values and social institutions. In general, advocates maintained that the introduction of movies, radio, and television would serve society well. The new media would allow men to do those things they most wanted done, would strengthen the institutions which society had erected to realize its values. Innovation gave support to those things and ideas held to be necessary, worthwhile, and desirable. Opponents took the opposite position. To them innovation threatened values, weakened institutions. Tradition, stability, and order were the victims of change. New problems were created, old ones intensified. What men most feared, said their critics, the movies, radio, and television would cause to happen.

There remain to be considered three other broad categories of argument. The first of these is argument from comparison.

Notes

1. Comm, 24 Mr '50, p. 621.

2. WW, My '10, p. 12876; CCom, 8 Je '07, p. 295; Sur, 3 Ap '09, p. 8.

3. Lip, O '09, p. 458.

4. HW, 30 Jl '10, p. 12; Dial, 16 F '14, p. 129; CO, D '15, p. 405. See also, RR, Mr '12, p. 329; AmMag, Ap '14, p. 48; Out, 3 Mr '15, p. 498; NAR, N '21, p. 624.

5. CO, Mr '25, p. 330.

6. NR, 5 F '30, p. 298.

7. NAR, Summer '37, p. 231.

8. Scrib, Jl '29, p. 7. See also, Scrib, Mr '37, p. 74.

9. Out, 26 S '28, p. 865; Col, 25 Ag '28, p. 12; NAR, O '28, p. 430.

10. SEP, 16 F '29, p. 150.

11. Nat, 27 Mr '29, p. 365; Col, 25 My '29, p. 48; Out, 23 O '29, p. 293. See also, LD, 25 S '26, p. 28; Nat, 10 O '28, p. 360; Out, 5 D '28, p. 1270; Col, 23 F '29, p. 42; SEP, 9 Mr '29, p. 132; Scrib, Ap '29, p. 373; Nat, 26 Je '29, p. 772; SEP, 20 Jl '29, p. 20; TA, S '29, p. 652; SEP, 21 S '29, p. 136.

12. Out, 31 D '30, p. 693; Scrib, F '35, p. 85; RD, Ja '41, p. 63.

13. AmMag, Mr '48, p. 44; NB, Je '49, p. 41; SR, 17 Je '50, p. 10; Time, 28 My '51, p. 100; SEP, 19 Ja '52, p. 18.

14. USN, 2 S '55, p. 43. See also, Col, 16 S '22, p. 3; SEP, 21 S '29, p. 140; RR, Je '35, p. 54; RR, Ag '36, p. 4; SEP, 28 S '40, p. 25; Nwk, 1 N '48, p. 52; GH, Ja '49, p. 4; USN, 7 Ja '49, p. 24; SRL, 26 Ag '50, p. 8; SEP, 2 F '52, p. 102; Comm, 6 Jl '51, p. 300; TA, Ag '51, p. 10; Nat, 13 O '51, p. 300; SEP, 26 Je '52, p. 122; Atlan, O '53, p. 57.

15. Nat, 30 N '46, p. 618; AmMag, Mr '48, p. 45; Nwk, 20 D '48, p. 53; Time 7 F '49, p. 70; SEP, 2 F '52, p. 100; USN, 2 S '55, p. 39. See also, SR, 5 Je '48, p. 6; NR, 7 Je '48, p. 20; NB, Je '49, p. 44; SA, S '49, p. 26; BW, 27 D '52, p. 27; NR, 26 Ap '54, p. 22; NR, 28 N '55, p. 20.

16. LD, 23 Ag '24, p. 32; Ind, 17 O '12, p. 890; LD, 4 F '22, p. 32; Out, 15 Mr '22, p. 410; Comm, 13 Ag '30, p. 381; LD, 27 Ja '33, p. 35; SSoc, 3 D '38, p. 724; CC, 2 F '49, p. 143; Mus, Je '29, p. 17; CO, Ag '24, p. 202; RR, N '27, p. 518; Etude, S '31, p. 615; Out, 16 O '29, p. 276; LD, 9 Jl '32, p. 35; LD, 16 Jl '32, p. 32; AmMag, Mr '48, p. 45; NR, 7 Je '48, p. 20; Nwk, 20 N '50, p. 60; Comm, 8 Je '51, p. 204; Comm, 14 S '51, p. 541; SEP, 19 Je '52, p. 18; Nwk, 8 Je '53, p. 67; USN, 2 S '55, p. 43; NR, 7 Je '48, p. 20.

17. LD, 4 O '13, p. 576.

18. LD, 4 O '13, p. 577.

19. Cent, Je '24, p. 149.

20. NR, 13 Ag '30, p. 357; CC, 8 Ap '31, p. 479.

21. Scholastic Teacher, 1 N '50, p. 21T.

22. HM, N '31, p. 718; Atlan, My '37, p. 539; SR, 19 F '44, p. 28.

23. SG, Mr '47, p. 187.

24. BHG, Mr '37, p. 96; SR, 25 N '50, p. 10; SSoc, 15 D '51, p. 369.

25. Comm, 14 N '48, p. 139; SD, My '50, p. 36.

26. CC, 22 Ja '30, p. 112; CC, 15 Ja '30, p. 76.

27. Col, 23 N '29, p. 11; BHG, Mr '37, p. 98; Rot, N '38, p. 12.

28. SD, O '49, p. 25; Nwk, 26 D '49, p. 36.

29. Comm, 24 My '50, p. 621; Nat, 22 Jl '50, p. 87; SS, 20 S '50, p. 20; WHC, N '50, p. 71; Scholastic Teacher, 1 N '50, p. 21T; SR, 25 N '50, p. 9; CC, 26 D '51, p. 68; USN, 2 S '55, pp. 36, 41, 45-48.

30. NR, 19 Mr '24, p. 92.

31. USN, 23 Je '50, p. 14.

32. Comm, 6 O '50, p. 622.

33. NR, 9 My '55, p. 13; 13 My '55, p. 141.

34. SEP, 20 My '39, p. 106.

35. Time, 21 Jl '52, p. 40.

36. SR, 6 D '52, p. 58; Comm, 4 F '55, p. 469; USN, 5 S '55, p. 37.

37. RR, S '24, p. 237; HM, N '52, p. 28; LD, 9 Ag '24, p. 11; NR, 3 S '24, p. 9.

38. Time, 21 Jl '52, p. 38.

39. Nat, 16 Ag '52, p. 132.

40. Nat, 16 Ag '52, p. 132. See also, USN, 2 S '55, p. 37.

41. NR, 2 My '55, p. 8; SR, 26 F '49, p. 26; NR, 1 D '52, p. 13; SR, 6 D '52, p. 58; SA, My '53, p. 46.

42. NR, 2 My '55, p. 8; SR, 15 Mr '52, p. 31. See also, Atlan, Mr '49, p. 36.

43. USN, 23 Je '50, p. 14.

44. NR, 9 My '55, p. 12.

45. NR, 9 My '55, p. 12; Comm, 13 My '55, p. 141.

46. NR, 23 My '28, p. 6.

47. NR, 1 D '52, p. 13; NR, 9 My '55, p. 12.

48. USN, 23 Je '50, p. 14.

49. Nat, 15 N '52, p. 449.

50. NR, 1 D '52, p. 13.

51. USN, 2 S '55, p. 37; USN, 23 Je '50, p. 14; Comm, 6 O '50, p. 622; NR, 17 D '51, p. 5; AmMag, Ap '52, p. 111.

52. SR, 6 D '52, p. 17; Nat, 15 N '52, p. 449; SR, 6 D '52, p. 57; Nwk, 19 S '55, p. 39; Comm, 13 My '55, p. 141.

53. SR, 6 D '52, p. 17. See also, NR, 1 D '52, p. 14; NR, q My '55, p. 7; Comm, 13 My '55, p. 141.

54. Comm, 13 My '55, p. 141.

55. NR, 17 D '51, p. 5; NR, 9 My '55, p. 15; Comm, 13 My '55, p. 141; Nwk, 18 F '52, p. 68. See also, NR, 2 My '55, p. 7.

56. NR, 17 D '51, p. 5; AmMag, Ap '52, pp. 111-112.

57. WT, O '08, p. 1052; CO, O '23, p. 471; Time, 7 F '49, p. 70.

58. CO, S '14, p. 192.

59. AmMag, Jl '22, p. 65.

60. Lip, O '09, p. 454.

61. Out, 28 My '24, p. 131.

62. GH, Ag '10, p. 184; Ind, 5 Mr '17, p. 427.

63. CC, 22 Ja '30, p. 112.

64. CC, 24 My '33, p. 689.

65. Nat, 25 Mr '25, p. 325; Forum, Mr '29, p. 170.

66. USN, 2 S '55, p. 48.

67. SR, 25 N '50, p. 9; ParM, D '48, p. 64; AmMerc, D '54, p. 81; SD, O '49, p. 24; USN, 2 S '55, p. 41.

68. USN, 2 S '55, p. 48.

69. AmMerc, D '54, p. 81; SR, 25 N '50, p. 50.

70. SEP, 9 Mr '46, p. 9.

71. NB, Je '49, p. 42.

72. SR, 26 Ag '50, p. 7. See also, SD, Ap '45, p. 27; ParM, D '48, p. 42.

73. Lip, O '09, p. 458.

74. WW, My '10, p. 12876.

75. Over, Je '21, p. 550; WW, F '11, p. 14020.

76. IW, O '15, p. 235.

77. Nat, 27 Mr '29, p. 365; Scrib, Mr '37, p. 28. See also, SA, 12 Ag '11, p. 156; RR, Mr '12, p. 336; Ind, 17 O '12, p. 890; Ind, 17 Jl '13, p. 144; Lip, Ag '13, p. 191; Over, Mr '14, p. 274; CO, S '14, p. 176; CO, Je '20, p. 794; NAR, Jl '20, p. 81; NR, 1 Ap '31, p. 174; NAR, Summer '37, p. 231.

78. RR, Mr '12, p. 329; SEP, 6 D '24, p. 78; Scrib, Mr '37, p. 19; NAR, Mr '29, p. 303; HM, D '28, p. 112. See also, AmMerc, Ap '33, p. 417; SA, 12 Ag '11, p. 156; Scrib, Mr '37, p. 19; NAR, Summer '37, p. 231.

79. Comm, 7 My '30, p. 23.

80. RR, Mr '12, p. 332.

81. Over, Je '12, p. 551.

82. CO, D '15, p. 405.

83. AmMag, D '15, pp. 32-33; CO, Je '20, p. 794.

84. Nat, 27 Mr '29, p. 365; SEP, 20 Jl '29, p. 20. See also, Comm, 21 My '30, p. 71; AmMerc, Ap '33, p. 417; Scrib, Mr '37, p. 27; NAR, Summer '37, pp. 233, 236.

85. TM, Ja '30, p. 30. See also, Ind, 17 Jl '13, p. 142; Over, Mr '14, p. 273; AmMag, O '14, p. 96; NAR, Jl '20, p. 83; IW, Ja '16, p. 662; Col, 23 N '29, p. 11.

86. NAR, Jl '20, p. 81; CO, Je '20, p. 794; IW, Ja '16, p. 661; Out, 18 S '29, p. 115; NAR, Summer '37, p. 232; Scrib, Mr '37, p. 26. See also, NAR, O '28, p. 430; Nat, 10 O '28, p. 360; HM, D '28, p. 112; NAR, Mr '29, p. 303; Nat, Ag '30, p. 216; GH, Ja '49, p. 4.

87. NR, 9 Mr '27, p. 73; NAR, O '28, p. 428; Nat, 10 O '28, p. 360; HM, N '28, p. 708; Out, 5 D '28, p. 1270. See also, Col, 23 F '29, p. 26; SEP, 23 Ja '32, p. 10.

88. HM, N '28, p. 707; Out, 5 D '28, p. 1270; Comm, 29 My '29, p. 104.

89. SA, S '26, p. 209; Out, 5 D '28, p. 1270. See also, Col, 25 Ag '29, p. 12; NAR, O '28, p. 428.

90. HM, N '28, p. 709.

91. Out, 5 D '28, p. 1272; Col, 23 F '29, p. 42; Comm, 21 My '30, p. 71; Nat, 27 My '31, p. 590.

92. Col, 23 F '29, p. 28; Out, 23 O '29, p. 292; NAR, Ag '33, p. 146; SEP, 23 Ag '30, p. 117.

93. NR, 8 Ag '28, p. 306.

94. Out, 5 D '28, p. 1270; SEP, 21 S '29, p. 136.

95. SEP, 21 S '29, p. 136.

96. NR, 10 D '30, p. 103.

97. Nat, 26 S '28, p. 286.

98. NAR, O '28, p. 434.

99. NAR, O '28, p. 434. See also, Col, 25 Ag '28, p. 47; Nat, 26 S '28, p. 286; Scrib, Ap '29, p. 368; SEP, 23 Ja '32, p. 10; NO, S '33, p. 22; NAR, My '32, p. 448; Col, 23 N '29, p. 11; Col, 23 F '29, pp. 28, 42.

100. NAR, My '32, p. 448.

101. LD, 1 S '28, p. 19.

102. Scrib, Jl '29, p. 7.

103. HM, S '29, p. 454; Scrib, F '35, p. 82; RR, Ag '36, p. 4; SEP, 28 S '40, p. 25.

104. NB, Jl '47, p. 75; Nwk, 20 D '48, p. 53

105. SEP, 2 F '52, p. 102. See also, Atlan, My '37, p. 533; SR, 21 F '42, p. 4; Time, 7 F '49, p. 70; CC, 11 My '49, p. 591; Etude, Je '49, p. 342.

106. Time, 28 My '51, p. 100; SEP, 19 Je '52, pp. 18, 19. See also, TA, Ag '51, p. 10.

107. USN, 7 Ja '49, p. 24; SEP, 7 F '53, p. 112; Etude, Je '49, p. 324; HB, F '50, p. 126; SR, 17 Je '50, p. 34; SEP, 26 Ja '52, p. 119; Comm, 23 O '53, p. 65; USN, 5 Mr '54, p. 41.

108. USN, 7 Ja '49, p. 24; SEP, 2 F '52, p. 102; NB, 7 S '42, p. 283.

109. LD, 1 S '28, p. 19; HM, S '29, p. 454; SEP, 27 Jl '29, p. 12; RR, Je '35, p. 54.

110. Atlan, My '37, p. 533; RR, Ag '36, p. 4; SR, 21 F '42, p. 16.

111. NB, Jl '47, p. 75; Nwk, 27 D '48, p. 44; CC, 11 My '49, p. 591.

112. NR, 23 Ja '50, p. 21.

113. NR, 26 Ap '54, p. 22.

114. Scrib, F '37, p. 64; SR, 5 Je '48, p. 6; BW, 27 D '52, p. 27; Nat, 25 D '48, p. 724; SEP, 2 F '52, p. 101.

115. Ind, 25 S '26, p. 359; NAR, Mr '29, p. 303; Mus, My '29, p. 34; NR, 30 Mr '42, p. 426.

116. Mus, My '29, p. 34.

117. SEP, 9 Mr '29, p. 18; NAR, Mr '29, p. 305; Mus, Je '29, p. 17; LD, 3 My '24, p. 30; SEP, 6 D '24, p. 78.

118. RR, N '27, p. 518; Mus, Je '29, p. 17; Out, 9 Ap '24, p. 605; LD, 3 My '24, p. 30; CO, Ag '24, p. 202; SEP, 6 D '24, p. 78.

119. NAR, Mr '29, p. 305.

120. Educa, F '15, p. 361; Bookm, Mr '19, p. 42; NR, 10 N '26, p. 343; SG, Mr '47, p. 187.

121. SR, 5 Je '48, p. 6.

122. Time, 7 F '49, p. 70; SR, 26 Ag '50, p. 8.

123. SS, 20 S '50, p. 21; Comm, 18 Ja '52, p. 366; USN, 2 '55, pp. 36, 40; SNL, 26 N '55, p. 344.

124. USN, 2 S '55, p. 45.

125. USN, 2 S '55, p. 46.

126. USN, 2 S '55, p. 46.

127. HM, S '34, p. 472.

128. Col, 26 Je '15, p. 23; Ind, 9 Jl '27, p. 33; NR, 7 My '30, p. 314; Out, 31 D '30, p. 692; Scrib, My '31, p. 490; NO, Jl '33, p. 17; Nat, 12 Je '35, p. 677; SR, 21 F '42, p. 16; AmMerc, Jl '41, p. 61; CC, 22 N '33, p. 1462; Comm, 28 S '34, p. 499; HM, N '52, p. 33; Time, 7 F '49, p. 70; USN, 2 S '55, p. 39.

129. Comm, 8 Je '51, p. 204.

130. Comm, 6 Jl '51, p. 300; Comm, 14 S '51, p. 541.

131. SR, 14 Je '47, p. 26; Educa, O '50, p. 127; SR, 25 N '50, p. 9. See also, Nat, 22 Jl '50, p. 87; SSoc, 15 D '51, p. 369; ParM, D '52, p. 36.

132. Forum, Mr '29, p. 170; WHC, N '50, p. 71; GH, N '50, p. 265; USN, 2 S '55, p. 36; SR, 26 Ag '50, p. 8; NB, Je '49, p. 41.

Chapter VI

ARGUMENT FROM COMPARISON
Advocacy and Attack

The second genre of argument employed in the agitation over
the introduction of motion pictures, radio, and television was
comparative. These arguments, with their emphasis on similarity
and dissimilarity, were used approximately half as often as the
arguments from cause. They were used by advocates and attackers
alike to define the place of the new media in the social order,
to show the relation of the media to the value and institutional
systems, to evaluate the performance of new inventions, and to
predict the consequences of their introduction.

Various kinds of comparisons can be identified in the discourse. For this analysis they are grouped roughly in the order
of their complexity, from the simplest to the most complicated.
First to be considered are the simple statements of likeness, the
comparative assertions. These are followed by comparisons in which
predominant values ascribed to the media are weighed and evaluated.
The third type of comparison deals with advantage and disadvantage,
and the fourth with the potential of the media as opposed to their
performance in practice. I discuss in fifth place the intra-media
comparisons, arguments in which the media are tested by measuring

their present performance against that of the past. Finally, the
chapter ends with analogical argument, the most sophisticated of
the comparisons.

Comparative Assertion

In the simplest and most frequent of the arguments from comparison, promoters and critics appraised the new media by asserting
their comparability to past inventions and familiar institutions.
To praise the new thing, its promoters said it was like other
things which were already accepted as good and valuable; i. e.,
the motion picture is like the theatre. To blame, critics linked
the unknown, by comparison, to something commonly believed to be
bad; i. e., the motion picture is like the dime novel.

Typically, these comparisons are brief, often made in a single
sentence, seldom developed past the level of assertion. They depend
upon readers' acceptance of common judgments about the goodness
or badness of things past; the audience, for example, can be counted
upon to accept the theatre as good. The comparison thus focuses
on the new, the untested, the undecided. The argument serves to
formulate an estimation of the new, to test how it measures up in
comparison to the familiar, to assign it a place in the social
scheme.

Various levels of comparison may be distinguished in promoters'
assertions about the new media. The first, in which the terms of
the comparisons were strongest, stressed the superiority of motion
pictures, radio, and television. The new media were not merely
as good as their predecessors, they were better. The comparative
adjectives were better, more potent, more varied and more intelligent, more complete, and more valuable. Movies, radio, and TV
were described as able to reach more people, as having the ability
to teach more, as having distinct advantages over, as the inventor's
greatest contribution, the most revolutionary instruments ever to
be developed.

Sometimes the new media were measured against a general class
of familiar good things. One writer, for example, compared radio
to recent inventions, concluding that radio was superior to all
of them.

> None of the other miracles of applied science has begun
> to appeal to the public imagination as has the development
> of radio. Nor is it likely that any of the inventions
> of this century will exercise a commensurate influence
> on human thought and manners of living.[1]

Other writers said the new mass media were better than any other
means for the transmission of intelligence, more effective than
all other moral media, "the greatest single force shaping the
American character," superior to former means of entertainment,
more important than other news media, more efficient than other

forms of communication, more valuable than previous means for education, more varied than other modes of expression, offering as
Saturday Review put it with television approaching, the promise
of a "glowing future when we will all have an educational, cultural,
and entertainment device in our homes ten times as effective as
anything we have now."[2]   Advocates depended upon the audience to
insert the specific terms in the comparisons, and ended their
descriptions with the suggestion that the new media were superior
to all things formerly held to be good and desirable.

When the comparisons were made specific, radio, television,
and motion pictures were most frequently named superior to printing,
the newspaper, and the stage, the three oldest and most respected
of the former media. Scientific American, for example, asserted
that "motion pictures present in a single minute more than can
be portrayed in a chapter of printed material." Saturday Evening
Post named television "the greatest advance in the educational
field for both children and adults since the Middle Ages, when
invention of moveable type paved the way for mass printing of
books and magazines and newspapers." Independent said that "the
moving picture shows are in general superior, both artistically
and morally, to the vauseville and melodrama that they have driven
out of business."[3]   These comments are typical of the comparisons
which promoters offered as they sought to carve a place for their

new media. Supposing that the worth of the new media could be
demonstrated most clearly if the standards for measurement were
stringent, advocates tested the new against the strongest and most
respected of the old forces.

Other comparisons measured the new media against a variety
of particular, but less prestigeous social goods. Motion pictures
were, by comparison, superior to other media in the war effort.
Radio, talkies, and television were named an improvement over the
silent screen, as in this <u>Scribner's</u> comment about radio:

> The printing-press and the motion-picture stand out as
> epoch-marking instruments in telling the world what the
> world is doing. But radio broadcasting harks back to
> the primitive, the direct appeal by word of mouth, giving
> it new power as yet unmeasured.[4]

American films were judged better than foreign films, and the
American system of broadcasting was deemed superior to that of
England and Europe. Movies, radio, and television were compared
favorably to the traditional educational lecture. And movies and
television were held to be better in education than radio. For
example, James Rorty said in <u>Harper's Monthly</u> in 1931 that "a
percentage of informed people, both educators and engineers, are
of the opinion that as an educational instrumentality, sound pictures have greater potentialities than radio." When politics was
considered, <u>Review of Reviews</u> said, for instance, that "there is
no other single method of campaigning on a great scale that can

now be compared for effectiveness and for cheapness with radio

broadcasting." Television later took the place of radio in the

comparison. Television was also compared to radio and print as

a means for advertising, and found superior. John Crosby, for

example, said advertisers found that an hour of television was

better than a full page in a newspaper and that the potency of TV

advertising was "generally rated three times that of radio."

In other comparisons, the new media were asserted to be superior

to the telephone, the telegraph, the automobile, magazines, news-

reels, the phonograph, and all other "past fads." Radio was even

expected to "do more for promoting world peace than all the recip-

rocal trade treaties ever seen in the dreams of Cordell Hull."[5]

Thus, promoters argued in their comparisons that the new media were

better than whatever society had formerly considered to be its

best.

The second level of comparison stressed the similarities of

the new media and other good things. Instead of asserting the su-

periority of the new, promoters said movies, radio, and television

were like former media, as good as things which were valued, held

as important a place as respected institutions. The arguments

on this level were fewer, but the objects to which the new was

compared were the same as in the former category. Movies, radio,

and television were said to be on a plane with printing, newspapers,

schools, drama, the automobile, and the home. Advocates of television said students learned as much from a lesson on TV as from the same presentation in a classroom. Commonweal argued that "radio is as important an agency of communication as the printing press." And television was described by U. S. News as another service given the American public, equal to the newspaper, to magazines, and to the radio. Mary Pickford said motion pictures held "a foremost place alongside the forces that are shaping the world's progress." A writer for Scribner's compared the mass entertainment of the movies to the entertainment provided by Shakespeare's theatre. When the morality of films came under fire, one of their defenders argued that "the moral standard of the moving picture film is quite as high as the standard of the fiction and poetry in our public library." A Saturday Evening Post editorial compared the universality of the movies to that of the Twenty-third Psalm. Radio was named the greatest medium for national unity since the railroad and the telegraph. Sarnoff said the radio was a public service equal to the automobile. And Christian Century compared religious radio to the work of the missionary.[6] Through comparison, advocates here named the new media the equals of the old.

A third mode of comparative assertion ranked the new media above most existing agencies for social benefit, but reserved the place of primary importance for something other than movies, radio, or television. Most commonly, printing was named the medium of

greatest influence and value. For example, the United States
Commissioner of Education named movies "the most revolutionary
instrument introduced in education since the printing-press."
A writer for Saturday Evening Post believed "that the development
of radio telephony will be only a little less important in its
effect on our lives than the invention of printing." Speaking
in the early days of the medium, Richard B. Hull, director of the
nation's first educational television station, said that "when
you see what the educational possibilities of television are, even
as demonstrated in our limited way, you know that here is an instrument for progress second only to the printing press." Operating in
the same mode of comparison, the Chairman of the National Board
of Censorship of Motion Pictures (The National Board of Review)
claimed that "next to the daily press and the school the movie is
probable the most influential educational and recreational agency
in our daily life." Harper's said that "excepting the home, the
press, and the schoolroom, the movie has been called the most
potent existing factor in the shaping of our national mind and
morals."[7] Unwilling to commit themselves completely to the superiority of the new, these authors qualified their response by ranking
the new media below only the most valued of the present institutions.

When advocates found it necessary to answer charges about the deleterious effects of the new media, they also turned to comparative assertion. They argued, in essence, that the media were no worse than many of society's accepted practices and institutions.

These justifying assertions compared the new media with a number of familiar amusements which enjoyed wide acceptance. Movies, as early as 1911, were defended as no more dangerous than the dime novel, an unusual comparison considering the generally low estate of the yellow back at the time. It was Harper's which said, with approval, that "the motion picture show has in it, of course, the elements of the dime novel and the cheap short story." This comparison was less unusual twenty five years later, after the intervention of amusements which not only superseded the dime novels but softened memories of them. Then one spokesman for broadcasting asserted that children's programs were merely the modern replacement for five cent weeklies, and another dismissed parental concern with the comment that there was no more to fear in the programs than there had been in the dime novels of fifty years before. Radio programs were also defended as no worse than most children's literature, ghost stories, and "the mystery thrillers at the movies even today." Children's television programs were compared, by their defenders, to other familiar stories. One industry executive argued, for example, that TV was no worse than fairy tales, asserting that

"Mother Goose is full of acts of violence." The violence which radio played upon was justified by comparing it to the violence apparent in Greek tragedy, specifically the blinding of Oedipus, and the bloody make-believe "which made Macbeth a hit with the Elizabethans." The violence of the movies, their "trinity of love, sex, and crime," was excused on the basis of its likeness to serious drama "from Aeschylus to O'Neill." Extending the comparison, and admitting that "some pictures today are crude, untrue, and inartistic," William deMille went on to excuse the industry by pointing to "the same percentage of unexcellence . . . in the arts of the novelist, the dramatist, the painter, and the music-ian." Some people, said America, had even defended pictures by claiming the screen was no more lurid than many Biblical stories.[8]

These justifications of the new media are roughly equivalent to advocates' assertions that movies, radio, and television were of the same genre as things previously accepted. There is, how-ever, in the statement that the new is no worse than the old a clear, yet implicit, criticism of the old, a suggestion that the established modes, while acceptable or popular, are not all that one might wish them to be. The new media might thus be termed acceptable simply because they were the lesser of the evils, al-though this judgment never became an open consideration in the

comparisons. Commonly, movies, radio, and television were termed
acceptable because they were no worse than things long tolerated.

Comparative assertions were not limited to positions of advocacy and defense, but were also employed by opponents of radio,
television, and motion pictures. These critics, first of all,
developed a body of counter-comparisons which made use of the same
bases the advocates had employed, but led to opposing conclusions.
Hence, the new media were compared again to printing, to drama,
to telephone and telegraph, to newspapers, to political techniques,
to other forms of recreation, and to social institutions. This
time, however, they were judged inferior to the objects against
which they were tested.

Several examples will illustrate this type of comparative
argument. Motion pictures were judged inferior to the stage, even
to the popular drama to which advocates had compared them. In an
unusually long and sophisticated series of comparisons, Olivia
Howard Dunbar argued in Harper's that

> in comparison with the popular drama that it has succeeded
> and supplanted, the motion picture of course provides
> little or no emotional outlet. It is far from attempting
> to 'purge with pity and terror' the casual multitudes
> that it attracts. In most cases the interest that it
> excites, when it excites any, is shallow, fleeting, two-
> dimensional, like the pictures themselves. It offers
> no illusion and no mystery.[9]

A writer for Ladies Home Journal thought movies inferior to other
forms of recreation for children because the films allowed no

physical activity and were shown in physical surroundings that were "the worst possible from the standpoint of recreational needs." American radio was measured against foreign programs, and New Republic asserted that when our programs were compared with those of the English, their programs were "far superior to those in the United States." Television was expected by skeptics to "add little to the best things now available on the air." While it might "make prima donnas of conductors it won't improve Bach," and it was considered to add little to "the great occasions of the air, the national hook-ups for presidential messages or international broadcasts."[10] The new media were thought to be not as good as those to which they were compared. The new did not measure up well when critics devised the comparisons.

A second level of comparison common to critics stressed the similarities of the new media to things writers generally disapproved. That is, movies, radio, and television were said to be like, similar to, or as bad as the dime novel, melodrama, the domestic pages of the tabloids, lantern-slide advertising, pulp magazines, B-pictures, risqué novels, smallpox, medicine shows, bull fights, comic strips, comic books, corner gossip, burlesque, prize fights, magazine fiction, and the other vulgar media.

The most common of these comparisons linked movies and the dime novel. Claudy asserted in 1909 that the moving picture "is nothing less than a very live dime novel in short and condensed, but very spicy, form." Walter Prichard Eaton carried on the comparison in 1915 in his comment that "the movies today are the substitutes, for millions of young folks and adults, for the nickel-shockers or the yellowbacks boys used to buy by the hundreds of thousands, and for the dime novels and 'Fireside Companions' of an elder day."[11] It was the contention of Dorothy C. Fox in Outlook in 1921 that

> if a statistical record could be made of the nation of
> the pictures shown, it would undoubtedly reveal the fact
> that the bulk of the filmed stories are nothing more or
> less than the adventures of the Diamond Dicks and Jesse
> Jameses of twenty years ago, vitalized and visualized
> for vastly larger audiences than ever could have been
> reached by the paper-covered detective and wild west
> stories of those days.[12]

Instead of the dime novel, some writers compared movies to the risqué novel, as in this statement from Outlook in which a Y. M. C. A. secretary said movies exhibited "a morbid, demoralizing interest, exactly similar, only of greater magnitude, to that of the risque novel." Radio was compared to the domestic pages of the tabloids, to pulp magazines, and to comic strips, all of which had served to exemplify evil when the dime novel had become history and therefore respectable. By the time television became popular, the comic book was the new source of unease. As would be expected, it and television were compared as equivalent influences.[13]

Writers seeking to denigrate the new media compared them to
any agency or influence which they thought represented social evil,
bad taste, or impropriety. <u>Christian Century</u> said, for example,
that if the government had a bureau to promote the sale of American
pictures abroad, it might as well create a bureau to spread smallpox. <u>Outlook</u>, arguing editorially in 1914 that movies were dangerous
for children, capped the argument with this comparison: "Hundreds
of Americans have written fluently about the brutalizing effect of
the Spanish bull-fight; American children in the most receptive age
are being familiarized with scenes of cruelty which are repulsive
to every normal-minded man or woman." <u>Better Homes and Gardens</u>
contended that "seeing a movie is as great a nervous strain on a
child as being kept up until midnight." Radio was said by <u>Nation</u>
to be a "medium comparable to corner gossip"; by <u>Commonweal</u> to be
the modern equivalent of the old-fashioned medicine show; by <u>Cur-
rent Opinion</u> to be equal to any of the forces competing with the
church; and by <u>Christian Century</u> to deal in the kind of livery
stable humor formerly kept to burlesque and night-club acts. The
talkies, trading on "sex, crime, booze, and lurid high-society
cutups," were said to be as bad as the silents. Television was
equated with the least acceptable parts of the present system,
"warmed-over radio," Hollywood's B pictures, and comic books.[14]

Finally, in the strongest of their comparisons, critics called the new media worse than the evils of the present system. In this context, motion pictures were named "the crown and summit of all the influences demoralizing the country today, not even the saloon being an exception." _Independent_ predicted that "the latest form of popular entertainment, the moving picture show, is liable to be more of a menace to health than any of the popular amusements of recent years." Pictures were labeled more offensive to good morals and to good taste than objectionable books, because what might only be alluded to in a book, the birth of a baby or an attack on a woman, was spelled out in a film. The "baneful influence of the old yellow-backed 'Nick Carter' was multiplied a thousandfold" by the movies. And, said a writer in _North American Review_, because the movies encouraged apathy they were "more demoralizing than Bolshevism to the proletariat and intellectuals alike."[15]

Similar comparisons were developed to assess radio. It was named "the greatest menace to concert going that has ever appeared." Compared to the automobile and the airplane, "the menace of the radio is a thousand times greater," said a writer for _New Republic_. Like its predecessors, radio was compared to the dime novel: "By its power to play on the ear with horror effects, /radio/ exercises a far stronger influence than did the dime-shockers of the 'Eighties."[16]

Talkies were considered a more dangerous influence than either radio or the silents. For one thing, talkies were thought to do more damage to language than radio was capable of. Talkies were more of a threat to the stage than silents had been. But of special concern were the new moral problems raised by the introduction of talking. Speech made the medium more subtle, and at the same time made it more offensive to the moralists. For one thing, it was possible "to have characters say many things in rapid conversation which could not have been shown either in action or in unmistakable subtitles in black and white." Or a character might begin a familiar story--"Did you hear the one about the farmer's daughter and the . . ."--then lapse into a whisper. Speech could be slurred to cover material banned from the silent titles. Silence could also be used in the talkies to heighten the suggestiveness of some scenes. For instance, the famous Cagney line, delivered as he carried a girl into a bedroom, "I'm going to give you an experience you'll never forget," was followed by silence and a fade-out.[17] Immorality was reinforced by innovation, and the new medium was judged worse than the ones before it.

Television was accompanied by comparisons which also classed it with the worst of society's influences. Christian Century said, for example, that "the child with a television set will see more gun-toting in one year in television movies than his parents have

seen on the screen in a lifetime." Norman Cousins in 1949 argued
that "the terror comic strips were bad enough, but they are rapidly
on the way to playing squeaky second fiddles to television as prime
movers in juvenile misconduct and delinquency." John Crosby's
favorite characterization of television was that it delivered five
times the wallop of radio and demanded five times the attention
in return. And it was the conclusion of the Senate Subcommittee
to Investigate Juvenile Delinquency in 1955 that "there is reason
to believe that television crime programs are potentially much
more injurious to children and young people than motion pictures,
radio, or comic books."[18] If these influences were undesirable,
television was even more undesirable.

Comparative assertions of the kind examined here serve as a
means for evaluating innovation in terms of things with which
society is familiar and about which judgment has been passed.
Advocates used these comparisons to argue that the new media
were like other good things, therefore predicting that the new
would be as good as the old and thus hoping to gain acceptance
for the new. Critics weighed the new against former hurtful things,
and in so doing warned of similar dangers to come.

The range of comparisons can be described as falling into
place along a continuum. At one end are the comparisons chosen
for strongest advocacy: the new is better than past goods.

Following them are positions of moderate advocacy: the new is as
good as past good things; the new is as good as most past good
things. In defense, a middle position, advocates argued that the
new was no worse than other accepted media. The weakest of the
attackers' comparisons, also a middle position, tested the new
against the same goods described by advocates, but judged the
new media to be inferior to the objects of comparison. Strengthening
the attack, and moving toward a polar position, critics turned to
social evils for their comparisons, arguing that the new media were
like known evils of past and present. Then in the strongest position
of attack, critics offered the counterpart of the strongest defense
argument: the new is worse than known social evils. The two poles
thus represent the arguments that the new is better/worse than known
good/evil. Other positions of comparison fall within these limits.

The analysis of these evaluative comparisons not only serves
to describe the workings of the argument, but as in causal argument,
serves to indicate what it was that society valued and feared.
Apparent in the comparisons, for example, is the great value placed
on printing, for statements about printing were the most common
reference point for both attackers and advocates. But likewise
valued were newspapers, the stage, and even motion pictures and
radio. In general, advocates sought to link the new with anything
they thought the reader would accept as socially valuable. Attackers

on the other hand, still worrying about dangers to children, threats
to morality, damages to institutions, and subversion of values,
stressed the similitude of the new and all agencies which were said
to have caused such damage in the past.

It is interesting that neither side thought it necessary to prove
the validity of their comparisons, but rather depended upon common
understandings about the goodness and evil of institutions to support
the connections drawn. Just as writers using causal argument assumed
consensus about values and institutions, so these writers presumed that
readers held generally similar opinions about the institutions and
media to which they compared movies, TV, and radio. Hence, a writer
might refer to the damage caused by the dime novel, confident that
his statement would find acceptance. The comparisons were maintained
at the level of assertion; there was no need to prove the case.

Weighing of Values

Another form of argument used for assessment of the new media
involved a comparison and weighing of values. Having associated
the new media with value terms--"profit," "morality," "freedom,"
"intellect"--advocates and opponents named certain of these values
characterisitic of the media, weighed the values against each other,
and made judgments about the media in terms of the
weighing. That is, for example, a critic might argue that

radio was characterized by an emphasis on <u>quantity</u> rather than <u>quality</u>, the two value terms having been placed in a position of being weighed against each other. <u>Quantity</u>, which the opponent presumed to be a thing of lesser good than <u>quality</u>, was named the principal concern of radio, and the medium was found wanting because of this negative association. A number of these comparisons, in which the media are evaluated on the basis of their predominant values, are apparent in the total argument.

This kind of comparative assessment was used most commonly by opponents of the new media. And of all the comparisons opponents set up, one third compared <u>profit</u> and some higher value. By definition, <u>profit</u> was made to serve as a devil term, the negative in the comparison, and the media were called harmful because they were characterized by <u>profit</u> as a motive or an end. Presuming that the values were mutually exclusive, critics of motion pictures named <u>profit</u> as opposing <u>morality</u>, <u>finer</u> <u>sensibilities</u>, <u>beneficial</u> <u>emotions</u>, <u>religion</u>, <u>education</u>, <u>home</u>, <u>children's</u> <u>minds</u>, <u>decency</u>, <u>clean</u> <u>pictures</u>, or <u>an</u> <u>accurate</u> <u>picture</u> of <u>America</u>. In the comparison, <u>profit</u> was judged inferior to these higher ends or values; movies because they were characteristically profit seeking, were likewise assessed negatively. In connection with radio, <u>profit</u> was opposed most often to <u>public</u> <u>service</u>, as in the comment by Charles Siepmann that commercial radio would survive the Second World War "only if

the natural and necessary incentive of profit is subordinated to
the public interest as a criterion of policy." Other opponents of
radio weighed profit against good programs and concern for children.
When television's critics used profit in the comparison, they weighed
it against the good programs which might be available if the situation were not one of the "simplest economics."[19]

Profit was but one of the negative values used for testing the
new media. In other circumstances, motion pictures suffered a
negative judgment because they depended upon popularity as opposed
to excellence, because their artistic progress did not measure up
to their technical progress, because they valued sex appeal over
talent, because they stressed immoral conduct instead of cultural
enrichment. The paired values which served to measure radio were
these: monopoly vs. education and freedom; numbers vs. character;
violence vs. service; and public acclaim vs. public service. Television was attacked because "almost all attempts at novelty, origi-
nality, or exploration of any sort are ruthlessly stifled by the
exigent need to Play It Safe"; because, while it might do an occasional program of spectacular importance, "TV spends the better
part of its regular season mired in the muck of mediocrity"; because
of its emphasis on crime as opposed to the things which give a
child inspiration, which enrich his life; or because of the standardization of taste which threatened to destroy individuality.[20]

Thus, by presenting the values in comparative terms, and by associating the new media with the less desirable of the values, attackers
made a judgment of the media.

Advocates also argued from a comparison of values in defense
of the media. Like attackers, supporters of pictures balanced
profit against morality and service, conceding that money alone
was insufficient justification for the media. American Magazine,
for example, associated intelligence and social spirit with a better
class of picture operator, commenting that "there is a little more
immediate profit, perhaps, to the shady and dangerous exhibit, but
the exhibitor with a sound business head will let that go." Similarly, supporters of radio named monopoly undesirable, two of them
going so far as to favor government control over control by business.
Both competition and democracy in the industry, however, were more
desirable than either government control or monopoly. In motion
pictures, self regulation was weighed against government control,
and the two were taken to demonstrate the extremes in possible
solutions. And pictures were justified, finally, on the grounds
that it was better to have movies than either poor drama on the
stage or no theatre at all.[21]

Spokesmen for radio, apparently sensing a choice between
stupidity and sensuality, defended radio on the grounds that the
former was preferable to the latter. This was Gilbert Seldes'

position in 1927 when he commented that although a greater part
of broadcasting was "subtabloid intellectually," it had escaped
the exploitation of sex common to other media. Another writer,
ten years later, allowed that while radio programs might be poor
in quality and vulgar in tone, "only at most infrequent intervals
is a charge of immorality raised against them." Other arguments
occasionally grew out of the contrasts between the youth of radio
as opposed to the maturity of other media, youth serving as an
excuse for poor programming; the contrast between the contribution
to the art of broadcasting by commercial people as opposed to
educators; and the contrast between the entertainment function of
radio and its educational and scientific potential.[22]

Spokesmen for television turned for support several times to
comparisons of cost. The equation of the high cost of television
and good results from the medium appeared in connection with both
religion and politics. Christian Century, for instance, said that
while television programs would be vastly more costly than radio
shows, "considering the greater influence of what is received by
the eye and ear as compared to what is received by the ear alone,
the church cannot afford to sleep while this new industry grows
into a giant." When Thomas E. Dewey used a telethon type of presentation in his 1951 campaign, Newsweek concluded that "television
is expensive (Dewey's final day cost $17,500) but it was worth it

in showing off a candidate at his relaxed best." With the cost
of the endeavor weighed against the results obtained, television
was judged worth the extra money. Money was not always considered
an advantage, however. In the early days of television
American Magazine argued that there was one distinct advantage to
the lack of money for elaborate production on television--producers
were forced to be imaginative. Implicit here is the suggestion
that with sufficient money imagination is stifled and that hardship
is the breeder of creativity. Finally, television's spokesmen
recognized the commonplace that popularity and excellence are in-
compatible. It was Seldes who argued in 1937 that while television
was to be a popular art it could also attain excellence. One did
not of necessity exclude the other.[23]

The technique of weighing values was used less frequently
by advocates than by attackers, probably because advocates sensed
that it worked less well for them than for the opposition. Critics
were able to point up clear cut and striking contrasts in their
choices of value terms, could play upon the extremes apparent in
the alternatives, and could use some of the conventional value
contrasts--profit vs. service, public vs. private, quality vs.
quantity--to support their case. Advocates were forced to devise
many of their comparisons from less extreme alternatives, or even
from pairs of terms in which both were undesirable but one less

undesirable than the other. For example, consider Seldes' choice between stupidity and sensuality, or the concession that films were vulgar but not immoral. Advocates, moreover, could not simply reverse the pairings of the attackers, for to do so would be to deny what common knowledge said was true of the media. Movies, radio, and television were geared to the mass audience, they were profit making, they were the public arts, they had for many years dealt with stories of social extremes. Advocates could hardly deny common knowledge and yet retain their credibility. Thus the technique of weighing values, used to demonstrate the place of the new media in the value system and consequently to evaluate the media, was principally a strategy of attack. It served better to denigrate than to praise.

Eye-Ear Comparisons

Related to the comparisons of values were comparisons of the relative importance of the eye and the ear as a means for learning. Advocates of silent motion pictures, faced with the problem of promoting an educational medium which had no real facility for language, turned to these comparisons for support of their position. They judged the eye to be the superior organ for acquisition of information, and on this ground promoted films for teaching. A writer for Outlook asserted, for example, that

> most knowledge of importance is knowledge that can be
> gained through the eyes. The preference of a child for
> the picture book rather than for the printed page is
> evidence of the general preference humanity has for
> using the eyesight rather than the imagination or
> reasoning faculty.[24]

Current Opinion predicted in an editorial in 1922 that films would

have great success in teaching because "impressions received through

the eye, psychologists tell us, are stronger than any other sort

(except odors!)." Independent explained the appeal of films on the

grounds that "seeing is believing," and Thomas Edison testified

in 1925 before government hearings about motion pictures that

"90% of all knowledge is gained through the eye." Even as late

as 1933, after the advent of talking pictures, the Religious Edu-

cation Secretary of the Congregational Church in Illinois still

argued that it was "universally recognized that motion pictures

offer an unparalled aid to education, all educators recognizing

that the gateway of the eye is one of the most important avenues

of instruction."[25]

These comparisons allowed promoters of films to minimize

traditional educational methods which relied upon both visual and

non-visual teaching techniques. If it were true that the eye

accounted for most learning, and the motion picture appealed to the

eye, then obviously films were a superior means for education. The

argument apparently had some basis in psychological opinion, as

advocates occasionally mentioned, but it also depended greatly

upon an intuitive response to the notion of primacy of vision and
upon reinforcement from the commonplace that a picture is worth
a thousand words.

Opponents of pictures picked up the assertions about the
superiority of the eye as a channel for learning and on this basis
concluded that pictures were indeed potent sources for harmful
information. This was the contention of an anonymous movie producer who did a series of articles for Collier's in 1922 about the
dangers of films. He argued that because in pictures youngsters
saw ideas and ideals distorted and life misrepresented, their
"ideas and ideals and taste and character and conduct" were damaged.
"And more," he wrote, "we receive impressions most readily, most
indelibly through the eye." Similarly, Fred Eastman argued in
Christian Century that children retained 90 per cent of what they
learned visually from the screen as opposed to 70 per cent retained
from other sources.26 His conclusion was that pictures were a more
dangerous moral influence than other media.

In another variation on the eye-ear comparison, a writer for
Ladies Home Journal questioned movies as a source for recreation
because of their primarily visual appeal. He held that "recent
studies" showed the ear to be more important for recreation than
the eye. "Attention," he concluded, "is much better concentrated
on the hearing than on the sight, and . . . therefore a much more

complete diversion of mind is obtained in that way."27 The comparison could thus serve either side; its application depended upon the individual writer's interpretation of the data.

Radio, with its aural appeal, led to a new evaluation of the importance of the ear both in learning and in persuasion. At the same time that supporters of pictures were asserting the primacy of the eye, supporters of radio were arguing for the ear. When radio broadcasting was beginning in 1922, the Chairman of the Board of R. C. A. explained radio's importance on the basis of its appeal to the ear. Contrasting listening to reading, the latter a skill which involved effort and training, he said that

> the radiophone suffers from none of these disadvantages.
> We all have ears and do not have to be taught how to
> use them. We can be reached through them without special
> effort on our part. The ear has always been the means
> for reaching and swaying people most easily. Now we have
> a means of reaching the ears of the whole world at once.28

H. V. Kaltenborn, with no evidence to go on apart from his status as a broadcaster, asserted in 1926 that radio had a great opportunity in education because "education comes more easily through the ear than through the eye." In 1931 he claimed that radio rivaled "the press in directing public thought, because the average citizen is much more responsive to what he hears than to what he reads." A similar point of view was expressed by a member of the Board of Governors of the B. B. C. who said of radio in Harper's Monthly that "here, we know, is a mysterious, new force, among the most potent in the world if, as I incline to think, the younger

generation is more directly accessible through its ears than through

its eyes, whether those eyes are directed to the visual images,

as in the films, or to the printed words of books and newspapers."[29]

Opponents of radio, like opponents of pictures, occasionally

turned to the eye-ear comparisons for material. Several of the

supporters of radio had suggested that radio was popular because

listening was more of a natural function of man than reading. A

spokesman for newspapers, opposing radio, took up this line of

thought, inverted it, and made it an argument in her favor, asserting

that

> it is a psychological truth that the ear is the lazy
> man's way of learning; the eye the intelligent man's
> way. That is why gossip spreads faster than the printed
> word; it is why radio, for better or worse, has become
> the powerful influence that it is in America today.[30]

Again, interpretation established the tone of the argument, and

made it an instrument for the attack.

Concurrently, then, spokesmen for radio were talking about

the primacy of the ear while spokesmen for motion pictures argued

from the primacy of the eye as a channel for information. The

argument suggests there was no clear cut or commonly known evidence

favoring either side. Consequently, unhampered by the necessity

for conforming to what was generally understood to be true, advo-

cates were free to interpret the influence of the media in terms

of their own commit ment. This led to the contradictions apparent
in the positions.

The eye-ear controversey extended into the promotion of television. In general, advocates of the medium argued that it would
be valuable because it added clearly superior visual appeals to
the aural stimulation of radio. For example, a writer for Saturday
Evening Post argued in 1939 that the public would welcome television
because of its eye appeal for "the eye is the important organ; the
ear is an inferior one. If you doubt it, just ask yourself the
question whether or not you would rather lose your sight or your
hearing."[31] Saturday Review argued in 1942 that the public was
being hurt because television, then operational in some parts of
the country, was being withheld from the general public. This was
the argument:

> Tests have shown that of all the senses, vision accounts
> for ninety per cent of all our learning, and the other
> four contribute a mere ten per cent when combined. Keep-
> ing back this means of sending sound and pictures through
> the air is hurting the public as much as keeping back
> vitamins or anesthesia would have hurt, had the medical
> profession, for some reasons of self-interest, decided
> to hold back new products or developments in its own
> field.[32]

When television broadcasting began, industry people were said
to be aware of the greater impact of the visual materials as compared to sound alone, and advertisers were happy with the results
of their visual appeals. Television was by 1950 accepted as a new

visual medium, its success attributed to the fact that "the eye
is 85% more retentive than the ear." Because of its visual emphasis, television was judged superior to all former media. (The
advocates ignored the similar visual and aural appeal of the talking
pictures as they spoke of the new combination introduced with
television.) As Parent's Magazine said, in reference to education,
television has tremendous power for good because children "not only
give it their undivided attention, but they learn visually as well
as orally."33

Television, while it combined visual and aural appeals, was
taken by its advocates to be a demonstration of the superiority
of the eye as a means for acquiring information. The descriptions
of it as having "eye appeal," as a "visual medium," as possessing
"visual impact," also served to make a judgment about television,
for they linked the medium with the superior sense. The discussions
about the eye and the ear in television marked at least a temporary
end ot this line of comparison. Advocates after 1950 turned their
attention to other matters, opponents never took up the eye-ear
arguments, and the question was discarded, very little changed in
form or substance, after some thirty-five years.

Advantage-Disadvantage Comparisons

Related to the eye-ear comparisons and the weighing of values
are arguments in which promoters and critics compared the relative
advantages and disadvantages of the new media. That is, promoters
argued that while there were both advantages and disadvantages
arising from innovation, the advantages of the new outweighed the
disadvantages. Critics took the other side, arguing that there
were more or greater disadvantages than there were advantages. Like
the other comparisons, these served to assess the media, to praise
or to blame depending on the point of view of the arguer.

This kind of argument allowed writers for both sides to relate
their cases to the knowledge and experience of the audience, to
examine the new media in terms of the value system, to recognize
common lines of attack and defense, and to minimize or refute
familiar contentions of the opposition. For example, in their
early days, motion pictures were commonly believed to hurt the
eyes. A promoter of that period, who felt constrained to recognize
the charge but who had no readily available refutation, could
minimize the danger by calling the damage to the eyes a minor
disadvantage in contrast to greater services performed by the
movies. This is how Scribner's handled the situation in 1909.

> No longer is the magic lantern a nursery plaything!
> Men deal with it, it deals with men. Some would have
> us believe that homes are corrupted thereby, and that

> children steal in order to raise the price of admission.
> If it breaks homes it mends them too. But yesterday
> we read of brothers brought together through its bene-
> ficient agency--brothers separated from childhood. The
> one recognized the other--the prodigal--as he swung by
> in a file of sailors, parading in San Francisco--all
> this, of course, upon the screen. 'That's Harry himself!'
> exclaimed the older brother; whom it is good to know for
> a prosperous merchant, who will make life easier for the
> seaman now.
>
> If the moving-picture shows can unite families,
> what matter if they <u>are</u> a bit hard on the eyes, and
> sometimes almost as vulgar as the contemporary stage
> itself?[34]

In this example, the motion picture was judged acceptable.

The service it performed was considered highly valuable, while

the harm it did was made to seem relatively insignificant. Hence,

the comparison favored the advocate, because the good effects

were more important than the harmful ones. This ranking of effects

is characteristic of the advantage-disadvantage comparisons. Pre-

suming an implicit hierarchy of values consonant with the reader's

system of beliefs, advocates or opponents showed by comparing the

effects where they lay on the scales of values. Just as the pro-

moter sought to show that the greater good and lesser evil resulted

from the medium, the attackers devised comparisons between the

greater evil and the lesser good.

Advocates employed two variations on the advantage-disadvantage

comparison. The first of these plays upon the apparent fairminded-

ness of the argument. Promoters said that there were both advantages

and disadvantages in the new media, as there were to all things, and that the bad would have to be taken with the good. Implicit in the argument, however, is the assumption that the badness of the thing is not great enough to outweigh the good. The comparison, despite its appearance of neutrality, is slanted toward advocacy.

This use of comparison is exemplified in Literary Digest's assertion that "while some of the moving pictures are teaching crime others are teaching practical ethics by showing the value of clean milk." Similarly, radio preaching was said to be advantageous because the radio congregation numbered from 500,000 to 2,000,000, more people than could be reached in a lifetime by other means, and at the same time disadvantageous because it offered no personal contact, no means for gesturing, no force of personality as did face-to-face speaking. Radio also was said to be a poor way to educate children but a good one for adults. Television, said American Mercury, had made serious inroads on the amount of money radio people were willing to spend on good music, but "in exchange, it is giving the people all over the country a chance to see opera." After the Kefauver hearings had been televised, America reprinted an article from the Georgetown Law Review which said that while the hearings gave the public a great practical education in "direct democracy" their purpose was sometimes distorted as participants played to the "mass audience."35 Using this form of comparison advocates recognized that there was both bad and good in what the

new media offered. At the same time, they suggested that the bad
would have to be accepted in order to gain the good, and excused
the new media on the grounds that the disadvantages were not severe
enough to negate the good. Implicit in the comparison, then, was
argument favoring the new mass media.

The apparently neutral comparisons account for only about
one-third of the advocates' arguments from advantages and disadvantages.[36] The other two-thirds took the position that the advantages clearly outweighed the disadvantages.

These comparisons were called up in the general advocacy of
movies and in response to particular criticisms of the medium.
When calls for censorship of films were first issued, Harper's
Weekly came to their defense with the comment that while the usual
indictments of movies "were true in many instances, . . . yet
they were far from presenting an entirely truthful picture of the
business. Mixed with the evil influences were a great majority
of good ones." When a new color process was introduced for films
in 1910, Outlook commented on this "eighth wonder of the world,
. . . the instantaneous photographing of moving objects in natural
color." Having described some of the films, Outlook concluded that
"against the undoubted harm that has come to some children who have
loved the moving-picture show not wisely but too well should be
set the awakening of the imagination that must come from seeing

pictures such as these under proper auspices." When the Vitaphone
process was introduced, Literary Digest commented that it might be
hard on the musician's union but great for the public.[37] This line
of argument is probably best exemplified, however, by a statement
from Harper's in 1919.

> Pleasure generally has its concomitant disadvantages,
> and the film has not always brought unadulterated sweet-
> ness and light to the communities it gladdened. Some
> incipient vampires and some potential crooks of tender
> age may have had their ambitions fired by the pictures.
> . . . In any case, no philosophic observer can fail to
> acknowledge how greatly the pictures have contributed
> to the vivacity, to the bearableness, of our national
> existence.[38]

The foregoing are samples of the comparisons devised by advocates of pictures. In addition to these, they contrasted benefits
to education, crime prevention, low cost, entertainment of the
deaf, and general social uplift to the need to build fireproof
projection booths, knowledge of sex, a lack of great drama in
films, harm to the eyes, and other unspecified dangers. Films,
in all the comparisons were of benefit to the greatest number or
associated with the greater good.

Similar comparisons were devised by the promoters and defenders
of radio. For example, they said that while radio might take time
formerly given to thinking and reduce the amount of conversation,
it would lead to a better world. It might hurt reading, but it
would serve the nation's needs better than books had done. While

network radio might hurt the small radio station, it would provide
better programming for the general public. And, the defenders
said, if some radios shows had hurt children, most programs offered
them valuable information. "Even in the children's thrillers there
are certain positive values," namely their emphasis on "qualities
of honesty, truthfulness, loyalty, fair dealings, courage, and respect
for authority and for their elders."39

Television, too, caused both good and evil, but for the advocates the advantages outweighed the disadvantages. The advantage
most often cited was togetherness in the family, the same thing
which brought praise for films in 1909, which was contrasted to
damage to reading, loss of other amusements, and disruption of
household routines. But in addition, if television hurt minor
league baseball, it helped the majors; it was fraught with poor
shows, but it brought the President into the living room; it exposed
children to crime, but it made them aware of their world as nothing
else could do; it hurt the amusement industry, but it was a source
of great new entertainment. And even though television had caused
meal times to be shifted to accomodate programs and had led to later
bedtimes, experience proved that "it is a powerful new medium for
educating our children, and stimulating them to ask questions."40
The good in it outweighed the bad.

The same techniques of comparison was used by opponents of the
media. For them, however, the disadvantages outweighed the advantages. They argued that the problems raised by innovation were
of greater magnitude that the benefits created by it; that if good
were done, it was for special interests and the majority suffered;
if social goals were achieved, it was for only a short time and
that in the long run society would suffer. The critics who used
this pattern of argumentation presumed a hierarchy of values like
that of the advocates, but their interpretation of the compared
situations weighted the argument in favor of the negative.

Opponents of motion pictures argued that while movies had
done good things, their most common results were evil. Speaking of
the exportation of American films, and the commercial advantages
gained from them, Christian Century asked, for example,

> but if, along with these commendable /commercial7 results,
> they poison the minds of Europeans against American cul-
> ture and misrepresent our ideals and character, is the
> net result a liability or an asset? What will it profit
> the United States to gain the whole world of trade and
> lose its own soul?[41]

Admitting that pictures had transformed the world for millions of
people, the head of the Department of Science at a Birmingham,
Alabama, high school argued in a long comparison that their disadvantages were greater than the good they did. Children's health
was damaged by watching even educational films, children copied the

dress and the manners of the stars in commercial pictures and

their inhibitions against nudity were weakened.

> Other objections to the attending of children have been
> that the movie develops a craze and an abnormal appetite
> for the sensational, the grotesque, and the bizarre, and
> that the mind is kept keyed up to a condition of trying
> to realize such conditions in everyday life; that such
> interests interfere with the child's wholesome love for
> outdoor sports and recreation, and destroy his love for
> good reading.
> The tendency of children to imitate the daring deeds
> seen upon the screen has been illustrated in nearly every
> court in the land. Train wrecks, robberies, murders,
> thefts, runaways, and other forms of juvenile delinquency
> have been traced directly to some particular film. The
> imitation is not confined to young boys and girls, but
> extends even through adolescence and to adults.[42]

Other critics of movies contended that newsreels might broaden

the viewer's understanding of his world, but that the sex pictures

shown with them were morally harmful; that immigrants might learn

about America from educational pictures, and about crime and sex

from the commercial movies; that pictures might spread drama about

the land, but that the drama they showed was mediocre if not harm-

ful. Contrasted, too, were advantages to the actor and damage to

the theatre; the interesting stories in pictures and the loss of

healthful recreation; knowledge about other lands with disrespect

for adults; and films' ability to attract crowds at the expense

of other, more desirable forms of entertainment.[43]

The comparisons of this type made in regard to radio were

fewer in number, but typical of the general pattern. That is,

opponents argued that while radio might give a few artists new popularity, it hurt concert bookings in general. Radio might help
the immediate war effort, but its war tactics could cause long-range
harm for the nation. Radio had done "splendid things," but in so
doing destroyed the quiet of the home, kept people from thinking,
created unfair competition for other amusements, and ignored its
responsibility for social education. Radio, like other new inventions had seemed to be the answer to pressing social needs, but when
put into service had been the cause of problems more serious than
those it was supposed to correct.[44]

The argument about television is well summarized by this
comment from a mother: "I'm sure Sylvia learns a lot from TV,
but I wonder if it's good for her eyes." Other children learned
much about their world, but their health and their school work
were weakened in the process. Vast new audiences were created
for sports on television, but at the same time crowds were drained
from major league ball parks, minor league franchises had to be
transferred out of television areas, and "the box-office for high-
school and small-college games has suffered crippling blows."[45]
Television, in fulfilling many of the dreams of its promoters and
the predictions of its advocates, had also caused problems which,
critics said, were even more serious than those caused earlier
by either movies or radio.

The comparison of advantages and disadvantages, depending upon the interpretation of the effects cited, worked in favor of either the critics or the promoters, and the pattern of argument was used by both sides. Hence, the same effect, the changes in minor league baseball attributable to television, for example, could be interpreted to support either side. Advocates dismissed the importance of the minor leagues by stressing the advantages to the majors, while critics did the reverse. Each side used the comparison to assure audiences they were aware of the problem, and after that either to refute the charge, to minimize it, or to confirm it. Moreover, in using this two-sided presentation the arguers strengthened their ethical appeal, taking on an appearance of tolerance, giving the impression of willingness to consider both sides of the issue and to judge the case solely on its merits.

Presumed in the comparison was a hierarchy of values to which the argument related, and which was assumed to be consistent with the belief system of the audience. Hence, writers could praise films and television for having brought families together and be reasonably certain that readers would accept this effect as one of the ultimate goods. It was, for example, a greater good than regularity in family routines, which in other contexts was also held out as an example of a good thing. When the two virtues, togetherness and regularity, were compared, togetherness was chosen to represent a superior position in the hierarchy.

There was, however, a lack of consensus about the place of many values in such a hierarchical system, just as there was uncertainty about the effects of the mass media. This is apparent in the pairs of advantages and disadvantages chosen for the argument. It could be assumed that if there were agreement about the values, then some of them would be repeated in the comparisons. This mode of argument was used eighty-nine times in all, and in no two cases was the same pair of values repeated. The choice of terms in the comparison and the ranking of values within the system depended, apparently, on the individual writer's analysis of the concerns and values of his audience, upon his perception of the influence of the media, and upon his special interests. This variety of influences could well account for the inconsistency of the comparisons.

Prediction-Practice Comparisons

Another form of evaluative comparison, this one used primarily by opponents of the new media, contrasted predictions about movies, radio, and television to what the media had done in practice. The ideal image of the new devices was compared with the real image developed from their application. Theoretical statements about what the media could do were contrasted with what they had done. The promises of the promoters were measured by the operation of the media when they were put into use.

The tone of the argument will be best illustrated with some examples of the general potential-practice comparisons which critics of all three media devised. This kind of test was applied to motion pictures while they were still in their infancy. C. H. Claudy said in 1908 that the movies were not fulfilling their potential:

> A great agent for good, a means of education unrivaled, a source of much innocent and inexpensive pleasure, the moving picture show has come to mean, as a rule, a pandering to the lowest tastes, a misinterpretation of life as it really is, as harmful and more accessible than the dime novel, and the telling of a lie, constantly and universally, not only in fake pictures it produces, but in the way in which the true pictures are run.[46]

The movies were called "the world's worst failure" in 1921 because they failed to live up to their potential.[47] Then, five years after the talkies replaced the silents, Gilbert Seldes had this to say about the new medium:

> The talking picture has utterly confounded the pessimists and won over the die-hard enthusiasts for the silent moving pictures; the entertainment it provides is more varied and more intelligent than that of the silent picture; and it has a vitality and an obscure faith which makes it often superior to the stage. Yet--
> In five years the talking picture has not produced a single work of the highest order of importance; it has floundered in ignorance of its own capacities; and at the present moment it is in grave danger of sinking to the level of monotonous, moderately satisfactory production.[48]

Despite the good things it had done, the talking picture had failed to achieve the theoretical goals Seldes and others had set for it.

Radio, likewise, failed to measure up to what advocates had predicted for it or what people in general hoped it would become. A writer for _Forum_ recalled in 1929 that five years earlier the public had been told that radio was going to enrich culture and generally broaden American life.

> And now we know definitely what we have got in radio
> --just another disintegrating toy. Just another medium
> --like the newspapers, the magazines, the billboards,
> and the mailbox--for advertisers to use in pestering us.
> A blatant signboard erected in the living room.[49]

New Republic in 1945 spoke of radio's failure to find a significant place in society.

> For anyone interested in radio as a social force, as an
> important means of information and entertainment, the
> present situation is disconcerting. Radio is certainly
> getting no better, and many people believe it is getting
> worse. The high hopes which were held a quarter of a
> century ago, when broadcasting was born, have been
> gravely disappointed. The radio has become increasingly
> a device to sell goods by any means, fair or foul, while
> the question of usefulness to the public is more and more
> neglected.[50]

The potential of radio, according to its detractors, had gone unrealized.

The same case was made against television. One of the first to use the argument was Norman Cousins in _Saturday Review_. He said in 1949 that television, "the supreme triumph of invention, the dream of the ages," after a year of full-time operation had simply not worked out. It was, he said, "still light years away in any truly vital and creative approach to the fabulous possibilities waiting to be recognized and realized." Any speculation about television "must begin with the hard truth that right now it is being murdered in the cradle." Television, said others after more experience with it, "couldn't be worse." Its endless possibilities for greatness went unexplored, its potential remained unrealized. Television itself was "nothing more than a triumph of mediocrity."[51]

These are samples of the general arguments from lost opportunities which were used in the evaluation of the new media. More frequently, critics talked of particular areas in which the movies, radio, and television had failed to live up to their potential. For example, movies failed to achieve the level of dramatic art predicted for them, failed to perform as expected in recreation, and did not live up to their potential in the areas of social service, universal communication, intellectual communication, culture, morality, national leadership, and international understanding. Pictures failed, moreover, to reinforce the value system, to represent us well abroad, to tell the truth about drinking, to spread English around the world, to properly inspire the younger generation, or to make progress consistent with their capabilities. Radio was a disappointment in its work with politics, news reporting, entertainment, social service, religion, music, culture, and children's programs. It, too, failed as a means for intellectual communication and as a stimulus to good taste. And, as Commonweal said, "no one can deny that the radio has fallen far short of what it might be as an instrument for progress." Television suffered the same weaknesses as the others. In addition to its failures with regard to religion, politics, drama, culture, public service, and children's programming, it also failed to provide live broadcasts from around the world, to use the great writers available to it, to give the viewer a choice in programming, or to help Hollywood regain its footing.52

Most important, the new media did not achieve their potential in education. This was the most frequently mentioned failure in all of the potential-practice comparisons. (Three-quarters of all the arguments dealt with it.) Recall, for example, Claudy's suggestion that movies had not served education as he thought they should. Others said the same thing about pictures, and also about radio and television.

Part of the responsibility for the failure of the mass media in education lay with the media. That is, as Claudy pointed out in 1908, although the movie could serve useful educational purposes, "the effect is largely destroyed by the absurd speed with which the pictures are thrown upon the screen." There was a problem, too, in getting enough of the right kind of films for educational use. Henry Wysham Lanier called attention to this problem in 1914, commenting that while "film manufacturers are educating about five

million American children a day along highly undesirable lines,"
there were too few films made by educators for use in school. Then,
too, there was not "a really satisfactory projecting machine at a
reasonable price (and incidentally a film that will not char or
burn, and will not permit the stopping of the machine for clari-
fying an explanation)." These kinds of films for teaching, and
a scarcity of reliable projection equipment for school use plagued
both educators and film makers for the first forty years of the
movie's existence. But more frequently mentioned as a matter for
concern was what the commercial films were teaching. As various
writers pointed out from its earliest days, the screen was, in
fact, "one of the most powerful single instruments in the education of our population."53 The problem lay in what was learned
from it. Too often the lessons contradicted society's prevailing
affirmative values. Motion pictures could be used for education,
but the industry had not used them that way.

The same complaints were made about broadcasting. New Republic
said in 1930 that for ten years the public had been told that radio
was a mighty device for educating young and old, but most attempts
to use it to do so had failed. As Everett Case, acting secretary
of the NBC Advisory Council for Education, said a month later,
"Whatever the ultimate possibilities of radio as a medium for education, broadcasters and educators will both admit, I think, that

little progress has been made toward their realization." The specific

charges were familiar ones. There were too few educational programs

to suit the critics. What programs there were were ineptly done,

dull, and uninteresting. The educational stations which were on

the air had to compete for space on the broadcast spectrum with

commercial interests, and if they got a frequency were then ham-

pered by inexperience and too little money to operate. On the

other hand, educational programs carried by commercial stations

were assigned the least desirable broadcast times. Even H. V.

Kaltenborn, radio's defender, commented on the latter problem,

noting in 1931 that educational programs were "rarely heard on

the air during the popular evening hours when they might conflict

with the sock sellers who sponsor Dick and Mick, the Wear Forever

Duo."54 Radio, said the critics of the medium, did not give edu-

cation a fair chance.

The potential-practice comparisons were used far less frequently

to evaluate television's work with education than they had been

with either movies or radio. One reason is that television had not

been in operation long enough before 1955 to make such comparison

profitable. The medium, as far as education was concerned, was

still in the prediction stage; as the vice-chairman of the FCC

said, "The potentialities of television in the field of education

are nothing less than breathtaking." Even so, there were occasional suggestions that television in education was not working out as well as its advocates had said it would. Cousins, for example, said as early as 1949 that there were fewer educational, or public service, programs than there should be. Saul Carson called attention to the growing battle between commercial interests and educational broadcasters for channel allocations. A writer for Education implied in 1951 that the schools weren't having much to do with TV and that they should use it more. Nation warned that educators must not let the opportunity to use TV slip away, as they had with radio, for "the impact of TV on our thinking and living habits is much too great to permit educational programming to depend upon the beneficence of TV station owners." And New Republic told in 1953 how commercial broadcasters in Illinois opposed university telecasting on the grounds that it "would create 'a propaganda mill for bureaucratic officeholders' into which they pictured subversives infiltrating to 'hasten the creation of the totalitarian state.'" Still, however, in 1955 educational TV was called the "greatest advance in the educational field for both children and adults since the Middle Ages" and the invention of moveable type. At the same time, writers noted that there was no rush on the part of educators to pick up the 257 channels set aside by the FCC for non-commercial educational stations.[55] If past performance is an accurate predictor, it can be assumed that educational television will eventually be faced with the charge that it had never realized its potential.

The responsibility for the failure of the mass media in education was shared by the educators themselves. Writers who used the potential-practice comparisons pointed out, for example, that even when educational movies were available, teachers did not use them nor did school administrators encourage their use. Recall, too, that Edison said he discontinued his experiments with educational talking films "when the educators failed to respond." Even after the Second World War, American Mercury reported, fewer than one-fifth of the public schools were equipped with so much as a sound picture projector.[56] Educators' attitudes about education by radio seemed similar to their attitudes about pictures. Speaking of the problem, Levering Tyson, director of the National Advisory Council on Radio in Education, said in 1934 that

> educators have been provided with an instrument the perfection of which was a significant event in social history. They have paid cursory attention to it, and a certain kind of lip-service. I suppose that when moveable type was invented, many years passed before the thinkers of the time were able to forsee the uses to which books, magazines and newspapers might be put in a culture of the future.[57]

With television in the offing writers recalled the failure of the educators in connection with radio, and warned against allowing history to repeat itself.[58] The critics of education were clearly suspicious that if educators were allowed to go their own way,

they would do do no more with television than they had done before
with radio and the movies. Both the media themselves and the educators charged with using them were thus held responsible for the
failure of the movies, radio, and television to realize their
greatest potential in education.

Reflected in the potential-practice comparisons are the concerns
with which we have seen the advocates and opponents dealing through
causal argument. Here, however, the new media were tested by comparing their performance in practice to their potential service to
society's institutions and values. Critics argued that the media
had failed to support fully society's notions of what was necessary,
worthwhile, and desirable. Not only were judgments of the media
made in the comparisons, but this mode of argument permitted criticism of the institutions through their representatives. As I showed
in the last chapter, opponents of the media, even though they were
dissatisfied with social institutions, were hesitant to criticize
them directly. This was particularly true of the church and the
school. The comparison, however, offered a means by which opponents
could point to the failure of institutions and their representatives
without offering explicit criticism of the institution itself.
For example, where a critic might not argue openly against education,
he could point to the failures of educators in the use of radio or
movies and thereby suggest that the institution itself was slow to

adapt to change. The same situation existed in connection with the
church, and here too critics of the new media argued that church
people failed to make good use of movies, radio, and television.
The comparisons of potential with practice thus permitted evaluation
of the media and of the institutions they were presumed to serve.

Some of the critics employed a variation on the potential-
practice comparison to judge the work of Will Hays and the
M. P. P. D. A. After his appointment, Hays promised that he would
work for "the attaining and maintaining, for the motion picture
industry, a high educational, moral, and business plane"; that the
industry would assume new responsibility for protecting "that
sacred thing, the mind of a child, . . . that clean and virgin
thing, that unmarked state"; and that producers would make "certain
that all films which are sent abroad, wherever they may go, shall
correctly portray American life, ideals, and opportunities."59
Writers for the New York Times Magazine, Commonweal, Outlook, and
Christian Century, presuming that Hays had power to regulate the
movie industry, tested his promises against practices of the industry. Hays' success was measured in terms of his statements about
the movies.

Critics' objections related to all of Hays' promises. He was,
in effect, condemned in his own words. For example, Current Opinion,
quoting the New York Times Magazine, argued that movies with their

emphasis on crime and violence did in fact misrepresent American life
and aspirations to people in other countries. Commonweal commented
in 1930 that if the Hays Office was the channel through which churches
and civic organizations could make known their wishes about movies,
if the current films represented the "flowering of the industry
under the great moral and educational influence of Mr. Hays," then
"our conclusion is that the channel needs dredging." Christian
Century for four years argued that industry practices contradicted
the promises of Hays, that the general run of pictures in 1930
was "little or no better than it was eight years ago." Movies continued to deal with crime, violence, and sex; still led children to
violate the standards of moral behavior generally espoused; and
distorted the American image abroad. Hays, said these attackers,
had not lived up to his promises. "Behind a Presbyterian false
front, /movie makers7 have gone merrily on making money out of
muck."60

Hays, like the movies he represented, was judged on the basis
of the comparison between what was said and what was done. Per-
sonifying causes, critics charged Hays with responsibility for the
actions of pictures. Assuming that good and honest men do not
renege on promises, critics challenged Hays' credibility as well
as his ability to do the job for which he was hired. Varying the

terms, the potential-practice comparison was thus applicable to
the judgment of men and their work.

The argument from comparison of potential to practice was used
also, though not frequently, by the supporters of the new media.
For them it served two functions. First, it was refutative. That
is, the comparison answered predictions of the critics, advocates
arguing that the evils feared from innovation had not materialized
in practice. Second, the comparisons served to excuse the media
for failing to achieve their expected potential. Movies and radio,
said their supporters, had not worked out as well as predicted
because of the influence of outside forces. It was not the fault
of the media, but of someone or something else.

The refutative comparisons were related to theatre, religion,
the foreign market for films, music, and politics. Advocates maintained that the damage predicted for each institution was denied
by practice. New Republic, for example, argued in 1915 that the
critics who predicted that movies would end the spoken drama were not
"trustworthy oracles." Legitimate drama continued to flourish
despite the attraction of the pictures, said the magazine, "and it
is now generally recognized that the prophecy of its early extinction was a foolish one." Review of Reviews said radio had not
hurt religion, but instead had brought church services to invalids
and to people isolated by distance. Neither had talkies killed

the foreign market for American pictures. Nor was music hurt appreciably by either radio or pictures. In fact, said North American Review in 1929, "We are right now in the midst of a full market in musical appreciation." Concerts were sold out, thousands of boys and girls were preparing themselves for musical careers, hundreds of schools had orchestras, and "half of the 20,000,000 children in our schools study music as a school subject." Finally, advocates claimed that TV had not done the damage to politics that attackers had predicted. Sponsorship of political programs did not bias the coverage, television did not influence the candidate selection at the 1952 conventions, nor did the use of TV "make the transformation of political debates into gigantic fund-raising contests almost inevitable."[61] Thus, the potential-practice comparisons, while they were not used very often by advocates, became for them a means for refutation. Using the categories established by the critics, defenders offered a reinterpretation of the effects of the media. Experience proved, they said, that the fears of the critics were unwarranted.

Advocates also used the potential-practice comparison to shift responsibility for predicted or actual failure away from the media. Most often this argument was applied to movies in education. Friends of the medium argued, as critics did, that institutional representatives had used films badly, that the producers of educational

material had failed, or that educational pictures faced unexpected
obstacles in the audience. That is, films for teaching were limited
by the intelligence of the audience; film makers did not make
educational films interesting; the range of subjects for filmed
instruction was unexpectedly limited in practice; or, as Edison
said in 1914, even when films were available teachers would not
go to the trouble of using them. Norman Corwin argued in 1942
that radio had not achieved its expected potential in either education or propaganda because neither users nor producers knew
enough about it in these contexts. "The painful truth," he wrote,
"is that neither our government nor the industry of radio itself
seems fully awake to the potentialities." And a similar argument
was used to explain the failure of religious radio. A writer for
Christian Century, Charles M. Crowe, said in 1944 that "in spite
of the fact that radio affords the most powerful medium of mass
influence in history, with opportunity to reach a vast heterogeneous
audience untouched by conventional church activities, its use by
religious leaders has been lamentably unintelligent and ineffective." Religious leaders, he concluded, "must learn how to utilize
. . . radio instead of complaining that radio is a competition for
the people's interest or looking upon it as a toy of doubtful value
to the church."[62]

In this variation on the argument, advocates conceded that the potential of the media had not been realized, but shifted the responsibility to some outside agency. The potential remained, they said, but the use of the instrument was faulty. The media and their users were treated separately in the argument. Adding the causal explanation to the comparison, advocates turned the comparison into a defense of the media in question. The argument, however, was used only occasionally.

The comparisons of potential to practice could thus serve both attackers and advocates. It was used, however, most extensively by the former, who pointed to the discrepancies between what promoters said about the media and what movies, radio, and television did when put into practice. Drawing the comparisons out of the value system, critics charged, in effect, that the new media failed to implement society's prevailing values or to support its institutions. Advocates, on the other hand, either interpreted the comparison to their advantage, arguing that effects in practice were not as serious as critics' predictions had made them out to be, or added a qualifying statement to the comparison and so shifted responsibility away from the medium and onto the use made of it.

A comment is warranted on the applicability of the line of argument. This kind of potential-practice comparison would appear to be useful in many contexts, especially for purposes of denigration.

Any device, idea, or person, of which certain results were expected, could be judged on the basis of whether or not the predictions were borne out in practice. Failure to achieve predicted good could be taken as a fault; achievement of predicted evil could likewise count against the person or thing so judged. Less spectacular, but equally applicable, would be the confirmation of predicted good results or the failure to do the harm expected. Although the comparison would seem to be useful in many circumstances of judgment, the writers concerned with movies, radio, and television apparently did not consider it one of their strongest arguments.

Intra-Media Comparisons

Advocates and attackers also evaluated the new media on the basis of their own past performance. Each medium was tested against itself, through time, and measured in terms of its own past failures or accomplishments. In these comparisons the promoters maintained that the medium, at a given point in time, was better than it had been in the past. Movies, they said, were better than ever. The same line of argument was used by attackers who said, as Christian Century did of the movies in 1930, that the media were deteriorating, getting worse than they had been before. This kind of comparison was used first by defenders of movies and was carried over into both radio and television.

This line of argument can be applied to various dimensions of any medium. That is, it can relate to technical considerations, to moral concerns, to aesthetic problems, to influences on health, to any of the areas in which the medium is supposed to have an influence. It was first used, however, to demonstrate that the movies were less of a moral problem in 1908 than they had been in 1903. John Collier, reporting a survey of cheap amusements in Manhattan conducted in 1908 by the Women's Municipal League and the People's Institute, said that five years earlier the nickelodeon was "often a carnival of vulgarity, suggestiveness, and violence, the fit subject for police regulation," and deserving of its bad name. But, he went on, "during the present investigation a visit to more than two hundred nickelodeons has not detected one immoral or indecent picture, or one indecent feature of any sort."63 Movies had improved, and readers were offered assurance that no longer was there need for concern. The present was an improvement over the past.

For the next ten years, other writers noted improvement in the technical quality of pictures, in the educational features produced, in the artistic quality of the movies, in the stories used as film vehicles, and in the level of taste exhibited on the screen. When Current Opinion began its movie department in 1917, its editor said that the magazine

aims to follow the development of the motion picture
into a vital art. In its first phenomenal and ill-
regulated stages, it has borne along with it, like a
young freshlet, an apalling amount of debris. The
waters are already clearing and a real concerted effort
is being made to place the movement on a higher plane.[64]

And Otis Skinner in 1920 echoed the notion that the movie was indeed

better than before, suggesting

let us rejoice that its distributors are sending forth a
cleaner, saner product. There has been too much pandering
to the salacious to be wholesome. . . . Things are changing,
thanks to censorship and a realization that perhaps the
masses have finer emotions than some at first imagined.
. . . By and large, I believe that the moving picture
is now setting the purveyors of modern dramatic fare a
very worthy example.[65]

The theme that motion pictures were improving was adopted by

Will Hays for his advocacy and became one of his common topics. From

the time of his appointment, Hays assured all who would listen that

better pictures were either here or on the way. For example, he said

in Collier's in 1922 that

if the public cannot see, even this soon, a larger number
of excellent moving pictures shown on the screens, with
high standards of art, directorship, morals, and other
elements that make good pictures, than ever before, then
we have been standing still. The only measurement I know
is better pictures and the increasing number of them.[66]

The next year Hays said that movie producers,

continuing this new drive for the best possible pictures,
measuring up toward what the standards should be--a standard which many pictures already had achieved--earnestly
asking the public's cooperation, and desiring, from every
possible standpoint, selfish and unselfish, to move in
the right direction, they have brought out, and are
bringing out, a series of pictures which we are hoping

will attract the public's attention, as evidence both of
good faith and ability to accomplish, and as an augury
for still better things to which every effort shall be
directed. The better pictures are here.[67]

And in 1927, Hays promised again that "the trend is upward, the

aims and the purposes are high."[68] Compared to the past, pictures

were continually improving. Each year marked the achievement of

a higher plateau.

By 1934, even Christian Century, claiming credit for cleaning

up the movies, joined in praise for improved pictures. Better

films are coming it said; even Billboard and Variety "are hopeful

enough to believe that the producers have been finally convinced

that the American people as a whole want something better than crime,

passion, and nakedness."[69] The next year, after looking at the

latest production schedule, Christian Century said that

never in the history of motion pictures have the prospects been so rosy for movies of high quality. Never
before has Hollywood been so well equipped in actors,
directors, designers, and technicians. If these pictures
are produced with honesty and sincerity, and if the programs in which they appear are free from the cheap and
tawdry variety of 'short' and from propaganda-weighted
newsreels, this prodigal industry will be rendering to
the world some part of the cultural ministry its genuine
friends have sought for it.[70]

Argument from this comparison of time present to time past

as a means for defending motion pictures went on until the end of

the period with which I am concerned. For half a century, on an

average of at least once a year, advocates assured readers that the

motion pictures at that moment were better than the motion pictures
of the past. Movies, they said, were now less objectionable morally,
better technically, more artistic, less hard on the eyes, more
educational, more intellectual, more concerned with the social and
economic problems of the times, better for children, more closely
related to great literature, and of greater service to democracy
than any pictures of the past. Arthur Mayer put the argument typically when he said in 1950, in the face of television's predicted
decimation of the motion picture industry, that movies are better
than ever, "but there is good reason to believe that they are going
to get even better than that."71

Similar arguments were used in the defense of radio. Each time
the medium was used in politics someone argued that the latest
application was better than anything gone before. The entertainment
provided by radio was said to be getting progressively better, as
were the educational programs, the cultural programs, the musical
programs, the public service programs, and the children's programs.
In 1926, David Sarnoff talked of the "golden age of radio." In
1927, Review of Reviews said radio was "constantly improving" its
programs and its techniques. In 1931, H. V. Kaltenborn pointed
to the many improvements in radio broadcasting from its early days,
1925.72 In all of these, radio's present performance was compared
explicitly or implicitly, to its performance in the past. And this

was the way Harriet Van Horne defended radio in 1952. She said
that

> from a state quite properly described as moribund, deca-
> dent and all-washed-up, radio has emerged this past season
> as a lively new source of entertainment and information.
> Intellectually its programs are on a higher level. There
> is more 'serious music' available and more serious talk.
> The old fears and nice-Nelly anxieties are being outgrown.
> People now say 'hell' on the radio. They discuss venereal
> disease and drug addiction. They read lengthy selections
> from classical literature. They debate politics in a
> manner that would have caused continuity acceptance
> (i. e., the censor) to fall down in a faint five or ten
> years ago.73

It was her conclusion in 1952, just as writers had concluded since

1922, that "it looks as if radio is growing up." Radio, like the

movies, was better than ever.

Past-present comparisons about television related first to

technical innovation in the medium. In 1926, for example, E. F. W.

Alexanderson, television consultant for GE and RCA, announced the

development of a new television projector. With the new machine,

he said, "it is now possible to see objects in motion by radio

better than it has ever been done in the past." Two years later

a moving image was sent from London to New York, and Bell Labs

managed to televise a tennis match. Each improvement elicited

praise for the medium and comparisons with the past. Then, in 1939,

TV was used to open the World's Fair, an accomplishment greater

than any of the past. Looking back to the early days, 1939, when

television was crude and its image dim, Atlantic said in 1945 that

in contrast, the public could soon expect "magnified images of
adjustable size, pictures in perfect focus, and then the transmission of color over the air waves."[74] Each year, the technical
side of television looked better to its advoctes than it had the
year before.

Once television's technical proficiency was demonstrated and
programming was undertaken, writers compared its most recent performance to that of the past. The topics were familiar, but never
was the defense as firm as it had been with radio or movies. For
example, television's programming in 1944 was described as consisting "for the most part of ancient travel films, cookery classes,
puppet shows, second rate vaudeville acts (jugglers, magicians,
etc.), and radio news commentaries in which the audience has the
dubious privilege of seeing as well as hearing the newscaster."
The material was expected to improve after the war. By 1949 television was said to have "exhibited almost every known type of
entertainment, from the classic ballet to knockabout burlesque
acts." Television's coverage of politics, its work with education,
its treatment of news and special events were judged to be getting
better as the medium matured, but the greatest share of air time
was devoted to entertainment. Consequently, its advocates were
never as enthusiastic about its progress as spokesmen for radio
and movies had been. Entertainment alone was not sufficient grounds

for justification of the medium. There was by 1955 a strong feeling that television was not doing as well as it might.[75] Attackers, as I will show later, found more grounds for argument in what television hadn't done, or in what it had done badly, than advocates found in its improvement.

There is in these present-past comparisons not only an assessment of the present state of the art, but a prediction of the future performance of television, radio, and movies. Advocates suggest in the argument that if the media had gotten better over the years past, the improvement would continue into the future. If the present were better than the past, the future should be better than the present. The argument thus confirmed advocates' predictions about the brave new world to be introduced by the mass media. Part of that world had arrived; the changes already observed were a demonstration that the predicted benefits were in the process of realization. Hence, there was an implicit appeal to progress in the descriptions of the changing courses of the media as well as an explicit link to social betterment. The advocates created an optimistic argument. Appealing to the notion that we live in the best of ages, they predicted a better age to come. The new mass media were not only good things in themselves, but the means to a brighter future.

If advocates of the new media were optimists, attackers were
pessimists. Where spokesmen for the media had emphasized the beneficial changes from past to present, critics argued that the media
were getting worse, that the past was better than the present.
The argument was used for the same purposes that advocates had
used it, to test the media and to predict their future course, but
it was employed far less frequently by the critics than by the
promoters.

When the line of argument was applied to movies it was very
nearly the exclusive property of Christian Century or its writers.
Only twice did the argument appear outside this publication. Once,
in 1929, a writer for Commonweal, in an article dealing principally
with radio, mentioned in passing that "with the better class of
suitable fiction well-nigh exhausted, trite threadbare plots, dependent upon sex interest or murder thrills" had become the predominant materials of the movies. No longer did Hollywood make
films like The Birth of a Nation, Broken Blossoms, or The Last
Laugh. When the Hollywood production list was announced for 1933,
Nation commented that films such as My Lips Betray, Moonlight and
Pretzels, The Woman I Stole, and He Knew His Women were evidence
that the movie situation was deteriorating.[76] Pictures were worse
than they had been.

Christian Century sustained the line of argument in its attacks.
Opening the campaign of 1930, Eastman used the presumed deterioration
of the movies as justification for attacking them. It was his contention and the opinion of Christian Century readers, that "the
movies are as bad or worse than they were then /before Hays took
office7 and that they constitute nothing short of a menace to the
mental and moral life of America." In elaborating his case, Eastman
argued that "pictures the last year have been more objectionable
from the standpoint of immorality and criminality than ever before."77
This became the theme of the Christian Century campaigns, the problem
on which their efforts focused. For three years the publication
maintained the position that movies were worse than ever. Its
writers abandoned the arguments only when Christian Century began
taking credit for improving the movies. After 1934 they argued
that movies are better than they were before, and Christian Century
is responsible for the change.

Critics of radio spoke from a wider range of sources and
for a longer period of time, but their argument was like that of
Christian Century. They claimed that radio was deteriorating in
the areas of music broadcasting, public service, and education.
Music was one of the first services for which radio was praised,
but by 1931 critics registered dissatisfaction with much of the

music heard on the air. For example, writing in <u>Outlook</u> <u>and</u> <u>Inde-</u>
<u>dendent</u>, Marshall Kernochan said that

> as recently as two years ago, good music was frequently
> to be heard on the air. Today it is rare, and audible
> only during the few minutes which the advertiser feels
> to be the minimum that will secure attention for his
> sales talk. . . . /Except for the "General Electric
> Hour," the "Atwater Kent Hour," and the Sunday symphony/,
> song recitals are now mostly made up of ballads and an
> occasional hackneyed classic. Choral music fares a
> trifle better; but chamber music, once plentiful, has
> become nearly as extinct as the dodo, and, even in its
> pitifully few appearances, is likely to be broken off
> abruptly in the middle of a piece because the time has
> been preempted by So and So's tooth paste.[78]

B. H. Haggin took up the argument in <u>New</u> <u>Republic</u> four years later,

charging that while most good music might be heard on the air now,

it was mostly concentrated on Sundays and there was none to be

heard on the weekdays. A similar criticism of radio was offered

again in 1951, Florence Norton claiming in <u>American</u> <u>Mercury</u> that

there was "four times less good music on the air" than there had

been a few years ago. As evidence she cited the loss to listeners

of the Boston Symphony in 1947, "Invitation to Music" in 1948,

and the CBS symphony in 1950. The present situation in music was

judged in each case to be worse than the practices of the past.

Following the Second World War, when discussions of ETV were be-

ginning, Senator Benton called upon the example of radio to support

his position that commercial sponsorship and education do not mix.

Benton claimed that educational radio on a newwork level had gotten

steadily worse, the networks doing a poorer job of it in 1940 than
in 1930, worse in 1950 than in 1940.[79] The attitude of these critics
about radio, and its trend toward insignificance, is perhaps best
reflected in New Republic's summary of the situation.

> For anyone interested in radio as a social force,
> as an important means of information and entertainment,
> the present situation is disconcerting. Radio is certainly
> getting no better, and many people believe it is getting
> worse. The high hopes which were held a quarter of a
> century ago, when broadcasting was born, have been gravely
> disappointed. The radio has become increasingly a device
> to sell goods by any means, fair or foul, while the question
> of usefulness to the public is more and more neglected.[80]

Radio, in the eyes of these critics, had not improved with maturity.
Television, like radio and movies, was characterized by its detractors
as getting worse instead of better as the years passed. This line
of argument proved more of a fertile field for opponents than it
had for advocates. Critics said, in the first place, that televsion
in 1949 and 1950 was in its golden age, that it would never again
provide such diversified or satisfactory service as in those years.
This was the position of both Gilbert Seldes and Charles Siepmann.
Seldes, for example, said in 1949 that even though "nearly everything
now on the air was tried or planned five years ago, and in several
respects current programs lag behind those of the last days of the
war," the current offerings were as good as any to follow. It was
Siepmann who characterized the present as the golden age. He argued
that in five, ten, or fifteen years sponsors would be driven to a

lower common denominator to attract the mass audience, and in so
doing would destroy the present good of the medium.[81] Compared
to the probable future, the present was judged good and acceptable.

Other writers took a more conventional stance and argued that
the present was not as good as the past, or that the problems of
TV were growing more serious as time passed. Christian Century,
for example, was worried about the abandonment of intellectual
programs for children in order "to make way for the cheaper stuff
which sponsors seem to prefer." Color was accepted as an inevitable
development in the medium, but Theatre Arts and Saturday Evening Post
saw it causing commercials to be even more of a nuisance and bloody
children's programs to be more of a threat than they had been.
Walter Goodman, writing for New Republic, was convinced that the
increased use of political TV predicted for 1956 meant that "the
inequities and uncertainties which have appeared in previous election years may be expected to appear again--more unequal and less
certain than ever." But of greatest concern was children's programming, namely "the glaring absence of worth-while children's
programs from television station and network schedules today."
As America said, "the good shows for youngsters that have appeared
on the video horizon inevitably have been replaced by inferior
productions." Both Robert Louis Shayon in Saturday Review and
Al Toffler in Nation warned readers that the amount of crime and

violence in children's programs had increased significantly over the years and had reached the point in 1954 and 1955 where it constituted a serious threat to the welfare of the nation. The core of evidence from which the argument was drawn was the 1954 report of the National Association for Better Television and Radio which concluded that "today, crime programs are being produced specifically for television in a volume approximately four times greater than in 1951." And all the while, as U. S. News noted in 1955, the proportion of entertainment to information programs was slipping toward entertainment. "If anything, the trend is toward a higher content of entertainment and a lower slice of information."[82] The indications were clear to attackers; television was not only less intellectual, more of a nuisance, more of a problem in politics, and more dangerous to children than in the past, it was also committed more than ever to the fallacy that entertainment for its own sake was a good thing as well as a moneymaker. There was more in television to worry the critics than there had been for the advocates to praise.

In general, however, the comparison of present with past was used less frequently by critics than by advocates. While the comparison could be used to assess the current state of the media and to predict the character of movies, radio, and television in the future, opponents found stronger and more spectacular grounds on which to build arguments. For example, they could point to new problems caused for society's institutions, denials of the value system, damage to most areas about which people are concerned. The comparisons contained less rhetorical potential for them than for the advocates. Advocates, by comparison, could confirm their predictions about the media, demonstrate the growth of the arts, and give films and broadcasting the sanction of progress. The argument promised more for them, and consequently appeared more often in their repertory.

Analogy

There remain to be examined the arguments from analogy, the longest, least direct, and most sophisticated of the comparisons. Grouped together here are the comparisons which call attention to relationships among the media, to similarities between circumstances, to parallels in events past and present; which often involve four terms; and in which relationships can frequently be expressed as ratios. These comparisons allow writers to draw inferences about the behavior of one medium from the performance of another, to judge one medium by measuring it against others of the same class, and to predict the consequences of innovation through an examination of the known or presumed consequences of past innovation.

Prediction of consequences

Both promoters and critics of the new media used the argument from analogy to make predictions about the consequences of innovation. Presuming that history does   repeat itself, and that much can be learned about the new and unfamiliar by looking to the past, writers commenting on the new media often chose examples from the past in order to draw conclusions about the present and the future. Advocates developed two lines of argument from this mode of comparison. First, they argued that the new media would prove beneficial for society, as other innovations had in the past. Second, defenders offered assurance that the new media would not damage social institutions: the institutions had survived innovation in the past; they would survive it now.

Reasoning analogically, supporters of the new media predicted new good for society. If books, the radio, the talkies, and the theatre had served society well, as advocates presumed they had, the new media would serve equally well, for they are like the old. This line of argument was used in various situations, one of which was the introduction of Independent's new motion picture review column in 1914. Recalling the value of printing and books, the writer argued that "now in the same way the moving picture does for drama what printing did for literature, that is, it brings it within the reach of multitudes through a process of mechanical manifolding."

As printing extended literature, so the motion picture extended
the drama. With the coming of talkies, William deMille argued that
the new form would lead audiences to appreciate the spoken word,
just as silent pictures had led them to appreciate finer values
in drama. Jesse Lasky, also writing in praise of talkies, argued
that just as silent pictures had influenced fashion in clothing,
so the talkie would "have its wide and deep effect upon the voices
of the nation; . . . the speech of the screen heroine /will/ find
echo on the tongue of her audience." Moreover, he said,

> the synchronized picture will create an enormous appetite
> for the best in music. It will influence the music-
> cultural growth of the nation just as surely as the silent
> pictures have given us a better theater.

Television, as radio and concert tours had been before it, was
expected to be a great stimulus to the study of music. Said David
Sarnoff of the newest medium, "It is probable that television
drama of high calibre and produced by first-rate artists, will
materially raise the level of dramatic taste of the nation, just
as aural broadcasting has raised the level of musical appreciation."
And television was to "stimulate sports attendance in the long
haul just as radio has done."[83]

The new media would perform as their predecessors had. If
radio had influenced national life in some praise-worthy direction,
television would also. If silent films had done good, talkies
would do even more good. The examples of the past provided grounds

for comparison, and demonstrated, if nothing else, that the media had the capacity to influence society. The predictions formulated from the comparison went on to assert that the new would serve values and institutions for which society had great affection.

In their second line of argument from analogy, advocates assured readers that the new media would damage neither valued institutions not established media. The theatre, the church, and musical performances by live artists had survived a variety of threats in the past; they would survive the coming of movies, radio, and television. Movies and radio, in turn, judging from the examples of the past, would survive television.

This line of argument was used most often to assure readers of the stability of the theatre, an institution which critics had predicted would survive neither movies, radio, nor talkies. Each time its defenders sought to minimize the danger, they argued on the basis of past experience that the theatre would endure despite increased competition. Current Opinion, for example, contended that the theatre was not endangered by the silent pictures.

> An art some twenty-five hundred years old cannot con-
> ceivably perish as suddenly as the managers predict.
> When a crisis in the spoken drama supervenes, the tendency
> of the business men of the theater is to look for external
> causes. Some time ago it was the automobile. Then it
> was the auction bridge and the tango. Now it is the
> motion pictures. It must be a frail virtue that succumbs
> before every fad of the moment.[84]

When talking pictures were demonstrated in 1913, Walter Prichard
Eaton turned again to the example of the past to calm the fears
that the theatre could not survive the new threat. Just as the
phonograph did not end grand opera, singing lessons, concerts,
singing teachers, music schools, and Caruso singing, just as photography had not decreased travel, the number of painters, or gate
receipts at art museums, the combining of the phonograph and the
picture machine posed no threat to the stage. "Just why we should
think that the increase of motion pictures is going to have a
different result, a disastrous result, is hard to see."[85] When
Brady predicted the death of the drama because of radio, which
had joined the silent pictures in attracting people away from the
theatre, Outlook replied that

> the general experience with inventions and improvements
> is that the new never entirely supplants the old. We
> venture to predict that in improved form the movies and
> the radio will continue to have a big place in American
> life, while at the same time the speaking play will main-
> tain its hold. There are many different kinds of enjoy-
> ment and of tastes. There seems to be plenty of room
> for all these forms of pleasure taking.[86]

When talkies were finally introduced in the late 1920's, defenders
of the theatre, reasoning analogically, denied again that it would
die. Peggy Wood, an actress turned writer, said that "I think the
theater--that is what we now call the legitimate theater--will
survive; it has survived so much before now that even inventions
cannot kill it." And Nation reacted to George Bernard Shaw's

predictions of the death of the theatre with this comment: "That

the poor old theater is completely done for we cannot believe; the

reports of its death have been exaggerated too often."[87] For all

these writers, the example of the past held hope for the future.

The theatre had never yet been hurt mortally; in all probability

it would survive the present crisis.

The longevity of the theatre in the face of change offered

encouragement to spokesmen for other institutions. With television

at hand, Milton McKay argued in Saturday Evening Post from the

experience of the theatre:

> When talking pictures came in, there were Jeramiahs who
> foresaw the death of the legitimate theater. It got
> pretty sick, but survived. It is the belief of this
> reporter that movies and movie theaters will also sur-
> vive, although they may be different, but there are
> never enough talented entertainers to go around.[88]

But there was evidence from places other than the theatre confirming

the stability of established institutions. Writers judged each

new threat in terms of ones which were safely past. For example,

when attackers predicted that with the coming of talkies the machine

would replace the living artist, a writer for North American Review

turned to the history of the radio and the phonograph for rebuttal.

> No device, contraption or machine ever invented, or still
> to be invneted, will displace such artists as Kreisler,
> Paderewski, Casals and Galli-Curci, nor will machine
> productions supersede the performances of such orchestras
> as the Philharmonic in New York, and the Boston and Phila-
> delphia Symphonies. Nor will they take from Messers.

Arturo Toscanini, Serge Koussevitzky and Leopold Stokowski,
who are virtuoso conductors, their daily bread. Those
who thought that the phonograph and the radio would displace the artists have learned to the contrary.[89]

His experience with the past led Bennett Cerf to deny that books

and reading would be displaced by television. He said that

> when I first became a publisher myself, in 1923, it was
> motion pictures and cheap automobiles that had doomed
> the book business, to hear my confreres tell it, with
> that dreaded new monster radio about to deliver the
> coup de grace. During the Wall Street Boom people were
> 'too busy speculating to read books'; after the crash
> they were 'too depressed.' It was always something.
> And yet, you may have observed, the book business has
> survived handsomely. The answer is that despite all
> and any distractions there will always be millions of
> Americans who want to read good books--and, praise be,
> their number is growing. In my opinion, television
> will not only fail to hurt the book business, but actually
> may improve it.[90]

Reasoning from the past, advertisers claimed television wouldn't

run radio out of business any more than radio ran its competition

out of business in the 1930's; Sam Goldwyn said television would

hurt movies no more than radio had hurt the theatre; and a publication

of the Presbyterian church, replying to predictions of radio's

damage to the church, argued that "no scientific invention of

the past has essentially harmed the church, and it need not be

feared that the wireless telephone will prove destructive of what

has thus far survived the force of the inevitable needs of human

nature and the inherent character of the Holy Spirit's ministry

to man."[91] Presuming that if harm had not been caused by similar circumstances in the past, it would not be caused now, advocates used arguments from analogy to refute predictions of damage from innovation. Choosing examples which confirmed their beliefs, spokesmen for the new media assured readers that movies, radio, and television would harm none of society's institutions. Innovation, as the past had demonstrated, was safe; tradition would not suffer because of it.

Writers critical of the new media turned also to analogy to assess the consequences of innovation. Taking a stance opposite to that of the supporters, arguing from the position that past innovations had often been harmful, critics predicted that what had happened once would probably happen again. Where the circumstances of past and present were comparable, the troubles of the past were apt to be repeated in the present. And the evidence indicated that the new media were indeed going the way of the old; undesirable patterns of the past were appearing again. Consequently, their opponents warned against the dangerous influence of motion pictures, radio, and television.

Some of the critics argued that the talkies, radio, and television were going the way of their predecessors. The same sets of conditions which had caused earlier media to fail society, if not to harm it, were recreated with the introduction of each medium. For example, shortly after talkies were introduced, Alexander Bakshy expressed his disappointment in their reception by intellectuals,

warning of the consequences if those people ignored talkies as they

had ignored the silents. He said that

> it is a sad reflection on the limitations of intellec-
> tuals and artists all over the world to see history
> repeat itself in the contemptuous resentment with which
> they are greeting the arrival of the talking picture.
> Just as twenty years ago when the silent movie began to
> stir the world, so today the patrons of art and the
> theater refuse to see in the talking pictures anything
> but another vulgar product of our machine civilization.
> . . . Thus . . . the talking picture is apparently doomed
> to grope blindly for several years before it reaches
> anything that may be properly described as an original
> form of drama.92

The difficulties of the movies were carried over to the radio.

Writers worried about the direction broadcasting was taking, warned

that it was following the path of the movies. New Republic, for

example, commented in 1924 that too frequently on radio "the making

of programs is in the hands of underpaid individuals, picked up

at haphazard, usually musicians or men whose primary interest is

in music," or businessmen whose first interest was in the commercial

end of broadcasting. This was dangerously reminiscent of the early

days of movies.

> The development of motion pictures in the United States
> was held back half a decade because at first it was in
> the control of fly-by-nights, adventurers, and reformed
> push-cart peddlers, not one in a hundred of whom had reached
> the social level where one takes one's hat off indoors.
> Radio broadcasting seems threatened by the same fate, and
> for somewhat the same reason: because a remarkable new
> educational device has suddenly developed as a sort of
> by-product of industry and is therefore in the hands of

business men not only ignorant of its proper use, but indifferent as to whether it is used properly or not.[93]

Ten years later Harper's said "having reached substantially the same stage of development as the movies in 1911-12, the broadcasting art seems to have congealed at that point." If the intellectuals and the visionaries did not come to its rescue, radio would duplicate the record of the movies, never to achieve the good of which it was capable.[94]

Television inherited the problems of both radio and movies, and the failures of these media were envisioned for it. Once again, the new was going the faulted way of the old. For example, the commercial powers which had controlled radio were said to be leading television down the same path to mediocrity: "the big guns in television are the same big guns that in radio have been most guilty of advertising excesses." The advertisers who "bastardized the great cultural force of radio," were in control of television and it was "following slavishly in the economic footsteps of radio." The intellectuals who had ignored radio were ignoring TV. The educators who failed with radio and the movies were heading toward failure with television. The church, which "largely missed her opportunity in radio . . . is now well on the way to missing it in television." Television which at first presented good children's programs by 1950 was beginning to turn out the kinds of things to which parents had objected in both movies and radio.[95] Television, like the past it copied, was plagued

with the myth of the twelve-year-old mind. It was, said Norman

Cousins,

> the same old story: the grotesque perpetuation of the
> fable about the intelligence of the *Average American*
> --that is somewhere on the level of the twelve-year-
> old child. This billion-dollar blunder has already come
> close to putting the skids under Hollywood, has devita-
> lized and disfigured much of radio, and has wrecked some
> of the largest pulp magazines in America. Despite the
> evidence, TV is apparently using the same bubble for its
> foundation.[96]

Television was following the lead of radio, taking five years to

acquire intelligence and ten to devise its own materials. With

television, said Gilbert Seldes, "we seem to be watching, for the

hundredth time, the traditional development of an American art

enterprise: an incredible ingenuity in the mechanism, great skill

in the production techniques--and stale, unrewarding, contrived,

and imitative banality for the total result."[97]

The new media were repeating the failures of the ones which

had preceded them. The same problems which had plagued the movies

were apparent in radio; those of radio were passed in turn to

television. The causal factors which had prevented the matura-

tion of the earlier media were at work in the later ones. There

was no reason, said critics, to expect the last in the line to be

of more benefit than the first. As one had failed society, so

would the others.

But the critics were not concerned merely with the failures
of the new media. They also argued that movies, radio, and television,
since each was following the course set by the first in the line,
would have similarly harmful effects on society's values and its
institutions. The fears of the critics were foreshadowed in the
defense arguments we examined earlier. Like advocates, writers
warning against innovation feared that the theatre would be destroyed. For instance, Gilbert Seldes stated the warning in con-
ditional terms in 1928, arguing that if the newly introduced talkies
had enough power to end the silents, they had enough to end the
theatre also. He claimed that

> the effect of the new movies on the stage will depend
> largely on its effects on the old movie. According to
> enthusiasts, the silent movie is doomed. I would say
> that in that case the stage, although it has nothing what-
> ever in common with the silent movie, will also go under.
> If the talking movie can undrmine one, it can undermine
> the other.98

W. A. Brady, the theatrical producer, Outlook reported, assuming
that radio and the movies were comparable in their influence, argued
that radio

> may be a menace to the theater and declares that the
> movie already has injured the legitimate stage a great
> deal--not in New York City, to be sure, but in smaller
> cities throughout the country. He thinks that the radio
> may even injure the movie, and he paints a picture of
> a group of people seated in a room, enjoying free of
> charge a performance over the radio, of which he says,
> 'I can only describe it as gorgeous,' and asking, 'Why
> in the world should we go to the theater and pay money?'99

Television, too, was expected to damage the theatre, working the
same kind of harm on it that movies, talkies, and radio had already
begun. John Dos Passos said, for example, that while he didn't
know what television would do to the theatre, he knew it would be
worse than the talkies, and the talkies were eating up the stage.
Recall, too, R. E. Sherwood's argument that as radio had taken the
audience for theatre, television would lead to the closing of
both picture houses and legitimate theatres.[100] If past inventions
had hurt the theatre, new inventions of a similar type would also
be a cause of harm to it.

Working analogically, other spokesmen for the status quo warned
against the effects of television on institutions and media already
established. For example, William Morris of the William Morris
Agency, an early user of television, predicted in 1939 that television "may eventually displace the talking pictures, as the talkies
wiped out the silents." Review of Reviews said even earlier that
"when practical television arrives it means the dump-heap for radio
sets, just as surely as the talking picture displaced the silent
film."[101] In 1937, Val Gielgud wrote in Theatre Arts that

> with the shadow of television rapidly lengthening upon
> the horizon, the entire problem of the future of broad-
> casting is thrown into the melting-pot. We remember the
> parallel case of what happened to the cinema, the mom-
> ent that the lush strains of 'Sonny Boy' startled the ears
> of the world. . . . And, by obvious analogy, it is simply
> imitating the ostrich to pretend that, once television has

> become universally attainable and reasonably cheap, it
> will not make simple sound-broadcasting as out of date
> as The Great Train Robbery.[102]

Then in 1952 Saturday Evening Post commented that "what movies

did to vaudeville, TV is doing to radio." Newspapers, too were

predicted to suffer. Commonweal, noting that radio had already

damaged the newspaper, predicted by implication that television

would follow the same course. The story of damage to the newspaper,

it said, was not finished. "Television is ahead. What that will

do to the newspaper worker nobody can forsee." Isabelle Keating

was more specific in Harper's, however. She said that "the experi-

ence of the weekly papers when dailies entered the field may be an

index to the fate" of most newspapers when television arrived,

the experience of the past being used to predict the consequences

of future innovation.[103]

Analogy of the same order also was used to predict economic

and moral damage. For example, the situation of the motion picture

theatre musician at the advent of talkies was said to be the same

as that of the telegrapher when the automatic telegraphic printer

came in. "When every theatre in the country is fitted for sound,

when the dahned music of a single orchestra of excellent musicians

can be heard simutaneously in every hamlet in the land, when every

picture is made with music accompaniment and has a specially written

score--when this happens the fiddler will go the way of the colorful

but economically outmoded telegrapher." When the opponents of the
white slave films sought to demonstrate that there was danger in
the pictures, they turned to analogy. Mrs. Barclay Hazard, assuming
that if movies could cause boys to run away from home or to attempt
to burn their playmates at the stake, then the white slave films
could just as easily lead girls into lives of prostitution.[104]

Argument from analogy was thus used to make predictions about
the consequences of innovation. Arguing from the experience of the
past, both advocates and attackers pointed to the probability of
similar occurrences in either present or future. There is in this
argument a strong causal element. When writers predicted that the
new media would affect society in the same way inventions of the
past had exerted their influence, they were arguing causally within
the framework of the analogical mode. Not having sufficient experience with the new media to point to observed effects, perhaps not
having evidence of the influence immediately available, they turned
to analogy in order to project the causal relationships from one
set of circumstances to another. They said, for example, if movies
caused damage to the theatre, an effect most people were familiar
with, television, which as yet was untried and with which people
were unfamiliar, will cause damage to movies, which are similar
in many ways to the theatre. The function of the analogy is to
establish a predictive causal relationship. It should be noted, too,

that these arguments are attached to the same reference points as
the arguments we have examined before. That is, the new media were
related by both attackers and advocates to the value and institutional
systems. This time the method for making the relationship was
analogy, but once again innovation was assessed on the basis of its
influence on things society held to be necessary, worthwhile, and
desirable.

Historical parallels

Many of the arguments from analogy point to similarities
between past and present. Some of them, as I have shown, function
causally. Others, the ones to be examined now, suppress the causal
relationships which may lie within the argument and stress instead
the historical parallels. The present is like the past, they say;
and consequences follow. Argument from this presumption served
two purposes for the advocates: it gave them a method by which
to minimize or discount the charges of the critics, and it was a
means for offering reassurance about the current state of affairs.

Discounting

A strategy of discounting or minimizing was adopted by advocates to deal with the predictions of critics. Turning to history,
they argued that what was said in the disparagement of movies, radio,
or television were merely the things always said about new inventions,

that the arguments were not unique to the present situation, that

common knowledge denied that the effects would be as serious as

they had been painted. They evaluated the argument of the oppo-

sition and dismissed it as insignificant.

This kind of analogical argument was used to defend films.

It was developed during the attacks of the 1920's, when the morality

of movies came under fire again. One of those who used it was

Charles D. Isaacson. He began by redefining the focus of the

dispute, shifting the argument from a question of morality to one

of innovation. He then argued that the charges against films were

merely reflections of the normal resistance to change. They were

no different from the arguments used to oppose the telephone,

electricity, steamboats, sewing machines, railroads, rubber pro-

ducts, and even the newspaper.

> It was against the dicta of the church, the state, and
> all authorities that the newspaper came into existence.
> Type was a joke. Printing was considered an indecent
> affair. People didn't want to read, they didn't know
> how to read.[105]

The inventions Isaacson named, everyone knew, had come to be social

and economic necessities. In this context, the attacks on movies

was meaningless, and their future bright. Similarly, William

DeMille dismissed charges against the motion picture with the

comment that "like many other new things it has been denounced as

crude, untrue, inartistic, and debasing to the youth of the land."

The audience, in this case, was left to supply the details to fill
out the argument. When the musician's union objected to talkies
on the grounds they would dehumanize music, a writer favoring the
new invention argued in North American Review that the union's
arguments, "these strabismic apothegems, are of the same genre as
the myopic view of the reactionaries of another century who saw in
the industrial revolution a dehumanization of civilization." Again,
predictions of disaster were disproved in the course of history,
and the present argument was suggested to be as foolish as the
earlier one had been. Finally, when Jesse Lasky announced that
the silent film was dead, one of its defenders commented in Collier's
that he could recall his father predicting that the telephone would
end retail shopping; that the phonograph would displace live musicians; that radio would eliminate the telephone, the telegraph, and
the phonograph; that 16 inch guns were going to end war; and that
motion pictures were going to end the stage. "Now, speakies are
going to end the silent drama."[106] The conclusion was obvious.
The argument, while it worked most of the time, was highly dependent
upon the arguer's perceptivity and his caution in its application.

Supporters of radio said that the arguments against it were
merely commonplaces. The fears that radio would destroy peace,
quiet, and thought, or would cause international unrest were dismissed with the observation that they were "the fears of a crochety

generation that is passing."[107] Marion Spitzer reminded readers of

the Saturday Evening Post in 1924 that when theatrical groups said

something must be done about radio or the "whole structure of theater

would collapse," this was

> an exact repetition of the attitude of theatrical pro-
> ducers when the movies first became popular. Everyone
> was sure that the speaking stage was well on the way to
> limbo, that it would not be long before theaters other
> than movie houses would be traditions of the dim past,
> and that the human voice on stage would be nothing but
> a remote myth.[108]

Then twenty-five years later, when the children's programs came under

fire for a third time, Library Journal commented that "the attacks

made upon children's programs in terms of their psychological

effects, particularly upon the stories used in the programs, is

reminiscent of the attacks which were made earlier upon the movies

prepared for children and upon the so-called 'children's literature'

which appeared in children's story books."[109] The arguments presumed

to have been meaningless the first time they were used, were dis-

counted by the supporters of radio when they were applied again.

Moreover, since history had not borne out the validity of the pre-

dictions in time past, there was no reason to consider them authen-

tic in the present.

Writers favoring television employed the same technique of

discounting. For example, a writer for Saturday Review argued in

1942 that the complaints then heard about television's influence

on the movies were the same ones which had been raised when theatre

people predicted that movies and radio would be the death of the
legitimate stage. When, nearly ten years later, opponents of television asked where the money was coming from for ETV on a national
scale, Saturday Review commented that this was the same "taunt
that was hurled a hundred years ago against the dream of free
public education for all children." If it was a good thing, the
money would be found, as it had always been found before.[110]

In addition there was a subtle variation in the argument about
television. Some of the writers who were generally favorable to
the innovation, suggested that it would do damage as well as good,
or that the dreams for it merely reflected the hopes always held
for new inventions. That is, Alva Johnson, writing in the Saturday Evening Post in 1939, pointed out that the then current debate
about television and movies was much like the discussion of talkies
and silents in 1928. In that case, of course, the new displaced
the old. Later, George Marek, writing in Good Housekeeping, contended
that the extravagant claims made for television were merely indicative of the stage it was in, "the National-Craze stage; /when/ the
invention becomes the popular national toy." At this time, as the
arguments of the moment seemed to prove, "the invention is expected
to solve international problems, virtually remake human beings,
and do wonders for culture." Although he believed TV a hopeful
invention, Marek concluded that it, "like radio, will have to pander

and proselytize, offer good and bad."[111]   What had happened before,
said these writers, would happen again; what was said before, the
others argued, would be said again.

Supporters tended to discount the customary statements of
alarm, to minimize the importance of arguments which appeared to
be a part of the conventional rhetoric. The cries of "Wolf!
Wolf!" had been heard before, but the wolf had never materialized.
The fears which history demonstrated to be specious were called
upon to serve in defense of innovation. But it must be recognized,
too, that good sense guided advocates' choice of examples. Recall
that they most often referred to the stage, which had never failed
despite predictions to the contrary, and to the other media and
institutions which remained strong in the face of competition.
These examples, familiar ones, pointed out the discrepancy between
critics' predictions and the historical fact. At the same time,
advocates generally avoided mention of the case of silent films,
destroyed by innovation within the medium.

Reassurance

The other function of the argument from historical parallels
was to offer reassurance. Advocates of radio and television used
examples from the past to demonstrate that things would work out
all right with the new media, they would find their place as other

inventions had, and society would be none the worse, and probably better, for it.

For example, a writer for Saturday Evening Post argued in 1924 that radio's growth paralleled that of the movies and the "mechanical music dispenser," the phonograph. Both had caused an uproar in their youth, but were soon accepted. Radio would follow their pattern "and settle down eventually into a recognized, well established, separate branch of the theater, with its own public, its own personnel and its own technic." The publisher of The Musician likewise recalled that when the phonograph and the player piano appeared musicians were violent in their opposition to the new machines. Now they opposed radio and movies with equal violence, while the phonograph and the player piano were accepted as aids to music. The implication of the argument was clear. And the same kind of defense was used for radio's childrens programs. The editor of The Publisher's Auxiliary, writing in Rotarian, said that "fifty years ago the dime novel was the pet horror of a whole generation of conscientious parents. Then came the 'funny papers'. . . . Now we have the radio."[112] Children had survived past threats; they would, in all probability, survive even the radio. Each inno-vation, even those thought at first to be dangerous, were assimilated and proved in the end to be advantageous.

This line of argument was first used in connection with television in 1927. Then Walter Davenport turned to historical example to demonstrate the possibility of television's eventual practical realization.

> Still, they said, 'Fulton's Folly' would never be practical.
> They said that nothing would come of Morse's tick-tack.
> And the public laughed at the first motor-car and told
> the driver to 'get a horse.'
> Radio 'wasn't possible' a few years ago, but today
> they are beginning to turn out small tubes which will
> eliminate your radio's batteries.
> That being the case, it would be silly to predict
> that we shall never have television in a small, compact
> plant--say no larger than a small radio cabinet--and,
> sitting comfortably in our own home, see and hear a
> football game, a prize fight or what not even though it
> be in progress a thousand miles away.[113]

By recalling similar circumstances in the past, Davenport offered a kind of predictive assurance that television would be made practical. Later, after TV broadcasting was begun, other promoters argued it would follow radio's course of development, that people would react to television much as they had reacted to radio, that movies would learn to adapt to it just as newspapers had adapted to radio, and that reading would be as safe from TV as it had been from movies and radio. As Commonweal said,

> history proves that human beings can learn to get along
> well with almost anything. Human resilience is proving
> itself even now. The students have worked out techni-
> ques for doing homework and watching video simultaneous-
> ly.[114]

Thus, not only did history confirm the probability for success of new inventions; it also offered assurance that new things, like the old ones before them, would be absorbed into the social pattern with little disruption of the way of life sanctioned by tradition.

The argument from historical parallel relies upon the presumption that history is repetitive, that events of the past will probably be repeated under comparable circumstances. Advocates used it to predict that the new media would behave much as the old had behaved; they would be accepted in society to gain a valued place there. In addition, advocates used it to show that the predictions of the opposition were unimportant, not only because history had failed to confirm them, but also because they were merely the same arguments which had been used to oppose innovation in the past. The argument was not generated by the particular circumstances, they said, and was not characterized by the specificity of immediate concern. It was equally applicable in a variety of circumstances, and depended for its direction merely upon the choice of examples and the users' interpretation of them. The familiarity of the argument weakened it. The few writers who perceived the argument as a commonplace of attack dismissed it on this ground.

Similitude

The last kind of analogy to be examined I call similitude. Comparisons of this type call attention to similarities between

media, between effects, between circumstances, between proposed
solutions, and between events. They are not as time bound as the
ones just discussed, nor do they attempt to establish a causal relationship. They are a way of commenting on the new, a way of
making a judgment about it, a way of predicting its course. They
are most closely related to the comparative assertions which opened
this chapter, but the comparisons here are less direct than the
former, longer, and generally more sophisticated.

This line of argument was applied, in a number of variations
to the defense of movies. First, advocates used it to classify
motion pictures as similar to other good and accepted things.
Scientific American, for example, compared the commercial value
of the motion picture to that of the bicycle. The bicycle first,
and now in 1901 the motion picture, "originally designed as a mere
toy," had become instruments "of practical utility in the great
world of commerce." One of the most original of the comparisons
was devised by Newton A. Fuessle in 1921. He argued that motion
pictures' critics did not give the new art enough time to develop,
did not allow for a period of normal growth. For example, he said,
look at Beethoven, Homer, Michelangelo, and Shakespeare who did
not become successful immediately. The motion picture therefore
should be given a chance to grow up before being attacked. Another
writer for Outlook compared movies to the Elizabethan theatre, and

cited a number of parallels to demonstrate that the two institutions were indeed similar.[115]

The argument was used to predict adoption of the medium. In 1922, when interest renewed for a time in educational pictures, Current Opinion told of the many new teaching techniques possible with films, and concluded that movies were indeed a new short cut to power and knowledge. In the past every such short cut had been adopted by education. Therefore, speaking of pictures in education, "their ultimate use is as inevitable as the sunrise."[116]

The argument was used to chide critics for failing "to appreciate the illimitable artistic, the illimitable social, possibilities of the moving picture." To ignore the "incalculably potential" appeals to human mentality and imagination in the pictures "is, for actors or publicists or educators or playwrights, to go on thinking in terms of gas after the discovery of the electric light." Others said the thinking was equivalent to selling coal oil in the days of electricity.[117]

The argument was used to justify and excuse the early failures of the movie industry. Will Hays, for example, said movies were like other respected industries, and had had the same kind of beginnings. The crowded early years of the pictures were "in some respects, a chaos," and at the same time "like an Arabian nights story," he wrote. When the movie was introduced,

when keen men saw the commercial possibilities in it,
they set out in feverish haste on the world-old quest
for gold, just as the Forty-niners did when the word came
from Sutter's Hill that sent them around Cape Horn and
overland across desert, mountain, and plain, undaunted
by peril, hardship, or savage. Picture pioneers set out
to dig gold just as men went to get it in Alaska when the
Klondike flashed the golden invitation to the spirit of
adventure.

Consequently, both danger and irresponsibility were typical of

the days of the gold rush, and of the early years of other now

respectable industries. As Hays said,

the pioneer in any business is always a romantic figure,
his conduct frequently does not measure up to the best
boarding-school standards. Force and trickery and even
homicide were common incidents in the opening of yester-
day's oil fields, and in the mighty struggle for supremacy of the railroads of the country.

There was fierce competition in these early industries, and in the

movies. The rush for expansion was so great "that there was neither

time nor the proper mood to consider adequately the moral and

educational responsibility" in these great new things.

But those days are over. At the end of this period
of incredibly compressed physical, mechanical, financial,
and artistic development, the pioneers have caught their
second breath. They find themselves the responsible
leaders and custodians of one of the greatest industries
in the world, with limitless commercial possibilities
and perhaps more income than all the public utilities
in the country combined. The business is seeking and
finding a firm anchor, in the same way that banking and
manufacturing and other mercantile enterprises have done.
Sober business men, with vision clarified, old rivals
now seeing their common interest, know better than anyone else the future of the business, as well as the
future of society, demands better and still better pictures.[118]

The movies, Hays said, were now like other respectable industries.
Like them, pictures had lost their way for a time, but had emerged
stable and responsible. A new definition of pictures emerged from
the comparisons, a new image was created for them. Hays asked that
the early failures be excused, and that pictures be judged by the
same standards applied to other business.

Critics of pictures called them similar to things of which
society disapproved. One writer for Collier's said, for example,
that never would we allow our children to be taught by incompetents
in school. Yet the movies were a kind of school, conducted by
incompetents, in which "we allow our children, and go ourselves,
to watch photoplays produced on such a low scale of intelligence
that our own untrained minds can detect their weaknesses and obvious absurdities." When crime pictures were begun again after the
Christian Century and Legion of Decency campaigns, this time with
policemen or G-men the heroes, opponents argued that these were
merely the same old films in a new mold, a device for getting around
the regulating agencies.[119]

The arguments from similitude put at the disposal of critics
a sophisticated and socially acceptable form of invective. For
example, when the film industry defended movies on the grounds
they took several months to make and cost a lot to produce, and
therefore must be good, a writer for Outlook commented that the

argument was foolish. Brewerys cost a lot, too, and took time and

care to produce their product. Like the movies, brewerys had yet

to produce anything of beauty.[120] Christian Century used such

arguments to place movies in the same class as the brothel and

the saloon, which probably were to Christian Century and its readers

the most intensely distasteful of society's evils. Evaluating pic-

tures, one of Christian Century's, Clifford G Twombly, said that

> America sometimes makes excuse for Hollywood on the
> grounds that foreign nations must enjoy these /immoral7
> pictures or else they would not patronize them! . . .
> It is an argument that could be used equally well by
> the keepers of brothels. People willing to traffic in
> a certain line of goods can always do a lively business
> with the unhappy human race, but they should be content
> with gold for payment and should not clamor for respect.[121]

Speaking of the same line of defense for pictures--foreigners liked

them or wouldn't buy them--Fred Eastman said the argument deserved

to be used by the keeper of a saloon or a disorderly house.[122]

Writers who wanted to castigate films in the strongest and most

unsavory terms available to them, found in the argument from simi-

litude a means for making their point unquestionably clear.

Arguments from similitude also were employed in the promotion

and defense of broadcasting. For example, when broadcasters found

they could no longer get talented artists to work without pay,

Outlook suggested that radio would have to adopt the solution

discovered by the phonograph industry. That is, radio would "have

to reach out for talent that is at present beyond their means,"

paying the finest performers in the field for their appearances
on the air. When objections were raised to children spending too
much time listening to radio, the practice was defended by a psychology professor from Wesleyan University who said that a boy's
playing the radio, listening to snatches of programs from here and
there, was no worse than his sister spending her time playing popular songs on the piano. Levering Tyson in 1936 compared the status of radio with that of printing. Just as the people of the Middle
Ages did not realize for a long time, what a marvelous tool for
learning they had in printing, "today we are in an analogous position in respect to various mechanical aids to learning, of which
the radio-telephonic devices are the most spectacular." The realization of the place of broadcasting was only beginning but like
printing it would also be accepted in time.[123]

Supporters of television said that it would not be faced with
the same kind of problems which had beset radio in its early days.
As C. Francis Jenkins said in 1929, "Unlike radio broadcasting,
television will come to a waiting and friendly public, for the
pioneer work for this new invention was accomplished in the early
struggle of radio." When television failed to develop as quickly
as promoters of the late 1930's thought it should, one of them,
blaming movies, newspapers, and the telecasters themselves for the
delay, argued that "keeping back this means of sending sound and

pictures through the air is hurting the public as much as keeping
back vitamins or anesthesia would have hurt, had the medical pro-
fession, for some reasons of self-interest, decided to hold back
new products or developments in its own field." The ground was
prepared for ETV with denials of similitude. That is, I. Keith
Tyler, Chairman of the Joint Committee on Educational Television,
argued that educational television should not be judged on the
basis of radio's failure. "The evidence is clear that school
educators are looking with much greater interest toward television."
After the Kefauver report on television and juvenile delinquency
was issued, a writer for Nation sought to place broadcasters' attacks
which the comic book publishers had mounted in response to attempts
to clean up their industry.[124]

The arguments from similitude functioned in much the same
way as the simpler comparative assertions. They established a
context for the new media, showed what they were like, connected
them with known good or evil, showed them to be like past inventions which had worked out well or badly, and explained or justified
the reasons for failures along the way. In the process, the comparisons served as means for assessment of the media. As before,
the new was judged in terms of what was already known. The variety
of topics can be explained both on the basis of the arguers' interests
--they wrote of matters which concerned them and which they assumed

to interest the audience--and on the basis of the freedom offered
by this kind of analogy. The comparisons here were not so strict
as those demanded in other forms of analogy; arguers could link
things and ideas which were not so closely related as one might
expect in other modes of comparison. In this sense, the arguments
from similitude worked in much the same way as figurative analogy.
They give the writers broad limits within which to structure their
comparisons. At the same time, they offered an interesting means
of evaluation.

Two further applications of analogical arguments should be
noted before concluding the discussion of it. First, advocates
used it to predict new applications for the media. That is, one
writer argued that if television had been a success in England,
it could be used in the United States. Another said that since
the commercials and the dramatic programs on TV had such a great
appeal for children, the medium should be highly effective in
religious broadcasting. Similarly, Outlook commented that "the
very potency of the motion picture in degrading taste and corrupting morals is the measure of its potency as a force for recreation,
enlightenment, and education." Second, analogical arguments were
employed by supporters of regulation who argued, for example, that
if other countries had the right to prohibit children going to
films, we should have the same right; if the government could pass

laws to insure the purity of food and drugs, it should also have
the power to regulate the content of pictures; if the post office
could regulate advertising or prohibit the use of the mail to
defraud, other agencies should have the right to regulate radio.
Writers opposed to regulation argued, on the other hand, that since
other media were not restricted, pictures should not be, and that
since movies were neither foodstuffs nor drugs, the analogy was
invalid.[125] All of these writers, of course, were pointing to
similarities for the purpose of making decisions and judgments,
just as the others had done who used analogy. The process was the
same; the arguments merely served another end here.

Analogy thus operates as the most sophisticated species of
the genre of comparative argument. Its particular value in the
controversy over movies, radio, and television lay in its adapta-
bility to illuminating the unknown through the known, to making
connections between past and present, to showing the similarities
between apparently dissimilar things, and to establishing relationships which are not available from the comparatively simple and
direct causal arguments. Lacking experience with the new media,
without direct evidence from which effects could be inferred, writers
turned to analogical argument to describe and evaluate innovation.
Consider, for example, the rhetorical problem of the writers concerned about television from 1912 until 1939, when there were

frequent unsupported predictions about the medium but no substantial grounds from which to argue. No one knew what television would do, because it had never been tried outside the laboratory. Hence both attackers and defenders turned to analogical argument. Reasoning that TV would work like radio and like motion pictures, they argued that it would have the same effects as the past media. Cases for and against television were built to a large extent from the experience of the past and from knowledge of related media. The analogical argument thus provided an instrument for suasion when unsupported prediction was thought insufficient and causal data unavailable.

Despite its apparent value, this form of reasoning was never used as frequently as the other comparisons nor as often as the argument from cause. Writers, it seems, accepted it as second best, as a means for support to be used when causal argument was not available. Analogy was indirect, there was a distance between the elements, which could weaken the clarity of the relationship. Causal argument, on the other hand, was direct and close-knit; the lines of influence could be made clearly apparent and relatively simple. The first choice was argument from cause. Analogy was less popular, presumed to be less persuasive to a general audience, and so less often used than the other forms.

When it was used, however, it was an interesting, varied, and flexible instrument. Moreover, it served many of the same functions

as the other arguments which have been examined so far. Like other
arguments from comparison and those from cause, it was employed by
both advocates and opponents to assign the new media their places
in the social order, to evaluate their impact on society, and to
predict their future courses. Hence, arguments from comparison,
like those from cause, functioned to illuminate the relationships
between innovation and the values and institutions held by society
to be necessary, worthwhile, and desirable.

NOTES

1. CC, 11 Mr '31, p. 340.

2. CL, S '08, p. 328; WT, O '08, p. 1052; RR, S '10, p. 7; WT, O '10, p. 1132; Ind, 13 F '13, p. 354; WW, My '13, p. 40; Ind, 6 Ap '14, p. 8; Out, 22 Ag '14, p. 968; HW, 2 Ja '15, p. 8; HM, Ja '19, p. 183; WW, Ja '21, p. 251; CO, Mr '23, p. 331; Scrib, Ap '23, p. 410; LA, 22 S '23, p. 568; Nat, 23 Jl '24, p. 90; Col, 3 Ja '25, p. 40; SEP, 28 Mr '25, p. 47; RR, Ja '26, p. 33; PE, O '26, p. 175; Out, 18 Ap '28, p. 616; Scrib, My '28, p. 626; Forum, Ap '29, p. 214; SA, Je '29, p. 527; Nat, 18 S '29, p. 291; NR 23 O '29, p. 259; PE, F '30, p. 640; Nat, 19 N '30, p. 547; CC, 11 Mr '31, p. 340; Scrib, My '31, p. 498; SEP, 20 My '39, p. 104; SR, 21 F '42, p. 13; Nwk, 20 D '43, p. 68; SEP, 9 Mr '46, p. 10; TA, Ap '49, p. 47; NB, Je '49, p. 41; TA, F '51, p. 48; SR, 25 Ag '51, p. 31; SNL, 27 S '52, p. 200; RD, F '53, p. 146; NR, 18 Ja '54, p. 7; SEP, 12 Mr '55, p. 137; USN, 2 S '55, p. 43.

3. SA, 26 Ag '16, p. 193; SEP, 12 Mr '55, p. 33; Ind, 29 S '10, p. 713; LD, 21 Jl '06, p. 80; HW, 16 S '11, p. 6; HW, 18 Ja '13, p. 20; Ind, 6 Ap '14, p. 8; Ind, 11 O '15, p. 43; HM, Ag '17, p. 349; Ind, 24 Ja '20, p. 152; RR, Jl '20, p. 107; Col, 8 Ap '22, p. 4; Col, 10 Je '22, p. 18; Scrib, Ap '23, p. 410; Scrib, S '24, p. 231; Col, 21 F '25, p. 20; PE, O '26, p. 178; Nat, 5 D '28, p. 601; Forum, Ap '29, p. 214; NAR, Ap '29, p. 432; PE, Jl '29, p. 57; NR, 23 O '29, p. 258; LA, 1 Ag '30, p.669; Scrib, My '31, p. 498; RR, Mr '32, p. 31; SSoc, 22 Ag '36, p. 231; Nat, 12 N '38, p. 498; NB, Je '49, p. 72; HW, 24 Ag '07, p. 1247; HW, 13 N '09, p. 9; Ind, 13 F '13, p. 354; HW, 6 Je '14, p. 20; Ind, 11 D '16, p. 448; RR, Ja '20, p. 103; NAR, Jl '20, p. 90; RR, Ap '27, p. 34; Comm, 22 Ja '30, p. 335; LA, 1 Jl '30, p. 555; Scrib, F '35, p. 81; NR, 22 S '37, p. 184; SEP, 15 Ap '22, p. 144; NR, 19 Mr '24, p. 91; Ind, 29 Mr '24, p. 171; NR, 8 O '24, p. 136; SEP, 28 Mr '25, p. 47; Ind, 18 S '26, p. 326; Ind, 9 Jl '27, p. 33; RR, Jl '28, p. 87; HM, S '34, p. 463; Comm, 28 S '34, p. 499; Nat, 12 Je '35, p. 667; SR, 4 Jl '42, p. 6; AmMerc, Jl '44, p. 63; SR, 9 Ag '52, p. 20; HM, N '52, p. 28.

4. CC, 24 S '41, p. 1173; Scrib, Ap '23, p. 410. See also, SEP, 3 D '27, p. 46; Out, 18 S '29, p. 1151; SR, 24 Je '33, p. 661; Scrib, F '35, p. 81; NR, 22 S '37, p. 184; PMech, S '39, p. 322; AmMerc, Jl '44, p. 63.

5. Out, 17 Ja '14, p. 121; Col, 8 Ap '22, p. 3; Col, 10 Je '22, p. 9; CO, Mr '23, p. 330; Nat, 2 Ja '24, p. 5; LD, 12 Ja '24, p. 26; NR, 19 Mr '24, p. 91; Out, 25 N '25, p. 474; Ind, 9 Jl '27, p. 33; RR, D '28, p. 577; SEP, 2 F '29, p. 141; NAR, Ap '29, p. 433; Scrib, Jl '29, p. 3; LA, 1 Ag '30, p. 669; NR, 24 S '30, p. 154; HM, N '31, p. 725; RR, Mr '32, p. 31; HM, Ap '33, p. 557; Comm, 28 S '34, p. 499; SSoc, 22 Ag '36, p. 225; SEP, 20 My '39, p. 104; AAA, Ja '41, p. 148; SR, 19 F '44, p. 30; SS, 18 Mr '46, p. 20; NR, 21 Je '48, p. 27; Nwk, 27 D '48, p. 44; GH, Ja '49, p. 4; NB, Je '49, p. 41; SR, 17 Je '33, p. 34; SR, 26 Ag '50, p. 14; NR, 13 N '50, p. 61; SR, 25 Ag '51, p. 31; HM, N '52, p. 28.

6. Scrib, Jl '09, p. 122; Ind, 29 S '10, p. 713; Ind, 13 F '13, p. 356; AmMag, Jl '13, p. 102; Nat, 28 Ag, p. 193; Ind, 6 Ap '14, p. 8; Out, 20 Je '14, p. 412; RR, Jl '14, p. 104; HW, 2 Ja '15, p. 7; CO, Ap '22, p. 507; Col, 8 Ap '22, p. 3; SEP, 15 Ap '22, p. 144; SA, Je '22, p. 376; CO, Jl '22, p. 69; Scrib, Ap '23, p. 410; Out, 19 Mr '24, p. 465; Forum, Je '24, p. 770; RR, Ap '27, p. 397; SEP, 26 Je '26, p. 28; SEP, 14 Ag '26, p. 145; Out, 20 Ap '27, p. 488; LD, 23 Ap '27, p. 7; Comm, 10 Ap '29, p. 652; Col, 25 My '29, p. 8; Comm, 7 My '30, p. 23; RR, Jl '30, p. 90; LA, 1 Jl '30, p. 555; SEP, 23 Ag '30, p. 118; Comm, 13 D '35, p. 178; Time, 23 My '38, p. 25; CC, 8 Ja '47, p. 36; NB, Jl '47, p. 74; CC, 10 S '47, p. 1079; RD, F '53, p. 148; USN, 2 S '55, pp. 38, 42; Nat, 5 N '55, p. 379.

7. SSoc, 4 Ja '41, p. 16; SEP, 15 Ap '22, p. 144; RD, F '53, p. 148; Out, 20 Je '14, p. 413; HW, 2 Ja '15, p. 7. See also, CO, Je '15, p. 411; Col, 8 Ap '22, p. 3; SEP, 15 Ap '22, p. 144; RR, Ap '27, p. 393; Scrib, S '24, p. 231; Comm, 10 Ap '29, p. 652; PE, Jl '29, p. 57; SEP, 12 Mr '55, p. 33.

8. HW, 16 S '11, p. 6; Educa, D '36, p. 215; Rot, N '38, p. 13; LJ, 15 F '45, p. 175; WHC, F '47, p. 117; Time, 1 N '54, p. 64; HB, O '47, p. 274; Nat, 5 Jl '33, p. 26; NAR, S '20, p. 391; Scrib, S '24, p. 321; Amer, 5 Je '54, p. 279.

9. HW, 18 Ja '13, p. 22.

10. LHJ, F '24, p. 40; Comm, 6 O '50, p. 622; NR, 24 Je '31, p. 140; NR, 2 D '31, p. 71. See also, PE, O '08, p. 161; AmMag, S '13, p. 60; Out, 14 F, p. 348; NR, 14 Ag '15, p. 51; CO, D '15, p. 405; NAR, Mr '17, p. 451; NAR, Jl '20, p. 83; RR, My '21, p. 555; NAR, N '21, p. 624; LA, 22 S '23, p. 568; NR, 19 Mr '24, p. 92; Out, 28 My '24, p. 131; LA, 15 N '27, p. 993; Nat, 26 S '28, p. 286; Comm, 29 My '29, p. 105; PE, Ag '29, p. 74; Out, 16 Jl '30, p. 409; Comm, 13 Ag '30, p. 381; NR, 13 Ag '30, p. 357; RR. S '30, p. 66; HM, N '31, p. 718; LA, Ap '23, p. 183; CC, 3 My '33, p. 592; Scrib, F '35, p. 84; RR, Je '35, p. 52; Col, 26 O '35, p. 38; NR, 17 My '39, p. 43; NR, 19 F '40, p. 237; NR, 26 F '51, p. 18; SR, 6 D '52, p. 59; Nat, 14 Mr '53, p. 235; NR, 18 Ja '54, p. 7; Nat, 15 O '55, p. 234.

11. PE, Mr '09, p. 121; AmMag, D '15, p. 64.

12. Out, 24 Ag '21, p. 660.

13. Out, 14 F '14, p. 346; NR, 23 Mr '27, p. 140; Nat, 25 Mr '25, p. 325; Comm, 14 Ap '39, p. 678; Nat, 26 Ap '47, p. 481; Nat, 15 O '55, p. 324. See also, PE, Mr '09, p. 121; GH, Ag '10, p. 148; CO, O '15, p. 244; NAR, Jl '20, p. 83; Bookm, Mr '19, p. 42; LD, 22 Ap '16, p. 1169; Col, 16 S '22, p. 3; LHJ, F '24, p. 214; Nat, 26 S '28, p. 286; Comm, 10 Je '31, p. 143; CC, 17 Mr '34, p. 325; Rot, N '38, p. 59.

14. CC, 29 Ja '30, p. 146; Out, 28 O '14, p. 449; BHG, Mr '37, p. 78; Nat, 12 Je '35, p. 667; Comm, 15 Ap '38, p. 686; CC, 4 My '32, p. 564; CO, '23, p. 471; CC, 12 Ap '50, p. 452; CC, 18 Je '30, p. 775; Nat, 5 Ag '31, p. 142; Time, 5 F '51, p. 51; CC, 2 F '49, p. 143; SEP, 26 Ja '52, p. 119; Nat, 15 O '55, p. 324.

15. GH, Ag '10, p. 184; Ind, 17 Mr '10, p. 591; WW, Ja '21, p. 257; Bookm, My '21, p. 244; NAR, N '21, p. 625; HM, Ja '26, p. 160.

16. CO, Ag '24, p. 202; NR, 23 Mr '27, p. 140; AmMerc, 6 Jl '38, p. 295.

17. Comm, 10 Ap '29, p. 653; RR, Mr '12, p. 335; Out, 25 D '29, p. 645; Scrib, F '35, p. 84.

18. CC, 2 F '49, p. 143; SR, 24 D '49, p. 20; HB, F '50, p. 125; USN, 2 S '55, pp. 75-76. See also, Comm, 14 N '48, p. 138; SA, S '49, p. 26; Nat, 22 Jl '50, p. 87; HB, Ag '50, p. 119; Comm, 4 Ag '50, p. 406; SR, 26 Ag '50, p. 29; Educa, O '50, p. 126.

19. RR, D '08, p. 744; Out, 3 D '10, p. 767; GH, Ag '10, p. 185; HW, 16 S '11, p. 6; RR, F '22, p. 214; Col, 17 O, '25, p. 15; Col, 16 Ja '26, p. 6; PE, O '26, p. 179; NR, 6 Jl '27, p. 178; CC, 15 Ja '30, p. 76; CC, 5 F '30, p. 173; CC, 12 F '30, p. 202; CC, 13 Ag '30, p. 978; CC, 22 O '30, p. 1271; Scrib, My '31, p. 491; CC, 17 My '33, p. 655; CC, 24 My '33, p. 690; SR, 24 Je '33, p. 661; NAR, S '33, p. 207; SSoc, 16 S '39, p. 372; NR, 12 Ja '42, p. 48; NR, 26 F '45, p. 296; CC, 8 Ja '47, p. 36; Nat, 22 Jl '50, p. 87; NR, 1 N '54, p. 14.

20. RR, D '08, p. 161; Nat, 6 My '15, p. 486; NAR, Jl '20, p. 83; Nat, 23 Jl '24, p. 91; Col, 16 Ja '26, p. 6; AAA, N '26, p. 151; RR, N '27, p. 523; Col, 25 Ag '28, p. 48; Nat, 26 S '28, p. 286; CC, 15 Ja '30, p. 77; ParM, F '30, p. 11; RR, Mr '32, p. 35; LD 13 My '33, p. 17; CC, 31 My '33, p. 720; NAR, S '33, p. 208; Nat, 10 O '34, p. 410; Atlan, My '37, p. 541; NR, 22 S '37, p. 138; SSoc, 3 D '38, p. 721; HB, F '50, p. 125; SEP, 2 F '52, p. 115; TA, D '51, p. 17; SR, 2 Ag '52, p. 30; SR, 14 Ag '54, p. 25.

21. AmMag, Ag '13, p. 93; PE, O '26, p. 179; CC, 22 Ap '31, p. 549; Nat, 3 Ap '43, p. 486; Scrib, My '31, p. 491; RR, Mr '32, p. 35; HW, 6 Je '14, p. 20; Out, 18 S '29, p. 115.

22. NR, 23 Mr '27, p. 140; Educa D '36, p. 214; SEP, 6 D '24, p. 74; SA, D '22, p. 379; NR, 3 O '34, p. 202.

23. CC, 2 F '49, p. 143; Nwk, 18 Ap '49, p. 78; Nwk, 20 N '50, p. 61; AmMag, Mr '48, p. 107; Atlan, My '37, p. 541.

24. Out, 22 Ag '14, p. 968.

25. CO, D '22, p. 707; Ind, 6 Ja '23, p. 6; Out, 25 N '25, p. 474; CC, 25 Ja '33, p. 124. See also, PE, Ap '19, p. 178; LA, 22 S '23, p. 569; Col, 26 O '35, p. 38.

26. Col, 16 S '22, p. 3; CC, 10 My '33, p. 620.

27. LHJ, F '24, p. 40.

28. Col, 8 Ap '22, p. 4.

29. Cent, O '26, p. 670; Scrib, My '31, p. 489; HM, D '34, p. 59.

30. HM, S '34, p. 465.

31. SEP, 20 My '39, p. 104.

32. SR, 21 F '42, p. 17.

33. SEP, 16 Mr '46, p. 23; ParM, Ja '49, p. 27; Etude, Je '49, p. 341; HB, F '50, p. 126; ParM, N '49, p. 58.

34. Scrib, Jl '09, p. 122.

35. LD, 3 S '10, p. 343; RR, F '25, pp. 203-204; CC, Ap '31, p. 480; AmMerc, Jl '51, p. 115; Amer, 26 Je '54, p. 329.

36. Advocates used the advantage-disadvantage comparisons fifty-four times. Of these, nineteen of the arguments can be called "apparently neutral." For comparisons of this type, in addition to those cited above, see: CCom, 11 Ap '08, p. 75; Out, 27 N '09, p. 710; Over, Mr '14, p. 273; SEP, 4 Je '21, p. 21; Out, 15 Mr '22, p. 410; SEP, 15 Ap '22, p. 6; Ind, 23 My '25, p. 548; HM, Ja '26, p. 165; Col, 25 Ag '28, p. 48; Out, 16 Jl '30, p. 436; Comm, 17 F '32, p. 421; GH, Ja '46, p. 4; Comm, 4 Ag '50, p. 406; ParM, D '52, p. 74.

37. HW, 30 Jl '10, p. 13; Out, D '10, p. 768; LD, 25 S '26, p. 28.

38. HM, Ja '19, p. 185.

39. Educa, D '36, p. 215; NAR, Ap '25, p. 433; NR, 26 O '27, p. 352; Rot, N '30, p. 60.

40. ParM, D '48, p. 67. The other advantage-disadvantage comparisons employed by advocates may be found in the following: Scrib, Jl '09, p. 121; TW, Mr '13, p. 21; LD, 4 O '13, p. 577; Nat, 6 Ag '14, p. 154; CO, Ag '18, p. 99; Educa, D '19, p. 203; Col, 23 F '29, p. 42; Scrib, Jl '29, p. 3; NAR, Jl '30, p. 128; LA, Mr '35, p. 91; NAR, Mr '36, p. 49; BHG, Mr '37, p. 78; Etude, Ag '41, p. 524; SD, Ap '45, p. 27; BHG, N '45, p. 23; NB, Jl '47, p. 37; Col, 27 S '47, p. 32; NB, Je '49, p. 42; USN, 2 S '55, p. 45; SNL, 26 N '55, p. 344.

41. CC, 29 Ja '30, p. 147.

42. Educa, D '19, pp. 204, 207-209.

43. LD, 3 Ag '12, p. 190; AmMag, Ag '13, p. 93; WW, Ja '21, p. 257; Educa, D '19, p. 208; LHJ, F '24, p. 40; HM, S '24, p. 425; HM, Ja '26, p. 159; HM, N '28, p. 708; Nat, 18 S '29, p. 291; TM, Ja '30, p. 30; CC, 15 Ja '30, p. 76; CC, 29 Ja '30, p. 147; CC, 24 My '33, p. 688; NAR, Summer '37, p. 236; SSoc, 3 D '38, p. 724.

44. Nat, 29 Mr '22, p. 362; Col, 8 Ap '22, p. 23; NR, 23 Ap '24, p. 228; LD, 3 My '24, p. 30; NR, 26 O '27, p. 251; LD, 3 N '28, p. 29; NR, 12 Ja '42, p. 48; CC, 27 My '42, p. 694.

45. SD, O '49, p. 25; SR, 25 N '50, p. 9; SEP, 2 F '52, p. 102; ParM, D '52, p. 37.

46. PE, O '08, p. 161.

47. Out, 23 F '21, p. 292.

48. Scrib, F '35, p. 81.

49. Forum, Mr '29, p. 169.

50. NR, 26 F '45, p. 296.

51. SR, 24 D '49, p. 20; TA, My '51, pp. 43, 96.

52. PE, O '08, p. 744; RR, S '10, p. 317; Out, 13 Jl '12,
p. 598; AmMag, Ag '13, p. 92; Out, 20 Je '14, p. 387; Out, 28 O
'14, p. 449; NR, 1 My '15, p. 329; WW, Ja '21, p. 254; Out, 19 Ja
'21, p. 104; Out, 23 F '21, p. 292; NAR, N '21, p. 620; Out, 16 My
'23, p. 882; Col, 10 Je '22, p. 18; Col, 30 S '22, p. 11; CO, D '22,
p. 207; LA, 22 S '23, p. 567; NR, 23 Ap '24, p. 228; CO, Jl '24,
p. 74; LD, 9 Ag '24, p. 11; Col, 23 Ag '24, p. 10; NR, 8 O '24,
p. 135; Nat, 25 Mr '25, p. 325; RR, N '25, p. 523; HM, Ja '26, p. 165;
Col, 16 Ja '26, p. 6; NR, 26 O '27, p. 251; Nat, 10 O '28, p. 360;
LD, 3 N '28, p. 29; Forum, Mr '29, p. 169; Nat, 5 Je '29, p. 670;
CC, 15 Ja '30, p. 75; Nat, 22 Ja '30, p. 107; CC, 29 Ja '30, p. 146;
ParM, F '30, p. 11; Out, 28 My '30, p. 137; Out, 16 Jl '30, p. 435;
CC, 28 Ja '31, p. 128; ParM, N '31, p. 52; HM, N '31, p. 714;
SA, My '32, p. 284; Scrib, My '33, p. 315; SR, 24 Je '33, p. 661;
NR, 3 Ja '34, p. 209; CC, 17 Mr '34, p. 327; Scrib, Jl '34, p. 43;
Scrib, F '35, p. 81; NR, 10 Jl '35, p. 251; AmMerc, Ag '35, p. 481;
Scrib, Mr '37, p. 72; AmMerc, 6 Jl '38, p. 296; Rot, N '38, p. 12;
CC, 16 F '44, p. 197; NR, 3 Jl '44, p. 11; CC, 23 Ag '44, p. 974;
NR, 26 F '45, p. 296; SG, Ag '45, p. 345; TA, Ja '46, p. 56; Comm,
14 Je '46, p. 204; NR, 3 F '47, p. 10; Atlan, Ap '47, p. 68; CC,
10 S '47, p. 1079; SEP, 10 Ja '48, p. 20; NR, 31 Ja '49, p. 11;
Atlan, Mr '49, p. 35; NR, 31 O '49, p. 21; SR, 24 D '49, p. 20;
NR, 26 F '51, p. 18; TA, My '51, p. 43; Educa, Je '51, p. 601;
SR, 23 Je '51, p. 31; Comm, 6 Jl '51, p. 300; TA, S '51, p. 52;
TA, D '51, p. 17; SR, 6 D '52, p. 59; Comm, 19 D '52, p. 271;
Comm, 23 O '53, p. 65; NR, 1 N '54, p. 14; Time, 14 Mr '55, p. 56.

53. RR, O '08, p. 744; CO, D '22, p. 708; SA, Je '29, p. 526.
See also, PE, O '08, p. 162; WT, O '08, p. 1054; GH, Ag '10, p. 185;
RR, S '10, p. 317; Out, 13 Jl '12, p. 598; Educa, Je '13, p. 625;
AmMag, Ag '13, p. 92; Out, 14 F '14, p. 346; Nat, 6 Ag '14, p. 154;
RR, D '14, p. 725; WW, Ja '21, p. 254; Out, 16 My '23, p. 882;
Col, 21 F '25, p. 20; HM, Ja '26, p. 160; ParM, F '30, p. 11;
CC, 5 F '30, p. 173; CC, 12 F '30, p. 202; CC, 28 Ja '31, p. 128;
Nat, 5 Ag '31, p. 142; ParM, N '31, p. 52; CC, 13 Ap '32, p. 481;
CC, 25 Ja '33, p. 124; CC, 3 My '33, p. 592; SR, 24 Je '33, p. 661;
AmMerc, Ja '47, p. 36; CC, 8 Ja '47, p. 36; SG, Mr '47, p. 188.

54. NR, 13 Ag '30, p. 357; NR, 24 S '30, p. 154; Scrib, My '31,
p. 492; CC, 8 Ap '31, p. 478; Comm, 29 Je '32, p. 230; SR, 14 Je
'47, p. 27. See also, RR, N '25, p. 592; NR, 26 O '27, p. 251;
RR, N '27, p. 523; AmMag, Ja '29, p. 100; RR, N '30, p. 91; CC,
15 Ap '31, p. 512; CC, 22 Ap '31, p. 545; HM, S '32, p. 468; Comm,
25 My '34, p. 101; NR, 17 Mr '37, p. 189; Rot, N '38, p. 59; SEP,
10 Ja '48, p. 20.

55. SR, 26 Ag '50, p. 29; SR, 24 D '49, p. 20; NR, 11 D '50, p. 31; NR, 26 F '51, pp. 18-24; Educa, Je '51, p. 600; Nat, 13 O '51, p. 298; NR, 17 Ag '53, p. 11; SEP, 12 Mr '55, p. 32.

56. CO, D '22, p. 708; Col, 21 F '25, p. 20; AmMerc, Ja '47, p. 36.

57. Comm, 25 My '34, p. 101.

58. NR, D '50, p. 31; Time, 5 F '51, p. 51; NR, 26 F '51, p. 18.

59. Out, 11 Ap '28, p. 576; Col, 2 D, p. 11.

60. CO, Jl '24, p. 74; Comm, 8 Ja '30, p. 270; CC, 5 F '30, p. 175. See also, CC, 22 Ja '30, p. 112; Out, 16 Ap '30, p. 612; CC, 22 O '30, p. 1270; CC, 13 Ap '32, p. 482; CC, 7 Je '33, p. 752.

61. NR, 14 Ag '15, p. 51; CO, D '15, p. 405; RR, F '25, p. 126; Comm, 22 Ja '30, p. 335; NAR, Mr '29, p. 305; Comm, 13 My '55, p. 141; SR, 6 D '52, p. 17.

62. Out, 22 Ag '14, p. 968; NR, 1 My, p. 329; Nat, 6 Ag '14, p. 154; HW, 16 S '11, p. 6; Educa, D '19, p. 204; SR, 4 Jl '42, p. 6; CC, 23 Ag '44, p. 974.

63. CCom, 11 Ap '08, p. 74.

64. CO, Mr '17, p. 185.

65. NAR, S '20, p. 391.

66. Col, 2 D '22, p. 10.

67. RR, Ja '23, p. 79.

68. RR, Ap '27, p. 398.

69. CC, 4 N '34, p. 1447.

70. CC, 31 Jl '35, p. 982.

71. SR, 17 Je 50, p. 38. See also, PE, Mr '09, p. 119;
AmMag, S '09, p. 499; PE, F '10, p. 79; WW, My '10, p. 12876;
HW, 30, Jl '10, p. 12; Out, 24 Jl '11, p. 382; Ind, 11 Ja '12,
p. 108; CO, Je '14, p. 438; Out, 27 Je '14, p. 445; Out, 22 Ag
'14, p. 970; AmMag, O '14, p. 44; HW, 2 Ja '15, p. 8; Col, 26 Je
'15, p. 22; Ind, 28 F '16, p. 311; Ind, 11 D '16, p. 448; CO,
Mr '17, p. 185; Ind, 23.F '18, p. 328; CO, Je '18, p. 403; Col,
28 F '20, p. 36; HM, Ja '19, p. 194; NAR, Jl '20, p. 88; SEP,
7 Ag '20, p. 34; NAR, S '20, p. 387; Out, 26 Ja '21, p. 136; SEP,
4 Je '21, p. 94; SEP, 18 Mr '22, p. 150; CO, Ap '22, p. 507; Col
21 O '22, p. 12; Col, 2 D '22, p. 10; CO, Je '23, p. 733; Out,
19 S '23, p. 105; Ind, 15 S '23, p. 114; Out, 23 Jl '24, p. 426;
Scrib, S '24, p. 231; Out, 10 D '24, p. 596; Col 7 F '25, p. 10;
SEP, 7 N '25, p. 154; PE, O '26, p. 179; SA, My '27, p. 343; RR,
Ap '27, p. 397; Col, 25 My '29, p. 8; SA, Je '29, p. 527; SEP,
15 Je '29, p. 50; HM, S '29, p. 460; RR, Mr '32, p. 63; RR, Mr
'32, p. 31; NAR, My '32, p. 448; NO, S '33, p. 24; CC, 4 N '34,
p. 144; CC, 31 Jl '35, p. 982; BHG, Mr '37, p. 96; SSoc, 3 D '38,
p. 723; AmMag, My '39, p. 82; Nat, 20 Ap '40, p. 511; CC, 24 S
'41, p. 1173; NR, 7 S '42, p. 284; NR, 3 Ja '44, p. 16; Nat, 3 F
'45, p. 123; BHG, N '45, p. 74; SR, 17 Je '50, p. 34; Comm, 19 D
'52, p. 279; USN, 5 Mr '54, p. 41.

72. SEP, 14 Ag '26, p. 103; RR, N '27, p. 521; Scrib, My
'31, p. 490.

73. TA, My '52, p. 36. See also, Ind, 12 Jl '19, p. 64;
CO, My '21, p. 449; SA, 4 Je '21, p. 449; IW, F '22, p. 948; CO,
Mr '22, p. 404; Out, 15 Mr '22, p. 410; IW, Ap '22, p. 308; RR,
Ap '22, p. 400; Col, 8 Ap '22, p. 3; SEP, 15 Ap '22, p. 141; SA,
D '22, p. 379; Scrib, Ap '23, p. 415; Ind, 15 S '23, p. 114; CO,
My '24, p. 731; SEP, 17 My '24, p. 10; Nat, 9 Jl '24, p. 34; Col,
23 Ag '24, p. 10; Out, 14 Ja '25, p. 48; SEP, 18 Ap '25, p. 185;
SA, D '25, p. 421; SEP, 14 Ag '26, p. 103; RR, N '27, p. 521;
Col, 24 S '27, p. 9; Scrib, My '28, p. 626; NR, 23 My '28, p. 6;
SEP, 30 Je '28, p. 11; RR, N '28 p. 495; RR, D '28, p. 577; Out,
24 Ap '29, p. 675; Nat, 5 Je '29, p. 671; RR, S '30, p. 67; Comm,
29 Je '32, p. 230; HM, S '32, p. 468; LD, 7 Ja '33, p. 16; Scrib,
O '34, p. 244; NAR, Mr '36, p. 51; SSoc, 22 Ag '36, p. 233; Educa,
D '36, p. 216; BHG, Mr '37, p. 97; NAR, Summer '38, p. 302; Rot,
N '38, p. 61; Atlan, Ap '41, p. 460; Nat, 3 Ap '43, p. 30; SR,
19 F '44, p. 29; LJ, 15 F '45, p. 175; BHG, N '45, p. 73; Comm, 14
Je '46, p. 205; Nat, 2 N '46, p. 502.

74. Out, 29 D '26, p. 549; Ind, 25 F '28, p. 172; Out, 1 Ag
'28, p. 526; SEP, 28 S '40, p. 24; Atlan, D '45, p. 132.

75. AmMerc, Jl '44, p. 61; Etude, Je '49, p. 341; USN, 2 S '55, p. 36. See also, SA, Mr '28, p. 246; SA, O '28, p. 358; SA, Je '29, p. 527; SA, D '29, p. 487; LA, Mr '31, p. 95; AmMerc, My '39, p. 15; SEP, 28 S '40, p. 25; Atlan, Ap '41, p. 460; AmMerc, Jl '44, p. 61; Nat, 29 Jl '44, p. 67; SD, Jl '45, p. 34; Atlan, D '45, p. 132; SEP, 9 Mr '46, p. 134; SEP, 16 Mr '46, p. 94; NR, 7 Je '48, p. 16; Nwk, 1 N '48, p. 52; ParM, D '48, p. 67; Nwk, 20 D '48, p. 53; ParM, Ja '49, p. 73; Etude, Je '49, p. 341; USN, 23 Je '50, p. 14; Comm, 4 Ag '50, p. 406; WHC, N '50, p. 71; TA, Ag '51, p. 11; LJ, 15 F '52, p. 305; USN, 2 S '55, p. 42; Nat, 15 O '55, p. 323; SNL, 26 N '55, p. 344.

76. Comm, 10 Ap '29, p. 653; Nat, 9 Ag '33, p. 146.

77. CC, 15 Ja '30, p. 75; CC, 13 Ap '32, p. 481; ParM, N '31, p. 53.

78. Out, 22 Ap '31, p. 561.

79. NR, 10 Jl '35, p. 251; AmMerc, Jl '51, p. 111; SR, 25 Ag '51, p. 8.

80. NR, 26 F '45, p. 296.

81. Atlan, Mr '49, p. 35; NR, 26 F '51, p. 20; SR, 25 Ag '51, p. 8.

82. CC, 26 D '51, p. 1499; TA, My '51, p. 43; SEP, 7 Jl '51, p. 12; NR, 9 My '55, p. 15; Amer, 21 Mr '53, p. 689; Nat, 15 O '55, p. 323; SR, 31 Jl '54, p. 36; USN, 2 S '55, p. 39.

83. Ind, 6 Ap '14, p. 8; Scrib, Ap '29, p. 373; Col, 25 My '29, p. 9; Etude, S '31, p. 615; PMech, S '39, p. 324; Col, 27 S '47, p. 32. See also, Lip, Ag '13, p. 191; AmMag, S '13, p. 59; CO, Je '18, p. 403; NAR, Mr '29, p. 305; SEP, 21 S '29, p. 136; AmMag, Mr '48, p. 45; HB, F '50, p. 126.

84. CO, D '15, p. 405.

85. AmMag, S '13, p. 59.

86. Out, 14 Ja '25, p. 48.

87. SEP, 20 Jl '29, p. 82; Nat, 27 Ag '30, p. 216. See also, AmMag, S '13, p. 59; CO, D '15, p. 405; LD, 4 F '22, p. 32; Out, 14 Ja '25, p. 48; PMech, N '28, p. 882; HM, D '28, p. 112; SEP, 20 Jl '29, p. 82; Scrib, Mr '37, p. 16; Nat, 27 Ag '30, p. 216; LA, N '30, p. 298.

88. SEP, 2 F '52, p. 102.

89. NAR, Mr '29, p. 304.

90. SR, 26 F '49, p. 4.

91. Cent, Je '24, p. 149; PMech, N '28, p. 822; LD, 4 F '22, p. 32; BW, 27 D '52, p. 27; USN, 5 Mr '54, p. 39.

92. Nat, 20 F '29, p. 236. See also, Out, 3 Mr '15, p. 499.

93. NR, 8 O '24, p. 136.

94. HM, Ap '34, p. 577. See also, CC, 15 Ap '31, p. 514; HM, '31, p. 722; CC, 4 My '32, p. 564; Nat, 2 Ja '24, p. 5.

95. NR, 31 O '49, p. 20; Nat, 30 N '46, p. 618; SR, 26 Ag '50, p. 29; NR, 30 Ja '50, p. 29; Time, 5 F '51, p. 51; CC, 2 F '49, p. 142; HB, F '50, p. 125; LD, 1 S '28, p. 19.

96. SR, 24 D '49, p. 20.

97. NR, 2 D '31, p. 71; Atlan, Mr '49, p. 36. See also, LD, 1 S '28, p. 19; SEP, 20 My '39, p. 20; NR, 2 D '31, p. 71; Nat, 30 N '46, p. 618; ParM, Ja '49, p. 27; CC, 2 F '49, p. 142; Atlan, Mr '49, p. 36; NR, 31 O '49, p. 20; SR, 24 D '49, p. 20; NR, 30 Ja '50, p. 29; HB, F '50, p. 125; SR, 26 Ag '50, p. 29; Time, 5 F '51, p. 51; SR, 25 N '50, p. 10; SR, 25 Ag '51, p. 8; Nwk, 8 Je '53, p. 67.

98. HM, N '28, pp. 710-711.

99. Out, 14 Ja '25, p. 48.

100. NR, 1 Ap '31, p. 174; Scrib, Jl '29, p. 7.

101. SEP, 20 My '39, p. 20; RR, Ag '36, p. 4.

102. TA, F '37, p. 108.

103. SEP, 2 F '52, p. 30; Comm, 28 S '34, p. 500; HM, S '34, p. 472.

104. NAR, Mr '29, p. 307; Out, 14 F '14, p. 349.

105. Col, 28 F '20, p. 35.

106. Scrib, S '24, p. 231; NAR, Mr '29, p. 305; Col, 23 F '29, p. 26. See also, Out, 17 Ja '14, p. 121; CO, D '15, p. 405; SEP, 8 Ap '22, p. 157; Ind, 1 S '28, p. 210; Out, 18 S '29, p. 115; NAR, Summer '37, p. 231.

107. Nat, 29 Mr '22, p. 362.

108. SEP, 6 D '24, p. 74.

109. LJ, 15 F '45, p. 175.

110. SR, 21 F '42, p. 4; SR, 25 Ag '51, p. 31.

111. SEP, 20 My '39, p. 105; GH, Ja '49, p. 4.

112. SEP, 6 D '24, p. 74; Mus, Je '29, p. 18; Rot, N '38, p. 13.

113. Col, 23 Jl '27, p. 43.

114. Comm, 24 Mr '50, p. 622, LD, 1 S '28, p. 19; SA, Je '29, p. 527; Atlan, My '37, p. 541; SEP, 20 My '29, p. 104; NR, 26 Je '44, p. 842; Col 27 S '47, p. 30; GH, Ja '49, p. 143; HB, F '50, p. 125; NR, 26 F '51, p. 18; Nat, 13 O '51, p. 300; Nat, 5 N '55, p. 379.

115. SA, 30 Mr '01, p. 196; Out 26 Ja '21, p. 136; Out, 4 Ja '22, p. 29.

116. CO, D '22, p. 708.

117. NR, 1 My '15, p. 329.

118. RR, Ja '23, p. 66. See also, Col, 2 D '22, p. 10; RR, Ap '27, pp. 395, 398.

119. Col, 7 O '22, p. 13; Nat, 12 Je '35, p. 696; SR, 2 O '54, p. 43.

120. Out, 23 F '21, p. 292.

121. CC, 13 Ap '32, p. 482.

122. CC, 7 Je '33, p. 752.

123. Out, 9 Ap '24, p. 604; Col, 14 Je '24, p. 20; SSoc, 22 Ag '36, p. 231.

124. SEP, 27 Jl '29, p. 133; SR, 21 F '42, p. 17; NR, 26 F '51, p. 20; Nat, 15 O '55, p. 323.

125. Atlan, D '45, p. 130; CC, 2 F '49, p. 143; Ind, 13 F '13, p. 353; Out, 20 Je '14, p. 387; RR, S '10, p. 320; GH, Ag '10, p. 185; Out, 16 Jl '10, p. 542; WW, Ja '21, p. 260; Out, 16 My '23, p. 883; Scrib, My '31, p. 646; SEP, 15 Ap '22, p. 6; CO, My '21, p. 652; CO, Mr '21, p. 362; Out, 24 Je '11, p. 382; RR, Ap '27, p. 393.

CHAPTER VII

ARGUMENT FROM ASSOCIATION

Advocacy and Attack

It is appropriate to begin this chapter with a series of
maxims, for they illustrate the kind of argument with which it
deals. Just as like attracts like, birds of a feather flock together, and a man is known by the company he keeps, so were the
new mass media judged on the basis of their adoption by social
institutions, their acceptance by the public, and the things said
about them by persons of known reputation. These arguments differ
from those we have seen before, because in the earlier ones, both
causal and comparative, the media were assessed on the grounds
of their influences on society. In the arguments from association,
the media are evaluated on the basis of society's acceptance of
them and its opinions about them. Hence, when advocates reported
that movies were used by churches, they expected judgments about
the institution to be transferred to the medium. When supporters
told how the public was enthusiastic about the movies, they made
the public's acclaim serve as evidence in favor of the medium. When
well known people were quoted in behalf of pictures, their reputations as well as their statements stood in support of the medium.
In the analysis which follows, I will discuss the arguments as they

grow out of the three kinds of association suggested here: institutional association, public acceptance, and testimony.

Institutional Association

Advocates of motion pictures, radio, and television pointed
often to the uses which various institutions were making of the new
mass media. Movies, they said, were used in churches, in the
schools, or in the government. Radio was a valuable tool for the
politician, for the law officer, or for the preacher. Television
was adopted by colleges and universities, was useful in hospitals,
and was an asset to the home. Their point was clear: if the movies,
radio, and television were good enough for the institutions which
society had founded to realize its values, the media themselves
were obviously good and valuable. In being adopted as auxiliaries by
the agencies to which society had given its sanction, the new media
were in turn worthy of approval.

Soon after each new medium was introduced, its spokesmen sought
ways to demonstrate that it had gained acceptance by respected
agencies and institutions. For example, in 1906 World's Work,
telling how stop motion photography in motion pictures could be
used to show the life cycle of a plant in a few minutes, said that
under the sponsorship of the "Scientists in the Department of
Agriculture . . . an 'education train' shall be sent out to tour

the country, to tell by 'moving pictures' and lectures, what the

government is doing for the farmers."[1] Charities and The Commons

reported the following year that

> it is interesting to know that Hull House is opening
> a five cent theater. It is to be strictly up to date
> and the experiment will run for three months. A Catholic
> church in Chicago is introducing moving pictures and
> entertainment for its people.[2]

In 1909, Harper's Weekly concluded that there was no doubt but that

movies had a great future "as an institution of amusement and

education," and that

> the government is already using the moving picture for
> certain purposes. For instance, a set of pictures was
> recently taken at the Newport Naval Station showing
> interesting and pleasurable phases of the apprentice's
> life. These will be reproduced, together with a descrip-
> tive lecture, at the various enlistment bureaus.[3]

By 1913, Carl Holliday reported in World's Work that "the state

of Texas recently bought a large number of projecting machines to

be used throughout its school system; such cities as New York,

Chicago, Cleveland, and Detroit make frequent use of motion pic-

tures to instruct their children." Moreover, he said, the "faculty

of the University of Rochester recently introduced a four-year

course in the art and science of cinematography." Added to the

list the year following were Harvard, Cornell, Pennsylvania, Wis-

consin, and Minnesota. Further evidence of the legitmacy of the new

medium was supplied by a later Holliday article for Independent in

which he contended not only that motion pictures were "a movement

that cannot be ignored by the progressive church," but that already
pictures had been brought into some of "the most conservative
churches in America," and then "not only into the Sunday School
but into the Church Auditorium." The argument was climaxed with
the announcement that "even the Pope has consented to appear in
moving pictures, and his image may now be seen by thousands of
devout Catholics who never dared to hope for such a privilege."
Motion pictures were said also to have come to the aid of science
with their slow motion, micro-photography, X-ray, and electric-
spark photos. Films had preserved a moving record of the eclipse of
the sun so that scientists, rather than attempting to make all of
their observations at the moment, could go back and study the
permanent record of the event at their leisure. When he sought
defense for the motion pictures against charges of immorality,
Will Hays not only promised better days ahead, but called attention
to the composition of his "Public Relations Committee" of the
M. P. P. D. A. Working there were representatives of the American
Federation of Labor, the Y. M. C. A., the Y. W. C. A., Camp Fire
Girls, the Girls Scouts, the National Catholic Welfare Council,
the Boy Scouts, and the Russell Sage Foundation. The movie industry
and the agencies represented were working together for a common
end.[4] Motion pictures, said their supporters, were of service to

the most respected of social institutions and were associated with
society's most important agencies for good.

The pattern was similar in the promotion of radio. In addition
to telling how it had brought new entertainment, information, and
culture into the home, and how it had been used in broadcasting
church services, classes in schools and college, weather information,
market reports, and political speeches, radio's advocates spoke of
some of its more esoteric applications. For instance, radio had
been adopted as a weapon against crime by the police departments
of Detroit, Chicago, Cleveland, "and nearly a dozen other cities."
Detroit alone had 35 radio cars by 1929, and their crews had made
1,300 arrests in an eighteen month period, some of them within
thirty to sixty seconds after the "orders were flung through the
air." Eight years earlier, however, the United States Bureau of
Fisheries was sending out to the fishing fleets radio reports of
fish sighted from an airplane over the ocean. Large stores, with
branches in both New York and Philadelphia, had used radio to link
the two locations. Newspapers by 1922 had begun to use radio to
broadcast their headline bulletins. Great industries, the business
leaders of the country, "the companies that . . . have attained
and hold that position because they make a systematic business
of looking ahead," were constantly engaged in experimentation to
improve radio broadcasting equipment. The New Deal was said by

1939 to be using the radio so extensively--3000 local station broadcasts a week by the Department of the Interior, the Department of Agriculture on 322 stations six days a week, 500 county agents on the air weekly, 450 weekly WPA programs by transcription, and some 746 other live broadcasts by government officials during the year--that this governmental use of the medium was threatening to crowd out other programs. The only salvation of broadcasting, said Scribner's, was that the medium had always been in the hands of "far sighted people."[5]

Although television had been predicted for a quarter of a century before it was used to open the World's Fair in 1939, the arguments from association were sparse until after the Second World War when the medium finally got fully under way. This is not to say there were none before that, however. Saturday Evening Post reported in 1940 that the opening day of the Dodger's season had been televised "as a contribution to science," that the movie people were televising scenes from the rehearsals for current films, and that Monsignor Fulton J. Sheen had preached a sermon in praise of television. Then, by 1944, American Mercury reported that some newspapers, seeking to get in on the ground floor, had applied for television channels.[6]

The argument from institutional association, however, is predicated upon experience, and so was not begun in earnest until after

the war. Churches were in the forefront of institutions to be reported using the medium. They turned to it first, not to propagate
their message but to draw people into the church houses and social
rooms, thus away from the bars where the first sets were installed.7
For the same reason, to attract TV fans, night clubs bought sets
and "big hotels like New York's Pennsylvania and New Yorker have
installed special 'television suites' calculated to attract trave-
lers from hinterlands still beyond television's range." As early
as 1947 Collier's reported that

> fifty-five Philadelphia firehouses are installing sets
> for neighborhood children, and, incidentally, for the
> firemen themselves between alarms. Receivers are boons
> to veterans and other shut-ins in hospitals who other-
> wise might never see an outside spectacle. Even several
> convents are now wired for sight as well as sound.8

By 1949, schools in Philadelphia, Chicago, and Baltimore had already
begun experiments with "video learning," and Minneapolis, St. Louis,
and New York City were added within a year. At the same time the
Veteran's Administration was using television, said promoters of
the medium, to demonstrate, by showing them at work on the job,
that partially disabled veterans were good workers. Politicians
turned to the new medium in 1948, and by 1954 Walter Goodman reported
television was being used by nearly every candidate. By 1955 the
use of television was reported to be widespread in schools, and
U. S. News said that "religious groups, which feared TV would keep
people away from church, are trying to make it an aid, just as

educators are doing." Not only did advertisers recognize the value
of television, as evidenced by their use of it, but industry had
turned to television as a medium for in-service training of employ-
ees.[9] Agencies which were respected for their contributions to the
social order, or for their ability to recognize a good thing when
it comes along, adopted television as an instrument to further
their ends. The selection of the medium, said its supporters,
demonstrated its value.

In a sense this kind of argument from association is a form
of testimony about the value of new things. Respected institutions
and successful businesses, in demonstrating their acceptance of
movies, radio, or TV by employing them, can be assumed to be giving
approval to the media. The institutions are showing by their
example that innovation can be counted on to help achieve society's
goals. This, at least, was the point of view taken by advocates
when they used the argument. Most often promoters argued from the
use of the new media by religion and education, the two institutions
which apparently they considered most prestigious. Next most
frequently they talked of the uses of the media by politicians and
by agencies of the government. These were followed by references
to business, the family, law enforcement, newspapers, science, and
the miscellaneous applications.[10]

I have been describing here the explicit arguments from association in which advocates clearly stated the institutional-media relationship. A similar connection is implied in many of the arguments we have looked at before. Consider, for example, the causal arguments. There advocates argued that the new media would have a variety of beneficial effects on social institutions; at the same time an association between the media and the institutions is presumed. The influence could not work without it. The relationship is not stated, but certainly the new media gain stature from their association. If nothing else, they can be judged important because they have the capacity to influence prestige institutions. But more important, favorable impressions of the institutions are transferred to the media because of the relationship between them.

So far the emphasis has been on beneficial, prestige institutions. The argument from association is not limited to them, however. Advocates, as they did on occasion, could also demonstrate the importance of the new media by reference to their use by institutions, or men, which were disapproved or feared. For example, when Mussolini forbade English language talkies in Italy, Commonweal took this as a demonstration of the importance of the medium. If Mussolini disliked it, it must be good. This use of the argument was unusual, however. More commonly, writers turned to it to demonstrate the importance of radio, pointing to the highly effective use of the medium in dictatorships. Support for this argument was supplied in July of 1934, when Austrian Nazis seized the state radio station in their attempted overthrow of the government. As supporters of radio assessed the situation, this was clear evidence of the importance of the medium. As a writer for Harper's said, "In any contemporary revolution the broadcasting station may be the key position, as the Nazi putsch in Vienna recently proved." Other writers told of the uses made of radio by Hitler, Mussolini, and Stalin, the representatives of world dictatorships. Sir Thomas Inskip, according to Review of Reviews, went so far as to claim that "dictators have only become possible through the invention of the microphone."[11] With the United States approaching the Second World War, the argument was applied also to movies. Arguing for greater use of films for propaganda, Margaret Frakes wrote in Christian Century that no nation could afford to be without propaganda films.

> More dramatic than newspaper or radio, and more effective
> because of the public's tendency to trust implicitly when
> it 'sees with its own eyes,' the screen was one of the
> first agencies to be controlled and utilized by the dic-
> tator regimes in their rise to power. . . . The lesson
> can hardly be lost on American producers.[12]

If the media had been effective for our enemies, they could be equally effective for us. Their use by undesirable institutions of acknowledged success and power demonstrated their importance.

By associations of this negative sort, advocates commented on the
place of the media in society.

The argument from institutional association should be available
as much to attackers as to advocates. It did not work this way
in practice, however. Attackers, either because they chose to
work along other lines or because they had difficulty finding strong
negative institutional images with which to connect the media, seldom
used the line of argument. They pointed a few times to the actions
of theatrical producers, concert managers, and motion picture
people in forbidding their stars to work in the competing media,
suggesting that if they disapprove we should also. Once, Nation
told how the Associated Press forbade members to supply material to
broadcasters. New Outlook, taking a dim view of "big business,"
argued in 1933 that radio was dangerous because it was part of the
"Power Trust." And in 1943, Nation objected to the "economic
monopoly" which it said was in control of the motion picture industry.[13] More commonly, however, critics of the media ignored the
argument from institutional association as a possible line of
attack.

One form of this kind of associative argument was used by
both attackers and defenders. In substance it is the same as the
others, but its method is different. The method could be called
argument by accumulation, because in it writers listed institutions,

either valuable or harmful, and in the list included the name of one of the new media. The goods or evils were accumulated, and the unknown was slipped in among them. Naming the new in series with things already judged good or evil, writers assumed that the common assessment of the familiar would appear to apply also to the new.

A good example of this species of associative argument is provided by an anonymous film producer who wrote a series of articles for Collier's in the early 1920's. It was his contention that the movie was an important but dangerous factor in the national life. To support this evaluation, he argued that where formerly he spoke of the power of the press, the power of the school, the power of the church, and the power of the government as conditioning influences in society, it was now necessary to "add the power of the movies" to the list. By association, movies took on the qualities of the institutions named previously. Using the same kind of argument, William DeMille spoke in favor of the motion picture, commenting that it had "grown to a degree which makes it as much a part of modern life as is the daily press, of more national importance than the legitimate stage, it even compares with the church in the number of its devotees; and more than the church it stimulates public interest in its personnel and the details of its management." Other supporters made lists which included the home, the school, the press, and the movies. Later lists brought together

the church, the school, motion pictures, and radio, as the "major
forms through which we express what is common in our hopes, interests,
and activities." When attackers employed this argument from accumulation they suggested, as a writer to Christian Century did, that
"if the state is to continue to punish racketeering, bootlegging,
theft and murder, then let it ban pictures that promote these."
Outlook said, on the other hand, that as long as the public spent
more time in bridge and golf than "in chasing out of town the rum
runner, bootleggers, crooked politicians, and crime pictures, our
present discussion must remain academic."[14]

In each of the arguments there is a strong element of comparison, for readers are asked to measure the unknown against the
record of the known. The method, however, is one of association,
for the new is caused to seem like the old by being named in close
connection with them. Like the other arguments from association,
this one leads to a judgment about the new media.

Despite its occasional use by attackers, the argument from
institutional association was more popular for praise than for
denigration. It was apparently easier to find good institutions
from which to make the associations than it was to find bad ones.
Advocates found a variety of examples from which to build their
cases. The media, they said, were widely used by desirable institutions; this use was taken as evidence that the media worked for

the same ends as the institutions by which they were employed. Moreover, the adoption of the media by favored institutions was taken
as evidence that the media were acceptable and desirable in themselves. If the church used television, TV could not be all bad;
if schools used movies, films must have some value to them; if
politicians found it useful, radio must be effective. The new
media were judged by their associations; they were known by their
friends.

Public Acceptance

The arguments to be examined now relate to the public's reaction to the new mass media. In these arguments, advocates and
attackers talk of the growth of the media, favorable and unfavorable
public reactions to them, and their popularity or unpopularity.
The argument served to point out for readers the reactions of their
peers to movies, radio, and television, and to evaluate the media
in terms of public acceptance.

The advocates argued first that the new media were popular;
that is, the public approved of them and responded enthusiastically
to them. As C. H. Claudy said,"in recent years none has made such
headway or so completely taken hold of public favor as the moving
picture." Attendance figures bore out this observation, Literary
Digest reporting, for example, that movies drew a daily attendance

of four million during 1908, or more than one billion admissions

for the year. In 1912, W. D. Howells called movies the most uni-

versally accepted of modern amusements.[15] Just before the First

World War, Homer Croy observed in Harper's that

> no other force in history has risen so quickly nor come
> into such intimate touch with so many people as the
> motion pictures. It took printing two hundred years
> to come into the daily lives of the people; motion pic-
> tures have taken twenty.[16]

The theme of the popularity of pictures was reasserted by Otis

Skinner in 1920, as he called movies "the most popular recreation

in the world today." Will Hays carried on the notion, reminding

readers in 1923 that "in a little over twenty years, the motion

picture has grown from a mere idea until to-day it is the princi-

pal amusement of the great majority of our people, and the sole

amusement of millions and millions." The year that talkies were

introduced, C. B. Neblette argued in Photo-Era that the growth of

the movie industry was an "eloquent indication" of its acceptance

by the grateful American public. In that year, he said, there were

"nearly 20,000 motion picture houses in these United States with

an average weekly attendance of approximately 50,000,000 or nearly

one-half of the total population."[17]

Sound pictures were justified on the grounds of public demand

for them. As William de Mille said, "Its popular success as enter-

tainment has been instantaneous." And as Jesse Lasky observed in

1929, the public wanted sound pictures, and no picture succeeds and no producer survives "who does not correctly measure the public's appetite." By 1929 there were 3000 first run houses wired for sound, 5000 predicted for 1930, and "the patronage of the cinema theaters has increased twenty-five per cent." By 1937, Fred Eastman, satisfied now that the motion picture industry could serve the best interests of the public, argued that the movies were both a popular and an important national amusement. There were, he said, 16,000 theaters in the country, with an average weekly attendance of 88,000,000. The movies were the amusement of the nation.[18]

Promoters of radio turned, as had the spokesmen for pictures, to arguments from popularity. "None of the other miracles of applied science has begun to appeal to the public imagination as has the development of radio," said one of them. Even in 1921, the Dempsey-Carpentier fight was heard by some 300,000 "ear witnesses." In six months time 500,000 receivers were sold, and the manufacturers could not keep up with the demand. Bruce Barton said in 1922 that "radio enthusiasm is spreading through the nation like whooping cough through a kindergarten; it has taken the place of prohibition as the foremost topic of dinner-party conversation." Radio grew in little more than a year, said its promoters, from a plaything for amateur electricians to a national necessity. By 1923, it had "an audience even now compelling attention for its

overwhelming size, and growing fast into 'a great multitude which
no man could number.'"[19]

    Television, said its promoters, was the most popular new
medium ever to be introduced. In its adolescent years after the
Second World War, when public demand for sets far exceeded the
supply, television salesmen found themselves "loaded with doctor's
certificates from rheumatics, arthritics, women with child and
a sprinkling of hastily self-convinced hypochondriacs," all of whom
declared a need for television sets. In Chicago, the number of television sets rose from 125 to 100,000 in a twenty-eight month period. Christian Century reported that in New York, when the popular
children's shows first came on the air, "the streets are empty of
children." Television, said Harland Manchester, had grown from an
insignificant amusement "which would do little more than destroy
the peace of barrooms and supplement radio in the homes of the
well-heeled" into a national medium serving a million homes by
1949.[20] By 1955 there were only sixteen million families who
did not have sets. Said U. S. News:

> On an average evening, twice as many set owners will
> be watching TV as are engaged any other form of enter-
> tainment or leisure activity, such as movie-going, card
> playing, or reading. Seven out of 10 American children
> watch TV between 6 and 8 o'clock most evenings.[21]

Television had caught the fancy of the public like no other amusement before it.

In founding their advocacy on popularity, promoters assumed
that what was popular was good. Public acceptance was an overt
demonstration of the value of the new inventions. The argument
suggests that if the American people had taken the new media into
their homes, had spent as much time with them as with any other
form of amusement, then the new media could not be harmful. The
public, advocates imply, would not be deluded, would not stand
for something which was dangerous to them. But there were other
demonstrations of the worth of movies, radio, and television in
this argument from popularity. The growth of the media was one
of them, for it could be assumed that expansion was one of the
measures of worth. The large size of the media was another, for
experience suggested that size was a concomitant of goodness. Hence,
advocates in their arguments point to popularity as the hallmark
of quality, growth as evidence of goodness, and size as a measure
of worth. The new media, in advocates' terms, were sanctioned by
public demand.

Opponents, as would be expected, also argued from the public
response to movies, radio, and television. They made no effort
to deny the popularity of the new media or to challenge the fact
that movies, radio, and television had grown phenomenally in their
relatively short lifetimes. Instead, their arguments offered an
implicit challenge to popularity as a criterion for judgment.

Critics developed two lines of attack from this presumption. First, they argued that while the media were popular, the audience to which they appealed was undesirable. Second, they contended that the better elements of society, the people from whom the media should seek judgment, were dissatisfied with mass entertainment.

Critics' attitudes about the audience have already been explored to some extent. In other contexts we have seen the media judged harshly because they did appeal to what was labeled "the mass audience." This argument, cast in the framework of association, reflects the same attitudes as those evident before. For example, recall that very early in their history pictures were attacked because their audiences were made up of "shirking housewives and truant children," and because "three-fourths of the spectators are always men," even in the middle of the day. Children who went to movies were exposed to the "undesirables of many kinds . . . /who/ haunted them," and girls who attended the white slave pictures often encountered the class of men who could "afford two hours of an afternoon at the moving picture show" and who "seemed to gloat over the horrors portrayed" on the screen. The movies, said their critics, "are being produced for the morons of America." As William Allen White observed, "The movies generally have no message for intelligent people." The movies, with their vast appeal, had their greatest influence among "the ignorant and the poor," the class for whom

they were produced.[22]

Complaints of the same nature were directed to broadcasting.

Radio was said to appeal to the most suggestible strata in the popu-

lation, to those of lowest intelligence and least ambition. Tele-

vision, both in its commercials and in the entertainment offered,

was thought to be directed to the morons among the general popu-

lation. There was little in it for anyone "educated to read, trained

to be critical, exposed to the theatre."[23] Television's average

viewer--

> the mean to whom all TV shows are beamed--is a retired
> plumber's helper, nesting in some dark cubicle in Brook-
> lyn or The Bronx. After dinner, it is his pleasure to
> take off his shoes, light up his pipe, and settle down
> to an eveing of fisticuffs and gunshots.
>   Qualitatively, this Average Viewer is seen as demanding
> nothing. He just likes the picture to keep moving.[24]

If this was the mass audience to whom the media appealed, the cri-

terion of popularity was a faulty one. The audience who made the

greatest use of the mass entertainment and apparently approved of

the fare offered it was hardly a desirable one.

The audience who counted, said critics of the media, did not

approve of what they were offered, were dissatisfied and disgusted

with what they found on the screen or on the air. The first "hue

and cry from one end of the land to the other against the moving

picture shows" was raised on the grounds of their morality. But

there were other grounds, too. The novelty of films was wearing off,
and perceptive audiences were growing tired of "simple emotions
and transparent plots." The audience of better quality, said
Collier's in 1921, "wants the pictures to get better, wants real
intelligence to be displayed in the making of films." The public,
the genuine audience, was no longer impressed with how much a
picture cost; they wanted "realism" instead. This was the analysis
of Heywood Broun. Even children, when they were asked, said they
did not like the kind of films Hollywood put out. Intelligent
people were aware of the character of films, said Christian Century,
and the extent of their concern was indicated by requests for
100,000 reprints of the Eastman articles on the motion pictures.25

Opponents of radio, like those of the movies, argued that the
audience, in some cases even the mass audience but most often
special groups, did not like what they were getting over the air.
By 1931, New Republic said that "there are growing signs of dissatisfaction with the outrageously inferior character of much
broadcasting today, and particularly with the perpetual sales talk
which has become more and more insistent as times have grown harder."
The listening public, said Lee DeForest, was becoming more critical
of program quality "and more lukewarm to what is being offered
them." Listeners, said Commonweal, were refusing to turn on their
radios because of the "flood of inane crooning and jazz . . . and

the prostitution of the radio to ignoble advertising--promoted by
astrologers, chewing-gum makers, stocks and bonds peddlers, real
estate agents and a welter of other 'high pressure salesmen,'
offering things good, bad and indifferent." Educated people,
thinking people, music lovers, parents, and children were dissatisfied with what they heard or did not hear on the air. Their complaints, especially those related to the children's programs and the
crime features, were voiced through women's groups, Child Study
Clubs, the American Legion Auxiliary, the P. T. A., and the Women's
National Radio Committee.26 Radio was not meeting the needs of
its listeners and there was a growing disenchantment among them.
Even the mass audience, said critics, was beginning to rebel.

Professional critics of television spoke out against much of
the entertainment on the air, parents expressed concern about
crime and violence, educators complained that the medium did less
than it could in their field. But, at least in the period through
1955, there was relatively little argument about the public's
disenchantment with the TV. There were occasional comments.
Christian Century said in 1952 that people who had had television
for a time were tiring of it: "In regions where TV has been in
operation for a year or more there are already hundreds, probably
thousands, of sets which are hardly turned on from one week to the
next." Saturday Review said that "scarcely half of the current set

owners will concede that they are 'satisfied' with present television
programming; and various minorities--especially mothers of young
children--are up in arms over some of the shows." America commented
in 1953 that "parents, educators, child psychologists and editorial
writers, all have a common concern these days: . . . the glaring
absence of worth-while children's programs from television station
and network schedules today." The National Association for Better
Radio and Television reported its concern about crime and violence.
And housewives were reported by U. S. News to feel they had wasted
their evenings watching "these dreadful quiz programs or the other
inferior stuff." As one of those interviewed said, "I particularly resent the commercials, which surely are directed toward
morons. You get awfully tired of being talked to as if you were
twelve years old mentally." But balanced against reports such as
these were figures which indicated that the average amount of television viewing was going up instead of down.[27]

Although they were unimpressed with the quality of the programs,
and disenchanted with the general run of television audiences,
opponents of the medium did not often turn to the argument about
audience dissatisfaction in their attack on TV. Perhaps the medium
was too young by 1955 for the argument to seem plausible, perhaps
critics found other grounds which seemed to yield more forceful

opposition. Nevertheless, this line of argument was less used in
connection with television than with the other two media.

In using the arguments from public response, opponents of the
media attempted to counter assertions of advocates about the popularity of movies, radio, and television. Popularity, they implied,
was insufficient grounds for judgment of the media, for they were
popular with the wrong people. They were the mass media, the media
which appealed to an unintelligent, uncritical audience. The prestige audiences, on the other hand, were suspicious of the media,
if not opposed to them. Thinking people resented what they saw and
heard. Readers of the periodicals were obviously in the latter
group--at least this was the implication of the opponents. If this
were true, the example of their peers would lead the readers to take
a position counter to the media. Just as the promoters had suggested
that the readers get on the bandwagon with everybody else, the
opponents played on the notion that the reader should join the
people who set themselves apart from the masses. Since they could
not deny that the media were popular, critics challenged popularity
as valid ground for judgment.

Before leaving the arguments from peer group association,
let us return for a moment to the promoters. The arguments by the
opposition, their attacks on the appeals of the media to the masses
and their challenge to popularity as a standard, led advocates to

devise a new line of defense for motion pictures, a line which was
carried over into the advocacy of radio and television. Promoters
argued, in sum, that they did appeal to the general audience, but
that this audience wanted only the best and insisted on getting it.
The argument redefined the character of the general audience, and
endowed it with qualities favorable to the media. This was the
second line of argument advanced by the advocates.

Defenders of pictures said, in effect, that they did give the
public what it wanted, and that what the public wanted was good and
uplifting entertainment. The argument was used by Otis Skinner in
1929, when he wrote that pictures were getting better "thanks to
censorship and a realization that perhaps the masses have finer
emotions than some at first imagined." Will Hays picked up the
line of argument, dropped the reference to censorship, and made it
one of the primary arguments in his defense of films. Hays argued
that "the American people want--and must have--nothing but good
pictures." One of the most indecent films ever to be offered the
American people was a rank failure, contrary to the predictions of
its producer. The American people, said Hays, "won't pay for
dirt, if they know that what they are going to see is dirt." But
neither would they pay for the typical "goody-goody film." Somewhere
between the extremes of smut and saccharinity "is the something

good and fine, on which we can set our standard," a standard consistent with the American character.[28]

> The motion picture industry accepts the challenge in
> the demand of the American people for a higher quality
> of art. . . . We accept the challenge in the righteous
> demand of the American mother that the entertainment
> and amusement of that youth shall be worthy of its value
> as a most potent factor in the country's future.[29]

Hays' theme was echoed by other spokesmen for the picture industry in the years following. As one said, pictures are improving "because the public is demanding" stories which show "faith--devotion, loyalty to a country, a cause, or a person," the themes which express the American temper and its values.[30] Pictures, according to these advocates, provided a kind of entertainment consistent with the good character of the audience.

This line of argument was used by promoters of radio, who apparently adopted it from the defense of pictures. For example, in 1924, a writer for Saturday Evening Post argued that radio would find it necessary, as pictures had, to give the public high quality entertainment. As he said, "give the public the best and the public will find some way of lining up at the box-office." Other promoters of the new medium told how radio audiences demanded precision in pronunciation, had rejected jazz in favor of classics, and according to the early Crossley surveys, tuned out programs when they were of low quality.[31]

While the line of argument was used occasionally in the promotion of television, it did not play a major role in the introduction or justification of the medium. When it was used, it was
like the arguments for radio. That is, for example, a writer for
Nation's Business argued that television was "perhaps the most en-
grossing gadget ever invented, but its long-term future will depend
on the quality of its programs."[32] The public television sought
would accept only the best in entertainment.

The argument from redefinition of the character of the mass
audience served to deny assertions of critics about the users of
the media. It was also a means for refutation of the common notion
that the popular arts were necessarily bad. By claiming a higher
standard for their audiences, spokesmen could improve the image
of the media. This line of defense also took the edge off the
critics' charges that the media's philosophy of giving the audience
what it wanted was unacceptable. If the new definition of the
audience was accepted, media spokesmen could agree that they did
give the audience what it wanted, for the audience demanded quality
entertainment. In this sense, the argument shifted the responsibility for program quality away from the media and onto the audience.

The argument from public acceptance worked like the other
arguments from association we have examined before. The media
were presumed to take on the character of the people who used them.

If advocates first presumptions were acceptable, that popularity
was an indication of goodness and that the judgment of the mass
audience was valid, then the new media were shown to be a good thing.
If, as opponents claimed, the media were suited best for the ignorant
and the lazy, then the argument served the opposition. The line of
argument, like many of the others we have seen, depended for its
direction upon the meanings and values inserted in it by those who
employed it. This argument from peer group association functioned
as another means for making a judgment about the new, and assessing
its place in the social order.

Testimony

The last kinds of associative argument to be examined draw
their influence from the reputations and special knowledge of
individuals. These are the arguments in which men testify, either
by their actions or by their statements, to the worth or danger
of the new mass media. Two forms of this argument from individual
association can be found in the agitation over movies, radio, and
television. First, famous people lent their reputations to the
supporters of the media. That is, advocates called attention to
the associations between prestigious individuals and new devices.
Second, in testimony in the conventional sense, advocates and
attackers drew support from the opinions of authoritative individuals.

In the analysis of arguments already undertaken we have seen a number of examples of the first type of individual association, a form of testimonial. The arguments about legitimate actors going to the motion picture from the stage were of this species, as were the comments about preachers, the educators, the doctors who made use of the new media in their special fields. The most common of these associations drew from the reputation of Thomas Edison, who was accepted as the inventor of the motion picture. For some forty years, the name Edison was employed consistently to suggest the unquestionable worth of the movie.

The arguments from prestige association work very simply, as do the arguments from institutional association. By linking the medium with a person of acknowledged reputation, a favorable judgment is made about the medium. That is, if Thomas Edison made it, it must be good. Other writers told, for example, how the President used the radio to talk to the whole nation, and an editor of the Fox News Reels claimed that "no week passes but what the President sees a newsreel." Readers of <u>Scientific American</u> were told in 1925 how the most famous concert artists in the country were appearing on the radio. Famous actors and actresses were named who had deserted the stage for the screen, and the names of famous theatrical producers--Daniel Frohman, Klaw and Erlanger, John Cort, Al H. Woods, the Shuberts, and even Belasco--were connected with

the new venture. Great writers--Edmond Rostand, D'annunzio, Barrie,
Maeterlinck, Henry Arthur Jones, Elmer Rice, Rupert Hughes, and
Mary Roberts Rinehart--were said to be turning out plays for the
motion pictures. The nation's poets had been represented on radio.
As Senior Scholastic said in 1946, "It is small wonder that poets
like Archibald MacLeish, Stephen Vincent Benet, Carl Sandburg,
Maxwell Anderson, Norman Corwin, Edna St. Vincent Millay, John
LaTouche, Norman Rosten, A. M. Sullivan and many others have turned
to the radio with renewed hope for poetry." As early as 1939,
successful playwrights--Owen Davis, Clare Kummer, Max Gordon, and
Rogers and Hart--were reported to be writing for television.
Politicians of the stature of Robert Taft turned to television
in their campaigns. And television coverage of the conventions
was so good by 1952 that Walter Lippmann stayed away from the hall,
"for the first time in as long as he can remember," and covered
the event via a borrowed TV set.33

The associations of these individuals with the new media was
used by promoters as arguments in favor of movies, radio, and
television. If people like Taft, the President, Lippmann, Carl
Sandburg, or Thomas Edison gave the new media their approval by
using them, then the new devices were undoubtedly good for society.

The same style of argument could be employed by attackers, who
might demonstrate that evil men or people of bad reputation employed

the new media. This style of attack is suggested in the argument
that some motion picture operators in the early days preyed on young
viewers; in Eastman's comment that in the picture industry "90
per cent of the upper strata of control is Jewish"; in references
to the use of radio by Huey Long and Father Coughlin; in articles
about the use of broadcasting by Hitler, Mussolini, and Stalin;
and in some of the extreme charges against advertising practices
in both radio and television.[34] In the main, however, opponents
of the media chose other means for their opposition and avoided
this form of attack. It was used much more frequently by the
advocates.

The second type of individual association involves testimony.
Both advocates and attackers called upon the statements of other
people, usually well known or specially qualified, to support their
assertions about the media. An analysis of the use of testimony
in this controversy indicates that it is equally applicable within
all the forms of argument, and that arguers considered it useful
in nearly every rhetorical situation. That is, testimony was used
to support assertions about causality, as material from which to
construct comparisons, in pointing out associations, and in making
definitions. In addition, advocates and attackers introduced
authoritative statements in their discussion of most of the issues
taken up in the dispute. Testimony was a handy and widely used
method of support; only assertion was used more often.

The use of testimony in the controversy can be illustrated
with three articles in which the writers made extensive use of this
form of proof. The first is by Carl Holliday in World's Work for
May 1913. He argued that the motion picture was a valuable teaching
tool, and in supporting his claim quoted "the Reverend Herbert Jump,
Oakland, California, in a recent lecture at the University of
California"; Thomas Edison; Professor Hugo Münsterberg of Harvard;
"Beerbohm Tree, the most famous of English actors"; "the Reverend
Robert Burdette"; "members of the Academie Francaise"; the "Prus-
sian authorities"; and "Chairman George P. Fraser, of the Detroit
Public Health League." In addition, statements about the use of
pictures in education were quoted from "Prof. Milton Fairchild
of Baltimore, Maryland"; Thomas Edison again; "Prof. Arthur G.
Balcom, supervisor of lectures for the Newark Board of Education";
"Mr. Milton C. Cooper, district superintendent of schools in Philadelphia"; and Superintendent Martindale, of Detroit." Holliday,
moreover, cited numerous instances in which both well known people
and institutions had made use of the new educational tool.[35]

The second example is Fred Eastman's article, "Our children
and the Movies," in Christian Century for January 22, 1930. In
it, Eastman drew heavily from Alice Miller Mitchell's Children and
Movies, but also quoted the Child Welfare Committee of the League
of Nations; the Chicago Motion Picture Censorship Board; crimi-
nologists attending the International Prison Congress in London;

sociological studies in New York, Chicago, and Cleveland; "Professor Edward A. Ross, a Wisconsin sociologist"; and Professor E. W. Burgess of the department of sociology at the University of Chicago. Reported, too, were the opinions of parents and teachers about the influence of the movies on children they knew, and statements by juvenile delinquents about the effects of movies on their behavior.[36]

The third article to be used as an example is Robert Lewis Shayon's "The Pied Piper of Video" in Saturday Review for November 25, 1950, a commentary on the influence of television on children. As evidence Shayon submitted a poll of parents taken by Paul Witty of Northwestern University; a survey by the United Parents Association of New York; a poll conducted by Tide magazine of the opinions of leaders in advertising, marketing, and public relations about the influence of the media on children; a letter from a private school operator in Melrose, Massachusetts; a quotation by Wilbur Schramm in Journalism Quarterly; a survey of the television viewing behavior of New York high school students; the opinions of high school students about television; autobiographical statements from 373 elementary school children collected by the director of Hunter College Elementary School; and a quotation from Charles A Siepmann's Radio, Television, and Society.[37]

These articles are atypical in two ways: all use more evidence than many of the articles surveyed, and all use a high proportion

of testimony. Nevertheless, the articles represent a trend in the
use of testimony, a shift from reliance upon opinion testimony
to reliance upon factual testimony. The article by Holliday depends
primarily upon the opinions of various authority figures. Eastman,
while he quotes authorities, tends to favor evidence from empirical
examination. Shayon, finally, tends mostly to evidence gathered
from polls, surveys, and samples of one kind and another. This
general shift in the use of testimony may be observed over the course
of the controversy.

One may speculate on the causes for the shift. First, there
is the possibility that Holliday perceived his audience as more
likely to accept authority than factual data, and Shayon to see
his as more susceptible to fact than to opinion. But there is a
more probable explanation in the availability of evidence to the
writers. Holliday did not have the kind of evidence available to
him that Eastman and Shayon did. He could not quote samples which
had not yet been devised. And there is the possibility, finally,
of a general social trend over a period of some forty years away
from reliance on "mere opinion," even from an authoritarian figure,
to an emphasis on fact and "scientific" proof.

In general, writers called upon the testimony of someone else
when they needed backing for what they had said. Therefore, in
addition to the factual testimony provided by the various studies

of audience behavior, writers for both sides turned to doctors for information about the effects of the media on health; politicians to talk about politics; educators to talk about education. And in addition certain people of very high status, who were well known, were apparently considered qualified to talk on a variety of subjects. Thomas Edison was one of them, Lee DeForest another. Ministers, college professors, and psychologists, were also given more freedom of field than some of the other people from whom testimony was taken. In the main, however, writers apparently picked for testimony those people who supported their position and whose word would be taken by the anticipated readers of the piece.

Arguments from personal association, like the other forms of associative argument, were used to define the place of the media in society and to make decisions about their worth. The people who talked about the media, the people and institutions who used them, offered a commentary on the new in society. If the new media were approved by persons of high status and institutions of acknowledged importance, the new media were thought well of. Compared to the arguments from cause and from comparison, the arguments from association are a relatively simple means for persuasion. Perhaps their simplicity made the arguers suspicious of them, for they were never used as frequently as the other forms of argument.

Notes

1. WW, Je '06, p. 7690.

2. CCom, 8 Je '07, p. 297.

3. HW, 13 N '09, p. 9.

4. WW, My '13, pp. 39-40; Out, 22 Ag '14, p. 970; Ind, 13 F '13, pp. 354, 356; PE, 0 '26, p. 178; Col, 2 D '22, p. 10. See also, WW, F '11, p. 14031.

5. SEP, 7 D '29, p. 68; AmMag, Jl '21, p. 32; AmMag, Je '22, p. 72; SEP, 11 F '39, p. 9; Scrib, My '28, p. 629.

6. SEP, 28 S '40, pp. 37, 39; AmMerc, Jl '44, p. 61.

7. Nwk, 27 0 '47, p. 82.

8. Col, 27 S '47, p. 30.

9. Nwk, 28 My '49, p. 81; SS, 20 S '50, p. 21; ST, 1 N '50, p. 21T; NB, Je '49, p. 37; USN, 23 Je '50, p. 15; NR, 2 My '55, p. 9; USN, 2 S '55, p. 43; SEP, 12 Mr '55, p. 33.

10. Religion: CCom, 11 Ap '08, p. 75; Ind, 13 F '13, p. 354; Nat, 6 Ap '14, p. 154; RR, D '14, p. 727; Ind, 28 F '15, p. 311; CO, F '20, p. 226; LD, 17 Je '22, p. 27; Scrib, Ap '23, p. 415; CO, Mr '25, p. 343; PE, Jl '29, p. 46; RR, My '30, p. 92; LD, 27 D '30, p. 18; CC, 21 0 '31, p. 1301; RR, Mr '32, p. 31; CC, 9 Jl '37, p. 745; SEP, 28 S '40, p. 39; Col, 27 S '47, p. 30; Nwk, 27 0 '47, p. 82; SEP, 25 S '48, p. 172; Nwk, 18 Ap '49, p. 78; USN, 2 S '55, p. 43. Education: WW. My '13, p. 46; Out, 22 Ag '14, p. 968; HW, 11 D '15, p. 574; HW, 25 D '15, p. 620; Ind, 28 F '16, p. 311; LD, 29 Ja '21, p. 35; CO, Ap '22, p. 507; SEP, 15 Ap '22, p. 142; LD, 13 My 22, p. 28; Scrib, Ap '23, p. 415; Col, 3 Ja '25, p. 40; Cent, 0 '26, p. 670; RR, Ap '27, p. 398; AmMag, Ja '29, p. 100; PE, F '29, p. 101; PE, Jl '29, p. 57; SR, 24 Je '33, p. 661; Nwk, 6 Jl '35, p. 26; Atlan, Mr '36, p. 358; PMech, S '39, p. 325; AAA, Ja '41, p. 151; BHG, N '45, p. 73; AmMag, 7 S '42, p. 41; Col, 27 S '47, p. 30; Nwk, 28 My '49, p. 81; SS, 20 S '50, p. 21; ST, 1 N '50, p. 21T; USN, 2 S '55, p. 42. Politics: AmMag, Je '22, p. 72; RR, S '24, p. 237; AmMag, N '28, p15; Scrib, My '31, p.490; NR, 17 Mr '37, p. 189; Life, 29 Ap '40, p. 36; Nwk, 1 N '48, p. 52; USN, 23 Je '50, p. 14; Nwk, 18 F '52, p. 67; NR, 1 D '52, p. 14; NR, 2 My '55, p. 9; NR, 9 My '55, p. 13;

Nwk, 19 S '55, p. 39. Government: HW, 13 N '09, p. 9; WW, F '11, p. 14031; RR, Ja '12, p. 22; AmMag, Jl '21, p. 32; SA, D '21, p. 104; RR, Ja '22, p. 102; CO, Mr '22, p. 404; Col, 8 Ap '21, p. 18; Ind, 18 S '26, p. 325; CC, 9 Jl '37, p. 746; SEP, 11 F '39, p. 8; NB, Je '49, p. 74. Business: HW, 13 N '09, p. 9; AmMag, Jl '21, p. 32; AmMag, Je '22, p. 72; NAR, Summer '38, p. 309; Nwk, 20 D '43, p. 68; Col, 27 S '47, p. 32; Etude, Je '49, p. 341; SEP, 12 Mr '55, p. 33. Family: CCom, 11 Ap '08, p. 75; Ind, 28 F '16, p. 311; HM, Ja '19, p. 185; RR, Ja '23, p. 52; Nat, 23 Jl '24, p. 90; Col, 6 F '26, p. 8; Etude, Je '37, p. 359. Law enforcement: WW, My '13, p. 44; AmMag, Je '22, p. 72; RR, D '25, p. 646; SEP, 7 D '29, p. 68. Newspapers: Nat, 24 D '24, p. 699; AmMerc, Jl '44, p. 61. Science: HW, 11 D '55, p. 574; PE, O '26, p. 178. Miscellaneous: CCom, 8 Je '07, p. 297; WW, F '11, p. 14031; RR, Ja '12, p. 22; WW, My '13, p. 44; Col, 2 D '22, p. 10; AC, S '24, p. 246; Out, 25 N '25, p. 474; Scrib, My '28, p. 628; CC, 15 Ap '31, p. 512; Nat, 30 N '46, p. 618; Col, 27 S '47, p. 30; USN, 2 S '55, p. 48.

11. Comm, 22 Ja '30, p. 334; HM, D '34, p. 59; SEP, 1 D '34, p. 8; SSoc, 22 Ag '36, p. 233; Nat, 9 My '34, p. 531; SR, 4 Jl '42, p. 6; RR, F '37, p. 38. See also, CC, 24 S '41, p. 1173; SR, 14 Je '47, p. 27; CC, 2 F '49, p. 142.

12. CC, 24 S '41, p. 1173.

13. Nat, 24 D '24, p. 699; NO, Jl '33, p. 20; Nat, 3 Ap '43, p. 484.

14. Col, 16 S '22, p. 3; Scrib, Mr '27, p. 311; HW, 9 Ja '15, p. 39; RR, Mr '32, p. 31; CC, 15 Ja '30, p. 76; Out, 29 Jl '31, p. 414. See also, Out, 11 Ap '28, p. 576.

15. RR, D '08, p. 744; LD, 22 My '09, p. 882; HM, S '12, p. 635.

16. HM, Ag '17, p. 349.

17. NAR, S '20, p. 391; RR, Ja '23, p. 65; PE, O '26, p. 176. See also, AmMag, S '09, p. 498; WW, My '10, p. 12876; HW, 30 Jl '10, p. 12; WW, F '11, p. 14020; SA, 12 Ag '11, p. 156; Dial, 16 F '14, p. 129; NAR, S '20, p. 391; Out, 19 S '23, p. 106; Ind, 6 F '08, p. 306; WT, O '08, p. 1053; CCom, 6 Mr '09, p. 1038; Lip, O '09, p. 454; WW, My '10, p. 12876; Out, 24 Je '11, p. 441; HW, 16 S '11, p. 6; Over, Je '12, p. 551; Nat, 28 Ag '13, p. 193; CO, S '14, p. 176; Col, 26 Je '15, p. 22; Ind, 11 D '16, p. 448; SA, 13 Ja '17, p. 56; CO, Mr '17, p. 185; HM, Ja '19, p. 184; CO, Ap '22, p. 507; Nat, 2 Ja '24, p. 5; Col, 3 My '24, p. 28; RR, Ap '27, p. 394;

Ind, 12 Je '26, p. 689; RR, Mr '32, p. 32; CC, 31 Jl '35, p. 982.

18. Scrib, Ap '29, p. 367; Col, 25 My '29, p. 8; TA, S '29,
p. 651; CC, 12 My '37, p. 618. See also, Out, 26 S '28, p. 865;
SEP, 9 Mr '29, p. 18; Comm, 21 My '30, p. 73; Comm, 13 Ag '30, p.
381; CC, 12 My '37, p. 617.

19. CC, 11 Mr '31, p. 340; SA, D '21, p. 104; SEP, 15 Ap '22,
p. 6; CO, My '22, p. 684; AmMag, Je '22, p. 13; Scrib, Ap '23, p. 416.
See also, LA, 16 D 1899, p. 699; Out, 15 Mr '22, p. 410; Col, 8 Ap '21,
p. 3; Nat, 29 Mr '22, p. 361; RR, S '22, p. 303; SA, Ap '23, p. 242;
Nat, 2 Ja '24, p. 5; NR, 8 0 '24, p. 135; RR, N '27, p. 521; Scrib,
My '28, p. 631; RR, Jl '29, p. 142; Scrib, My '31, p. 494; CC, 11 Mr
'31, p. 340; HM, Ap '33, p. 554; SEP, 11 F '39, p. 8; Educ, Je '40,
p. 609.

20. Col, 27 S '47, p. 30; CC, 2 F '49, p. 143; NB, Je '49,
p. 41.

21. USN, 2 S '55, p. 37. See also, SEP, 28 S '40, p. 37; SEP,
16 Mr '46, p. 94; Nat, 30 N '46, p. 618; NB, Jl '47, p. 37; AmMag, Mr
'48, p. 105; Nwk, 27 D '48, p. 45; GH, Ja '49, p. 4; CC, 2 F '49,
p. 142; NR, 26 F '51, p. 18; Time, 21 Jl '53, p. 38; USN, 2 S '55,
p. 37.

22. HW, 18 Ja '13, p. 20; HW, 24 Ag '07, p. 1246; Out, 14 F
'14, p. 346; CC, 15 Ja '30, p. 76; Col, 16 Ja '26, p. 5; Comm,
13 Ag '30, p. 381. See also, AmMag, Ag '13, p. 93; Ind, 31 Ja '25,
p. 115; LA, 31 0 '25, p. 255.

23. NR, 19 F '40, p. 236; NR, 3 0 '34, p. 201; TA, Je '52,
p. 46; USN, 2 S '55, p. 46; SR, 11 S '54, p. 46.

24. TA, Je '52, p. 46. See also, USN, 2 S '55, p. 46.

25. Out, 13 Jl '12, p. 598; NR, 14 Ag '15, p. 51; Col, 8 0
'21, p. 21; Col, 11 F '22, p. 16; Out, 24 Ag '21, p. 660; CC, 15 Ja
'30, p. 76; CC, 18 Je '30, p. 774. See also, Nat, 6 My '15, p. 487;
NAR, N '20, p. 640; Col, 30 S '22, p. 12; HM, S '24, p. 428; HM,
N '28, p. 711; SEP, 21 S '29, p. 22; CC, 21 My '30, p. 646; CC,
17 Mr '34, p. 326; Comm, 13 Ag '30, p. 381; CC, 21 0 '31, p. 1301;
ParM, N '31, p. 20; NAR, Ag '33, p. 145; Nat, 20 Ap '40, p. 511.

26. NR, 24 Je '31, p. 139; Out, 21 Ja '31, p. 87; Comm,
17 F '32, p. 421. See also, Cent, Je '24, p. 149; Out, 22 Ap '31,
p. 561; NR, 24 Je '31, p. 139; Out, Jl '33, p. 19; HM, Ap '34, p. 576;

Scrib, O '34, p. 246; Nwk, 1 D '34, p. 27; Atlan, Mr '36, p. 358; Nwk, 8 N '37, p. 26; AAA, Ja '41, p. 12; Nat, 9 F '46, p. 171; Comm, 14 Je '46, p. 204; SR, 8 F '47, p. 26; HB, O '47, p. 274; CC, 12 Ap '50, p. 452.

27. CC, 28 My '52, p. 637; SR, 26 Ag '50, p. 30; Amer, 21 Mr '53, p. 689; USN, 2 S '55, pp. 39, 46. See also, TA, Je '52, p. 46; CC, 14 Ja '53, p. 36; SEP, 12 Mr '55, p. 33.

28. NAR, S '20, p. 391; RR, Ja '23, p. 74; Col, 2 D '22, p. 11.

29. RR, Ja '23, p. 80.

30. Col, 7 F '25, p. 10. See also, Ind, 18 S '26, p. 326; PE, O '26, p. 175; RR, Ap '27, p. 396; PE, F '29, p. 103; SEP, 19 Jl '30, p. 31; SEP, 1 Ag '31, p. 20; NO, F '35, p. 15.

31. SEP, 17 My '24, p. 109; Col, 3 Jl '26, p. 16; Ind, 23 My '25, p. 584; CC, 11 Mr '31, p. 343. See also, NR, 8 O '24, p. 136; SEP, 6 D '24, p. 82; Scrib, My '28, p. 625; NR, 24 Je '31, p. 139; HM, S '32, p. 469.

32. NB, Je '49, p. 42; SR, 21 F '42, p. 17.

33. Col, 24 S '27, p. 9; Ind, 18 S '26, p. 326; SA, D '25, p. 421; Lip, Ag '13, p. 191; Ind, 17 Jl '13, p. 143; Col, 12 Ap '13, p. 11; Out, 27 N '09, p. 710; HW, 13 N '09, p. 9; RR, S '10, p. 319; CO, S '14, p. 176; CO, Mr '17, p. 185; NAR, Jl '20, p. 90; NAR, S '20, p. 390; SS, 6 Mr '46, p. 20; SEP, 20 My '39, p. 107; Time, 21 Jl '52, p. 58. See also, AmMag, S '09, p. 500; LD, 3 Ag '12, p. 190; AmMag, Jl '13, p. 102; AmMag, O '14, p. 44; Nat, 27 Mr '29, p. 365; Comm, 21 My '30, p. 73; SEP, 14 F '53, p. 25; USN, 23 Je '50, p. 14; USN, 2 S '55, p. 44.

34. HM, S '12, p. 634; CC, 5 F '30, p. 173.

35. WW, My '13, pp. 39-49.

36. CC, 22 Ja '30, pp. 110-112.

37. SR, 25 N '50, pp. 9-11, 49-51.

CHAPTER VIII

ARGUMENT FROM DEFINITION

Advocacy and Attack

Our discussion of the genres of argument identifiable in the controversy over motion pictures, radio, and television ends with a consideration of arguments from definition. Such arguments, the least frequent of the four genres, were used by promoters and attackers to characterize the new media, to offer persuasive descriptions of them, and to show how they were useful or harmful.

Two modes of definition are apparent in the agitation. The first is definition from value terms. Spokesmen for the media described them in the god terms we have seen used before in the argument. Motion pictures, for example, were labeled a form of education. The word chosen for the definition implied a judgment of the thing defined and supplied a connotation favorable to acceptance. Opponents, predictably, chose terms of negative connotation for their definitions. To them, instead of being an educator, radio was a "blatant signboard erected in the living room." The definitions in themselves were persuasive and were intended to influence the reception of the new media.[1] The second mode of definition described the new media as neutral tools. That is, motion pictures, radio, and television were but transmitters of the message, instruments for good or ill depending

upon the wise or foolish use made of them by society. These two
modes of definition served to place the new media in a social context, to locate them in categories which were understood from past
experience, and to identify their social functions.

Definitions from Value Terms

I discussed in Chapter Two the difficulties faced by advocates in defending movies, radio, and television as means for
entertainment. Amusement for its own sake was never considered
acceptable grounds for advocacy, even though entertainment was
the primary function of the new media. The same problems are
apparent in the definitions. Here again entertainment, while it
was recognized as one function of the media, was never given as
the sole defining term. Always another dimension was added. Most
commonly, the new media were defined as serving to please and to
teach. That is, movies and broadcasting were new forms of entertainment and education.

This mode of definition was introduced by George Parsons
Lathrop in his first article about the movies. Recall that he
said the kinetograph, while opening "very large resources . . .
in the way of simply amusement," was also to "become very useful
for instruction in sundry directions." This theme was used in the
defense of movies in licensing hearings in 1907, when the pictures

were described as "edifying, educational, and amusing." By 1908,
Robert Thorne Haines said in _Photo-Era_ of the movie that "to pleasure
and amusement it has largely contributed; for educational purposes
its value is acknowledged."[2]

Long after the movies were well established, when there was
no longer need of definition merely to tell what the medium was,
what it looked like, or what it did, promoters continued to define
movies as both entertainment and education. The definitions were
used rhetorically, to establish the bases for judgment, to give the
movies respectability. As Hays said in 1923, the motion picture
"is the principal amusement of the great majority of all our people
and the sole amusement of millions and millions." But, he added,
the movie was more than amusement: "it is an instrument and means
for immeasurable education and moral influence; and we must not forget that even as we serve the leisure hours of the people with the
right diversion so do we rivet the girders of society."[3] Perhaps
most characteristic of this definition of motion pictures is a
statement from Martin Quigley, the editor of _Motion Picture Herald_,
who argued in 1938 that

> granting that the first business of theatrical films is
> to entertain, we hold that they actually and inevitably
> do more than entertain. For they subtly influence the
> movie patron's emotional attitudes, his behavior patterns
> and his character values. This is the very essence of
> education.[4]

Radio and television, too, were defined as entertainment and
education. A spokesman for Westinghouse said in 1922, for example,
that "radio possesses possibilities of entertainment and instruction not yet comprehended even by those who are familiar with wireless developments to date." The chief function of radio, said the
science editor of the New York Times, was the simultaneous entertainment and instruction of millions. Radio, said the President of
RCA, meant entertainment and education for the millions. Television,
said the Washington Post in 1928, would open up new dimensions
"for the instruction and amusement of the public." After television
had been used to transmit the Republican National Convention from
Philadelphia to New York in 1940, David Sarnoff characterized the
medium as eventually the nation's "principal source of entertainment,
education, and news." In 1946, Scholastic said that "on its mark and
rarin' to go, television is set to open a whole new age of entertainment and education." And when a doctor sought to reassure readers
of House Beautiful that television would not harm their eyes, he
suggested they forget their fears "and enjoy a new privilege, which
will mean more pleasure in the home, a new vehicle for teaching,
a richer entertainment."[5]

In all of these characterizing statements, entertainment was
buttressed with education. But although entertainment-education
was the most common form of multiple definition, promoters of movies

called them also an instrument of science, a social force, a political tool, a new business, and an aid to religion. Television, too,
was more than entertainment; it was art, a medium of culture, an
instrument of science, a political tool, and a source of news. As
Gilbert Seldes said, "Television has the great opportunity of
becoming a fully integrated medium of commerce, communication, and
diversion."[6] In all of the definitions, entertainment was excused
because it was but one function of the new media. The new inventions also served more important ends.

An occasional variation on the entertainment-education definitions should also be considered here. The line of argument was
suggested in Quigley's comment that movies, because of their subtle
influences on attitudes and values, while they seemed only to entertain, inevitably did more than that. This capacity of the films
led George Bernard Shaw to comment that

> the cinematograph begins educating people when the pro-
> jection lantern begins clicking, and does not stop until
> it leaves off. . . . And it is educating you far more
> effectively when you think it's only amusing than when
> it is avowedly instructing you in the habits of lobsters.[7]

Later, C. B. Neblette argued in Photo-Era that the motion picture,
in what were apparently only entertainment films, had "opened the
eyes of the American people to the romantic history of the North
American continent." William de Mille argued that "under the
guise of entertainment" the motion picture was a new art and an

important social force. Similarly, Edgar Dale of Ohio State University held that the entertainment and education functions of motion pictures could not be separated. For example, he said, films such as The Story of Louis Pasteur, The Life of Emile Zola, and Dead End, while they were entertaining and pleasant to watch also "provided social insight that illuminated problems of human conduct."[8]

Radio, too, was said to be teaching when it seemed only to amuse. For example, Grace Johnson, director of Women's and Children's Programs for the Blue Network, argued in 1945 that the radio serials, which were then under fire, "taught while entertaining, just as did the writers of the classics for children." A similar line of defense was offered by a writer for Better Homes and Gardens for comics, radio, and movies. She argued that these media were making "learning of all kinds easy and pleasant." The child might seem to be unduly absorbed in the stories he saw or heard, but "all the time, without realizing it, he is learning about the world he is going to have to cope with one day, and he is being handed the tools with which to build his life there."[9]

Movies and radio were thus defined as educational agencies although they seemed only to amuse. Their function was to make learning enjoyable, knowledge desirable, and teaching pleasing. Education was given a coating of entertainment. The amusement was defined as a means to a higher end. On that ground it was excusable.

The foregoing definitions made explicit reference to entertainment as one facet of the new media. In other definitions advocates ignored entertainment and talked instead of other valuable functions of the new inventions. Movies, they said, were a new form of   art, a new social force, a new kind of theatre, a second educational system, a true universal language, a public service, a recreative school, and "one of the chief contributions of science to education." Movies, moreover, were a good business. As William Berchtold said in North American Review in 1939, "The motion picture could be an art or a science or a great educational medium or a business; it is all four, but principally it is a business." Radio was named a means for education, a business, a public service; an instrument for mass appeal, communication, culture, and the exchange of ideas; a public utility, a social mirror, "a common human necessity," "a war necessity and a peace asset." What was television? It was a spreader of culture, a new form of theatre, "a new art form," a sales medium, a new industry, a scientific miracle, and "the ultimate goal of communication."[10]

The new media were thus defined in value terms which advocates presumed would lead to more ready acceptance than if films and broadcasting were left to be considered merely new amusement devices. The new inventions were to be and to do the things we as a nation admired. If we respected education, they educated; if we thought well of business, they were businesses; if we placed high value on the arts, they were arts; if we were awed by science, they were both a product of science and its tool. The definitions endowed the new inventions with admirable properties, suggested the laudable functions to which the media might be put, and placed the new in classifications of good things sanctioned by experience.

In another sense the definitions told readers how to evaluate the new media. Writers who linked entertainment with some other value concept asked readers not to dismiss movies, radio, and television merely as entertainment, but to judge them on the basis of their dual functions as entertainer and cultural agent. The new inventions, said their advocates, were more important than they might first appear, for in addition to amusing they served ends for which society held great respect. Moreover, one could not expect to judge a business, an art, an agency of government, the theatre, or scientific progress by a single system of standards. The criteria must change for each one. This, in effect, was what promoters asked for the media: that they be judged according to the functions defined for them. Hence, movies might be thought highly successful as a business, but a failure as an art. Nevertheless, if the promoter managed to argue from the position that movies were a business and not an art, then the medium would be judged acceptable. Definition, in this case and in others, was important in structuring

the criteria, setting up the ground rules, for the evaluation of
the media. At the same time, the rhetorical definitions in the
naming of the media drew upon common understandings about what was
good and valuable. By definition, advocates placed the new inventions in a class with other good things.

Opponents of movies argued less frequently from definition
than did the advocates. In general, however, they dealt with the
same topics. For example, where advocates named pictures a new kind
of theatre, writers dissatisfied with the medium denied that it was
a form of dramatic art. As Harold Trowbridge Pulsifer said in 1921,
dramatic art should deal, as Aristophanes and Shakespeare did,
with life; movies, despite their technical capacity, failed to do
so. Films did not satisfy his criteria for drama. For another
reason, because films in 1924 could not transmit the words of the
playwright, George Bernard Shaw denied that silent films were properly classified as drama. Brander Matthews likewise developed
a long argument from definition in order to demonstrate not only
that motion pictures were outside the realm of drama but also to
defend his contention that while movies might destroy the theatre,
they could never hurt the drama. As he said, in drama "the eyes
and ears of the spectators must be entertained while the mind is
being satisfied and the feelings being moved." Motion pictures
could satisfy the criteria on neither technical nor artistic grounds.

When talkies were introduced, the question was raised of whether or not they were an art. Two writers denied that they were, because talkies were merely a reproduction of reality whereas art was a modification of nature. Finally, movies were said to be a form of dope, a narcotic for the emotions.[11]

Opponents of radio, as we have already seen, called the medium a "blatant signboard." Others referred to it as a fad, "a disintegrating toy," and "America's prize sideshow." Lee DeForest was said to have called the medium he invented "a laughing stock of intelligence, surely a stench in the nostrils of the gods of the ionosphere." Gilbert Seldes said that despite claims made to the contrary radio in 1931 was devoted pretty much to unimportant and uninspired entertainment. Others claimed that no matter how it was defined, radio would never be a satisfactory medium for education. There were the continuing arguments about what was or was not classical music, and about the kinds of pieces which could be defined as "good music." Some writers defined radio as merely another source for advertising. On the other hand, Stuart Chase claimed in 1928 that radio would never survive as a medium for direct advertising because the public would not stand for it. Finally, when public control for radio channels was proposed by the National Congress of Parents and Teachers, the proposal was rejected as socialism.[12]

Television, as we have observed in other contexts, was defined
as a time trap, a medium for "commercial entertainment," a huckster
in the living room, a triumph of mediocrity, and an electronic
nursemaid.[13]

In general, the argument from definition was less popular
with opponents than with advocates. The technique, however, was
the same for both sides. That is, advocates defined the new media
in terms they assumed to carry favorable connotations; opponents
chose negative terms and used them for derogation. These rhetorical
definitions, which named the new media in value terms, served as
another means for placing innovation in a social context, for
showing its relationship to familiar things, and for making an
assessment of it.

Neutral Tool Definitions

The second major type of definition advanced by their opponents
and supporters referred to the new media as neutral, therefore
susceptible to the manipulations of their users. The movies, radio,
or television were not necessarily means for education, politics,
or culture, neither were they of themselves harmful moral influences, threats to children, or dangers to the theatre. Each medium
could be any of these, depending upon how well or badly it was

employed. The particular definitions of the media lay with those who controlled them and with those who watched or listened to them.

This line of definition was introduced in the discussion of movies by C. H. Claudy in 1908 as he spoke of "the degredation of the motion-picture." As he said, the opportunities of films for good or bad are endless, but "as a general rule, they are taken up on the bad side." Harper's Weekly, on the other hand, observed in 1911 that "any form of amusement which takes so great a hold on the people, especially on the children, must be a great power for good or for evil." Harper's stressed in its argument the good, but at the same time warned of the potential dangers of the medium.[14] The argument was applied to the educational use of films in 1913 when Leonard P. Ayres of the Russell Sage Foundation said this about Edison's plan to teach with pictures:

> Every tool can be misused. The more effective it is when
> rightly handled, the greater is its capacity for damage
> when unskilfully wielded. The new motion pictures are
> an educational tool of great potential value, and while
> their dangers and limitations are real, they are not
> inherent or unavoidable.[15]

One of the most sophisticated defenses of motion pictures from the neutral tool definition was developed by Francis Hackett in New Republic in 1915, at a time when there was growing dissatisfaction with the moral tone of some of the movie stories. He argued that any mechanical invention could be used for either good or evil, and that the machine should not be condemned because of the use

made of it. For example, he said,

> a safety match is an admirable little thing, but not
> when the baby eats it. A laundry pin serves its humble
> purpose in the world, but not when the baby swallows
> it. Dynamite can be employed to blow men to smithereens,
> but it can also be employed to blow rocks to smithereens.
> One of the ugliest murders of modern times was the Phoenix
> Park murder, but it was only by a cruel irony that Lord
> Frederick Cavendish was stabbed to death with the finest
> surgeon's operating knives. The man who bought those
> knives had often put similar ones to a purpose diamet-
> rically opposite. If the demon in man can pervert his
> own instruments, it is a feeble argument against the
> instruments.[16]

It was Hackett's conclusion that because of their failure to see

beyond the uses to which movies had been put in the past, their

opponents failed "to appreciate the illimitable artistic, the

illimitable social, possibilities of the moving picture."

The motion picture, said other writers who defined it as a

machine subject to man's manipulations, had the capability to

do either general good or extensive evil in society. It might be

used to show the best in man or to expose him at his worst. It

could create international understanding or cause disputes among

nations. It could lead its viewers to support conventional morality

or it could lead them to crime. What movies contained depended

upon the wisdom and social conscience of the men who made them.

Their eventual influences, however, depended upon the wisdom and

stability of the people who watched them. The responsibility for

movies, therefore, was divided between producer and audience. The
machine itself, the medium, could not be blamed for the consequences.

Radio was characterized by Daniel Frohman as "an instrument
of the gods that is sometimes the work of the devil." This is
apt summary of these definitional arguments about broadcasting.
As Stanley Frost said in Collier's in 1922, radio was able to
"do more than any other agency in spreading mutual understanding
to all sections of the country, to unifying our thoughts, ideals,
and purposes, to making us a strong and well-knit people," if we
would but let it. Unfortunately, he said, "there is stubborn resistance in many human souls to being benefitted, and we may want to
limit the radio to jazz." The machine was capable of serving man
well; man's use of the tool was questionable. When complaints about
programming were heard in the late 1920's, Gilbert Seldes reminded
readers of New Republic, as had the spokesman for movies ten years
earlier, that radio was "an instrument and we can hardly despise
the instrument because we do not know to what good use to put it."[17]

Radio for more than twenty years was often defined by its promoters and its opponents as a neutral tool subject to man's wise
or unwise use. Broadcasting could bring both opportunity or menace
to politics. The radio could be used to teach religious tolerance
or to spread suspicion and intolerance.

Things heard on the air were a "real and potent force for good or
for evil in our cultural development." "As a result of radio broadcasting," said James Rorty in Harper's, "there will probably develop
during the twentieth century either chaos or a world order of civilization." Radio could work to support the dictator or could be used
in a democracy "to stimulate thinking and inform the intelligence."
"For good or ill," said a writer for School and Society, "the radio
is an influential partner of the school in the business of educating
children." Radio's value depended upon the people who created its
programs and upon the people who listened to them. As Better Homes
and Gardens said in 1945, "It seems to be pretty much up to the
individual home and parents, therefore, whether radio is a curse
or a boon."18

Television was defined in similar fashion both at its introduction and after it was established. It would be, said one writer
in 1936, either an instrument of public enlightenment or a weapon
of destruction. Which end it served would depend upon those who
used it. Looking ahead to greater use of television following the
Second World War, Robert Conly said in 1944 that "like all great
technical advances, its value will not be inherent in itself, but
will depend on the wisdom with which it is used." After extensive
telecasting was begun, other writers commented that television could
be a wonderful improvement in the home if parents and children used

it well. The medium was described as "one of the most significant teaching aids ever to come within reach of the educator." On the other hand, it was "up to the educator to provide the guidance and assistance necessary to bring its vast educational potentialities to fruition." FCC Commissioner Frieda B. Hennock said in 1951 that "television can do either tremendous good or incalculable harm." For the sake of the children who had been captured by it, "we must see to it that this powerful medium is also used for cultural advancement--for education as well as entertainment." After television had been demonstrated to be a facile political instrument in 1952, Clifford C. Durr, a former member of the FCC, called TV a tool which with equal impact could "inform or confuse, educate or degrade, challenge the emotions of people or exploit them." Similarly, Paul Seabury of the Department of Government and Public Law at Columbia University said of television in politics that "turned to high moral and educative purpose, we have seen that it can uplift; turned to sordid expediency, sloganeering, and manipulation, it can do great damage to our political processes."[19] It was the opinion of Christian Century in 1955 that

> atomic power is not the only giant let loose on this
> generation whose potentialities for good or evil have
> still to be measured. Consider, as another, television.
> No one can as yet even begin to comprehend what effect
> this electronic marvel will have on the remaining years
> of this century.[20]

Unlike the definitions with which this chapter began, these ascribed no set function to the media and endowed them at first with neither laudable nor offensive characteristics. The media themselves were described as neuter, inarticulate, unresponsive without men to guide and use them. The character of innovation was determined by the use to which it was put.

The arguments from neutral tool definitions offered advocates and opponents certain advantages over the value definitions. In the first place, definitions of neutrality permitted writers to characterize the media without committing themselves to particular functions. The media, they suggested, could do nearly anything their users wanted them to do. People writing about the media could thus take an apparently neutral stance with respect to the new machines. This, if nothing else, gave their argument an appearance of fairmindedness and objectivity. In the second place, the definitions of the media as neutral tools, as the examples cited show, were often accompanied by a description of possible applications. Usually these presented striking two-valued contrasts between the potential good and evil ends to which innovation might be applied. Hence, implicit in the definition was a call to rally on the side of good against the forces of evil. Finally, and probably most important, defined as neutral tools motion pictures, radio, and television were freed from responsibility for their effects. The media were but vehicles for communications of various kinds; they were not themselves accountable for the uses to which they were put. The instrument, as some writers said, was not at fault if it was used badly. Responsibility was thus shifted away from the media to some other agency. Commonly, attackers charged that producers were responsible for the faults of films and that advertisers were to blame for the failures of broadcasting. Carrying the responsibility one step further and shifting it again, as the industry spokesmen often did, the blame lay not in the industry at all but with the public, the set owners and the movie goers. One was always at liberty to turn off the TV or to stay home from the movies.

I have said nothing here about the purely technical descriptions of the new media which also might be considered a form of definition. These descriptions accompanied the first announcements of the new machines and appeared whenever an important technical change was announced. They were not continued after the public could be assumed to be acquainted with the new media. The other forms of definition, however, were continued throughout the course of the dispute.

The arguments from definition served functions similar to the other arguments we have examined. They were used to demonstrate the similarities between the unfamiliar and the familiar, to suggest the place of the new media in society, and to describe their

characteristic functions. The definitions were a form of persuasive introduction; a means for setting limits on the expectations
for movies, radio, and television; and a way of establishing the
limits of responsibility for the new. Like the other arguments
in the controversy over motion pictures, radio, and television,
these were used to demonstrate the relationship between innovation
and the things and ideas held by society to be necessary, worthwhile,
and desirable.

Notes

1. For a discussion of other uses of these persuasive defi-nitions see: Charles L. Stevenson, Ethics and Language (New Haven: Yale University Press, 1944), pp. 206-226.

2. HW, 13 Je 1891, p. 447; HW, 24 Ag '07, p. 1246; PE, N '08, p. 231.

3. RR, Ja '23, p. 65.

4. CC, 27 Ap '38, p. 521. See also, HW, 30 Jl '10, p. 12; Ind, 11 Ja '12, p. 109; Lip, Ag '13, p. 194; CO, Ag '14, p. 105; CO, Ap '22, p. 507; LA, 22 S '23, p. 569; SA, Jl '26, p. 53; PE, O '26, p. 177; Scrib, Mr '27, p. 311; Nat, 3 Ap '43, p. 485.

5. SEP, 15 Ap '22, p. 141; Forum, Je '24, p. 764; RR, Ja '26, p. 33; LD, 1 S '28, p. 19; AAA, Ja '41, p. 151; SS, 18 Mr '46, p. 3; HB, Ag '50, p. 115. See also, SA, D '21, p. 105; RR, Ja '23, p. 52; SEP, 17 My '24, p. 11; RR, F '27, p. 183; SEP, 9 Je '28, p. 160; NAR, S '35, p. 313; CC, 22 Ap '31, p. 550; LA, Ap '35, p. 179; Educa, D '36, p. 216; SEP, 6 My '39, p. 8; AmMerc, Jl '44, p. 63; LJ, 15 F '45, p. 175; BHG, N '45, p. 75; ParM, Ja '49, p. 27; Atlan, Mr '49, p. 34.

6. Atlan, Mr '49, p. 34.

7. CO, Ag '14, p. 105.

8. PE, O '26, p. 177; Scrib, Mr '27, p. 311; CC, 27 Ap '38, p. 521.

9. LJ, 15 F '45, p. 175; BHG, N '45, p. 75.

10. NAR, D '39, p. 504. See also, Motion Pictures: CCom, 11 Ap '08, p. 75; WT, O '08, p. 1052; CCom, 6 Mr '09, p. 1038; Scrib, Jl '09, p. 122; AmMag, S '09, p. 498; Out, 27 N '09, p. 704; Ind, 29 S '10, p. 715; Col, 18 Jl '14, p. 11; RR, D '14, p. 726; LD, 22 Ap '16, p. 1171; Ind, 11 D '16, p. 448; HM, Ja '19, p. 183; NAR, Jl '20, p. 89; Out, 26 Ja '21, p. 136; CO, Ag '22, p. 157; HM, Ja '26, p. 164; Out, 18 Ag '26, p. 526; PE, O '26, p. 180; LA, 1 Ja '27, p. 82; Scrib, Ag '28, p. 160; Nat, 5 D '28, p. 602; RR, Mr '32, p. 31; LD, 21 Jl '34, p. 24; CC, 12 My '37, p. 617; NAR, D '39, p. 504. Radio: RR, Ap '22, p. 396; Col, 8 Ap '22, p. 4; SEP, 15 Ap '22, p. 144; IW, Je '22, p. 500; Col, 10 Je '22, p. 18; RR, Ag '22, p. 170; Nat, 2 Ja '24, p. 5; AmMerc, Mr '24, p. 212; Ind, 29 Mr '24, p. 171:

SEP, 17 My '24, p. 107; Forum, Je '24, p. 764; Col, 24 S '27, p. 9; SEP, 3 D '27, p. 48; Forum, Ap '29, p. 215; Comm, 10 Ap '29, p. 652; RR, Jl '29, p. 142; Scrib, My '31, p. 489; Comm, 29 Je '32, p. 229; Nat, 9 My '34, p. 531; SSoc, 22 Ag '36, p. 231; SEP, 11 F '39, p. 8; LJ, 15 F '45, p. 175. Television: Scrib, Jl '29, p. 11; SSoc, 22 Ag '36, p. 232; Col, 18 Mr '39, p. 72; SEP, 28 S '40, p. 25; Nat, 29 Jl '44, p. 127; CC, 2 F '49, p. 142; NR, 21 N '49, p. 20; SS, 20 S '50, p. 21; SEP, 22 Mr '55, p. 137.

11. Out, 19 Ja ' 21, p. 104; HM, S '24, p. 428; NAR, Mr '17, pp. 447-449; Ind, 25 S '26, p. 359; SEP, 21 S '29, p. 136; LA, 22 S '23, p. 568.

12. Forum, Mr '29, p. 169; RR, D '32, p. 60; NR, 3 F '47, p. 10; CO, My '22, p. 650; NR, 20 My '31, p. 20; HM, S '32, p. 472; Nat, 5 Je '29, p. 670; Nat, 28 D '46, p. 767; NR, 26 O '27, p. 251; Out, 18 Ap '28, p. 619; HM, N '31, p. 724.

13. SR, 24 D '49, p. 20; SR, 11 S '54, p. 46; TA, My '51, p. 43; SS, 20 S '50, p. 20.

14. PE, O '08, p. 161; HW, 16 S '11, p. 6.

15. LD, 4 O '13, p. 576.

16. NR, 1 My '15, p. 329; See also, CCom, 6 Mr '09, p. 1038; Out, 24 Je '11, p. 381; Out, 17 Ja '14, p. 121; WW, Ja '21, p. 254; LD, 7 My '21, p. 19; Col, 16 S '22, p. 3; Col, 23 S '22, p. 11, LHJ, F '24, p. 214; HM, Ja '26, p. 165; Ind, 18 S '26, p. 326; PE, Ag '29, p. 74; Comm, 13 Ag '30, p. 381; Comm, 5 My '33, p. 20; NR, 18 Ap '34, p. 373; BHG, Mr '37, p. 78; CC, 27 Ap '38, p. 521; Comm, 22 Ja '54, p. 392.

17. Comm, 13 D '35, p. 176; Col, 10 Je '22, p. 18; NR, 23 Mr '27, p. 140.

18. Nat, 29 Mr '22, p. 362; Nat, 2 Ja '25, p. 5; Out, 19 Mr '24, p. 465; Out, 28 My '24, p. 131; Nat, 23 Jl '24, p. 91; HM, Ja '26, p. 165; Comm, 10 Ap '29, p. 652; Scrib, My '31, p. 498; HM, N '31, p. 716; HM, D '34, p. 59; Comm, 13 D '35, p. 176; NAR, Mr '36, p. 56; SSoc, 22 Ag '36, p. 236; RR, F '37, p. 38; SSoc, 16 S '39, p. 369; BHG, N '45, p. 23.

19. SSoc, 22 Ag '36, p. 236; AmMerc, Jl '44, p. 63; SD, O '49, p. 25; ParM, N '49, p. 45; NR, 21 N '49, p. 20; SS, 20 S '50, p. 21; WHC, N '50, p. 71; GH, N '50, p. 264; ST, 1 N '50, p. 21T; NR, 26 F '51, p. 18; Comm, 18 Ja '52, p. 366; Nat, 15 N '52, p. 448; NR, 1 D '52, p. 12; AmMerc, D '54, p. 80; ParM, D '54, p. 80; CC, 2 F '55, p. 131.

20. CC, 2 F '55, p. 131.

CHAPTER IX

CONCLUSIONS

The motion pictures, radio, and television, from the time of their introduction and their immediate adoption as the new modes for popular entertainment, have been the subjects of frequent and persistent controversy. They have been hailed by their friends as the greatest advances in communications since the invention of the printing press and as means for accomplishing society's most desired ends. At the same time, movies, then radio, and most recently television have been labeled the crown and summit of the demoralizing influences of the present age--a threat to most of the ideas and institutions men hold to be necessary, worthwhile, and desirable. The agitation about the effects of the new media provided the substance for this investigation.

My purpose has been to identify and analyze the genres and lines of argument which were used in promoting, evaluating, and attacking motion pictures, radio, and television over a period of some sixty-five years. This is, therefore, first of all, a study of arguments about innovation, an examination of discourse written in praise and denigration of new things. The method is historical and analytical. The materials are drawn from some 1000 articles published in seventy popular periodicals between 1891 and 1955. The study illumines the rhetorical problems in a situation of innovation and adds at the same time to our understanding of the workings of popular persuasion. Through examination of the development of the media and the arguments about them, the study also adds a further dimension to the history of motion pictures, radio, and television.

Because of the emphasis on the particular working methods of the arguers, the analysis of data was undertaken so as to extract from the total discourse the general modes of argument, the patterns apparent in the lines of argument, the persistent concerns of the arguers, their recurrent themes, and their common strategies. The material was expected to speak for itself. I attempted, so far as possible, to avoid structuring the argument through my analysis of it. That is, first concern went to the particular character of this agitation, and as a result certain of the traditional patterns of analysis were given a second place. The question which guided the analysis was: What happened in the dispute? Consequently, what emerges from this system is a working classification of public argument. What has resulted, therefore, is not a technical description of argumentation nor a tight philosophical system for the classification of discourse. It is, instead, an account of the practice of popular persuasion.

In light of the length of the study, it is desirable to review the material before drawing conclusions about it. What follows first, therefore, is a rather extensive summary of the argument.

Four predominant modes of reasoning are apparent in the discourse: those from cause, from comparison, from association, and
from definition. These I refer to as the genres of argument, for
they are the largest classes into which the arguments tend to fall.
Within these genres appear the individual lines of argument, those
formulations of particular appeals cast into familiar patterns
by which men commonly justify their judgments of value. Within
the genre, causal, for example, one line of argument asserts that
radio will be beneficial to politics by bringing political speakers
into closer touch with the electorate. The genre identifies the
fundamental mode into which the argument is cast, and the line
of argument is the particular means by which the mode of reasoning
is made applicable to the case at hand.

The most numerous arguments were causal. This is to be expected because of the nature of the dispute, for it was the effects
of the media rather than their intrinsic worth which was at issue.
Moreover, causal arguments are forceful, direct, clear-cut, and
relatively simple. The line of influence is clearly focused and
the movement of the argument easy to follow. This mode of argument provided broad opportunity for the advocates who pointed out
the many positive influences of the new media as well as for the
attackers who played upon the nation's fears. Because of its

simplicity and versatility, causal argument was perhaps thought
to be the most appropriate means for this assault upon the public
mind.

In this analysis, the causal arguments were classified according to their reference to either social values or institutions.
Considered first were arguments which related to the value system.
So far as was possible, both advocates and attackers attempted
to demonstrate that motion pictures, radio, and television influenced the shared judgments on which men guided their behavior
and structured their society.

Advocates argued that values would be complemented, strengthened, and extended. Motion pictures, radio, and television would
provide entertainment that was socially useful, would broaden
man's vision of his world, would bring him knowledge and acquaint
him with culture. The media would serve the nation at home and
abroad, record its history, make its artists immortal, and strength-
en its economy. The new inventions would extend democracy and
bring world peace. They would reinforce morality and promote good
health. Whatever men respected or held dear the new media would
support.

The media, said their advocates, offered a new opportunity
for correcting weaknesses in present society and provided new means
for realizing national dreams. Ideal democracy, exemplified by
the town meeting, might be restored to practice on a national level.

People who were formerly apathetic about politics would seek active involvement once they were made participants in the democratic process via radio. Class distinctions would be leveled. The nation would find new unity through communication, and the isolation of the individual citizen would be ended. No longer need universal education remain only a dream. Through pictures, radio, and TV all people would have equal opportunity for amusement, education, and culture. The introduction of the new media offered a second chance to mend the faults and flaws of the past.

When, on the other hand, opponents argued from values, they predicted wide-ranging damage to generally accepted standards, goals, and ideals. The value system itself, they said, was undermined, and false values were substituted for those tested by time and experience. Innovation was labeled a threat to culture, a cause of war, and dangerous to the nation and its reputation. The entertainment offered by the media was shoddy and unrealistic, and was dictated by the whims of the masses. The mass media were dangerous to health, both mental and physical. But most important, the movies, radio, and television were immoral. That is, they dealt too much with crime, violence, and (especially the movies) sex. Children were unnecessarily exposed to brutality and sensuality. Instructed in sex on the screen and crime over the air, children were inspired to imitate the lessons they had

learned. The arguments from morality constituted the most persistent of all the attacks on the media.

Like arguments from values, arguments from the influences
of the media on social institutions served both advocates and
attackers. As part of their argument, advocates assured readers
that nothing presently valued would be disrupted by the introduction
of new communications. Tradition would survive and all that was
good in the present system would be preserved. In addition to
offering this reassurance, advocates argued that social institutions would benefit directly from innovation. New audiences
would be created for all institutions which depended upon public
support. Schools and churches were given new techniques for dis-
seminating their messages and new tools to use in their work.
Political speechmaking was to be improved, political campaigns
were to be made more efficient, and the electorate was to become
better informed about politics than ever before in history. Family
bonds would be strengthened as the members enjoyed together the
new education and entertainment. The home was to be restored as
the center for family recreation. Even the old modes of commercial entertainment, for which the new media offered direct competition, were said to profit from the introduction of television,
radio, and movies.

Advocates, however, could not ignore the competition between
the new and the old and were obliged to account for the fact that

movies, radio, and TV had caused modifications in established
institutions. In order to maintain their position that innovation was good for society, therefore, promoters argued from a
pattern of concession. They agreed that the new media had proved
damaging, but added one of three qualifications: the damage was
only temporary and things would soon return to normal; damage
had been done only to institutions which were undesirable in the
first place; or, even though institution were forced to change,
the changes would be ultimately beneficial. What was apparently
harmful was interpreted by advocates to be beneficial in the long
run.

Opponents of motion pictures, radio, and television argued
that just as social values had suffered because of innovation, so
too would society's insitutions be damaged. Audiences for all
other amusements and for any of the institutions which depended
upon popular support would be decimated. The educational system was weakened because the use of the media was inconsistent
with accepted educational theory, schools were forced to take
on new duties to make up for the skills that children lost or
never learned, and the children themselves did badly in their
studies because of the time they spent at movies or with radio
and television. Familiar political traditions were uprooted by
electronics, new criteria were established for candidate selection,
the political demagogue was given a new tool, and politics was

made a rich man's game. Churches faced not only loss of their congregations but usurpation of their functions. Motion pictures fostered attitudes in conflict with traditional beliefs about home and family; radio and television disrupted household routines and family relationships. Hurt most severely, however, were other forms of entertainment. Its supporters predicted that the theatre would fold because of the movies. Radio cut into the time people formerly gave to movies, concerts, reading, and sports. Talkies laid waste the silents. Television, in turn, threatened to cripple or to destroy most other amusements; neither movies, radio, reading, sports, concerts, conversation, nor children's play were safe from its influences. In all of these arguments, the presumption lay with the existing institution and on the side of tradition. Innovation was viewed as a threat to be resisted.

The second genre comprises arguments from comparison. These arguments are found approximately half as frequently as those from cause. Advocates and attackers used them to characterize the new media, to define the place of the new in the established order, to assess their performance, and to predict the consequences of innovation. The comparisons were used in many cases to complement causal argument, but they were employed most commonly either when causal argument was unavailable or when it was desirable to draw inferences and establish relationships which were not possible in arguments from cause. The particular value of the comparisons lay in their ability to illuminate the unknown through the known, to show relationships through time and across media, and to demonstrate the similarities between apparently dissimilar things.

The simplest of the comparisons, the unelaborated assertions of similarity, were used most frequently. Advocates claimed that the new media were like or better than familiar good things. Movies, radio, and television were like the theatre, were as significant as printing and as important in the national life as schools, automobiles, and newspapers. Defenders argued that movies, radio, and television were no worse than the theatre, the dime novel, each other, or the other mass media. On the other side, critics of the new inventions said they were as bad as, if not worse than, the dime novel, the theatre, tabloids, pulp magazines, comic books, corner gossip, burlesque, and prize fights. Moreover, radio was worse than the silent films, talkies were worse than either the silents or radio, and television was judged the worst of all. These assertions represent almost all degrees of comparison.

A second form of comparison involved a weighing of the predominant values ascribed to each medium. Motion pictures, for example, were described as motivated by profit, which was used in this context as a term of denigration. Profit, the term most frequently used as the negative in the comparisons, was weighed against such values as morality, education, the home, or decency.

In connection with broadcasting, _profit_ was balanced against _public service_, _good programs_, and _concern for children_. In their comparisons, attackers called into play many of the conventional pairs of contrasting values: _quality-quantity_; _public-private_; _popularity-excellence_; or _private gain-public service_. Advocates devised their comparisons from less extreme alternatives and in some cases, to blunt an attack, from pairs of terms in which both were abusive but one less so than the other. For example, films were _stupid_ but not _sensual_ and _vulgar_ but not _immoral_. The strategy of weighing values was used much less frequently by advocates than by attackers.

Similar to the comparisons of values were the eye-ear comparisons devised for explaining the appeals of the media. When defending silent films advocates argued that the eye was the superior organ for learning and for persuasion. However, when radio was introduced, its defenders found the ear superior. Advocates simply shifted their interpretation of the predominant sense in order to adjust to the primary mode of communication for each medium. Television, which combined the appeals to eye and ear, was named superior to either silent films or radio.

Advocates and attackers also compared the relative advantages and disadvantages of the media. Advocates held that although there were both advantages and disadvantages, the advantages outweighed the disadvantages. Early in the history of films, for example, promoters argued that while the eyes might become tired from watching movies, the good that pictures did outweighed the momentary discomfort. Later, the crime programs on television were excused on the basis of the medium's service in bringing the family together for recreation. Opponents took the reverse position, arguing, for example, that while radio might bring a few artists new popularity, it was generally harmful to programs of live music and to concerts. This technique allowed both sides to recognize the faults and virtues of the new media, and by interpretation either to minimize dangers or discount strengths.

Another type of comparison contrasted predictions about motion pictures, radio, and television to the performance of the media in practice. Opponents argued that the new instruments had never achieved their potential, had not lived up to the promises that promoters made for them. Radio, for example, promoted as a means for broadening culture, an instrument for intellectual communication, a reporter of the news, a new mode of popular education, and a vehicle for the finest of entertainment, was said by its detractors in 1929 to have become merely another "disintegrating toy." This argument is typical. Throughout the courses of the media there is in evidence continuing tension between what the media did and what their promoters and attackers hoped they might do. There were many areas in which movies, radio, and television failed to achieve the level of performance expected of them, but the failure of principal concern was in education. Neither motion pictures nor radio (the argument had not yet been applied to television in 1955) worked out as well in education as either promoters or detractors thought they should. Attackers used the argument to point up the failure of the media. Defenders used it occasionally to shift the blame from the media to the people responsible for them. Teachers, for instance, were said not to have used educational films even when they were available; radio programs produced by educators were said to have been dull and pedantic. The line of argument, however, was used most frequently by the opponents.

In other cases advocates and attackers evaluated the media by comparing their present performance to that of the past. These comparisons are best illustrated with the slogan that movies are better than ever, for this was the line of argument employed by their defenders. For half a century, on an average of at least once a year, advocates assured readers that the motion pictures at that moment were better--i.e., less objectionable morally, better technically, more artistic, more educational, more intellectual, more appropriate for children--than any pictures of the past. Time, said advocates, was the solution; eventually the motion picture would do all that its advocates had promised. The same promise was held out for radio and television, for their promoters also used this line of argument. Attackers, predictably took the opposing side. They claimed that the media were deteriorating as the years passed. Each new season brought more crime and less

culture, more entertainment and less education, more commercials

and less public service. Motion pictures in 1930 were said to be

worse than they had been before Will Hays took over. Television

was said to have been in its golden age in 1949. The future, to

the attackers, held little hope. Movies, radio, and television,

judged on the basis of their performance in the past, were worse

than ever.

The arguments from analogy were the most sophisticated of the

comparisons. That is, they contain at least four terms, are less

direct than the other comparisons, often deal with relationships

which are not immediately recognizable as similar, and allow their

users relatively greater freedom and creativity. Analogical argu-

ments were used to predict the consequences of innovation, to

point up the parallelism in events past and present, and to demon-

strate similarities among the media and between effects, circum-

stances, and proposed solutions.

Analogical arguments treating the consequences of innovation

were used by both advocates and attackers. Advocates argued that

since the new media were like good things of the past, the new

would serve as well as the old had served. That is, for example,

if printing, radio, the talkies, and the theatre were valued,

television should be similarly valued, for it was like those things.

It would continue the good which they had begun. Attackers, on

the other hand, predicted that the problems of the past were apt
to be repeated in the present. The new media would almost certainly perform like their predecessors. Each new medium, therefore, was predicted to do damage similar to that done by the
ones before it. If talkies had the power to kill the silents,
said some writers, they also were capable of ending the stage.
Radio would be harmful to children just as movies had been. Television was expected to "eventually displace the talking pictures,
as the talkies wiped out the silents." Arguing analogically,
turning to the experience of the past, both advocates and attackers
pointed to the probability of similar occurrences in either present or future. Analogy here served to establish a predictive
causal argument.

Arguments from the consequences of innovation and from historical parallels were used by advocates to offer reassurance
about the safety of traditional institutions and to demonstrate
that the new media would assume their places in society with a
minimum of disruption. Seeking to discount assertions about the
dangers of new inventions, advocates argued that institutions which
had survived the threats of the past would survive the competition
of motion pictures, radio, and television. The theatre, the church,
concerts by live artists, books and reading, and even motion pictures and radio when threatened by TV were thus declared safe from
the latest threat of innovation. Moreover, judging from the experience

of times past, the new media after an initial flurry of resistance, would be accepted as valuable new services. Almost every other invention of consequence, said spokesmen for the media, even those thought at first to be dangerous, were soon assimilated into society and proved in the end to be advantageous to man. There was no reason to believe the pattern would change.

The arguments from historical parallels also provided advocates a means for discounting or minimizing the predictions of critics. Turning to history, spokesmen for the new media argued that what was said in disparagement of movies, radio and television were merely the commonplaces which were always heard when new inventions were announced. The recurrent laments that the theatre was dying because of the competition of movies, for example, were labeled a familiar and repetitious theme. As such, it and other arguments like it, were dismissed as inconsequential. The arguments had been heard too often before; the experience of history denied their validity. This kind of minimizing was not often used, however. For the most part, writers ignored the repetitious nature of the arguments and the extensive use of commonplaces in the agitation. Only occasionally did the participants in the controversy comment in this fashion on its character.

Other analogical arguments dealt primarily with the similarities between events, circumstances, solutions, and media. These arguments, extended versions of the comparative assertions mentioned

earlier, were used by advocates to point up the likenesses between the media and things which society had already accepted,
to show that solutions employed in the past were available to
the new media, and to justify and excuse the failures of motion
pictures, radio, and television. Attackers used them to compare
the media to familiar social evils, to show that one medium was
as bad as another, and as a socially accepted form of invective.

The third genre contains arguments from association. Here
the new media were judged on the basis of the people and institutions who employed or supported them. Pointing to the use of
movies, radio, and television in religion, education, politics,
government, business, law enforcement, or the home, advocates
argued that such employment was indicative of the worth of the
new inventions. The institutions which society had erected to
realize its values demonstrated their approval of the media by
using them. Such approval was offered by advocates as evidence
of the value and importance of the media. On the other hand, they
also argued that the importance of the media was demonstrated in
their use by powerful, but dangerous institutions. For example,
the worth of radio was said to be clearly apparent in the use
of the medium by the Nazis in the period before the Second World
War.

Public acceptance was also made a criterion in the judgment
of the media. Promoters talked of the popularity of the new

entertainments, telling how people flocked to see the movies, how listening to the radio was the most popular of national pastimes, and how manufacturers could not make enough television sets to satisfy the demand for them. Advocates, expressing confidence in the good judgment, good taste, and good sense of the public, argued that the media were valuable because the public liked them. Attackers responded by challenging popularity as an acceptable standard for judgment, arguing that movies, radio, and television appealed only to the great uncritical mass, the lowest common denominator of good taste and discrimination. There was nothing in the media, said their critics, for the intelligent audience. Advocates replied to these attacks with praise for the character of the audience and with promises that movies, radio, and television would give their publics nothing but the best in information, culture, and entertainment.

Arguments from association were also based upon the reputations of individuals and their testimony about the media. Advocates told, for instance, how important people were associated with the new media. For a number of years, Thomas Edison's name was invoked in support of motion pictures. In the early days, appearances of famous stage players on the screen were used as evidence of the new stature of the art. At other times, writers favoring the three media told how preachers, educators, doctors, government officials, poets, politicians, and playwrights made use

of television, radio, or movies. At the same time, opponents
spoke of the unsavory people connected with the three industries.

Testimony was a common means of support for both advocates
and attackers. It was used frequently, in connection with all
issues and within all genres of argument. In form, testimony
ranged from statements by prestige individuals to reports of social
and psychological research. One trend in the use of opinion evidence over the course of the agitation should be noted. In the
early part of the period, writers tended to rely upon the opinions of various authority figures. As reports of research on the
effects of the mass media became available, this kind of evidence
from empirical investigation became the favorite means for support
of argument. Testimony from individuals was given a second place
following the Second World War.

Included in the fourth genre are arguments from definition,
of which two modes were employed in the agitation. Most common
were the definitions from value terms. Motion pictures, radio,
and television were defined in the god terms which have appeared
frequently in the course of this discussion. These rhetorical
definitions named the media sources for education, culture, information, news, and public service. They were called new forms
of theatre, adjuncts to religion, political tools, new businesses,
new arts, and new sales media. Their function as entertainers
was never used as the sole defining term. Always another dimension

was added to justify the entertainment; most commonly the second

term was education. Opponents, who did not argue from definition

as frequently as advocates, either challenged the definitions which

had been offered--for example, that motion pictures were a

legitimate form of drama--or defined the media in terms of deroga-

tion.

The second mode of definition referred to the media as neutral

tools. Motion pictures, radio, and television were, after all,

machines. As such they were capable of a variety of functions,

depending upon the wisdom with which they were employed. Hence,

the media could serve either good or evil, and the responsibility

for their effects were shifted to the men who controlled them and

to the public who used them.

These four genre represent the basic modes of reasoning char-

acteristic of the controversy over motion pictures, radio, and

television. In illustrating the lines of argument which appeared

within them, I have attempted to preserve the character and tone

of the originals, so far as this is possible in summary form. I

have also noted in passing some of the recurrent themes, concerns,

and strategies typical of the agitation.

I have not yet mentioned the participants in the dispute.

Some five hundred different authors are responsible for seven

hundred of the articles surveyed; the remaining articles and edi-

torials are unsigned. A minority of the writers, however, not more

than fifty at most, served as leaders in the dispute, catalysts
for the agitation. They called attention to new developments
and new problems within the media, often began or renewed the
agitation, and established the general pattern and tone of the
argument. George Parsons Lathrop served this function at the
beginning of the dispute; following him in support of films were
William Inglis, a writer for Harper's Weekly, and Walter Prichard
Eaton, the drama critic and author. Early leaders in the agitation against films were C. H. Claudy, a writer for Photo-Era,
and William A. McKeever, professor of philosophy at Kansas State
Agricultural College. Thomas Edison was the principal spokesman
for films, especially in education, until Will Hays took over in
1922. Others whose names appeared frequently in the early defense
of pictures were William de Mille, the playwright brother of Cecil
B. de Mille, Richard Dana Skinner, one of the founders of Commonweal, and Otis Skinner, the actor. The chief opponent of motion
pictures after 1930 was Fred Eastman, Professor of Religious
Literature and Drama at the Chicago Theological Seminary and the
principal writer for Christian Century's movie series.

Radio was promoted by such people as Lee De Forest, the inventor, Waldemar Kaempffert, science editor of the New York Times,
M. H. Aylesworth, president of NBC, David Sarnoff, president and
chairman of the board of RCA, Graham McNamee, the announcer, H. V.
Kaltenborn, the news commentator, and Bruce Barton and Roy Durstine,

two of the founders of B.B.D. and O. The opposition, on the other hand, came mostly from spokesmen for reform groups, from some of the professional writers who were dissatisfied with the course of the medium, and from authors hired by the periodicals to do pieces on special topics of immediate concern.

After the coming of talkies much of the leadership in commentary about pictures, radio, and TV was taken over by the professional critics and columnists whose job it was to comment on the media. In this group are people such as Alexander Bakshy, Saul Carson, Walter Goodman, Lou Frankel, Robert Lewis Shayon, Gilbert Seldes, and John Crosby. The notable exception to this pattern, of course, was Norman Cousins, the editor of Saturday Review, who launched the attack on television.

Comparable patterns of support and opposition may be traced among the periodicals themselves. The singular example, of course, is the Protestant Christian Century's campaign to clean up the movies. The Catholic Commonweal also raised repeated objections to the moral state of the motion picture. Earlier, Outlook had persistently argued against the white slave films and had been a leader in the agitation over the moral climate of pictures following the First World War. The earliest objections to films, however, appeared in periodicals such as Good Housekeeping, Charities and The Commons, Photo-Era, and Review of Reviews. Despite their early objections to the pictures, however, both Photo-Era

and Review of Reviews later became consistent supporters of the
medium as were Harper's Weekly, Illustrated World, and Lippincott's.
The same sorts of loyalties are not exhibited for radio and television, however.

The majority of periodicals demonstrate a marked ambivalence
toward the media. Most of the magazines tended to favor or oppose
on the basis of the immediate issue. Thus Collier's, for example,
or even Saturday Review, might at the same time praise a medium
for one of its functions and attack it for another. Some of the
periodicals undertook individual campaigns for favorite concerns.
Nation and New Republic, for example, were outspoken in their
support of radio as a political medium. Later, Nation, Scribner's,
and New Republic led the forces opposed to the children's programs on radio. As would be expected, the special interest publications, the music magazines and the education journals, for
instance, talked mostly about matters of greatest concern to their
readers and judged the media on the basis of their influences on
these concerns. In the main, however, the total period of the
agitation considered, most periodicals carried about an equal number
of articles favoring and disfavoring the media. The exceptions to
this pattern are rare.

The predominant characteristic of the agitation about motion
pictures, radio, and television is its repetitiousness. Promoters
and attackers responded consistently and predictably to each new

situation of innovation and to each new eruption of argument. They greeted each new medium with the same predictions, evaluated each one on the basis of its effects on the same institutions and values, defined each one in the same terms. The lines of argument, changed only in their specific referents, were repeated on each new occasion for disputation. The patterns and strategies of the discourse remained constant. Each new agitation gave the appearance of being the one just past.

A certain amount of the repetition may be explained simply in terms of the experience of the arguers. Writers merely repeated the formulas and the patterns, the lines of argument and the commonplaces, with which they were familiar. Involved in a new dispute, faced with the task of writing an article about the movies, the individual turned to the kinds of things which were always said in such situations and selected the arguments which seemed suited to the immediate circumstances.

The repetitive nature of the argument may be accounted for also on the basis of the arguers' concerns with social values and institutions. The shared notions about what is necessary, worthwhile, and desirable are limited, as is the number of social institutions which have been erected to realize the values. The frequent references to these topics in the testing of the new media forced the argument into the familiar patterns.

Finally, the repetitive nature of the agitation may be further explained by examining the basic propositions, the ultimate terms, to which the arguers turned in making judgments. Certain of these terms, some of them referring to values and institutions, are used as the common reference points in the dispute. Both sides argue from them, but the terms themselves are not debatable. These are the god terms which refer to the sanctioned concepts society holds in highest regard and with which few men publicly express disagreement.

The number of these terms is even more limited than the values and institutions. Education, for example, is sanctioned, as are democracy, peace, culture, beauty, good health, morality, religion, home, and family. Similarly, science, progress, tradition, quality, and reality are held in high regard. These terms may be used not only to form judgments of the media, but also to assess social values and institutions. These are, as others have pointed out, the terms of ultimate rhetorical potency. Their counterparts, it should be noted, are the terms of ultimate derogation.

There are also certain concepts which appear to be tentatively sanctioned, yet have not been fully accepted as ultimate terms. One of these is politics. The effect of the media on politics was a persistent concern for both promoters and attackers, but politics as practiced was viewed with suspicion. Never

was politics, the institution, given unqualified approval. Neither
was entertainment without blemish, although it was referred to frequently in the argument and was used as one of the defining terms
for the new media. Entertainment was, obviously, the chief function
of the movies, radio, and television for most people. Yet writers
were never confident enough of entertainment to use it as the sole
defining term or as the single justification for the media. Always
entertainment was reinforced with some other more readily acceptable
term.

The unique position of references to children in this agitation deserves mention. Both advocates and attackers argued from
the influence of the media on children. Their arguments were
developed in the context of entertainment, education, morality,
social values, and religion, and the judgments of the media were
made on the grounds of their influences on children in these particular areas. The determining factor in the assessment was the
impact on the child. The same kind of concern was not exhibited
for adults. There was, however, a suggestion of this notion of
the necessity for protecting the person unable to fend for himself,
for example, in some of the arguments about the influence of the
media on immigrants, on illiterates, and on persons of low intelligence. There is, apparently, a partially developed sanction for
the general concept children. Even if not sanctioned, the concept
is unquestionably one of great rhetorical force.

The repetition in the argument can thus be accounted for on the grounds of limitations imposed on the arguer both by the nature of reasoning and by the culture in which he operates. His choices among methods for connecting ideas are relatively few. Likewise, the terms to which he may resort for judgment, in turn reflecting the cultural tradition and societal concerns, are limited in number. The arguers are thus found returning often to the same ideas, are observed couching their discourse in familiar patterns, as they set about testing the new. The argument thus often turns to reliance upon commonplaces and becomes a system of conventional responses to new situations.

The conventional and patterned qualities of the agitation are also observed in the movement of argument through stages. The discussion of each new invention was opened with a period of predictive argument. Promoters sought first of all to secure a favorable acceptance for the medium. They therefore attempted to minimize the novelty, the newness, of the new and to place it in a context of familiar and good things. The new object was defined in value terms and compared to other well known institutions. At the same time, promoters offered reassurance of the safety of innovation, promising that the new would not displace the old, nor destroy comfortable patterns and habits. Finally, promoters predicted that the new invention, when it arrived, would lead to wide ranging and important benefits to society, its values, and its institutions.

During this period of predictive assessment, other writers
pointed to the potential dangers of innovation. Their reaction
to the announcement of the new was one of apprehension. Taking
a position counter to that of the advocates, these opponents
argued that the media were disruptive and that they threatened
traditions, values, and institutions which were held in high regard.
The proposed new things, they said, would be an extension of the
familiar evils of the past.

This became the formula for the introduction of the new media.
The pattern is observable first in the arguments about movies.
Radio went through a somewhat longer period of prediction following
its first applications for communication in the last part of the
nineteenth century and before its adaptation to broadcasting in
1920. The arguments about television followed this pattern for
nearly forty years as new systems were announced and new speculations about the nature of the medium were begun. The stage ended
for television only with its emergence as a national medium in the
late 1940's.

The next stage in the argument about each medium was one of
evaluation. The first one was speculative; no one really knew
what the effects of the inventions would be. In the second stage,
the perceptible effects of the media were assessed, and defenders
and attackers talked of the observable impact of the media on society.
From the observations of the present, both sides turned to new

predictions about the future. Advocates continued to offer a brave
new world. They argued that the present was good, but the future
would be even better. Opponents took the reverse position and again
called attention both to immediately apparent threats and disruptions
and to probable dislocations extending into the future. The argument was focused on society's concerns, its values, and its institutions, and couched in the terms which in themselves are persuasive. Throughout the agitation this kind of evaluation and prediction
was called into service whenever there was cause to make judgments
about the media.

It should be evident that the "argument" over the new mass
media exhibits the general characteristics of popular persuasion.
In a strictly academic sense it is not argument, for there is little
of the quality of disciplined disputation in it. The common goals
are climates of approval or disapproval. Each side, however, goes
its own way through similar patterns to contrary ends. There is
little interaction among the arguers, there are few points of direct
clash, seldom even do the opponents acknowledge each other or attempt
to devise refutations for opposing arguments. Instead, the emphasis
is on reaching the public through the strategies of popular
appeal and on devices which will move the public to acceptance of
ideas. This is, in effect, a massive and persistent assault on the
public mind in contrary directions.

So far in this chapter I have dealt with the particular character of the agitation over motion pictures, radio, and television.
The analysis warrants generalization to the broader field of popular
argument, particularly that arising out of innovation.

Probably controversy about innovation of any public sort would
follow the broad patterns which have been identified here. That is,
other agitations would employ much the same genres and lines of argument which were used in connection with the new media. Moreover, I
would suppose that most new inventions and new ideas are greeted with
glowing promises about their future influences and with dire predictions
about their probable ill effects. Most promoters probably offer reas-
surances that the new will damage nothing which is held dear in the old
order. Similar values, institutions, and sanctions would undergird the
argument, provided it occurred in this culture and in our general period of history. The newcomer would be evaluated on the basis of its
influences on the things and ideas held to be necessary, worthwhile,
and desirable. Its friends would argue that it was presently doing
well, but would do better if only given enough time. Its enemies
would express regrets that the potential of the new had not been
realized. Finally, the people blamed for its presumed faults and
failures would argue that the responsibility was not theirs, but
lay elsewhere, probably with the public.

The genres of argument which have been identified here are
obviously broadly applicable in discourse. They identify the basic

modes of reasoning men use for making connections between ideas.
Hence, this method of collection into genres is a useful and
exhaustive system for the classification of argument. I would
expect these modes of argument to appear in all controversy about
people, things, and events of social concern. For instance, the
categories cause, comparison, association, and definition serve
well for classifying the arguments in a political campaign, for
in essence many of the proposals made in such a situation are
innovative. Similarly, the genres might be used for the assessment
of legislative debate. In other words, this method of looking at
argument provides a convenient system for the examination of the
basic modes of discourse.

Although it would be expected that these broad types of argument will appear in all discussions involving innovation, this is
not to say that they will necessarily appear in the same proportions.
It is probable that arguments about effects are primary concerns in
technological innovation. In other disputes, however, the emphasis
might well be placed on argument from definition or comparison. This
might be especially true when causality was not sharply defined or
in situations where there were no immediately apparent effects from
which to make judgments.

When available, however, causal argument is apparently thought
to be the most potent form. It was the genre to which the arguers
turned most consistently in the agitation just analyzed. It seems

to me significant that the comparative arguments were used often to predict a causal relationship. The comparisons, on the other hand, appear to allow the arguer a greater degree of freedom and permit greater creativity than the causal arguments in making connections. They are, however, much less direct in their movement.

Within the genres I have presented a virtually exhaustive list of the topics for argument about these innovations. The patterns into which ideas were cast in discussions of these new things, as well as the substance of the arguments, are all here. From this list, one might well predict the common lines of attack and defense which will appear in analogous situations. There is value in this sort of thing for the practitioner as well as for the student of discourse.

I mentioned above that this is a nearly exhaustive list of the topics. All of the social institutions were referred to at one time or another, as were most of the common social values. In addition, all of the social sanctions seem to have been employed in the discourse. The possibility obviously exists, however, that there are a number of topics which lie outside the realm of innovative argument, or which are used in periodicals other than the ones surveyed, and which are applicable in public discourse of this kind. One such argument, for example, might refer to supernatural sanction for innovation: God approves of this undertaking. The line of argument is potentially applicable in this dispute although it was not used in the magazines considered.

The values, institutions, and sanctions are also obviously applicable to broader areas of argument than have been observed in this discussion. They are the bases used for testing the new, and they furnish likewise the fundamental presumptions from which most argument springs. Embodied in them are the common notions through which modern democratic man rationalizes belief. As such, they serve as conditioners of the discourse. It would be expected that they would serve the same function in general public debate.

One of the topics which have considerable rhetorical force refers to children. Appeals from the effects of the new media on children, as I noted above, were important in judging motion pictures, radio, and television. Similar references would be expected in other public discourse, for the concern with children seems to be pervasive and rhetorically potent. Observation of general discourse suggests that in our society this is a widely used appeal in campaigns of many sorts.

Rhetorical invention in the type of argumentative situation considered here consists not so much in the creation of new arguments as in the selection of available topics for use in the particular discourse. The arguer is conditioned in his selection both by his own experience and by the limitations imposed on him by his culture, which supplies the presumptions on which the argument may be founded and the vocabulary in which it is expressed. The resources of invention are thus limited, as this study has indicated. Therefore, not only will the same lines of argument be repeated in any lengthy discourse, but the arguers will also return to the same themes and ideas to fill out their arguments. To put it another way, invention tends to run out in the long-term rhetorical situation, and the argument becomes more repetitious as it grows older.

Finally, this study adds substantially to the evidence of the belief in those who would form the public mind on broad fronts that persuasion grows not only out of the arguments which are formulated and the values from which appeals are drawn, but also from the insistent repetition of the same ideas. The massive presentation of suasory discourse, it is supposed, can hardly help having its influence; hearing the same argument, or reading it, a hundred times or more gives the appeal a kind of credibility not necessarily inherent in the substance. The mere weight of discourse may be in itself an important factor. There is evidence also that a point of exhaustion may be reached and may be tacitly, if not explicitly, recognized.

This investigation is, obviously, only a segment of the new look which is needed at the massive realities of rhetorical operation. It is a particular exploration of discourse on a large scale, exhaustive for the sources considered. The data it presents could be quantified for other dimensions of analysis. The frequency of the arguments from the various sanctions, for example, might be explored. Or the significance of the distribution of the arguments among the four genres might be investigated. It would be valuable, it seems to me, to examine more systematically the arguers' perceptions of the modes of argument available to them.

Various other more traditionally rhetorical analyses might also be undertaken. Worth investigating in this body of discourse are the points at which there is direct collision among the arguers, the issues on which this agitation takes on the character of more formal debate. Of interest, too, are the tendencies for the arguers, while seeking the same goals, to pursue them along different courses and through diverse methods. Although I have not done it with any diligence, it would be revealing to examine the particular lines of argument which are characteristic of the various periodicals and of the individual writers. Likewise, a close investigation of the time of appearance in the discourse of the various lines of argument and some analysis of the places where invention seems to break down would be worth undertaking.

There is, of course, an open field for study in the many other situations of innovation. Investigations of this type might be undertaken to examine the discourse surrounding the development of transportation, for example, or that connected with medical inventions, or with the introduction of new ideas, philosophies, or legislation.

From this and other studies of comparable scope we may come to a new synthesis, on the basis of historical practice, of the operating patterns in the behavior of popular argument, the form and features of popular persuasion as they are, and as they are changing.

BIBLIOGRAPHY

Primary Sources

The primary materials were drawn from a survey of the following periodicals as they are indexed in the Readers' Guide to Periodical Literature:

The American Magazine

The American Mercury

The American Review of Reviews

The Atlantic Monthly

The Christian Century

Collier's

The Commonweal

Current Opinion

Education

The Etude

The Forum

Harper's Magazine

Harper's Weekly

The Illustrated World

The Independent

The Literary Digest

The Living Age

The Nation

The New Republic

Newsweek

The North American Review

The Outlook

Parents' Magazine

Photo-Era

The Reader's Digest

The Saturday Evening Post

The Saturday Review

School and Society

Science Digest

Scientific American

Scribner's Magazine

Senior Scholastic

The Survey

Theatre Arts

Time

The United States News & World Report

The World's Work

Occasional articles from the following periodicals were also
employed in this investigation:

America

The American City

The Annals of the American Academy of Political and Social Sciences

Better Homes and Gardens

The Bookman

The Century

Changing Times

Charities and The Commons

Current Literature

The Dial

Everybody's Magazine

Good Housekeeping

House Beautiful

Ladies' Home Journal

Library Journal

Life

Lippincott's Monthly Magazine

Musical America

The Musician

Nation's Business

New Outlook

The Nineteenth Century and After

The Overland Monthly

Popular Mechanics Magazine

The Publishers' Weekly

The Rotarian

Scholastic Teacher

Science News Letter

Scientific American Supplement

Survey Graphic

Technical World

Theatre Magazine

Woman's Home Companion

The World Today

Secondary Sources

Books

Black, Edwin. Rhetorical Criticism. New York: Macmillan, 1965.

Head, Sydney. Broadcasting in America. Boston: Houghton-Mifflin, 1955.

Hendricks, Gordon. The Edison Motion Picture Myth. Berkeley: University of California Press, 1961.

Hertzler, Joyce Oramel. American Social Institutions. Boston: Allyn and Bacon, 1961.

Jacobs, Lewis. The Rise of the American Film. New York: Harcourt, Brace, 1939.

Klapper, Joseph T. The Effects of Mass Communication. Glencoe, Illinois: Free Press, 1960.

Peterson, Theodore B. Magazines in the Twentieth Century. Rev. ed.; Urbana: University of Illinois Press, 1958.

Schramm, Wilbur, ed. Mass Communications. Urbana: University of Illinois Press, 1960.

Stevenson, Charles L. Ethics and Language. New Haven: Yale University Press, 1944.

Dissertations

Donald N. Dedmon, "An Analysis of the Arguments in the Debate in
Congress on the Admission of Hawaii to the Union." Unpublished Ph.D. dissertation, University of Iowa, 1961.

Leland M. Griffin, "The Anti-Masonic Persuasion: A Study of Public
Address in the American Anti-Masonic Movement, 1826-1838."
Unpublished Ph.D. dissertation, Cornell University, 1950.

Robert Shepard Morgan, "The Television Code of the National Association of Broadcasters: The First Ten Years." Unpublished
Ph.D. dissertation, University of Iowa, 1964.

Todd G. Willy, "The Agitation in Parliment and England over Charles
George 'Chinese' Gordon and His Mission to the Soudan; January,
1884 to February, 1885." Unpublished Ph.D. dissertation,
University of Iowa, 1962.

The Arno Press Cinema Program

THE LITERATURE OF CINEMA

Series I & II

Agate, James. **Around Cinemas.** 1946.

Agate, James. **Around Cinemas.** (Second Series). 1948.

American Academy of Political and Social Science. **The Motion Picture in Its Economic and Social Aspects,** edited by Clyde L. King. **The Motion Picture Industry,** edited by Gordon S. Watkins. *The Annals,* November, 1926/1927.

L'Art Cinematographique, Nos. 1-8. 1926-1931.

Balcon, Michael, Ernest Lindgren, Forsyth Hardy and Roger Manvell. **Twenty Years of British Film, 1925-1945.** 1947.

Bardèche, Maurice and Robert Brasillach. **The History of Motion Pictures,** edited by Iris Barry. 1938.

Benoit-Levy, Jean. **The Art of the Motion Picture.** 1946.

Blumer, Herbert. **Movies and Conduct.** 1933.

Blumer, Herbert and Philip M. Hauser. **Movies, Delinquency, and Crime.** 1933.

Buckle, Gerard Fort. **The Mind and the Film.** 1926.

Carter, Huntly. **The New Spirit in the Cinema.** 1930.

Carter, Huntly. **The New Spirit in the Russian Theatre, 1917-1928.** 1929.

Carter, Huntly. **The New Theatre and Cinema of Soviet Russia.** 1924.

Charters, W. W. **Motion Pictures and Youth.** 1933.

Cinema Commission of Inquiry. **The Cinema: Its Present Position and Future Possibilities.** 1917.

Dale, Edgar. **Children's Attendance at Motion Pictures.** Dysinger, Wendell S. and Christian A. Ruckmick. **The Emotional Responses of Children to the Motion Picture Situation.** 1935.

Dale, Edgar. **The Content of Motion Pictures.** 1935.

Dale, Edgar. **How to Appreciate Motion Pictures.** 1937.

Dale, Edgar, Fannie W. Dunn, Charles F. Hoban, Jr., and Etta Schneider. **Motion Pictures in Education: A Summary of the Literature.** 1938.

Davy, Charles. **Footnotes to the Film.** 1938.

Dickinson, Thorold and Catherine De la Roche. **Soviet Cinema.** 1948.

Dickson, W. K. L., and Antonia Dickson. **History of the Kinetograph, Kinetoscope and Kinetophonograph.** 1895.

Forman, Henry James. **Our Movie Made Children.** 1935.

Freeburg, Victor Oscar. **The Art of Photoplay Making.** 1918.

Freeburg, Victor Oscar. **Pictorial Beauty on the Screen.** 1923.

Hall, Hal, editor. Cinematographic Annual, 2 vols. 1930/1931.

Hampton, Benjamin B. A History of the Movies. 1931.

Hardy, Forsyth. Scandinavian Film. 1952.

Hepworth, Cecil M. **Animated Photography: The A B C of the Cinematograph.** 1900.

Hoban, Charles F., Jr., and Edward B. Van Ormer. **Instructional Film Research 1918-1950.** 1950.

Holaday, Perry W. and George D. Stoddard. **Getting Ideas from the Movies.** 1933.

Hopwood, Henry V. **Living Pictures.** 1899.

Hulfish, David S. **Motion-Picture Work.** 1915.

Hunter, William. **Scrutiny of Cinema.** 1932.

Huntley, John. **British Film Music.** 1948.

Irwin, Will. **The House That Shadows Built.** 1928.

Jarratt, Vernon. **The Italian Cinema.** 1951.

Jenkins, C. Francis. **Animated Pictures.** 1898.

Lang, Edith and George West. **Musical Accompaniment of Moving Pictures.** 1920.

London, Kurt. **Film Music.** 1936.

Lutz, E [dwin] G [eorgé]. **The Motion-Picture Cameraman.** 1927.

Manvell, Roger. **Experiment in the Film.** 1949.

Marey, Etienne Jules. **Movement.** 1895.

Martin, Olga J. **Hollywood's Movie Commandments.** 1937.

Mayer, J. P. **Sociology of Film: Studies and Documents.** 1946. New Introduction by J. P. Mayer.

Münsterberg, Hugo. **The Photoplay: A Psychological Study.** 1916.
Nicoll, Allardyce. **Film and Theatre.** 1936.

Noble, Peter. **The Negro in Films.** 1949.

Peters, Charles C. **Motion Pictures and Standards of Morality.** 1933.

Peterson, Ruth C. and L. L. Thurstone. **Motion Pictures and the Social Attitudes of Children.** Shuttleworth, Frank K. and Mark A. May. **The Social Conduct and Attitudes of Movie Fans.** 1933.

Phillips, Henry Albert. **The Photodrama.** 1914.

Photoplay Research Society. **Opportunities in the Motion Picture Industry.** 1922.

Rapée, Erno. **Encyclopaedia of Music for Pictures.** 1925.

Rapée, Erno. **Motion Picture Moods for Pianists and Organists.** 1924.

Renshaw, Samuel, Vernon L. Miller and Dorothy P. Marquis. **Children's Sleep.** 1933.

Rosten, Leo C. **Hollywood: The Movie Colony, The Movie Makers.**
  1941.

Sadoul, Georges. **French Film.** 1953.

Screen Monographs I, 1923-1937. 1970.

Screen Monographs II, 1915-1930. 1970.

Sinclair, Upton. **Upton Sinclair Presents William Fox.** 1933.

Talbot, Frederick A. **Moving Pictures.** 1912.

Thorp, Margaret Farrand. **America at the Movies.** 1939.

Wollenberg, H. H. **Fifty Years of German Film.** 1948.

RELATED BOOKS AND PERIODICALS

Allister, Ray. **Friese-Greene: Close-Up of an Inventor.** 1948.

Art in Cinema: A Symposium of the Avant-Garde Film, edited by
  Frank Stauffacher. 1947.

The Art of Cinema: Selected Essays. New Foreword by
  George Amberg. 1971.

Balázs, Béla. **Theory of the Film.** 1952.

Barry, Iris. **Let's Go to the Movies.** 1926.

de Beauvoir, Simone. **Brigitte Bardot and the Lolita Syndrome.** 1960.

Carrick, Edward. **Art and Design in the British Film.** 1948.

Close Up. Vols. 1-10, 1927-1933 (all published).

Cogley, John. **Report on Blacklisting. Part I: The Movies.** 1956.

Eisenstein, S. M. **Que Viva Mexico!** 1951.

Experimental Cinema. 1930-1934 (all published).

Feldman, Joseph and Harry. **Dynamics of the Film.** 1952.

Film Daily Yearbook of Motion Pictures. Microfilm, 18 reels,
  35 mm. 1918-1969.

Film Daily Yearbook of Motion Pictures. 1970.

Film Daily Yearbook of Motion Pictures. (Wid's Year Book).
  3 vols., 1918-1922.

The Film Index: A Bibliography. Vol. I: The Film as Art. 1941.

Film Society Programmes. 1925-1939 (all published).

Films: A Quarterly of Discussion and Analysis. Nos. 1-4, 1939-1940
  (all published).

Flaherty, Frances Hubbard. **The Odyssey of a Film-Maker:
  Robert Flaherty's Story.** 1960.

General Bibliography of Motion Pictures, edited by Carl Vincent,
  Riccardo Redi, and Franco Venturini. 1953.

Hendricks, Gordon. **Origins of the American Film.** 1961-1966. New
  Introduction by Gordon Hendricks.

Hound and Horn: Essays on Cinema, 1928-1934. 1971.

Huff, Theodore. **Charlie Chaplin.** 1951.

Kahn, Gordon. **Hollywood on Trial.** 1948.

New York Times Film Reviews, 1913-1968. 1970.

Noble, Peter. **Hollywood Scapegoat: The Biography of Erich von Stroheim.** 1950.

Robson, E. W. and M. M. **The Film Answers Back.** 1939.

Seldes, Gilbert. **An Hour with the Movies and the Talkies.** 1929.

Weinberg, Herman G., editor. **Greed.** 1971.

Wollenberg, H. H. **Anatomy of the Film.** 1947.

Wright, Basil. **The Use of the Film.** 1948.

DISSERTATIONS ON FILM

Beaver, Frank Eugene. **Bosley Crowther:** Social Critic of the Film, **1940-1967.** First publication, 1974.

Benderson, Albert Edward. **Critical Approaches to Federico Fellini's "8½".** First publication, 1974

Berg, Charles Merrell. **An Investigation of the Motives For and Realization of Music to Accompany the American Silent Film, 1896-1927.** First publication, 1976

Blades, Joseph Dalton, Jr. **A Comparative Study of Selected American Film Critics, 1958-1974.** First publication, 1976

Cohen, Louis Harris. **The Cultural-Political Traditions and Developments of the Soviet Cinema: 1917-1972.** First publication, 1974

Dart, Peter. **Pudovkin's Films and Film Theory.** First publication, 1974

Davis, Robert Edward. **Response to Innovation:** A Study of Popular Argument About New Mass Media. First publication, 1976

Facey, Paul W. **The Legion of Decency:** A Sociological Analysis of the Emergence and Development of a Social Pressure Group. First publication, 1974

Karimi, A. M. **Toward a Definition of the American Film Noir (1941-1949).** First publication, 1976

Karpf, Stephen L. **The Gangster Film:** Emergence, Variation and Decay of a Genre, 1930-1940. First publication, 1973

Lounsbury, Myron O. **The Origins of American Film Criticism, 1909-1939.** First publication, 1974.

Lyons, Robert J[oseph]. **Michelangelo Antonioni's Neo-Realism:**
A World View. First publication, 1976

Lyons, Timothy James. **The Silent Partner:** The History of the
American Film Manufacturing Company, 1910-1921.
First publication, 1974

McLaughlin, Robert. **Broadway and Hollywood:** A History of Economic
Interaction. First publication, 1974

North, Joseph H. **The Early Development of the Motion Picture,
1887-1909.** First publication, 1973

Pryluck, Calvin. **Sources of Meaning in Motion Pictures and Television.**
First publication, 1976

Rimberg, John. **The Motion Picture in the Soviet Union, 1918-1952.**
First publication, 1973

Sands, Pierre N. **A Historical Study of the Academy of the Motion
Picture Arts and Sciences (1927-1947).** First publication, 1973

Shain, Russell Earl. **An Analysis of Motion Pictures About War
Released by the American Film Industry, 1939-1970.**
First publication, 1976

Stuart, Fredric. **The Effects of Television on the Motion Picture and
Radio Industries.** First publication, 1976

Wead, George. **Buster Keaton and the Dynamics of Visual Wit.**
First publication, 1976

Wolfe, Glenn J. **Vachel Lindsay:** The Poet as Film Theorist.
First publication, 1973

DATE DUE

Randall Library – UNCW

HN90.M3 D38 1976

NXWW

Davis / Response to innovation : a study of popula

304900216183.